A David Montgomery Reader

THE WORKING CLASS
IN AMERICAN HISTORY

For a list of books in the series, please see our website at www.press.uillinois.edu.

A David Montgomery Reader

Essays on Capitalism and Worker Resistance

DAVID MONTGOMERY

Edited by
SHELTON STROMQUIST
AND JAMES R. BARRETT

UNIVERSITY OF ILLINOIS PRESS
Urbana, Chicago, and Springfield

Manufactured in the United States of America
1 2 3 4 5 C P 5 4 3 2 1
∞ This book is printed on acid-free paper.

Library of Congress Cataloging-in-Publication Data
Names: Montgomery, David, 1927–2011, author. | Stromquist, Shelton, 1943– editor. | Barrett, James R., 1950– editor.
Title: A David Montgomery reader : essays on capitalism and worker resistance / David Montgomery ; edited by Shelton Stromquist and James R. Barrett.
Description: Urbana : University of Illinois Press, [2024] | Series: The working class in American history | Includes bibliographical references and index.
Identifiers: LCCN 2023054084 (print) | LCCN 2023054085 (ebook) | ISBN 9780252045905 (cloth) | ISBN 9780252088001 (paperback) | ISBN 9780252056796 (ebook)
Subjects: LCSH: Working class—United States—History. | Labor movement—United States—History. | Montgomery, David, 1927–2011. | BISAC: POLITICAL SCIENCE / Labor & Industrial Relations | HISTORY / United States / 20th Century
Classification: LCC HD8066 .M568 2024 (print) | LCC HD8066 (ebook) | DDC 305.5/620973—dc23/eng/20231221
LC record available at https://lccn.loc.gov/2023054084
LC ebook record available at https://lccn.loc.gov/2023054085

To Ann Mullin Stromquist

and the memory of Jenny Wong Barrett

Contents

Acknowledgments

Before all others, we wish to thank David Montgomery for the inspiration and intellectual guidance he provided to the field of labor history and the practitioners who followed in his footsteps, not the least his students at the University of Pittsburgh and Yale University, and legions of scholars and labor activists across the US and around the world, for whom in varied ways he was a mentor.

This collection is in memory of Marty Montgomery for her sharp wit, shrewd intelligence, and artistic talents. Over many years she offered hospitality, encouragement, stimulation, and abiding interest to David's students, their families, and their work. We thank Claude Montgomery and Ed Montgomery for their encouragement of our efforts and their interest in keeping David's intellectual legacy alive and their children, for whom David and Marty had that special love only grandparents can hold.

Jenny Barrett contributed her usual inspiration and encouragement and her own memories of David and Marty. Ann Stromquist encouraged us in this project and offered friendship and support to Marty in those difficult days and years after David's passing. Julie Greene gave valuable comments on the manuscript and advice about David's teaching at Yale. Two anonymous reviewers of the manuscript gave very helpful comments and advice. Kathy Oberdeck shared her memories of David and gave encouragement to this project.

For their help in collecting and securing permissions for photographs of David Montgomery at different stages of his life, we thank: Claude Montgomery and Ed Montgomery; Jon Butler, his former colleague at Yale; Michael Marsland from Yale; Cecelia Bucki and Dorothy Fennell, our fellow students of David's; Jonathan Kissam, UE Communications Director; Al Hart and Ron Flowers with the UE; Zachery Brodt with the UE Archives; Sharon Wood; Eric Fure-Slocum; and Leon Fink, Julie Greene, and Patrick Dixon with *Labor*.

At the University of Illinois Press we appreciate the encouragement and assistance of Alison Syring, Leigh Ann Cowan, Laurie Matheson, Tad Ringo and Tamira Butler-Likely. And at the Tamiment Library and Robert F. Wagner Archives, Kate Donovan helped facilitate access to David's as yet unprocessed papers, and Shannon O'Neill located additional materials in the collection and secured permission from New York University for the publication of previously unpublished essays. Pat Goodwin, Department Administrator, University of Iowa History Department, provided extraordinary help with the challenge of digitizing the essays and transforming them into publishable form.

A number of people provided support and encouragement in the early phases of this project, for which we are very grateful. They include Nelson Lichtenstein, David Roediger, Joe McCartin, Ellie Shermer, Leon Fink, Mike Rosenow, Peter Cole, Randi Storch, Donna Haverty-Stack, Adam Hodges, Will Cooley, Kathy Mapes, Eric Fure-Slocum, and Dennis Deslippe.

Publishers and editors graciously granted permission to reprint David's essays. We wish to thank Kris Inwood and *Social Science History*; Marjoleine Kars and *International Labor and Working-Class History*; Matthew Karush and the *Journal of Social History*; Aad Blok and the *International Review of Social History*; Boyd Cothran and the *Journal of the Gilded Age and Progressive Era*; Chris McKeen, Emily Redican-Bradford, and Cambridge University Press; Craig Phelan, Gerald Friedman, and *Labor History*; Anne Rasmussen, Lydie Rauzier, and *Le Mouvement Social*; the University of Illinois Press; Emma Thornton and Benjamin Irvin with the *Journal of American History*; Oxford University Press; Rick Halpern and Kate Alexander; Alice Essenpreis, and Springer Nature/Palgrave-Macmillan Press.

David Montgomery

A Biographical Sketch

Born in 1927 to middle-class parents in a comfortable home near Philadelphia, David Montgomery took an interest in issues of social class and inequality as early as his teen years. While playing football, running track, and excelling in his studies, he began to read the socialist press and followed local politics. His college years at Swarthmore were interrupted by a stint in the Army at the end of World War II, during which time he worked at the Los Alamos base radio station, an experience that had a profound effect on him. Surrounded by renowned scientists concerned about the future of nuclear weapons, he became active in the World Federalist movement, advocating for international control of atomic energy. Returning to Swarthmore in 1947, he read extensively in history and helped to lead the American Veterans Committee, engaging with Lincoln University students in integrating public facilities on the Pennsylvania border.[1]

After a brief stint studying political science and sociology at Columbia, Montgomery took a job in a New York City electrical manufacturing plant and joined the United Electrical Workers (UE) Local 475, where he was active in civil rights issues and served as shop chairman. He joined the Communist Party in late 1951 or early 1952, attracted by its activity in support of racial equality, peaceful coexistence, and social unionism. The main lesson he took away from these years was "an appreciation for the diversity of views and experiences among working people." He believed he became "much *less* doctrinaire . . . simply because of dealing with everyday life."[2]

Montgomery married another young activist, Martel Wilcher, and through her family he was introduced to a vibrant world of African American trade union and political activism in Chicago. In 1956, for what he described as personal reasons, he and Martel and their two young children, Edward and Claude, moved to Minneapolis where he worked as a skilled machinist in the large Honeywell plant, an experience that shaped his later studies of work and shop cultures. He left the Communist Party in 1957 but remained active in the Minnesota Farmer-Labor Party, the Teamsters Union, and the International Association of Machinists. When the Honeywell plant closed, Montgomery found himself blacklisted in a number of machine shops but managed to find work in a small shop. In 1960, he turned to graduate study in history at the University of Minnesota, where he studied with political scientist Mulford Sibley and historian David W. Noble, completing his PhD in record time in 1962. He took his first teaching position at the University of Pittsburgh the following year, where he was active in antiwar and labor circles. His first book, *Beyond Equality*, a revision of his dissertation, was published in 1967.

Montgomery joined the British socialist historian E. P. Thompson as a visiting professor at Warwick University in England from 1967 to 1969. Influenced by Thompson and *The Making of the English Working Class* (1963), he published a series of articles dealing with early industrialization in the United States. When he met to advise shop stewards at auto plants in Coventry, the Rootes Motor Company employed a detective and moved to have him deported as an "undesirable person" under the Subversive Aliens Act of 1919. His case later fueled a student movement at Warwick. This connection with workers' control issues in the United Kingdom, together with his own work experiences and contact with historians in England, France, and Italy, shaped his later work on workers' control in the United States and his interest in global and comparative history.[3]

In 1979, Montgomery published *Workers' Control in America: Studies in the History of Work, Technology, and Labor Struggles*, a collection of essays developed over the previous decade. His magnum opus, *The Fall of the House of Labor: The Workplace, the State, and American Labor Activism, 1865–1925*, would follow in 1987, and in 1993 he published *Citizen Worker: The Experience of Workers in the United States with Democracy and the Free Market During the Nineteenth Century*, originally a set of essays based on his Tanner Lectures at Oxford in 1991.

At Pittsburgh, Montgomery and his dozens of graduate students actively supported the struggles of university workers, coal miners, and auto and electrical workers. He moved to Yale University as Farnam Professor of History in 1979 where he was instrumental in support of graduate employee union organizing and the 1984 strike of the university's clerical and technical workers. In 1997, after training more than fifty graduate students in Pittsburgh and New Haven, he retired. Montgomery served as president of the Organization of American Historians from 1999 to 2000 and continued to speak at labor and academic meetings until his death on December 2, 2011.

Notes

1. James R. Barrett, "Class Act: An Interview with David Montgomery," *Labor: Studies in Working-Class History of the Americas* 1, no. 1 (Spring 2004): 23–28.

2. Ibid., quote, 32. See also, MARHO, "Interview with David Montgomery," in *Visions of History*, ed. Henry Abelove, et al. (New York: Pantheon, 1981), 169–81, and his discussion of his relationship with the Communist Party.

3. Ibid., 32–39; *Warwick University Ltd.: Industry, Management, and the Universities*, ed. E. P. Thompson (Harmondsworth, UK: Penguin, 1970); Bryan Palmer, *E.P. Thompson: Objections and Oppositions* (London: Verso, 1994), 109–11; on the relationship between Montgomery and E. P. Thompson see also, Shelton Stromquist, "Labor Historians and Traditions of Engaged Scholarship: Progressives, Insurgents, and the Making of a New Labor History," in *Civic Labors: Scholar Activism and Working-Class Studies*, eds. Dennis Deslippe, Eric Fure-Slocum, and John W. McKerley (Urbana: University of Illinois Press, 2016), 11–34.

David Montgomery with other United Electrical Workers (UE) Local 475 shopmates picketing the House Un-American Activities Committee hearings in Newark, NJ, 1955. (Courtesy of the United Electrical Workers)

For Socrates living example was as important as dialogue, study the complement of civic conduct. Today's commendable pursuit of mass education, coupled with the less estimable commercialization of life, has raised twin dangers of students concerned only with degrees and professors dedicated to the accumulation of publications, and transformed the Socratic ideal into a challenge to scholars.

David Montgomery
History

A collection of images of David speaking with students in his office, near the beginning of his career at the University of Pittsburgh, 1967. Office hours at both Pitt and Yale were nearly always crowded. (From "The Owl" yearbook of the University of Pittsburgh, Class of 1967.) (Courtesy of University of Pittsburgh Archives)

David in a mask playing a boss in "Circuit-Wise," a guerilla theater production in a protest at a class reunion, Yale, 1989. The reunion included Yale graduates who were the president and vice president of a local company, Circuit-Wise, organized by the UE but engaged in a four-year fight over a first contract. (Courtesy of the United Electrical Workers)

A characteristic photo of David, c. 1990. (Courtesy of Yale photographer Mike Marsland)

David standing in the midst of current and former graduate students at a conference celebrating him at Greensburg, PA, June 1993. Included are Steve Sapolsky, Joe White, Claude Montgomery, Peter Gottlieb, David Zonderman, Shel Stromquist, Dale Newman, Rob Ruck, Jenny Barrett, Xian Barrett, and others. (Courtesy of Rachele Lawton and the late Mark McColloch)

David and Martel Montgomery sitting by Lake Geneva, Switzerland, 1998. (Courtesy of Dorothy Fennell)

A portrait of David Montgomery at the time of his retirement from Yale. (Courtesy Yale University)

David and Martel Montgomery with grad students at a celebration for him at Yale (New Haven, June 2006), (clockwise from left) Bruce Laurie, Julie Greene, Kathy Oberdeck, Jim Barrett, Prudence Cumberbatch, Peter Rachleff, Horace Huntley, Shel Stromquist, and Cecelia Bucki. (Courtesy of Cecelia Bucki).

A gathering at the Labor and Working-Class History Association (LAWCHA) conference, Durham, NC, May 2007. David sitting with Mike Honey, Jim Green, and Alice Kessler Harris. (Courtesy of Shel Stromquist)

David speaking at the United Electrical Workers' Convention in 2009. He spoke at the UE's national conventions in 1966, 1973, 1975, and 2009, as well as at various regional and local meetings. (Courtesy of United Electrical Workers Union)

David speaking at a picnic event of the "Working-Class Worlds: Local and Global Perspectives" Conference, Iowa City, July 8, 2011, just a few months before his death in December 2011. (Courtesy of Sharon Wood)

Introduction

David Montgomery was a major architect of the "new labor history" and the broader transformation of American history "from the bottom up." But before his pioneering work as a historian of the working class, he was a trade union militant and political activist. His approach clearly reflected his own experiences on the shopfloor and as a Communist Party rank-and-filer for a time in the 1950s. A skilled machinist; a brilliant researcher, teacher, and writer; a labor and civil rights activist, he had an enormous impact on the past generation of students, activists, and scholars within and well beyond the field of working-class history. His books and articles constitute a vital part of the canon of American working-class history, a field he shaped and redefined from the 1960s until his death in 2011.

Beyond his own impressive scholarship, Montgomery influenced the field of working-class history in myriad ways. Mentoring more than fifty doctoral students, many of whom went on to make their own important scholarly contributions, he generously guided many others as well. He was one of the founding editors of the University of Illinois Press's "Working Class in American History" series, now with more than 160 volumes in print, and for many years, he edited the journal *International Labor and Working-Class History* (*ILWCH*). This editing and mentoring work literally laid the foundations for a pioneering approach to the study of working people in the United States and elsewhere. A practicing internationalist, he cultivated relations among labor historians in many parts of the world and took a comparative approach to the field long before the advent of what might be termed "the global turn." Maintaining his connections with the labor movement, he provided a link between the scholarly field and the men and women who organized and maintained that movement.

This collection of David Montgomery's essays provides a crucial window on the evolution of labor history during an especially creative period in which new ways of understanding the American working class and its history took shape. Montgomery recentered U.S. working-class history on the process of class formation in ways that gave new meaning to the complex nature of class identity in diverse American communities and workplaces. Through these essays and his influential books, he created a set of signposts that helped guide new research in the field toward a richer and deeper picture of a diverse and resilient working class capable of acting in new collective ways in the face of a powerful and a constantly evolving corporate capitalist order. This new approach created intellectual space for historians and other scholars as well as labor activists to affirm a history that did not fold their experience into a consensus understanding of America's past. Responding to critics, Montgomery emphasized the analytical approach that shaped his scholarship.

> The relations of production are the fibers which give coherence to the web of modern social interactions. To treat ethnicity and race as primordial realities and class as an ideological construct (or even as a phantom in the deluded brains of radical intellectuals) is to disguise the patterns of creation and distribution of wealth and power which distinguish our society from other historic configurations and which provide its relentlessly driving force of change. Without a grasp on the ways that class has shaped the actions of men and women in their making of history, we confine the study of social history to the reproduction of everyday patterns of human sustenance and interaction and leave the explanation of social and political change to those who write about policy decisions made by elites.[1]

Montgomery is widely recognized for his path-breaking books that in different ways defined new understandings of the impact of workers' lives and experience on major developments in American history. His first book, *Beyond Equality*, served as a lightning bolt in the field of Reconstruction history. Not only did he refocus attention northward, he shifted our gaze from the "radicals'" emphasis on guaranteeing political and civic equality to what lay "beyond equality," the claims of workers, as "wage-earners for life" and to their demands for a full measure of equality—economic rights, the eight-hour day, and a world they could still imagine, unscarred by the mark of "wage slavery." He did so without diminishing the importance of the radicals' essential fight to protect the civic and political equality of the newly emancipated slaves and African Americans' own claims to economic rights and to the land they had cultivated for generations. This was no mere footnote to Reconstruction historiography. It was an interpretive sea change that set the stage for a broader account of American history in which class and collective action were not marginal but the central theme and in which creating a "republic of labor" based on mutualism not acquisitiveness still seemed within the realm of possibility.

The originality of Montgomery's work was for many best exemplified in his "workers' control" studies. He and others found themselves turning sharply away from the Commons/Perlman "theory of the labor movement" in which skilled workers' job scarcity consciousness and their craft unions represented the "natural" and normal state of American labor. Drawing on his own shop-floor work experience and a close interrogation of nineteenth-century union minute books, contracts, and convention proceedings, Montgomery went to the roots of the world craft workers made and to the rules and standards by which they exercised shop-floor control of the production process. On the one hand, this led him to an ironic appreciation of the detailed work of the Commons school (reinforced by his own sense of craft pride, as a machinist and scholar). But on the other hand, he used that new understanding of the "craftsman's world" to identify outcomes that were quite different from the narrow solidarities and conservative trade unionism that Commons and his students had found normative. For him, the skilled workers' shop-floor control (and the frontal attack on it by "scientific managers") led to conflict, more inclusive solidarities, and the roots of a broader, syndicalist claim to "workers' control."

On the enlarged canvas he created for *The Fall of the House of Labor*, he repositioned his skilled craftsmen within a broader, more diverse working class that included the vast armies of unskilled immigrant and Black workers and factory operatives, both men and women who had come to populate industrial life. The struggles of skilled workers against the aggressive reorganization of work processes by scientific managers—those increasingly ubiquitous men in white coats with clipboards and stop watches—remained for him in many ways the central story. But his field of class vision—what E. P. Thompson once described as a magnetic field of force—now ranged more widely to the "frictions of daily life" in working-class communities, neighborhoods, and within families. It embraced young women garment workers, tenement house family labor producing everything from stogies to lace, the coal mine encounters of old and new immigrant miners, the railroad construction and maintenance crews populated by the newest immigrants—whether Asian or Italian. He reimagined a dynamic world of politics and collective action in which a militant minority on occasion pushed job actions into general strikes and political rebellion toward socialist consciousness. The impressive strikes of World War I and the postwar open shop era may have in their own contradictory ways paved the way for a "fall of the house of labor" as the postwar strikes collapsed in defeat and, in his words, as "becalmed and beleaguered trade unions of the 1920s . . . made their peace with a most undemocratic America." But some elements survived: the promise of wartime solidarities between skilled and unskilled, the memory of their collective actions, and a new consciousness that took up residence in unlikely places—in the ranks, for instance, of his beloved immigrant singing societies and in the sleeper cells of young, industrially conscious activists who covertly joined company unions and waited for their moment to organize anew.

For David, the story was never over. The house of labor had never finally and irreversibly fallen. Short-term defeats carried the seeds of renewed rebellion. Working-class activists of one generation passed on their lessons to the next. The forms of rebellion may never have been the same. The imprint of changed historical circumstances and new structural constraints would always shape new forms of struggle. But the notion that workers would acquiesce or that rebellion against the newest and most constraining forms of inequality would somehow become impossible was for Montgomery unimaginable and flew in the face of the detailed historical record of workers' self-activity he painstakingly reconstructed.

His accounting for that historical dynamic is ultimately his most enduring legacy—for his own students and for the social movements that followed. The emergence of the "occupy" movement in the very last months of his life, the ways in which it seized the political moment, embraced the rights of workers, and suddenly changed the terms of debate about inequality and democracy in America may have surprised some.[2] But, not David, we suspect.

As he reminded us in *The Fall of the House of Labor:*

> The history of American workers has not been a story of progressive ascent from oppression to securely established rights, nor has it offered us a past moment of democratic promise that was irretrievably snuffed out by the consolidation of modern capitalism. Their movement has grown only sporadically and through fierce struggles, been interrupted time and again just when it seemed to reach flood tide, overwhelmed its foes only to see them revive in new and more formidable shapes, and been forced to reassess what it thought it had already accomplished and begin again. The taproot of its resilience has been the workers' daily experience and the solidarities nurtured by that experience which have at best encompassed a lush variety of beliefs, loyalties, and activities within a common commitment to democratic direction of the country's economic and political life.[3]

In *Citizen Worker*, the volume based on his Tanner lectures at Oxford, Montgomery probed the tensions between law, popular democratic practices, and working-class self-activity on the one hand and the exigencies of the market system as it evolved, on the other. Enjoying both a wider franchise and greater civil liberties than in other capitalist countries, American workers, he argues, "obstructed bourgeois control of American life at every turn." Writing amid a discourse of neo-liberalism and libertarianism in the early 1990s,

Montgomery observed that "no two phrases come coupled more often than 'democracy' and 'a market economy.'"[4] Yet, drawing on critical legal theory, he argued the two were often at odds in the evolving American republic. The resulting study is sweeping in its scope. This tension between democratic values and those dictated by the market drove changes in vagrancy and other criminal laws, race relations, policing practices, poor relief, and political party ideologies.

The Essays

Over the course of his career, David Montgomery was an extraordinarily productive essayist. These essays, although widely read and influential at the time of their publication, have receded a bit from the prominent place they once occupied in the general awareness of his work. Their scope is remarkably wide-ranging. They sketched wider frontiers and signaled new directions that others would explore. They have a freshness and originality that reflect some of his most creative work, and, taken together, they provide valuable insights into the trajectory of labor history as a field of research in the United States.

The enduring importance of these essays lies not primarily in the historiographical context from which they sprang, but in their approach, broadly conceived, to understanding the history of workers and the persistence of class. They provide a framework for capturing the ebb and flow of social conflict in the United States. First, Montgomery understood from his own experience and from careful historical analysis that the experience of class formed an irreducible substratum of society but also a rich reservoir of ideas and strategies from which workers built and rebuilt movements to claim their democratic rights in the workplace and the community. Montgomery recognized that neither victories nor defeats were ever permanent, and "no historical resolution of the conflict between wage labor and capital . . . has enjoyed a permanent lease on life."[5] Second, he fully grasped the power of capital to shape and manage the contours of economic life and the state as enduring facts of life in the United States and around the globe. As he observed about his own work, "although my specialty is working-class history, the subject I am trying to get at is the history of capitalism."[6] In these essays and in his major monographs, he offered a new history of capitalism in which workers—enslaved and free, people of color and white, male and female—however coerced they may have been, remained in some fashion agents of their own lives and destinies, constructing solidarities from below, and playing a role, at times decisive, in shaping politics and economic institutions far beyond the local worlds in which they most often acted. Third, Montgomery's methods were grounded fundamentally in close attention to the intimate social relations of production and of community, neighborhood, and family life. If, as he wrote, "class conflict was the submerged shoal" in American life, its reality had to be documented "in the industrial towns of America, rather than in congressional debates." He sought then to find "the national patterns embedded in a mosaic of local histories."[7] While Marxism infused a general framework in his scholarship, it was in the gritty empiricism of local study that his work came to life. These essays represent in many ways the experimental forays of a historian sifting new evidence for the larger meanings it might offer. If he advanced "grand" generalizations, they were never unqualified or without contradiction.

This volume brings together many of Montgomery's most significant published articles with other essays and papers that have remained unpublished or appeared only in more obscure places. The unpublished essays sometimes convey bolder formulations than he allowed himself in the published work and, in this way, are particularly provocative. The collection focuses on the evolution of Montgomery's scholarly work over five decades, revealing the emergence of a distinctly powerful voice and approach. But the collection also includes some of his more explicitly political essays and unpublished lectures, gesturing to his important role as a labor intellectual and activist throughout these years. Four broad themes emerge from the essays: Working-Class Formation; The Social Relations of Production; The Diversity of the Working-Class Experience; and The Pervasiveness of Class.

Working-Class Formation

Following publication of *Beyond Equality*, Montgomery turned his attention to class formation in the early phases of industrialization in the United States. Like many, he was inspired by his association with E. P. Thompson at the University of Warwick, where he joined seminars in U.S., British, and comparative working-class history. He was influenced by James Hinton's research on the Shop Stewards' Movement and workers' control issues, by Thompson's work on the English crowd and work discipline, and by his students' research.[8] On the strength of this experience, Montgomery published a series of essays that grappled with the distinctive features of industrialization in the American context. His essay, "The Working Classes of the Pre-Industrial American City, 1780–1830," described the contours of a remarkably fluid capitalist marketplace in which the social relations of production were evolving and in which the boundaries between rural and urban worlds were fast dissolving with the appearance of new forms of production in both city and countryside.[9] Another essay, also republished here, provided a U.S. counterpoint to the story of class formation in England, in which cultural clashes between Catholics and Protestants, Irish and native-born, "fragmented the working class as a political force in ante-bellum Philadelphia and thereby created for historians the illusion of a society lacking in class conflict."[10] Unmasking that "illusion" became a major focus of his scholarship going forward. These and several other essays examine the cultural contours of the American working class before the Civil War and the boundaries between enslaved and wage labor.[11]

The Social Relations of Production

Montgomery brought to the study of work extraordinary insight into the culture and social power of skilled workers. This research involved the intimate reconstruction of the work rules by which skilled machinists enforced their own standards and ethical norms on the shopfloor. The emphasis on work was not entirely new. The first generation of labor historians, John R. Commons and Selig Perlman in particular, identified what Perlman called "scarcity consciousness," by which skilled workers defended their job territories, as the defining feature of the American labor movement. But Montgomery turned this concept on its head to emphasize the fundamentally collectivist nature of that trade union practice. Their codes of mutualistic behavior, their work rules, their sense of self-respect, and even the propriety and the festivity of their grand balls, evidenced forms of workers' control based on their power to set and enforce the rules. David Brody argued for continuity between Perlman's interpretation and Montgomery's, in effect between the Wisconsin School and what the historian Alan Dawley termed the "Pittsburgh School."[12] Montgomery did refocus attention on the world of work, however, he did so in ways that were fundamentally at odds with the conservative implications of Commons' and Perlman's conception of trade union practice.

The pivotal essay in which Montgomery reconceptualized the power and claims of skilled workers under assault from organized capital was a meticulous reconstruction of the work culture of nineteenth-century machinists.[13] But foreshadowing this carefully rendered case study of "workers' control" was an unpublished essay, a first draft of which he circulated in 1969 from England, in which he allowed himself to link traditions of skilled workers' control to a more expansive syndicalism—"the idea of direct workers' control of industry . . . through the union" as "a simple, logical extension of their daily trade union practice." He gave the idea a revolutionary twist by linking trade union "self-government" to the erosion of the power of capital and the idea of a "cooperative commonwealth" as a "world governed by union meetings." If the essay extended his argument further into a territory he was not prepared to fully defend, it nonetheless suggested more pointedly than his published work the potential "universal brotherhood of labor" with which on occasion skilled workers might align themselves.[14] Refinements but also complications of this argument may be found in a whole series of essays, including several in this collection. In "Labor and the Republic in Industrial America, 1860–1920," he sought to give fiber and substance to an evolving "house of labor" contending with the growing power of capital in the late nineteenth century and the early years of the new century. In the process he signaled the importance of labor historians' renewed attention to the Knights of Labor. But, poignantly he also conceptualized the sea changes underway in those *fin de siècle* decades. He argued that "class conflict had not subsided since the 1890s" nor had the working class "been won over to . . . the New Nationalism."

> It was the moral universality of the working class that had been ruptured, not its militancy. No single set of values, no commonly accepted vision of the redemption of the republic, any longer guided the many streams of working-class struggle into a single-minded flood of protest.[15]

The Diversity of the Working-Class Experience: Race, Gender, and Ethnicity

History yielded no "typical" working-class experience for Montgomery. It seemed vital to document the great diversity of this story in all aspects of life, and then to see how these diverse experiences related to broader narratives. His determination to document the complexity of working-class life is displayed most dramatically in the first three chapters of *The Fall of the House of Labor*, where he analyzed the work life and mentalities of skilled workers, common laborers, and factory operatives. This detailed examination of the workplace and community lent to his approach the "gritty" quality that many readers have observed and the "pointillist" methodology that he affirmed.[16]

The connections in his work between race, ethnicity, and other forms of social difference have not always been recognized, but they have been at the center of his scholarship from the outset. Such social differences could create divisions and even conflict, as they did in Philadelphia during early industrialization, and they certainly shaped the character of the labor movement in the United States throughout its history. Montgomery's deep awareness of race and racism as fundamental realities of American life and working-class experience are embedded in his work, from his early investigations of working-class cultural conflicts in the antebellum period to his documentation of the limits of Reconstruction, the racialization of immigrants, and the imperial reshuffling of class and race identities within the enduring project of capitalist global expansion.[17]

Montgomery's work often appears to neglect gendered interpretations of working-class experience. Yet, his early essays explicitly treat gender as a constitutive element in class identity. The distinctive worlds of male and female labor are compellingly delineated in "pre-industrial" manufacturing garrets of American cities, in cotton mill towns, and the familial divisions of labor. In his major work, *The Fall of the House of Labor*, gendered working-class identities emerge most clearly in the early chapters dealing with skilled metal trades workers, common laborers, and factory operatives, with discussions of women's experience figuring most prominently in the last of these. Reading in women's history helped him to develop his more expansive notion of class. "The work of feminist scholars, indeed the whole corpus of recent work on women's history, has been of central importance in getting me to think about what else is involved in class beyond the relations of production," Montgomery told interviewers in 1981. "If all we see is what's going on in the workplace, we are going to miss a great deal."[18]

The Pervasiveness of Class

Despite the obvious importance of the workplace in his research, the defining thrust of Montgomery's influence extended far more broadly in these essays and in his students' work. For Montgomery, the social relations of production may have been central, but class experience goes well beyond that. "Although the modern experience of class had its origin in the encounter with wage labor," he writes, "class consciousness permeated social discourse outside the workplace as well as within it. Married women caring for their children in bleak congested neighborhoods . . . were reminded of their class as regularly as their husbands, daughters, and sons in the factories. Children learned early the differences between their parents' attire, bearing, and patterns of speech and those of the gentlemen and ladies who seemed to move with such grace and ease through the corridors of power and the emporiums of abundance."[19]

For Montgomery, as the editors of *Labor Histories*, a collection of essays published in his honor, noted, "Class pervades all aspects of social experience—family and gender relations, neighborhood politics, race relations, and associational life; it infuses the realms of production and consumption, the work experience, family and community life, politics, social life, ideology, and culture in all its forms. Class and class consciousness in turn bear the imprint of the social relations of the workplace, the character of state policy, and gender, race, ethnicity, and region."[20] It is not simply the study of work but rather this capacious understanding of the diversity of class experience that may constitute Montgomery's most important and durable legacy to the field of labor history.[21]

Labor activists of all stripes animate Montgomery's evocation of this working-class milieu and play a central role in shaping historical change. He stressed that "class consciousness was more than the unmediated product of daily experience." It was a "project," and the key figures in this story are the "militant minority," those socialists, syndicalists, and union "progressives" in the early twentieth century and beyond who sought to "weld their work mates and neighbors into a self-aware and purposeful working class."[22] The significance of these activists had been obscured, Montgomery believed, as much by "history from the bottom up" as by any "fixation on great leaders." Though clearly fascinated with the rank-and-file movements and the strike wave of the 1970s, he was more skeptical of the notion that working-class militancy arose spontaneously from the daily experience of work and other aspects of working-class life. While he was certainly influenced by the labor activism he saw around him, he emphasized the role of a "militant minority" on the shop floor and in the neighborhood, perhaps a reflection of his own experiences as a Communist union militant in the postwar era.

Montgomery's determination to place workers at the center of US history led him to integrate his rich evocation of working-class life into a broader political context. His juxtaposition of common peoples' experiences with the sweeping social, economic, and political changes that remake societies and the struggle to define the causal relationship between these experiences and those changes—lends his work a compelling quality. No one who has read Montgomery's work or heard him construct such a narrative is likely to soon forget it.

Montgomery's final essays, represented here by "Empire, Race, and Working-Class Mobilizations" and "Workers' Movements in the United States Confront Imperialism: The Progressive Era Experience," are in some ways his most ambitious, prefiguring the "global turn" in some of the most recent writing in the field. Working within a Marxist framework, Montgomery's approach has always been transnational. One legacy of his Warwick years was a lasting involvement with the Social History Roundtable, which connected him to a range of European and American colleagues, including Joan Scott, Charles Tilly, Dorothy and Edward Thompson, Eric Hobsbawm, and Michelle Perrot. These discussions were explicitly comparative in nature.[23] Having projected working-class life onto the broad canvas of the evolving American nation state, he now demonstrated that workers were far more than cogs in the American and other empires. Their labor and activism shaped capitalism as it entered a new phase in its development and extended its reach around the world. As Julie Greene notes, "his intellectual vision was always shaped profoundly by the notion that global capitalism was the central context through which workers struggled, lived, resisted, and sometimes rebelled . . . in his later work he turned sharply toward a more rigorous exploration of global labor history and the ways that empire and global capitalism intersected with US labor and working-class history."[24]

For Montgomery, as for many who were inspired by his work, the past is also present. The crucible of workplace activism and political engagement that shaped his scholarship in the beginning continued to animate his work throughout his career. He spoke regularly to union conventions, especially the United Electrical Workers of America (UE); he organized picket line support for miners; and he was an outspoken public advocate for dining hall workers, clerical and technical workers, and teaching assistants in their organizing campaigns and their strikes at Yale. He was a regular commentator on developments in the labor movement. A few of those pieces are included here—some previously published, others now for the first time.[25]

David Montgomery's legacy, then, represents much more than the evolution of a remarkably rich research field. His work opened a new vantage point, from the bottom up, on American history writ large, illuminating in profoundly new ways aspects of industry and economy, law and politics, immigration and race relations, and the democratic traditions of the United States. These essays, along with his books, guided a generation of scholars to carry forward his insights into new territories, and they continue to provide such inspiration. In the process, his critical perspective on this history raised fundamental questions about the class nature of life in America. For him the challenge was always to look with a critical eye at "the propelling forces of historical change" and "to make the dynamics of our movement public knowledge once again."[26] In his view, rigorous historical analysis could never be divorced from engagement with the working class. As he said, "it's got to be shared with them." This was for him both a "personal commitment" and "crucial to any organized form of activity." Engaged scholarship "keeps us committed to our neighbors, to our fellow working people, and to others around the world in working-class struggles,"[27] and it is they who ultimately drive forward the promise of social and political transformation.

Notes

1. David Montgomery, "Class, Capitalism, and Contentment," *Labor History* 30, no. 1 (Winter 1989): 137.

2. Todd Gitlin, *Occupy Nation: The Roots, the Spirit, and the Promise of Occupy* (New York: IT Books, 2012).

3. David Montgomery, *The Fall of the House of Labor: the Workplace, the State, and American Labor Activism, 1865–1925* (New York: Cambridge University Press, 1987), 7–8.

4. David Montgomery, *Citizen Worker: The Experience of Workers in the United States with Democracy and the Free Market during the Nineteenth Century* (New York: Cambridge University Press, 1993), quotes on 6, 11.

5. Montgomery, *The Fall of the House of Labor*, 464.

6. "David Montgomery Interview," in MARHO, *Visions of History*, ed. Henry Abelove, et al. (New York: Pantheon, 1983), 176.

7. David Montgomery, *Beyond Equality: Labor and the Radical Republicans, 1862–1872* (Urbana: University of Illinois Press, 1967), x.

8. James Hinton, *The First Shop Stewards' Movement* (London: G. Allen & Unwin, 1973); E. P. Thompson, "The Moral Economy of the English Crowd in

the Eighteenth Century," *Past and Present*, no. 50 (1971): 76–136; E. P. Thompson, "Time, Work Discipline, and Industrial Capitalism," *Past & Present*, no. 38 (1967): 56–97; James R. Barrett, "Class Act: An Interview with David Montgomery," *Labor: Studies in Working-Class History of the Americas* 1, no. 1 (2004): 38–40.

9. David Montgomery, "The Working Classes of the Pre-industrial American City, 1780–1830," *Labor History* 9 (Winter 1968): 3–22.

10. David Montgomery, "The Shuttle and the Cross: Weavers and Artisans in the Kensington Riots of 1844," *Journal of Social History* 5 (Summer 1972): 411–46.

11. See in particular, David Montgomery, "Social Attitudes of American workers in the 1840s," (previously unpublished) and "Wage Labor, Bondage, and Citizenship in Nineteenth-Century America," *International Labor and Working-Class History (ILWCH)*, 48 (Fall 1995): 6–27.

12. David Brody, "Reconciling the Old Labor History and the New," *Pacific Historical Review*, 62 (February 1993): 14–15; Alan Dawley, "The Worker's Brain Under the Historian's Cap," *Radical History Review*, 40 (January 1988): 101–14.

13. David Montgomery, "Workers' Control of Machine Production in the Nineteenth-Century," *Labor History* 17 (Fall 1976): 485–509.

14. David Montgomery, "Trade Union Practice and the Origins of Syndicalist Theory," previously unpublished essay, included in this collection, see below. Jim Green recalled that Montgomery sent him a version of this paper from England in 1969, where he had first delivered it. James R. Green, "David Montgomery, Scholar," OAH Plenary Session, "David Montgomery—Labor Historian, Activist, Teacher, Mentor," OAH Annual Meeting, Milwaukee, WI, April 20, 2012, http://www.lawcha.org/2015/08/30/david-montgomery-1927–2011/

15. Quotation from David Montgomery, "Labor and the Republic in Industrial America, 1860–1920," *Le Mouvement Social* 111 (April–June 1980): 211; also, David Montgomery, "Strikes in Nineteenth-Century America," *Social Science History* 4 (Winter 1980): 81–104; David Montgomery, "The 'New Unionism' and the Transformation of Workers' Consciousness in America, 1909–22," *Journal of Social History* 7, no. 4 (Summer 1974): 510–29.

16. Barrett, "Class Act," 49.

17. See the essays in this collection that grapple with the intersections of race, class, and imperialism. David Montgomery, "Wage Labor, Bondage, and Citizenship in Nineteenth Century America," *International Labor and Working Class History* 48 (Fall 1995): 6–27; David Montgomery, "Racism, Immigrants, and Political Reform," *Journal of American History* 87 (March 2001): 1253–74; David Montgomery, "Empire, Race, and Working-Class Mobilizations," in *Racializing Class, Classifying Race: Labour and Difference in Britain, the USA and Africa*, eds. Peter Alexander and Rick Halpern (London: Palgrave Macmillan, 1999).

18. MARHO, "David Montgomery interview," 177.

19. Montgomery, *The Fall of the House of Labor*, 1–2.

20. *Labor Histories: Class, Politics, and the Working Class Experience*, eds. Eric Arnesen, Julie Greene, Bruce Laurie (Urbana: University of Illinois Press, 1998).

21. Shelton Stromquist, "David Montgomery: A Labor Historian's Legacies," *The Journal of the Gilded Age and Progressive Era* 13, no. 2 (April 2014): 258, 276.

22. Montgomery, *The Fall of the House of Labor*, 2.

23. Barrett, "Class Act," 37–38.

24. On the global turn in working class history, see Marcel Van der Linden, "The 'Globalization' of Labor and Working-Class History and Its Consequences" and the responses, *International Labor and Working Class History* 65 (April 2004): 136–56; and on this aspect of Montgomery's work, Julie Greene, "The Global Montgomery: Assessing the Place of the World in David Montgomery's Historical Writing," *Labor: Studies in Working Class History of the Americas* 10, no. 1 (March 2013): 57–63, quote, 57.

25. David Montgomery, "What's Happening to the American Worker," *Radical America* pamphlet, Madison, Wisconsin, 1970; David Montgomery, "Yesterday's Wisdom: Changing Situations and New Initiatives in the American Labor Movement," unpub. mss 1990; David Montgomery, "Working Peoples' Response to Past Depressions," *Workers in Hard Times: a Long View of Economic Crises*, eds. Leon Fink, Joseph A. McCartin, and Joan Sangster (Urbana: University of Illinois Press, 2014).

26. MARHO, "David Montgomery Interview," 180.

27. Quoted in Shelton Stromquist, "Labor Historians and Traditions of Engaged Scholarship: Progressives, Insurgents, and the Making of a New Labor History," 11, and David Montgomery, "Epilogue: Carry It On! Creative Research and Social Action," 270, in *Civic Labors: Scholar Activism and Working Class Studies*, eds. Dennis Deslippe, Eric Fure-Slocum, and John W. McKerley, (Urbana: University of Illinois Press, 2016).

PART I

Writing the People's History

David Montgomery's first venture into writing about the history of the working class, was, by his own account, part of a collective effort to tell a people's history of Minnesota on the occasion of the state's centennial.[1] It was a history, not surprisingly, that the Chamber of Commerce had chosen to ignore. As he recalled, the group of contributors gathered together by Meridel LeSueur did not see themselves writing a history "for the working people. We *were* the working people of Minnesota writing about ourselves."[2]

At the time, Montgomery was a rank-and-file activist working as a machinist at the Honeywell Corporation in Minneapolis. He was on the rebound from membership in the Communist Party that he had come to feel was increasingly out of touch with the working class. Still vulnerable to the blacklist, he contributed to *The People Together: One Hundred Years of Minnesota, 1858–1958* under the pseudonym Amos Flaherty, and he focused on one of the high points in Minnesota labor history, "The Great Northern Strike of 1894: When Gene Debs Beat Jim Hill." By all accounts his first published piece of labor history, Montgomery's essay brought to life in vivid narrative prose a key moment of victory in the rise of the American Railway Union that set the stage for the massive Pullman boycott and general railway strike that would ensue a little more than a month later.

For David Montgomery, the path to becoming a historian was not foreordained. He loved the camaraderie of his factory work, where "the sense that an injury to one was an injury to all ran through the whole department." But blacklisted by 1960, he turned to graduate work in history. "Becoming a historian was *not* my first choice. I had to do something, so I took the second-best choice that was around then."[3]

Cover of *The People Together* (Minneapolis: The People's Centennial Book Committee, 1958).

Notes

1. Meridel LeSueur, ed., *The People Together: A Century Speaks* (Minneapolis: The People's Centennial Book Committee, 1958).
2. "David Montgomery Interview," in MARHO, *Visions of History*, ed. Henry Abelove, et al. (New York: Pantheon, 1983), 176.
3. Ibid., 175–76.

CHAPTER 1

The Great Northern Strike of 1894

When Gene Debs Beat Jim Hill

From *The People Together: A Century Speaks* (Minneapolis: The People's Centennial Book Committee, 1958), written under the pseudonym Amos Flaherty.

Spring 1894 was brutal for the people of Minnesota, as it was for the nation.

Layoffs came, and one round of wage cuts after another. Bankruptcy was the order of the day among farmers and small businessmen. Only the great nationwide trusts grew.

Here in the Northwest a new kind of empire was being erected, based on wheat, and tied together by steel track. In 1879, James J. Hill had taken over and expanded the St. Paul, Minneapolis and Manitoba line. With the strategy of a general waging a campaign, as soon as he completed a stretch of track he consolidated his rear by bringing in farmers, livestock, and seed. As one railroad after another folded in the depression, Hill was ready. He and J. P. Morgan of the First National Bank bought out their rivals until the whole Northwest lay at their feet. The great wealth of a veritable empire flowed out over the railroads Hill owned, and the monarch "Empire Builder" exacted his tribute from every bushel of wheat and ton of cargo.

Great Northern net income had zoomed to over five million dollars, or 43% of gross earnings in 1893, up $700,000 from the previous year. For 1894 the rate of profit was 40%. In January, 1894, Great Northern slashed wages for the second time, and in March announced a third round of cuts, a total slash of from 6% to 33%.

What could the railroad workers do? Another cut was unthinkable, yet to fight meant a strike, and never had the railroad workers beaten a major line in a strike!

Great Northern strikers receiving coffee and bread at Blackfeet Reservation in Montana.

Organized railroad men were in separate and warring Brotherhoods. An effort led by Eugene V. Debs to unite the Brotherhoods into a Supreme Council had been defeated, as had been his attempt at unity during the firemen's year-long strike on the Burlington. Debs, then Secretary of the Firemen's Brotherhood and editor of the *Locomotive Fireman's Magazine*, had brought his own Brotherhood from imminent ruin to considerable strength. He had helped organize several other crafts in cities and towns throughout the country. Now he saw these organizations being either broken in strikes or meekly accepting wage cuts.

Out of these experiences, an answer began to emerge—the bold and new concept of industrial union organization.

Thus in June of 1893 a national convention to found the American Railway Union was called by Debs, Howard of the Conductors, Kelliher of the Carmen, and Rogers of the Trainmen. Their object: to bring all railroad workers, skilled and unskilled, together in one body to face the companies.

Railroad workers flocked to join individually, and in entire lodges of the Brotherhoods. Within a year there were 150,000 members; the previous total membership of all the Brotherhoods was only 90,000. By March, 1894, the union estimated that on the Great Northern 80% of the workers east of Minot and 90% of those west had signed up.

At this point, Hill ordered the third round of wage cuts, already approved by the Brotherhood leaders, to take effect on April 11. Hill began to round up unemployed workers to take the places of those he feared might strike.

Emboldened by the success of the ARU in blocking a wage cut on the Union Pacific by negotiations and without a strike, the Great Northern workers were ready for action. Switchmen in Helena struck on their own, and in one day won their demands.

In the West the men were in no mood to wait until they were fired and replaced by scabs or to let the company make the first move. On April 14 they walked out demanding the wages prior to the first cut be restored.

Within a day the strike was solid from Larimore, N. D. to Spokane.

"Not a wheel is turning on the Great Northern system," said the *Tribune*, perhaps with unconscious irony, "the new men, who were expected to take the places of the strikers, are sidetracked at Devil's Lake."

The strike swept east. At every point the union rallied local unions, farmers, and businessmen—all subjects of J. J. Hill—to its support. Mass meetings were addressed not only by union officers, but by mayors and businessmen. Owners of boarding houses signed pledges not to feed scabs. By April 16 traffic was stopped at Fargo. On the 17th, 1,000 men stopped two passenger trains at St. Cloud. The same day Breckenridge was closed up, as well as Willmar.

The ring was closing on the Twin Cities. There the yards were active and trains moved out. The ARU locals in St. Paul and Minneapolis had scarcely 400 members. The locals held enthusiastic meetings and voted to strike; but they did not go out. Vice President Howard explained that, "As long as the men remain on duty in the Twin Cities there is no chance to put any scabs at work here and they can't be used to much advantage west of here."

Excitement in the St. Paul yards was intense. With traffic slow and work slack men stood in groups arguing the big question: how to win unity with the men who remained loyal to the Brotherhoods?

On April 19 a second problem was added. The company countered with a court injunction against "strikers and all other persons from interfering, by force or threats or intimidation, with the business of the company, or with its property or employees."

Federal marshals went out to every point along the line to read the order. The issue came to a head in St. Cloud where 20 armed marshals came with the order. Their train was stopped and President Foster of the local union advised his members not to be alarmed. "Use no violence and we shall not be molested. Their injunction is not a warrant for arrest."

Although Foster and the local leaders were arrested, no train moved. Their example spread. Several days later in Willmar 500 strikers stopped a train armed with marshals. The *Pioneer Press* reported the incident in this way:

"Marshall Bede addressed the strikers again warning them of what they are doing, telling them the courts are incorruptable and that 'Thank God the courts and our women are still virtuous.' He managed to work the men into good humor but that counts for nothing, as the strikers are determined to stop traffic and they have succeeded . . . At this hour Bede, his deputies,

Eugene V. Debs

and your correspondent are helpless in the town of Willmar and don't know when they will get out. . . . The place bears the appearance of a holiday, and all the women and children are on the streets joining in the general uproar."

So died the injunction. Order was maintained at all points.

The problem of unity with the Brotherhoods was far more knotty. In the Twin Cities the large Brotherhood membership was reluctant to throw over its old organizations even though they had all negotiated contracts accepting the wage cuts.

At the outset, Hill had counted on the Brotherhood leaders for help in controlling their members. Brotherhood men who sympathized with the strike even feared expulsion from their unions. The position of the Brotherhoods was, however, extremely weak. Only two had put the new contract to a vote of their membership. Both had been voted down. The demands of the ARU were clearly the demands of a majority of Brotherhood members.

It was perhaps on this point that the personal contribution of Debs was the greatest. For almost a week Debs was in the Twin Cities, but spoke at no meetings. Instead he was seen visiting one officer or leader of the local Brotherhoods after another, many old friends. On the 18th he had a conference with Arthur and Sargent, national heads of the engineers and firemen.

On the same day the Brotherhood leaders in a meeting with Hill refused to take part in organizing strike-breaking. They agreed only to keep their own members at work.

The next day Debs made his first speech in St. Paul at Labor Hall, calling for the unity of all labor and an independent political party, and pointing out that the Chicago-Great Western had just rescinded a 10% wage cut on its line as a result of this strike.' At the meeting 300 new members joined and a call for strike was again voted.

Debs declared to the press on April 20 that wages, not recognition of the ARU, was the strike issue. The Brotherhoods responded with a joint declaration that they would not work with scabs.

At this point Hill sent his aide Sam Hill to see Governor Knute Nelson. According to Sam Hill, he asked for arbitration by three Minneapolis businessmen, since he trusted no one in St. Paul. Nelson sent a letter to Debs asking for such a meeting and called the union leader to his office where he denounced the strike leader as an "agitator stirring up strife among peaceful and contented workingmen." Debs replied, "You can't bluff me. I can see clear through you and your game. You wear Jim Hill's collar. I don't. You are acting under his orders. I am here to fight him. I absolutely refuse to order the strikers back to work."

A meeting between the ARU committee and the company was finally agreed to for April 25. A thunderous rally in St. Paul the day before rejected the Governor's demand to go back to work and arbitrate.

Debs was ready to meet Hill.

It was eleven days after the strike had begun that the first negotiating session was held. A committee of 33 men from the ARU, including Debs, Howard, and Rogers, met with representatives from the company. Despite the injunction, all lines were closed from St. Cloud and Willmar west. In the Twin Cities the men had declared their readiness to strike and the Brotherhoods moved to a position of support.

After the initial sparring the session settled into a two-man show. Debs and Hill faced each other, each armed with a thoroughly detailed knowledge of every question at hand, and each determined in his stand. To complete the picture, the meeting was open to the press. The union demanded restoration of the 1893 wage schedule, switchmen in Great Falls and Helena to receive the same pay as those in Butte, management to sign the schedules, in any future cut-backs hours to be reduced before men are laid off, and no prejudice against any strikers.

Hill countered by insisting that the ARU did not represent the men, rejecting Debs' offer of a vote. He held that he had contracts with the Brotherhoods, but would meet with any group of men, including the ARU, to discuss grievances after the men had gone back to work.

When the meeting broke up on these stands Hill gave the union a written proposal for arbitration with the Brotherhoods present after the men had returned to work. Debs rejected it declaring, "Efforts have been made ever since this trouble started to divide the organization and make trouble between the Union and the Brotherhoods. I understand such to be the policy of the company . . . My idea is that in raising the question of representation you have sought to evade the issue."

His stand was underscored by Young of the Switchmen who summarized the situation thus: "The A. R. U. is not representing all the employees, but its officers are assisting them. That is all."

"The Fight Between the Railroad and the Union is on!" declared the *Pioneer Press* the next day. On the front page it blasted the union for "having refused the fairest and most generous proposition ever offered by a railroad president" to dissatisfied employees. It called on the men to return to work and claimed, "The company has shaken itself free from the conflict which must now be waged between the labor organizations alone."

At noon all ARU members on the Great Northern were called out. Traffic in the Twin Cities came to a halt. So complete was the stoppage of yardmen in St. Paul that no other lines moved. The St. Paul Trades and Labor Assembly passed a resolution denouncing Hill and calling for all possible aid to the strikers.

On the next day, Saturday, Mayor Eustis of Minneapolis called a meeting of 125 representatives from the commercial clubs of St. Paul and Minneapolis. The business interests of Minneapolis, especially the millers, were no longer in full harmony with Hill. Having lost contact with the wheat areas for 16 days their main interest was to end the strike. They backed Hill as long as it seemed that the strike might be broken. At this time they and Mayor Eustis began to work hard for a settlement. Debs was invited to speak at the meeting and with great diplomacy he presented the case of the strikers.

Hill had but two weapons remaining, a public campaign to make the union agree to return to work and arbitrate, spearheaded by the *Pioneer Press*, and second, a last effort to break the hard-won unity with the Brotherhoods. To do this he called in representatives Nolan and Uptergrove of the engineers and firemen and restored their former wages on the ground that the scheduled reduction for the Trainmen had never actually gone into effect, so they should not be made to suffer.

Although Nolan stated that he had not asked for this action, they signed an agreement to this effect. The agreement was denounced at a mass ARU rally in Minneapolis as traitorous to the movement, and St. Paul Brotherhood men voted to continue the strike until the demands of all classes were met.

At the same meeting Mayor Eustis pleaded for arbitration. He was greeted with applause, complimented the men, and compared Debs and Howard to Grant and Sheridan. But arbitration on the company's terms was voted down.

The company was now frustrated on all sides. Debs offered to negotiate in the presence of a board from the commercial club of Minneapolis who could act as mediators. Hill rejected the proposal as impractical. The next day, May 1, just such a meeting took place.

At the outset Hill stated that the reductions for all the Brotherhoods were rescinded. He then agreed that since this was the normal time of year for posting wage rates for laborers, the rates to be posted were $1.25 a day east of Minot and $1.50 west of there, agreeing thereby to the union's demand. These groups comprised 19 out of 20 of the Great Northern workers.

For other grades the board awarded: "90% of the differences in wages in controversy were amicably settled between the company and its employees . . . 75 percent of the reduction in wages made since Aug. 1, 1893 of all classes of men whose claims were submitted to us should be restored."

Signed: Chas. Pillsbury (Chm.) . . .

On May 1, 1894, more than 1500 men returned to work on the Great Northern system. The trains would roll again as usual. But Minnesota could never be the same again. The workers had *won for themselves a total of $146,000 a month more in wages*. They had defeated a major railroad in a strike for the first time in our history!

The ARU was not to accomplish its mission of industrial unionism. Scarcely eight days after the Great Northern victory it became locked in its mortal combat with the Pullman Company. All the forces of reaction were thrown at the union, Debs jailed, and the union stamped out in the industry. Refusing to die, the ARU reorganized itself into a political party, the Social Democracy of America, later to become the Socialist Party.

Beyond this, the strikers brought the idea of farmer-labor unity beyond a mere dream. They had actually beaten the common enemy. They had pointed the path followed by all labor in the 1930s, and had produced the future leaders and workers for Minnesota's great contribution to America, farmer-labor political unity.

As for Debs, he spoke for himself when he returned home to Terre Haute:

"My glory, my friends, consists in the gladness which I know will be brought into the little cottage homes of the humble trackmen among the hills in the West . . . In all my life I have never felt so highly honored as I did when leaving

St. Paul on my way home. As our train pulled out of the yards the token of esteem, which I prize far more highly than all the others, was in seeing the old trackmen, men whose frames were bent with years of grinding toil, who receive the pittance of from 80¢ to $1 a day, leaning on their shovels and lifting their hats to me in appreciation of my humble assistance."

PART II

Working-Class Formation

Early in his academic career, David Montgomery evidenced a deep interest in workers' self-activity but also the institutional and cultural barriers to working-class formation that marked the American experience. These themes would shape his scholarship going forward. Drawing on his own political and trade union work in the 1950s and on the opportunity to develop a comparative perspective that came with his two-year (1967–69) sojourn in England as a colleague of E. P. Thompson at Warwick University, Montgomery turned his attention to the experience of early industrialization in the American context. After publication of *Beyond Equality*, he had accepted a position as a visiting lecturer in Thompson's program on "social and labor history" and imbibed deeply a new cultural approach to working-class formation that carried Thompson's imprint. Over the next several years, much of his research and teaching engaged the problems of American working-class formation in the early phases of industrialization. While the comparisons with Thompson's work on England were rarely explicit, the implications were obvious.

In an essay published while he taught at Warwick, Montgomery explored the social landscape of the pre-industrial city in the United States and the distinctive experience of its working classes (plural) in shifting and unstable labor markets where old norms and expectations were constantly being called into question. Early American cities became magnets for half-trained migrants from the countryside, skilled immigrant craftsmen, ex-slaves, itinerant laborers, and a new factory labor force of women and children. These urban spaces had a polyglot and unstable quality that offered opportunity for craftsmen while foreshadowing dilution, wage instability, and attacks on their trade unions which employers saw as "conspiracies." Montgomery noted that American historians "have yet to probe the culture of the American mechanic," as Thompson had done "for his British counterparts." And he suggested that "we have rushed ahead to evaluate labor's response to industrialism without first ascertaining labor's pre-industrial behavior and attitudes."[1]

It was precisely to an examination of "the cultural and intellectual life of the working classes of this period" to which he turned his attention.[2] All three of the other essays in this section mark off in specific ways the distinctive American experience of class formation in the first half of the nineteenth century. An unpublished essay, very likely a conference paper, explored the "social attitudes of American workers in the 1840s" and examined the widening gap between a middle-class ideology of the "self-made" man and the reality of deepening and enduring poverty that most antebellum working people faced. While many workers remained resistant to the entreaties of evangelical reformers who sought to "improve" them, the culture of evangelical Protestantism did make inroads among working people, especially in the aftermath of economic hardship, and sharpened divisions along ethnic and religious lines.

Having sketched the contours of cultural conflict within the working class, Montgomery turned his sights to a specific case that illuminated how profoundly those conflicts disrupted class alignments in the American context. Drawing on some of the methods and sources of the "new social history" (and some studies by his new colleagues at the University of Pittsburgh), he chose a case study of cultural conflict in the Irish Catholic handloom weaving neighborhoods of Kensington (Philadelphia) to illuminate the sharp divide between class polarization of workers and employers, on the one hand, and, on the other, workers' political behavior, where "they consistently failed to exhibit a class consciousness." The remarkable solidarity between native and immigrant, Protestant and Catholic workers evidenced in the rise of the General Trades Union and in the general strike of 1835 largely collapsed in the depression years that followed. The predominantly Irish handloom weavers now stood alone in their depression-era strikes against their masters. The bitter and violent clashes that followed in the mid-1840s pitted Protestants against Catholics and enlisted workers on both sides. In Montgomery's richly detailed account, Protestant evangelism "fragmented the working class as a political force" but also "created for historians the illusion of a society lacking in class conflict."[3]

Years later (in 1995), Montgomery returned in "Wage Labor, Bondage, and Citizenship in Nineteenth-Century America" to the question of American workers' political engagement. By then he could draw on a rich body of "new labor history" studies that highlighted the racial and gendered experience of nineteenth-century workers. Central to his analysis lay the paradox of workers' increasing power at the ballot box—most evident in northern state and local elections—accompanied by the enhanced coercive power of the state and the judiciary, over workers' lives, including the regulation of poor relief, vagrancy, labor contracts, and, in the South, the fundamental political and economic rights of African American workers. But, as in so much of his scholarship, Montgomery emphasized working peoples' capacity, as agents of their own rights claims, to devise new ways to resist employer and state coercion.

Notes

1. David Montgomery, "The Working Classes of the Pre-industrial American City, 1780–1830," *Labor History* 9 (Winter 1968): 21–22.
2. *Ibid.*, 20.
3. David Montgomery, "The Shuttle and the Cross: Weavers and Artisans in the Kensington Riots of 1844," *Journal of Social History* 5 (Summer 1972): 411, 439.

CHAPTER 2

The Working Classes of the Pre-Industrial American City, 1780–1830

From *Labor History* 9 (Winter 1968): 3–22

In the years since Raymond W. Goldsmith submitted to Congress his statistical findings on the rise of per capita income in the United States many economic historians have come to date the beginnings of sustained industrial growth at some time during the 1830s.[1] This chronology has provided historians of the working class with a significant benchmark to guide their own research and analysis. Among other things it raises questions concerning the sources, size, and character of the labor supply which was at hand before the acceleration of economic growth and the ideological baggage (attitudes, customs, institutions) which the available workers carried with them when they entered the industrial era. The objective of this article is to suggest some parameters for both sets of questions derived from an examination of the working classes in the young nation's four northern cities: Boston, New York, Philadelphia, and Baltimore.

During the five decades before 1830 these cities were essentially depots for trans-oceanic shipping, and their labor force was largely tied to maritime commerce. Surrounding each of them was "a vast scene of household manufacturing" where, wrote Alexander Hamilton, country folk produced clothing, shoes, and other necessities, "in many instances, to an extent not only sufficient for the supply of the families in which they are made, but for sale, and even, in some cases, for exportation."[2] Such a countryside Albert Gallatin found twenty years later in New Hampshire, where the average farmer's house had at least one spinning wheel, and every second house boasted a loom on which from 100 to 600 yards of saleable cloth were woven annually (at a time when journeymen weavers in their homes averaged only 829 yards per year and factory looms, 1,111 yards).[3] Most manufacturing, in other words, was carried on outside of the major cities. By 1820 some 12 percent of the nation's labor force was engaged in manufacturing and construction, and 28 percent in all non-agricultural occupations, but at that time the residents of these cities and their contiguous suburbs totaled only 356,452, or 3.7 percent of the American people.[4]

The merchant elite of these communities, furthermore, was concerned not so much with hiring labor as with vending the produce of labor, both agricultural and mechanical. Mathew Carey went so far as to accuse the merchants of hostility toward manufacturing interests, of striving "to impress upon the public mind, that the national prosperity depended almost altogether on commerce; that the protection of manufactures by duties on imports was impolitic and unjust."[5] Understandably the broadsides of Carey, Gallatin, Tench Coxe, and other promoters of manufacturing bore the aspect of appeals to the dominant agricultural and commercial interests of the land to pay some heed to the needs of industry and to believe that the growth of domestic manufactures could take place without depriving farmers and merchants of either manpower or customers. But Carey's conception of the merchant as industry's relentless foe slighted the encouragement offered manufacturing by the commercial city itself. The concentration of population in seaports required by a growing flow of commerce prevented urban residents from producing their own necessities in the fashion of farm families. It generated a social division of labor within the city itself and hence a need for sedentary artisans. The accumulation of merchant fortunes, furthermore, created a demand for luxury goods and thus for expert craftsmen: for silversmiths, goldbeaters, clockmakers, wig and peruke makers, printers of books and journals, tailors, and cordwainers familiar with European fashions and capable of reproducing them. By the end of the eighteenth century, moreover, seaboard merchants had opened a substantial oceanic trade in shoes, clothing, barrels, and ironwares with the regions of slave plantations. This trade encouraged the development of both the putting-out system and the early efforts toward factory organization of production.

Although most manufacturing was carried on outside the great urban centers, the seaport itself, therefore, generated a demand for labor in production as well as trade. In the eighteenth century most manufacture had been performed in the workshops of mechanics who, with the aid of family, apprentices, and occasional journeymen, made the wares they vended themselves.[6] The printer, for example, was usually a bookseller and a journalist as well, in the manner of Mathew Carey, who in the 1790s composed his own editorials in type and then hawked the paper about Philadelphia. Only after 1810 did urban newspapers gravitate into the hands of publishers who were not printers but, in the language of the journeymen, "speculators on the labor of printers" who installed "hireling editors" to write the columns printers now set in type.[7]

The colonial conception of a journeyman as tomorrow's master mechanic was neither dead nor fully obsolete by 1820, for vertical mobility was still remarkable. Among the early members of the Franklin Typographical Association of New York, a trade society of journeymen founded in 1799, were David Bruce, the future owner of the city's largest printing shop and a pioneer typefounder; Thurlow Weed, a future boss of state politics; Samuel Woodworth, the poet of "Old Oaken Bucket" fame; and Peter Force, America's most eminent historical archivist.[8] Two of the master shoemakers who testified against the cordwainers union in Philadelphia's 1805 conspiracy trial were former journeymen and union members, as were two of the employers at the similar Pittsburgh trial ten years later.[9] But by the first two decades of the nineteenth century the emergence of distinct societies of journeymen and of masters among printers, tailors, shoemakers, carpenters, stone cutters, and other trades in every seaport indicated a new awareness of distinct class interests. The seventeen benevolent societies of Philadelphia carpenters, ship masters, stone cutters, and other trades listed by James Mease in 1811 were clearly organizations of master mechanics. Their initiation fees ranging from $10 up and their annual dues of four or five dollars contrast remarkably with the one dollar initiation and the 25 cents monthly dues (waived after ten years' membership) charged by that city's printers union.[10] Societies of journeymen that sought to combine benevolent functions with the enforcement of union wage scales ultimately found it necessary to either expel members who had risen to the rank of employers, or to succumb to the urgings of "alimoners" in their midst and abandon the effort to regulate trade conditions. Thus the printers' organizations in Philadelphia and Boston during the 1820s converted themselves into friendly societies open to employers and workmen alike, while the New York society, bent on controlling wages and aware that "the interests of the journeymen are separate and in some respects opposite to those of the employers," resolved in 1817 "that when any member of this society shall become an employing printer he shall be considered without the limits of this society."[11]

The myth of harmonious personal relationships among masters, journeymen, and apprentices in a setting of domestic paternalism may be quite anachronistic when applied to post-Revolutionary decades. Ian Quimby's study of apprentice contracts in eighteenth-century Philadelphia revealed a persistent erosion of filial duties and loyalties by the emerging ethos of commercialism. The mutual moral obligations of apprentices and masters in such matters as work expected of the boy, and the education and clothing due him were converted over the course of the century into money values and specified in ever-increasing detail in the contracts.[12] The experience of cabinetmakers, furthermore, suggests that journeymen seldom remained long enough with any master to develop a sense of personal attachment. The journeymen of

Samuel Ashton's Philadelphia cabinet shop between 1795 and 1803 averaged scarcely six months in his employ. So rapid was the turnover of craftsmen that, though Ashton rarely needed more than five workmen at a time, forty-nine different men worked for him during those eight years.[13] Under such circumstances class antagonisms based on chronic disputes over wages could be quite consistent with a high level of upward social mobility.

By the 1820s, therefore, the urban working classes comprised recognizable and self-conscious elements of urban society. The "classes . . . who are wholly dependent upon wages," wrote Reverend Joseph Tuckerman, "are very numerous" and, he continued:

> would, indeed, be numerous, if we looked for them among only those who have no trade, and who are generally distinguished alone, as labouring men. This large division includes shop, market, and other porters; carmen; those who are employed in lading, and unlading vessels; wood-sawyers; hod carriers; house servants; those employed by mechanics in a single branch of their business; and multitudes, who are men and women of any work, occasionally required in families, as washing, scouring, etc.; or on the wharves, or in the streets of the city. Besides these, the number is great of those, who are journeymen, and many of whom will never be anything but journeymen, in the various mechanic arts; and considerable numbers are also employed in the different departments of large manufactories, who possess no capital; and who know, and will continue to know, little or nothing in any other department of these establishments, except that in which they are themselves employed. All these, in the strictest sense, and in the common acceptation of the term, are dependent on the wages which they obtain for their services.[14]

Tuckerman's definition of the wage-earning classes suggests that journeymen, mechanics, casual laborers, and factory operatives must be analyzed separately. Even though many mechanics would "never be anything but journeymen," they enjoyed the highest incomes and status of any wage earners and were psychologically the most firmly wedded to the social values and practices of the traditional artisan. Apprenticeship was the historic route of access to "the art and mysteries" of any trade, and the journeymen of this period strove to bar any other avenue of entry. The Philadelphia Typographical Society, which sought with occasional success to reserve all printing positions in town for its own members, excluded from membership anyone "who shall not have served an apprenticeship satisfactory to the board of directors" of the union, and subsequently tried to keep from the presses anyone who had "broken into the trade" after he was twenty-one years old.[15] Both the income and the honor associated with the printer's art were thus to be reserved to those who elected to ply it when they first attained the age of productive manhood at fifteen or sixteen years old. Altogether Philadelphia's complete records of apprentices bound between October 1771 and October 1773 revealed 1,075 youths apprenticed to sixty-eight trades (including many girls indentured to learn "housewifery"). Ten percent of them were to learn the cordwainer's art, and the trades of tailor, mariner, carpenter, and cooper followed shoemaking in order of preference.[16]

Sons of mechanics apprenticed to trades were supplemented by those of farmers who, for example, constituted the bulk of Massachusetts' supply of shoemakers,[17] and in Baltimore by young slaves. The emancipation of northern slaves meant the eclipse of Negro apprenticeship in most urban trades elsewhere. Because the training of slave craftsmen had rarely been complete, freed Negro artisans, who faced intense animosity from white craftsmen and had lost the protection of their masters, rarely survived in positions where they could train apprentices of their own race, and even fewer whites would engage black youth for training.[18] The influx of white farm boys to urban trades, on the other hand, was inhibited by that "desire of being an independent proprietor of land" which Alexander Hamilton believed would always keep small the numbers of those "who would be diverted from it towards manufacturers."[19] Youths who did elect urban trades, furthermore, often fled their apprenticeships after only a year or two of service and, to the great distress of established journeymen, easily found employment as half-trained workmen at substandard wages. The supply of labor was thus rapidly increased at the expense of its quality. The founding of mechanics' institutes (vocational schools) in every major northern city in the 1820s bears witness to the breakdown of traditional apprenticeship training.[20]

The fact remains that residents of rural areas in the Northeast were being lured toward the city, just as others were migrating westward, and frequently such migrants had been craftsmen, rather than (or as well as) farmers. In every decade between 1790 and 1840, the population of all four cities under review grew at a rate substantially above the 33 percent to 36 percent growth for the nation as a whole, with two exceptions: both Philadelphia and New York grew at less than the national rate between 1810 and 1820, and Baltimore's increase after 1820 was chronically below the national pace.[21] This urbanization of native Americans was supplemented by the arrival of European immigrants, but the extent of the trans-oceanic contribution to the growth of these seaports is difficult to measure. Although newcomers to America totaled 400,000 between 1790 and 1830, with 1801–1807, 1816, and 1828–1830 being the years of greatest influx, the bulk of them came not to the American seaport but through it.[22] It was the demand for farm laborers in the hinterland which produced, for example, the large-scale trafficking in redemptioners Frances Wright witnessed in the Philadelphia of 1818.[23]

Among the immigrants who tarried in the city, however, were many skilled mechanics. British emigrants and British trade union practices (complete to the oaths sworn over union scales and the trappings of secrecy necessitated in the old country by the Combination Acts but retained here as a matter of custom) showed up in every conspiracy trial of union journeymen. When the prosecutor charged Philadelphia cordwainers in 1805 with "crimes" committed by union members a decade earlier, the defense replied with only slight exaggeration that none of the journeymen on trial had been in America when those acts were committed.[24] Stocking weavers in Germantown and Kensington outside of Philadelphia had almost all learned their trade in Leicester or Nottingham or the Rhineland. Linen weavers had poured out of northern Ireland in the early 1770s and again at the close of the American Revolution, many of them coming to the new republic. In 1784 alone 11,000 passengers embarked from Dublin, most of them emigrants of this type.[25]

An extreme case of immigrants' providing an industry with its skilled labor was offered by the thousand or so carpet weavers in the country in the early 1830s, at least nine-tenths of whom were Scots, largely from Kilmarnock and Ayr. So well did these mechanics know each other that when sixty-three of them struck the Thompsonville Carpet Manufacturing Company in Connecticut, they quickly assembled, compiled from memory a list of the eleven other principal carpet manufactories in the nation, wrote personal letters to friends in each of them explaining the dispute, notified the Blue Bonnet Tavern in New York City, which served as the country's hiring hall for carpet weavers, to divert men from the struck plant, and dispatched an appeal to the *Old Countryman* in that city to warn off any Scots not reached by the other methods.[26]

Such incidents suggest the hypothesis that America was then a land of opportunity for handicraftsmen whose skills were being undermined by the industrial revolution in England but still in high demand in the more backward American economy. True, the number of handloom weavers and stockingers working in England continued to grow rapidly down to 1820 and perhaps beyond, despite the unmistakable deterioration of income and status in those trades. Many older craftsmen, Arthur Redford found, moved to manufacturing cities in England, there continuing to ply their obsolete trades while depending increasingly on the earnings of their factory-employed children.[27] The Scottish carpet weavers brought to trial in Connecticut for their strike, however, were remarkably young men, twenty-two years of age or less. The presumption is that the craftsman-immigrant tended to be neither the daring innovator nor the veteran artisan who could not quit his obsolescent trade but the mobile youth who spurned Briton's factory for the possibility of plying the (to him) preferable family trade in a new location. This hypothesis is consistent with Hamilton's belief that "the disparity" between the "dearness of labor" in America and that in England was "much less in regard to artificers and manufacturers, than in regard to country labourers," a belief recently concurred in by H.J. Habakkuk and Stuart Bruchey.[28] During the first two decades of the nineteenth century, skilled tradesmen in England engaged in "honourable work" (a high quality work not yet subjected to a division of labor and deterioration of apprenticeship standards) looked upon 30s. weekly ($7.50) as an expected income, while some earned £3 and over. Such a 30s. standard fell below the $8.25 of an American shoemaker or the $9 a more seasonal carpenter might ordinarily have expected when working at union standards by precisely the differential of 12 percent–20 percent in America's favor which J. Leander Bishop found for glass workers.[29] True, American workmen paid considerably fewer taxes than their English counterparts, and as D. B. Warden observed of Philadelphia, "Smiths, shoemakers, weavers, and tailors have generally one or two acres of land, which afford pasture for a cow, fuel, and esculent plants."[30] But such bucolic benefits were by no means unknown to English weavers, croppers, and shoemakers, most of whom still worked in their cottages in rural villages.

Far more extreme was the contrast between the American municipal or canal laborer's expectation of some $4.50 a week (often paid partly in board) and the earnings of the English casual laborer, which then ranged from perhaps 11s. weekly in cotton factories to ls. a day for wheelbarrow men in Birmingham. Taking 10s. (i.e., $2.50) as good weekly pay for such laborers in the second decade of the century, the unskilled American enjoyed a premium of 80 percent over his British counterpart.[31] That the wage differential was less rather than greater for the artisan than for casual labor is thus evident even without investigation of the real values of money wages in the two countries. Yet British craftsmen did migrate, spurred by the deteriorating conditions in their trades at home and lured, as one emigrant manual declared, by the openings in American trades left by "the strong emulation of the *cute* native Yankee to elevate himself above the common labour class."[32]

Whether graduates of American or British apprenticeships, urban tradesmen were both geographically mobile enough and sufficiently well informed about the state of the labor market elsewhere to maintain rather uniform wage standards throughout the northeastern cities. When Philadelphia shoemakers demanded a schedule of prices based on $4 a pair for back strap boots in October 1805, they were aware that the New York union had established precisely that scale in March. Similarly, when Pittsburgh shoemakers unionized at the end of that decade, they quickly drove up their prices from 75 cents below the Philadelphia wage to parity with it—but when they sought a scale higher than Philadelphia's, they were roundly defeated by their masters.[33] Both the New York and Washington societies of printers undertook—by correspondence with their counterparts in Philadelphia, Baltimore, Boston, and Albany—to establish uniform scales, and all these societies exchanged "rat lists" with each other, so that typographers who violated union rules and standards could not find refuge in other communities.[34] At times employers cooperated with these efforts of the journeymen, as did master printers in New York in 1815, or, more dramatically, the master weavers of Baltimore, who in 1829 did everything in their power to ostracize a fellow employer for slashing his journeymen's wages below the city norm.[35]

Although the mechanic was ranked by Tuckerman within the wage-earning classes, there is little evidence that prior to the 1830s he either identified himself with "the poor" or felt in any way alienated from the existing social order. Despite the absence from common American parlance of the rigid British distinction between "honourable" and "dishonourable" work, only the scale of the New York shoemakers out of all the union price lists which have been preserved from that period (mainly those of printers, shoemakers, tailors, and weavers) included a specified wage for coarse work, partially completed work, or the work of helpers. While the Pittsburgh shoemakers' union did explicitly deem coarse work "out of society" and posed no objections to non-members performing such tasks, there is no such clear evidence from any of the seaport cities. It is remarkable, however, that the prosecutor in the New York shoemakers' trial, while conceding that many journeymen were not members, insisted that "all the best workmen were of the society." Similarly Philadelphia shoemakers considered themselves fully unionized between 1798 and 1804, when their society had 100 to 150 members, while the city directory for 1798 listed 292 shoemakers and cordwainers.[36] A plausible inference is that cheap shoes for slaves and for auction sale, which did not appear in the union's scale of prices, were deliberately relegated to inferior workmen whom the society made no effort to recruit.

The mechanics proudly preserved an ideological heritage blended of Ben Franklin's maxims and Tom Paine's "rights of man." The best local legal talent defended their societies in the several conspiracy trials to which they were subjected, as witness Philadelphia's shoemakers enlisting Caesar Rodney, whom President Jefferson was soon to appoint Attorney General of the United States. When seventeen years earlier that city's mechanics had paraded with their masters in joyous celebration of the ratification of the federal constitution, they had borne such emblems as "the weavers' flag, a rampant lion in a green field, holding a shuttle in his dexter paw—motto, '*may the government* protect us,'" the boat builders' flag (atop the thirty-three-foot schooner *Federal Union* drawn down Market Street for the occasion) bearing "an axe and an adze crossing each other—motto, 'by these we live,'" or the bricklayers' flag, with "the federal city rising out of a forest, workmen building it, and the sun illuminating it," motto, "'*both buildings and rulers are the works of our hands.*'" At the close of the procession, bakers distributed bread to the poor, victuallers slew their "two stately oxen" and gave away the meat, and millers provided the needy with flour.[37] The best the printers could do was to read the destitute a poem, but clearly the citizen craftsmen were dispensers, not recipients, of charity.

Very different was the outlook of the impoverished residents of the Rittenhouse Square vicinity, who petitioned the Philadelphia city council in 1830 to halt the dumping in the square of offal swept from neighboring streets, "which being in heaps, occasions numerous ponds of stagnant and putrescent water in the immediate spots, which in summer send forth pestilential vapours wafted by every breeze to the dwellings of your petitioners, whose only comfort, health, is thus destroyed." These poor argued that "being of the working class, their whole time is indispensably employed in various labour to maintain their families," so that sickness is "a scourge the most severe."[38] Here was a group whose annual incomes ranged far closer to $200 than to $400 or $425 expected by craftsmen, a group who Reverend Tuckerman feared "have lived, and to a great extent are living, as a *caste*—cut off from those in more favoured circumstances; and doomed to find their pleasures, and sympathy in their suffering, alone among themselves."[39]

The seaport poor were by no means a new phenomenon at the end of the 1820s. James Henretta has clearly traced their emergence in eighteenth-century Boston as a function of the growth of overseas commerce. He discovered from the Boston tax rolls of 1687 that only 14 percent of the adult male population of the city, that is, 188 men, were neither "dependent" nor owners of property. In contrast to them stood the 17 percent of the adult males who as servants, apprentices, or participants in family home enterprise were classified as dependent. The propertied classes numbered 1,036 (69 percent of the adult males) and included 521 poor craftsmen, 275 artisans of the "middling sort" with two or three journeymen apiece, and the wealthier tradesmen, professionals, and merchants. By 1771 only 10 percent of the adult males were dependent in the traditional sense, while 29 percent were neither dependent nor propertied. These were wage earners in the full meaning of the term, and while the city's population had doubled between the two counts, their number had increased fourfold. They ranged in occupation from seamen and longshoremen at one end of the scale to journeymen at the other, but, while the latter ranked close to the small property-holding mechanic, the division of wealth between the upper and lower halves of property owners was far sharper than had been the case in the seventeenth century.[40]

Most day laborers participated directly in transportation and commerce. It was the demand for seamen, longshoremen, carters, and domestic servants which absorbed unskilled wage earners already in the eighteenth century. By the early nineteenth century, construction work, wood cutting, and road building employed many, while thousands of Philadelphia's poor, Mathew Carey found, "travel hundreds of miles in quest of employment on canals at 62½, 75 and 87½ cents per day, paying a dollar and a half or two dollars per week for their board, leaving families behind, depending on them for support."[41] By 1830 Carey estimated "labourers, hodmen, seamstresses, families of workmen on canals and rail-roads" at 40 percent of the working classes and 25 percent of the total population of Philadelphia.[42]

Many laborers reached the city from the farm by way of the sea. The merchant fleet of Massachusetts, wrote Samuel Eliot Morison, "was manned by successive waves of adventure-seeking boys, and officered by such of them as determined to make the sea their calling." The great majority on the crew lists professed "to be native-born Yankees, and probably were."[43] Seamen would register with federal revenue agents after 1796 and receive, for a fee of 25 cents, papers certifying their United States citizenship. Between that year and 1812, 106,757 seamen collected their papers, and of them only 1,530, or 1.4 percent were naturalized citizens. The registrations reported for the years after 1808 were certainly still incomplete, for district revenue collectors were very tardy in submitting their reports to Washington. The fact that registration was heaviest in years such as 1797 and 1805, when the danger of British impressment was most severe, indicates that enrollment was never very thorough.[44] These figures, nevertheless, can suggest the large number of native Americans who took to the sea.

So high were the rates of promotion, death, and desertion that the man who spent more than twelve years before the mast was rare indeed. No other occupation offered an unskilled farm boy so great an opportunity to rise quickly in wealth and standing—or to topple from yardarm into the cold Atlantic. Few seamen dwelt long in any port, but while ashore they augmented the local casual labor supply significantly. Illustrative of their role was young Charles Erskine, whose mother moved to Boston in the early 1820s after his father (a currier) had deserted her. Playing about the docks, Erskine heard the tales of sailors and through them was lured to sea. Between voyages he and his mates earned their keep ashore by whatever employment was available wherever they happened to be. He once helped construct an aqueduct in Washington and at another time worked in a Philadelphia hook and eye factory.[45]

In marked contrast to the artisan's tendency to ply for life the trade he had learned in his adolescence, the laborer was the epitome of versatility. To move from to sea to canal digging to hod carrying to factory work was well within the realm of possibility. Many of the half-trained journeymen and "botches" who bedevilled mechanics' efforts to retain high quality and wage standards were of this sort. New England's first factory to use cotton spinning machinery, founded in Beverly, Massachusetts, in 1787, wasted precious quantities of material in training its workmen, then was driven close to ruin when it had to raise wages to prevent its partly-taught employees from deserting to rival firms. Mercifully, perhaps, the factory burned down in 1808.[46] A happier experience with such labor was reported by a cotton mill near Providence, which employed fifty-three workers in the factory and 125 on putting-out by 1810. The owners, reported Albert Gallatin, at first suffered "in being put to much expense by English workmen, who pretended to much more knowledge in the business than they really possessed." But the phony Samuel Slaters were discharged, "and Americans, as apprentices, &c. are getting the art very fast," though the company did not anticipate dividends "for a considerable time."[47]

The fact that machine operatives could be trained made the "factory controversy" of this period focus not on the fate of the workers, as was to be the case in the 1830s and 1840s, but on the potential impact of manufacturing upon the nation's supply of farm labor. Wages of farm hands, Henry Carey reported, were higher in the vicinity of the cities than in more rustic settings.[48] Whether this differential in money wages was a sign of competition from urban employments or simply an indication that the market economy was more mature near the cities (that a smaller portion of the farm laborer's income was paid in kind and more in cash than was the case to the West) is not clear. Whichever it meant, advocates of governmental aid to manufactures from Coxe through Carey felt obliged to echo Hamilton's famous assurance that manufacturing would not attract able-bodied men away from the land, that it would rather "afford occasional and extra employment to industrious individuals and families," through which farmers could profit by the home produce of their wives and daughters, and provide steady employment for "persons who would otherwise be idle, and in many cases a burthen on the community," and render women and children "more useful, and the latter more early useful . . . than they should otherwise be."[49]

At this period, therefore, it was impossible to speak of the factory labor force without directing attention to women, children, and charitable institutions. This was the case long before the mills of Lowell arose. Philadelphia's first large-scale use of spinning jennies was undertaken by the United Company of Philadelphia for Promoting American Manufactures, founded by patriotic subscriptions in 1775. By the late 1780s it employed 400 women, most of them recruited from the city's poor rolls. Despite the pride with which the Society displayed a jenny of eighty spindles in the Federal Procession of 1788, and boasted that the woman operating it was "a native of and instructed in this city," the company's building was destroyed by an arsonist only two years later.[50] Newly-inaugurated President Washington found a similar labor force when he visited a Boston sail duck factory. Here pairs of little girls spun and wove flax from eight in the morning until six at night, but their demeanor favorably impressed the President, who described them as "daughters of decayed families" and "girls of character—none others are admitted."[51]

Two decades later the Secretary of the Treasury reported that eighty-seven cotton mills then in operation or about to commence operations in the United States needed a labor force of about 500 men and 3,500 women and children.[52]

Such a work force was for Gallatin proof positive that manufacturing need not lure men from the farm. Tench Coxe agreed:

> Female aid in manufactures, which prevents the diversion of men and boys from agriculture, has greatly increased. Children are employed, as well as the infirm and the crippled. The asylums of the poor and unfortunate, and the penitentiaries of indiscretion and immorality are improved and aided by the employment and profits of manufactures.[53]

The markets of seamstresses were especially crowded with unmarried and widowed women, not to speak of those whose husbands were "travelling"—in the informal divorce procedure of the day. When such women bid on sewing work, they competed with both married women trying to supplement their own families' meager incomes and recipients of work relief. While female operatives in Philadelphia factories earned two or three dollars a week in the 1820s, seamstresses rarely surpassed $1.25, and the city's home relief system helped keep those earnings low. In slack seasons so many women applied to the Provident Society and other charities for work to tide them over that the scale offered by almshouses became, during the 1820s, the standard price offered by private firms. Thus the US War Department offered seamstresses 12½ cents a shirt, the very wage given by the Provident Society. In reply to a plea that such a price reduced the seamstresses "to the degradation of pauperism," the Secretary of War termed the subject "of such delicacy, and so intimately connected with the manufacturing interests, and the general prices of this kind of labour in the city of Philadelphia" that he dared not change his Department's practice.[54]

While the seamstress stood with one foot in the poor house, this was not the case with the weaver, for in the urban areas most cloth was still put out to families with handlooms. The city and county of Philadelphia in 1809 produced 65,326 yards of cloth in its six factories on both hand and power looms, but its home production amounted to 233,232 yards.[55] Furthermore, the spinning mills, while they continued to be staffed primarily by women and children, tended to free themselves by the second decade of the century from dependence on public charities. The reason is that unmarried women, widows, and orphaned families gravitated toward them by free choice.

Especially was this the case in New England, where the textile mill became a means of emancipation for the "maiden aunts" who lived with so many of the region's families. In Massachusetts the 1810 male population under the age of sixteen outnumbered females of the same age in the ratio of 104 to 100. Between the ages of sixteen and forty-five, however, the proportions were reversed. During the marrying season (ages sixteen through twenty-five) there were 103 women for every 100 men, but in the post twenty-six age of the spinster, women outnumbered men by a ratio of 107 to 100. And Massachusetts had 3,335 more women of that age than it had men.[56] Theirs was the choice, at best, of boarding with parents, or a married sister, or entering a mill. Since the loss of males was a result of the westward movement, it would seem that, as far as New England's early textile industry is concerned, the famous "safety-valve" worked in reverse. The migration of men to the West created a surplus of female labor in the East.

Neither New York State nor Pennsylvania exhibited such an imbalance of the sexes, for both were receiving substantial immigration, and considerable westward movement still occurred within their boundaries. But within the cities of New York and Philadelphia free white women between the ages of sixteen and twenty-five sharply outnumbered the men of the same age. The New York ratio in 1820, for example, was 119 women to 100 men in that age bracket, while in Philadelphia women of this marriageable age outnumbered men 122 to 100. Similarly, the Boston ratio was 127 to 100, and that of Baltimore 108 to 100.[57] Although the terrible toll of childbirth, among other hazards, more than corrected the balance of the sexes in all four cities after the age of twenty-six, each of the seaports was naturally provided with a sizeable force of women for whom there was no prospect of marriage and for whom entry into the labor market was a necessity.

Each of these groups of city workers of the pre-industrial epoch (journeymen mechanics, male laborers, and women) merits careful historical study. Little new work has been done in this area since David J. Saposs contributed his chapters to John R. Commons' *History of Labour in the United States* in 1917, and because of this deficiency the labor historian's view of this period has fallen seriously out of phase with that of the economic historian. For example, Saposs' contention that "the wages of the unskilled were going up while those of the skilled were kept down by the merchant-capitalist" in the century's first two decades finds no support in the wage data of this article or in recent economic studies.[58]

The problem assumes considerable significance in the light of George Rogers Taylor's hypothesis that per capita income in America declined rather steadily between 1807 and the early 1830s.[59] The impact of such a trend could logically have been different for mechanics, for factory operatives, for casual laborers, and for women sewing in their rented rooms. Only specific studies of particular groups of workers can yield conclusive data on the standard of living. Jackson Turner Main and James Henretta have shown that enough evidence exists in tax rolls, judicial records, and the press of the eighteenth century to enable the historian to reconstruct patterns of property and income distribution quite clearly.[60] Their work challenges other historians to trace the evolution of these patterns in early nineteenth century city life and to reduce their reliance on impressionistic evidence.

Still greater is the need for research into the cultural and intellectual life of the working classes of this period. We need to know what the urban poor expected of life, how they reacted to the commercial ethos of their cities, and how they conceived their relationship to the governing merchant elites. Were they, as some historians have recently portrayed the poor of Naples or London, simultaneously devoted to the traditional social order, aware of their power as a mob, confident the city would care for them in times of want, and, profoundly hostile toward the emerging impersonal and amoral market economy?[61] Was it such a mentality which made some 200 assembled New York sailors, idled by the embargo, respond obediently when Mayor Marinus Willet commanded them to disperse, with assurances that the embargo was "the *Captain's Orders*," and that the city would "do everything possible for your relief"?[62] Such questions cannot yet be answered because a fixation on the clash of "agrarian" and "industrial" values has distracted us from exploring pre-industrial urban values and customs.

Similarly American historians have yet to probe the culture of the American mechanic as, say, E. P. Thompson did for his British counterpart. Our concern has been either with the journeyman's economic circumstances (where there is still much to be learned) or with whether he voted for Andrew Jackson (and may we be spared that debate for a while). Because the mechanics were frequently organized and far more articulate than the urban poor, research into the mind of the journeyman should prove relatively easy. The ideas suggested in this article need careful testing, to begin with, and beyond them lie several major issues for research. How open was economic mobility for the journeymen, and what changes did the post-Revolutionary generation experience in this regard? Why did this class provide most of the country's early nineteenth century adherents to deism, and just how widespread and significant was infidelity among them?[63] What new circumstances made craftsmen in every major city between 1827 and 1837 expand the horizons of their concern beyond the limits of their own trades, create city Trades' Unions as new institutions to fuse the efforts of the several crafts, undertake unprecedented united action with the unskilled laborers, giving rise to something worthy of the name labor movement?

These problems suggest that we have rushed ahead to evaluate labor's response to industrialism without first ascertaining labor's pre-industrial behavior and attitudes. In exploring the shock of change after the Civil War our attention has been directed half a century too late, and our concern with the fate of agrarian values has led us to ignore the impact of the spreading factory system on the cultural heritage of urban America's lower orders.

Notes

Reprinted courtesy of *Labor History.*

1. U.S. Congress, Joint Economic Committee, *Hearings* [*on*] *Employment, Growth and Price Levels,* "Part 2-Historical and Comparative Rates of Production,

Productivity, and Prices," 86th Cong., 1st Sess., 1959, 230–279; George Rogers Taylor, "The National Economy Before and After the Civil War," in *Economic Change in the Civil War Era*, eds. David T. Gilchrist and W. David Lewis (Greenville, Del., 1965), 1–22; Douglass C. North, *Growth and Welfare in the American Past* (Englewood Cliffs, NJ, 1966), 15–17, 75–89; Robert Gallman, "Commodity Output, 1839–1899," in *Trends in the American Economy in the Nineteenth Century, National Bureau of Economic Research Studies in Income and Wealth Volume Twenty-Four* (Princeton, NJ, 1960), 13–67. Stuart Bruchey finds indices of significant industrial growth before the 1830s, *The Roots of American Economic Growth, 1607–1861, An Essay in Social Causation* (New York, 1965), 76–91.

2. Alexander Hamilton, "Report on Manufactures," in Hamilton, *Papers on Public Credit, Commerce, and Finance*, ed. Samuel McKee, Jr. (Indianapolis and New York, 1957), 222.

3. Albert Gallatin, "Manufactures," *American State Papers*, Finance, II, 434–435.

4. Figures on distribution of labor force are calculated from U.S. Department of Commerce, Bureau of the Census, *Historical Statistics of the United States, 1789–1945* (Washington, D.C., 1949), 29. Population figures for city and suburban areas are taken from those presented by Professor Everett S. Lee at the 1966 Eleutherian Mills-Hagley Foundation Conference on the Growth of Seaport Cities, 1790–1825.

5. Mathew Carey, *Autobiography* (Research Classics, Number One, Brooklyn, 1942), 95.

6. See Carl Bridenbaugh, *Colonial Craftsman* (New York, 1950); Richard B. Morris, *Government and Labor in Early America* (New York, 1946); Staughton Lynd and Alfred Young, "After Carl Becker: The Mechanics and New York City Politics, 1774–1801," *Labor History*, V (Fall, 1964), 215–224.

7. Carey, *Autobiography*, 11–25; Ethelbert Stewart, "Documentary History of the Early Organization of Printers," in U.S. Department of Commerce and Labor, *Bulletin of the Bureau of Labor*, No. 61 (Washington, DC, 1905), 912.

8. George A. Stevens, *New York Typographical Union No. 6* (Albany, 1913), 38, 81–102.

9. *Commonwealth v. Pullis*, in John R. Commons, *et al, Documentary History of American Industrial Society* (10 vols., Cleveland, 1910), III, 59–248; *Commonwealth v. Morrow*, in *ibid.*, IV, 15–88.

10. Thomas Wilson, *Picture of Philadelphia, for 1824, Containing the "Picture of Philadelphia, for 1811, by James Mease, M.D." with All Its Improvements since that Period* (Philadelphia, 1823), 267–276; Stewart, 943.

11. Stevens *op. cit.*, 76.

12. Ian M.G. Quimby, "Apprenticeship in Colonial Philadelphia," (unpublished Master's Thesis, University of Delaware, 1963), 60–63.

13. Morrison H. Heckshel, "The Organization and Practice of Philadelphia Cabinetmaking Establishments, 1790–1820" (unpublished Master's Thesis, University of Delaware, 1964), 22–25.

14. Joseph Tuckerman, *An Essay on the Wages Paid to Females for Their Labour* (Philadelphia, 1830), 8.

15. Stewart *op. cit.*, 877, 943.
16. Quimby *op. cit.*, 30.
17. Blanche Evans Hazard, *Organization of the Boot and Shoe Industry in Massachusetts before 1875* (Cambridge, Mass., 1921), 322–323.
18. Leonard Price Stavisky, "The Negro Artisan in the South Atlantic States, 1800–1860: A Study of Status and Economic Opportunity with Special Reference to Charleston" (unpublished PhD dissertation, Columbia University, 1958), 16–22; Morris *op. cit.*, 182–188; Leon Litwack, *North of Slavery. The Negro in the Free States, 1790–1860* (Chicago, 1961), 153–162.
19. Hamilton *op. cit.*, 203.
20. See Bruchey *op. cit.*, 188–189.
21. Everett S. Lee, figures on urban population growth presented at the 1966 Eleutherian Mills-Hagley Foundation Conference on the Growth of Seaport Cities, 1790–1825. See also D.B. Warden, *Statistical, Political, and Historical Account of the United States of North America* (3 vols., Edinburgh, 1819), I, xiii. Between 1775 and 1790 the growth rates of these cities had fallen well behind the national rate. George Rogers Taylor, "American Economic Growth before 1840: An Exploratory Essay," *Journal of Economic History*, XXIV (Dec., 1964), 439.
22. *Historical Statistics of the United States*, 34; Curtis P. Nettels, *Emergence of a National Economy, 1775–1815* (New York, 1962), 133; Marcus Lee Hansen, *Atlantic Migration, 1607–1860* (Harper Torchbook edition, New York, 1961), 84; E.P. Thompson, *Making of the English Working Class* (New York, 1966), 430–432.
23. Frances Wright, *Views of Society and Manners in America*, ed. Paul R. Baker (Cambridge, Mass., 1963), 240–241. Compare the observations of Johann David Schoepf in Baltimore in 1783. *Travels in the Confederation*, translated and edited by Alfred J. Morrison (2 vols., Philadelphia, 1911), I, 339–340.
24. Commons, *Documentary History*, III, 108.
25. Edwin T. Freedley, *Philadelphia and Its Manufactures* (Philadelphia, 1858), 241–242; Arthur Redford, *Labour Migration in England 1800–1850*, edited and revised by W.H. Chaloner (Manchester, 1964), 166–167.
26. *Thompsonville Carpet Manufacturing Company vs. William Taylor* in Commons, *Documentary History*, IV-Supplement, 16–125.
27. Thompson, *op. cit.*, 279–296; Redford *op. cit.*, 186.
28. Hamilton, *op. cit.*, 208; H.J. Habakkuk, *American and British Technology in the Nineteenth Century: The Search for Labour-Saving Inventions* (Cambridge, 1962), 21–43; Bruchey *op. cit.*, 162–164.
29. J. Leander Bishop, *History of American Manufactures from 1680–1860* (2 vols., Philadelphia, 1864), I, 242. For a description of "honourable work" in England see Thompson, 234–268.
30. Warden *op. cit.*, II, 107.
31. For data on wages of unskilled labor see Mathew Carey, *Appeal to the Wealthy of the Land* (Philadelphia, 1833), 17; Warden, II, 85; Christopher Roberts, *The Middlesex Canal* (Cambridge, Mass., 1938), 78–82. For comparable wages in England see Thompson, 310, 313; Redford, 39.

32. Patrick Matthew, *Emigration Fields. North America, The Cape, Australia, and New Zealand* (Edinburgh and London, 1839), 40.

33. Commons, *Documentary History*, III, 106, 368–369; *ibid.*, IV, 34.

34. Stewart, *op. cit.*, 866, 871–872, 877, 881, 886, 888. Compare the efforts of Philadelphia's union curriers, Leonard Bernstein, "The Working People of Philadelphia from Colonial Times to the General Strike of 1835," *Pennsylvania Magazine of History and Biography*, LXXIV (July, 1950), 325.

35. Stewart, *op. cit.*, 877; "Report of the Trial of the Journeymen Weavers in Baltimore City Court," in Commons, *Documentary History*, IV, 269–272.

36. *Ibid.*, III, 368–370; *ibid.*, III, 72–81, 84–85; *ibid.*, IV, 28–40; Cornelius Wm. Stafford, *Philadelphia City Directory for 1798.*

37. *American Museum*, IV, (July 1788), 57–78.

38. Samuel Hazard, ed., *Register of Pennsylvania*, V (Feb. 20, 1830), 124. Rittenhouse Square became a wealthy neighborhood only after 1850. See Nathaniel Burt, *The Perennial Philadelphians. The Anatomy of an American Aristocracy* (Boston and Toronto, 1963), 531.

39. Tuckerman, *op. cit.*, 25.

40. James A. Henretta, "Economic Development and Social Structure in Colonial Boston," *William and Mary Quarterly*, Third Series, XXII (Jan., 1965), 75–92. See also Jackson Turner Main, *Social Structure of Revolutionary America* (Princeton, 1965), 37–40.

41. Carey, *Appeal*, II. On canal laborers see William A. Sullivan, *Industrial Worker in Pennsylvania 1800–1840* (Harrisburg, 1955), 71–73.

42. Carey, *Appeal*, 7.

43. Samuel Eliot Morison, *The Maritime History of Massachusetts 1783–1860* (Sentry Edition, Boston, 1961), 106, 108.

44. *American State Papers*, Commerce & Navigation, I, 955, 968; Act of May 28, 1796, *Public Statutes at Large of the United States of America* (17 vols., Boston, 1850), I, 477.

45. See J. Grey Jewell, *Among Our Sailors* (New York, 1874), 1–50; Charles Erskine, *Twenty Years before the Mast* (Philadelphia, 1896), 2–9, 272.

46. Bishop, *op. cit.*, I, 399–401.

47. Gallatin, *op. cit.*, 434.

48. Henry C. Carey, *Essay on the Rate of Wages: with an Examination of the Causes of the Differences in the Conditions of the Labouring Population throughout the World* (Philadelphia, 1835), 91.

49. Hamilton, *op. cit.*, 193.

50. Bishop, *op. cit.*, I, 384–387; *American Museum*, V (July, 1788), 60.

51. Edward Everett, *Mount Vernon Papers* (New York, 1860), 112.

52. Gallatin, *op. cit.*, 427.

53. Tench Coxe, *A Statement of the Arts and Manufactures of the United States of America, for the Year 1810* (Philadelphia, 1814), xiv.

54. Exchange of correspondence with the Secretary of War, printed in Matthew Carey, *Appeal to Common Sense and Common Justice* (Philadelphia, 1822), xii–xiii.

On the role of charities in fixing urban wage levels see Mathew Carey, *Essays on the Public Charities of Philadelphia* (Philadelphia, 1829), 18–19; Benjamin J. Klebaner, "The Home Relief Controversy in Philadelphia, 1782–1861," *Pennsylvania Magazine of History and Biography*, LXXIVII (Oct., 1954), 420.

55. Coxe, *op. cit.*, 44.

56. Warden, *op. cit.*, I, 200.

57. The ratios are calculated from statistics presented by Everett S. Lee at the 1966 Eleutherian Mills-Hagley Foundation Conference on the Growth of Seaport Cities, 1790–1825.

58. John R. Commons, et al, *History of Labour in the United States* (4 vols., New York, 1918–1938), I, 105. *cf.*, Sullivan, *op. cit.*, 31, 72–73.

59. Taylor, "American Economic Growth before 1840," 437.

60. See note 40.

61. See E.J. Hobsbawn, *Primitive Rebels. Studies in Archaic Forms of Social Movement in the 19th and 20th Centuries* (New York, 1965), 108–125; Thompson, 55–76.

62. George Daitsman, "Labor and the Welfare State in Early New York," *Labor History*, IV (Fall, 1963), 250.

63. See Herbert M. Morais, *Deism in Eighteenth Century America* (New York, 1934); Albert Post, *Popular Freethought in America, 1825–1850* (New York, 1943); Lewis Masquerier, *Sociology: Or, the Reconstruction of Society* (New York, 1877).

CHAPTER 3

Social Attitudes of American Workers in the 1840s

Unpublished paper, c. 1970–71, David Montgomery Papers, New York University, Tamiment Library and Robert F. Wagner Labor Archives

The America of the 1840s tantalizes historians with a number of intriguing paradoxes. Not the least among them is the juxtaposition of what historians have been fond of calling the "Age of the Common Man" with the spawning of a sizeable propertyless proletariat. If today's historian is less aware of that paradox than were contemporaries, he finds himself confronted with another, equally perplexing form of the same problem. This was the decade to which W.W. Rostow awarded the notorious label, "the take-off period" of American economic growth. Statistically inclined economic historians of the type of Douglass North and Robert E. Gallman, though they may agree on little else, do concur in the findings that sometime around 1839 per capita income leapt abruptly upward, and that part of this process was a Great Leap Forward in manufacturing output. Yet this leap occurred in the midst of drastic reductions of wages. This was true of the traditional handicrafts, where "Cat-Gut Bosses" devastated the traditional standards of such honorable trades as printing, weaving, hat making, furniture making, and shoemaking in order to meet intensely competitive markets for their wares. In the language of the craftsmen, their trades were left "all foul." It was also true for factory operatives. James Montgomery, the observant Scottish mill owner, noted that the depression which closed the 1830s tended both to level out the wages paid by competing American textile mills and to make New England piece rates equal to those he paid in Glasgow, through reductions of as much as 30%. Not only did manufacturing output rise 53% during the five years of under-employment and depressed wages and prices between 1839 and 1844, but workers' real incomes failed to rise when prices revived (and manufacturing output soared another 68%) during the next five years. Here, it seems, was a classical counterpoint of progress and poverty.

Society at that time offered the wage earner two justifications for his anomalous position. The first was that, unlike the European worker sentenced from birth to poverty and servitude, the American had been blessed with birth in a "nation of workers" where all white men possessed equal opportunities in the race for fame and fortune. In the words of Calvin Colton (a minister of the gospel, like most of the nation's writers on political economy at the time): "in this country, labor occupies a *high social and political position*. It is never *compelled* to work for wages fixed by employers, because there is always open to it the *alternative* of working *on its own hook*."

Hence the ideal type of American was the self-made man, and since every man worth his salt was bound to rise in station, the industrial wage earner was seen in some sense as a beginner in the world—as a youth, an immigrant, a new arrival in town. "If any continue through life in the condition of the hired laborer," explained Abraham Lincoln, "it is not the fault of the system, but because of either a dependent nature which prefers it, or improvidence, folly, or singular misfortune." Within the gospel of equality, in other words, there lurked a gratuitous insult to the workingman. His poverty was the consequence of his own moral failing. Drink, prostitution, and gambling are the "crushers" of the workingmen, declared Horace Greeley, not the capitalists.

The second justification contained implications which contradicted those of the first. If the poverty of the workers was their own fault, it behooved them to endure their lot in honest and humble silence. The common schools used William H. McGuffey's *Second Reader* to drill their pupils in such lessons as that about "the good boy whose parents are poor"—

> When he sees little boys and girls riding on pretty horses, or in coaches, or walking with ladies and gentlemen, and having on very fine clothes, he does not envy them, nor wish to be like them.
>
> He says, "I have often been told, and I have read, that it is God who makes some poor, and others rich; that the rich have many troubles which we know nothing of; and that the poor, if they are but good, may be very happy: indeed, I think that when I am good, nobody can be happier than I am.

But according to the doctrine of the self-made man, such honorable behavior (except in cases of "singular misfortune") should have sent the lad flying up the social ladder. Perhaps this is why similar moral exhortation in religious journals was so often entitled "lessons for apprentices." Be that as it may, the workers were instructed simultaneously in the desirability of virtuous endurance of poverty and the certainty of escape by the virtuous from poverty. Thus the model employer was one who coupled moral with industrial discipline. The

Reverend Henry A. Miles of Lowell, in his elaborate tribute to the mills of his towns, noted with pleasure that the books of one factory recorded dishonorable discharges for thinning cloth, worthless character, irregular attendance at work, improper conduct in town, reading in the mill, intemperance, and profanity. All such cases concluded with the notation "name sent round," assuring the reverend that "Such persons obtain no more employment throughout the city."

Neither the cult of the self-made man nor the glory of virtuous poverty could be quite convincing to the workingman—though each of these notions left its strong imprint on his thinking. The few careful studies of economic mobility in mid-nineteenth century factory towns which have been made have all concluded that the number of industrial wage earners who actually rose to the ranks of employers was pitifully small. Those who left industry to become self-employed in store-keeping, professions, or politics were more numerous, and those whose sons escaped by such routes were a significant number, but still by no means the norm. Following the career of every laborer in Newburyport, Massachusetts, through the census schedules of 1850, 1860, and 1870, Stephen Thernstrom found that less than one-twentieth of them rose to middle class occupations. "More often than not," Thernstrom concluded, "the unskilled Newburyport workman remained an unskilled laborer throughout this period; more often than not the son of such a man became a semiskilled worker."

Success for the worker, then, as a matter of fact, consisted of training his son for a somewhat better job than the father's *within the factory*, and of acquiring some real estate—a house. Modest though these goals might seem in the land of the self-made man, they were themselves mutually antagonistic to a significant degree. Saving for a house meant sacrificing the education of the children, since it meant sending all members of the family out to work. This need may account in part for the fact that at legislative hearings on child labor in Massachusetts and Pennsylvania during the 1830s and '40s, more concern about the schooling of working class children was expressed by professional educators, and even by some manufacturers, than by the operatives who testified. To be more precise, the proposal to prohibit child labor and compel school attendance was favored by middle class reformers of the Horace Mann type. Workers more commonly asked that hours of labor be reduced and wages increased *for the whole family*. The appeal of the Manayunk Working People's Committee revealed their priorities when it argued that if its members enjoyed leisure time and a decent income, "we might then live comfortable, and place our children at some public school, where they might receive instruction, sufficient to carry them with propriety through life."

Under the traditional apprentice system, education of the workman's child had been the responsibility of the *master*. Apprentice contracts of the eighteenth and early nineteenth century were quite explicit regarding the instruction to be given the youth, and from the 1750s onward schools for poor youth flourished in the cities as a means of providing the academic instruction promised in such indentures. But the collapse of the apprentice system in the 1820s and '30s had put an end to such obligations, while the spreading use of unindentured children in workshops and factories in the forties placed the youth in the labor market as a free laborer—as his father's competitor. Hence while workmen's organizations demanded free and so-called equal education for their children, poor fathers themselves were sorely tempted to exploit their children, whose wages legally belonged to the head of the family. In fact, the level of wages paid in such industries as textiles made such exploitation indispensable.

No matter how many members of their families went to the mills, however, the majority of workmen at this time did not even succeed in acquiring the desired real estate. Thernstrom found that 78% of the laborers who remained in Newburyport from 1850 through 1870 had bought houses (and used their much-touted savings accounts to store up the annual mortgage payment); but he also found that only 35% of the laborers of 1850 had remained in the city during the ensuing twenty years.

Studying the changes in industrialization wrought in Northampton, Massachusetts, between 1800 and 1850, Robert W. Dougherty discovered that, in contrast to the 23% of the town's adult males who owned no real estate in 1800, by 1850 63% were unpropertied. His conclusions, in fact, are very helpful in our effort to deal with the paradoxical rise of a proletariat in the Age of Equality. Among the persons who did own property, writes Dougherty, its distribution was indeed broader in the industrial town of 1850 than it had been in the farming village of 1800. "The change which had occurred was not so much in the distribution of property as it was in the entry of a large unpropertied group into town." Transients, he found, amounted to almost one-half of the adult population.

My own examination of the 1840 tax rolls of the cotton spinning and weaving town of Manayunk, near Philadelphia, revealed that very few workers there owned any real estate. The great bulk of them were assessed for personal property only, at a somewhat standard figure of $30 worth, though many laborers were rated at the minimum level possible, $25. The ownership of real estate was common only among smiths, who tended to operate their own forges, and among carpenters and masons, who evidently built their own houses.

But as for the great concern of middle class ideology, the accumulation of a "competence"—for the vast majority of the working class it was a will-o'-the-whisp. They were consumption-minded. Reformers and evangelists might have been shocked by seamstresses and mill girls wasting their earnings in the attempt one of them described to "reproduce in muslin and calico the gaudy vulgarisms which the unrefined wealthy flaunt along Broadway in silk and velvet." But what should those women have saved—and for what could they realistically have saved? Workers who took the gospel of wealth seriously tended to want their wealth immediately. Their attitude appalled the English Chartist James Burns when he briefly plied his trade in New York. "In the old country, I have never witnessed anything so disgustingly disagreeable as this selfishness of the American hat makers," he wrote. They "gobble" up each others' work, labor "like horses with the lash continually over them," "drink like savages," engage in ceaseless conflict with their bosses over prices, and "as soon as they made their money, they spent it, and in a manner which showed that they were thoroughly regardless of the contingencies of health or continued employment."

What could have horrified the good parson more than the parody of the swells put on by New York's Bowery B'hoy? Up the Bowery he strolled in the evenings or on Sunday, to the theater where three popular plays were performed each evening—dressed, in the words of one observer, in "a high beaver hat, with the nap divided and brushed in opposite directions, the hair on the back of his head clipped close, while in front the temple locks were curled and greased . . . a smooth face, a gaudy silk neck cloth, black frock-coat, full pantaloons, turned up at the bottom over heavy boots for service in slaughterhouses and at fires." On his arm strolled the gaily bedecked girl for whom he was ready to fight chivalrously in the twinkling of an eye. And the fight always came: for the honor of their ladies the troops of Bowery B'hoys whooped their battle cry, "Lam him," and charged into the nightly fray.

Such behavior is so far removed from the gospel of virtuous poverty that one is lead to inquire if the voice of the preacher ever reached the tenements and boardinghouses of the workers. In fact, both remote mining communities and workmen's quarters of the great seaports were the despair of evangelists. Robert Baird lamented: "Open infidelity . . . has descended to the lower ranks. It now burrows in the narrow streets, and lanes, and purlieus of our large cities and towns, where it finds its proper aliment—the ignorant and the vicious to mislead and destroy." Revivalist Albert Barnes concurred. The "lower stratum of society . . . that dense and dark mass, the population of the alleys and cellars, and garrets—the ignorant, the degraded, the grossly sensual, the idle, the worthless—the refuse of society," he argued, "are not in a condition where revivals of religion can be expected such as I am advocating."

In fact the last faint traces of the nation's once-proud heritage of Deism were found in farming villages far removed from the centers of civilization (generally in universalist or Swedenborgian guise) and among the city poor. Organized infidelity, noteworthy for its remarkable coupling of a stern moral code with scornful hostility to the clergy, had been an important ideological component of the revolt of the city artisans in the 1830s. William Heighton had issued his call for a union of the Philadelphia trades at the universalist church pastored by Abner Kneeland, the nation's best known Painite. In New York City the Moral Philanthropists of Tammany Hall, ignoring hostile admonitions to "go back to their shopboards," had both carried on the Religion of Nature and provided a link between the trades unions and the radical wing of the Democratic Party. Their secular caste of mind had become an enduring part of the Locofoco ideology.

Though that artisans' movement was dead in the forties, big city Democrats carried on the secularist crusade against pietistic bigotry, prohibition laws, and Sabbatarianism which, they exclaimed, "would make your house a prison." Mike Walsh and George Wilkes, heroes of the Bowery B'hoys and spokesmen of what they called the "Subterranean Democracy" had no equals in the art of ridiculing pious mill owners who "clamor about the wrongs and outrages of the Southern slaves," while preaching holy resignation to the "white wage slaves of the North."

Radical German workmen, led by Hermann Kriege and Wilhelm Weitling, imbued as they were with the *Freidenker* heritage of their own country, naturally gravitated toward this Locofoco group—Kriege soon becoming a regular functionary of Tammany Hall. Catholic immigrants, be they German or Irish, found shelter behind the secularists' resistance to *Protestant* enthusiasm and also joined the fold.

Ironically it was here among the dregs of big city life—in those "cancers on the body politic" Thomas Jefferson had most feared—that his doctrine, "a wise and frugal government, which shall restrain men from injuring one another, leaving them otherwise free to manage their own affairs, and shall not tax from the mouth of labor, the bread it has earned," enjoyed a popular devotion more ardent than was to be found anywhere else in the land. This political outlook, well supplemented by their rabid racism, prodded Walsh and Wilkes into political alliance with John C. Calhoun and the ultras of the South in the early forties. Theirs was the mentality of the sailor in Herman Melville's *Redburn*, who contrasted the joys of his princely sojourn among the natives of Madagascar with the woes he suffered in "snivilization": "You don't see any Methodists chaps feelin' dreadful about their souls; you don't see any darned beggars and pesky constables in *Madagasky*, I tell ye; and none o' them kings there gets their big toes pinched by the gout. Blast Ameriky, I say."

Small wonder the Protestant clergy of the day sent their Missionaries to Madagascar and wrote off the city poor as unworthy of their efforts. The Reverend Ashael Nettleton, a foe of revival methods, warned that it was *not* judicious "by impassioned discourses, addressed to the sympathies of our nature, to raise this class of feelings to flame" or to ignore "the danger, in the large cities, of permitting undisciplined people to assemble promiscuously." Revivalist Albert Barnes replied that his meetings were not intended for "that dark mass," but were successful only where people "are the best educated, and where they are most sober in their lives, most virtuous and industrious and regular in their attendance on the house of God."

If Edward Thompson is correct in his judgment that Wesleyan Methodism in England was peculiarly "a religion *for* the poor" (as distinct from the Dissent of Bunyan which he sees as a religion *of* the poor), then America was remarkably different from England in this respect. Methodism, and its revivalist counterparts in other denominations, were religions of and for the middle class. Their official spokesmen consciously and studiously spurned the urban poor.

Protestant churches as institutions suffered irredeemably from success. As the most prominent members of their urban congregations prospered, rose in the world and moved uptown, the churches responded by fixing pew rents (legalized even by the Methodist General Conference in 1852) and moving uptown with them. A survey of New York City's 25 Methodist churches in 1846 (two of which already charged pew rents) described 17 of them (boasting 9571 members in all) as having "a substantial brick edifice" or a "handsome and commodious house of worship" or "a prosperous congregation," while three of the remainder were special mission churches for sailors, and the remaining five poorly endowed chapels claimed only 524 members among them.

As the churches migrated away from the poor, they left behind only an occasional mission, or a valiant tract society agent carrying Bibles from door to door though the slums. And the latter were the first to declare that the congested living of the poor made a mockery of Victorian prudery. In fact they easily projected their own carefully repressed appetites onto the workers, concluding from the ubiquity of grog shops in lower class neighborhoods that all their residents were drunken and lustful: One New York missionary gave classic expression to such sentiments when he declared of the slums: "Every house was a filthy brothel, the resort of persons of every age, color, and nationality." Similarly when some Pittsburgh Baptists did venture to bring the poor into their church, they were roundly criticized by the American Missionary Association for making "untimely efforts: administering the sacraments of the church of Christ to the openly vile, such as Sabbath breakers, licentious persons, and drunkards."

Even the fires of revivalism in the Pentecostal Year (1858) burned uptown, not in the working-class quarters. The nondenominational prayer meetings which generated such enthusiasm in every major city met at noon hour in the commercial center of town and were called by their organizers "businessmen's revival meetings." The Young Men's Christian Association, the most significant institutional outgrowth of that revival, defined its own area of work when it appealed to businessmen for funds to help render the youth it touched, "better men, better clerks, better salesmen, better cashiers, better agents, better creditors, and better in every way, whether as friends of your family, suitors of your daughters, husbands to your loved and cherished ones, fathers of your families, officers in your banks, directors in your railroad companies, aldermen in your Council, and officers in your churches."

Yet the working class did *not* go untouched by this wave of revivalist enthusiasm. In the first place hundreds of thousands of wage earners were caught up in its negative thrust: anti-Catholicism. Complaints of the Catholic clergy against use of the King James version of the Bible in common schools, coupled with their demands for state aid to parochial schools, roused nativists to a militant assault on the Catholic Church as the foe of republican education, and on politicians who courted Catholic votes (generally Democrats) as corrupters of the body politic. With the battle cry "an open Bible and a pure ballot box" they swept to control of local offices and Congressional seats in New York and Philadelphia in 1844.

Their rise in Philadelphia was climaxed by two fierce riots, one in early May and the other in July of that year. The first broke out in the suburb of Kensington, which contained a large closely-knit community of handloom weavers, constituted almost entirely of Irish emigrants of the 1820s. A demagogic lawyer and temperance publicist, Lewis C. Levin, foremost leader of the nativists was staging a rally in the midst of Kensington to denounce "Popish interference in the elective franchise," when a sudden rainstorm forced him and his followers into the shelter of the market house. There Levin tried to resume his speech, and his effort enraged the Irish who were shopping for their day's groceries. Furiously the Irish assaulted the nativists, killing one of them and wounding seven others.

The next morning Levin's paper raised its followers with the cry, "Another St. Bartholomew's day is begun in the streets of Philadelphia." Reasoning that the best way to avoid such a massacre was to slaughter the Catholics first, a vast assemblage of Protestants marched north from Philadelphia for two days of shooting and pillaging in Kensington. Quickly assembled troops made only a half-hearted effort to restrain the tumult but devoted themselves primarily to safeguarding arsenals and Catholic institutions. The pattern of destruction made it clear that the rioters' target was the colony of weavers. Weavers' cottages and outbuildings were burned to the ground. Their residents were described by one journalist as "Men with their wives, and often six or seven children, trudging fearfully through the streets with small bundles, seeking refuge they knew not where."

Throughout the previous decade these weavers had been waging a furious struggle against the degradation of their trade. Their stand-out in 1836 had been provided $1000 in aid by the Philadelphia Trades' Union, but since the collapse of that organization they had continued alone. By 1843 they were resorting to vitriol, the slashing of scab-made chains, and assaults on factories housing power looms, all in vain resistance to the relentless decline of their piece rates. Kensington was in the hands of the military at some point in every year from 1841 on.

Now, in the wake of the riots, with the army requiring its special permission for any public gatherings, Kensington manufacturers hastened to cut wages once again. Though the army command did permit a county temperance convention and even ward nativist meetings in Kensington itself, it would not allow the weavers to assemble. The only recourse of the weavers' committee was to publish a notice in local newspapers advising members of the trade to seek work from "the more honorable employers, in the southern part of the city," who were still paying the previously established scale. Though the number of handloom weavers in Philadelphia county continued to rise until 1860, never again did workers in this trade play the militant role for which they had been noted before May 1844. Their back had been broken.

Then, who were the nativists? The rolls of their martyrs and the lists of ward officers published in their journal makes the answer remarkably clear. Their top leaders were lawyers, publishers, and merchants—men whose political ambitions were rewarded by a meteoric rise to power, to the astonishment of established Whig and Democratic politicians, and to the horror of the city's elite, who were terrified by the nativists' violent tactics. But the ward club activists were ship carpenters and caulkers, riggers, blacksmiths, tailors, house carpenters, printers, chairmakers—all of them from the traditional trades of the American seaport. Not one weaver was among them. They represented the same occupational groups as had sparked the Revolutionary Sons of Liberty and brought to life the Trades Union of the 1830s. In fact, their most formidable political stronghold was the suburb of Southwark, birthplace of the citywide artisans' movement in 1827.

My survey of the manuscript census schedules of 1850 for Kensington itself (the earliest census recording the type of information I needed) revealed that workmen in these trades were in fact almost all Philadelphia born. These craftsmen, long associated by family and by trade with the historic activities of Philadelphia as a *seaport*, reacted violently against the incursion of this new *manufacturing* community into their midst. Having devoted themselves in the previous decade to the cause of establishing the state's common schools, they now turned to defending those schools against Popish corruption. Their psychology is understandable. Yet how remarkable it is that trades which had supported each other with ardor in the Trades' Union of the 1830s and together acclaimed that they knew no Jew or Gentile, Christian or infidel—only the equal rights of man—should have been combatting each other violently on cultural grounds less than ten years later.

Clearly the voice of militant Protestantism *did* reach the workers, especially those of old Calvinist American stock, despite the disdainful attitude of the churches. It is also clear that (in good American fashion) politicians marched in where preachers feared to tread. And such politicians rallied working-class followers with a markedly evangelical rhetoric. Those temperance orators who entered the political arena, appealing for votes to curb demon rum, often enjoyed a warm response from constituencies of native born, Protestant workingmen. Both Henry Wilson of Natick and Nathaniel Banks of Lowell began their political ascents in just this way in 1840—and soon found themselves advocating prohibition laws, the ten-hour day, and defense of the republic against the Catholic menace.

As the names of Lowell and Natick suggest, it was especially in smaller mill towns that such constituencies were to be found. But most American manufacturing was carried on in just such towns, not in the port cities. In mining villages and iron rolling towns throughout Pennsylvania and Ohio the Welsh Calvinist Methodist church, made up there entirely of workers, enforced a moral code far more rigorous than that of middle-class congregations. In New England, Freewill Baptist and Methodist chapels with poorly educated worker- and farmer-preachers, held many operatives and mechanics who had migrated from the surrounding countryside in the fold. Yankee shoemakers, whether they were still found in New Hampshire villages or had migrated to dismal quarters in New York City, were notorious for their sobriety and their devotion to church. If they abandoned the ancestral fold of the Congregationalists (as many did), it was usually to become Methodists.

The Second Advent frenzy sparked by William Miller, after spreading slowly for several years through the New England hill country and smoldering in Boston and New York during the early depression years, burst into flame among the city poor after the cholera epidemic of 1842. In fact, the so-called "excesses" of Millerism strongly influenced the decision of respectable revivalists to shun the slums thereafter. And in Lowell, where mill owners required church attendance of all their operatives, many young women overacted the part. Company agents complained to Reverend Miles that girls were exhausting themselves through "a too frequent attendance, in times of religious excitement especially, upon evening meetings, at the churches or vestries."

The religion of these mill town operatives may best be described as a primitive revivalism. Its rejection of predestination in favor of the doctrine of "free agency" was akin to the teachings of Wesley—and to the main currents of middle-class revivalism. But in the churches of the workers the fire of God's anger and the flames of Hell burned far more hotly than they did in the sermons of Charles G. Finney or the Pentecostal revivalists of 1858, let alone the insipid pap of Moody and Sanky. In the hands of lower-class advocates, furthermore, the attitude of religion toward the virtuous resignation of the poor became decidedly ambivalent. On the one hand the journal of the Freewill Baptists argued that "the evils (workers) suffer and the vices they contract are chiefly of their own choosing . . . They are as completely the master of their own persons and property as any other class of men." On the other hand, the same journal advocated the founding of a workers' paper—"without the name"—to resist company regulations which injured health or morals, doing so through the preaching of virtue, rather than discontent.

Other workers found in the Bible itself the language to express their discontent. The Massachusetts Ten Hour Convention called it "God's will to abridge man's daily labor." Operatives of Peterboro, New Hampshire, protested against their employers' introduction of the practice of lighting up the mills before breakfast to stretch the working day in this language: "Although the evening and the morning is spoken of in the Scripture, no mention is made of an evening in the morning. We therefore conclude that the practice of lighting up our factories in the morning, and thereby making two evenings in every twenty-four hours, is not only oppressive but unscriptual."

But note that while the faith of these workers to some degree resembled the social gospel of the future in its conviction that Christian behavior could bridge the gulf between labor and capital, it also struck a sharper note. "The cries of them which have been shamefully oppressed," declared the Fall River Mechanics, "have entered into the ears of the Lord of Sabaoth." Enough of the Bunyanesque strain had survived in their thinking to keep alive the Lord of Hosts who smites the Christian's powerful enemies.

Finally, this cast of mind helped link Yankee workmen to the middle-class reformers in their vicinity—especially in New England. Sarah Bagley, leader of the Ten Hour Campaign in Massachusetts, to take but one example, was a Sunday school teacher and a regular attender at Lowell Institute lectures after her hours at the spinning frame. Her activities brought her into contact with the intellectual luminaries of her state. Workers of her type were drawn, not toward the champions of free trade and slavery, as had been the case with the Locofoco followers of Mike Walsh, nor even toward the cracking of Catholic skulls, like Levin's partisans, but toward the anti-slavery movement.

As Thomas Wentworth Higginson recalled the early forties, workers consumed with "the Second Advent delusions just then flourishing," were the very heart of the abolitionist movement in New England, which, he continued, "was not, like our modern civil service reform, strongest in the educated class, but was predominantly a people's movement . . . far stronger for a time in the factories and shoe-shops than in the pulpits or colleges."

In short, during the 1840s the Locofoco strain and the Primitive Revivalist strain of working-class endeavor were moving in mutually contradictory directions. Trade unions of the fifties tried to resolve this problem by banning all political and religious topics from their meetings. But it was not until the Civil War had disposed finally of the slavery issue and relegated the nativist crusade to comparative obscurity that a national movement of workers could appear. That movement, in turn, was enriched by both streams of its cultural inheritance.

CHAPTER 4

The Shuttle and the Cross

Weavers and Artisans in the Kensington Riots of 1844

Journal of Social History 5 (Summer 1972): 411–46

American workers in the nineteenth century engaged in economic conflicts with their employers as fierce as any known to the industrial world, yet in their political behavior they consistently failed to exhibit a class-consciousness. This paradox was evident as early as 1844, when nativist parties triumphed at the polls in Philadelphia, Boston and New York. At the close of a decade and a half of hotly contested strikes and severe economic hardship climaxed by the bitter depression of 1837–43, working men had divided their votes along ethnic lines. The greater part of them were swept up into an enthusiastic political movement whose negative reference group was not the capitalists, but Roman Catholics. Other workers found their enemy in evangelical Protestantism.

Analysis of the nativist movement and of the bloody riots it spawned in the Philadelphia area suggests that the political behavior of American workingmen in the 1840s was fashioned not so much by the economic impact of industrialization as by the workers' reactions to the political demands made by evangelical Protestantism: the moral content of education, liquor licensing and prohibition, Sabbath closing and the suppression of popular "lewd and tumultuous" conduct. Such moral policing as evangelists demanded was in turn urgently needed by the new industrialists, to be sure, for it promised them a disciplined labor force, pacing its toil and its very life cycle to the requirements of the machine and the clock, respectful of property and orderly in its demeanor.[1] Because the responses of various groups of workers to these evangelical issues were determined by their religious outlooks, rather than their economic conditions, however, the working classes were fragmented on election day. Class interests were most clearly evident in trade union activity and in tensions *within* the political parties over questions like the legal ten-hour day.

Such issues, rising directly from the economic impact of industrialization, set working class against middle class. The pattern of cultural politics generated by the religious impact of industrialization, on the other hand, attached workers to the political leadership of the middle classes of their particular ethnic groups. The counterpoint of class and ethnic conflict in working-class life was clearly visible in Kensington, a manufacturing suburb of Philadelphia, where crowds of Irishmen and native Americans battled each other for four days in May 1844. While the city proper contained some of the most advanced iron rolling mills, machine shops and locomotive works in the country, only 54 percent of its 16,600 working adults were listed in manufacturing and trades by the census of 1840. Commerce, navigation, and the learned professions absorbed the rest. By way of contrast, in Kensington 89 percent of the labor force of slightly under 3,000 people was classified in manufacturing and trades.[2] Few really wealthy men lived there. The richest residents were master weavers, shoemakers, vitualers, gunsmiths, and ship builders whose holdings census takers in 1850 assessed mostly between $2,000 and $10,000. By the Delaware River waterfront one could find the old Pennsylvania Wainwright family, lumber dealers and co-owners of two large piers. Jonathan Wainwright's real estate holdings valued at $20,000 in 1850 were remarkably large for Kensington, yet his wealth was surpassed by that of the acknowledged leader of the Catholic community, boss weaver Hugh Clark. Michael Keenan, another Catholic master weaver, whose houses were burned by rioters in 1844, estimated his real estate at $18,000 in 1850. Only the most prosperous of the Vandusens, a large clan of lumber merchants, ship builders and ship carpenters who helped lead the Protestant cause, approached this level of wealth.[3]

This was a community of working men and women, and among them that division of labor which Adam Smith termed the mainspring of economic growth was evident in profusion.[4] Interspersed with the larger occupational categories were solitary cloth measurers, artificial limb makers, tooth manufacturers, bird stuffers, lime burners and saw handle makers, not to mention two perfumers, a drum maker and a "comedean." More important, the major occupations encompassed superior craftsmen whose style of work had changed little since the eighteenth century (butchers, cabinet makers, ship carpenters), some factory operatives (in metals and glass works), swarms of outworkers (weaving, tailoring and shoemaking) and the inevitable impoverished laborers, carters, draymen and boatmen.

With the notable exception of the weavers, most of the workmen had been born in the United States. In fact, the manuscript census returns of 1850, the first to record age, occupation and birthplace for each individual, indicate that most were native Pennsylvanians. In contrast to the heavily immigrant weaving areas, concentrated in the second and fifth wards of 1844, the waterfront first, third and fourth wards with their vast tracts of lumberyards, furniture shops, shipbuilding facilities and fishermen's wharves were the special domain of the natives. Alongside only five Englishmen and four Irishmen who worked in shipyard trades could be found 433 Americans. Many of their neighbors on the Delaware's shore worked at one of the two paternalistically managed glass works, where more than 70 percent of the employees were native born.[5] Not only were 92 of the 103 fishermen Pennsylvanian by birth, but they shared among themselves only a handful of family names.

Shoemaking, one of Kensington's largest occupations in 1850, involved 343 natives, 128 Germans, 70 Irishmen, 19 Englishmen, 3 Frenchmen, 2 Scots and a Dutchman. In the newer metal trades of the same area—machinists, boiler makers, molders and rolling mill hands—more than half were Pennsylvanians, and 63 percent were Americans, though numerous Englishmen were to be found in their ranks. Among tailors, on the other hand, German immigrants were preponderant; and in the ranks of cabinet makers Germans almost equaled the natives in number. At the bottom of the occupational ladder, the laborers included 405 Irishmen, 99 Germans, and 205 natives.[6]

Among the wage earners were many young recent arrivals in Kensington. The town's population almost doubled between 1840 and 1850, on top of an increase of 88 percent during the twenties and 66 percent in the thirties.[7] Many of the residents lived in boardinghouses, kept mostly by widows or by workingmen's wives. In the home of a New York-born bootmaker dwelt three young families (his own and those of two youthful locally born machinists) and no fewer than four other machinists, one pattern maker, two blacksmiths, two iron molders and a stray cigar maker. All the boarders were Americans in their twenties, except for a molder and a machinist from England.[8] An inn, not far from this menagerie of metallurgists, bore a more cosmopolitan aspect. In addition to the owner's family, it housed an Irish hostler and his 18-year-old wife, an English bartender and his blacksmith compatriot, a painter, a ship carpenter, an accountant, a house carpenter and a cordwainer—all from Pennsylvania—a ship carpenter and a ship joiner from New York state, another ship carpenter from Vermont, and a house carpenter who had come up from Maryland.[9]

Kensington's main industry was weaving, both cotton cloth and, to a lesser extent, woolen. Its output, combined with that of other suburbs like Manayunk and Moyamensing, helped keep Philadelphia County the leading textile producing region of the country down to the Civil War. After the city of Philadelphia had absorbed these suburbs by the consolidation act of 1854, it boasted 260 separate cotton and woolen factories which was more, its champions claimed, than any other city in the world.[10] But most of its weaving was not carried on in these factories. Weaving was basically a cottage industry, based on the putting-out system and the use of handlooms. As early as 1827 the local Society of Weavers boasted, probably with some exaggeration, that 104 warping mills in the region supplied about 4,500 weavers. On the eve of the Civil War Edwin Freedley estimated that 6,000 handloom frames were in use in the county.[11]

Kensington alone had 2,238 weavers when the 1850 census was taken.[12] During the preceding decade some rooms used for cloth weaving and more of those used for carpet weaving had "assumed more of a 'factory' air, and a few really important establishments [had begun] their career."[13] Some large manufacturers put out yarn to as many as 100 weavers each, while many more supplied but half a dozen cottages. Spools of yarn for the journeymen's shuttles were wound either by their own families or by women and children employed by the master. In that case the master passed on the cost of winding to the journeyman at a rate of 75 cents a week, a rate which remained quite constant from the 1820s through the 1840s.[14] For the most part as Edwin T. Freedley observed, "the persons engaged in the production have no practical concern with the ten-hour system, or the factory system, or even with the solar system. They work at such hours as they choose in their own homes, and their industry is mainly regulated by the state of the larder."[15] A starker description by the contemporary novelist, George Lippard, suggested perhaps luridly, but nonetheless accurately, that the "state of the larder" was usually far from good: "Here we behold a house of time-worn brick, there a toppling frame; on every side the crash of looms, urged by weary hands even at this hour, disturbs the silence of the night."[16]

The neighborhood Lippard described surrounded the Nanny Goat Market, storm center of the great riots of 1844. In that neighborhood the census takers of 1850 confirmed the literary images of Lippard and Freedley. They found, for example, an Irish-born master weaver, Alexander Myers, living with his American wife and three small children, as well as a laborer and his wife who performed domestic service. Six Irish weavers with their families tenanted the surrounding buildings. The whole complex was valued at some $3,000.[17] Not far off lived Jacob Hopes, who similarly had come from Ireland early in the 1830s, married an American woman and now boarded seven single men, all weavers and presumably his journeymen.[18] John Lavery, another boss weaver, had lost in the 1844 riots a $2,000 establishment described by a metropolitan newspaper as "a large and handsome brick house with brick back buildings." The journeyman weaver, whose $150 two-story frame house next door was also wrecked, was a tenant as were the weaver residents of the next eight houses burned down the street.[19]

As these few examples suggest, both masters and workmen in the weaving business were predominantly Irish. In fact, 78 percent of the weavers were of Irish birth. In wards three and six (of 1850), where 70 percent of the town's weavers dwelt, 85 percent of them were Irish. The 5 percent who were born in America and the 9 percent born in England seem to have been largely children of Irish immigrants.[20] The ages of the weavers' oldest children born in the United States indicate that the parents came to Kensington in two great waves, one about 1828–33 and the second in the latter half of the forties, after the riot of 1844.[21]

Although the immigrant weavers seem to have been predominantly Roman Catholic, there was a significant Protestant minority among them. The precise division cannot be known because the census takers specified the religion of no one but clergymen. Just to the east of Second Street, the north-south axis of the weaving district, lived many Irish weavers with such names as Montgomery, Campbell, McTaige and Stewart. Though it is always dubious to guess an Irishman's faith by his family name, firmer evidence of Protestantism lies in the presence among these weavers of a Presbyterian minister. a Methodist minister and an Irish-born agent of the American Tract Society. One Presbyterian preacher shared the home of an Irish boss weaver, William Wallace. Two Catholic priests, presumably serving the large St. Michael's Church, were their close neighbors.[22] In a word, Catholics and Protestants were found in almost random dispersal among both boss and journeyman weavers, but almost all were Irish. Their ethnic cohesiveness was epitomized by the case of Bernard Sherry, a master weaver who lost one frame and three brick houses inhabited by his journeymen during the riot. After his buildings had been burned, Sherry was arrested on charges of having armed his workmen to defend them against the nativists.[23]

The ethnic cohesiveness of the weaving community did not preclude sharp economic conflict within it. From the end of the 1820s through the 1840s, the weavers fought a running battle against the constantly recurring efforts of their countrymen masters to reduce piece rates. When times were hard, as they were in 1833–34 or in 1837, or desperate as they were from 1839 to 1843, the masters claimed the fierce competition of the market compelled them to lower prices for weaving. When times were good, as in the flourishing years of 1835–36, the same masters argued that the high price of cotton threatened to wipe out profits if production costs did not fall. The dilemma of American hand weavers was precisely what Frederick Engels described in England at the same time: "One class of woven goods after another is annexed by the power-loom, and hand-weaving is the last refuge of workers thrown out of employment in other branches, so that the trade is always overcrowded."[24] Well might the Royal Commission on Handloom Weavers of 1838 warn British workers "to flee from the trade, and to beware of leading their children into it, as they would beware of the commission of the most atrocious of crimes."[25] But the supply of weavers stubbornly refused to fall. From the manufacturing towns of Yorkshire to the banks of the Delaware River, the rural poverty of Ireland kept the weaving cottages full from the late 1820s onward.[26]

In 1827 an English emigrant warned weavers of Yorkshire not to expect to improve their lot by coming to America. In Philadelphia, he wrote, a "smart weaver . . . by a fair week's work of 12 hours per day" would do well to acquire gross earnings of $4.50 a week. Some did no better than $4.00.[27] A press statement of master weavers the same year claimed $5.00 as a weekly average for journeymen.[28] There seemed general agreement throughout this period that 100 yards of three shuttle gingham was something of a standard week's work, 120 yards the fruit of an extremely intensive week's application. From the late twenties through the mid-thirties, prices paid to journeymen hovered around 4 cents a yard for this rather common style of cloth. If a weaver had a family, their work at spooling could save the journeyman a charge of 75 cents weekly and possibly, with enough children, earn a pittance more for the household by winding spools for the use of other journeymen who had no children. Customarily part of the worker's pay was given in store goods rather than cash.

Wages were fixed by agreements negotiated each spring and fall between the manufacturers and a committee representing the weavers. Kensington and Moyamensing rates were governed by separate but usually similar scales at least from the mid-1830s on.[29] Often the agreements were reached only after severe strikes, and during the 1830s these conflicts brought the weavers into affiliation with the General Trades' Union of the City and County of Philadelphia, an assembly of delegates from all the organized trades of the area. During the weavers' strike in the fall of 1836 their societies received $1,500 in aid from the Trades' Union.[30] In turn the weavers contributed one of the most prominent leaders of the local workers' movement, John Ferral. To accommodate both immigrants and the native American craftsmen the Trades' Union banned from its midst all "party, political, or religious sectarian" questions. "The followers of Christ acknowledge a time for all things," explained the American-born saddler John Crossin on behalf of the Trades' Union, and "we do the same."[31]

As the depression of 1839–43 deepened, weavers' strikes became increasingly violent. The basic gingham scale (which was used as the yardstick throughout this discussion) was cut to 3 cents a yard in 1841, yet scabs were available in abundance especially from the most recent immigrants. From August of 1842 until January of the next year Kensington weavers refused to work at the fall scale offered by their employers. When some workers broke ranks, stalwarts staged parades of 150 to 500 participants through the streets, entered the houses of non-strikers and hurled their unfinished chains into bonfires in the streets. Early in November they dispersed a meeting of their masters by threatening to tear down the house where it was taking place, and two months later a sheriff's posse attempting to arrest some strikers was routed by a charge of over 400 weavers armed with muskets and brickbats. Three military companies arrived during the night, and in their presence the workers and masters reached agreement on a scale which left hundreds of families living on less than three dollars a week.[32]

A strike in the spring of 1843 won a small raise, which was celebrated by a massive unity parade of Kensington and Moyamensing weavers.[33] That August improving market conditions, optimism over the new tariff, and a very effective one-month strike allowed the Kensington weavers to negotiate an enormous raise—to 5¼ cents a yard for the standard gingham. When three of the largest employers refused to accede to the new scale and demanded that other masters support them in continuing to resist, the employers' conference broke up in a brawl.[34] As the early glimmerings of returning prosperity shone over the land, the weavers' incomes actually moved upwards.

The trend did not last long. The following May saw the Kensington weaving district gutted by nativist rioters. Ten days after the disturbance, the handloom weavers' committee announced that a number of manufacturers, "willing to take advantage of the then existing circumstances to enrich themselves," had reduced "our wages at a time when it is uncalled for by the markets" and when journeymen could not respond because the authorities had banned all meetings. The committee spoke the truth. The basic gingham price had been slashed from 5¼ cents a yard back to 3¼ cents.[35]

The key to the weavers' downfall lay in the fact that no longer did they enjoy the support of the other workmen of Philadelphia. Quite the contrary; the final defeat had come in the wake of actual physical assault by other workers, for the most part native-born Protestant artisans. The central problem for this study, therefore, is to explain the rift between the weavers and their fellow workmen of Philadelphia County.

During the 1830s all groups of Philadelphia workmen—Protestant and Catholic, native and immigrant, superior craftsmen, outworkers, factory operatives and laborers—had been caught up in an awakening of class solidarity as significant as any in American history. The formation of the General Trades' Union, which included delegates from some 50 organized trade societies by 1836, and the successful general strike for the ten-hour day in 1835 epitomized this movement.[36] With revenues of $400 to $500 a month from its constituent unions, the Trades' Union could boast early in 1836: "Within the last six months more than one half of the Societies in the Union have struck, and no instance is known where a Society has struck, under the sanction of the Union, and failed in that strike."[37] Most significant of all, these successful strikes were conducted by workers who ranged in status from laborers and factory operatives at one end of the scale to bookbinders and jewelers at the other. Even journeymen cabinet makers (whose primary concerns were to collect debts due them from merchants and to halt competition from auction sales) and butchers and victuallers (struggling to hold down stall rent charged by the city and impede the "shaving" practices of cattle dealers) participated in the Trades' Union.[38]

From the ranks of these diverse groups, the Trades' Union could summon up what a local paper called "one of the largest meetings ever held in this city," conducted "with strict order and propriety" to protest the conviction of striking coal heavers, who were among the poorest but also the most militant of the city's working people. The rally demanded the defeat of Mayor John Swift for "the false imprisonment and unconstitutional bail [he] demanded of the Schuylkill laborers whose only crime consisted in asking 25 cents per day addition to former wages."[39]

Many prominent workingmen plunged into the county's political struggles, for the most part supporting the anti-bank wing of the Democratic Party. Ferral of the weavers, Benjamin Sewell the tanner, William Thompson the carpenter, William English, William Gilmore and Samuel Thompson, all shoemakers, and Edward A. Penniman and Joshua Fletcher of the coachmakers were but some of the Trades' Union leaders who promoted Henry A. Muhlenberg's gubernatorial campaign as an anti-monopoly Democrat, sent their champion Lemuel Paynter to Congress from the Southwark area (the manufacturing suburb to the south of Philadelphia which was the birthplace of the artisans' movement), and helped maintain a consistent Democratic majority of almost two to one in Kensington elections.[40] After the depression struck, they organized mass rallies to support President Van Buren's Independent Treasury scheme, demand resumption of specie payments and suppression of "shin plaster" small notes by banks and dispatched committees to visit each of the city's banks with these demands.[41] Ferral proudly boasted to Senator James Buchanan that "the working classes" had frustrated the efforts of pro-bank "shin plaster democrats" to dominate the local party. He concluded that "all is well with the bone and sinew" who had rededicated the Democratic organization to the "emancipation of our Country from the bondage in which it is at present held by chartered Monopolists."[42]

At the very time Ferral wrote, however, the impact of the depression was relentlessly undermining the working-class cohesiveness which the Trades' Union had built up on both the economic and political fronts. As a prominent Philadelphian confided to his diary in the summer of 1842: "The streets seem deserted, the largest houses are shut up and to rent, there is no business, there is no money, no confidence & little hope, property is sold every day by the sheriff at a 4th of the estimated value of a few years ago, nobody can pay debts, the miseries of poverty are felt by both rich & poor. . . ."[43] In this setting most trade societies collapsed, and the General Trades' Union disintegrated with the evaporation of its once munificent treasury.

With the demise of the Trades' Union, Philadelphia lacked any institution uniting the Catholic weaver, the Methodist shoemaker and the Presbyterian ship carpenter as members of a common working class. Strikes became as uncommon as they were hopeless, except among the handloom weavers. Artisan struggles of other types excited the county. In the spring of 1839, for example, the butchers waged a brilliantly executed campaign against "shaver" cattle dealers. Through great public fanfare they enlisted the support of their impoverished customers behind the butchers' concerted refusal to pay more than 10 cents a hundredweight for live cattle.[44] The next year shoemakers set up a committee to aid their Boston counterparts then being prosecuted in the famous case of *Commonwealth v. Hunt.*[45]

From August to October 1842, a Workingmen's Convention met weekly, organized ward clubs and staged street meetings throughout the county to protest unemployment and "to guard their more indigent brethren against the inclemancies of the coming winter." An Equal Rights Party which was launched by the movement, however, failed abysmally at the polls.[46]

When prominent mechanics convened a series of meetings during January and February of 1839 in an effort to revive their trades movement, laborers, factory operatives and even the struggling weavers were conspicuously absent. An address signed by well-known spokesmen of the coach makers, shoemakers, painters, bricklayers, tailors, cabinet makers and others blamed the economic crisis on "corrupt legislation," stressed the theme of self-help and made its chief demand "a system of education which shall teach every child in the Commonwealth his duty and interests as a citizen and freeman." It argued that "the old system of pecuniary benefits through the assistance of Trades' Unions seems to have fallen into disrepute" and criticized the "old Union" for "indiscriminate association of all the Trades without any regard to their assimilation or affinity."[47]

It was precisely by making strikes futile, destroying the Trades' Union beyond even hope of resurrection and stimulating this new emphasis on self-improvement that the depression opened the way for the rise of nativism among the artisans. By magnifying the importance to artisans of the temperance and public education movements, these developments set their aspirations on a collision course with those of Catholic immigrants.

The temperance movement paved the way. Like the stress on education, it involved nothing new to artisan culture. In his eloquent pleas for working-class unity at the founding of the Mechanics Union of Trade Associations in 1827, William Heighton had implored his fellow craftsmen to put aside their "drinking, gaming, and frolicking," and devote themselves to self-education.[48] Almost 40 years before that a commentator describing the gathering of 17,000 Philadelphians, proudly arrayed by trades to celebrate the newly-adopted federal constitution, had attributed their orderliness to their drinking nothing but "American Beer and Cyder," and admonished his readers to "despise SPIRITOUS LIQUORS, as *Anti-Federal*, and to consider them as companions to all those vices, that are calculated to dishonor and enslave our country."[49]

The depression cast this traditional artisan virtue in a new light. The hard times made temperance societies with middle-class evangelical leadership ubiquitous in the manufacturing districts, infused a new sense of crusading militancy into their ranks and made them an integral part of artisan life. When the Journeymen House Carpenters prepared their futile strike for a wage increase in March 1839, they appealed publicly for help from the "friends of temperance," arguing that under current wages carpenters "are frequently driven by poverty and care to intemperance, to dispel for a season, the horrid gloom which envelopes their homes," thereby "encompassing their families with misery."[50] The Temperance Society responded with a public letter endorsing the carpenters' demands and calling upon them to make total abstinence a condition of membership in their society.[51] By 1842–43 the temperance societies in almost every ward were supplemented by others organized on trade lines, like the Cordwainers' Beneficial Temperance Association. A new labor-for-labor exchange, The First Co-operative Labor Association of Philadelphia, met in a city temperance house.[52]

In 1838 the movement acquired a new leader of increasing prominence named Lewis C. Levin. This Charleston-born lawyer, described by Alexander McClure as "one of the most brilliant and unscrupulous orators I have ever heard," both lectured for the cause and edited the *Temperance Advocate.*[53] In January 1842, he attracted attention to a new temperance society in the waterfront woodworking district of Kensington, which then had only 15 members, by staging a spectacular bonfire of booze obtained from a converted saloon keeper before the eyes of thousands of spectators. Gathering as much of his audience as would fit into a nearby church, he blamed drunkenness on "the prodigality of the mushroom aristocracy of the country," appealed to the "steady habits of old times" and demanded that the public be allowed to vote on whether taverns should be tolerated in neighborhoods.[54]

It was this demand for popular control of liquor licensing which brought the temperance movement with its new evangelical leadership and artisan base into the political arena.[55] There its impact blended with that of an even more emotionally-charged controversy over reading the Bible in the common schools.

There is no end of irony in the Bible-reading issue, and most of it stems from the fact that two very divergent groups had been involved in the struggle for free public education in Philadelphia in the 1820s and 1830s. One group was the artisans, starting with those involved in the Mechanics' Union of Trade Associations, founded in 1827 with the quest for "equal education" one of its foremost goals. "The original element of *despotism,*" argued one of its reports," is a **MONOPOLY** OF TALENT." The republican alternative, it contended, was the extension of the same education to all citizens "as a matter of right."[56] This theme was repeated at the 1836 Trades' Union mass meeting in defense of the coal heavers. Resolutions adopted there denounced government grants "to colleges, academies and seminaries, where the children of the wealthy alone are taught, that they may move in the same sphere of life as their parents," while "our children are destined to hereditary bondage, in consequence of the prevailing ignorance of the poorer classes."[57] Similarly the artisans' convention of 1839 demanded a "levelling system . . . of education," in the belief that "intelligence is a passport everywhere."[58] That artisan devotion to education was not simply rhetorical is suggested by a list of the students admitted from the city's common schools to its select Central High School in 1844. Of the 90 students admitted that year, 37 were sons of artisans and four were sons of laborers. Together they almost equaled in number the children of merchants, manufacturers and professional men admitted. Not one weaver's child was on the list.[59]

The other, and ultimately more effective promoter of free public education, was a band of paternalistic merchants and professional men, largely old Federalists, led by Roberts Vaux and Samuel Breck. These men spoke not of "levelling education" to emancipate the working man, but of "universal education" as "a powerful check on vice," to use the words of Governor Wolf's message in support of the Public School Bill which became law in 1834.[60]

Prominent evangelists endorsed this effort. Albert Barnes, the "New School" leader of Philadelphia's First Presbyterian Church, took a comprehensive view of the problem when he warned that "the lower stratum of society . . . that dense and dark mass, the population of alleys and cellars, and garrets—the ignorant, the degraded, the grossly sensual, the idle, the worthless—the refuse of society . . . are not in a condition where revivals of religion can be expected such as I am advocating." The remedy, he suggested, was to elevate "that dark mass" by closing the city's "fountains of poison," placing the Bible in the homes of the poor, providing them "self-denying instruction," and ensuring that "these hordes of wandering and wretched children [are] to be gathered into schools and taught."[61]

More secular objectives for the same crusade were expressed by the Reverend Orville Dewey of Massachusetts in a review of two new elementary school textbooks. Dewey saw "combinations of the employed to procure higher wages" and "political workingmen's parties" as threats to "tear up every social institution by the roots, and leave nothing behind but disorder, waste, and ruin." The remedy for such evils lay in looking "to the very power which has given the impulse to control it. That power, undoubtedly, is education" of the common people. To fulfill its function of preserving social order, education must above all be moral, Dewey concluded. "Conscience," and he repeated, "conscience is our safeguard!"[62]

It was fine to have available such spelling lessons as "Obedience to superiors is requisite in all society; it is consistent with propriety and adds to general convenience,"[63] but what better text for the safeguarding conscience was available than the Bible? The study of the scriptures was seen by these reformers not as peripheral to the purposes of the common schools, but central.

Now every good American Protestant knew that the volume God had written personally was that authorized by King James. To the Roman Catholic clergy, however, that translation was anathema. Its use in classrooms endangered the very souls of Catholic pupils. The dramatic expansion of the common school system in Philadelphia County in the decade following the 1834 act added urgency to the issue. All the while Protestants simply found Catholic objections incomprehensible. "We have never discovered anything in that book, the reading of which we could suppose would injure the morals of either Catholic children or their parents!" wrote one indignant Protestant.[64]

Bishop Francis Patrick Kenrick of Philadelphia fought relentlessly and skillfully to protect his Catholic flock from the Protestant Bible. He realized that the Protestant clergy were adamant and very vocal in their insistence that the Bible remain in the schools. He also realized that news of the burning of King James Bibles by a Catholic missionary priest in a small town in upstate New York and of Bishop John Hughes' call to New York City's Catholics to form a separate political party around the Bible issue had inflamed Philadelphia's Protestant establishment. Consequently Bishop Kenrick issued a discreet but firm public appeal to the Board of Controllers of the Pennsylvania common schools to allow Catholic children to use their own version of the Bible in class and to be excused from other religious instruction. He was partially successful. The Board of Controllers ruled in January 1843, that children whose "parents were conscientiously opposed" might be excused from class during Bible readings.[65]

Agitation over the Bible in schools, like the excitement over liquor licensing, aroused both Catholic and Protestant workingmen with several important consequences. The first was the rise of Democratic politicians in Kensington and similar towns who were closely tied to the Irish weavers, but who defended them on cultural, rather than economic grounds. Leaders of the stripe of John Ferral, who had fought manufacturers and bankers in the political arena, were shunted aside by men like Hugh Clark, a boss weaver who fought "Puritan fanaticism." Born in Ireland in 1796, Clark came to the United States around 1813 and by 1827 was a member of the masters' Society of Weavers. His brother Patrick was a tavern keeper, and Hugh himself was a police magistrate of such prominence in the Catholic community that Protestant rioters made a point of sacking both of their homes and tavern in 1844. When listed by the census-takers six years later, Hugh was an alderman and manufacturer, the owner of $30,000 of real estate, more than was reported by any other individual in the town. With him lived his 70-year-old mother and his two younger brothers, both weavers. Next door dwelt Patrick, who had replaced his lost tavern with a dyeing establishment valued at $6,700.[66] Here was the political leader of Kensington's Irish weavers, a man who opposed them in a succession of bitter strikes, then mounted the hustings to champion their right to a drink and the consciences of their children.

Second, Democratic artisans, among them some of the party's most consistent anti-monopolists, reacted angrily to the new prominence of Irish ethnic politics in their party. A revolt of the self-styled "Incorruptibles" against Clark's nomination for County Treasurer in 1841 split the Democratic Party and helped defeat Clark in his own home town.[67] Two years later an insurrection was mounted by Thomas Grover, Lemuel Paynter and William D. Kelley, the leaders of the artisan wing of the Democratic Party in Southwark, against the party's nomination of an Irishman for that district's Congressional seat. The result again was victory for the Whigs.[68] The whole Incorruptible movement was remarkably similar to the struggle in Williamsburg (Brooklyn) which the emigre Irish Chartist and land reformer Thomas A. Devyr described in his memoirs. Furiously opposing Catholic sectarian politics in the name of the local Democratic Party's Jacksonian economic program, Devyr found himself denounced by his fellow Irishmen and hailed by the nativists.[69]

Third, the cleavages opened in Democratic ranks by the issues of liquor and schools tempted prominent Whigs to try to strike bargains with Democrats like Clark in order to capture county offices. In fact, nativist publicists charged that Whig lust for such votes lay behind the decision of the Whig-dominated Board of Controllers of the common schools to accede to Bishop Kenrick's demand on the Bible reading question. Whether or not there was any truth in that charge, it is certain that when Morton McMichael ran for sheriff on the Whig ticket in 1843 he received considerable support from Irish Catholics out to avenge their recent defeats at the hands of native Democrats. An open letter in the press from "A NATURALIZED CITIZEN; A DEMOCRAT AND AN IRISHMAN FOREVER" accused the Democratic party of proscribing Irish candidates both in 1841 and in the current Congressional elections in Southwark. The remedy it proposed was for Irishmen to vote Whig so that they could later return to the chastised Democratic fold. "The Whig County Ticket," it claimed, "is made up of known and ardent friends of Ireland, and is headed with the name of Morton McMichael, who, like General Jackson, is the son of Irish parents, and, like him, every inch an Irishman!"[70] Enough Irish voters heeded the advice of "A NATURALIZED CITIZEN" that McMichael won the election, carrying even Kensington by almost 200 votes, while the Democrats, as usual, handily won every other office in that town.[71]

Finally, the success of Catholic sectarian politics and the Bishop's partial victory on the school issue account for the overnight mushrooming of the American Republican Party, a political movement to exclude immigrants from the suffrage and to defend the use of the King James Bible in schools. American

Republican clubs had been operating in nearby Spring Garden since the end of the 1830s, and for more than a decade itinerant ministers, spellbound by the Romish menace, had been peddling the *Awful Disclosures of Maria Monk* about the county. They had little to show for their pains, though one had been arrested on charges of selling pornography in the guise of anti-Catholic literature. The school controversy, however, had united 94 leading clergymen of the city in a common pledge to strengthen Protestant education and "awaken the attention of the community to the dangers which . . . threaten these United States from the assaults of Romanism."[72] The American Tract Society took up the battle cry and launched a national crusade to save the nation from the "spiritual despotism" of Rome.[73] The whole Protestant edifice of churches, Bible societies, temperance societies, and missionary agencies was thus interposed against Catholic electoral maneuvers in the name of "nonsectarian politics" at the very moment when those maneuvers were enjoying some success. Lewis Levin stepped over from the temperance movement to take command of the American Republican Party and led it with such skill that within one year it was in full control of the political life of the county.

The meteoric rise of the American Republican movement cannot be understood as a capitalist conspiracy to divide and crush the workers, even though it was portrayed in precisely this way by George Lippard's contemporary novel *The Nazarene,* and it did enable the master weavers to destroy the union of their journeymen. To be sure, it enjoyed widespread but ordinarily tacit sympathy from the old Quaker elite of Philadelphia. Many of them shared the sentiment which Sidney G. Fisher confided to his diary:

> This movement of the "native" party is decidedly conservative, because by excluding foreigners so much democracy is excluded, so much of the rabble, so much ignorance & brutality from political power. The natural ally of this party are the Whigs. Their object harmonizes with the instincts & secret wishes & opinions of the Whigs.[74]

Nevertheless, the American Republicans themselves were decidedly not upper class in leadership or following. Levin surrounded himself with out-of-office Whig politicians who opposed their party's 1843 deal with the Catholics and Democrats of the Incorruptible camp. To their ranks he added an imposing array of minor publishers, attorneys, ministers of the gospel and a few master craftsmen as the leading cadres of his party. Among them were an ex-colonel, C. J. Jack, who sought to prove during the riots that a big city can have its village idiot, and Charles Naylor, a Southwark lawyer and former Whig Congressman from the northern suburbs, whom Fisher described as "partially deranged."[75] Thomas Grover, the wharf builder, and Lemuel Paynter, whom Grover had helped put in Congress a decade earlier as spokesman of Southwark's artisans, were well known but hardly upper class. Only William

B. Reed, of all the prominent nativists, had personal ties to the First Families, being a nephew of John Sergeant. But Reed's involvement in bribery scandals connected with the Bank of the United States had not only cost him a Congressional seat; it also left him in disgrace with his fellow gentlemen.[76]

The following these men gathered can be identified from the lists of nativists injured or arrested in the riots and from the rolls of ward club officers printed in their newspaper *Native American.* This enumeration provides almost as many occupations as it does names of individuals, but the trades which appear more than once give a clue to the nature of the rest. They are victualler, butcher, cordwainer, merchant and ship carpenter. All these occupations were not only dominated by native Americans but were also the traditional trades and crafts of an American seaport.

In Kensington itself, the candidates nominated by the American Republicans for the February elections following the riots (1845) included a tax collector, a carpenter, a blacksmith, a tailor, a carter and a cabinetmaker. In the two wards where the party ran strongest, its candidates were an alderman and former combmaker, two ship carpenters, a chair maker, a brass worker and a victualler.[77] The tightly knit community of Kensington fishermen not only supplied a candidate for that election, but marched as a body in the American Republicans' grand parade of July 4, 1844.[78]

In short, during 1844 the American Republicans mobilized not only the electoral support but the active participation of Protestant artisans in Kensington, Southwark and other industrial suburbs. Superior tradesmen abounded at the movement's secondary levels of leadership: cabinet makers, ship carpenters, butchers and victuallers, whose occupations had as yet suffered little erosion of traditional status and practices from burgeoning industrialization. Their conspicuous support to the top leadership of professional men and small proprietors gave the American Republican clubs an eerie resemblance to a resurrected Sons of Liberty three generations out of date. Less numerous but still evident among the activists were such building tradesmen as carpenters and bricklayers, and such workmen enmeshed in the putting-out system as shoemakers and tailors, who often suffered from the new competitive development of the economy almost as bitterly as the weavers, and who had contributed extraordinary strength to the General Trades' Union of the thirties.[79]

While all these workmen shared the animosity against Roman Catholicism which pervaded Anglo-Saxon culture, it is difficult to determine just how fully they were incorporated into the institutional structure of organized Protestantism. The upper classes of the time tended to scoff that most of the rioters would not know the difference between a Protestant and a Catholic Bible if they were confronted with the two books. Leading evangelists of the age, furthermore, not only disdained to preach to the lower classes, but agreed with Albert Barnes that workingmen were by and large incapable of genuine religious experience.[80] On the other hand, four Protestant churches (Episcopalian, Baptist, Presbyterian and Unitarian) were substantial enough to appear on a Kensington map of 1850, and the census takers of that year were to uncover no fewer than 16 Protestant ministers in town.

There is no way of knowing the nature of the congregations served by each of these preachers, but perhaps some meaningful guess can be made on the basis of the character of the neighborhoods in which they resided. Six of the preachers were found among substantial home-owning tradesmen and small employers near the waterfront, or in one case in the rustic outskirts of the weaving district. One of them did not specify his denomination. The others were a New Light Baptist, an Old Light Baptist, a Presbyterian and two Methodists (one of which was a very young man with very prosperous neighbors). The Episcopalian priest lived among poor laborers and weavers but probably because that was where his large church was situated. A Presbyterian, a Reformed Presbyterian and a Methodist lived among Irish weavers, as has already been pointed out.

The remaining six lived among poorer workmen of various occupations. One was a German who gave no affiliation. Another was an Irish-born Old School Presbyterian. Near him lived a 19-year-old Primitive Methodist, whose father was a Pennsylvania-born carpenter. Two others were Methodists, one Irish and one native Pennsylvanian, both living among shoemakers, tailors and carpenters. The last was William Metcalf, a 70-year-old Bible Christian ("ranting Bryantite") from England who lived in a pocket of native- and English-born workmen in the midst of the largest weaving ward.[81] It is probable that these men represented the world of popular sects or "store front churches," which is as elusive to the historian as it was central to the culture of the working classes.

It appears, then, that Protestantism was a vital force in the ideology of these workingmen. Through its influence they could be attached to the middle-class leadership of a political party whose negative reference group was the Catholic immigrant, provided those leaders draped the movement with the most cherished symbols of artisan culture. Lewis Levin played to the values, the hopes and the anxieties of his audience of artisans with unerring aim. His paper, the *Native American,* displayed Longfellow's *Village Blacksmith* and with equal emphasis acclaimed the continuing "march of improvement."[82] The evils of the times were attributed to the behavior of the corrupt politician, who had allied himself with foreign-born voters, alien to America's egalitarian traditions and subject in their voting behavior to the discipline of the Roman Catholic church. The American Republicans promised to reintroduce into politics the sense of personal honor once exemplified by the Revolutionary Founding Fathers, to win the "entire separation of sectarianism from Politics" and to secure both objectives through "AN OPEN BIBLE and a PURE BALLOT BOX!"[83]

Kensington soon provided the nativists an ideal battleground for their cause. While Bishop Kenrick tried to soothe Protestant fears with statement after statement denying any desire to deprive Protestant school children of their King James Bible, magistrate Hugh Clark himself authorized a Kensington teacher to omit Bible reading altogether in her overwhelmingly Catholic class. American Republicans responded by dispatching emissaries to the weaving town to demand the culprit's resignation. At first the meetings attracted more Catholic hecklers than Protestant supporters, and two local American Republicans who tried to organize a club in the middle of the weaving district were prevented by their neighbors from holding a meeting.[84] Inspired by their party's triumph in the April elections in New York City, however, the nativists did stage an open air rally addressed by S.R. Cramer, a Philadelphia carpenter and publisher of the *Native American,* on a Friday evening early in May within a block of a Catholic church, only to see the speaker driven from his platform by about a hundred angry Catholics.[85]

The following Monday, May 6, Levin himself accompanied Cramer to the scene of Friday's debacle to avenge the insult. Tensions were already running high when a heavy rain drove the nativists across the street to the shelter of the Nanny Goat Market. There Levin ascended some packing boxes in the midst of Irish shoppers to hold forth on "the deleterious effects of Popish interference in the elective franchise." Hardly had he begun when the marketers assaulted him and his followers with vegetables, fists and bricks. Rallying their forces, the nativists charged the Irish in the streets, then assaulted the Hibernia Hose House and two weavers' cottages from which, they later claimed, they had been fired upon. Gunfire was soon general on both sides; but because the Protestants were in the open and the Irish snipers inside, the heavy casualties were suffered by the nativist side: four badly beaten, seven shot, and a Morocco dresser's apprentice, George Shiffler, killed.[86]

By mid-evening both sides had swelled to great crowds, freely shooting at each other. Protestant reinforcements from Philadelphia fought their way north along Second Avenue into the weaving district. Two more nativists, a blind maker and the son of a salt merchant, were killed and an Irish captive severely beaten in a battle which, quite appropriately, found Catholics firing from behind the walls of a seminary while the nativists barricaded themselves across the street in a temperance grocery store.[87]

"Another St. Bartholomew's day is begun in the streets of Philadelphia," editorialized the *Native American* the next day, while Colonel Jack rallied Protestants to march from Philadelphia and Southwark north to Kensington, armed with fife and drum, torch and musket, to exorcise the menace of Popish bigotry. By early afternoon the town was locked in pitched battle. Nativists charged from building to building burning and sacking the homes and back buildings of weavers John Lavery, Matthew Quinn, Barnard Sherry, Owen

McCulloch, Michael Keenan, Hugh Devlin and John Mellon. Two carpet manufactories and the homes and stock of peddler Patrick McGee and tailor Thomas Sheridan were put to the torch. In all, some 30 buildings were ablaze by the time troops arrived escorting firemen into the town.[88]

On Wednesday, more than 3,000 troops, complete with artillery, placed Kensington under martial law. Sheriff McMichael tried to secure his political future by demanding that the troops shoot no one, save in self-defense, and restrict themselves to guarding the property of the Roman Catholic church. In this setting, bands of nativists, mostly boys, searched Irish homes for arms and beat the owners of houses where weapons were found. Despite the presence of soldiers, Protestants set fire to St. Michael's Church in Kensington and to St. Augustine's Church in Philadelphia along the route north to Kensington, as well as Hugh Clark's house and his brother's tavern.[89] Not until Thursday was the town smoldering quietly, with refugees trudging aimlessly about and small bands of boys looting. Public meetings were banned everywhere in the county, and troops dispersed anything that faintly resembled a demonstration as far away as Southwark and Moyamensing.[90]

The weavers' community had been gutted. General George Cadwalader's successful defense of the city's cathedral and, later in July, of St. Philip's Church in Southwark, was to earn him the praise and thanks of Bishop Kenrick; but the army had been unable to protect the cottages or even the lives of the weavers. In fact, it had little will to do so; the soldiers visibly sympathized with the nativists.[91]

Judging from the names of the victims, it seems that the rioters burned the homes of Protestant as well as Catholic weavers. Although American Republican rhetoric identified Roman Catholicism as the enemy, the nativist rioters made the weaving community as a whole their target. Conversely, there is no evidence of participation by Protestant weavers in the American Republican movement before the riot. It is true that the first American Republican shot in the Nanny Goat Market, former constable Patrick Fisher, was a Protestant Irishman and that four years later a weavers' spokesman charged that the riot had been "incited by North of Ireland Orangemen." But the three Irishmen who led the first American Republican club in Kensington were a flour dealer, a rope maker and an undertaker-cabinetmaker.[92] Possibly the common wage struggles and the single union organization of Protestant and Catholic weavers generated a group solidarity which rendered these particular Protestants impervious to the American Republican appeal. Only as avenging mobs stormed toward their homes did some Protestants understandably begin to post American flags, or better yet, mastheads from the paper *Native American*, in their windows to convert the crowd from angry shouts to loud cheers.[93]

Despite the familiarity of clashes between Orangemen and Catholics to Irishmen on both sides of the Atlantic, it does seem that there were Irish

Protestants among that significant minority of workingmen who remained loyal Democrats in defiance of the new trend to sectarian politics. A Protestant lad from County Antrim could write home to his father after the riots that he despised the nativists, was "a Democrat out and out, and takes the platform for the cause against Monarchy and aristocracy."[94] The persistent vitality of the Repeal Association in Philadelphia, in which both Hugh Clark and William D. Kelley participated even though they were on opposite sides of the "Incorruptible" fence at the time, testifies to the resilience of the eighteenth-century Irish heritage of Catholic-Dissenter cooperation against the Anglican Establishment. On the fourth of July 1841, the Repealers had turned out 1,860 participants for a parade led by the Montgomery Hibernia Greens, a rifle company of Protestants which three years later was to find itself brutally attacked by nativists in Southwark.[95] When President Tyler, ostracized from the Whig Party, set out to build a Democratic base, his son Robert became president of the Philadelphia Repeal Association.[96] Consequently, while there were Irish Protestant activists among the American Republicans, it is understandable that the party at times denounced all Irishmen and doubly understandable that Levin sometimes identified the Repeal Association as his main enemy.[97]

Clearly there were other workmen who found the nativist movement unattractive. The Democratic vote throughout the county remained far larger in 1844 than could be accounted for by Catholics alone. Shoemakers, tailors and laborers appear in the rolls of American Republican activists but in numbers far smaller than their proportion of the labor force. Factory operatives are conspicuously absent, though one should study a mill town like Manayunk before passing judgment on their role. Such shoemakers' leaders as Samuel Thompson, William English, and William Gilmore, who had entered politics as Democrats in the 1830s, remained Democrats through the forties. Like William D. Kelley and the land reformer-novelist George Lippard, who attributed the riots to a joint conspiracy of Calvinist bankers and Rome to destroy American democracy, these men denounced both sides in the sectarian controversies which raged about them. They were the genuine Locofocos, political foes of capitalists, evangelists, and priests alike, and at least some of them still adhered publicly to the Painite Rationalism which had been so widespread among workingmen's leaders in the 1830s. Their working-class following, that minority which was neither nativist nor immigrant, needs and deserves a historical study all its own.[98]

Neither Repealers nor Locofocos, however, could stop American Republican artisans from securing control of local politics in the wake of the Kensington riot. Large numbers of nativists enlisted in the armed citizen guards raised to protect Catholic buildings and police Kensington, a service for which they were highly praised by Major General Patterson. They saw to it that 13 of the 19 men arrested for disturbances in Kensington had unmistakably Irish names and, later in July when Protestants were to fight the army in Southwark, that volunteers *en masse* refused to turn out.[99]

While the weavers and all others were strictly forbidden by military orders to assemble, General Patterson was persuaded to allow a public meeting of the Washington Temperance Society nine days after the end of the riot. Nine days after the temperance meeting, he permitted a gathering of the American Republicans in the second ward of Kensington itself and sent along troops of the second brigade to protect it. By mid-June all bans had been lifted and a memorial service for eight nativists killed in the riots was held in Kensington's Brickmakers' Methodist Protestant Church. A soiree at the Christian Home Missionary Society of Philadelphia the same evening raised funds for families of the Protestant martyrs.[100] The report of the Grand Jury of the Court of Quarter Sessions investigating the riot placed all the blame on the Catholics, Magistrate Clark and Sheriff McMichael.[101] All the while, American Republican rallies of ever-growing size were being held throughout the county; and Levin trumpeted charges that "persons of wealth" were financing the arming of Catholics with "splendid rifles and warlike munitions" for their "Guy Fawkes plots and infernal machinations." "Burn no churches, even if your fathers were murdered before your eyes," he advised, but defeat the enemy at the polls.[102]

Independence Day provided the occasion for a long-heralded manifestation by the nativists of their power and their determination to "sweep the demagogues" from office. Whether the parade numbered the 30,000 participants claimed by the *Native American* or the 4,500 Colonel A. R. Pleasonton noted in his diary, it must have been impressive. The pageantry and symbolism were of the same pattern displayed in artisans' demonstrations from the welcoming of the Federal Constitution in 1788 to the July Fourth processions of trades' unions in the 1830s. All delegations were gaily bedecked, many with their trade insignia. A Temple of Liberty was drawn at the front of the parade, and replicas of Washington, the Declaration of Independence and the Bible were everywhere to be seen. Widows and orphans of the Kensington martyrs held a special place of honor. Even two blacks were allowed to participate in this celebration of Protestant liberties—as water carriers for the other marchers.[103]

The nativists had every reason to be exultant. Despite blistering verbal assaults to which they were subjected by leading spokesmen of both the Whigs and the Democrats, they carried the fall elections in all the manufacturing suburbs. Levin was sent to Congress from Southwark and his colleague J.H. Campbell from the district which included Kensington. One state senate seat and those of the eight county representatives in the state house, all of which had formerly been filled by Democrats, were taken by American Republicans. The county commissioner's office was handily captured by Thomas Grover. Everywhere the pattern of voting was the same. Democratic tallies fell off sharply, and almost all former Whig votes went American Republican.[104] No longer was the commercial city the stronghold of the Whigs and the manufacturing county that of the Democrats as had long been the case. American Republican endorsement of two Whig candidates, Henry Clay for President and Joseph Markle for Governor, allowed both men to carry with ease the city and county alike.[105]

In local elections the following February the nativists strengthened their political grip on the county. In the five wards of Southwark, all of them once solidly Democratic, the American Republicans' share of the total vote cast ran from a low of 63.2 percent to a high of 71.8 percent. In Kensington, where the Whigs fielded no candidates of their own and native-born Democrats clung to their traditional party in far greater numbers than their Southwark counterparts, the contest was somewhat less one-sided. The fourth ward, and even the fifth, where most of the fighting had taken place, went to the nativists in what their press hailed as a "Waterloo sweep." In the first and third wards American Republican candidates were narrowly defeated (in the former by only two votes). Of special interest is the second ward, situated directly on the line of march from Philadelphia to the Nanny Goat Market. Alderman Boileau of this erstwhile bastion of anti-bank Democrats switched his affiliation from the Democratic to the American Republican party and was handily re-elected.[106]

The route by which the nativists attained this level of political power had involved them in more street fighting, as well as electioneering. The conflict which raged in the vicinity of St. Philip de Neri Church in Southwark between Friday, July 5, and Monday, July 8, took a considerably greater toll of lives, though not of property, than had the riot in Kensington. Southwark was an American Republican stronghold, a community of traditional seaport craftsmen, laborers and sailors. An assault by more than a thousand of its residents on St. Philip's Church, following the rumor that Catholics were caching arms there, precipitated a direct clash between the nativists and the troops. No Catholics were involved in the fighting which ensued. Nativist leaders sought ardently, though in vain, to fend off violence. On the other hand, though soldiers frequently proved reluctant to fire at the crowd and troops of the Markle Rifles actually deserted the church to fraternize with those storming it, their commanders were clearly determined to put a forceful end to rioting once and for all. Generals Patterson and Cadwalader demanded that city officials give them a free hand, not the restraints under which they had served in Kensington; and they got their way.[107]

Although there is not the space here for a narrative of the battle, two aspects of the encounter are of importance. First, the behavior of Philadelphia's social elite showed that while they might have sympathized with the nativists' proclaimed objectives, they were aghast at the mob forces which nativism had unleashed. Even before the Southwark riot the *Public Ledger* had drawn the editorial lesson from Kensington that soldiers should not fire *over* the heads of rioters but *at them.* Joseph R. Ingersoll had written to General Cadwalader that "the population of a large town is always excitable," so that a "power must exist to check its first outbreak, and it must be both willing and able to do so effectually. A strong preventive police is cheaper than indemnity for destroyed churches," he argued. Especially in "a country like ours where the people are supreme," there should be a "paid police on a basis which would always be in action—like Sir Robert Peel's men in England."[108]

After the Southwark fighting, scores of the city's "members of the bar, merchants, & men of education & property,"[109] among them Horace Binney, John Sergeant, Joseph R. Ingersoll and Sidney Fisher, met at Evans Tavern and addressed a memorial to the Governor praising the performance of the military forces. "Religion and politics have nothing whatever to do with such men as have been acting in these scenes, nor such men with them," they wrote. "The rioters are men cast off from all respect for law, or for our institutions, and are ready for arson, for murder, for rapine. . . ." To quell such activities, they recommended the quartering of a permanent military regiment in the city.[110]

Secondly, for the mass of Philadelphia's voters, the Southwark battle had cast the American Republicans in a heroic role, as embattled American workmen courageously defending their homes against invading troops. The cannonades of grape shot and the cavalry charges of the soldiers had been answered by three cannons used with considerable success by the citizens. By early Monday morning, when the exhausted troops found themselves at last patrolling empty streets, 15 of their number had been wounded, four more dangerously lacerated and two lay dead. Fallen civilians were estimated by J.H. Lee at 50, though there is little firm evidence to support his guess. Threats of a mob assembling for renewed assault later Monday induced governmental authorities to withdraw the battered troops and allow the American Republican leaders themselves to pacify the town. No one else could control the populace.[111]

The perspective of the next ten years helps one judge the significance of these tumultuous events. The First Families got their uniformed, professional police force, with a permanent military establishment of 1,350 cavalry, infantry and artillerymen to stand in reserve.[112] For a full decade, furthermore, they fended off a drive led by Morton McMichael, who now allied himself with the nativists, to consolidate the suburbs with the city. Fear that popular demagogues would dominate the larger unit prompted Horace Binney to rally municipal bondholders against the absorption of Kensington and Southwark into Philadelphia until the next nativist upsurge, the Know-Nothings, overwhelmed them.[113]

The handloom weavers were never to recover the wages with which they had entered 1844. Several subsequent strikes, based more in Moyamensing than in Kensington, failed to rescue their trade from the economic obsolescence and overcrowding which haunted it in this decade from Pennsylvania to Yorkshire and Silesia.[114] However, in contrast, Hugh Clark, Michael Keenan and other master weavers recovered quickly and progressed to greater fortunes.

The American Republicans' electoral strength began to wither within two years after 1844, as one office after another returned to the Whigs or Democrats. But there was no resurgence of class cohesiveness in the political behavior of workingmen. On election days Protestant and Catholic workingmen continued to align themselves not with each other, but with employers of their respective ethnic groups.[115]

Although the economic impact of industrialization was felt in quite different ways and involved remarkably different rates of change for factory operatives, outworkers and the many varieties of craftsmen, all these groups shared common interests enough to allow them to act as a class in support of trade union efforts and such political demands as the legal ten-hour day. This unity had been the driving force behind the urban radicalism of the 1830s. Quite different was the impact of the ideology of modernization by which a new sense of social order and discipline was imposed on the industrializing community. Because major elements of this ideology were transmitted through the political demands of evangelical Protestantism, above all liquor licensing and the moral content of public education, the responses of workingmen to modernization varied with their own religious beliefs. No political conflicts of the age touched the daily lives of the people more intimately than these issues. By their very nature, evangelical demands fragmented the working class as a political force in ante-bellum Philadelphia and thereby created for historians the illusion of a society lacking in class conflict.

Notes

Reprinted courtesy of Oxford University Press and the *Journal of Social History.*

1. See Liston Pope, *Millhands and Preachers, A Study of Gastonia* (New Haven, 1942); E.P. Thompson, "Time, Work-Discipline, and Industrial Capitalism," *Past and Present*, no. 38 (December 1967): 56–91. Lee Benson, *The Concept of Jacksonian Democracy* (Princeton, 1961) is the classic work on "ethnocultural" determinants of American political behavior, but the book shows no awareness of the interaction between those determinants and class relations in the setting of industrialization.

2. U.S. Census Office, *Sixth Census or Enumeration of the Inhabitants of the United States . . . in 1840* (Washington, 1841), 151.

3. U.S. National Archives, 1850 Census Population Schedules. Pennsylvania (microfilm rolls 806–7), 4th ward, dwellings 72, 74, 78 (p. 245); 3rd ward, dwellings 621–22 (p. 170), 1071 (p. 205); 5th ward, p. 324. Hereafter these schedules will be cited as 7th Census MSS.

4. Adam Smith, *An Inquiry into the Nature and Causes of the Wealth of Nations* (London, 1822), Book I, chap. 1.

5. See T.W. Dyott, *An Exposition of the System of Moral and Mental Labor Established at the Glass Factory of Dyottville* (Philadelphia, 1833) for a description of this works when it employed about 400 people. The calculation of nativity of glass workers is mine, from 7th Census MSS.

6. All figures are calculated from 7th Census MSS.

7. *Sixth Census*, 151; Sam Bass Warner, Jr., *The Private City: Philadelphia in Three Periods of Its Growth* (Philadelphia, 1968), 51.

8. 7th Census MSS, 2nd ward, dwelling 757, p. 106.

9. *Ibid.*, 1st ward, dwelling 682, p. 41.

10. Edwin T. Freedley, *Philadelphia and Its Manufactures* (Philadelphia, 1858), 234, 250–51.

11. Samuel Hazard, ed., *The Register of Pennsylvania*, I (January 1828), 28 (hereinafter cited as *HR*); Freedley, 250–54.

12. My count from 7th Census MSS.

13. Pennsylvania Bureau of Industrial Statistics, *Report*, XVII (1889), 4D (hereinafter cited as *Pa. Bis*).

14. *HR*, I (Jan., 1828), 28; letter of "One Who Knows, and a Weaver" to *Spirit of the Times*, Sept. 13, 1848; "Meeting of the Weavers," *Philadelphia Public Ledger*, March 2, 1845 (hereinafter cited as *PPL*).

15. Freedley, 241–42.

16. George Lippard, *The Nazarene; or, The Last of the Washingtonians, A Revelation of Philadelphia, New York, and Washington, in the Year 1844* (Philadelphia, 1846), 168.

17. 7th Census MSS, 2nd ward, dwellings 98–102, pp. 63–64.

18. *Ibid.*, 3rd ward, dwelling 1329, p. 231. The date of emigration in this and later cases is guessed from the age of the oldest child born in America.

19. *PPL*, May 11, 1844.

20. My count from 7th Census MSS. Of 2,238 weavers, 1,758 were born in Ireland. Of the weavers not born in Ireland 204 were English, 114 American, and 105 German by birth. The rest were from Scotland (55), France (2), and Switzerland (1). Of the 114 born in the U.S., 33 were clearly sons of Irish immigrants, as were many of those born in England. The 3rd and 6th wards of 1850 were made from the 5th ward of 1844, focal point of the riots, as was the rural 7th ward.

21. A significant but smaller peak of immigration was reached between 1836 and 1838.

22. 7th Census MSS, 6th ward, dwellings 70 (p. 406), 103 (p. 408), 96 (p. 408), 528 (p. 440).

23. *PPL*, May 11, 1844.

24. Frederick Engels, *The Condition of the Working-Class in England in 1844* (translated by Florence Kelley Wischnewetzky, London, 1892), 140.

25. Quoted in Asa Briggs, ed., *Chartist Studies* (London, 1962), 8–9.

26. Engels, 93, 138–40, 183–84; E.P. Thompson, *The Making of the English Working Class* (London, 1963), 296, 431; A. Redford, *Labour Migration in England, 1800–1850* (Manchester, 1964), 144–64. See also K.H. Connell, *The Population of Ireland, 1750–1845* (Oxford, 1950).

27. An Intelligent Emigrant at Philadelphia, *A Letter on the Present State of the Labouring Classes in America* (Bury, 1827), 5–6.

28. *HR*, I (Jan., 1828), 28.

29. Carpet weavers' assemblies of the Knights of Labor continued this practice in Kensington into the 1870s. See *Pa. Bis*, XVII (1889), 18D-19D; Terence V. Powderly, *Thirty Years of Labor*, 1859–1889 (Columbus, 1889), 183.

30. John R. Commons, et al., *A Documentary History of American Industrial Society* (Cleveland, 1910), V, 351, 377, 384.

31. *Ibid.*, V, 391.

32. *Pa. Bis*, VIII (1880–81), 266–68.

33. *PPL*, June 6, 1843.

34. Letter of "One Who Knows, and a Weaver" to *Spirit of the Times*, Sept. 13, 1848; *Pa. Bis*, VIII (1880–81), 269; *PPL*, Aug. 11, 16, 1843. This rate may have been as much as one cent per yard higher than the season's scale in Moyamensing, but a march of weavers from that town to Kensington failed to inspire a sympathy strike there. See *PPL*, Aug. 12, 15, 16, 1843; "Meeting of the Weavers," *ibid.*, March 2, 1845.

35. *PPL*, May 24, 1844; "One Who Knows, and a Weaver" to *Spirit of the Times*, Sept. 13, 1848. In 1848 Freedley was to find the going rate no higher than three cents. Freedley, 254.

36. See Commons, *Documentary History*, V, 325–92; William A. Sullivan, *The Industrial Worker in Pennsylvania, 1800–1840* (Harrisburg, 1955), 133–36; Leonard Bernstein, "The Working People of Philadelphia from Colonial Times to the General Strike of 1835," *Pennsylvania Magazine of History and Biography*, LXXIV (July, 1950), 322–39.

37. Commons, *Documentary History*, V, 390.

38. On the special demands of cabinet makers, see *PPL*, Oct. 15, 1841; Sept. 4, 1843. On those of butchers, see *PPL*, May 9, 1839.

39. *PPL*, Aug. 25, 1836.

40. Bruce G. Laurie, "The Working People of Philadelphia, 1827–1853" (unpublished doctoral dissertation, University of Pittsburgh, 1971), 79–90, 253–65; Sullivan, 196–207; Warner, 90–91. On Kensington votes see *PPL* Oct. 14, 1837; Oct. 12, 1839.

41. *PPL*, April 28, Sept. 8, 1838.

42. John Ferrall to James Buchanan, Feb. 19, 1838 (Buchanan Papers, Box 92, Historical Society of Pennsylvania).

43. Sidney G. Fisher, *A Philadelphia Perspective, The Diary of Sidney George Fisher Covering the Years 1834–1871*, ed. Nicholas B. Wainwright (Philadelphia, 1967), 134–35.

44. *PPL*, May 9, 1839.

45. *PPL*, Nov. 21, 1840.

46. *PPL*, Aug. 1, 8, 13, Sept. 16, Oct. 19, 24, 1842.

47. E.A. Penniman, etc., *An Address to the Workingmen of the City and County of Philadelphia* (Philadelphia, 1839), 2, 3. On the mechanics' meetings see John

R. Commons, *et al., History of Labour in the United States* (4 Vols., New York, 1918–35), I, 469–71.

48. William Heighton, *An Address Delivered Before the Mechanics and Working Classes, Generally of the City and County of Philadelphia* (Philadelphia, 1827), 13. See also Heighton, *An Address to the Members of Trade Societies and to the Working Classes Generally* (Philadelphia, 1827).

49. *American Museum*, IV (July, 1788), 78.

50. *PPL*, March 22, 1839.

51. *PPL*, March 29, 1839.

52. *PPL*, Feb. 21, 1842; Dec. 13, 1843. Artisans supporting Whig candidates had organized their efforts in temperance halls as early as 1838. See the account of the Naylor meeting, *PPL*, Sept. 24, 1838.

53. A.K. McClure, *Old Time Notes of Pennsylvania* (2 vols., Philadelphia, 1905), I, 89. On Levin see *Dictionary of American Biography* (New York, 1937), VI, 200–201 (hereinafter cited as *D.A.B.*).

54. *PPL*, Jan 24, 1842.

55. For a good discussion of the transition from temperance to prohibition see Joseph Gusfield, *Symbolic Crusade: Status Politics and the American Temperance Movement* (Urbana, Ill., 1963).

56. Report of the Joint Committee on the Common Schools, New York *Daily Sentinel*, Feb. 20, 22, 1830.

57. *PPL*, Aug. 25, 1836.

58. Penniman, 2.

59. *PPL*, July 10, 1844.

60. Warren F. Hewitt, "Samuel Breck and the Pennsylvania School Law of 1834," *Pennsylvania History*, I (April, 1934), 63–75; Joseph J. McCadden, "Roberts Vaux and His Associates in the Pennsylvania Society for the Promotion of Public Schools," *ibid.*, III (Jan., 1936), 1–8; Warner, 111–23. The quotation from Wolf is in Hewitt, 68.

61. Albert Barnes, *Sermons on Revivals* (New York, 1841), 155–57. See also Timothy L. Smith, "Protestant Schooling and American Nationality, 1800–1850," *Journal of American History*, LIII (March, 1967), 679–95.

62. (Orville Dewey), "Popular Education. I. The Political Class Book . . . by WILLIAM SULLIVAN . . . 2. The Moral Class Book . . . by the SAME . . ." *North American Review* XXXVI (Jan., 1833), 73–99. The quotations are on pp. 81 and 96.

63. B. Brandneth, *A New System for the Instruction of Youth* (New York, 1836), quoted in Ruth Elson, *Guardians of Tradition* (Lincoln, Nebraska, 1964), 102.

64. J.H. Lee, *History of the American Party in Politics: Embracing a Complete History of the Philadelphia Riots in May and July, 1844* (Philadelphia, 1855), 29–30. On the expansion of the schools during 1834–44, see Warner, I, 17–18. On anti-Catholic bias in school textbooks, see Elson, 47–55, 123–28.

65. Hugh J. Nolan, *The Most Reverend Francis Patrick Kenrick, Third Bishop of Philadelphia, 1830–1851* (Washington, DC, 1948), 289–96; Ray A. Billington, *The Protestant Crusade, 1800–1860* (New York, 1938), 142–66; Lee, 17–21. On Bishop

Hughes in New York see Charles H. Haswell, *Reminiscences of an Octogenarian of the City of New York* (New York, 1897), 372–75; Thomas A. Devyr, *The Odd Book of the Nineteenth Century* (Greenpoint, NY, 1882), American Section, 33–38; Anna E. Carroll, *The Great American Battle; Or, The Contest between Christianity and Political Romanism* (New York and Auburn, 1856), *passim.*

66. 7th Census MSS, 3rd ward, dwellings 621–22, p. 170; *PPL*, May 11, 1844; *HR*, I (Jan., 1928), 28; letter of "A NATURALIZED CITIZEN: A DEMOCRAT AND AN IRISHMAN FOREVER" to *PPL*, Oct. 7, 1843.

67. *PPL*, Oct. 14, 1841. Plankenton, the Whig candidate, carried Kensington with 852 votes. Clark came second with 821. Faunce, the Incorruptible, got 679 votes.

68. *PPL*, Oct. 12, 1843.

69. Devyr, American Section, 35–38.

70. *PPL*, Oct. 7, 1843. For the American Republicans' accusations of conspiracy between Bishop Kenrick and Whigs on the Board of Controllers, see Lee, 17–21; Billington, 214, n. 49.

71. *PPL*, Oct. 12, 1843. Charges of collusion in this election between McMichael and the Catholics were commonplace at the time of the riots. See the *Address of the American Republicans* (Cadwalader Collection, folder May 22-June 29, 1844, Historical Society of Pennsylvania, hereinafter cited as CC); George Cadwalader to J.R. Ingersoll, May 24, 1844 (CC); Grand Jury Report, *PPL*, June 17, 1844.

72. Lee, 31–32; Billington, 182–84. The quotation is from Billington, 183.

73. Clifford S. Griffin, "Religious Benevolence as Social Control, 1815–1860," *Mississippi Valley Historical Review*, XLIV (Dec., 1957), 423–44.

74. Fisher, 177. On the anti-Catholic attitudes of the upper classes, see P. Kenny, "The Anti-Catholic Riots in Philadelphia in 1844," *American Catholic Historical Researches*, XIII (1896), 50–64; Joseph Ripka's testimony, *Journal of the Senate of Pennsylvania* (1838), II, 357–58.

75. On Jack, see his letter to *Native American* (hereinafter cited as *NA)*, Aug. 2, 1844. On Naylor see U.S. Congress, 81st Cong., 2nd sess., House Doc. 607, *Biographical Directory of the American Congress* (Washington, 1950), 1379; Fisher, 172.

76. *D.A.B.*, VIII, 461–62; McClure, I, 89–91; Fisher, 125.

77. The names of activists are taken from Grand Jury of the County of Philadelphia Minute Book, Sept. 2-Oct. 23, 1844; list of American Republican casualties in, *NA*, May 7, 1844; article on May 6 rally, *ibid.*; North Ward officers, *ibid.*; Fifth Ward Southwark officers, *NA*, April 23, 1844; Kensington candidates, *NA*, Feb. 22, 1845. The best source for occupations was McElroy's *Philadelphia Directory* for 1843 and 1844.

78. The candidate was Charles Bakeoven. *NA*, Feb. 22, 1845. On the parade, see Lee, 155.

79. It is noteworthy, however, that despite the strength of Methodism and temperance among shoemakers, their most prominent spokesmen in political life, William English, William Gilmore, Israel Young and Samuel Thompson, remained Democrats through the 1840s.

80. This thesis is well argued in Teresa L. Bradley, "The Response of Evangelical Protestantism to the Urban Working Class, 1830–1860," unpublished M.A. paper, University of Pittsburgh History Department Library.

81. 7th Census MSS: 1st ward, J.C. Lyons (O.S. Presbyterian), George W. Brindle (Primitive Methodist); 2nd ward, C. Hummel (no denomination), Francis Hoffman (Methodist); 3d ward, William Metcalf (Bible Church), John Shields (Methodist); 4th ward, David Dailey (Methodist), William Paulin (O.L. Baptist), George Hand (N.L. Baptist); 5th ward, George Chandler (Presbyterian), Alfred Cookman (Methodist), John G. Maxwell (Presbyterian); 6th ward, John G. Wilson (Methodist Protestant), Thomas Flavell (Reformed Presbyterian), Robert Black (Presbyterian); 7th ward, Daniel Gaston (no denomination).

82. See editorial and article on Kensington industry, *NA*, Sept. 16, 1844. Longfellow's poem appeared in *NA*, July 30, 1844.

83. *NA*, Sept. 16, 1844. The argument that immigration depressed American wages was a latecomer to American Republican editorializing. See *NA*, Nov. 29, 1844.

84. Billington, 221–24; Lee, 40–46.

85. Lee, 42–64; *PPL*, May 4, 1844. On the New York elections see Carroll, 264–65; Haswell, 409–10.

86. *PPL*, May 7, 1844; *NA*, May 7, 1844; Lee, 48–65.

87. *PPL*, May 7, 8, 9, 1884; *NA*, May 7, 1844; Lee, 63–66.

88. *NA*, May 7, 1844; *PPL*, May 8, 11, 1844; Lee, 71–78.

89. *PPL*, May 9, 1844; Lee, 78–89; Cadwalader notebook, "Suppression of Riots," 8–16, 19, 62–64 (CC); Col. A. R. Pleasonton to Gen. Patterson, May 8, 1844 (CC); Tho. T. Firth to Col. A.R. Pleasonton, May 8, 1844 (CC); Order No. 6, May 9, 1844 (CC).

90. *PPL*, May 9, 11, 1844; Order No. 7, May 10, 1844 (CC).

91. Francis Patrick Kenrick (Bishop) to Brigadier General George Cadwalader, July 29, 1844 (CC). On the behavior of troops, see Brig. Gen. H. Hubbell to Cadwalader, dated "20 minutes to noon" (CC); Col. Pleasonton to Gen. Cadwalader, May 20, 1844, (Cadwalader notebook, 62–64); *PPL*, May 9, 1844; General August Pleasonton Diary, 1838–1844, 422–23 (Historical Society of Pennsylvania); Fisher, 173.

92. On Irish-born American Republicans, see Lee, 54, 71–72. On the Orangemen charge, see "One Who Knows, and a Weaver" to *Spirit of the Times*, Sept. 13, 1848.

93. *PPL*, May 11, 1844. In Moyamensing two leaders of the weavers' union were prominent American Republicans. See Laurie, 269.

94. Robert Smith to James Smith, Aug. 14, 1844 (Record D1828/25, Public Record Office of Northern Ireland).

95. *PPL*, March 13, July 7, 1841; Jan. 21, Feb. 23, 1842. On the fate of the Montgomery Hibernia Greens in Southwark see Capt. John B. Calahan to Gen. Cadwalader, July 11, 1844 (CC). On political collaboration between Ulster Presbyterians and Catholics in Ireland, see Owen Dudley Edwards, *The Sins of Our Fathers: Roots of Conflict in Northern Ireland* (Dublin, 1970), 74–78, 221–24. It is

remarkable that religious conflict in Ireland grew more intense in the early 1840s just as it did in America. Still the Orange Lodge of Stewardstown enlisted as a body in the Repeal Association, to the delight of Philadelphia Repealers. *PPL*, Aug. 15, 1843.

96. Fisher, 170–71.

97. Lee, 105.

98. On Kelley, see *NA*, Sept. 16, 1844. On Lippard, see *The Nazarene*; (anon.,) *The Life and Choice Writings of George Lippard* (New York, 1855). For evidence of continuing Rationalist meetings, see notices in *PPL*, Feb. 19, 1842. For the politics of the shoemakers' spokesmen, see Laurie, 253–65. Lee Benson, interestingly, finds Locofocoism in New York most pronounced among voters of old Pennsylvania Scotch-Irish and German stock. Benson, 184.

99. Order No. 19, May 13, 1844 (CC); *PPL*, May 9, 1844; Fisher, 167, 173; Edward Hurst to Alderman Snyder, May 10, 1844 (CC); Grand Jury of the County of Philadelphia Minute Book, Sept. 2-Oct. 23, 1844.

100. Order No. 20, May 14, 1844 (CC); pass slip initialed G.C., May 19, 1844 (CC); Geo. Cadwalader to Gen. Patterson, May 19, 1844 (CC); *PPL*, May 28, 1844; *NA*, June 15, 1844.

101. *PPL*, June 17, 1844. Col. C. J. Jack was charged with embracery for a letter he sent to the Grand Jury. *PPL*, May 30, June 10, 1844.

102. *NA*, June 25, 1844. The quotations are all from Levin editorials in the Philadelphia *Sun*, May 11–13, reproduced in Lee, 104–9.

103. *NA*, July 6, 1844; Pleasonton Diary, 417. For examples of earlier artisans' parades see *American Museum*, IV (July, 1788), 57–78; Frederick Robinson, *An Oration Delivered before the Trades Union of Boston and Vicinity* (Boston, 1834), 32.

104. *PPL*, Oct. 12, 14, 1844. For examples of major party attacks on the American Republicans as instigators of violence, see the speeches of William Seward and William D. Kelley, *NA*, Aug. 10, Sept. 16, 1844. For an excellent summary of the editorial attitudes of Philadelphia newspapers toward American Republicans, see Lee, 103–30.

105. *PPL*, Oct. 12, 14, 1844.

106. Laurie, 266; *NA*, Feb. 22, 1845.

107. Brig. Gen. Geo. Cadwalader to Major General Patterson, July 19, 1844 (draft report in CC); Capt. John B. Calahan to Gen. Cadwalader, July 11, 1844; Calahan to Cadwalader, July 7, 1844 (CC); Pleasanton Diary, 418–24; Col. C.J. Jack to *NA*, Aug. 2, 1844; Geo. Cadwalader to J.R. Ingersoll, May 24, 1844 (CC); Col. Pleasanton to Gen. Cadwalader, May 20, 1844 (Cadwalader notebook, 62–63); Cadwalader notebook, 70–71.

108. *PPL*, May 13, 1844; J.R. Ingersoll to Gen. Cadwalader, May 20, 1844 (CC).

109. Fisher, 174.

110. *United States Gazette*, July 12, 1844: letter of Horace Binney et al, *loc. cit.*, July 11, 1844 (clippings in CC); Fisher, 174.

111. Cadwalader to Patterson, July 19, 1844 (draft report in CC); Lee, 174–77; Fisher, 172–73.

112. Gen. Cadwalader to Select and Common Councils, Sept. 26, 1844 (CC); Ellis P. Oberholtzer, *Philadelphia: A History of the City and Its People* (4 vols., Philadelphia, 1911), II, 496–97.

113. Warner, 152–57; Fisher, 179.

114. See "One Who Knows, and a Weaver" to *Spirit of the Times*, Sept. 13, 1848; Freedley, 254.

115. See David Montgomery, *Beyond Equality: Labor and the Radical Republicans, 1862–1872* (New York, 1967), 42–44 and *passim.*

CHAPTER 5

Wage Labor, Bondage, and Citizenship in Nineteenth-Century America

From *International Labor and Working-Class History* 48 (Fall 1995): 6–27

Both the content and the boundaries of citizenship were contested terrain in the United States throughout the nineteenth century. The claims of working people to active participation in the polity were draped in the rhetoric to which the ardent revolutionary and future attorney general of Massachusetts, James Sullivan, had given vigorous, though commonplace, expression during the turbulent spring of 1776:

> a very great number of the people of this Colony have at all times been bound by Laws to which they were never in a Capacity to Consent not having estate worth 40/per annum & c . . . Why a man is supposed to consent to the acts of a Society of which in this respect he is absolutely an Excommunicate, none but a lawyer well dabbled in the feudal Sistem can tell.[1]

The demands of the "excommunicates" and strictures of lawyers "well dabbled in the feudal Sistem" were to clash vigorously during the republic's formative decades. The evolution of that conflict revealed a paradox, which this article will explore. Political democracy expanded significantly after the 1790s, providing wage earners freedom of association and a capacity to influence their government—especially their local government—that they clearly treasured. Nevertheless, the ability of elected officials to shape social and economic life was tightly circumscribed. As L. Ray Gunn put it in his excellent discussion of New York State's political reforms of the 1840s, "the economy was effectively insulated from democratic control."[2]

But the title of Gunn's book, *The Decline of Authority*, is misleading. Restricted government did not mean weak or unobtrusive government. On the contrary, the coercive power of the state, as found in its judiciary, its municipal police, and its military forces, grew steadily. The growing police powers exercised by state and local government were used—in sum—to change the personal and collective behavior of working people from that permitted by eighteenth-century market systems to that seen in the lifestyles and time-discipline necessary and suitable to industrial capitalism. Governmental coercion thus underwrote new forms of subordination, which contrasted sharply with the equality in human interactions, moral independence, and ability to participate in shaping the polity that workers associated with citizenship.

As Christopher Tomlins has argued persuasively, the meaning of *police*, as expressed in the new functions that repressed popular behavior while liberating market activity, involved an extensive transformation of the concept from its older and broader usage. In the colonies, and especially in New England with its network of town governments, local authorities had pursued the maintenance of social peace in the absence of standing armed forces. Maintaining roads, training and outfitting militia, assisting the indigent (often by binding them out to service), stabilizing the price of bread in the cities, and regulating the quality of major exports (like lumber and fish in New England or tobacco in the Chesapeake Bay area) had provided basic elements of this quest. The rise of plebeian influence in local governments after the Revolution evoked the prospect that such extensive powers might be exercised as the local majority desired.[3] And the possibility that such majorities might include many individuals "who have no permanent stake in the city; men who can pack up their all in a knapsack, or carry them in their pockets" to another town (as the attorney prosecuting the Philadelphia shoemakers put it in 1806) made that prospect ominous to the men of substantial property, who had historically managed town affairs.[4]

It did not prove possible simply to exclude men of little or no wealth from the electorate. On the contrary, between the 1770s and the 1840s every northern state except Rhode Island redefined its voting qualifications so as to incorporate virtually all adult white males. Alexis de Tocqueville grasped the dynamics of the complex process by which partisan divisions in the ranks of the "higher orders" after the Revolution had led "each of their several members to follow his own interest; and as it was impossible to wring the power from the hands of a people which they did not detest sufficiently to brave, their only aim was to secure its good will at any price." The consequence was that "the most democratic laws were . . . voted by the very men whose interests they impaired." No less aristocratic a state than Maryland led the way, amending its state constitution in 1801 to abolish property qualifications for voting and require ballots to be cast in secret.[5]

The changes were justified by the rhetoric of equal rights and popular sovereignty, which conformed neatly to the everyday experience of the large rural smallholding element of the population and may well have encountered relatively weak resistance outside of Rhode Island because the wage-earners' numbers remained quite unthreatening in comparison to those of small proprietors. Indeed, in New England most wage earners were sons and daughters of local landowners. Tocqueville's observation that most of the gentry "did not detest" the people "sufficiently to brave" them is especially apt. A comparison with the venomous hostility displayed by Southern plantation owners toward the enfranchisement of their former slaves in 1867–68 underscores the fact that a significant portion of the gentry, assembling under the Jeffersonian banner, was prepared to advance its own political fortunes by soliciting the votes of humble white farmers and artisans.

For champions of a free-market economy, however, the duties of citizenship were both more universal in scope and more fundamental to the republican order than were its rights. The obligation to uphold and obey the law fell upon all free inhabitants, even in the view of those who considered admission to the electorate a privilege. Boston's Federalist attorney Peter Oxenbridge Thatcher called for "a simple, united and energetic government under the gravest and wisest of citizens" that could restore the "orderly distribution of duties."[6]

The distinction between duties and rights was especially evident to free women. The plasticity of the early republic did not extend to the inclusion of women in the active citizenry, though the possibility did become part of public debate. Women were subject to criminal prosecution for violations of the law, paid taxes, and could be charged with treason. They could sue in civil courts and could and often did press criminal charges against other women and men, especially before local magistrates.[7] In all states, however, the common law placed married women under the coverture of their husbands. In the words of the prestigious legal commentator Tapping Reeve, the marriage contract gave the husband dominion over everything his wife had acquired by "labor, service, or act," as well as over the "person of his wife."[8]

The capacity of married women to own property in their own names began to be recognized by Northern state legislatures after New York led the way in 1846, and by Southern states during Reconstruction. Married women's entitlement to wages they had earned by their own labor was also secured by statute in two-thirds of the states by 1877. Moreover, courts became increasingly sympathetic to the claims of women, who protested that their husbands had abused their authority. Not until the 1890s did women win the right to vote in more than school-board elections and to serve on juries, and then only in four states of the far West. The writings of Mrs. E. W. P. Packard championing the causes of married women and patients in mental institutions were so widely read during the 1870s as to earn her a small fortune in royalties, but it was in vain that she argued that "Wives are not mere things, they are a part of society. They ought to be citizens. They feel as men do, and want to be allowed to be free moral agents as much as they do."[9]

Workers' Quest for Citizenship

The struggle for universal manhood suffrage that raged with special fury in Rhode Island between 1832 and 1842 is significant, not only because it culminated in a brief and futile attempt to challenge the authority of the established government with an elected People's Convention, but also because it revealed the positive content that working people lent to the concept of citizenship. Because of the early industrialization of the Blackstone River Valley, Rhode Island was the only state in which the manufacturing population outnumbered the farming population in 1840. Its workers demanded not only the right to vote for legislators and governors but also the right to participate in town government, from both of which landholding qualifications had barred them. The resolutions adopted by their conventions and rallies also revealed how they intended that the police powers of a democratically elected government should be employed: They called for a legal ten-hour day, direct election of all public officials, abolition of imprisonment for debt, and equal and universal education. The public humiliation and beating of a teenaged factory operative by her overseer because she had "refused to obey [his] directions" was held up at meeting after meeting as an illustration of why workers needed full citizenship.[10]

The outcome of the Rhode Island struggle was also portentous. After state authorities had forcefully suppressed the People's Convention movement, they convoked their own constitutional convention, which abolished property requirements for native-born men but retained them for the many workingmen who had been born abroad. During the 1850s Massachusetts, Pennsylvania, and other industrial states also restricted the political rights of immigrants through residency requirements and literacy tests and through the requirement that the five-year process of naturalization be completed before voting privileges could be extended. In contrast, most Midwestern states allowed immigrants to vote as soon as they had declared their intention to become citizens. The practice of reducing the workingclass vote by restricting immigrants' access to the ballot reached its extreme form in the case of the Chinese, who were barred from becoming citizens at all, first by state law in California and then by federal statute after 1882.[11]

The example of Rhode Island suggests that male wage earners linked their claims to citizenship to a refusal to be bound to the service of any master, and also to freedom to promote their collective well-being through their own associations. When the Jeffersonian attorney William Sampson defended the shoemakers of New York, who had been charged in 1809 with forming "an unlawful club and combination," he seized the occasion to excoriate the British legacy of hunting down absconding laborers, incarcerating them, and punishing persons who harbored them. A legal code that classified the "lower orders" as "servants, labourers, artificers, and beggars," he thundered, "is surely not American!" The eighteenth-century conspiracy indictments against combinations of workers in England had been based on medieval statues of laborers and artificers, which, Sampson claimed, were not only alien to the spirit of a republic where "no man is subject, and no man lord and master," but also "were never in force in the United States of America, not when they were colonies, and certainly not since."[12]

Sampson's arguments remind us that, as the nineteenth century began, hired labor coexisted with and was often overshadowed by slavery, indentured servitude, apprenticeship, and other forms of bound labor. Merchant capital had accommodated the production of commodities through a variety of labor systems, ranging from the total subjugation of the slave to such autonomy among artisans and yeomen as was seldom to be found in either previous or subsequent human experience. Moreover, the largest concentrations of wage earners had been found among merchant seamen, who were subject to physical punishments and for whom quitting during the period for which they had signed on constituted the criminal offense of desertion.

By the 1820s, however, the swelling ranks of men and women dependent on wages for their livelihood and on rental for their dwellings had made wage contracts so commonplace that legal commentators devoted close attention to their relationship to other types of contracts. Jurists elaborated the meaning of wage contracts in ways that secured the worker's right to quit, but also read an obligation to obey employers into the acceptance of employment. Indentured servitude had virtually disappeared by the census of 1850, and a few years after that enumeration the number of wage earners ten years of age and older for the first time surpassed the number of slaves over ten years of age.[13]

This was the rapidly changing context within which male wage earners became part of the active citizenry whose votes were courted by office-seekers. White immigrants were among those courted—to the disgust of nativists. Moreover, the Jeffersonian conviction that people best solved their problems by forming their own associations encouraged an exuberant diversity in civil society and provided workers with a widely recognized justification for assembling in trade unions, short-hour leagues, cooperatives, workingmen's parties, working-girls' clubs, and ethnic self-help societies, parishes, gymnastic associations, singing societies, and nationalist clubs. Workers used both their claims on government and their rights to act without interference from government in their battle against the inequities of the labor market. When Judge Ogden Edwards instructed a jury hearing the case against the journeymen tailors of New York, he asked them "whether any body of men could raise their crests in this land of law, and control others by self-organized combination." Rhode Island's fiery workers' leader Seth Luther replied: "We can, and do, tell the learned judge that 'self-constituted societies' *do* exist, *must* exist, and *shall* exist, even if we have to defend ourselves with the bayonet's burnished point."[14]

Nevertheless, the Jeffersonian republic was a slave republic. The very government to which white workers turned in defense of their liberties long upheld the bondage of black workers. African Americans engaged in their own battle for citizenship, and the outcome of that battle in the middle decades of the century had an enduring impact on the meaning of democracy for all workers. Well before that time, however, the slave base of the republic had also infused the thinking of white people with a racial definition of political rights. All states outside of New England either barred black men from voting or retained property qualifications for them until the Fifteenth Amendment to the federal Constitution was adopted in 1870. Moreover, public processions by African Americans to claim or celebrate their liberties in the manner so commonplace among whites were routinely subjected to physical assault.

Such annual carnivals as Negro Election Day in New England, Pinkster in New York, and General Training Day in New Jersey, in which black men and women had celebrated under the usually benign eye of whites, disappeared with the gradual emancipation of the slaves in those states. In their place arose urban processions of black men, featuring marshals, uniforms, and banners, commemorating the abolition of the Atlantic slave trade, emancipation in the British West Indies, or the statutory end of slavery in the home state. Shane White has argued that these parades bore a "confrontational edge" and were staged deliberately on days associated with British antislavery measures, or on July 5th, rather than the 4th (when whites routinely drove blacks away from Independence Day celebrations). Although the black processions were savagely caricatured by the white press and often assaulted by white youths, they continued until the Civil War as defiant manifestations by those who remained "excommunicates."[15]

Workers' Use of Suffrage

Despite the exclusion of women, African Americans, Chinese, and many European immigrants from active citizenship, it would be a serious mistake to underestimate the unusual character and the importance of popular participation in American government. Of the major industrial countries in the 1880s only France had extended voting rights to virtually all its adult male population while also securing freedom of the press and of association for its working people. The United States had opened the franchise to propertyless white males in the Northern states between the 1790s and the 1840s and to black males in the Southern states in the 1860s.

Struggles for voting rights and against autocracy shaped the most massive class confrontations in nineteenth-century Europe. At the turn of the century that conflict triggered many general strikes. Austria, Italy, Belgium, the Netherlands, Norway, Sweden, Spain, Russia, and Finland all produced huge mobilizations of workers demanding one man, one vote (in the Finnish case, one person, one vote) during the first decade of the twentieth century. Only in the aftermath of those struggles could the secretary of the Socialist International write with misplaced confidence: "no one doubts that within a few years democracy will triumph in all countries of European civilization."[16]

The gradual but steady collapse of property barriers to voting that Tocqueville had noted prepared the way for the unprecedented nationwide leap in actual voter participation in the presidential election of 1840. It was an occasion, recalled the triumphant Indiana Whig activist George Julian, when "mass-meetings of the people, such as had never been dreamed of before, became the order of the day. The people took the work of politics into their own keeping, and the leaders became followers."[17]

From then on male wage earners were mustered into election campaigns and public spectacles by the Democrats, Whigs, Know Nothings, and Republicans, not to mention the many labor-reform parties. Even though barriers to voting by noncitizens and transients abounded in the northeastern states, between 92 and 94 percent of all adult males in the country were citizens after the citizenship of African Americans was formally recognized. In every presidential election after the Fifteenth Amendment (from 1872 through 1896) between two-thirds and three-fourths of the country's adult males cast ballots—the highest level of male voting involvement in the country's history.

Moreover, the importance of the way in which elections incorporated working people into the polity is disguised by the condescending tone of Julian's recollection. The pageantry of processions, serenades, bonfires, and election-day gatherings not only mobilized workers for their parties but also symbolically defined the social boundaries of the nation. Patriotism was trumpeted by all processions of vote seekers. Flags, soldiers, war heroes, and stirring march music were indispensable. The many formal processions were masculine rituals, with women restricted to ceremonial or allegorical roles (in contrast to their appearance in temperance and trade union processions as marchers). As Jean H. Baker has argued persuasively, partisan ceremonies and the public schools reinforced each other's indoctrination in the wondrous heritage and awesome might of a republic, which coupled individual advancement to community bondings and obligations. The rhetoric and symbolism of elections articulated the terms on which propertyless men took part in the governance of the republic.[18]

Although the influence of working-class voters on local government had become evident in many manufacturing towns by the 1850s, it was especially important during the last two decades of the century. In fact, the clout workers could exert on the major parties in any locality was directly proportional to the level of organization accomplished there by the trade unions and the Knights of Labor. It also helped if the concentration of wage earners was large, and Democrats appeared more likely to favor labor's demands if the town had many Germans. A close and unstable balance of power between the major parties often made both of them more attentive to workers' voices, and the presence of an effective Greenback-Labor or Socialist Labor party in the community made them much more attentive.

It is misleading to consider working-class politics only as an adjunct to union struggles. To be sure, every one of the five successful mobilizations of workers in municipal politics of the 1880s studied by Leon Fink was made possible by a strong presence of the Knights of Labor and trade unions in local manufacturing and construction. The focal point of political struggle, however, was the workers' effort to rescue their cities from the squalor and neglect produced by free-market capitalism. The town officials elected by the United Labor party of Rochester, New Hampshire, did little to alter the structure of government, but they did shift municipal expenditures away from private claims for public favors into increased appropriations for schools, poor relief, a reading room, and road paving, all of which had suffered long neglect. The story was similar in every other case Fink examined. While the coercive power of government had roused the anger of labor organizations, the diminished scope of governmental action, where social priorities had been fixed by market economics, had left urban life a shambles, except for those individuals with sufficient wealth to provide for themselves. In Kansas City, Kansas, where Mayor Thomas Hannan had channeled labor's strength into the Republican fold, thus facilitating a most unusual alliance between white and black workers, his administration wrung the funds needed for parks, a library, and a sewer system from the city's businesses. The regime of Detroit's Mayor Hazen Pingree, which provides something of a model of what could and could not be done by municipal government, focused its energies on cheap, accessible public transportation and on assistance to the unemployed.[19]

The huge vote garnered by Henry George's campaign for mayor of New York in 1886 represented for many reformers the high-water mark of that decade's labor struggles. The Declaration of Principles, drafted by George and adopted by a conference of 175 labor organizations launching his campaign, contended that

> the enormous value which the presence of a million and a half of people gives to the land of this city belongs properly to the whole community; that it should not go to the enrichment of individuals and corporations, but it should be taken in taxation and applied to the improvement and beautifying of the city, to the promotion of the health, comfort, education, and recreation of its people, needs of a great metropolis.[20]

George's election campaign involved women far more actively than did campaigns of the major parties. Women solicited many of the thirty thousand signatures that he demanded as a precondition of his candidacy, collected pennies to cover campaign expenses, and appeared in large numbers at both neighborhood "tailgate speeches" and mass rallies. Here was an electoral effort that modified the social boundaries of citizenship: It was neighborhood-based; its demands touched the lives of women with households to manage and children to nurture as well as those of men and women who earned wages outside of their homes.[21]

Black Republicans

The connection between citizenship and struggles at the point of production was especially clear for rural black workers in the South. As early as the fall of 1865, when pardoned former slave-holders reclaimed their estates in the South Carolina coastal region behind the arms of federal soldiers, it was clear that no distribution of estates was going to follow the emancipation of the slaves. Some form of wage masquerading as a share of the crop became commonplace as early as the 1866 season, because share payment did not oblige the employer to turn any money over to the worker until the crop was in, and the practice also gave the worker an interest in the size of the harvest. Always at issue, however, was the question of whose labor the planter had hired with that share: that of one person or that of an entire family. Moreover, intensive cultivation of the cash crop was best encouraged by placing many croppers on small lots. That practice maximized the return to the planter at the expense of the worker's standard of living. Battles over the number of families working a plantation could not be separated from disputes over the size of garden plots and the grazing area for livestock to which workers were entitled, or indeed from controversies over whether things other than cotton raised on the plantation belonged to the planter or to the worker.

In short, even on the resuscitated plantation the former slave sought to rent land by paying its owner a portion of the crop, while the employer sought to hire labor time in exchange for that same share. Black workers quickly learned to pledge each other not to work for less than the terms to which they had agreed among themselves. Their most effective instrument was the paramilitary club, which brought men and women from various plantations together, often on Saturday market days. In response to planters' claims that six days' labor was owed, and to Black Code prohibitions against the bearing of arms by African Americans, the freedmen argued to U.S. military authorities that theirs were patriotic gatherings associated with the defense of the United States and often featuring drills by black army veterans. After the Reconstruction Acts of 1867 these armed contingents openly affiliated with the Union Leagues and became the most effective agencies for mobilizing Republican votes in the countryside.[22]

To put it another way, the enfranchisement of black voters by the 1867 Reconstruction Acts grafted the new state Republican parties directly onto existing networks of solidarity which rural laborers had fashioned in daily struggles around the terms under which they would work for wages. In urban areas (especially Richmond and New Orleans) mutual-aid societies and black trade unions played similar roles.

In preparation for elections of delegates to state constitutional conventions required by the Reconstruction Acts and in the subsequent balloting for state officials, Republican activists toured the Southern countryside. Among them were more than eighty "colored itinerant lecturers" financed by the party's Congressional Committee. They were welcomed by Union League clubs, which were made up not only of black field and household workers but often of beleaguered local white loyalists as well. Local economic grievances blended with state and national governmental issues in clubs' discussions. In fact, it can be said that the distinction between economic and political questions, which was then so finely drawn by white trade unionists and socialists, made no sense in African-American organizations.[23]

Southern conservatives regained power through strategies that also combined electoral and paramilitary action. "Old men in the Tax Unions and young men in the Rifle Clubs" was the battle cry of South Carolina's Redeemers in 1876.[24] The victors shattered Republican political organizations, wreaking especially bloody vengeance on party activists and on Union Leagues. They effectively suppressed the counter pressures of workers' solidarities in all districts but those where the African-American population was most dense. They placed local sheriffs and magistrates directly under the authority of the white-supremacist state governments. And they festooned the statute books with legislation regulating in detail the issues of everyday confrontation between planters and workers: vagrancy, enticement, and criminal surety laws; laws restricting hunting rights and enclosing unimproved lands; laws declaring thefts of livestock or sales of standing crops to be felonies; laws giving the landlord or merchant-creditor first lien on the crop; and laws for leasing out to labor the thousands of African Americans sentenced under the new statutes. Open disenfranchisement followed. The defeated Republican Albion Tourgee observed: "The lords of the soil are the lords of the labor still."[25]

The door to citizenship for African Americans was partially pried open once again during the 1880s and 1890s, thanks in large measure to the emergence of Independent and Populist movements among discontented white farmers. Although the candidates of those movements were often overt white supremacists, Morgan Kousser argues that they openly appealed for black votes and called for a "free vote and fair count," thereby "legitimizing the race's participation in politics, sanctioning biracial alliances, and accustoming many white leaders to politicking in the black community." Blacks responded with very specific demands, such as the laws they wrung from the Readjuster-dominated legislature of Virginia by 1883 abolishing public whipping posts, repealing the state's poll tax, increasing funds for education, and permitting black men to serve on juries. A black majority on the city council of Danville reshaped the police force before a bloody assault on the town by white Democrats in 1883 helped their party sweep the polls in the state election and instituted a regime of disfranchisement and segregation. By 1900 that pattern prevailed throughout the South.[26]

Restricting Democracy for the Free Market

For at least a century to follow, the South provided a powerful bulwark against working-class demands in the federal government and in both major parties. But when we turn our attention to the industrial North, we find a different political dynamic. In the North the most effective agency for circumventing the voting power of working people was the judiciary. In the industrial regions, unlike the rural South, elected legislators played a very minor role in determining the legal meaning of the labor contract. The courts played a decisive role. They did so under the guidance of commentaries written by learned members of the legal profession. Even their vocabulary would have mystified or enraged the people gathered at election festivities. It reeked of terms like "master and servant" and "baron and femme." In the epoch of the Revolution Benjamin Rush had asked, "Do not men use Latin and Greek as scuttlefish emit their ink, on purpose to conceal themselves from intercourse with the common people?"[27]

Important judicial decisions focused on the right to quit. As early as 1808 lawyers argued about whether the law of master and servant found in Britain's Tudor Code applied in the United States. That law imposed criminal sanctions against workers who left their employment without the master's permission. Wage earners who "absconded" from their master's service could be jailed, as could slaves, indentured servants, and apprentices.[28] In 1823 the British Parliament renewed the law's provision that abandoning work could lead to criminal prosecution before a justice of the peace and a sentence of up to three months at hard labor, after which the workers still owed their masters all contracted labor time. In one English county studied by Douglas Hay and Paul Craven, "130 men and women were imprisoned under master and servant for every one imprisoned" under the more famous Combination Acts. Daphne Simon has calculated that during the 1860s an average of 10,000 men and women in England and Wales were prosecuted each year for leaving their jobs, most of them agricultural laborers, household workers, miners, and workers in potteries and cutlery trades.[29]

In the United States the end of criminal punishment for quitting (or what lawyers called specific enforcement of contracts) was tied up with growing popular revulsion against indentured servitude for whites. In 1821 the Supreme Court of Indiana issued a ringing declaration: Forcing a woman against her will to perform labor on a master's premises and under his direction is slavery, and slavery is illegal in Indiana. Three decades later immigrant glass workers from England went on strike in that state to force their employer to cancel the debts they owed for their passage to America. In Illinois, Pennsylvania, and especially Maryland, however, indentured servitude continued a desultory existence until the Thirteenth Amendment explicitly banned any "involuntary servitude."[30]

Monetary sanctions replaced criminal prosecution. In 1824 a Massachusetts court ruled that a worker leaving before he had completed the terms of a contract was entitled to no money whatever—not even for the period already worked. Over the next decades most courts softened that punishment, but they did authorize employers to withhold wages, usually for two weeks or a month, and to refuse to turn over that pay to someone who quit without giving the notice required by company rules.

Thus, two legal principles emerged side by side. The first was, in the words of Tennessee's Supreme Court in 1884: "Either party may terminate the service, for any cause, good or bad, or without cause, and the other cannot complain in law." Along with the employer's power to jail an "absconding servant" went any right of a worker to protest in court against dismissal. Throwing farm laborers too ill to work out of the house became perfectly legal. So did firing a railroad employee who bought something at a store where his company had forbidden him to trade. The Supreme Court even ruled unconstitutional a federal statute that would have punished an employer who fired a worker for voting.[31]

The second was that anyone accepting employment for wages was legally bound to obey whatever rules the employer might devise for the job. Courts in Massachusetts, Pennsylvania, and New York decided during the 1870s and 1880s that rules posted by a company became part of the contract between employer and employee. Even if the rules were not explicit, decided a New York Court of Appeals, workers "entered into the contract with the knowledge of the established usages of the employment." Established practices could even overrule acts of the legislature: Despite the fact that the state's law had declared eight hours a day's work in 1867, a scowman was bound by the custom of the docks—ten hours.[32]

Factory regulations, sometimes posted, more often simply understood, required workers to be at their machines from first whistle to last, to abstain from conversation, to complete assigned tasks and quotas of output, to give two weeks' notice or more of intention to quit, to refrain from joining unions, and to act with deference and obedience toward "superiors." Such rules were often flouted, to be sure, but the employers' sanctions of dismissal, humiliation, fines, blacklists, and evictions from company-owned housing were reinforced by the workers' own need for income. Conversely, customs and usages of the trade that ran counter to an employer's rules or practices enjoyed no legal sanction. They were often defended by the workers' collective action and enshrined in trade-union rules. Union enforcement of those rules, however, could and did bring union members before the courts charged with conspiracy to injure an employer or to obstruct commerce. When the legislature of Massachusetts prohibited employers from fining workers for failing to meet company standards, the state Supreme Court quickly ruled the statute unconstitutional. When unions fined an employer for violations of union rules, they were guilty of extortion.[33]

In the second half of the century, as judicial embellishment of the law of a free-market system reached its perfection, the courts moved against both legislation won by the labor movement and workers' efforts to regulate wage contracts collectively. Miners' unions had wrung some statute regulating conditions in coal mines out of the Pennsylvania legislature almost every year between 1868 and 1881. Checkweighmen were permitted and later required at mines, safety regulations and inspections were mandated, payment was allowed only in lawful money, company stores were forbidden, and a state hospital was established for the anthracite region.

During the 1880s and 1890s the scope of unions' legislative demands expanded. In various industrial states unions lobbied successfully for bills creating state bureaus of labor statistics, restricting child labor, providing free textbooks for public schools, outlawing the importation of strikebreakers or armed guards from out of state, obliging factories to construct fire escapes, prohibiting home or tenement-house manufacturing, restricting manufacturing or printing or mining by convict labor, installing railroad safety appliances, limiting the work days of women in factories to ten hours, forbidding employers to punish their workers with fines, making Labor Day an official holiday, and regulating terms of apprenticeship.[34]

Most of the measures enacted proved impossible to enforce. When statutes did threaten to impinge on companies' control of their own business affairs, the courts usually found them unconstitutional. William Forbath has catalogued sixty state labor laws invalidated by courts between 1881 and 1900. Most of them, not surprisingly, dealt with coal mining. Others had restricted hours of labor, outlawed workplace fines, prohibited dismissal for union membership or voting, required union labor on public works, or allowed workers suing employers to be awarded attorneys' fees. Important measures that were upheld often were construed so narrowly as to nullify their intended effect. For example, although two-thirds of all states had enacted laws by 1877 securing married women's claims to wages they had earned themselves, the courts limited that protection to what the women had clearly acquired outside of the household. As Amy Stanley has written: "Taking in boarders, nursing the sick, canning fruit, working [at home] as a seamstress for five dollars a week, running a hotel—such diverse enterprises were all deemed part of the domestic labor the wife owed as the 'helpmate of her husband'," and to which any enforcement of her claim might result in "frauds upon the creditors."[35]

The courts also threw their weight decisively against efforts by workers' organizations to impose social standards through their own collective action in the market. The city-wide boycott, by which all residents were mobilized to "leave severely alone" a particular firm that persecuted or defied its own workers, had developed by the mid-1880s into the most effective weapon of the Knights of Labor. While workers defended their hundreds of local boycotts as the sort of private arrangements to promote the common welfare that were favored by America's Jeffersonian legacy, courts prohibited them precisely because their motivation was not self-interested but "sympathetic." By introducing community moral standards into economic behavior, judges charged, boycotts were "combinations of irresponsible cabals or cliques" that threatened to bring "an end of government."[36]

Citizenship, Police Powers, and Policing

The coercive power of government over the citizenry expanded at the same time that the ability of elected officials to shape economic life was restricted. Judicial action against unions and against legislation that would have used the police powers of the states to uphold standards of social justice and community well-being in economic life constituted the negative side of the process by which market activity was sheltered from democratically elected legislatures and from the actions of "self-constituted societies" of working people. The active component of the same process was the application of the state's coercive power not only to the collective action of employees, but also to the individual behavior of those who were not at work. Although the courts had ended criminal punishment of men and women who quit a particular boss, the law punished with increasing severity anyone who had no boss at all. Punishment for vagrancy had been increased by several states during the 1850s, and the new uniformed municipal police forces had from time to time conducted dragnet arrests of people found in the streets without visible occupations. In 1877, however, a conference of boards of public charities had agreed that new, uniform state legislation was needed to prevent people from begging and wandering about without employment.[37]

Tramp Acts were soon adopted by forty of the forty-four states. The acts shifted the emphasis in the definition of the crime from begging to wandering without work. In addition, they converted deeds that were misdemeanors when committed by others into felonies when perpetrated by tramps, and they provided that state governments would reimburse localities for the expenses of incarcerating tramps. Sidney Harring's study of Buffalo revealed that police there arrested more than two thousand people each year under New York's tramp law between 1891 and 1897, including Jack London, who had ridden the rails to see Niagara Falls. They seized 4,716 people as tramps in 1894 alone, in addition to even greater numbers charged under the older vagrancy and drunk-and-disorderly rubrics.[38]

Labor organizations denounced the measures as new fugitive slave laws and they sought to provide their own facilities for those whom Samuel Gompers defined as "workingmen who for a time have become superfluous in society, men rather, whom the employing class have made superfluous." During the depression of the 1870s workingmen in municipal office sometimes spurned the wandering poor, while soliciting government aid for "worthy citizens," who, said cigar makers' leader Fred Blend of Evansville, Indiana, "had lived here for many years, and whom the hard times and scarcity of work has driven to poverty." Faced with the depression of the 1890s, however, trade unions worked directly with city governments in such cities as Chicago and Denver to feed and house all unemployed, and demonstrators in Boston demanded "municipal factories where the unemployed can work for themselves." Populist Governor Lorenzo Lewelling of Kansas declared his state's tramp act unconstitutional, and he ordered the police not to molest people without homes or jobs. "The right to go freely from place to place in search of employment, or even in obedience of a mere whim," his circular proclaimed, "is part of that personal liberty guaranteed by the Constitution of the United States to every human being on American soil."[39]

Those views made little impression on the judiciary. A commentary on criminal law from the 1890s made two complementary tenets of the law of the free market in labor crystal clear. The learned Joel Bishop wrote: "there is, in just principle, nothing which a government has more clearly the right to do than to compel the lazy to work; and there is nothing more absolutely beyond its jurisdiction than to fix the price of labor."[40]

Regulation of personal conduct to satisfy the needs of the market for wage labor also involved changing the relation of government to poor relief. Eighteenth-century practices of town or county assistance to needy families, holding down the costs of necessities, and binding out the indigent came under persistent attack from elite reformers from the 1810s through the 1890s. The reformers' basic objectives were to privatize poor relief for all except the physically infirm, to exclude recipients of relief from the electorate, and to use private control to impose a work ethic on the recipients.

There never has been a clear line of demarcation between public and private charity in North America. Moreover, the history of poor relief is filled with plans and legislation that boldly promised fundamental reforms in the treatment of the poor, but which in practice turned out to have changed little or nothing. Refusal by the poor to enter workhouses and the abundance of ethnic, religious, women's, and fraternal aid societies provided alternative sources of assistance that frustrated the most determined efforts of elite reformers at controlling poor relief.

Poor relief was also an arena of social and political activity in which women were especially prominent, both as recipients and as donors. Consequently, gender profoundly shaped the everyday experience of class in the distribution of public charity. Conversely, public charity ranked among the most important instruments of class rule in the democratic polity. There is space here for only a few remarks about this important topic.

A rapidly rising tide of urban poverty in the 1810s and 1820s provoked widespread controversy over the costs and purposes of poor relief. "Patrician confidence in urban benevolence faltered before the pressing demands of the poor during and after the War of 1812," writes Christine Stansell. "By 1817, it had all but collapsed."[41] Thousands of urban residents who were dependent on the capricious wages of maritime, construction, and portage work routinely became supplicants for donations of goods or money to individuals who were not residents of almshouses ("outdoor relief"). For poor women, who commonly pursued a variety of employments throughout the year, outdoor relief became a basic element of their incomes, and even the almshouse was a temporary shelter to which they flocked when all else failed.

Critics of existing relief practices echoed the sentiments of the economist Thomas Cooper: "It is not the suppression of poverty that is wanted, so much as the suppression of idleness, extravagance, dissipation, drunkenness, and vice, which are uniformly the parents of poverty." Like other groups, New York's Society for the Prevention of Pauperism sought to speed the reduction of outdoor relief by taking action against the dissolute habits of the poor. The city's Common Council followed suit in 1817, slashing its grants to private charities, which it accused of promiscuous almsgiving.[42]

The same council session summoned the state to end outdoor relief. It also abolished the most familiar historic protection of the living standards of the poor: the assize of bread. The practice by which magistrates had calibrated the price and the size of a loaf of bread according to the current price of wheat had actually been discontinued, subsequently resumed, and only fitfully enforced since the beginning of the century. As a symbol of the authorities' historic duty to restrain profiteering in the necessities of life and protect the welfare of working people, however, it had not lost its grip. In New York its abolition also came hard on the heels of a campaign by the mayor and council to stamp out the people's custom of letting their hogs feed in the streets. While sympathetic lawyers appealed in vain to the common law in defense of poor people's pigs, angry crowds of white and black women continued into the 1830s to assault police who were "stealing their hogs."[43]

The battle over the cost of living faced by the poor resurfaced angrily in the flour riots of 1837. Crowds, contemptuously described by the *Journal of Commerce* as "the very *canaille* of the city . . . several of them colored people, not a few of them noted thieves, and some of them foreigners of the lowest description," hurled barrels of flour out of Eli Hart's store in protest against exorbitant bread prices, echoing an earlier petition to the council for a restoration of the assize. The *Journal of Commerce* replied: "We say, let every man look out for himself. If you weigh the loaf, you know what it weighs, but if it is stamped with the weight, you do not know." Two weeks later it added: "Price is the regulator of consumption. If there is a scarcity it draws supplies from a distance and deals out for consumption with a sparing hand." The *Evening Star* reassured the poor: "if they are in want, the public authorities, on application, will relieve their wants."[44]

Free markets, a safety net of abstemious relief to the worthy poor, and the suppression of "idleness" and "dissipation" thus framed the historic alternative to working people's claims to benevolence from the rich and from town magistrates. To reach their goal philanthropists like Charles Loring Brace, Josephine Shaw Lowell, and Frederick Law Olmsted sought not simply to share authority with elected officers of the cities, but also to usurp public control of relief disbursement. They persuasively portrayed politics as the seedbed of corruption and privately directed benevolence as the nation's salvation. City officials dispensed relief to win voters' favor, the reformers charged. Their powers posed the greatest menace of all to poor-relief reformers, because tax-based benevolence threatened, as the *Chicago Tribune* editorialized in 1874, to make the city "an organized robber" that would use the votes of the many to transfer "the sweat and toil of the thrifty and self-denying" to "the idle, the improvident, the spendthrifts, and the drones of society."[45]

The quest of workers to avoid submission to private charity took many forms and constituted a major component of their struggle to articulate their citizenship. Mutual insurance against the perils of unemployment, incapacity, and death was provided by scores of fraternal lodges, many based on nationality, and some, like the half-million-member-strong Odd Fellows, international in scope. All of them shared the desire, so clearly expressed by the Odd Fellows, to guard members and their families "against what is most to be dread in these unavoidable ills of life," while preserving "the feeling of equality, and the dignity of a *man*." As one lodge member expressed it: "when a poor man receives a benefit, the heart is not made sick and the feelings crushed and degraded by the thought that it is bestowed because he is poor."[46]

Many trade unions also provided similar benefits to their members. Adolph Strasser, an enthusiastic advocate of such benefits, argued that they both instilled a sense of discipline and commitment into the members (because failure to make a single payment could sacrifice everything the worker had invested) and cultivated support for the unions from "our wives, who because they are ordinarily less idealistic and more egotistical than the man, look upon participation in associations, which offer no material benefit, as unnecessary and as a waste of time and money." Correspondingly, accessibility of such funds would undergird the members' manliness (*Männlichkeit*) by easing the pressures to accept employment at any wage or even to scab.[47]

Just as workers turned to "self-constituted societies" to secure a material basis for their moral independence, so they also made diverse and imaginative uses of the machinery of government, over which the suffrage gave them some influence. At the municipal level, incessant protests from the working class prevented the permanent removal of poor relief from control by elected officials. That protest most often took the form of action: individuals and families refusing to enter almshouses, asking for overnight accommodations in police stations, cajoling and threatening visitors from benevolent agencies who determined eligibility, and at times joining in large public demonstrations demanding relief. Despite the outrage of organized philanthropists, many city officials agreed with the views expressed by Mayor William Shenton of New Haven that "humanity should prompt a liberal provision for giving [the unemployed] a partial employment until our industries assume their normal condition." The city should rotate jobs weekly, he explained. "To keep one set of men continually at work, to the exclusion of others equally worthy at a time like this, is morally wrong."[48]

Shenton's position revealed that what Tomlins called the traditional view of government's "police" role remained much alive in the popular imagination forty years after New York's flour riots of 1837. By the end of the depression of 1873–78, however, the advocates of free-market economics, an abstemious safety net of privately administered relief to the "worthy poor," and forceful repression of "idleness" and "vice" could look back upon a decade of arduous campaigning with satisfaction. The privatization movement had spread to urban areas throughout the North. In New York City all municipal outdoor relief except coal distribution had been terminated in 1874, and even the distribution of coal to the needy was halted in 1879. Not until the great depression of the 1890s (and later the crises of 1908 and 1913–15) overwhelmed the capacities of private charities did their leaders cautiously turn back to city and state governments for resources to help them care for the needy and dampen social unrest.[49]

The Crisis of Free-Market Democracy

In short, male white workers had successfully claimed the right to give their consent to the laws that governed the community by participating in the selection of legislators and administrators. Conflicts within the elite after the Revolution led to an extension of the suffrage to a populace most notables "did not detest sufficiently to brave." Only where slavery prevailed and in Rhode Island, the most industrialized state, did most workingmen remain "excommunicates" from the polity. Moreover, even in the relatively homogeneous towns of New England, immigrants, who were deemed to have "no permanent stake in the community," faced significant barriers to voting. By the last four decades of the century, however, workingmen were eagerly incorporated into the political culture of the land and exerted a highly visible influence on the elections and municipal government of many industrial towns and cities and also, temporarily, on the state governments of the South. They laid claim to both the police powers of the states and freedom of association to advance their collective well-being. Their citizenship envisaged active participation by all males in a polity where, as William Sampson had promised, "no man is subject, and no man lord and master."

In the South, claims by former slaves to such citizenship were forcefully repressed. Upper-class resistance in industrial states took the different course of constricting the domain of governmental authority while strengthening the capacity of government to restrain and reshape the individual and collective behavior of the working class. Judicial bodies and the legal profession played a decisive role in defining the doctrine of "freedom of contract" in such a way as to assure that the wage contract implied obedience to the employer. Vagrancy law and the privatization of poor relief were crafted to secure that those who had no employer were at least subject to the supervision of police and of philanthropic institutions.

The depression at the end of the century upset more than just the campaign to remove poor relief from the hands of elected officials. As Karl Polanyi wrote: "the idea of a self-adjusting market implied a stark utopia. Such an institution could not exist for any length of time without annihilating the human and natural substance of society." Confronted with class conflict on a titanic scale, utter exhaustion of the relief funds of private agencies, and the patent inability of the domestic market to consume all that modern industry had produced, the leaders of business, government, and intellectual life set out on their own quest for social and governmental mechanisms to regulate economic life. In the famous words of Walter Lippmann's book of 1914, society faced the alternatives of "drift or mastery" concerning the forces it had created.[50]

In contrast to the nineteenth-century effort to insulate the economy from democratic government, twentieth-century progressives and later New Dealers expanded the administrative capacity of government to solve economic problems; and that effort renewed and redefined the contest over the meaning of citizenship for workers. The nation-state emerged as the agency for stabilizing national economies and integrating conflicting social groups in those industrial powers that exercised mastery over the other peoples of the globe. The meaning of citizenship in workers' lives was refashioned to emphasize obligations of loyal service in international conflict and entitlements, by which government mended some of the social damage wrought by industrial life.

By the 1990s, however, twentieth-century claims of citizenship were as much in dispute as those to which workers had been devoted a hundred years earlier.

Notes

Reprinted courtesy of Cambridge University Press and *International Labor and Working-Class History.*

1. Sullivan to Elbridge Gerry, May 6, 1776, quoted in Linda K. Kerber, "The Paradox of Women's Citizenship in the Early Republic: The Case of *Martin vs. Massachusetts*, 1805," *American Historical Review* 97 (April 1992): 367.

2. L. Ray Gunn, *The Decline of Authority: Public Economic Policy and Political Development in New York, 1800–1860* (Ithaca, 1988), 9.

3. Christopher L. Tomlins, *Law, Labor, and Ideology in the Early American Republic* (Cambridge, 1993), 32–93; Michael Zuckerman, *Peaceable Kingdoms; New England Towns in the 18th Century* (New York, 1970); Joshua Wilson, "Electing 'Suitable Persons': Authority, Politics, and Leadership in York, Maine, 1783–1820" (senior essay, Yale University, 1994), 6–21; Charles G. Sydnor, *American Revolutionaries in the Making: Political Practices in Washington's Virginia* (New York, 1962), 78–85.

4. Quoted in Tomlins, *Law, Labor, and Ideology*, 132.

5. Alexis de Tocqueville, *Democracy in America*, trans. Henry Reeve (New York, 1838), 38; Carl B. Swisher, *Roger B. Taney* (New York, 1935), 47–48.

6. Peter Oxenbridge Thatcher, *An Address to the Members of the Massachusetts Charitable Fire Society May 31, 1805*, quoted in Tomlins, *Law, Labor, and Ideology*, 94.

7. Allen Steinberg, *The Transformation of Criminal Justice: Philadelphia, 1800–1880* (Chapel Hill, 1989), 52.

8. Tapping Reeve, *The Law of Baron and Femme, of Parent and Child, Guardian and Ward, Master and Servant and of the Powers of the Courts of Chancery* (Albany, NY, 1862), 482; Linda K. Kerber, *Women of the Republic: Intellect and Ideology in Revolutionary America* (Chapel Hill, 1980), 119–27.

9. Amy Dru Stanley, "Contract Rights in the Age of Emancipation: Wage Labor and Marriage After the Civil War" (PhD diss., Yale University, 1990), 283–303; Michael Grossberg, *Governing the Hearth: Law and Family in Nineteenth Century America* (Chapel Hill, 1985); E. P. W. Packard, *The Great Drama: or, the Millennial Harbinger*, 4 vols. (Hartford, 1878–79), I, 320; Barbara Sapinsley, *The Private War of Mrs. Packard* (New York, 1991); Myra Samuels Himelhoch with Arthur H.

Shaffer, "Elizabeth Packard: Nineteenth-Century Crusader for the Rights of Mental Patients," *Journal of American Studies* 13 (1979): 343–75.

10. David Montgomery, *Citizen Worker: The Experience of Workers in the United States with Democracy and the Free Market during the Nineteenth Century* (Cambridge, 1993), 17–21.

11. Ibid., 20–21; Edna Bonacich, "Asian Labor in the Development of California and Hawaii," in *Labor Immigration under Capitalism: Asian Workers in the United States before World War II*, eds. Lucy Cheng and Edna Bonacich (Berkeley, 1984), 162–65.

12. John R. Commons, et al., *Documentary History of American Industrial Society*, 10 vols. (Cleveland, 1910–11) 3, 252, 257, 261, 278.

13. Slaves accounted for 23 percent of the nation's labor force over nine years of age in 1850 and 21 percent in 1860. Although the number of wage earners is difficult to calculate precisely from census data, the labor force in manufacturing, construction, mining, transportation, and domestic service accounted for 21 percent of the total in 1850 and 23 percent in 1860. U.S. Department of Commerce, Bureau of the Census, *Historical Statistics of the United States. Colonial Times to 1970*, 2 vols. (Washington, DC, 1975), I, 139.

14. Tomlins, *Law, Labor, and Ideology*, 162, 198.

15. Shane White, "'It was a Proud Day': African Americans, Festivals, and Parades in the North, 1741–1834," *Journal of American History* 81 (June 1994): 13–50; David R. Roediger, *The Wages of Whiteness: Race and the Making of the American Working Class* (London, 1991); Alexander Saxton, *The Rise and Fall of the White Republic: Class Politics and Mass Culture in Nineteenth Century America* (London, 1990); Jean H. Baker, *Affairs of Party: The Political Culture of Northern Democrats in the Mid-Nineteenth Century* (Ithaca, 1983); Susan G. Davis, *Parades and Power: Street Theater in Nineteenth-Century Philadelphia* (Philadelphia, 1986), 46; Paul A. Gilje, *Road to Mobocracy: Popular Disorder in New York City, 1763–1834* (Chapel Hill, 1987), 153–58, 162–70; Frank J. Webb, *The Garies and Their Friends* (London, 1857).

16. Dick Geary, *European Labor Protest, 1848–1939* (London, 1981), 59–65, 103–18; David Blackburn and Geoff Eley, *Peculiarities of German History: Bourgeois Society and Politics in Nineteenth-Century Germany* (New York, 1984), 256–57, 275; Geoff Eley, *Reshaping the German Right: Radical Nationalism and Political Change after Bismarck* (New Haven, 1980), 21–24; Marcel van der Linden and Jurgen Rojahn, eds., *The Formation of Labour Movements, 1870–1914* (Leiden, 1990); Göran Therborn, "The Rule of Capital and the Rise of Democracy," *New Left Review* 103 (May–June 1977): 11–17; Emile Vandervelde, *Socialism versus the State*, trans. Charles H. Kerr (Chicago, 1919), 61. Vandervelde wrote this important book in 1914.

17. George W. Julian, *Political Recollections* (Chicago, 1884), 16.

18. Davis, *Parades and Power*, 47, 149, 157; Michael E. McGerr, *The Decline of Popular Politics: The American North, 1865–1928* (New York, 1986); Baker, *Affairs of Party*, 71–107. See also, Paula Baker, "The Domestication of Politics: Women and American Political Society, 1780–1920," *American Historical Review* 89 (June 1984): 620–47; Mary H. Blewett, *Men, Women, and Work: Class, Gender, and Protest in the New England Shoe Industry, 1780–1910* (Urbana, 1988), 130–62.

19. Leon Fink, *Workingmen's Democracy: The Knights of Labor and American Politics* (Urbana, 1983); Melvin G. Holli, *Reform in Detroit: Hazen S. Pingree and Urban Politics* (New York, 1969). See also Lawrence M. Lipin, *Producers, Proletarians, and Politicians: Workers and Party Politics in Evansville and New Albany, Indiana, 1850–87* (Urbana, 1994); Richard J. Oestreicher, *Solidarity and Fragmentation: Working People and Class Consciousness in Detroit, 1875–1900* (Urbana, 1986); Richard Schneirov, "The Knights of Labor in the Chicago Labor Movement and Municipal Politics, 1877–1887" (PhD diss., Northern Illinois University, 1984).

20. Peter A. Speek, *The Singletax and the Labor Movement* (Madison, 1917), 68.

21. David Scobey, "Boycotting the Politics Factory: Labor Radicalism and the New York City Mayoral Election of 1884 [sic.]," *Radical History Review* 28–30 (1984): 280–325 (quotation 311); Speek, *Singletax and the Labor Movement*, 101–104; Louis F. Post, *The Prophet of San Francisco: Personal Memories and Interpretations of Henry George* (New York, 1930), 73, 76, 78, 86.

22. Julie Saville, *The Work of Reconstruction: From Slave to Wage Laborer in South Carolina, 1860–1870* (Cambridge, 1994), 143–88; Michael W. Fitzgerald, "'To Give Our Votes to the Party': Black Political Agitation and Agricultural Change in Alabama, 1865–1870," *Journal of American History* 76 (September 1989): 489–505; Gerald D. Jaynes, *Branches without Roots: Genesis of the Black Working Class in the American South* (New York, 1986), 45–53. For a wartime offer of one-quarter of the crop, see Ira Berlin et al., *Freedom: A Documentary History of Emancipation, 1861–1867* (Cambridge, 1982), vol. 2, 327.

23. Eric Foner, *Reconstruction: America's Unfinished Revolution, 1863–1877* (New York, 1988), 283–91; Peter J. Rachleff, *Black Labor in the South: Richmond, Virginia, 1865–1890* (Philadelphia, 1984), 39–51; Fitzgerald, "'To Give Our Votes to the Party,'" 495–505.

24. Francis B. Simkins and Robert H. Woody, *South Carolina During Reconstruction* (Chapel Hill, 1932), 184; Robert J. Norrell, *Reaping the Whirlwind: The Civil Rights Movement in Tuskegee* (New York, 1985), 3–11.

25. [Albion Tourgee], *A Fool's Errand by One of the Fools* (New York, 1880), 342.

26. J. Morgan Kousser, *The Shaping of Southern Politics: Suffrage Restrictions and the Establishment of the One-Party South* (New Haven, 1974), 26, 41, 93; James Tice Moore, *Two Paths to the New South: The Virginia Debt Controversy, 1870–1883* (Lexington, KY, 1974), 104, 116; Luther P. Jackson, *Negro Office-Holders in Virginia, 1865–1895* (Norfolk, VA, 1945), 79–81.

27. Rush to John Adams, July 21, 1789, quoted in Kerber, *Women of the Republic*, 218.

28. Albert Matthews, "Hired Man and Help," *Publications of the Colonial Society of Massachusetts*, vol. 5 (Transactions, 1897, 1898), 234; Richard B. Morris, *Government and Labor in Early America* (New York, 1946), 1–18.

29. Douglas Hay and Paul Craven, "Master and Servant in England and the Empire: A Comparative Study," *Labour/Le Travail* 31 (Spring 1993): 176; Daphne Simon, "Master and Servant," in *Democracy and the Labor Movement*, ed. John Saville (London, 1954), 160–200. The statistics on prosecutions are on 160.

30. Montgomery, *Citizen Worker*, 31–39; New Albany, Indiana, *Ledger-Standard*, July 10, 1873, cited in Lipin, *Producers, Proletarians, and Politicians*, 215.

31. *Stark v. Parker*, 19 Mass. (2 Pick.) 267; *Payne v. The Western Atlantic Railroad Company*, 81 Tenn. 507; William E. Forbath, *Law and the Shaping of the American Labor Movement* (Cambridge, Mass., 1991), 185.

32. *McCarthy v. Mayor, Aldermen and Commonality of the City of New York*, 96 NY 1, 7 (1884), quoted in Stanley, "Contract Rights," 62.

33. On company rules and union rules, see David Montgomery, *Fall of the House of Labor: The Workplace, the State, and American Labor Activism, 1865–1925* (Cambridge, 1987), 9–44, 148–70, 203–13. On imprisonment of union delegates who fined employers for violating union rules, see *New York v. Hughes*, 137 NY 29 (1893), and the discussion of plumbers' union fines in *John Swinton's Paper*, August 22, 1886. *Conseils de prud'hommes* in France did give legal sanction to customs of the trade which ran counter to employers' rules. Alain Cotereau, "Justice et injustice ordinaire sur les lieux de travail d'apres les audiences prud'homales (1806–1866)," *Le Mouvement Social* 141 (October–December 1987): 25–60.

34. The full scope of union lobbying has yet to be examined by historians, and Victoria Hattam's categorical distinction between the lobbying objectives of the Knights and that of the unions is misleading. Hattam, *Labor Visions and State Power: The Origins of Business Unionism in the United States* (Princeton, 1993). For a partial list of union-supported legislative demands, see "Michael McKettrick," *Labor Leader*, October 24, 1891; Knights of Labor, *Proceedings of D.A. 16 held at Scranton, July 28th and 29th 1890* (manuscript, no pagination, Powderly Papers, reel 66). On arbitration laws, see Gerald Friedman, "Worker Militancy and Its Consequences: Political Responses to Labor Unrest in the United States, 1877–1914," *International Labor and Working-Class History* 40 (Fall 1991): 8–9. On nineteenth-century protective legislation for women, see Alice Kessler-Harris, *Out to Work: A History of Wage Earning Women in the United States* (New York, 1982), 180–94; Kathryn Kish Sklar, *Florence Kelley and Women's Political Culture*, vol. 1, *Doing the Nation's Work, 1830–1900* (New Haven, 1995), 171–285.

35. Forbath, *Law and the Shaping of the American Labor Movement*, 38n, 177–87; Stanley, "Contract Rights," 283–303. Quotation on 302.

36. Norman J. Ware, *The Labor Movement in the United States, 1860–1895* (New York, 1929), 334–45; Mary C. Grimes, *The Knights in Fiction: Two Labor Novels of the 1880s* (Urbana, 1986), 44; *Crump v. Commonwealth*, 84 VA 927, 946 (1888), quoted in Forbath, *Law and the Shaping of the American Labor Movement*, 84.

37. Paul T. Ringenbach, *Tramps and Reformers, 1873–1916: The Discovery of Unemployment in New York* (Westport, Conn., 1973), 20–23; Amy Dru Stanley, "'Beggars Can't Be Choosers': Compulsion and Contract in Postbellum America," *Journal of American History* 78 (March 1992): 1277.

38. Sidney L. Harring, "Class Conflict and the Suppression of Tramps in Buffalo, 1892–1894," *Law and Society Review* 11 (Summer 1977): 873–911. The New York statute is quoted on 881; Ringenbach, *Tramps and Reformers*, 22–23.

39. New York *Gewerkschafts-Zeitung*, April 15, 1879; Stuart B. Kaufman, ed., *The Samuel Gompers Papers*, 4 vols. (Urbana, 1986–91), vol. 1, 342; Lipin, *Producers, Proletarians, and Politicians*, 151; Carlos C. Closson, Jr., "The Unemployed in American Cities," *Quarterly Journal of Economics* 8 (January 1894): 168–217, 257–58;

Alexander Keyssar, *Out of Work: The First Century of Unemployment in Massachusetts* (Cambridge, 1986), 349; "The Tramp Circular," in Lawrence Goodwyn, *Democratic Promise: The Populist Moment in America* (New York, 1976), 597–99, quotation 598.

40. Joel Bishop, *New Commentaries on the Criminal Law*, 2 vols. (Chicago, 1892), vol. I, 273–74.

41. Christine Stansell, *City of Women: Sex and Class in New York, 1789–1860* (New York, 1986), 32.

42. Cooper, *Lectures on the Elements of Political Economy* (Columbia, SC, 1826), 260, quoted in David Harris, *Socialist Origins in the United States: American Forerunners of Marx, 1817–1842* (Assen, Netherlands, 1966), 26n; Stansell, *City of Women*, 33–35, quotation 35.

43. Stansell, *City of Women*, 35; Gary B. Nash, *The Urban Crucible: Social Change, Political Consciousness and the Origins of the American Revolution* (Cambridge, Mass., 1979), 130; Hendrick Hartog, *Public Property and Private Power: The Corporation of the City of New York in American Law, 1730–1870* (Chapel Hill, 1983), 140–42, 151–52; Gilje, *Road to Mobocracy*, 228–30.

44. *Journal of Commerce*, February 1, 14, 18, 1837; *Evening Star*, February 15, 1837. I am indebted to Elizabeth Basch for these references. Cf. the dignified depiction of the protests in Fitzwilliam Byrdsall, *The History of the Loco-Foco or Equal Rights Party* (New York, 1842), 99–113.

45. Ringenbach, *Tramps and Reformers*, 15; *Chicago Tribune*, January 2, 1874, quoted in Karen Lynn Sawislak, "Smoldering City: Class, Ethnicity, and Politics in Chicago at the Time of the Great Fire, 1867–1871" (PhD diss., Yale University, 1990), 313.

46. August Sartorius von Waltershausen, "*Das Hilfskassenwesen in Nordamerika*," *Jahrbücher* and *Nationalökonomie und Statistik*, Neue Folge, Bd. 10 (1885), 112–14; *Western Odd Fellows Magazine* 3 (July 1854): 6, quoted in Lipin, *Producers, Proletarians, and Politcians*, 37.

47. *Die Gewerkschafts-Zeitung*, March 15, 1880. My translation of the text: "[Die Unterstützungskassen . . . erwecken das Interesse] selbst das unserer Frauen, die sonst gewöhnlich, weil weniger idealistisch und mehr egoistisch wie der Mann, die Theilnahme an Vereinigungen, die keine materiellen Vortheile bieten, als unnütz und als Zeit und GeldVerschwendung betrachten."

48. Mayor's Address, *City Year Book for New Haven, 1877* (New Haven, 1878), 23.

49. Ringenbach, *Tramps and Reformers*, 83, 93–97.

50. Karl Polanyi, *The Great Transformation* (New York, 1944), 3; Walter Lippmann, *Drift and Mastery: An Attempt to Diagnose the Current Unrest* (New York, 1914).

PART III

Mutualism and Contention

Strikes, Immigrants, and Working-Class Consciousness in the Nineteenth Century

These essays bring together the histories of migration and class struggle. Historians once looked upon immigrant workers as an obstacle to organization and a brake on strike activity. On the contrary, Montgomery argues, they were often at the heart of the great and little conflicts that made American industrial relations among the most contentious in the world. And they helped fuel late nineteenth-century social and political reform movements like the Henry George campaign.

Turning to a quintessentially proletarian form of protest in an essay on nineteenth-century strikes, Montgomery observed that there was no "natural history" of the strike, but strikes did indeed evolve between the early nineteenth and the late twentieth centuries—from what the British historian E. J. Hobsbawm characterized as "collective bargaining by riot"[1] through the mass strikes of the early twentieth century, in which immigrant workers were the main protagonists, into the carefully planned actions later in that same century. If the form of the strike evolved, so too did its aims, from the often-spontaneous actions of early industrialization, over wages, through the movement for shorter hours in the late nineteenth century, to the "control strikes" of the early twentieth. While disputing explanatory frameworks reliant on "modernization" theories, he remained interested nonetheless in "what the long-term evolution of strike behavior reveals about the changing consciousness of workers." What he terms "control strikes" suggests a desire to generate power at the point of production and to shape the work process itself. Sympathy strikes show a worldview and aspirations that crossed occupational lines and embraced workers as a social class. General strikes, which became more common in the World War I era, often involved broader political aims, threatening the power structure in a particular city or region. Ultimately, for Montgomery, strikes must be understood in the historically contingent "context of the changing totality of class conflicts."

Behind these strike movements lay an ideological evolution deeply related to profound structural changes in American capitalism. In "Labor and the Republic" Montgomery charted the emergence in the working class of a mutualist ethic and, what he terms, a "moral universality," powerfully embodied in the Knights of Labor critique of the "wages system" and in the collective actions of working people themselves. Although the twentieth century witnessed sharp rises in strikes and more violent employer and state resistance, Montgomery noted important changes in the new century. With the changing structure of American capitalism, a new, more diverse working class emerged as did new bourgeois strategies. "It was the moral universality of the working class that had been ruptured, not its militancy." Even if workers did not champion Teddy Roosevelt's "new nationalism," neither did they any longer embrace a "commonly accepted vision of the redemption of the Republic" or see the convergence of "many streams of working-class struggle into a single-minded flood of protest." Socialist and syndicalist opposition remained but now more isolated. In significant ways, this essay foreshadowed arguments he would develop more fully in *The Fall of the House of Labor*.

In 2000, Montgomery delivered his presidential address to the Organization of American Historians (OAH) in the context of a boycott of the St. Louis conference hotel accused of both racial discrimination and unfair labor practices. He and the OAH executive committee led a march of historians to a nearby church where he delivered this address from the pulpit. In that ambitiously synthetic talk, "Racism, Immigrants, and Political Reform," he argued for the close fit between the emergence of a working-class politics on the one hand, and on the other, immigrant political agitation and the freedom struggles of African Americans in and after Reconstruction. Strikingly characteristic of his approach is his movement from local reform movements and liberation struggles to the international economic, social, and political forces that shaped these movements. And in quintessentially Montgomery fashion, he argued,

> The struggles of migrants of every clime and complexion have transformed American life in every generation within limits set by that age. They remind us that capitalist economic development has relentlessly created social fomations from which popular struggles have sprung and subsequently wiped those formations off the face

of the earth, usually leaving the goals for which working people acted at best only partially realized, but never leaving society and politics unchanged.

Note

1. E. J. Hobsbawm, "The Machine Breakers," in Hobsbawm, *Labouring Men: Studies in the History of Labour* (New York: Anchor Books, 1967), 9.

CHAPTER 6

Strikes in Nineteenth-Century America

From *Social Science History* 4 (February 1980): 81–104

Strikes have always held great fascination for historians of the working class. Collective work stoppages tear the tissue of "normal life," and in doing so they provide historians with revealing glimpses of class relations and attitudes, which arise from but are disguised by the daily production and distribution of commodities. Because strikers have disobeyed social norms, which reflect capitalist ways of making and acquiring things and which are enforced by socially legitimized economic and legal sanctions, they must reorder relationships among themselves in accordance with their own social code and apply their own group sanctions to its violators.

In recent years many studies of strikes have analyzed particular episodes in detail, in an effort to shed light on the social relations of some epoch through local history.[1] An older tradition, running from Dacus through Brecher, examined a series of strikes in order to derive political lessons from them (how to dampen or fan the flames of discontent).[2] Occasionally, the study of strikes has been an exercise in group psychology, as in Hiller (1928) or Gouldner (1954).[3] A few books have scrutinized strikes with the purpose of learning the best strategy and tactics to recommend to future strikers—a form of investigation which has not won much academic acclaim.[4]

This article is not directly concerned with any of these problems, worthy as they all may be, but rather with what the long-term evolution of strike behavior reveals about the changing consciousness of workers. To reach this objective, I will first review critically the conceptual frameworks which different scholars have used to analyze strike behavior, then survey the statistical and other data on nineteenth-century strikes that are already available in governmental and other sources, and finally apply some of the more useful concepts to the available data in an attempt to develop a general theory of the evolution of consciousness of American workers, as seen in their conduct of strikes. This theory will have to deal with the problems of when strikes emerged as the most significant form of urban popular protest, what groups of workers were most prominent in strike activity, how those workers transformed the ways in which and the issues over which they conducted strikes, and the relationship their strikes had to social and political conflicts outside the realm of industrial relations. I will argue that, although definite patterns of evolution in strike behavior are evident in the nineteenth century, no "natural history of the strike," which abstracts industrial conflict from other aspects of class struggle, can adequately link strike statistics to the problem of consciousness.

A pioneering work on the subject appeared in 1939: Griffin's *Strikes: A Study in Quantitative Economics*. Griffin correlated various series of economic data with the comprehensive statistics that the U.S. Commissioner of Labor had collected on American strikes between 1881 and 1905, the Department of Labor's figures for the period after 1915, and the much less adequate state data from the intervening years. He concluded, among other things, that defensive strikes tended to cluster in periods of economic crisis and meet with defeat, while strikes in times of economic buoyancy usually represented aggressive efforts by workers to improve their conditions and began on dates and in seasons of the workers' choosing (such as a springtime Monday after payday). To this clear evidence of a certain rationality in workers' conduct of strikes, Griffin added the observations that the tendency of workers to unionize grew more rapidly than their participation in strikes, and that the most highly unionized occupations were also the most strike prone. He also noted that, though the moving average of the number of workers involved in strikes each year formed a steadily rising line, there were years of extreme deviation from that trend. Strike participation in 1886, 1894, 1903, 1912, 1913, and every year between 1916 and 1922 leapt high above the trend line. No correlation with business cycles could adequately explain those leaps.

More recent efforts to formulate a general theory of strike development have been informed by modernization theory. Ross traced "the natural history of the strike" and concluded that in "the hands of the business union the strike has not only been invested with rationality, strategy, and discipline but has also been adjusted to the economic and political mores of the community."[5] Similarly, Kerr et al. argued that "worker protest in the course of industrialization tends to peak relatively early and to decline in intensity thereafter."[6]

In Kerr's view the process of modernization leads to a pluralistic integration of society, as "the unlimited individual" emerges from the traditional cocoon of the socially "isolated group" to "find protection from domination from any source in the multiplicity of organizations" in which he or she is involved. This formula was actually a prescription for social policy, rather than a description of the course of historical development. In fact, the famous analysis of U.S. strike data for the period 1927 to 1941 and comparable data from other countries offered by Kerr and Siegel in 1954, identified certain "industrial environments" in which a "high propensity to strike" persisted obstinately. These environments were characterized by large homogeneous masses of socially segregated workers engaged in tough and unpleasant jobs. Nevertheless, the authors' tone was optimistic. The integration of "the worker and his associations, and the employers, as fully as possible into the general society," was not only their remedy for strikes and "ideological thinking" alike, but also the historic destination of that inexorable process called industrialization.[7]

The notion that strikes once represented a far graver challenge to American capitalism than they do now is one which many American historians find attractive. Gutman and his followers, while not sharing Kerr's social values, have also located the mainspring of working-class militancy and ideology in "pre-industrial" customs and practices. They have noted a lengthy persistence of resistance to "the imperatives of industrial society" in this land of immigrants and also envisaged the last three decades of the nineteenth century as an epoch in which popular support made such resistance especially effective.[8] In their view the quantitative study of strikes can disguise important qualitative differences in the nature and significance of strikes between one period and another.

When one turns from quantitative to qualitative changes in strike behavior, however, neither econometric studies nor attempts to cast "the natural history of the strike" into the mold of modernization offer very clear guidance. At this point several less grandiose, more specific concepts deserve consideration. They have been suggested by Tilly, Hobsbawm, and Perrot in their studies of French and British strikes.

Tilly contends that before the middle of the century the strike was not the primary weapon of "protest" employed by French working people. The riot, and at times the armed rising, were more significant. It was only after 1850 that the workplace became the main location of struggle for the urban populace; even in the middle of the century there were important occasions when workers walked off their jobs, not so much to persuade their employers as to be where the action was—in the streets. Moreover, much of the research of Tilly and his students has turned on the proposition that some workers were much better situated to remedy their grievances through strikes than were others. The connection between work roles and the relative capacities of different groups of workers to mobilize for action is thus presented as a matter of great importance in the analysis of strikes.[9]

Finally, in collaboration with Shorter, Tilly developed a general interpretation of French strikes, which envisaged them as essentially a form of political struggle. Those who lacked established access to power in "the polity" struck to influence it on their own behalf.[10] This formulation is as unconvincing as it is vague. In fact, any attempt to discern a single underlying meaning in all strikes is dubious. Nevertheless, one must consider whether some strikes or strike waves may have a very different political significance than others.

In short, the American historian can borrow three significant questions from Tilly: When did strikes displace older forms of popular struggle? What groups of workers were best situated to mobilize strikes effectively? Which strikes represented efforts by workers to challenge or reshape "the polity" itself, as distinct from simply wringing concessions from employers?

Hobsbawm addressed himself to the continuities and discontinuities, which Griffin and others had already detected, in the evolution of strikes. Scrutinizing those moments when the struggles of British workers reached levels far above what long-term trends would have predicted, he found that "the size of the 'leaps' bears no apparent relation to the size of the cyclical up- or down-swing in which it occurs, at any rate after 1850."[11] He suggests that the leaps occurred when large numbers of workers suffered tangible declines in their living standards over the course of the downswing and the subsequent upturn of the business cycle, or else when the intensity of work was increasing noticeably. Unfortunately, both of these hypotheses are too mechanistic to provide a complete explanation. But another of his conclusions provides a more promising line of investigation, namely, that the distinctive quality of "leaps" in strike activity was the participation of groups of workers who had not been prominent before. Even large strikes of workers who had traditionally been highly unionized, Hobsbawm argued, might have much less impact on the rest of the working class than a strike by previously unorganized dockers, for example.[12]

An important element of continuity, in his view, was the gradual process whereby workers "learned the rules of the game." Although this concept, to which Hobsbawm often returns in his writings, bears a superficial resemblance to the image of modernization projected by Ross and Kerr to the concept of "sophistication" favored by Stearns[13] there is a significant difference. Hobsbawm describes not a process of accommodation to "a new social order," but rather one of learning to combat the new order more effectively. "The habit of industrial solidarity must be learned, like that of working a regular week," he wrote, and "so must the common sense of demanding concessions when conditions are favorable, not when hunger suggests. There is thus a natural time-lag, before workers become an 'effective' labor movement."[14] This argument flies so defiantly in the face of all theories which associate militancy with the novelty of industrial experience or with the strength of preindustrial customs and values that it deserves our closest attention.

Perrot approaches the subject somewhat differently in her definitive study of French strikes in the 1870s and 1880s. Her book is unique in the abundance of provocative insights it offers, but two of her points are particularly relevant here. First, she discusses in minute detail the growing importance of calculation and deliberation in the behavior of French strikers. On the basis of econometric correlations, which are more sophisticated than those of Griffin, she finds behavioral evidence that workers conceived of their own social position in ways quite different than either the preindustrial poor or the bourgeoisie. She concluded:

> The strike is a weapon of conquest, the major instrument of a working class more and more desirous and capable of improving its lot (above all its pay), more and more fascinated by the possibilities of the strike. This extension continues across, and against, all phases of the economic cycle.[15]

Second, for Perrot the strike was not only a tactic for pressuring employers, but also means of expression for the workers involved. On strike they repudiated (if only for a moment) the lot in which capitalism had placed them, fled the confines of "the prison" in which they toiled, manifested their own images of themselves and their forces, conducted a modern-day festival of the poor. The rush out the gates, the songs they favored, the symbolic violence, the parades, and the oratory all bore witness to those aspects of the strike which cannot be subjected to statistical correlations. The converse of the growing precision, and hence negotiability, of strike demands (in all but revolutionary moments) is found in those qualities of strikes which cannot be couched in the form of demands, let alone be won in the terms of settlement. Mediating between the curves of economic change and those of strike participation was the evolving consciousness of workers, the question of quality to which Gutman has also drawn our attention.[16]

We find ourselves, therefore, not with a single hypothesis to test, but with a fistful of provocative suggestions. Trying to fit them into a coherent theory, which may help in the analysis of nineteenth-century American strikes, we encounter a formidable problem of evidence. The strike statistics collected by the U.S. Commissioner of Labor for the years 1881 to 1905 are, on the whole, both comprehensive and reliable. Although only portions of the raw data are available in various annual reports, the figures tabulated in 1906 do provide clear evidence concerning the number, size, and location of strikes, as well as their outcomes, their relationship to union organization, and the major issues involved. The statistical series record 36,757 strikes, which involved a total of 6,728,048 strikers (roughly three times the amount of strike activity in France during the same years).[17] There are also many state and federal reports on specific strikes that took place during these years.

No such tabulation has ever been attempted for strikes before 1881 in this country. That lack poses serious problems for this article, because the changes in strike behavior which are revealed in the statistics of the 1881–1905 period seem to be less relevant to the questions posed by Tilly, Hobsbawm, and Perrot than would the contrast between that period taken as a whole and the decades before it. Furthermore, because no comprehensive reporting of earlier strikes exists, it is possible for our image of them to be unduly influenced by the very large and dramatic strikes, such as the Massachusetts shoe workers' walkout of 1860, or the Chicago strike for the eight-hour day in May 1867—not to mention the great strikes of July 1877, which textbooks routinely portray as the genesis of labor history.

It is necessary, therefore, to rely on memoirs and press reports of these early years, state labor bureau reports from the 1860s and 1870s, and a very sketchy survey attempted by the federal commissioner in 1887. Fortunately, in 1881 the Pennsylvania Bureau of Industrial Statistics compiled a review of that state's strikes since 1835.[18] It is far from complete, recording only 152 strikes. Nevertheless, it does provide very useful insights into general patterns of strike development. Moreover, the importance of Pennsylvania in the history of the country's strikes lends special value to this compilation. Of all strikes recorded during the 1881–1905 period, one-fourth took place in that state. It seems advisable, therefore, to rely on the Pennsylvania study as a basic source for analyzing developments before 1881, to be supplemented by scattered evidence from other states during the same years.[19]

The first impressions gleaned from these data are that Tilly's conception of the gradual emergence of the strike as the most significant form of urban popular struggle around the middle of the nineteenth century and Hobsbawm's notion of "learning the rules of the game" can both be employed fruitfully in the American context. Until the mid-1840s, far more working people expressed their grievances through riots than through strikes. Protests against high prices, the malpractices of banks, railroad construction along populated streets, racial and religious foes, and abolitionist meetings frequently brought angry crowds into the streets of the major cities. The neighborhood, rather than the workplace, was the locale of these crowd activities, they were seldom directed against the crowd's employers, the crowds themselves represented a *mélange* of social elements, and some outrage against traditional popular customs and values provided the motif. The prevalence of the putting-out system in weaving and clothing manufacture tended to convert even wage strikes in those occupations into neighborhood movements, often characterized by violent crowd action.[20]

To be sure, there were strikes. Journeyman artisans had engaged in wage struggles and attempts to compel masters to employ only members of their societies since the 1790s; in fact, the seaport cities had experienced frequent strikes by journeymen between 1804 and 1815. Moreover, the years 1834 to 1836 had witnessed the first "leap" in strike activity (in Hobsbawm's sense). Trade societies in major cities undertook joint actions for the first time, while laborers and weavers, who had seldom struck in earlier years, now did so frequently. The rapidly rising cost of living produced more wage struggles than food riots (though both occurred), and enthusiasm for the ten-hour day generated unprecedented working-class unity, especially in Philadelphia. Nevertheless, this activity subsided rapidly during the depression of 1837–1843, and subsequent strikes were characteristically undertaken by isolated, small groups of journeymen—in fact, often by minute groups, as the rapidly growing division of labor made many handicrafts more and more specialized—while riots became bigger and better than ever.[21]

Two significant turning points then appeared in the 1840s and the 1860s. After 1845 strikes spread gradually but perceptibly beyond the big cities and the artisanal trades, slowly displaced or else became the source of riots, and showed some evidence of the aggressive attitude toward wages that Perrot discerned by the 1870s in France. Most notably, such journeymen as carpenters, tailors, shoemakers, and printers, who had long dominated the strike scene, were joined after 1845 by members of new occupations: coal miners, iron molders, rolling mill hands, mule spinners and power loom weavers in textile mills, and construction gangs (those whom the British call "navvies" and the French *terrassiers*, but for whom there is interestingly no American word other than "ditch diggers").

The very names of the new actors betray the impact of rapid industrialization. In these disputes workers were clearly arrayed against employers, and large enterprises were often the scenes of the action. Although a vast strike movement in the early months of 1850 recalled those of 1835 and 1836 (especially in New York City, where rallies of thousands of tailors and building tradesmen were addressed in both English and German, vowed to form cooperative leagues, and demanded that a room of the city hall be turned over to the use of their central committee), the two decades following 1845 are best understood not as another "leap," but as a major transition period in the locus and nature of popular struggles.[22] Although trade unions made important efforts during these years to resurrect apprenticeship under their own control and to devise new work rules (such as the molders' limitation of helpers to one per craftsman and the window glass blowers' stint of 48 boxes per week), conditions, and hours were seldom explicit strike issues.[23] Moreover, the steady rise in the cost of living imparted such a defensive quality to the constant demands for wage increases as to make one reluctant to conclude that many workers yet thought it possible to *improve* their living standards through strikes. Also, the strikes of factory operatives were often very violent. Women were especially prominent in the crowd activity which strikes produced, not only when the women were on strike themselves, as in the textile stoppages of 1845 and 1848 near Pittsburgh, but also when their husbands' jobs were taken by scabs, as in that city's rolling mill walkout of 1850.[24]

In short, the growing importance of strikes between 1845 and 1865 was evident in the gradual transition from neighborhood to workplace as the locus of mobilization in popular protest and the replacement of community grievances by wage demands as the cause of confrontation, as well as in the prominence of new types of workers in strikes. The next three decades witnessed a gradual change in the way workers conducted strikes, and especially an increasing importance of unions in organizing strikes and defining demands. Strikes without unions remained numerous, to be sure. More than half of all strikes in 1881 and 1882 involved no union, and a similar proportion probably obtained during the preceding two decades (except in the union upsurge of 1869–1874). Crowd action was more and more often connected to strikes (though not always, as New York's bloody confrontation between Irish Catholics and Orangemen on 12 July 1871 shows), and a hallmark of the large strikes of the period was a march by hundreds of people from factory to factory, shutting down the machinery and calling everyone out from work. Sabotage was commonplace, though it could assume quite polite forms. Railroad workers, for example, might extract all coupling pins from a train and throw them into a nearby canal, then graciously carry the luggage of stranded passengers to the nearest depot. Scabs were often attacked physically, but were almost never killed, except when they were blacks or Chinese. The most common cause of bloodshed was soldiers' firing into a crowd.

Nevertheless, with two important qualifications to be noted below, strikers were "learning the rules of the game" in significant ways. A large body of workers familiar with the exigencies of industrial capitalism, and led by activists who were largely of a second generation of urban-industrial workers devised new and often effective forms of solidarity based on their occupations or places of work.[25] They were also clearly convinced that they could improve their own lives by collective efforts and were determined to try. Six characteristics of this development deserve brief mention.

First, union organization throve in all but the most depressed phases of the economy's development, and six out of every ten strikes between 1881 and 1905 were conducted by unions. With unions came an increasingly deliberate use of the strike weapon: careful timing, prior accumulation of funds, simultaneous closing of entire market areas (or alternatively, the use of rolling strikes to minimize the worker's loss of income), and victimization payments for discharged militants when no way to win their reinstatement was evident. One major development appeared during the upsurge of unionism of 1869–1874, when unions increasingly negotiated wage scales with employers, rather than declaring them unilaterally, as had formerly been the general practice. In other words, the tendency of workers to strike only as a "*dernier ressort*" (a favorite phrase of the 1860s), to confer authority on delegates from their ranks to "treat with" employers, and to marshal their forces carefully before walking out (then called "acting conservatively") was at least as important as the growing number of strikes.

Table 1. Propensity to Strike by Industry, 1881–1905

Industry	Strikers/Workers	Strikers/Strikes
Meat packing	.185	684
Mining	.133	475
Clothing	.065	329
Tobacco	.054	134
Street car	.042	394
Leather & shoes	.031	85
Construction	.026	96
Metallurgy	.025	150
Textiles	.023	189
Team & freight handling	.017	272
Railroads	.012	229
Printing	.012	44
All industries	.026	183

Sources: U.S. Commissioner of Labor, *Twenty-First Annual Report* (Washington, DC: Government Printing Office, 1906) and U.S. Bureau of the Census, *Sixteenth Census of the United States. Population—Comparative Occupational Statistics for the United States, 1870–1940* (Washington, DC: Government Printing Office, 1940).

Second, although union organization most frequently followed the lines of craft (even most Knights of Labor local assemblies in industries such as shoes, meat packing, and textiles, where they organized all grades, followed craft lines and were coordinated by a district assembly acting as a joint board), large enterprises played a major role in strike activity. A rank ordering of workers' propensities to strike in different industries can be calculated by dividing the average number of strikers per year in the period 1881 to 1905 in a given industry by the number of people employed in it in 1900. The resulting scale departs at several points from the twentieth-century rankings of Siegel and Kerr and, at the very least, suggests that socially "isolated masses" could be found as readily in metropolitan as in rustic settings.

The twelve industries that led the strike procession are listed in Table 1. It is worth noting that the ratio of strikers to employees for all industries by this formula is .026, exactly that for the building trades, which produced by far the largest number of strikes (four times more than their nearest rival, mining). The contrast between the large number of strikes by building workers and the relatively small total number of strikers reveals how small most strikes in construction were, as well as the importance of the large enterprise in generating big strikes. The massive concentration of meat packing in half a dozen companies grouped around a few stockyards, especially those of Chicago, accounts for that industry's salient position.

Third, unionized workers learned to coordinate their struggles on both the local and national levels. Much has been written about the growth of international unions and the Knights of Labor. In fact, historians tend to treat American labor exclusively in terms of its rise and fall.[26] This emphasis obscures the crucial role of central labor unions, which were comparable to Italy's *camera del lavoro* and France's *bourses du travail.* The assistance they provided strikers who had no unions or only frail unions of their own was especially significant between 1878 and 1883. They were also important centers of socialist agitation among workers and of the labor press.[27]

Fourth, aided by these citywide and national organizations, strikers began to demand uniform wage scales from many competing employers, that is, to impose some order on capitalism from below. For example, the coal miners whose employers shipped by water to Pittsburgh shut down the mines of three counties in 1859 to demand payment by the ton, as weighed at the pit-mouth, rather than by the quite elastic measurement of the car, which then prevailed. In 1873 they again struck the same area to demand compliance by their owners with a new law limiting the size of the screens over which coal passed before it was weighed. Between 1879 and 1882 they fought with some success for a master arbitration agreement to cover the entire region, then broadened their sights in 1885 with the "Pittsburgh Scale," which was supposed to encompass the whole Central Competitive Field, west into Illinois. The great strike of 1897 finally accomplished that grandiose objective.[28]

Miners were not the only workers who struck in an effort to standardize wages over large market regions. The iron molders' eastern strikes of 1866 and 1867, those of the Knights of St. Crispin in the shoe factories of Lynn and Philadelphia in 1870 and 1871, the movement of Philadelphia's building workers in 1869 for uniformity among, as well as within, crafts and, of course, the national stove molders' scale agreement of 1890, all testify to the workers' keen awareness of the mechanics of capitalist competition. They also dramatize the folly of the present historiographical vogue, which depicts the activities of the elite as creative or "cosmopolitan," while subsuming all activities of workers under such labels as "protest," "parochial," or "antimodern."

Fifth, the more highly unionized workers became, the less often they made wages the central issue in their strikes. When less than half of the country's strikes were union-led, as in 1881 and 1882, close to 80% of their strikes concerned wage demands, as shown in Table 2. When the percentage of strikes ordered by unions rose to 75, as in 1891 or 1902, the number of strikes over wages fell to less than half of the total. Struggles to enforce union rules, to protect members from victimization, and to win formal recognition of delegates came with unionization. The number of lockouts rose correspondingly; they were used almost exclusively against unionized workers.

Union work rules and strikes to enforce them provide important evidence concerning the consciousness of the more skilled and urbanized members of the working class. By carefully limiting individual output, prohibiting subcontracting, regulating apprenticeship, fixing the division of labor between

Table 2. Strike Trends, 1881–1905

Year	Number of Strikes (1)	Workers Involved (,000) (2)	Percent Wage Strikes (3)	Percent Ordered by Unions (4)	Percent Sympathy Strikes (5)	Number Sympathy Strikes (6)
1881	471	101	79.8	47.3	0.8	2
1882	454	121	75.4	48.5	0.9	3
1883	478	122	77.2	56.7	0.6	2
1884	443	117	74.1	54.2	2.0	6
1885	645	139	72.9	55.3	3.1	20
1886	1432	407	63.0	53.3	2.9	37
1887	1436	273	54.8	66.3	4.7	71
1888	906	103	55.2	68.1	3.8	34
1889	1075	205	59.0	67.3	6.1	67
1890	1833	286	50.9	71.3	9.9	188
1891	1717	245	48.9	74.8	11.5	204
1892	1298	164	50.4	70.7	8.9	117
1893	1305	195	58.8	69.4	4.5	62
1894	1349	505	63.7	62.8	8.8	120
1895	1215	286	69.6	54.2	0.6	7
1896	1026	184	57.6	64.6	0.6	7
1897	1078	333	66.2	55.3	0.7	9
1898	1056	182	63.0	60.4	0.8	9
1899	1797	308	59.4	62.0	1.5	29
1900	1779	400	59.0	65.4	1.5	29
1901	2924	396	46.6	75.9	2.4	71
1902	3162	553	51.2	78.2	2.6	87
1903	3494	532	51.5	78.8	2.4	88
1904	2307	376	42.2	82.1	3.7	93
1905	2077	176	44.5	74.7	2.7	61

Sources: The number of strikes and the number of workers involved (1 and 2) are taken from U.S. Commissioner of Labor, *Twenty-First Annual Report* (1906), 15. Wage strikes as a percentage of all strikes (3) is from J. H. Griffin, *Strikes* (1939), 76. The percentage of strikes ordered by unions, the percentage of all strikes represented by sympathetic strikes, and the number of sympathetic strikes (4, 5, and 6) are from Florence Peterson, *Strikes in the United States, 1880–1936* (1937), 32, 33.

journeyman and helper, and proscribing acts by which one worker might "undermine" a workmate, these rules codified working-class ethical norms, which were profoundly at odds with the acquisitive individualism of the upper and middle classes. The workers who made such rules considered them indispensable to the protection of their earnings and enforced them wherever possible by the sanctions of fines and ostracism against those workers who followed the moral code of the bourgeoisie. By the early 1890s more than one-fifth of all strikes were openly contests over whose rules and ethical standards should govern the workplace: those of the boss or those of the craftsmen.[29]

Sixth, as the power struggle in the workplace reached a crescendo in the early 1890s, the number of sympathetic strikes rose to the highest level in the country's history. In 1891 more than 11% of all strikes were deliberately called by unionized workers to assist embattled workers of another trade.[30] Courts and legislatures bestirred themselves to criminalize such behavior over the next two decades. As a contemporary study observed, however, the likelihood of sympathetic strikes was "least in those cases where the dispute concerns conditions of employment such as wages and hours, and greatest in regard to disputes which involve questions of unionism, the employment of only union men, the recognition of the union, etc."[31]

In short, it is meaningful to speak of American workers "learning the rules of the game" between the 1860s and 1890s. Two qualifications must be appended to this assertion, however, to distinguish it from the conceptions of "rationality" and "modernization" offered by Ross and Kerr. First, this process neither involved an adjustment by workers "to the economic and political mores of the community," as Ross suggested,[32] nor did it bear out Kerr et al.'s argument that "worker protest in the course of industrialization tends to peak relatively early and to decline in intensity thereafter." On the contrary, strikes not only became more deliberate over the years, but also more numerous and larger. They showed not only that workers had rejected the strictures of the dominant political economy against conscious, collective action in the marketplace, but also that the more workers became familiar with industrial life the more effectively and openly they challenged the pretensions of their employers to mastery over "their own" workplaces, as well as the ethic of acquisitive individualism, through which the "mores of the community" legitimized those pretensions.[33]

Second, the history of strikes did not progress in a straight line of "natural" development, any more than do other sorts of human experience. To think only of maturing patterns of strike behavior, as modified by the ebb and flow of business cycles, is to assume that the social and political parameters of work stoppages remained constant. They did not. On the contrary, there were important differences in the nature of class struggle before and after 1877. Only in the later period could the workers' growing understanding of the use of strikes decisively shape their character.

During the 1860s and 1870s the pervasive and violent conflict between a reforming bourgeoisie, which laid claim to the "sovereign powers of the nation" and the "internal social polity" of the South, which, to quote Confederate Vice-President Alexander Stephens, rested upon "the subordination of the African race,"[34] destroyed all semblance of consensus within the political elite and unleashed the open employment of armed forces in domestic politics for more than two decades. In this context many strikes vaulted over the confines implicit in the notions of "economic" or "industrial" disputes to contest the objectives and powers of the state itself.[35]

An editorial published in a leading labor newspaper during the closing months of the Civil War placed the workers' struggles clearly in this larger political context:

> An oligarchy at the South, holding in its grasp the destinies of millions of the human race, and made mad by their lust for additional power, and, from the very nature of things, antagonist to free labor, has struck a blow at the National life, and men stand appalled at the magnitude of the struggle. And here at the North, where every village, town, and hamlet gives evidence of the industry of our people; where we have through our institutions instilled into our minds and fixed in our hearts a sacred love of liberty, an oligarchy, comparatively small, strikes a blow at the independence, nay, the very manhood of the industrial classes, when it denies their right to combine for mutual protection and advancement . . . All this talk about Republican equality and the rights of man is as water spilled upon sand, if the right of the laboring man to govern those affairs which pertain to his political, social, and moral standing in society be denied him.[36]

Conversely, employers were likely to perceive trade unions or strikes as challenges to their tenuous political hegemony. Thus, a Pennsylvania coal operator, petitioning President Lincoln to dispatch a "military force of several thousand men" and impose martial law on the coal regions, mustered every sort of behavior by "a large majority of the coal operatives" into a single "law-defying" array:

> They are so numerous that they have the whole community in terror of them. They dictate the prices for their work, and if the employers don't accede, they destroy and burn coal breakers, houses, and prevent those disposed from working. They resist the draft and are organized into societies for this purpose. The life of no Union [pro-government] man is secure among them, and the murder of such a citizen is almost a nightly occurrence. The civil authorities make no effort to arrest this state of things. . . . [They] seem to have too much sympathy for these very men.[37]

This context of Civil War and Reconstruction infused the two largest strike movements of the epoch, those of 1863 and 1877, with an insurrectionary quality. The New York draft riots of 1863, which began as a contagious strike, were the most violent and bloodily suppressed popular rising in the country's history. Five regiments of the Army of the Potomac were dispatched from the Gettysburg front to recapture New York City. The target of the crowd's wrath was nothing less than the two-year-old Republican regime and all its works—emancipation, conscription, taxation, and the coercive authority now wielded by bourgeois reformers in the national government.[38] Although the strikes of 1877 were less sanguinary, they were more widespread, covering the whole East-West belt serviced by the railroad trunk lines. The character of those strikes varied between one locality and another, to be sure, but everywhere the first target of the crowd's fury was the interlocking directorate of railroad executives, military officers, and political officials, which constituted the apex of the country's new power structure.[39]

This epoch was also the heyday of the strikers' march: the moving torrent of men, women, and children closing every workplace in its path. This contagious form of strike was very different than the deliberate, organized effort toward which union behavior was then evolving. Even strikes which began in highly structured and disciplined form, like Chicago's citywide strike for the eight-hour day in May 1867, could be converted abruptly into a sequence of angry marches without apparent structure or leadership.[40]

The significant differences between the insurrections of 1863 and 1877 are indicative of changing working-class consciousness during this epoch. The draft riots were saturated with racial hatred, ruthless attacks on blacks being the order of the day. In 1877 the lynch mob atmosphere was remarkably absent, except in California where Chinese were assaulted. Elsewhere the extensive participation of blacks and public fraternization between white and black strikers were outstanding. Moreover, the protests of 1877 pointed clearly and directly against the exploitation of labor by capital, while those of fourteen years earlier had been more complex and backward-looking. Finally, amid the apparent chaos of 1877, the careful observer detects innumerable meetings where workers assembled by workplace or trade to formulate demands, decide strategy, and elect leading committees. Although the workers' deliberations of 1877 had to take place quickly, they were ubiquitous. Self-organization on the spot was the hallmark of 1877, in contrast to the swirling crowds of 1863, guided by impulse, rumor, and furtive orators.

It is meaningful, therefore, to think of these strikes in Shorter and Tilly's terms, as efforts to "redefine the polity." Moreover, strikes of the 1860s and 1870s also exhibited this quality in two other ways. First, the political action of workers then involved not only lobbying, demonstrations, and petitions on behalf of desired legislation, but also large strikes to compel employers to obey the new laws, once they had been enacted. The strikes to enforce eight-hour day laws in Chicago (1867), Pennsylvania's coal mines (1868), and New York City (bricklayers in 1868 and general stoppage in 1872) illustrate this phenomenon, as does the strike by miners of the Pittsburgh area in 1873 to uphold the new screen law. Yankee employers, and state and federal courts, were no more inclined to consider legislation which violated "freedom of contract" as legitimate and binding than southern planters were in the case of tax and school legislation enacted by what they called "black and tan legislatures."

Lacking legitimacy in bourgeois eyes, such laws simply transferred the contest back to the point of production.

Second, the prominence of the struggle for the eight-hour day in the 1860s and early 1870s indicates that many workers considered it the central issue defining their place in reconstructed America. Although labor's spokesmen often borrowed from the language of bourgeois political economy in advocating this reform (arguing, for example, that shorter hours would raise the price of labor by reducing the available supply), they envisaged the contest above all as one which pit "the wages system" against "republican institutions." Its outcome would decide whether they and their children would live as drudges, creating wealth for others, or as free and active citizens of a democratic state, which their blood had saved on the battlefields.[41]

The struggle for the eight-hour day, therefore, combined high levels of calculation and organization with a vivid articulation of the antagonism between workers' aspirations to be free of domination by other men and the triumphant bourgeois regime, which secured that domination. The abundant oratory and pamphlet literature of the movement elaborated the meaning of class in American society with force and clarity. Similarly, the strike of 100,000 building, furniture, and metal workers in New York City under the direction of those industries' three Eight Hour Leagues in 1872 was among the century's most carefully planned and executed confrontations between labor and capital.[42] Like the more violent outbursts of 1863 and 1877, and like workers' attempts to enforce laws through strikes, the eight-hour day movement of the 1860s and 1870s defies comprehension exclusively in terms of economic trends or "learning the rules." All three were parts of a continuous, largely unsuccessful, effort by American workers to intervene on their own behalf in the reshaping of national social and political life in a period when no ideological consensus legitimized the state.

The withdrawal of federal troops from the South, the Molly Maguire hangings, and the great strikes of 1877 punctuated the close of this revolutionary epoch. By that time "New Departure" Democrats, "Stalwart" Republicans, and "Liberal" reformers all accepted the three formerly controversial constitutional amendments, which defined the rights of blacks and the nature of the federal system, as well as the restoration of southern "home rule." Though they squabbled angrily about local ethnic and religious controversies and conjured up divisive memories of the Civil War every election season, they all hailed private enterprise and constitutional government as the cornerstones of social progress. Thenceforth, trade union activity was legally tolerated, while the regulation of strikes (apart from those on railroads and at coal mines) was left to local police supervision, which the local voting strength of workers could often inhibit, and to the redress against picketing, boycotts, and "libelous" columns in the labor press, which employers could obtain on their own initiative from solicitous courts. Armed contingents of the labor movement were outlawed, and newly constructed armories stood silent watch over what one author of the time called "the volcano under the city."[43]

In this context strikes became sharply distinguished from political action, in fact and in the thinking of labor activists, despite the evident tendency of both forms of struggle to rise and subside together. The contests in which strikers of the 1880s and 1890s manifested their acquisition of "the habit of solidarity" developed along lines determined by the internal contradictions of laissez-faire capitalism itself. Although unionized craftsmen insidiously encroached upon their employers' workplace prerogatives in some industries, while in others they were defeated by lockouts or by technological innovations, these battles were fought out where the dominant ideology of the times said they should be: that is, within the factory. The legitimacy of the state was accepted, even celebrated, by most organized workers, despite their intense hostility to the power of business within the government. They carried their grievances to the state through petitions, mass meetings, election campaigns, and demonstrations, not through strikes. Only the small, though important, group of Social Revolutionaries aspired to "smash the state" through mass action and "propaganda by deed." In their minds only was a great strike, like that begun on 1 May 1886, envisaged as a rising against the social system. For others, including the trade unionists who initiated the 1 May movement, the strike was a calculated weapon to wring concessions from employers, and few strikers wished to rouse the lightly sleeping tiger of the state.

Nevertheless, the apolitical, self-help thrust of trade unionism itself generated a chronic challenge to the hegemony of acquisitive individualism (not to mention the domineering conduct of large business enterprise) in the form of the solid links forged by working-class experience between earnings, work rules, and a mutualistic ethical code. Even though the rhetoric of the labor movement evoked egalitarian traditions from the eighteenth century, and depicted big business as the subversive menace to "the civilization we have so laboriously evolved,"[44] it was evident that workers learning "the habit of industrial solidarity" were, to say the least, as much a force for social change as were the Pennsylvania Railroad and Carnegie Steel.

Consequently, two leaps of strike activity, which did not alter the direction in which strike practice was evolving but rather extended its scope dramatically, brought the soldiers back out of their barracks. The Great Upheaval of 1885–1887 lacked the insurrectionary quality of the events of July 1877, but it did show how the society could be shaken when large numbers of workers, who had previously played little or no role in labor struggles, abruptly became (in Perrot's world) "fascinated by the possibilities of the strike." There were more than three times as many strikes and strikers in 1886 as there had been in any year between 1881 and 1884. In addition to more than 900 walkouts over wages that year, there had been 286 strikes for the eight-hour day, including the citywide movements in Chicago and Milwaukee, which were dominated by laborers and factory operatives. For all the precipitous action of that year, however, 53% of the strikes were called by labor organizations, and strikes as large as those on the southwest railway lines and in the Chicago packing houses and the sympathy movement in support of New York's freight handlers, were all formally ordered by district officers of the Knights of Labor.

Nevertheless, as Perrot would suggest, the workers' self-expression was as revealing as their level of organization. Strikers poured forth pent-up fury, roaring approval of Social Revolutionary speakers who denied that workers owed any allegiance to a society that made them all outcasts, storming the fortifications of factories whose employees had failed to strike, and defiantly boasting their triumphs. Typical in this respect were the streetcar drivers of New York City, who paraded back to work past the horrified faculty of Columbia University in a column of trams, each sporting a red flag.[45] Hanging the Haymarket Martyrs provided polite society its psychic revenge for such insubordination.

Quite different were the two strikes that together were responsible for bringing out most of the half million strikers of 1894. The bituminous coal strike and the Pullman Boycott were the culmination of the development of nineteenth-century strike practice. The conduct of the mine and railroad unionists was the product of years of debate and experimentation within their own ranks, and their employers responded with their own highly perfected weapons of industrial conflict. Neither industry was new to unionism by any means. In stark contrast to the spontaneous and contagious walkouts on railroads, which had triggered the uprising of 1877, these strikes of 1894 were preceded by widespread organization, were centrally called and directed, and turned on the question of union power as the pivotal point of contention. The practice of sympathetic strikes, then in full flower, was employed on an unprecedented scale.

To be sure, these strikes were part of a general political crisis, but they were not a popular rising against the state. The leaders of both the American Railway Union and the American Federation of Labor summoned their members to change the government at the ballot box, not on the picket line.[46] The popular outcry against the plutocratic corruption of the republic, which attended the strikes, was a response to the unstinting support which the Cleveland Administration provided the railway executives and judicial decisions, which virtually made strikes by railroad workers illegal.[47]

To sum up, modernization theory is of no help in comprehending nineteenth-century strikes, and the Shorter-Tilly conception of strikes as an effort to change labor's position "in the polity" suggests a line of thinking which is useful only for the 1860s and 1870s. There is, however, an important sense in which strikes emerged in mid-century as the characteristic form of struggle of an industrial working class, were most effectively mobilized by certain definable bodies of workers, and evolved into increasingly deliberate and organized activities, as workers learned ways of using their collective power effectively within a capitalist economy. To grasp only that quality of calculation, as Perrot admonishes us, is to neglect another equally important aspect of strikes, i.e., their role as a moment of liberation from employers' discipline and bourgeois norms, of psychic release, and of self-direction for workers, which permits them to manifest their sentiments and their human potential in ways no opinion polls or voting behavior could ever reveal.

Nevertheless, only after 1877 were the social and political parameters of laissez-faire capitalism securely enough established to allow strikes to evolve along the lines dictated by maturing union practice. Even then the quantitative trends in strike behavior were interrupted by two leaps, which no econometric correlation could predict. That of 1886 conformed to Hobsbawm's thesis: It was dominated by an abrupt extension of strike and union activity to sections of the working class which had not previously been involved in them. That of 1894 did not conform to Hobsbawm's thesis: It was a direct outgrowth of decades of experience and discussion among some of the country's most frequently unionized workers.

What all these conclusions remind us, however, is that any attempt to formulate a positivistic "natural history of strikes" is doomed to failure. Strikes can only be understood in the context of the changing totality of class conflicts, of which they are a part.

Notes

Reprinted courtesy of Cambridge University Press and *Social Science History.*

For convenience, the citation system in this article has been changed from social science format to *Chicago Manual of Style.*

1. Herbert Gutman, "The Worker's Search for Power: Labor in the Gilded Age," 38–68 in H. W. Morgan, ed., *The Gilded Age: A Reappraisal* (Syracuse, NY: Syracuse Univ. Press, 1963); R. E. Ziegler, "The Limits of Power: The Amalgamated Association of Street Railway Employees in Houston, Texas, 1897–1905," *Labor History* 18 (Winter 1977): 71–90; H. B. Hammett, "Labor and Race: The Georgia Railroad Strike of 1909," *Labor History* 6 (Fall 1975): 470–485; J. T. Cumbler, "Labor, Capital, and Community: The Struggle for Power," *Labor History* 15 (Fall 1974): 395–415.

2. J. A. Dacus, *Annals of the Great Strikes in the United States* (Chicago: L. T. Palmer, 1877); J. Brecher, *Strike!* (San Francisco: Straight Arrow Books, 1972); W. H. Crook, *The General Strike: A Study of Labor's Tragic Weapon in Theory and Practice* (Chapel Hill: University of North Carolina Press, 1931).

3. E. T. Hiller, *The Strike: A Study in Collective Action* (Chicago: University of Chicago Press, 1928) or A. Gouldner, *Wildcat Strike* (Yellow Springs, OH: Antioch, 1954).

4. W. Z. Foster, *The Great Steel Strike and Its Lessons* (New York: B. W. Huebsch, 1920); W. Z. Foster, *American Trade Unionism: Principles and Organization, Strategy and Tactics* (New York: International Publishers, 1947); J. Steuben, *Strike Strategy* (New York: Gaer Associates, 1950); F. Dobbs, *Teamster Rebellion* (New York: Monad, 1972).

5. A. M. Ross, "The Natural History of the Strike," in *Industrial Conflict* eds. A. Kornhauser et al. (New York: McGraw-Hill, 1954), 23–36, quote, 32.

6. C. J. Kerr, J. T. Dunlop, F. H. Harbison, and C. A. Myers, *Industrialism and Industrial Man* (New York: Oxford University Press, 1964), 184.

7. The remedy proposed by Kerr and Siegel is equated with the course of social evolution in Kerr et al. (1964): 25–27, 66–68.

8. H. G. Gutman, *Work, Culture, and Society in Industrializing America: Essays in Working-Class and Social History* (New York: Knopf, 1976); M. A. Gordon, "The Labor Boycott in New York City, 1880–1886," *Labor History* 16 (Spring 1975): 184–229; L. Fink, "Workingmen's Democracy: The Knights of Labor in Local Politics, 1886–1896" (PhD dissertation, University of Rochester, 1977). The influence of ideological legacies from preindustrial days on working-class militancy is also stressed in A. Dawley, *Class and Community: The Industrial Revolution in Lynn* (Cambridge, MA: Harvard University Press, 1976).

9. C. Tilly, "The Changing Place of Collective Violence," 139–164 in *Essays in Theory and History: An Approach to the Social Sciences*, ed. M. Richter (Cambridge, MA: Harvard Univ. Press, 1970); M. Hanagan, "The Logic of Solidarity: Artisans and Industrial Workers in three French Towns, 1871–1914" (PhD dissertation, University of Michigan, 1978).

10. E. Shorter and C. Tilly, *Strikes in France, 1830–1968* (Cambridge, MA: Harvard University Press, 1974).

11. E. J. Hobsbawm, *Labouring Men: Studies in the History of Labour*. (London: Weidenfeld and Nicolson, 1964), 128.

12. Ibid.

13. P. N. Stearns, "Measuring the Evolution of Strike Movements," *International Review of Social History* 19 (Winter 1974): 1–27.

14. Hobsbawm, *Labouring Men*, 144.

15. M. Perrot, *Les Ouvriers en Greve: France 1871–1890* (Paris: Mouton, 1974), 64.

16. Perrot, *Les Ouvriers en Greve*, 102–103, 409–447, 547–644.

17. U.S. Commissioner of Labor, *Twenty-First Annual Report*, (Washington, DC: Government Printing Office, 1906), 15; Perrot, *Les Ouvriers en Greve*, 51.

18. *Annual Report of the Secretary of Internal Affairs of the Commonwealth of Pennsylvania: Part 3, Industrial Statistics*, Volume 9 (1880–1881) (Harrisburg, PA: Lane S. Hart, 1882), 262–389.

19. Useful information on strikes can be found also in Philip S. Foner, *History of the Labor Movement in the United States*, 4 volumes (New York: International

Publishers, 1947–1965), II; J. R. Commons, D. J. Saposs, H. L. Sumner, E. B. Mittelman, H. E. Hoagland, J. B. Andrews, S. Perlman, D. D. Lescohier, E. Brandeis, and P. Taft, et al. *History of Labor in the United States*, 4 volumes (New York: Macmillan, 1918–1935); N. J. Ware, *The Labor Movement in the United States, 1860–1895* (New York: D. Appleton, 1929); B. G. Laurie, "The Working People of Philadelphia, 1827–1853" (PhD dissertation, University of Pittsburgh, 1971); J. B. Curtis, "The Organized Few: Labor in Philadelphia, 1857–1873" (PhD dissertation, Bryn Mawr College, 1970); J. W. Bennett, "The Iron Workers of Woods Run and Johnstown: The Union Era" (PhD dissertation, University of Pittsburgh, 1977); and David Montgomery, *Beyond Equality: Labor and the Radical Republicans, 1862–1872* (New York: Knopf, 1967). Valuable early reports of state bureaus of labor statistics include those of Massachusetts, Ohio, and Pennsylvania.

20. L. L. Richards, *"Gentlemen of Property and Standing": Anti-Abolition Mobs in Jacksonian America* (New York: Oxford Univ. Press, 1970); J. T. Headley, *The Great Riots of New York, 1712 to 1873* (New York: E. B. Treat, 1873); M. Feldberg, "Urbanization as a Cause of Violence: Philadelphia as a Test Case," 53–70 in *The Peoples of Philadelphia*, eds. A. F. Davis and M. H. Haller (Philadelphia: Temple University Press, 1973); D. Montgomery, "The Shuttle and the Cross: Weavers and Artisans in the Kensington Riots of 1844," *Journal of Social History* 5 (Spring 1972): 411–446.

21. W. A. Sullivan, *The Industrial Worker in Pennsylvania, 1800–1840* (Harrisburg, PA: Pennsylvania Historical and Museum Commission, 1955); E. Pessen, *Most Uncommon Jacksonians: The Radical Leaders of the Early Labor Movement* (Albany: State University of New York Press, 1967); E. Pessen, "The Working Men's Movement of the Jacksonian Era." *Mississippi Valley Historical Review* 43 (December 1956): 428–443; W. Huggins, *Jacksonian Democracy and the Working Class* (Palo Alto, CA: Stanford University Press, 1960).

22. H. Schlüter, *Die Anfänge der deutschen Arbeiterbewegung in Amerika* (Stuttgart: J.H.W. Dietz, 1907); J. R. Commons, U. B. Phillips, E. A. Gilmore, H. L. Sumner, and J. B. Andrews, et al. *Documentary History of American Industrial Society* (Cleveland: Arthur H. Clark, 1910–1911): VIII, 296–309; C. N. Degler, "Labor in the Economy and Politics of New York City, 1850–1860: A Study of the Impact of Early Industrialism" (PhD dissertation, Columbia University, 1952); E. C. Wittke, *The Utopian Communist: A Biography of Wilhelm Weitling, Nineteenth-Century Reformer* (Baton Rouge: Louisiana State University Press, 1950).

23. Foner, *History of the Labor Movement in the United States*, I, 220–224; J. R. Commons, et al. *History of Labor in the United States*, II, 80–84.

24. Pennsylvania, *Annual Report*, 1882: 271–275; Philip S. Foner, *The Great Labor Uprising of 1877* (New York, Monad, 1977), 246–251; Monte A. Calvert, "The Allegheny City Cotton Mill Riot of 1848," *Western Pennsylvania Historical Magazine* (Summer): 97–133, 1963; J. Linaberger, "The Rolling Mill Riots of 1850," *Western Pennsylvania Historical Magazine* 47 (Winter 1964): 1–18.

25. Montgomery, *Beyond Equality*, 197–208; W. R. Van Tine, *The Making of a Labor Bureaucrat: Union Leadership in the United States, 1870–1920* (Amherst: U. of Massachusetts Press, 1973), 6–18.

26. Commons et al. *History of Labor in the United States*; G. N. Grob, *Workers and Utopia: A Study of Ideological Conflict in the American Labor Movement, 1865–1900* (Evanston, IL: Northwestern U. Press, 1961); Ware, *Labor Movement in the United States*; L. Ulman, *The Rise of the National Trade Union* (Cambridge, MA: Harvard U. Press, 1955).

27. Montgomery, *Beyond Equality*, 160–170; Gutman, *Work, Culture, and Society in Industrializing America*, 234–259; E. Aveling and E. M. Aveling, *The Working-Class Movement in America* (London: Swann Sonnenschein, 1891), 134–153; M. A. McLaurin, *Paternalism and Protest: Southern Cotton Mill Workers and Organized Labor, 1875–1905* (Westport, CT: Greenwood 1971), 68–119, 138–139; 1978: 52–79.

28. Pennsylvania, *Annual Report*, 1882, 277–278, 302–305, 372–381, 348–366; B. Ramirez, *When Workers Fight: The Politics of Industrial Relations in the Progressive Era, 1898–1916* (Westport, CT: Greenwood, 1978), 17–29; A. Roy, *A History of the Coal Miners of the United States* (Columbus, OH: J. L. Trauger, nd), 243–261.

29. D. Montgomery, "Workers' Control of Machine Production in the Nineteenth Century," *Labor History* 17 (Fall 1976): 485–509; A. Amsden and S. Brier, "Coal Miners on Strike: The Transformation of Strike Demands and the Formation of a National Union," *J. of Interdisciplinary History* 7 (Spring 1977): 583–616. Table 2 is reprinted from Montgomery (1976: 497) with the permission of *Labor History*.

30. For a revealing discussion of sympathetic strikes among coal miners, see K. A. Harvey, *The Best Dressed Miners: Life and Labor in the Maryland Coal Region, 1835–1910* (Ithaca, NY: Cornell U. Press, 1969), 278–296.

31. F. S. Hall, *Sympathetic Strikes and Sympathetic Lockouts* (New York: Columbia U. Press, 1898), 33.

32. A. M. Ross, "The Natural History of the Strike," 32.

33. C. Kerr, et al., *Industrialism and Industrial Man*, 164.

34. U.S. Congress, *Report of the Joint Committee on Reconstruction* (Washington, DC: Government Printing Office, 1866), Part 3, 160.

35. Montgomery, *Beyond Equality*; W.E.B. DuBois, *Black Reconstruction in America, 1860–1880* (New York: Harcourt Brace Jovanovich, 1935); C. V. Woodward, *Reunion and Reaction: The Compromise of 1877 and the End of Reconstruction* (Garden City, NY: Doubleday, 1956); E. B. Moore, *Social Origins of Dictatorship and Democracy: Lord and Peasant in the Making of the Modern World* (Boston: Beacon, 1966), 2; Dawley, *Class and Community*, 97–129 argues that the Civil War consolidated bourgeois political hegemony in Lynn.

36. *Boston Daily Evening Voice*, 1864.

37. U.S. War Department, "Chas. Albright to A. Lincoln," in *War of the Rebellion: A Compilation of the Official Records of the Union and Confederate Armies* Series 3, 1008–1009, November 9, 1863 (Washington, DC: Government Printing Office, 1900).

38. J. McCague, *The Second Rebellion: The Story of the New York City Draft Riots of 1863* (New York: Dial, 1968); Montgomery, *Beyond Equality*, 1967.

39. Foner, *Great Labor Uprising*; R. V. Bruce, *1877: Year of Violence* (Indianapolis: Bobbs-Merrill, 1959); D. T. Burbank, *Reign of the Rabble: The St. Louis General Strike*

of 1877 (New York: Augustus M. Kelley, 1966); J. A. Dacus, *Annals of the Great Strikes in the United States* (Chicago: L. T. Palmer, 1877); A. Saxton, *The Indispensable Enemy: Labor and the Anti-Chinese Movement in California* (Berkeley: U. of California Press, 1971), 113–121.

40. Montgomery, *Beyond Equality*, 306–311.

41. Montgomery, *Beyond Equality*, 230–360.

42. Montgomery, *Beyond Equality*, 323–334.

43. W. O. Stoddard, *The Volcano Under the City, by a Volunteer Special* (New York: Fords, Howard and Hulbert, 1887); H. David, *History of the Haymarket Affair* (New York: Farrar and Rinehart, 1936), 58.

44. American Federation of Labor, "An Appeal," in *Trade Unions: Their Origin and Objects, Influence and Efficacy*, W. Trant (New York: American Federation of Labor, 1888), 48.

45. R. Katz, "With Deleon Since '89," in *Daniel Deleon, The Man and His Works: A Symposium* (New York: Socialist Labor Party, 1919), 20.

46. J. Swinton, *A Momentous Question: The Respective Attitudes of Labor and Capital* (Philadelphia: Keller, 1895), 306–326.

47. G. G. Eggert, *Railroad Labor Disputes: The Beginnings of Federal Strike Policy* (Ann Arbor: U. of Michigan Press, 1967), 152–202.

CHAPTER 7

Labor and the Republic in Industrial America, 1860–1920

From *Le Mouvement Social* 111 (April–June 1980): 201–215

How did the rise of monopoly capitalism affect the political ideology of the American workers' movement? The question is difficult to answer, first, because there have always been conflicting currents of thought within the movement itself, and second, because most historical studies have been concerned with interpreting the lines of internal conflict at particular points in time, rather than searching for basic assumptions which the various parties to the debate shared at any moment, and comparing those assumptions with those which informed the thinking of later epochs. It has become common of late, however, for historians to detect in the rhetoric of American workers a deep and abiding faith in the republican institutions created in the eighteenth century, which guided the movement through its many forms until the depression of the 1890s, and then was somehow lost or transformed.[1]

The nature of that faith remains poorly defined, and just what became of it appears to be a complete mystery. The solution to the mystery may lie in a precise definition of the nineteenth-century faith itself. Fortunately, enough fine historical research is now available in recent studies of working-class culture, work practices, community life, and political action during the last decades of the century to allow us to attempt a definition and to speculate about the causes and main patterns of ideological change at the turn of the century.[2]

The problem, then, is to analyze shifts in the articulated ideology (or ideologies) of the workers' movement. To deal meaningfully with that problem, however, involves nothing less than an attempt, in however sketchy and speculative a manner, to understand the making and remaking of class consciousness in the years between the Civil War and the World War. During this entire epoch, as recent historical writings have so clearly shown, the beliefs and values of workers were rooted in plebeian traditions and in an ethic of mutuality, which daily experience nurtured at work, in the residential neighborhood, and to some extent in the family, as well as in the common experiences of subordination and deprivation that all working people shared. But class consciousness was more than the unmediated product of daily experience. It was also a project. Working-class activists (and some individuals from other social strata, who had linked their aspirations to the workers' struggles) consciously and persistently sought to foster a sense of unity and purposiveness among their fellow workers through the spoken and printed word, strikes, meetings, reading circles, military drill, dances, cooperatives, etc., and to promote through those activities widely shared analyses of society and of the path to "the emancipation of labor."

This project assumed different forms before and after the 1890s as a result of changes in both the type of capitalism that it confronted and the composition of the working class itself. Three basic features of American life during the last third of the nineteenth century decisively shaped the outlook of the labor movement: the political triumph of the northern bourgeoisie, chronic deflation, and nation-wide ascendency of capitalist relationships. Each of these must be examined in turn before we can grasp the distinctive characteristics of working-class consciousness in the heyday of competitive industrial capitalism.

It was during the decisive years between 1854 and 1877 that a new industrial bourgeoisie, which had already secured its political leadership over much of the North, forged a mass-based party, which won control of the federal government, defended the republic against an armed effort to divide it, uprooted the system of chattel slavery, temporarily encouraged the democratic aspirations of the Blacks of the South, and ultimately abandoned them in favor of an alliance with the emerging business leadership of the reconstructed states. It also beat back the efforts of a formidable post-war workers' movement to extend the process of social reconstruction northward—in the words of Ira Steward, to reconstruct "our dinner tables . . ., our dress, manners, education, morals, dwellings, and the whole Social System."[3]

Thus, the business and professional elements of the nation had come to dominate its political councils behind the facade of triumphant republicanism. But, as C. Vann Woodward revealed in his classic study *Reunion and Reaction*, the pinnacle of political power was occupied by an elite of railway executives, military commanders, and political power brokers. That elite was clearly the main target of popular wrath during the insurrectionary strikes, which swept across the country in July, 1877.[4]

The strikes of 1877 also highlighted the other two definitive features of the late nineteenth century. First, this was a deflationary period. From the late 1860s to the mid-1890s prices of both manufactured and agricultural wares tended to fall as output rose. Industrialists tried to reverse the trend by pricing pools, trusts, and other combinations, but the incessant alternation of boom and bust frustrated most of their efforts. More accessible to employers' control were the costs of production, which they strove tirelessly to reduce. Wage cuts, mechanization, dilution of skills. "Pluck me" stores, scrip payment, month-long pay periods, and fines were but some of the devices used in this chronic war against falling prices and falling profit rates. The America which captured the leading place among the world's manufacturing powers in 1883 was a land of ruthless competition.

Second, industrial capitalism became truly national (almost continental) in scope. The railroad lines, along which the strikes of 1877 spread, linked every corner of this vast country, just as telegraph lines and the daily press spread its news within hours of the event. On one hand, this meant that workers everywhere were enmeshed not only in wage relationships, but also in far-flung competitive markets. Hardly a corner of the land escaped the capitalist domain, which Frank Norris so appropriately labelled "the octopus." On the other hand, it meant that local conflicts readily became national news. Consider, for example, Sunday the 22nd of July 1877, when workers in towns as different and as remote from each other as Buffalo, Terre Haute, St. Louis, and San Francisco met in large assemblies and small to discuss the news of riotous strikes in Pittsburgh and Baltimore, and to decide what course of action they should themselves pursue the next day.

The triumph of the capitalist republic, a nationally integrated economy, and chronic deflation, then, decisively shaped working-class life and consciousness in the years 1860–1890. This setting produced both great diversity and elements of universality in the problems workers faced. The diversity arose from the fact that every industry and every trade experienced its own special forms of deflationary pressure on earnings and on work practices, as well as its own distinctive rhythm of opening and closing possibilities for individual advancement. Each ethnic, racial, sexual, and age grouping within the same industry might fare somewhat differently from each other. Each group had to devise its own particular forms and objectives of struggle as a result.

The common quality of these many struggles lay in the fact that each attempt to impose standard wage rates, regulate apprenticeship or hiring, devise and enforce union work rules, or resist fines and dismissals necessarily involved a conscious repudiation of the bourgeois ethic of acquisitive individualism. The workers' attempts to impose economic order (or some islands of economic order) on competitive, deflationary capitalism were futile unless they also involved a moral repudiation of the egotism which that system spawned and acclaimed. Consequently, the labor movement of the Gilded Age (and especially the Noble and Holy Order of the Knights of Labor) was a moral crusade—an effluence of lectures, pamphlets, secret rituals, boycotts, parades, ceremonies, and parties, all designed to instill a practical sense of the "universal brotherhood of labor."

This moral universality amid the particularities of the workers' daily sectoral struggles was the distinctive quality of late nineteenth century "labor reform." It was rooted in collective work practices (some customary, some quite new) by which workers defended their earnings and their dignity on the job.[5] It was reinforced by the necessity for working-class families to function as economic units for survival, and hence to suppress individualistic striving.[6] Moreover, the workers' mutualistic ethic had pre-capitalist sources, of which the labor reformers were well aware. The very name "Knights of Labor," and the Order's incessant appeal to "chivalry" against gluttonous commercialism underscore this romantic use of popular memories and traditions, just as did the medieval pageantry of anarchist parades, the ornate regalia of craft unions, and the invocation of crafts' patron saints by many workers whose ancestors had been Protestants for centuries.

In more than 15,000 local assemblies, which the Knights of Labor chartered in every part of the country during the 1880s, activists carefully cultivated a movement culture. Knights spurned saloons as meeting places (those dens of exclusively male sociability, where master brewers and ward politicians held sway) and substituted meetings and social gatherings for the whole family in a "producers" environment. They also taught workers to organize themselves apart from the institutions of bourgeois society, not only in trades assemblies, but also in sporting clubs, labor temples, and manufacturing and trading cooperatives. Their favorite punishment for infractions of their moral code was the boycott. Leaving a miscreant "severely alone" was far more than an economic sanction against unfair bosses. Its use was illustrated by women members in New York City, who resolved:

> whenever the Knights of Labor girls went to a picnic or ball, they were to tell all the brother Knights that none of the latter were to walk with a non-union girl in the opening promenade so long as a union girl was without a partner. Should any male Knight violate this rule, all the girl Knights are to step out of the promenade and boycott the entire crowd.[7]

Although the Knights never created a political party of their own, or even gave unequivocal support to a third party until 1894, when they joined with rebellious farmers in the People's Party, political action was essential to their movement. In the late seventies and early eighties local leaders of the Knights and of the Greenback Labor Party were virtually interchangeable in Pittsburgh, Richmond, Detroit, and many other towns. In the two years that followed the turbulent spring of 1886 local labor reform parties, which enjoyed strong electoral support in manufacturing towns and cities all over the country, exhibited a distinctly working-class variant of civic consciousness.[8] Although the local origins of this impulse gave rise to considerable programmatic diversity, it had a definite national character and significance. Grand Master Workman Uriah Stephens had explained its ideological thrust in 1871, when he said:

> Civil and religious liberty and theoretical equality before the law we already have in America. That was achieved for us by our revolutionary forefathers, and bequeathed by them as a sacred legacy to us, their descendants and successors. But an accursed slavery, a heaven-denounced tyranny, a degrading atheistic idolatry remains, has grown upon us, which it becomes our duty to destroy, to our posterity, to God and humanity, to destroy and utterly annihilate.[9]

"Abolition of the wages system" was the phrase used by virtually all Knights and trade unionists of these decades to describe the ultimate objective of their movement. In their minds, as the literature of the eight-hour day movement in the 1860s had made evident, the opposite of "wage slave" was "citizen."[10] The contrast between the condition of a factor of production and that of a participating member of society was drawn sharply by George McNeill in 1887. When the laborer is at work, wrote McNeill, "he belongs to the lower orders, and is continually under surveillance; when out of work he is an outlaw, a tramp . . ., the pariah of society." But with the triumph of labor reform, he dreamed:

> the now-dawning day shall witness a well-built, fully equipped manhood, using the morning hours in the duties and pleasures of the sunlit-home; taking his morning bath before his morning work, reading his morning paper in the well-equipped reading-room of the manufactory [. . .]. With the hours of work reduced to the minimum, the profits of his work increased to the maximum, he will be a man upon whom the honors and duties of civilization can safely rest.[11]

Two aspects of this vision of social reform deserve attention here. First, its goal could not be achieved without successful political struggle to redeem the republic from the corrupting power and "class legislation" of "the monopolists." Two particular demands which enjoyed ardent support among both Knights and trade unionists from the sixties through the nineties were the greenback plan (to substitute a government-controlled currency for private banking) and the abolition of monopoly power in land (either through the issuance of land titles for individual use only or through Henry George's "Single tax" on "the unearned increment" of rent).[12] Advocates of both reforms hoped to end the ability of the rich to enrich themselves further through the machinery of state and to restore the republic to its original egalitarian principles.

Second, the redemption of society from capitalism (the abolition of the wages system) was not envisaged by the Knights as basically a mission for the state. Through self-organization and self-help "the producing classes" were to organize their own associations, impose their own trade rules upon work, force capitalists to arbitrate industrial disputes, create their own cooperative enterprises, discipline exploiters and miscreants through the power of the boycott, educate themselves in political economy, and disseminate the morality of universal brotherhood throughout the land. Although these tasks could not be accomplished without redemption of the state, neither could they be accomplished by the state. The guiding principle was that which William Sylvis had preached to the Iron Molders Union in 1865: "*It is not what is done for people, but what people do for themselves, that acts upon their character and condition*."[13]

This was the belief of the mainstream of the post-Civil War labor movement, the faith espoused by most trade unionists and Knights down to the 1890s. For all the famous disagreements over such issues as strikes vs. arbitration, national craft organizations vs. city-wide solidarities of all workers, and secret vs. open unions, on which Grob, Ware, and other historians have lavished attention, the principles expressed by the Knights were those around which most working-class activists tried to mobilize their class in opposition to the dominance of industrial capitalism. Yankee labor reformers, Irish Land Leaguers, and British-born trade unionists all found common cause in this project.[14]

There were, however, two important variations to these themes of working-class radicalism, both of which were most deeply rooted in the neighborhoods and trades of German and Bohemian immigrants. The first envisaged political action to capture the machinery of state, transform it, and use it to uproot capitalism, as the essential task of the labor movement. The program of the Workingmen's Party of the United States demanded: "All industrial enterprises to be placed under the control of the Government as fast as practicable and operated by the free co-operative trade unions for the good of the whole people."[15] Only through communism, wrote Friedrich Sorge, could "the victory of *common* interests over hideous Egoism" be won. "Labor will then be acting according to a certain reasonable plan," he added, "and since, for that purpose, the use of the existing capital, comprising soil, houses, railways, shipping, manufactories, machines etc., will be necessary, those comparatively few possessors of all the wealth of the nations will have to be expropriated."[16]

The WPUS enrolled many English-speaking trade unionists and Knights, and through such papers as the *Labor Standard* of Paterson and the *Workingman's Map* of Indianapolis it provided an influential socialist voice for local labor struggles and central labor unions. During the July insurrection of 1877 its executive committee issued a call for workers to organize around the demands that the national government "take possession of and operate all the railroads and telegraph lines in the country" and establish an eight-hour day by legislation.[17] Its activists in Chicago and St. Louis organized and led the directing bodies of their cities' tumultuous strikes of the following week.[18] Nevertheless, those strikes and their aftermath did not elevate the party to the leadership of America's workers. On the contrary, they fragmented the party itself. Such important members as J.P. McDonnell, P.J. McGuire, and Adolph Strasser hurled themselves single-mindedly into the formation of trade unions, and they quit the party when it insisted on entering the electoral arena.[19] Those members who gave priority to political struggles changed the party's name to the Socialistic Labor Party at the end of 1877 and subsequently sought electoral victories through fusion with the Greenback Labor Party. That maneuver prompted Paul Grottkau to lead much of the German membership out in protest.[20]

The International Working People's Association, to which Grottkau and his comrades adhered after their secession from the SLP, emerged by the mid-1880s as the most influential movement among German immigrants of the midwestern cities. Between 1881 and 1890, 1,453,015 Germans entered the United States, and they provided large numbers of building laborers, lumber yard workers, and wagon drivers, as well as the predominant group of artisans in wood-working, tailoring, baking, brewing, and metal-working trades. Among them the anarcho-communists of the IWPA developed a vibrant network of institutions based on the needs of everyday life, but consciously antagonistic to bourgeois society: mutual benefit clubs, athletic and cultural associations, *Freidenker* schools, and trade unions. By the spring of 1886, 33 percent of all union members in Chicago were German (only 22.5 percent of all workers were), and the eleven largest unions in the city were affiliated with the IWPA's Central Labor Union, rather than with the Amalgamated Trades and Labor Union or with the Knights of Labor.[21]

In 1883 the IWPA had concluded that its mission was not to capture the state, but to smash it. Its famous leaders (Parsons, Spies, Fielden, Schwab, Grottkau etc.) envisaged their role not as organizers and strategists of the working class, but as its teachers—as editors, orators, poets, and dramatists, whose tutelage would help the workers find their own path to emancipation. They subjected bourgeois society to merciless ridicule through parades in the tradition of charivaris, poems and songs, which were travesties of familiar bourgeois art, and lampoons of prestigious gatherings of "high society," staged by swarms of ragged workers on the very scenes that were supposed to be dedicated to elegance. Here was the antagonistic counter culture against which bourgeois society took its revenge by the fierce police repression of May and June 1886, in Chicago and Milwaukee and by hanging the Haymarket martyrs.

All components of the labor movement (trade unions, Knights, SLP, IWPA, labor reform parties, and cooperatives) flourished simultaneously during the upsurge of strike activity and the renewed eight-hour day struggle of

1885–1886. Class-conscious activists then found themselves joined by hundreds of thousands of workers in picket lines, parades, rallies, and confrontations with police and troops. But the very scale of workers' struggles, which breathed such life into their class consciousness, also stimulated counter-moves by business and political leaders, which modified significantly the subsequent involvement of the working class with radicalism and with the state.

In part the bourgeois response was tactical; in part it reflected profound structural changes in the society itself. The new tactics involved a more systematic resistance to strikes, through employers' associations, court orders, private detective agencies, state militia, expanded use of lockouts, and massive discharge of defeated strikers. They also produced draconic enforcement of state legislation against tramps and the systematic reorganization of public charities and of commercial insurance, as alternatives to working-class self-help. Simultaneously urban political machines of the Democratic and Republican parties nominated candidates who styled themselves "friends of the workingman" and dispensed patronage jobs bountifully to prominent trade unionists and Knights. Chicago alone had some 400 labor leaders on its city payroll in the early 1890s. Subsequently, upper-class civic reformers launched crusades against such "corruption," the main effect of which was to reduce popular influence over city government drastically.[22]

Some effects of these strategies were quickly felt by the labor movement. Numerous strike defeats in large enterprises tended to reduce the ranks of unionized workers to the skilled crafts. While the Knights of Labor crumpled under the strain, the new American Federation of Labor championed the militant efforts of craftsmen to sustain their organizations, among which were more sympathetic strikes recorded than at any other period in American history. The vigorous support which the Socialist Labor Party lent to these unions restored its numbers and prestige, as is illustrated by the fact that Paul Grottkau rejoined the party after his term in prison for Milwaukee's May 1st events of 1886, and was dispatched by Samuel Gompers on a nation-wide speaking tour together with George McNeill to rouse workers for another attempt at the eight-hour day.[23]

Nevertheless, when the socialists attempted to commit the AF of L to a political program featuring collective ownership of the means of production, the Federation's officers successfully organized its 1894 convention against the effort. Most craft union leaders felt that they could fend for themselves in combat with their employers, but not against the government. President Weismann of the Bakers pointed to the recent Pullman strike and argued: "the governments of all countries up to date have been the great instruments of disintegration of the human race; and the movement, in developing our lines of freedom, should carefully avoid giving a tremendous power which today is in the hands of our enemies."[24]

Behind these new strategies of employers and politicians, however, were the beginnings of profound structural changes in the economy itself. Business' spasmodic efforts at trusts and pools gave way in the nineties to a merger movement sponsored by finance capital, which created the great corporations of the twentieth century. Through their trade associations businessmen themselves developed a more collectivist outlook, at the same time that they began to experiment with the use of governmental commissions to cope with their economic problems. Simultaneously the "octopus" of American capitalism extended its reach from a continental to a global scale. It drew into its domain not only the minerals and food products of the tropics, but also the labor power of the southern and eastern European peasantry. This development meant, first, that the composition of the working class itself was radically changed. Between 1900 and 1910, for example, more than two million Italians and a somewhat greater number of subjects of the Austrian Empire entered the United States. A comparison of the increase in the population of those groups in the US over that decade with the numbers who disembarked here reveals a turnover rate of 238 percent for the Italians and 281 percent for the "Austrians."[25] In short, southeastern Europe had become part of the American industrial economy.

Second, the nation's global role, combined with the re-composition of its working class, elevated both patriotism and racism to positions of decisive importance in the bourgeois ideology with which radicals had to contend. The new quality and significance of patriotism, for example, quickly revealed itself among workers. Although the frequent use of troops against strikers in the 1890s had inspired intense hostility toward militarism, illustrated by the American Railway Union's prohibition of membership to anyone who was enrolled in a state militia, an ardent admirer of the ARU, Youngstown's "puddler poet," Michael McGovern, wrote at the outbreak of the Spanish-American War:

> Your wealthy ones, who fear to fight,
> Make room for those who dare—
> Consign the flag—now threatened—to
> the fighting workingmen's care.[26]

During the next ten years the *Machinists' Monthly Journal*, which was edited by a Socialist, bedecked its pages increasingly with patriotic symbolism, until America's entry into the World War found its cover displaying little else than the American and Canadian flags. As early as 1908 its editor had demanded rapid naval construction to keep pace with England and Germany.[27] Eight years later the country's strongest union center, Chicago, witnessed the largest parade in its history to date, one dedicated to American "preparedness." Marching workers were ranked, not by the crafts of their unions, but by the industries for which they worked.[28] In Milwaukee the city's Socialist mayor reviewed the preparedness parade.[29]

But there was more than just patriotism to be seen in the events of 1916. The country was then gripped by the largest strike wave it had yet experienced. More than 600 strikes for the eight-hour day had begun on May 1, 1916 alone. Moreover, the Socialist-led Central Trades and Labor Union of St. Louis voted 133–42 against participating in the patriotic demonstration. In San Francisco, not only did most unions refuse to take part, but class tensions around the parade mounted to the point that a bomb was hurled into the marchers' ranks, and Tom Mooney and Warren Billings were arrested in that decade's counterpart of the Haymarket Affair.[30]

In other words, class conflict had not subsided since the 1890s and the working class had not been won over *en masse* to what Herbert Croly and Theodore Roosevelt called "the new nationalism." On the contrary, the sectoral struggles of workers involved more people than ever and often met more violent resistance from employers and the state than ever before. It was the moral universality of the working class that had been ruptured, not its militancy. No single set of values, no commonly accepted vision of the redemption of the republic, any longer guided the many streams of working-class struggle into a single-minded flood of protest.

Most notably the major leaders of the trade unions had set their faces fiercely against socialism. Numerous though Socialist Party members were in many unions, they were openly treated by Gompers and his associates as disloyal to the AF of L, and in fact secretary Morrison specifically instructed the Federation's field organizers to keep all Socialist officers under surveillance. Moreover, as the leadership of major unions became increasingly bureaucratized and professional, it set out to suppress sympathetic strikes, for the sake of secure contractual relations with employers. These developments culminated in the loyal adherence of the AF of L's heads to the National Civic Federation, and subsequently to the Wilson administration, in the efforts of those two groups to fit organized labor harmoniously into the new structure of American capitalism.[31]

In this setting the Socialist Party of America represented both the culmination of half a century's development of working-class radicalism and a distinctly minority movement, battling against new odds to keep alive George McNeill's vision of "the now-dawning day." The party had its origins in the confluence of SLP work within the trade unions and working-class Populism, which had been based on the Knights and the American Railway Union. It enjoyed a large following in many industrial towns, where it struggled to reorganize civil society around workers' needs. The spread of mass production methods and of scientific management and the intensity of the "open shop" assault against the unions, persuaded ever larger numbers of unionized craftsmen and women to follow Socialist leadership. Witness the union elections of 1911–1912, when socialist-backed candidates ousted the conservative presidents of the machinists', hatters', pattern makers', tailors', and sheet metal workers' unions. At the same time, the flurry of discussion in the commercial press about "the scientific reorganization" of the economy, the need to assert the "collective interests of the nation" over disruptive individualism, and the need for planning in a modern economy expanded the audience for socialist arguments.

To a solid core of German-born members, most of whom had been in the United States since the 1880s, the party now added thousands of Jewish garment workers, Finnish miners, and American-born machinists. Its appeal to workers to unite within the unions for "economic" struggles and around the party for the political battle to gain "the co-operative commonwealth" enjoyed visible success on both fronts. Moreover, the international movement of which the Socialists were so proudly a part seemed to supply the workers' answer to the global reach of capitalism—the invincible foe of imperialism, militarism, and war. Thus, despite the bitterness of the struggles it faced, the party's mood was buoyantly optimistic until August, 1914.[32]

Even before the Guns of August began to reap their bloody harvest, however, two interrelated problems had haunted and divided socialist ranks: capitalist collectivism and direct action. The first arose from the political and social reforms then being promoted by business and professional groups. Socialist writer John Macy warned his comrades in 1916 against dismissing "the new liberalism with too easy contempt." Capitalism's recent development, he explained, was "lifting above the line of privilege and security the skilled organized workmen" and "forming an ever-closer alliance between private and public capital, through the spuriously democratic device of government ownership."[33] Surveying the economic mobilization of the belligerent powers the next year, Ohio's Socialist leader Charles Ruthenberg argued that laissez-faire capitalism was being replaced by a profoundly anti-democratic form of collectivism. "Collectivism is the inevitable outcome of the existing system of production" he concluded in a way that almost reversed Sorge's emphasis of forty years earlier. "Democracy must be fought for and won through the power of the working class."[34] The economic thrust of the state's new role had been noted five years earlier by William English Walling: "The very essence of capitalist collectivism is that the share of the total profits which goes to the ruling class should not be decreased, and if possible, should be augmented."[35]

These thinkers shared a growing skepticism within the party's ranks that "the cooperative commonwealth" could be achieved by an accumulation of electoral triumphs, legislative reforms, and nationalization of industries. They found themselves increasingly attracted by such formulas as "direct action," "mass action," and "mass strikes," in their search for a pathway strategically linking workers' daily struggles to the overthrow of capitalism.[36] These formulas in turn reflected another feature of the new capitalism: the frequency, scale, and rebellious quality of its strikes. To cite but one example of this phenomenon: in April, 1917 the leaders of the AF of L forswore strikes in the wartime "national interest," but more workers struck that year than in any previous year of American history, and 67 of their strikes involved more than 10,000 workers each (14 more than in 1919).[37]

Moreover, though "militant minorities" of skilled English-speaking workers pressed radical demands in virtually every craft between 1909 and 1922, a special prominence in the wave of strikes was earned by the highly mobile recent immigrants in mass production industries. Radicalism sank such deep roots among them at this time that by the 1920s class consciousness and immigrant consciousness would be virtually co-extensive in centers of basic industry. Ethnic lodges and even churches provided important centers of self-organization for workers, whose working hours in the large mills were under strict surveillance and whose communities were governed by hostile municipal authorities. Moreover, internationalism assumed a new meaning, as recently arrived workers, speaking many languages and still linked by economic and personal ties to their native lands, joined forces in huge rallies and marches.[38]

The Industrial Workers of the World appreciated the significance of this development and based its strategy on the action of mass production workers from the start. Though many books have been written about the IWW, many aspects of its activity among immigrants remain to be explored. Consider, for example, the IWW allegiances of the predominantly Spanish marine firemen, whose union controlled the freighters of the United Fruit Company from 1913 to 1916, until the La Follette Seamen's Act excluded them from American ships;[39] the effective organization of Italian mine laborers in Pennsylvania's anthracite fields to "bore from within" the United Mine Workers in 1916;[40] and such offshoots of the IWW as the Allegheny Congenial Industrial Union in Pittsburgh's huge Westinghouse works.[41] But there is no need to say more about the IWW here, because most of its history is already well known. The point to be emphasized is the context in which the gospel of direct action (or mass action) arose: the strike had in fact become the main expression of working-class radicalism, and many of those using that weapon were not exclusively attached to any one nation-state.

Controversies within the Socialist Party over strategies to deal with "capitalist collectivism" and the revolutionary possibilities of mass strikes reached their boiling point with American participation in the war, the post-war strikes, and the revolutionary upsurge in Europe. In that context the party suffered major secessions in two opposite directions. One was the formation of numerous labor and farmer-labor parties, which emphasized electoral struggles for social reform, and in which ex-Socialists who had rallied to the patriotic banner during the war were especially prominent.[42] The other was the rapid coalescence of former adherents of the Socialist Party, the Socialist Labor Party, and the IWW into the Communist and Communist Labor Parties. The first manifesto of the Communist Party revealed its roots in the previous decade's experience, as well as the disruption of that decade's radical organizations:

> But there is a more vital tendency [than the creation of a Labor Party, it declared], the tendency of the workers to start mass strikes—strikes which are equally a revolt against the bureaucracy of the unions and the capitalists. The Communist Party will endeavor to broaden and deepen these strikes making them general and militant, developing the general political strike.[43]

Monopoly capitalism, therefore, fragmented the political ideology of the American workers' movement. By 1920 conflicting groups of workers fought each other, rhetorically armed with different fragments of what had formerly been a coherent vision of redeeming the republic. To summarize the argument: After the Civil War an incessant eruption of workers' struggles over a variety of sectoral demands and problems, with common roots in a deflationary phase of capitalist development, enabled conscious militants to inspire a sense of moral universality among "the producers," which directly challenged both the ethic of acquisitive individualism and "monopoly corruption" of the republic. The changing structure of American capitalism, the decomposition of the working class itself, and the new strategies of the bourgeoisie at the turn of the century did not destroy working-class militancy. They did disrupt the moral universality, which had given that militancy its nineteenth-century language.

In its place emerged a trade union leadership explicitly committed not only to reforming American capitalism by strictly trade union means, but also to defending the state against foreign foes and domestic revolutionaries alike. Arrayed against that dominant group were two minority currents of great importance: the Socialist Party and the direct-action movement, most clearly represented by the "IWW." The radicalism of these dissenters was necessarily both American and international. But the war and the nationalism of "capitalist collectivism" made it increasingly difficult for workers to champion both those loyalties at once.

Notes

Reprinted courtesy of *Le Mouvement Social.*

1. Paul Buhle, "The Knights of Labor in Rhode Island," *Radical History Review* (Spring 1978): 39–73; Howard B. Rock, *Artisans of the New Republic: The Tradesmen of New York City in the Age of Jefferson* (New York, 1979); George. B. Cotkin, "The Spencerian and Comtian Nexus in Gompers' Labor Philosophy: The Impact of Non-Marxian Evolutionary Thought," *Labor History* (Fall 1979): 510–523; Bruce Laurie, "The Working People of Philadelphia, 1827–1853" (unpublished PhD dissertation,

University of Pittsburgh, 1971); David Montgomery, "Labor in the Industrial Era," in *The American Worker*, ed. Richard B. Morris (Washington, DC, 1976). Standard works emphasizing conflicts within the movement include J.R. Commons et al., *History of Labor in the United States*, 4 vols. (New York, 1918–1935); Gerald N. Grob, *Workers and Utopia: A Study of Ideological Conflict in the American Labor Movement, 1865–1900* (Evanston, Ill., 1961); N.J. Ware, *The Labor Movement in the United States, 1860–1895* (New York and London, 1929).

2. See, for example, H.G. Gutman, *Work, Culture, and Society in Industrializing America: Essays in Working-Class and Social History* (New York, 1976); A. Dawley, *Class and Community: The Industrial Revolution in Lynn* (Cambridge, Mass., 1976); D. Walkowitz, *Worker City, Company Town: Iron and Cotton Worker Protest in Troy and Cohoes, New York, 1855–1884* (Urbana, Ill., 1978); D. Montgomery, *Workers' Control in America: Studies in the History of Work, Technology, and Labor Struggles* (New York and London, 1979).

3. Quoted in Montgomery, *Beyond Equality: Labor and the Radical Republicans, 1862–1872* (New York, 1967), ix.

4. C. Vann Woodward, *Reunion and Reaction: The Compromise of 1877 and the End of Reconstruction* (Garden City, New York, 1956); P.S. Foner, *The Great Labor Uprising of 1877* (New York, 1977).

5. D. Montgomery, *Workers' Control in America*, 9–31.

6. M.K. Simkovitch, *The City Worker's World in America* (New York, 1917); T.K. Hareven and R. Langenbach, *Amoskeag: Life and Work in an American Factory-City* (New York, 1978); T.K. Hareven, "Family Time and Historical Time," *Daedalus* (Spring 1977), 57–70.

7. *Argentine* (Kansas), *Labor Review*, Aug. 1, 1891. I am indebted to Susan Levine for this quotation. On the Knights' meeting places, see S. Levine, "The Knights of Labor Romantic Ideology"; D. Brundage, "The Producing Classes and the Saloon: Denver in the 1880s," (unpublished papers prepared for the 1979 Knights of Labor Symposium).

8. L. Fink, "Workingmen's Democracy: The Knights of Labor in Local Politics, 1886–1896" (unpublished PhD dissertation, University of Rochester, 1977); P.A. Speek, *The Singletax and the Labor Movement* (Madison, Wisconsin, 1917); A. Dawley, *Class and Community*.

9. Quoted in T.V. Powderly, *Thirty Years of Labor* (Columbus, 1890), 168.

10. D. Montgomery, *Beyond Equality*, 230–260.

11. G.E. McNeill, *The Labor Movement: The Problem of Today* (New York, 1887), 455, 466.

12. American Federation of Labor, *History, Encyclopedia, Reference Book* (Washington, 1919), 281; N.J. Ware, *The Labor Movement*.

13. J.C. Sylvis, *The Life, Speeches, Labors and Essays of William H. Sylvis* (Philadelphia, 1872), 169.

14. On Irish-American radicalism, see E. Foner, "Class, Ethnicity, and Radicalism in the Gilded Age: The Land League and Irish America," *Marxist Perspectives* (Summer 1978): 6–55; M.A. Gordon, "The Labor Boycott in New York City, 1884–1886," *Labor History* (Spring 1977): 184–229.

15. J.A. Dacus, *Annals of the Great Strikes in the United States* (Chicago, 1877), 86.

16. F.A. Sorge, *Socialism and the Worker* (London, 1884), 7, 11. The pamphlet was first published in New York in 1876.

17. *St. Louis Globe Democrat*, July 23, 1877.

18. D.T. Burbank, *Reign of the Rabble: The St. Louis General Strike of 1877* (New York, 1966); Foner, *1877*; L.E. Parsons, *Life of Albert Parsons, with a Brief History of the Labor Movement in America* (Chicago, 1889); M. Debouzy, "Gréve et violence de classe aux Etats-Unis en 1877," *Le Mouvement Social*, Janvier-Mars, 1978, 41–66.

19. Stuart B. Kaufman sees these men as the ideological founders of the A.F. of L. See *Samuel Gompers and the Origins of the American Federation of Labor, 1848–1896* (Westport, Connecticut, 1973).

20. L.E. Parsons, *Life of Albert Parsons*, xx.

21. H. Keil and H. Ickstadt, "Elemente einer Deutscher Arbeiterkultur in Chicago zwischen 1889 und 1890," *Geschichte und Gesellschaft*, 1979/Heft 1, 103–124; J.R. Commons, *History of Labor*, II, 386–394.

22. See E.E. Witte, *The Government in Labor Disputes*, New York, 1932; G.G. Eggert, *Railroad Labor Disputes: The Beginning of Federal Strike Policy* (Ann Arbor, Michigan, 1967); C.E. Bonnett, *Employers' Associations in the United States: A Study of Typical Associations* (New York, 1922); S.L. Harring, "Class Conflict and the Suppression of Tramps in Buffalo, 1892–1894," *Law & Society Review* (Summer 1977): 873–911; L.R. Fink, "The Uses of Political Power: Towards a Theory of the Labor Movement in the Era of the Knights of Labor"; F.G. Couvares, "Knights, Trade Unionists and Local Politics in Pittsburgh, 1867–1887"; R.J. Oestreicher, "The Limits of Labor Radicalism: Tom Barry and the Knights of Labor" (unpublished papers presented to the Knights of Labor Symposium, 1979); S.P. Hays, "The Politics of Reform in Municipal Government in the Progressive Era," *Pacific Northwest Quarterly* (October 1964): 157–169 ; C.M. Destler, *American Radicalism, 1865–1901* (New London, Connecticut, 1946); R.H. Wiebe, *Businessmen and Reform: A Study of the Progressive Movement* (Cambridge, Massachusetts, 1962).

23. J.R. Commons, *History of Labor*, II, 516.

24. A.F. of L., *A Verbatum Report of the Discussion on the Political Programme, at the Denver Convention of the American Federation of Labor, December 14, 15, 1894* (New York, 1895), 25. See also J.F. Finn, "A.F. of L. Leaders and the Question of Politics in the Early 1890s," *American Studies* (Fall 1973): 243–265.

25. My calculations from data in US Department of Commerce, Bureau of the Census, *Historical Statistics of the United States, Colonial Times to 1970*, 2 vols. (Washington, DC, 1975), 105, 117.

26. M. McGovern, *Labor Lyrics, and other Poems* (Youngstown, Ohio, 1899), 116.

27. *Machinists' Monthly Journal* (May 1908): 395–396.

28. *International Socialist Review* (July 1916): 7.

29. Ibid., November 1916, 267.

30. G.M. Fink, *Labor's Search for Political Order: The Political Behavior of the Missouri Labor Movement, 1890–1940* (Columbia, Mo., 1973), 61; *International Socialist Review* (October 1916): 216–217.

31. J. Weinstein, *The Corporate Ideal in the Liberal State, 1900–1918* (Boston, 1968); M. Green, *The National Civic Federation and the American Labor Movement, 1900–1925* (Washington, DC, 1956); B. Ramirez, *When Workers Fight: The Politics of Industrial Relations in the Progressive Era, 1898–1916* (Westport, Conn., 1978); D. Montgomery, *Workers' Control*, 48–90.

32. L. Fink, *Workingmen's Democracy*, 314–376; S.M. Miller, *Victor Berger and the Promise of Constructive Socialism, 1910–1920* (Westport, Conn., 1973); W.R. Van Tine, *The Making of a Labor Bureaucrat: Union Leadership in the United States, 1870–1920* (Amherst, 1973); G. Haupt, *Socialism and the Great War: The Collapse of the Second International* (Oxford, 1972). On the ethnic composition of the S.P., see C. Leinenweber, "The Class and Ethnic Bases of New York City Socialism, 1904–1915," *Labor History* 22 (1981): 31–56.

33. J. Macy, *Socialism in America* (Garden City, N.Y., 1916), 78.

34. C.E. Ruthenberg, *Are We Growing Toward Socialism?* (Cleveland, Ohio, 1917), 34.

35. W.E. Walling, *Socialism As It Is: A Survey of the World-Wide Revolutionary Movement* (New York, 1912), 115.

36. For numerous articles stressing direct action themes, see *New Review*, 1913 onward.

37. *Monthly Labor Review* (May 1922): 186.

38. G. Bock, P. Carpignano, B. Ramirez, *La formazione dell'operaio massa negli USA 1898/1922* (Milan, 1976); F. Fasce, "'Tra immigrazione e americanizzazione.'" Note per una storia della classe operaio americana, 1890–1920," *Miscelliatea Storiea Ligure*, 1978, 107–187; D. Montgomery, *Workers' Control.*

39. Interview with G.M. Pazos, Secretary-Treasurer, Marine Transport Workers, Industrial Union 100, IWW, Philadelphia, Pa., 4/9/19. Saposs Papers, State Historical Society of Wisconsin.

40. P.M. Lynch, "Pennsylvania Anthracite: A Forgotten IWW Venture, 1906–1916" (unpublished M.A. Thesis, Bloomsburg State College, 1974).

41. D. Kanitra, "The Westinghouse Strike of 1916" (unpublished M.A. Paper, University of Pittsburgh, 1971).

42. Little attention has been paid to this movement, but see J. Weinstein, *The Decline of Socialism in America, 1912–1925* (New York, 1967), 272–323.

43. Communist Party of America, *Manifesto and Program. Constitution. Report to the Communist International* (Chicago, 1919), 9.

CHAPTER 8

Racism, Immigrants, and Political Reform

From *Journal of American History* 87 (March 2001): 1253–1274

The theme of the ninety-third annual convention of the Organization of American Historians (OAH) was "The United States and the Wider World." Both that theme and the way the OAH's public protest against racism shaped the St. Louis convention prompt us to reconsider the overarching narrative within which United States history is ordinarily presented. This essay argues that it is misleading to present our country's history as the progressive fulfillment of democratic ideals, and it emphasizes the significance of the global context, especially of slavery and immigration, for the development of the country's economic, political, and intellectual life. The question of how and within what limits collective human action has shaped history informs all aspects of this discussion.

The OAH, St. Louis, and the Adam's Mark

Scarcely three months before the OAH convention was scheduled to open at the Adam's Mark Hotel, members of the OAH learned that the National Association for the Advancement of Colored People (NAACP), the United States Department of Justice, and the state of Florida had filed suit against the hotel chain for discrimination against and special surveillance of African American patrons in Daytona Beach. We also learned that an appeals court had previously found that testimony concerning employment discrimination at the St. Louis hotel, in the court's words, "supported a finding of outrageous conduct and an award of punitive damages."[1]

The executive board's decision to move all official convention business out of the hotel was based on the principle that the OAH could not fulfill its mission of encouraging the open exchange of the varied points of view and theoretical orientations found among its members if it met under circumstances that made any members feel unwelcome or unwilling to participate because of racial discrimination. The enthusiastic support of historians in St. Louis, the city's Board of Aldermen, and the administration of St. Louis University made it possible to hold a very successful convention at other locations within the city under these difficult circumstances. Moreover, the combined impact of these efforts helped make history: During the week before the convention the Adam's Mark management agreed to a consent decree providing for nondiscriminatory policies to be monitored by Project Equality of Kansas City, Missouri, and for payment of monetary relief totaling $8 million.[2]

The Mississippi Valley Historical Association, precursor of the OAH, addressed this question half a century ago. When New Orleans was designated the site for its 1952 convention, segregation was still unequivocally the law in that city. African American members, few as they then were, could attend sessions at convention hotels, but they could not sleep, dine, or socialize there. President Merle Curti informed the executive committee a year in advance of the scheduled meeting that he refused to deliver his scheduled presidential address in such a setting. He proposed to move the forthcoming convention to Chicago.

In marked contrast to the executive board's unanimity facing the St. Louis decision, in 1951 an adamant minority of officers angrily resisted the proposal to move, though they were not successful. The battle over segregated facilities continued for another two years, culminating in a referendum, which was phrased to evade the question of whether black members could reside at a convention hotel, and which revealed a sharply divided membership. The executive committee then settled the issue by voting to accept no invitations for convention facilities unless sponsors guaranteed that there would be no discrimination in meals *or* housing. The hotel under discussion at that time was in Topeka, Kansas. One month later the United States Supreme Court handed down its historic decision, *Brown v. Board of Education of Topeka*.[3]

Many members of the OAH at the beginning of the twenty-first century were not only offended by the conduct attributed to the Adam's Mark chain by the Department of Justice and the NAACP but also taken aback by the realization that such discrimination was still with us at the beginning of a new century, and thirty-five years after Congress enacted the Civil Rights Act of 1964.

The experience of this struggle reminds us of previous periods of retrogression in the basic liberties of peoples of color, and it bears directly on the "wider world" theme of the St. Louis convention. Placing United States history in a context defined by a worldwide capitalist economy enables us to grasp the human consequences of two decisive elements of global economic interactions:

North American slavery and the vast migration to the United States of people from Europe, Asia, and the Americas. Struggling to improve their own lives, often quite consciously within that world context, working people have left their own distinctive stamp on social and political life in the United States and on contests over the meaning of American nationality, which continue to unfold in our own time. Both the contributions of working people to the cause of political reform and the many defeats their efforts have suffered can best be understood by placing them in global context. As we consider those subjects, we can find guidance in the words of the late C. Vann Woodward.

> America has a history. It is only that the tragic aspects and ironic implications of that history have been obscured by the national legend of success and victory and by the perpetuation of infant illusions of innocence and virtue. . . . But she [America] desperately needs criticism from historians of her own who can penetrate the legend without destroying the ideal, who can dispel the illusion of pretended virtue without denying the genuine virtues.[4]

Retrogression

We are well aware that the hopes of freedom and of equal citizenship awakened in African American hearts during the 1780s and the 1860s were subsequently dashed. The decades following the revolutionary declaration that "All men are created equal," especially the 1790s, witnessed the renewal and expansion of slavery in the South, the enactment of the first federal fugitive slave law, and the exclusion of African Americans from industrial employment and from citizenship rights that accompanied the excruciatingly protracted demise of slavery in most of the North. Pennsylvania's supreme court made the limits of emancipation clear in 1837 when it ruled black men no longer eligible to vote in that state and explained: "no colored race was party to our social compact."[5]

Similarly, the last decades of the nineteenth century were marked by a steady retreat from Reconstruction's promise of racial equality. In 1870, when President Ulysses S. Grant announced the ratification of the Fifteenth Amendment, he took the then unusual step of adding his own commentary to the proclamation. Noting that only thirteen years earlier Chief Justice Roger B. Taney of the Supreme Court had asserted what he called the "fixed and universal principle in the civilized portion of the white race . . . that black men had no rights which the white man was bound to respect," Grant called the federal voting rights amendment "a measure of grander importance than any other one act of the kind from the foundation of our free Government to the present day."[6]

By that time, however, many of those northern whites who, like the *Nation*'s famous editor Edwin L. Godkin, applauded "the absolute civil and political equality of the colored man under our institutions and government" also protested that the articulation by former slaves, as well as by white workers, of "special interests and aims" was leading "ambitious politicians into follies of which the worst exploits of the great political deceivers of the present day afford but a very imperfect idea." Only four years after Grant's stirring proclamation, the Liberal Republican James Shepherd Pike published an influential denunciation of South Carolina's Republican regime, under the title *The Prostrate State*. The book argued that to permit propertyless black voters, not properly educated in the principles of personal conduct and free-market economics, to control the tax policies and expenditures of a state was to frighten off investment and hobble economic growth. To secure a successful free-market economy, wrote Pike, it was necessary for the federal government to end its support of the few remaining Republican regimes in the South and to cultivate instead an entrepreneurial spirit in the ranks of the old southern plantation and political elite. Only then would a rising tide lift all boats.[7]

Between 1873 and 1883 the Republican-controlled Supreme Court gradually but relentlessly narrowed the capacity of the federal government to protect the political and social rights of African Americans by rulings that reserved to state governments the authority to enforce the privileges and immunities of citizenship. The Fourteenth Amendment to the United States Constitution, it argued, had prohibited a state from "denying to any person within its jurisdiction equal protection of the laws," but the amendment did not "add anything to the rights which one citizen has under the Constitution against another." The citizen must look to the state government for protection against actions by other citizens that prevent him or her from assembling or voting or that lead to his or her murder or false imprisonment.[8]

The decisive formulation of this doctrine appeared in Justice Joseph P. Bradley's opinion striking down the public accommodation's provisions of the Civil Rights Act of 1875. Observing the long history of racial discrimination against free African Americans as guiding precedent and reasserting the argument that the federal government has no jurisdiction over social relations among citizens, Justice Bradley identified the "fundamental rights which are the essence of civil freedom" as the rights "to make and enforce contracts, to sue, be parties, give evidence, and to inherit, purchase, lease, sell and convey property." In words reminiscent of Godkin and Pike, Bradley explained,

> When a man has emerged from slavery, and by the aid of beneficent legislation has shaken off the inseparable concomitants of that state, there must be some stage in the progress of his elevation when he takes the rank of a mere citizen, and ceases to be the special favorite of the laws, and when his rights as a citizen are protected in the ordinary modes by which other men's rights are protected.[9]

The line of argument pursued by Godkin, Pike, and Bradley situated the end of federal protection of the civil and political rights of African Americans consistently within the framework of the defense of entrepreneurial independence from such legislation as, to them, represented the "special interests and aims" of propertyless voters. It also has a familiar ring for those who are attuned to the political and judicial discourse of our own time. Curbing federal authority, celebrating private arrangements, especially those of the marketplace, and casting a hostile eye upon what is called the awarding of special privileges to victims of past discrimination have all returned as guiding principles of public policy.[10]

Glenda Elizabeth Gilmore has shown how North Carolina, which had remained a beacon of racial progress (at least for black business and professional people) even after the early demise of its Republican regime, reversed course with terrifying speed at the end of the 1890s. Her account in *Gender and Jim Crow* provides an ominous warning to those who assume that once ensconced in law, civil rights can never be taken away. It took less than half a decade for North Carolina's governing Populist-Republican coalition to be replaced by a white supremacist regime, the city government of Wilmington to be overthrown violently, and the state to join the rest of the South in disfranchising black voters and imposing systematic legal segregation. By 1921 Carter G. Woodson could observe, "The citizenship of the Negro in this country is a fiction."[11]

The struggles that brought down the structure of legal segregation between the 1940s and the 1960s provide one of the most important and influential episodes in our country's history of genuine improvement in social life brought about by persistent and diverse grassroots efforts. Nevertheless, celebrating past victories for human liberation has all too often provided a means for denigrating subsequent attempts at further progress. Remembering the ways in which earlier African American struggles for emancipation were cut short provides an important warning against allowing the history of progress in civil rights to serve as a justification for inaction in our own times.

The International Context

Both this discussion of previous periods of retrogression in civil rights and the events surrounding our convention bear directly on the theme of the program: "The United States and the Wider World."

W. E. B. Du Bois wrote in 1906: "The Negro problem in America is but a local phase of a world problem." The world problem he had in mind was the consolidation of European and United States empires, all of which placed peoples of European ancestry in positions of domination over those Du Bois called "the darker . . . races in Asia and Africa, in America and the islands of the sea."[12] The domination of the globe by people of European origins had expanded steadily and undergone many changes during the preceding four hundred years. Those changes had brought with them corresponding transformations in the meanings of the human relationships we call race, which many papers at this convention have set out to clarify.

European states extended their power after 1500 by creating an international economy based on merchant capital, armed might, and fierce competition among themselves. Merchant capital financed the overseas shipment of commodities that had been produced by traditional relations of production in very diverse societies around the world. In this way European powers wove a mercantile web connecting many different preexisting social orders. But the same mercantile expansion also promoted a transatlantic commerce in slaves and in commodities that were cultivated and processed for export by slaves. The slave economies of the New World did not simply link together existing societies. On the contrary, they evicted or exterminated native populations and settled the land with plantations producing sugar, tobacco, rice, indigo, and cotton for use across the Atlantic Ocean. Like the later rise of industrial capitalism, plantation slavery generated a new social order.[13]

That transformation lies at the heart of United States history. During the 1950s and 1960s, economic historians oriented toward quantitative methods, most notably the future Nobel Prize winner Douglass C. North, demonstrated that the plantation economy generated well over half of United States exports before 1850, as well as the lion's share of the foreign exchange and investment capital used to finance the country's initial industrial growth. After 1810 the United States had more slaves than any other country in the world. Between independence and the Civil War, at least 125,000 new slaves were imported from Africa (counting only those who arrived legally), while more than a million slaves were moved from seaboard states to the booming region that stretched from southwestern Georgia to east Texas.[14]

Ira Berlin has argued that both the nature of slavery and the meanings imputed to race changed significantly between the 1620s and the 1820s and that they also varied from one region of the North American continent to another. There were "societies with slaves" in which chattel slaves were but one among diverse subordinate classes, some with members of European and Native American origin, but where slaves did not play a decisive role in wealth accumulation, for example, in the Chesapeake region before the 1660s or in the lower Mississippi Valley between 1730s and the 1780s. Quite different, he argues, were the "slave societies," such as both of those regions later represented. There the development of plantation economies and planters' acquisition of political dominance meant that "slavery stood at the center of economic production, and the master-slave relationship provided a model for all social relations."[15]

Back in the 1930s and 1940s, C. L. R. James, Eric Williams, and W. E. B. Du Bois reminded historians of labor and of immigration that African and African American slaves were actors of decisive importance in labor and immigration history. Plantation slaves were migrants, but their experience of migration was defined by the shattering brutality of the middle passage and by the fact that they came as property and that their descendants were destined to be the property of others. Just as the slaves' labors provided the foundation for colonial and antebellum economic growth, so defense and elaboration of their status as property provided a central element of the young nation's legal and constitutional framework.[16]

To put it bluntly, then, we must beware of starting our labor history courses with the strikes and the St. Louis commune of 1877 and of framing our histories of immigration exclusively with Frank Thistlethwaite's justly influential model of the 35 million Europeans who reached the United States after 1820. Long before the mills of Lowell were erected or Irish immigrants dug canals or artisans were converted into wage laborers, large concentrations of black propertyless workers were immigrants, from across the Atlantic or children of immigrants, toiled at fixed tasks under close supervision, and produced commodities sold for their masters' profits.[17]

It is also important, however, not only to incorporate slavery into our histories of immigration and labor but also to exercise care when we do so. The wide geographical areas from which slaves were drawn in Africa and the ways slaves were transshipped from ports of arrival in the New World rendered impossible anything resembling the chain migration patterns so characteristic of European and Asian immigrants. African Americans forged their identity as a nation *in America* where their lives were dominated by chattel slavery, even if not all were slaves. The European-dominated world economy was the matrix for African American life in yet other ways. Men and women of African ancestry who migrated voluntarily to the United States have played major roles in shaping African American political movements from colonial times onward, but especially during the twentieth century. Their stories constitute a much-neglected part of immigration history, for which the Thistlethwaite model provides little guidance.[18]

Moreover, the Atlantic economy, largely built around the slave trade and around commodities generated by slave labor, also nurtured a network of black, white, and brown maritime workers—wage laborers, slaves, tavern and shopkeepers, and artisans—that Paul Gilroy, Marcus Rediker, and Peter Linebaugh have shown us was saturated with rebellious and communitarian ideas very different from the teachings of John Locke. Just as many individuals who toiled on and around oceangoing vessels had direct encounters with Africa, Europe, the Caribbean, and North and South America, so their way of thinking about the black experience burst the conceptual confines of any one empire or nation-state.[19]

Consider but one familiar example: that of David Walker, whose mother was a slave and whose father a free black man in North Carolina and who came to Boston in the 1820s, where he was an agent for *Freedom's Journal.* Walker opened a slopshop (selling used and repaired clothing for sailors). It was from that shop that he distributed his *Appeal . . . To the Coloured Citizens of the World, but in particular, and very expressly, to Those of the United States of America*, often by sewing copies in the pockets and lining of jackets so that seamen might carry them to distant ports. Walker exemplified the diasporic vision that Robin D. G. Kelley has ably explored in his study of the writings of African American historians from the early nineteenth century to the present. Walker called on free blacks not only to seek "higher attainments than *wielding the razor* and *cleaning boots and shoes*" but also to deal with the "forever immovable *fact*, that your full glory and happiness, as well as those of all other coloured people under Heaven, shall never be fully consummated, but with the *entire emancipation of your enslaved brethren all over the world.*"[20]

This Pan-African vision of liberation coexisted with historic claims to the American soil and to the most inspiring parts of the American political and religious heritage, not only in the vigorous debates among African Americans but also within Walker's own thinking. He denounced colonizers, who would deport free blacks. He reproduced the unequivocal assertion of Bishop Richard Allen of the African Methodist Episcopal church:

> See the thousands of foreigners emigrating to America every year: and if there be ground sufficient for them to cultivate, and bread for them to eat, why would they wish to send the first *tillers* of the land away? This land which we have watered with our *tears* and *our blood*, is now our *mother country*, and we are well satisfied to stay where wisdom abounds and the gospel is free.[21]

The diasporic vision, the claim to citizenship, and the entitlement to the soil all surfaced vigorously when African Americans took action en masse during the Revolution and the Civil War. Their concerted flights from plantations, their negotiations with masters concerning terms of employment, and their wrangling for liberation with British, colonial, and, later, Union military forces have provided a healthy reminder to historians of the United States that effective political action can take forms other than voting.[22] Their voices projected political ideas that were richly informed by the controversies then raging among warring groups of whites but that also assumed a distinctive direction of their own. Among them were the anonymous leaflets found on the streets of New Orleans in 1865, signed only "A colored man." After describing the official war aims of the Union and of the Confederacy, one leaflet went on to ask, "what is the colored men fighting for"? Its answer was: "for our rights and liberty we care nothing about the union we have been in it Slaves over two hundred and fifty years." In a dazzling inversion of the political discourse then pronounced in Washington, the author concluded:

> we are the Blackest and bravest race the president says there is a wide Difference Between the black Race and the white race But we Say that white corn and yellow will mix by the taussels but the black and white Race must mix by the roots as they are so well mixed and has no taussels—freedom and liberty is the word with the Collered people.[23]

Local, National, and International

The anonymous author of that eloquent broadside reminds us of a second way the setting of our convention bears on the theme "The United States and the Wider World." Side by side with the legacy of slavery in the shaping of American history stands the convergence of peoples from many different climes and cultures. The meaning we impute to that convergence of peoples has been fashioned by recurrent conflicts over who is, or can be, an American. Those controversies have not focused only on African Americans. Moreover, the opposing sides in those conflicts have been influenced not only by events in the United States, as John Higham has demonstrated so well, but also by developments in the migrants' countries of origin and by the rise and demise of world empires.[24]

To understand the lives and struggles of working people, the power relationships they have both reproduced and challenged, and the varied identities they have manifested, we must learn to think on three interconnected levels: local, national, and global. The local setting is where men and women have pursued their personal goals in familiar contexts, identified friend and foe through everyday encounters, and forged, or failed to forge, collective action. This is why the best social history of the last generation (often to the exasperation of its critics) has concentrated research on particular localities. It is there that we can best scrutinize the panorama of economic relations and how identities "happen" amid historical change and conflict. But many practitioners of local studies have failed to confront the challenge of using their research to illuminate, and not to evade, the roles of the nation-state and of international economic relations in shaping local experience.[25]

The nation-state synthesis has long provided the favorite domain of historians, and for good reasons. State power and political mobilizations have played definitive roles in shaping the meaning of nationality, race, and class. As E. J. Hobsbawm has argued, nineteenth-century "national movements were expected to be movements for national *unification* or expansion," and they flourished in an epoch of international free-trade liberalism. America's

"Manifest Destiny" was surely no exception. Consider Susan Lee Johnson's splendid study of the southern goldfields during the California gold rush. It reveals not only the variety of peoples who encountered each other there (Yankees, southern whites, African Americans, Mexicans, Chileans, French, Miwoks, Yokuts, and Chinese—both Puntis and Hakkas) but also the decisive importance of Anglo-American domination of the machinery of state—primitive as it might have been—in defining ethnic hierarchies and economic opportunities and in assigning citizenship.[26]

All across the land between the 1830s and the 1850s, the convergence of unprecedented levels of immigration from Europe, conflicts over the geographic boundaries of chattel slavery, the annexation of half the territory of the Mexican republic, and the mobilization of mass electoral participation by national parties infused election campaigns with two conflicting definitions of American nationality. Democrats championed citizenship for anyone in the white race and exclusively for the white race within an expanding geographical domain and uninhibited global commerce, as well as a strictly secular and limited government that would leave property rights (including those in black slaves) and also religious practices and schools free of state direction but benefiting from state support. The unequivocal rejoinder came from the Know-Nothings and their American Republican precursors, who would have excluded aliens from public office, compelled all immigrants to live twenty-one years in republican America before they were eligible to join the body politic, nurtured the national economy, required lay ownership of all church properties, and provided public schooling for all, "subject to no sect" but with moral instruction informed by classroom use of the Bible.[27]

The victory of Union armies on the battlefields of the Civil War and the wartime struggles of the slaves, which effectively rendered impossible any compromise restoring the Union with slavery intact, enabled (indeed, compelled) the Republicans to enact a new national identity synthesis. It bestowed citizenship on "all persons born or naturalized in the United States, and subject to the jurisdiction thereof," and in 1870 legislation extended naturalization privileges "to aliens of African nativity and to persons of African descent" while providing penalties for voting by unnaturalized immigrants and pointedly *not* authorizing naturalization of Chinese. Congress rejected a proposal that it simply remove all references to race found in the existing Naturalization Act of 1790.[28] In short, the social and geographic boundaries defining the American nation were matters of political contestation so fierce as to be resolved only by prodigious bloodshed.

It is when we direct our imaginations toward the global level, however, that the distinctive character of the United States experience in inventing and reinventing ethnicity comes most clearly into focus. Although many other countries have received immigrants, the United States stands almost alone in defining itself as a "country of immigrants." It did not do so at the governmental and academic levels of discourse, however, until well into the twentieth century.

Ever since Frank Thistlethwaite delivered his magisterial 1960 paper on European population movements, historians have been forced to shift their focus from immigration to migration. Thistlethwaite reminded us that the overseas emigration of Europeans was an offshoot of a much larger movement of peoples within that continent, that two out of five Europeans who crossed the Atlantic did *not* go to the United States, and that a rising portion of those who did enter the United States before 1924 left again to return home. Among Italians, the largest national group of newcomers arriving in the United States after 1900, fully 60 percent returned to Italy. As Donna R. Gabaccia has phrased the argument: "Migrants became Italian Americans during years when state policy restricted their migrations as undesirable." The process of forming their new identity involved interaction among people from many different locales in southern Italy, the Anglo-American power structure, other immigrant neighbors, and subordinated peoples of color.[29]

Here was a case illustrating the conception of ethnicity advanced in 1992 by Kathleen Neils Conzen and her colleagues: "a process of construction or invention which incorporates, adapts, and amplifies preexisting communal solidarities, cultural attributes, and historical memories"—a process that is continually re-created in response to developments both in the United States and in the country of origin.[30] We need to focus our attention on those transnational interactions, as men and women shaped them in many local settings.

Moreover, a perspective that includes the wider world reminds us that patterns of migration as well as international flows of commodities and of capital have been fashioned as much by the imposing power of Gatling guns and dreadnoughts as by new techniques of production and communication and consumer demand. The destinations of migrants were determined by the shipping lanes, commodity needs, and legislation of industrializing powers. That is especially evident if we shift our attention away from Thistlethwaite's influential European paradigm and consider migration across the Pacific Ocean and within the Western Hemisphere. While 55 million Europeans migrated toward temperate zones between 1820 and 1920, a second broad current of transoceanic migrants, estimated by different historians at between 2 and 10 million people, moved primarily through equatorial zones. As Sidney Mintz pointed out in his great study of sugar and capitalism: "the link between sweated, tropical colonial labor and nonwhite labor was preserved, largely undisturbed by the end of slavery."[31]

That link proved especially important in the history of the far western states, of Alaska, and of Hawaii. By the 1870s a quarter of the work force of California was Chinese, and over the ensuing half century Japanese, Chinese, Koreans, and Filipinos came to dominate Hawaii's labor and political struggles. Starting with the act of 1882 banning entry of Chinese laborers, however, the doors admitting Asians to the mainland were systematically shut. The observation of the sociologist Nigel Harris that one hundred years ago "passports, visas, residence and work permits were not required" for travelers crossing international boundaries would have sounded like a cruel joke to Asians approaching the North American continent.[32]

Much of the best recent writing on immigration history has focused on the transnational networks fashioned by kinsfolk and neighbors that have escorted migrants to their destinations and nurtured a vast array of fraternal organizations, parishes, gymnastic clubs, newspapers, shops, and commemorations. Not only have those networks sheltered effective alternatives to the dominant institutions of the United States, they have also harbored political leaders whose activities encompassed the old country as well as the new. Thomas Masaryk, Jose Marti, Katayama Sen, Marcus Garvey, Ricardo Flores Magón, and many others come to mind. Exiled Irish revolutionaries of 1798, such as William James MacNeven, William Sampson, and John Binns, threw themselves into Jeffersonian politics from the moment of their arrival, without ever forgetting the Old Sod. Central to the history of Missouri is the role of German forty-eighters in promoting antislavery politics and providing a crucial military force to combat the state's secession—all as part and parcel of their continuing battle for a unified German republic. It has only been a few years since Father Jean-Bertrand Aristide generated similar political excitement in Haitian communities across the Northeast.[33]

Transnational networks were clearly evident during the strike wave of the mid-1880s, which labor historians have called the Great Upheaval, when workers fielded 180 local labor parties. The best-known such effort, Henry George's campaign for mayor of New York City in 1886, shows what can be learned from the scrutiny of immigrants' political action during the nineteenth century. The campaign was initiated by 175 local labor unions, which were enraged by police and judicial attacks against union strikes and boycotts. Nevertheless, as the "tailgate campaign" unfolded in working-class districts, it addressed much more than just the freedom to form unions. Campaign rhetoric focused (in the words of the insurgents' declaration of principles) on "the promotion of the health, comfort, education and recreation of [the city's] people, and the need for accessible mass transportation—issues that were later paramount for urban reformers of the Progressive Era.[34]

Henry George's economic theory offered an explanation of the shambles in which free-market growth left urban conditions while permitting the rich to buy their way out of the attendant squalor. This emphasis explains the appeal of the campaign to working-class women, who made themselves very visible in political mass meetings. In fact, George's secretary Louis Post later recalled that the thirty-four thousand signatures of male registered voters delivered to George by the unions to persuade him to run had been gathered mostly by women, who could not vote.[35]

The massive involvement of first-generation Irish and German immigrants in the campaign also produced a dramatic public schism in New York's Catholic parishes. The Reverend Edward McGlynn found in George's ideas a formula for bringing social life under the guidance of the Christian gospel and also for committing American Catholics, Protestants, and Jews to a common cause of social justice on this earth. Monsignor Thomas J. Preston, vicar-general of the New York Catholic archdiocese, proclaimed, on the contrary, that the church was "opposed to the candidacy of Mr. George," whose teachings "would prove the ruin of the workingmen he professes to befriend." When Archbishop Michael J. Corrigan removed McGlynn from his parish and later had him excommunicated, so many Catholic immigrants took to the streets in protest that the Cuban exile Jose Marti wrote: "Nothing happening today in the United States can compare in transcendence and interest to the struggle developing between the authorities of the Catholic Church and the Catholic people of New York."[36]

George's campaign attracted the support of many black New Yorkers, most notably Timothy Thomas Fortune, editor of the city's major African American newspaper, the *New York Age*. Indeed, Fortune drew on George's economic theory to single out "*the false system which makes the landlord possible*" as the fatal flaw in the postwar Republican program for Reconstruction. He summoned black and white laborers to stand together against their common oppressors.[37]

Similarly, the Irish Land League, fighting for tenant rights in the Irish countryside and in New York's tenements, often portrayed its battle as part of a worldwide struggle of oppressed peoples to defend their own access to the land against wealthy and often foreign monopolists. League partisans denounced the "human vultures" who were seizing the land of Native Americans in violation of treaty obligations, and they found kindred souls among Mexicans fighting for their land against bonanza ranches in the New Mexico territory, the *metis* of Manitoba battling under the leadership of Louis Riel against the whites overrunning their homeland, and peoples being colonized around the world. The 1879 founding meeting of the Land League in Connaught put its world view this way:

> From the China towers of Pekin to the round towers of Ireland, from the cabins of Connemara to the kraals of Kaffirland, from the wattled homes of the isles of Polynesia to the wigwams of North America, the cry is: "Down with invaders! Down with tyrants!" Every man to have his own land—every man to have his own home![38]

New York's immigrant-based urban reform movement disintegrated soon after the 1886 elections, with socialists and single taxers battling each other and both sides narrowing their immediate demands to trade-union questions (in effect, abandoning the immigrant women and voters who had urged them on). But the vision of government's proper role in correcting the failures and inequities of a market economy waxed even more influential in immigrant politics after 1900—in campaigns for municipal services, in the growing influence of socialism, and in the prominence of Protestant immigrants in local activities of the Bull Moose Republicans.[39]

The years 1916 to 1922 produced a strike wave that was far larger and longer lasting than that of the 1880s, though it has received much less attention from historians. Recent immigrants participated in strikes and unions on an unprecedented scale, while they were bombarded with conflicting ideological appeals from immigrant nationalists, government agencies cultivating patriotism toward the United States, business leaders promoting company loyalty, labor organizers advocating an "American style" of trade unionism, revolutionaries teaching class consciousness, and families urging them to send help or to come back home. The ravages of war in their countries of origin encouraged the belief that only social revolution could restore peace. High levels of employment stimulated by the war and revolutionary upheavals around the world whetted the appetites of working men and women for a better life. The eight-hour day emerged as the favorite embodiment of those aspirations.[40]

At no other time since independence had there been such distance between official and popular discourse. True, immigrant workers freely borrowed phrases and symbols from all the rhetoric that whirled about them. But they blended those phrases and symbols in ways that would confound historians who hunt for neat dichotomies or straightforward progress toward assimilation or modernization. Strikers often marched behind American flags, grouped by nationality, while singing "The International."[41]

They left us a rich record of their own words in many languages. They picked ideas from the ideology of citizenship, rights, and national self-determination, and they mixed that vocabulary with the language of class consciousness, of solidarity, of internationalism. They blended apocalyptic visions with clearly articulated trade-union demands. Through it all, an idyllic image of life on the land, back home, provided an irrepressible counterpoint.[42]

The soaring hopes expressed in that working-class discourse were decisively crushed during the immediate postwar years. Immigrants' thoughts then turned inward toward home, family, and respect among neighbors, leaving intensely politicized minorities in their midst, who staked their hopes on revolutions abroad. Moreover, they now found the language of American nationality turned against them. During the war, testified Rose and Grace Santora of Lawrence, Massachusetts, the "bosses then called all the Italians 'American people.' Now they are 'foreigners.'"[43]

Who Is an American?

The easy entry into the United States and other countries that people with European forebears had enjoyed for almost a century ended abruptly after 1918. In the words of Nigel Harris: "the world became fenced." While Congress recruited academic experts to help it determine what peoples were acceptable and in what numbers, the Ku Klux Klan rose briefly to become a formidable force in northern urban politics, claiming to defend the country's schools, government, and social conduct against the foreign Catholic menace.[44]

Militant affirmation of the country's Anglo-Saxon character both antedated and survived the meteoric rise and decline of the second Ku Klux Klan. Patriotic societies and flag-centered commemorations had sprouted up in the early 1890s, in reaction to labor's Great Upheaval and also to the solicitation of immigrant votes by William McKinley and other eminent Republicans.[45] They flourished during and after World War I and survived to galvanize opponents of the New Deal.

The Immigration Act of 1924 authorized a board of scholars to determine the proportion of each European nationality, not among recent immigrants, but "in the national blood" by enumerating the "national and linguistic stocks" found in 1790. The purpose of the exercise, which enjoyed the imprimatur of the American Council of Learned Societies, was to preserve American institutions by "continuing the blood of the United States in its present mixture." As Dr. Harry H. Laughlin of the Carnegie Institution of Washington testified in 1928, "The preservation of national institutions depends principally upon the conservation of the race which builds them."[46]

The bizarre scholarly effort of the Quota Board to trace the nation's bloodlines enjoyed ardent support within the faculties of Yale, Harvard, and Princeton universities, but it generated such angry quarrels among filiopietistic societies of British, Scandinavian, and German ancestry over who got here first as to jeopardize the prospects of Republican candidates for Congress, inducing President Calvin Coolidge and candidate Herbert Hoover to back away from legislating quotas and to place future control of immigration in the hands of the executive branch. The fierce identity politics of the 1920s also inspired leaders of ethnic groups ranked as undesirable by Congress to denounce the Anglo-Saxon bias of history textbooks and to demand in vain the inclusion of illustrious figures from their own nationalities in the pantheon of American history. Although a handful of midwestern historians, including George M. Stephenson, Theodore Blegen, and Carl Wittke, laid the foundations of scholarly study of immigration history, they were studiously ignored by the leading authorities of our profession.[47]

By the mid-1930s, however, the escalating influence of the urban working class in industrial and political life placed the discursive link between constitutional government and the "national blood" under siege. Between 1930 and

1934, the United States, under both Republican and Democratic administrations (despite their important differences) responded to the depression with much the same turn toward autarky evident elsewhere in the world: raising tariffs, leaving the gold standard, repatriating more than 365,000 Mexican immigrants, and deporting unprecedented numbers of Europeans, while several states restricted relief and public works employment to citizens. By the middle of the decade, however, important features of American political life differed remarkably from the national coalitions or open dictatorships prevalent in Europe. Party rivalries for office remained intense here, right-wing nationalism, however vigorous, was confined to the role of opposition, and official policy encouraged workers of all races in manufacturing and mining to unionize. The determination of Germany and Italy to redraw the map of Europe and Africa and of Japan to supplant European empires with a "new order in Greater East Asia," cast a pall of impending war over the entire decade.[48]

Many species of right-wing nationalism continued to make themselves well heard. The abiding appeal of Anglo-Saxon hegemony was evident in the immense popularity of Kenneth L. Roberts's novels deploring the American break with England in 1776. Far more virulent, but no less visible, was the rise of the German-American Bund and Italian, Croat, and Ukrainian fascist organizations, which espoused the national causes of their homelands while repudiating laissez-faire liberalism, and of the Christian Front, which solidified a vociferous anti-Semitic united front by 1938–1940. Nevertheless, a left-liberal alliance rooted in urban politics and the industrial union movement successfully reshaped the political agenda in Washington and in most industrial states and nurtured a rival form of popular patriotism that was linked to the causes of social reform at home and, as E. J. Hobsbawm has written, "emerged in the context of an international ideological civil war." A 57 percent increase in the presidential electorate between 1924 and 1936 had been generated primarily by the coming of age of immigrants' children and the naturalization of their parents. Voting patterns in the country's urban industrial centers congealed more clearly along class lines than ever before in the country's history. Amid the welter of what Michael Denning has aptly called "the competing populist rhetorics of the time," the new voters and the new unions inspired an outpouring of literary and artistic creativity rooted in working-class struggles and championing worldwide resistance to fascism.[49]

New Deal supporters nurtured a conception of "American" more capacious than that which prevailed in the Ivy League, though cleansed of the subversive challenge expressed by the strikers of 1919. Earl Robinson's "Ballad for Americans," which became instantly famous when Paul Robeson sang it on network radio in November 1939, epitomized this new sense of nationality. After he had narrated the role of ordinary people in national triumphs from the Revolution to the defeat of slavery, Robeson responded to insistent demands from the chorus to tell who he was with a long list of men's and women's mundane occupations and concluding: "All of them. I am the et ceteras. And the and so forths that do the work." That evoked the hostile response, "What are you trying to give us? Are you an American?" Robeson's reply earned instant and lasting fame:

> Am I an American? I'm just an Irish, Negro, Jewish, Italian, French, and English, Spanish, Russian, Chinese, Polish, Scotch, Hungarian, Litvak, Swedish, Finnish, Canadian, Greek and Turk, and Czech and double Czech American.[50]

Barbara D. Savage has enriched our understanding of the impact of immigrants on New Deal political and cultural life by studying network radio broadcasts promoted by the Roosevelt administration, such as the twenty-four-episode series *Americans All, Immigrants All.* As Savage wrote, "The show worked to fortify a sense of American patriotism among immigrants who for the first time heard the national government embracing and claiming them as valued and valuable citizens and attempting to erase the negative connotation attached to the word 'immigrant.'" Scriptwriters who placed a story of immigrants' toil, success, and contributions to the nation at the core of American patriotism borrowed heavily from labor movement rhetoric going back to the Civil War. Their image of America was a locus of battle—battle over belonging and battle over political and economic goals—not a set of established beliefs, rooted in the country's historic "mixture of blood," to which newcomers had to adapt.[51]

The New Deal's capacious image of America, which linked patriotism to the cause of social reform, had been evoked by millions of new urban voters and by a militant labor movement committed to transforming industrial and political life. By the end of the 1940s, however, representatives of the new white urban voting blocs were committed primarily to preserving their earlier gains, legislative restraints and political purges had sharply curtailed the militancy and aspirations of the union movement and minimized its allure for reform-minded intellectuals, while both major parties made containment of Communism their major proclaimed objective. In that context the New Deal reinvention of America could be melded into the conservative conception of a glorious national legacy to be defended against a foreign menace, and it was.[52]

In fact, the Republican party had offered a preview of this Fortress America image at the party's 1940 convention in Philadelphia. The first three days were devoted to patriotic prayers, pageants, and songs, dramatizing the legacy of 1776, which only a Republican victory at the polls could redeem from the Democrats' effort to impose on the country a third term for Franklin D. Roosevelt. The president had, in the introductory words of Harold Stassen, hobbled industry "by bureaucratic interference and dreamy-eyed governmental delays at every turn while the army and navy plead in vain for the release of restrictions so they can speed up defense" and had exposed the United States to a "fifth column of traitors." In that context there was even a place for an ecstatically received performance of the "Ballad for Americans" (to be sure, without Paul Robeson as soloist).[53]

Although the image of the United States as a "nation of nations" had been born of working people's struggles for social reform, the conservative consensus embraced it as a way of denigrating any further efforts to expand the scope of social welfare legislation, economic planning, and organized labor's influence. Moreover, even the writers of New Deal radio programs had declined to deal with the country's history of racial oppression. By dint of vigorous efforts, African American intellectuals did succeed in including "The Negro" as a final show of the series *Americans All, Immigrants All* but African Americans' demand for inclusion had been met by squeezing their history into the mold of immigrant progress. In much the same way, the New Deal provided economic gains for all working people but left the edifice of segregation standing, not only in the South but also in northern cities controlled by the new urban political coalitions. Similarly, as Barbara Savage wrote, the bitter history of exclusion of, and discrimination against, Asian Americans "made a celebratory history a particularly dishonest, artificial, and flawed construction." The enslavement of Africans had long been a fundamental feature of the economic and political order through which Europeans sought to fulfill their dreams, and even in the New Deal era, precious few people of European descent disputed the exclusion of Asians from our shores. But, as Ernest Renan wrote in 1882: "Forgetfulness and, I would say, even historical falsehoods are an essential factor in the formation of a nation, and so it is that the progress of historical studies is often a danger for the spirit of nationality."[54]

That is why it has been incumbent upon us to pursue rigorous historical research and in the same spirit to act together to thwart any resurgence of racist exclusion in our own day and age. The struggles of migrants of every clime and complexion have transformed American life in every generation within limits set by that age. They remind us that capitalist economic development has relentlessly created social formations from which popular struggles have sprung and subsequently wiped those formations off the face of the earth, usually leaving the goals for which working people acted at best only partially realized, but never leaving society and politics unchanged. They also remind us that not everything about our present "global economy" is without precedent.

Our own small part in making history links us to this legacy of popular action in the recurrent reinvention of our nation. But as we historians investigate yesterday's confrontations we must beware the traps laid by the myth of American success and innocence on one flank and by flag-waving celebration of causes with which we associate ourselves on the other. If our profession is to flourish in the present and help us all forge a better future, we must draw upon the contributions of all that rich variety of men and women that our country has known. Our collective investigation of America's past must not only be characterized by careful attention to each other's work but also be informed by honest, painstaking research and by conceptual frameworks that encompass and integrate struggle and change at the local, national, and global levels.

Notes

Reprinted courtesy of the *Journal of American History.*

This article is an expanded version of the presidential address delivered to the convention of the Organization of American Historians in St. Louis on March 31, 2000. I am deeply indebted to James R. Barrett, Barbara J. Fields, and John Higham for their comments on and criticisms of an earlier version.

1. "Justice Department Files Lawsuit against Adam's Mark Hotel Chain," press release, Dec. 16, 1999, *United States v. HBE Corporation* (M. D. Fla. 1999), http://www.usdoj.gov/cn/housing/caselist.htm; *Equal Employment Opportunities Commission v. HBE Corporation,* 135 F. 3d 543 (8th Cir. 1998), section VB, point 38.

2. "Justice Department Settles Lawsuit against the Adam's Mark Chain," press release, March 21, 2000, http://www.usdoj.gov/opa/pr/2000/March/134cr.htm; David Montgomery, "We Met in St. Louis," OAH Newsletter, 28 (May 2000), 1, 10.

3. Ray Allen Billington, "From Association to Organization: The OAH in the Bad Old Days," *Journal of American History* 65 (June 1978): 78–83; Thomas D. Clark, "Our Roots Flourished in the Valley," *ibid.*, 93–97; Howard K. Beale to Thomas D. Clark, Feb. 2, 1954 (in David Montgomery's possession). I am extremely grateful to professors William Preston and Gerda Ray for bringing the articles to my attention and making Beale's letter available to me. See also Howard K. Beale, "The Professional Historian: His Theory and His Practice," *Pacific Historical Review*, 12 (August 1953): 227–55. I am grateful to Professor John Higham for bringing this article to my attention.

4. C. Vann Woodward, *The Burden of Southern History* (1960; Baton Rouge, 1968), 209–10.

5. Ira Berlin, *Many Thousands Gone: The First Two Centuries of Slavery in North America* (Cambridge, Mass., 1998); Sylvia R. Frey, *Water from the Rock: Black Resistance in a Revolutionary Age* (Princeton, 1991); David B. Davis, "Significance of Excluding Slavery from the Old Northwest in 1787," *Indiana Magazine of History* 84 (March 1988): 75–89; Leon F. Litwack, *North of Slavery: The Negro in the Free States, 1790–1860* (Chicago, 1961); Barbara Jeanne Fields, *Slavery and Freedom on the Middle Ground: Maryland during the Nineteenth Century* (New Haven, 1985); Gary B. Nash, *Forging Freedom: The Freedmen of Philadelphia's Black Community, 1720–1840* (Cambridge, Mass., 1988); W. Jeffrey Bolster, *Black Jacks: African American Seamen in the Age of Sail* (Cambridge, Mass., 1997); David R. Roediger, *Wages of Whiteness: Race and the Making of the American Working Class* (London, 1991); *Hobbes v. Fogg*, 6 Watts 553 at 558 (1837).

6. James D. Richardson, ed., *A Compilation of the Messages and Papers of the Presidents, 1789–1897* (10 vols., Washington, 1897), VII, 55–56.

7. Edwin L. Godkin, "Classes in Politics," *Nation*, June 27, 1867, 519–20; James Shepherd Pike, *The Prostrate State: South Carolina Under Negro Government* (New York, 1874). On Pike's work, see Nancy Cohen, "Problem of Democracy in the Age of Capital: Reconstructing American Liberalism, 1865–1890" (PhD diss., Columbia University, 1995), 150–57. This line of argument is central to the interpretation of the Bourbon Redeemers in C. Vann Woodward, *Origins of the New South, 1877–1913* (Baton Rouge, 1951), and C. Vann Woodward, *Reunion and Reaction: The Compromise of 1877 and the End of Reconstruction* (Garden City, 1956). See also Scott Reynolds Nelson, *Iron Confederacies: Southern Railways, Klan Violence, and Reconstruction* (Chapel Hill, 1999), 163–82.

8. *United States v. Cruikshank*, 92 U.S. 542, 555 (1876).

9. *The Civil Rights Cases*, 109 U.S. 3, 22, 25 (1883).

10. Morgan Kousser, *Colorblind Injustice: Minority Voting Rights and the Undoing of the Second Reconstruction* (Chapel Hill, 1999). Neither the courts nor Congress has ever overturned the 1883 Civil Rights decision, according to Jack M. Balkin, a professor of constitutional law at Yale University. The civil rights laws of the 1960s used the interstate commerce clause of the Constitution as their basis, taking advantage of the expansion of federal power to regulate economic activity that the Supreme Court had authorized in the 1930s. *New York Times*, May 17, 2000, A23.

11. Glenda Elizabeth Gilmore, *Gender and Jim Crow: Women and the Politics of White Supremacy in North Carolina, 1896–1920* (Chapel Hill, 1996). For Carter G. Woodson's statement, see Robin D. G. Kelley, "'But a Local Phase of a World Problem': Black History's Global Vision, 1883–1950," *Journal of American History* 86 (December 1999): 1049. C. Vann Woodward, *Tom Watson: Agrarian Rebel* (New York, 1938). See also J. Morgan Kousser, *Shaping of Southern Politics: Suffrage Restriction and the Establishment of the One-Party South* (New Haven, 1974); Neil R. McMillen, *Dark Journey: Black Mississippians in the Age of Jim Crow* (Urbana, 1989); and Rayford W. Logan, *Negro in American Life and Thought: The Nadir, 1877–1901* (New York, 1954). Works that dispute Woodward by emphasizing the continuity of segregation and of political leadership in the post-Civil War South include Howard N. Rabinowitz, *Race Relations in the Urban South, 1865–1890* (Urbana, 1980); and Jonathan M. Wiener, *Social Origins of the New South: Alabama, 1860–1885* (Baton Rouge, 1978).

12. Kelley, "'But a Local Phase of a World Problem,'" 1054; W. E. Burghardt Du Bois, *The Souls of Black Folk: Essays and Sketches* (1903; Greenwich, 1961), 23.

13. Fernand Braudel, *Civilization and Capitalism, 15th-18th Century*, trans. Sian Reynolds (3 vols., New York, 1984), III; C. L. R. James, *Black Jacobins: Toussaint L'Ouverture and the San Domingo Revolution* (New York, 1963); Sidney W. Mintz, *Sweetness and Power: The Place of Sugar in Modern History* (New York, 1985); Eugene D. Genovese and Elizabeth Fox-Genovese, *Fruits of Merchant Capital: Slavery and Bourgeois Property in the Rise and Expansion of Capitalism* (New York, 1983).

14. Douglass C. North, *Economic Growth of the United States, 1790–1860* (New York, 1966), 62–96, 189–213; Robert William Fogel and Stanley L. Engerman, *Time*

on the Cross: The Economics of American Negro Slavery (Boston, 1974); William N. Parker, ed., *Trends in the American Economy in the Nineteenth Century* (Princeton, 1960); George Rogers Taylor, *Transportation Revolution* (New York, 1951). Internal slave trade figures are from Berlin, *Many Thousands Gone*, 308, 344, 359.

15. Berlin, *Many Thousands Gone*, 8.

16. *Ibid.*, 103; James, *Black Jacobins*; Eric Williams, *Capitalism and Slavery* (Chapel Hill, 1944); W. E. B. DuBois, *Black Reconstruction in America, 1860–1880* (New York, 1935).

17. For the classic formulation of this argument, see James, *Black Jacobins*, 392. On the St. Louis commune, see David T. Burbank, *Reign of the Rabble: The St. Louis General Strike of 1877* (New York, 1966); Philip S. Foner, *Great Labor Uprising of 1877* (New York, 1977), 157–87; and J. A. Dacus, *Annals of the Great Strikes in the United States* (Chicago, 1877), 352–405. Frank Thistlethwaite, "Migration from Europe Overseas in the Nineteenth and Twentieth Centuries," XI. *Congrés international des sciences historiques: Rapports (Eleventh International Congress of Historical Sciences: Reports)* (Stockholm, 1960), 32–60.

18. Berlin, *Many Thousands Gone*, 99–105. See also Albert J. Raboteau, *Slave Religion: The "Invisible Institution" in the Antebellum South* (New York, 1978); Peter H. Wood, *Black Majority: Negroes in Colonial South Carolina from 1670 through the Stono Rebellion* (New York, 1974); Michael A. Gomez, *Exchanging Our Country Marks: The Transformation of African Identities in the Colonial and Antebellum South* (Chapel Hill, 1998); and Sterling Stuckey, *Slave Culture: Nationalist Theory and the Foundations of Black America* (New York, 1987). Cf. Eugene D. Genovese, *Roll, Jordan, Roll: The World the Slaves Made* (New York, 1974). Winston James, *Holding Aloft the Banner of Ethiopia: Caribbean Radicalism in Early Twentieth-Century America* (London, 1998).

19. Paul Gilroy, *The Black Atlantic: Modernity and Double Consciousness* (Cambridge, Mass., 1993); Marcus Rediker, *Between the Devil and the Deep Blue Sea: Merchant Seamen, Pirates, and the Anglo-American Maritime World, 1700–1750* (New York, 1987), 201–53; Peter Linebaugh, *A Dish with One Spoon: The American Experience of Slavery and the Commons in the Transformation of Three Officers of the English Crown into Freedom Fighters for the United Irish* (Toledo, 1999).

20. Kelley, "'But a Local Phase of a World Problem'"; David Walker, *Appeal in Four Articles; Together with a Preamble, To the Coloured Citizens of the World, But in particular, and very expressly, to Those of the United States of America*, ed. Charles M. Wiltse (New York, 1965), 29, xiv.

21. Walker, *Appeal*, 57–58; Cf. Bayley Wyat, *A Freedman's Speech* (Philadelphia, 1867), quoted in Eric Foner, *Nothing but Freedom: Emancipation and Its Legacy* (Baton Rouge, 1983), 56. For the argument that black writers did not link their history and hopes to the United States, see Kelley, "'But a Local Phase of a World Problem,'" 1048.

22. Frey, *Water from the Rock*, 50–66, 108–205; Ira Berlin et al., eds., *Freedom: A Documentary History of Emancipation, 1861–1867*, series 1, vol. I: *The Destruction of Slavery* (New York, 1985); Ira Berlin et al., *Slaves No More: Three Essays on Emancipation and the Civil War* (New York, 1992).

23. Ira Berlin et al., eds., *Freedom: A Documentary History of Emancipation, 1861–1867, series 2: The Black Military Experience* (New York, 1982), 155, 157.

24. John Higham, "From Process to Structure: Formulations of American Immigration History," in *American Immigrants and Their Generations: Studies and Commentaries on the Hansen Thesis after Fifty Years*, ed. Peter Kivisto and Dag Blanck (Urbana, 1990); David Montgomery, "Nationalism, American Patriotism, and Class Consciousness among Immigrant Workers in the United States in the Epoch of World War I," in *"Struggle a Hard Battle": Essays on Working-Class Immigrants*, ed. Dirk Hoerder (DeKalb, 1986), 327–51; David Montgomery, "Empire, Race, and Working-Class Mobilizations," in *Racializing Class, Classifying Race: Labour and Difference in Britain, the USA, and Africa*, ed. Peter Alexander and Rick Halpern (London, 1999), 1–31.

25. For examples of local studies that have encompassed national and international dimensions, see Iver Bernstein, *New York City Draft Riots: Their Significance for American Society and Politics in the Age of the Civil War* (New York, 1990); Herbert G. Gutman, *Power and Culture: Essays on the American Working Class*, ed. Ira Berlin (New York, 1987); Christine Stansell, *City of Women: Sex and Class in New York, 1789–1860* (New York, 1986); Alexander Saxton, *The Indispensable Enemy: Labor and the Anti-Chinese Movement in California* (Berkeley, 1971); Karen Sawislak, *Smoldering City: Chicagoans and the Great Fire, 1871–1874* (Chicago, 1995); and Julie Saville, *The Work of Reconstruction: From Slave Labor to Wage Labor in South Carolina, 1860–1870* (New York, 1994).

26. E. J. Hobsbawm, *Nations and Nationalism since 1780: Programme, Myth, Reality* (New York, 1990), 25, 29, 33; Susan Lee Johnson, *Roaring Camp: The Social World of the California Gold Rush* (New York, 2000).

27. Jean Baker, *Affairs of Party: The Political Culture of Northern Democrats in the Mid-Nineteenth Century* (Ithaca, 1983); Tyler Gregory Anbinder, *Nativism and Slavery: The Northern Know-Nothings and the Politics of the 1850s* (New York, 1992); Daniel W. Howe, *Political Culture of American Whigs* (Chicago, 1979); R. Laurence Moore, "Bible Reading and Nonsectarian Schooling: The Failure of Religious Instruction in Nineteenth-Century Public Education," *Journal of American History* 86 (March 2000): 1581–99; David Montgomery, "The Shuttle and the Cross: Weavers and Artisans in the Kensington Riots of 1844," *Journal of Social History* 5 (Spring 1972): 411–46. For a lucid presentation of the Know-Nothing position, see Anna Ella Carroll, *The Great American Battle; or, The Contest between Christianity and Political Romanism* (New York, 1856). On the role of political parties in reinventing nationality and race, see Andrew Gyory, *Closing the Gate: Race, Politics, and the Chinese Exclusion Act* (Chapel Hill, 1998).

28. Edward McPherson, *Political History of the United States of America during the Period of Reconstruction* (Washington, 1875), 618–19; Gyory, *Closing the Gate*, 50–53; *Naturalization Act of 1790*, ch. 3, 1 Stat. 103 (1790). Although the best discussions of the naturalization act appear in writings on Asian Americans and white racism, congressional debates reveal that the primary concern of the authors of the law was to impede fraudulent or speedy naturalization by European immigrants. Postmodernist theories minimize conflicts and dialectical development within the

dominant discourse; see, for example, an otherwise insightful work: Matthew Frye Jacobson, *Whiteness of a Different Color: European Immigrants and the Alchemy of Race* (Cambridge, Mass., 1998), 39–43.

29. Thistlethwaite, "Migration from Europe Overseas"; Donna Gabaccia, "The 'Yellow Peril' and the 'Chinese of Europe': Global Perspectives on Race and Labor, 1815–1930," in *Migration, Migration History, History: Old Paradigms and New Perspectives*, eds. Jan Lucassen and Leo Lucassen (New York, 1997), 177–96; Rudolph J. Vecoli, "Foreword," in Marie Hall Ets, *Rosa: The Life of an Italian Immigrant* (Minneapolis, 1970), viii. Similar calculations of return rates can be found in David Montgomery, *Fall of the House of Labor: The Workplace, the State, and American Labor Activism, 1865–1925* (New York, 1987), 74. Donna R. Gabaccia, "Is Everywhere Nowhere? Nomads, Nations, and the Immigrant Paradigm of United States History," *Journal of American History* 86 (Dec. 1999): 1132.

30. Kathleen Neils Conzen et al., "The Invention of Ethnicity: A Perspective from the U.S.A.," *Journal of American Ethnic History* 12 (Fall 1992): 5.

31. Mintz, *Sweetness and Power*, 71; David Northrup, *Indentured Labor in the Age of Imperialism. 1834–1922* (New York, 1995), 8–9, 56–61, tables Al and A2; Stanley L. Engerman, "Servants to Slaves to Servants: Contract Labour and European Expansion," in *Colonialism and Migration: Indentured Labour before and after Slavery*, ed. P. C. Emmer (The Hague, 1986), 263–94; Hugh Tinker, *A New System of Slavery: The Export of Indian Labour Overseas, 1830–1920* (London, 1974).

32. Chinese Exclusion Act of May 6, 1882, 22 Stat. 58 (1882); Nigel Harris, *The New Untouchables: Immigration and the New World Worker* (London, 1995), 6; Eleanor C. Nordyke, *The Peopling of Hawaii* (Honolulu, 1977); Sucheng Chan, ed., *Entry Denied: Exclusion and the Chinese Community in America. 1882–1943* (Philadelphia, 1991); Ronald T. Takaki, *Strangers from a Different Shore: A History of Asian Americans* (New York, 1990); Lucie Cheng and Edna Bonacich, eds., *Labor Immigration under Capitalism: Asian Workers in the United States before World War II* (Berkeley, 1984).

33. On transoceanic networks, see Michael Hanagan, "Labor History and the New Migration History: A Review Essay," *International Labor and Working-Class History* 54 (Fall 1998): 57–79; Donna R. Gabaccia, "Worker Internationalism and Italian Labor Migration, 1870–1919," *ibid.*, 45 (Spring 1994), 63–79; Alejandro Portes, ed., *The Economic Sociology of Immigration: Essays on Networks, Ethnicity, and Entrepreneurship* (New York, 1995); Monika Glettler, *Pittsburg-Wien-Budapest: Programm und Praxis der Nationalitätenpolitik bei der Auswanderung der ungarischen Slowaken nach Amerika um 1900* (Pittsburgh-Vienna-Budapest: The program and practice of nationality policy concerning the emigration of Hungarian Slovaks to America around 1900) (Vienna, 1980); and Madeline Yuan-yin Hsu, "Living Abroad and Faring Well: Migration and Transnationalism in Taishan County, Guandong, 1904–1939" (PhD diss., Yale University, 1996). On Irish exiles of 1798, see Victor R. Greene, *American Immigrant Leaders, 1800–1910: Marginality and Identity* (Baltimore, 1987), 21–29; and John Binns, *Recollections of the Life of John Binns: Twenty-Nine Years in Europe and Fifty-Three in the United States* (Philadelphia, 1854). On Germans, see Bruce Levine, *The Spirit of 1848: German Immigrants, Labor Conflict,*

and the Coming of the Civil War (Urbana, 1992); Walter D. Kamphoefner, "St. Louis Germans and the Republican Party, 1818–1860," *Mid-America* 57 (April 1975): 69–88; and Jay Monaghan, *Civil War on the Western Border, 1854–1865* (Boston, 1955), 129–81.

34. Leon Fink, *Workingmen's Democracy: The Knights of Labor and American Politics* (Urbana, 1983); Peter A. Speek, *The Single Tax and the Labor Movement* (Madison, 1917), 68; David Scobey, "Boycotting the Politics Factory: Labor Radicalism and the New York City Mayoral Election of 1884," *Radical History Review* 28–30 (1984), 280–326. Melvin G. Holli's distinction between social reformers and structural Reformers among Progressives is helpful in situating Henry George historically. Melvin G. Holli, *The American Mayor: The Best and the Worst Big-City Leaders* (University Park, 1999), 59–61.

35. Henry George, *Progress and Poverty: An Inquiry into the Cause of Industrial Depressions and of Increase of Want with Increase of Wealth. A Remedy* (1885; New York, 1935); Henry George, *Social Problems* (London, 1931). On the prominence of women in the campaign, see Louis F. Post, *The Prophet of San Francisco: Personal Memories and Interpretations of Henry George* (New York, 1930), 73, 86.

36. Stephen Bell, *Rebel, Priest, and Prophet: A Biography of Dr. Edward McGlynn* (New York, 1937); Manuel S. "Jeff" Shanaberger, "Edward McGlynn: A Missionary Priest and His Social Gospel," *U.S. Catholic Historian* 13 (Summer 1995): 23–47. For Thomas J. Preston's statement, see Speek, *Single Tax and the Labor Movement*, 85. The argument that George's program would hurt workers had been a central theme of Abram S. Hewitt's campaign for mayor. See Henry George Jr., *The Life of Henry George* (New York, 1900), 473. José Martí, "El Cisma de los Catolicos de New York" (The Schism of the New York Catholics), in *Marti y la Iglesia Catolica Antologias Cubanas* (Marti and the Catholic church, Cuban anthologies) (Havana,. n.d.), 31. My translation from the Spanish original: "Nada de lo que sucede hoy en los Estados Unidos es comparable en transcendencia e interés, a la lucha empañada entre las autoridades de la Iglesia Católica y el pueblo católico de New York."

37. Timothy Thomas Fortune, *Black and White: Land, Labor, Politics in the South* (New York, 1884), 34–35, 174.

38. For the Land League's statement, see Theodore W. Moody, *Davitt and Irish Revolution, 1846–82* (New York, 1981), 289. See two editorials by Patrick Ford denouncing United States wars against the Sioux, *Irish World*, Sept. 23, 1876, 2. Robert J. Rosenbaum, *Mexicano Resistance in the Southwest: "The Sacred Right of Self-Preservation"* (Austin, 1981), 99–139. For Louis Riel's poem expressing his hopes for Irish American support, see Thomas Flanagan, *Louis "David" Riel: Prophet of the New World* (Toronto, 1996), 114. After the failure of Riel's 1885 insurrection, however, two Fenians to whom he had proposed joint armed action in 1878 declared to the press that they had laughed at his proposal. *Ibid.*, 108. The Land League of Homestead, Pennsylvania, welcomed into its ranks the first Poles to work in the mill in 1882 according to Paul Krause, *The Battle for Homestead 1880–1892: Politics, Culture, and Steel* (Pittsburgh, 1992), 221–22. Arif Dirlik has insightfully called place consciousness the "radical other" of global capitalism; see Grace Lee Boggs, "A Question of Place," *Monthly Review*, 52 (June 2000), 19.

39. On immigrants and municipal socialism, see Donald Pienkos, "Politics, Religion, and Change in Polish Milwaukee, 1900–1930," in *Politics and the Immigrant*, ed. George E. Pozzetta (New York, 1991), 178–209; Sally M. Miller, *Victor Berger and the Promise of Constructive Socialism, 1910–1920* (Westport, 1973); Cecelia E. Bucki, "The Pursuit of Political Power: Class, Ethnicity, and Municipal Politics in Interwar Bridgeport, 1915–1936" (PhD diss., University of Pittsburgh, 1991); and Mary Cygan, "Political and Cultural Leadership in an Immigrant Community: Polish-American Socialism, 1880–1950" (PhD diss., Northwestern University, 1989). On the less well studied immigrant participants in progressive Democratic and Republican urban politics, see Thomas M. Henderson, "Immigrant Politician: Salvatore Cotillo, Progressive Ethnic," *International Migration Review* 16 (Spring 1979): 81–102; A. William Hoglund, *Finnish Immigrants in America, 1880–1920* (Madison, 1960), 114–18; Gwendolyn Mink, *Old Labor and New Immigrants in American Political Development: Union, Party, and State, 1875–1920* (Ithaca, 1986), 226–27; Thomas Bell, *Out of This Furnace* (Pittsburgh, 1976), 187–90; and Thomas Kessner, *Fiorello La Guardia and the Rise of Modern New York* (New York, 1989).

40. P. K. Edwards, *Strikes in the United States; 1881–1974* (New York, 1981), 12–29; Montgomery, *Fall of the House of Labor*, 320–464; David Montgomery, "New Tendencies in Union Struggles in Europe and the United States, 1916–1922," in *Work, Community, and Power: The Experience of Labor in Europe and America, 1900–1925*, eds. James E. Cronin and Carmen Sirianni (Philadelphia, 1983), 88–116; Hobsbawm, *Nations and Nationalism*, 125–29; James R. Barrett, "Americanization from the Bottom Up: Immigration and the Remaking of the Working Class in the United States, 1880–1930," *Journal of American History* 79 (Dec. 1992): 996–1020; Ferdinando Fasce, *Una famiglia a stelle e strisce: Grande Guerra e cultura d'impresa in America* (A family under the stars and stripes: World War I and company culture in America) (Bologna, 1993); Gary Cross, *A Quest for Time: The Reduction of Work in Britain and France, 1840–1940* (Berkeley, 1984), 129–49.

41. Montgomery, "Nationalism, American Patriotism, and Class Consciousness," 327–51; James R. Barrett, *Work and Community in the Jungle: Chicago's Packinghouse Workers, 1894–1922* (Urbana, 1987), 188–239; David Goldberg, *A Tale of Three Cities: Labor Organization and Protest in Paterson, Passaic, and Lawrence, 1916–1921* (New Brunswick, 1998); James Gray Pope, "Labor's Constitution of Freedom," *Yale Law Journal* 106 (Jan. 1997): 941–1031; David A. Corbin, *Life, Work, and Rebellion in the Coal Fields: The Southwestern West Virginia Miners, 1880–1922* (Urbana, 1981), 236–52.

42. Montgomery, "Nationalism, American Patriotism, and Class Consciousness"; Steve Fraser, *Labor Will Rule: Sidney Hillman and the Rise of American Labor* (New York, 1991), 114–45; Fasce, *Una famiglia a stelle e strisce*, 127–222; Elizabeth McKillen, *Chicago Labor and the Quest for a Democratic Diplomacy, 1914–1924* (Ithaca, 1995).

43. Rose Santora and Grace Santora, statement concerning Wood Mill of the American Woolen Company, April 24, 1919, box 8, Anthony Capraro Papers (Immigration History Research Center, St. Paul, Minnesota).

44. Harris, *New Untouchables*, 86; John Higham, *Strangers in the Land: Patterns of American Nativism. 1860–1925* (New York, 1963), 164–330; Kenneth T. Jackson,

The Ku Klux Klan in the City, 1915–1930 (New York, 1967); Kathleen M. Blee, *Women of the Klan: Racism and Gender in the 1920s* (Berkeley, 1991).

45. Stuart McConnell, "Reading the Flag: A Reconsideration of the Patriotic Cults of the 1890s," in *Bonds of Affection: Americans Define Their Patriotism*, ed. John Bodnar (Princeton, 1996), 102–19.

46. U.S. Congress, House of Representatives, Committee on Immigration and Naturalization, *American History in Terms of Human Migration . . . Statement of Dr. Harry H. Laughlin*, 70 Cong., 1 sess., March 7, 1928, p. S; American Council of Learned Societies, "Report of the Committee on Linguistic and National Stocks in the Population of the United States," in *American Historical Association, Annual Report for the year 1931* (3 vols., Washington, 1932), I, 103–441; Mae M. Ngai, "The Architecture of Race in American Immigration Law: A Reexamination of the Immigration Act of 1924," *Journal of American History* 86 (June 1999): 67–92. I am indebted to Martha Ophir for her Yale University senior essay: Martha Ophir, "Searching for Americanism: The National Origins Controversy, 1924–1949," 1992 (in Montgomery's possession).

47. Ophir, "Searching for Americanism"; Rudolph J. Vecoli, "'Over the Years I Have Encountered the Hazards and Rewards That Await the Historian of Immigration': George Malcolm Stephenson and the Swedish American Community," in *Migration och mångfald: Essäer om Kulturkontakt och Minoritetsfrågor*, ed. Harald Runblom (Migration and diversity: Essays on cultural contact and minority questions) (Uppsala, 1999), 171–88. For a discussion of ethnic conflicts over history textbooks, see Jonathan Zimmerman, "'Each "Race" Could Have Its Heroes Sung': Ethnicity and the History Wars in the 1920s," *Journal of American History* 87 (June 2000): 92–111.

48. Eric J. Hobsbawm, *The Age of Extremes: A History of the World, 1914–1991* (New York, 1996), 85–141; Michael A. Bernstein, *The Great Depression: Delayed Recovery and Economic Change in America, 1929–1939* (New York, 1987), 184–206; Ellis W. Hawley, *The New Deal and the Problem of Monopoly: A Study in Economic Ambivalence* (Princeton, 1966); Francisco Balderrama and Raymond Rodriguez, *Decade of Betrayal: Mexican Repatriation in the 1930s* (Albuquerque, 1995); Camille Guerin-Gonzales, *Mexican Workers and American Dreams: Immigration, Repatriation, and California Farm Labor, 1900–1939* (New Brunswick, 1994), 78–109; Holly Marie Allen, "Fallen Women and Forgotten Men: Gendered Conceptions of Community, Home, and Nation, 1932–1945" (PhD diss., Yale University, 1997), 183; David Montgomery, "Labor and the Political Leadership of New Deal America," *International Review of Social History* 39 (December 1994): 335–60.

49. Kenneth L. Roberts, *Oliver Wiswell* (New York, 1940); Warren I. Susman, *Culture as History: The Transformation of American Society in the Twentieth Century* (New York, 1984), 161–71; Warren I. Susman, "The Thirties," in *The Development of an American Culture*, ed. Stanley Coben and Lorman Ratner (Englewood Cliffs, 1970), 179–218; Philip Jenkins, *Hoods and Shirts: The Extreme Right in Pennsylvania, 1925–1950* (Chapel Hill, 1997); Hobsbawm, *Nations and Nationalism*, 146; Richard Oestreicher, "Urban Working-Class Political Behavior and Theories of American Electoral Politics, 1870–1940," *Journal of American History* 74 (March

1988): 1257–86; Louis Adamic, *My America, 1928–1938* (New York, 1938); Michael Denning, *The Cultural Front: The Laboring of American Culture in the Twentieth Century* (New York, 1996), 126; Fraser, *Labor Will Rule*, 259–440.

50. Earl Robinson and John La Touche, "Ballad for Americans," program notes for First Concert, University of Minnesota Artists Course, Season 1940–1941 (in Montgomery's possession), 3–4; Martin Bauml Duberman, *Paul Robeson* (New York, 1988), 236–40. For an analysis of the "Ballad for Americans," see Denning, *Cultural Front*, 128–29. Warren Susman, *Culture as History*, 205.

51. Barbara D. Savage, *Broadcasting Freedom: Radio, War, and the Politics of Race, 1938–1948* (Chapel Hill, 1999), 58.

52. Samuel Lubell, *The Future of American Politics* (New York, 1965), 26–88; Daniel Bell, *The End of Ideology: On the Exhaustion of Political Ideas in the Fifties* (New York, 1962), 13–38; Nelson Lichtenstein, *The Most Dangerous Man in Detroit: Walter Reuther and the Fate of the American Labor Movement* (New York, 1995), 271–345; Elizabeth A. Fones-Wolf, *Selling Free Enterprise: The Business Assault on Labor and Liberalism, 1945–60* (Urbana, 1996); Thomas J. Sugrue, "Crabgrass-Roots Politics: Race, Rights, and the Reaction against Liberalism in the Urban North, 1940–1964," *Journal of American History* 82 (Sept. 1995): 551–78.

53. *Official Report of the Proceedings of the Twenty-Second Republican National Convention* (Washington, 1940), 53–143. On Harold Stassen's own 1938 election campaign, see Hyman Berman, "Political Antisemitism in Minnesota during the Great Depression," *Jewish Social Studies* 38 (Summer-Fall 1976): 247–64.

54. Savage, *Broadcasting Freedom*, 37–45, 32. For perceptive studies of Chinese American struggles to share in the New Deal, see Renqiu Yu, *To Save China, to Save Ourselves: The Chinese Hand Laundry Alliance of New York* (Philadelphia, 1993); and Judy Yung, *Unbound Feet: A Social History of Chinese Women in San Francisco* (Berkeley, 1995), 178–222. Cf. Lon Kurashige, "The Problem of Biculturalism: Japanese American Identity and Festival before World War II," *Journal of American History* 86 (March 2000): 1632–54. Ernest Renan, *Qu'est-ce qu'une nation?* (What is a nation?) (Paris, 1882), 7–8. My translation of "L'oubli et je dirai même l'erreur historique, sont un facteur de la formation d'une nation et c'est ainsi que le progrés des études historiques est souvent pour la nationalité un danger."

PART IV

Toward a History of Workers' Control

David Montgomery is perhaps best remembered for his studies of the workplace and the cultures that developed there. In probing the social relations of production in early industrialization and later with the advent of "scientific management" and mass production, he found in workers' experiences an elaborate culture of "mutualism." If managers emphasized "rationalized" production methods and capitalist efficiency, workers exercised their own forms of control based on values of craft pride and solidarity. Montgomery experimented with this theme in his unpublished paper, "Trade Union Practice and the Origins of Syndicalist Theory in the United States," first drafted during his stay in England. He drew on his own shopfloor experience and his encounters with British shop stewards and their history. He presented a later version of the paper to a University of Rochester workshop with his graduate students and those of Herbert Gutman in fall 1972. Here, he introduced the prophet of scientific management, Frederick Winslow Taylor, who, in pursuit of greater efficiency and profit, set out to dismantle the craftsman's control. Montgomery provocatively linked this tradition of control to syndicalist notions of power in the workplace. He suggested this might be understood as "a logical extension of their daily trade union practice." If he later felt he had "run too fast"[1] in conceptualizing the political implications of craftsmen's control, he never altogether abandoned the revolutionary implications of his nineteenth-century findings.

In "Workers Control of Machine Production," Montgomery showed how iron workers and other craftsmen exercised considerable control over work, often appealing to a gendered notion of "manliness" and a workplace ethical code. They may have been "autonomous craftsmen," but they were also "group-made men" who relied on a mutualist ethos to enforce their norms. If this was the "tap-root" of labor's strength in the struggle to control the shopfloor, workers also used "calculation and organization" in their strategic use of strikes, which on occasion could embrace all-grades unionism and sympathetic action. For Montgomery the story was never unilinear or without countervailing power, the most profound challenge of which in the early twentieth century was the spread of scientific management's direct attack on the prerogatives of skill. His conception of "workers' control" revised in significant ways the defensive posture of skilled workers' trade union practice as conceived in the Commons-Perlman tradition. In doing so he emphasized the fundamentally collectivist nature and potentially expansive claims of skilled workers' struggle for workplace control.

In "The 'New Unionism' and the Transformation of Workers' Consciousness," he documented a rising tide of labor conflict between 1909 and 1922 that saw the mingling of craftsmen's struggles to maintain and extend their control with the grievances and wage demands of less skilled workers that pushed labor conflict to ever higher levels during the war and immediate postwar years. "New unionism" expanded the struggle for control to involve unprecedented numbers of less skilled workers, now including women, new immigrants, and African Americans. The architecture of labor conflict that Montgomery sketched for these years placed a new factory labor force in textiles, garments, iron and steel, machinery, and munitions alongside skilled workers battling to retain control of the production process. With his characteristic attention to the gritty details of work processes and the peculiarities of individual trades and industries, Montgomery developed a new perspective on work and labor activism. In the wake of his studies, the politics of the workplace emerged as a major theme in labor history. But, so too did recognition of the importance of the unprecedented wave of labor conflict during and immediately after World War I.

Note

1. David Montgomery, "Workers' Control of Machine Production in the Nineteenth Century," *Labor History* 17 (Fall 1976): 489.

CHAPTER 9

Trade Union Practice and the Origins of Syndicalist Theory in the United States

Unpublished paper, c. 1969/1972, David Montgomery Papers, Tamiment Institute and Archives

The doctrines of revolutionary syndicalism have traditionally been identified in America with the Industrial Workers of the World. This is correct. The I.W.W. explicitly repudiated political action at its 1908 convention and placed its faith exclusively in direct action by workers economic organizations, culminating in the overthrow of capitalism by a general strike. The syndicalist bias had, in fact, been inherent in the group from its founding in 1905. William E. Trautmann, editor of the *Brewery Workers' Journal*, prime mover in the Chicago conference which brought the I.W.W. to life, and author of its *Industrial Union Manifesto*, declared at that time that his document was based on the principles of "revolutionary syndicalism" then widespread in Europe. The manifesto argued that "the growth and development of this organization will build up within itself the structure of an Industrial Democracy—a Workers' Co-operative Republic—which must finally burst the shell of capitalist government, and be the agency by which the working people will operate the industries, and appropriate the products to themselves."

Such ideas will be quite familiar to you. But there was a second dimension of I.W.W. theory quite different from the philosophy of the C.G.T., the syndicalists of Bucharest, or even Tom Mann and his followers in England and Wales—so different, in fact, that William D. Haywood declared after his visit to Europe that his I.W.W. did not preach syndicalism. Its doctrine, he said, was "industrialism."

The distinction lay in the fact that central to the theory of the I.W.W. was the view that trade union practices based on craft or skill were reactionary, had to be smashed, had to be replaced with a form of organization which united all workers in each industry, regardless of occupation, into a single fighting unit. The Wobblies subjected the trade union practices of the American Federation of Labor to a thorough critique and developed an alternative code of conduct of their own. The I.W.W. organized workers from the bottom up, enlisting first the unskilled and using their enthusiasm and power to pull the craftsmen into action. This meant it had to replace the craft unions' meticulous caution with dramatic, even flamboyant tactics. It scorned large strike funds, relying instead on mass appeals for aid, the workers' own spirit of sacrifice, and short strikes. It rejected written contracts, centralized leadership, and benefit funds—all hallmarks of the Federation. And it summoned the workers to leave the decrepit "American Separation of Labor" and join the new, revolutionary style union.

In other words, the I.W.W. was concerned with both the spirit and the form of trade union practice, and it attacked craft unions on both counts. The trade union, in its view was more than a defensive agency of the workers, it was to take over the governing power from the capitalists—to operate the economy and society of the socialist future. But, the Wobblies added, one could not breathe revolutionary élan into a reactionary body. The craft union was appropriate only to an aristocracy of labor, a privileged, conservative element within the working class.

All this is well known. I want to argue today that the I.W.W.'s conception of the trade union as both a revolutionary force and the basic unit of the socialist commonwealth to come were nothing new to the American workers in 1905. They had been commonplace already for 30 or 40 years and had arisen in the minds of the very craftsmen whom the I.W.W. was now scolding for their parochial views. The idea of direct workers' control of industry operated through the union came from the "aristocracy of labor" itself. It was a simple, logical extension of their daily trade union practice.

The heart of the matter is this: in the last four decades of the nineteenth century the industrial craftsmen exercised a significant degree of what today would be called workers' control. The means of production were in the hands of the employers, and therein lay their power. Control over the actual use of those implements in the productive process rested with the skilled workers. There was the source of their power, and of their ideology.

To see what I mean, let us glance through the minute books of lodge number 11 of the Rollers, Roughers, Catchers, and Hookers Union of the United States, located in Columbus, Ohio, for the years 1873–1875. These books, together with the records of the Amalgamated Association of Iron and Steel Workers, which was formed by a merger of the rollers union with those of the iron heaters and the iron puddlers in 1876, can be found in the papers of William Martin, who served as secretary to both organizations. In 1888 Martin also became a vice-president of the American Federation of Labor. Let us see what these records tell us about the practices of the iron rollers.

Iron rollers worked in teams—a rolling team usually consisting of 12 men. They were paid by the ton of iron rolled. When the Columbus Rolling Mill Company contracted to reheat and roll some railroad tracks in January, 1874, for example, the union elected a committee of four to consult with the plant superintendent about the price the workmen were to receive for the work. They agreed on a scale of $1.13 per ton, which the committee brought back to the lodge for its approval.

There followed an intriguing process. The members soon accepted the company offer, then turned to the major task of dividing the $1.13 among themselves. Each member stated his own price. When they were added up, the total was 3 3/4 cents higher than the company offer. By careful revision of the figures, each runback buggyman was cut 2 cents, and the gang buggyman given an extra 1/4 of a cent to settle the bill. By the final reckoning 19 1/4 cents went to the roller, 13 cents to the rougher up, 10 cents to the rougher down, 9 cents to the catcher, 8 1/4 cents to each of the four hookers, 5 cents each to the runout hooker and the two runback buggymen, and 13 3/4 cents to the gang buggyman, half of whose earnings were to be turned over to his non-union helper.

The payroll structure was thus devised without interference from the boss, in open meeting of all those involved (save the buggyman's helper). Similarly overtime and special work assignments were allocated by union decisions. On March 22, 1875, we find Brother Henry Meyers claiming the right as oldest hand to any extra turns at hooking which came open. His assertion precipitated a general discussion of the problem. Lodge president David Plant declared that Meyers had forfeited his claim to extra turns "on account of drinking" which led him to neglect his regular work. Controversy among the hookers as to who should "take the tongs" on "standing turns" and for "rough and tumble hooking" culminated in a general agreement to increase the hookers' share of tonnage rates, especially during the hot summer months, and to deputize a committee of hookers to devise a plan of job allocation, subject to the approval of the whole lodge at its next meeting.

Both hiring and promotion of workers were controlled by the rollers, as was also the case among puddlers and heaters. There was no apprenticeship in the rollers' trade. Instead, workmen began in such subordinate positions as hookers or buggymen and either worked their way up through the team to which they belonged, or dropped out—moving away during hard times, as laborers so often did. As late as the early twentieth century Article 27 section 22 of the Amalgamated's constitution specified: "all men are to have the privilege of hiring their own helpers without dictation from the management, and no member shall be permitted to discharge a helper, except for just cause, nor shall a member reduce the wages of a helper during the scale year." Similarly it was union rules which specified: "When a vacancy occurs in the boiling department, the oldest boiler, if he so desires, shall have the preference of the furnace so vacated," and that "Every member of this association is strictly prohibited from employing helpers at a boiling, puddling, or heating furnace under the age of fifteen years."

The fact that helpers belonged to the union and participated in its debates helped secure just enforcement of such rules. The rollers constitution specified that "all workmen in the mill who are capable of working around the rolls be taken into the union." Formation of the Amalgamated in 1876 made all tradesmen and their immediate helpers eligible for membership. But the Amalgamated was essentially a union of rollers, heaters and puddlers. It did not seek to recruit blast furnace crews and steel mill laborers. President John Jarrett of the Amalgamated snubbed such workers as "Hungarians, Poles, Italians, Bohemians, men that really didn't know the difference . . . between light work and heavy work, or good wages and bad wages." He considered such laborers "disgusting" and said, "those people can live where I think a decent man would die." His union was always exclusive, restricted to perhaps fifteen percent of the manual employees of America's iron and steel mills.

The decorum of union meetings matched the dignity and the grave responsibilities of the craftsmen. The minutes of the Columbus lodge reveal proceedings so formalized that most sessions must have been dreadfully boring. Parliamentary procedure was painstakingly followed until the gathering finally "by motion Closed in Peace and Harmony to meet" again on some specified date. On rare occasions a newly elected officer might offer a "tasty speech" on the "recent alarming onslaughts" of "Combined Capital," but such entertainment was uncommon. Officers were elected for six-month terms only, and grievances were regularly handled by ad hoc committees, rather than by a standing body of representatives.

Great diversion was once offered by a grand ball, staged New Year's Eve. For the 1873 entertainment 30 dances were planned, 20 square and 10 round. Members of the arrangements committee were to wear red, white, or blue roses, depending on their special assignments. And it was unanimously resolved that any member "Presenting himself at the Ball in Such a condition as be a hinderance or a nuicense to the guests Who may be Preasant Shall Be fined the Sum of 5 Dollars . . . and Should any Party or Parties conduct themselves in any improper way [they] Shall upon the Refunding of there money Be expelled from the Room."

Secretary Martin of this Columbus lodge was among the signers of an 1888 appeal of the new American Federation of Labor, which set forth the philosophy of direct democracy guiding these iron workers. Trade unions they saw as "the natural growth of natural laws" built by the wage earners themselves and based on their own experience, rather than upon "elaborate and exhaustive platforms of abstract principles." Their foundation was "the right of self-government, of the several trades." But the experience of defeats "in pitched battles against the superior forces of united capital" had taught the lesson of "unity of the working class"—of federation of all the trades in order to fight "to the bitter end the fast-coming grand struggle between Capital and Labor, involving the perpetuation of the civilization we have so laboriously evolved."

In short, the iron rollers through their union directed the process of production. They ran the factory. The boss bought the machinery and raw materials, sold the finished product, and set an aggregate price for the work of the craftsmen through negotiation with their representatives. That is all. And the union sought to extend its control even into that limited sphere. President Jarrett of the Amalgamated told a Senate committee in 1883 that a major cause of strikes in the trade was the persistent refusal of employers to prove they could not afford to pay higher wages by opening their books to the unions. "That is one of the things that we are trying to have the employers do," Jarrett explained, "show us their books, and show that they cannot afford the advance."

The actual role of these craftsmen in production, then, was the basis of their concept of "self-government" of their trades. But one must ask: were the rollers anachronistic? Were they unique?

Testimony that the rollers' control over the productive process was not unique, but common among industrial craftsmen, comes from the writings of the father of scientific management, Frederick Winslow Taylor. In his book *Principles of Scientific Management* written about 1905, Taylor called on *employers* to wrest control of their factories away from their workmen. He described business practice of the immediate past in this way:

> Now, in the best of the ordinary types of management, the managers recognize the fact that the 500 or 1000 workmen, included in the twenty to thirty trades, who are under them, possess this mass of traditional knowledge, a large part of which is not in the possession of the management. The management, of course, includes foremen and superintendents, who themselves have been in most cases first-class workers at their trades. And yet these foremen and superintendents know, better than anyone else, that their own knowledge and personal skill falls far short of the combined knowledge and dexterity of all the workmen under them. The most experienced managers therefore frankly place before their workmen the problem of doing the work in the best and most economical way. They recognize the task before them as that of inducing each workman to use his best endeavors, his hardest work, all his traditional knowledge, his skill, his ingenuity, and his good-will—in a word, his "initiative," so as to yield the largest possible return to his employer.

Taylor's description was accurate. The iron molder, the glass blower, the cooper, the cigar maker, the garment cutter, the brick layer, the carpenter, the locomotive engineer and conductor, the pipe fitter, the blacksmith, the printer, the tailor, the shoe laster—each of these craftsmen held the initiative in his work, was quite autonomous of the employers' control in the production process. Molders, glass blowers, potters, iron puddlers and some coal miners even hired their own helpers and often paid them out of their own earnings (though the unions opposed this practice). Several of these trades used sliding scales, which linked the piece rates of the workers directly to the market price of the product, so that even wages were independent of the employers. Unions usually favored this practice, especially in iron and coal, though in depressed times it worked to the disadvantage of the workers.

The American coal miner was the epitome of the autonomous workman, well into the twentieth century. Accompanied only by his laborer (or butty) at the coal face—in "his room"—rarely visited more than once a day by the foreman, the miner undercut, drilled, placed his charges, and blasted in his own way and at the tempo he determined. In some bituminous fields he even exercised the right to go home when he chose. More significantly, the flow of cars, pit props, and other materials needed by the miner was supervised in union mines by the elected pit committee. Time and again miners who left the pits for the safer and more regular work of factories, soon declared they felt like slaves in their new jobs and returned to the mines.

This quality of mining life was clearly described by Professor Carter Goodrich in his book *The Miner's Freedom*, published in 1925. One anecdote from that book illustrates the manner in which newcomers to the mines were taught how to behave properly. A Hungarian-born miner told Goodrich that on his first day in the pits in America he was toiling with his shovel as laborer for a miner when the foreman entered the room. To the Hungarian's astonishment, the miner told him: "Sit down, Frank." Fearfully glancing from the miner to the foreman, Frank sat down. The miner chattered with the foreman casually about various problems on the job, until the foreman left. Then the miner said to the Hungarian, "Don't you ever let me catch you working when a boss is around."

It was exactly this standard of behavior which Robert Frost captured in his poem "The Code":

> The hand that knows his business won't be told
> To do work better or faster—those two things.

The same code prevailed among machinists. Again Taylor has left us a vivid description of the bitter struggle he personally waged to master the machinists of Midvale Steel Company, when he was their foreman. Taylor assumed the employer should command, and so he saw the behavior of the workers only as recalcitrance, as disobedience. Their code required careful restriction of production in order to safeguard their own jobs, their piece rates, and their dignity. Taylor drove them unmercifully toward higher output, and in return the machinists heaped curses upon him, quit, called work stoppages, threatened to assault him, and sabotaged the machinery. Those who yielded to Taylor's threats or blandishments were ostracized and attacked by their fellow workmen.

Taylor's experience shows us that even without a union (for there was none at Midvale) skilled workmen had formidable powers of resistance. The massive study published by the U.S. Commissioner of Labor in 1904 on *Regulation and Restriction of Output* confirms the point. As Taylor himself concluded, the fact that the technology and the managerial methods of that time left the initiative in production with the craftsman put that worker in a strong position to oppose his employer. But only with a union could the craftsmen move from *resistance* to *control* of their trades. Resistance could be individual and spontaneous (though rooted in the workers' culture). Control was collective, organized, deliberate.

As we saw in the case of the iron rollers, the workers' control was embodied in a set of union rules, carefully adopted by the workers, determining how the process of production was to be carried out. That these rules could be very elaborate is illustrated by the following regulations enacted by the Coopers' Union of New York City in 1874:

> Hours of labor: 9 hours per day, being from 7 A.M. to 5 P.M. with one hour for lunch . . .
> No member shall be allowed to use country shaved hoops or straps . . .
> No members are allowed to use borrowed or old hoops . . .
> Wages for steady men, $4 per day; transient men, $4.50 (if discharged before Saturday night). For overtime, 80 cents per hour . . .
> Each shop employing one man steadily shall be entitled to one apprentice and no more . . .
> No person shall allow himself to be borrowed out from one employer to another . . .
> No member shall be allowed to work with any man who is not a member of the Cooper's Union . . .
> No member shall charge any more work for bosses than was actually done under penalty of $25 . . .

Please note that these rules were customarily adopted by the unions unilaterally. They were not negotiated but decided upon by the workers themselves. It was within the union that the problems of production were deliberated. It was the union which formulated and adopted the rules. It was the union which forced those rules on the employers.

If an employer resisted such "union law," no union members would work for him. Hence the unions fought tenaciously to close the shops to any craftsmen who were not members, though such efforts often brought them afoul of the law. In other words, the practice of "job control" for which the I.W.W. became so famous during its struggles of 1906 in Goldfield, Nevada, was well within the traditional form of craft behavior. But there was this enormous difference: at Goldfield the I.W.W. sought to include every worker in town within its membership and under its rules. Craft traditions, on the other hand, were always and necessarily exclusive. To preserve craft standards poorly trained workmen or those capable of doing only a part of the craft's work had to be excluded from membership. Also, the doors of admission were firmly barred to helpers and laborers (either by total prohibition or by some form of examination), lest employers use such workers to flood the labor market, dilute the skill requirements of the job, and pay less than union scale for work belonging to the craft to men who patently did not deserve journeymen's wages. The workers' control of craft union tradition was controlled by *a minority* of workers, by a privileged fifteen or twenty percent overall, in the name of labor, at times even at the expense of the laborers and helpers.

In some important instances union law succeeded in imposing order on the competitive chaos of entire industries. This was dramatically the case in Pennsylvania's anthracite coal fields between 1869 and 1874, and again in innumerable industries during the impressive A.F. of L. upsurge of 1898 to 1903. It was also the case in those battles waged against the practices of subcontracting by the iron puddlers and rollers, the iron molders, the mid-western coal miners, the carpenters of the big cities, and (much less successfully) the tailors between 1870 and 1890. In each case employers had encouraged craftsmen to act as small bosses, hiring several helpers of their own, paid from their own earnings. Such practices converted these crafts into sweated trades, with worker exploiting worker, all fiercely competing in markets glutted with both wares and hands. The battle to enforce union rules on employers and ambitious workmen alike in these trades played a major part in the creation and early growth of the A.F. of L. Because the rules for each trade could only be formulated by workers in that trade, the Federation made "craft autonomy" its central principle. The unifying demand of the whole movement, the struggle which established the A.F. of L. as a lasting feature of American life, was the rule it sought to impose on all trades—the eight-hour day.

I have portrayed late nineteenth century American trade unions as far more powerful and influential than most of you have imagined. I have meant to do so. They were also an important political force, especially in local government—but we have not time for that story today. Now I must qualify that picture of strength.

Although trade unions established local centers of great power (New York and Chicago between 1868 and 1874, Pittsburgh and San Francisco between 1878 and 1892, many mining communities in the 1880s), their position was never secure, always under fierce attack. The rapid progress of machinery and of the division of labor, combined with the relentless influx of new workers from Europe, Asia, and rural America posed chronic threats to union rules and union exclusiveness. The terrible economic depression of 1873–1878 devastated trade union membership, standards, and rules in every trade. That experience brought many shoemakers, miners, telegraphers, cigar makers, tailors and others to conclude that craft exclusiveness could no longer work, that trade unions were obsolete. Out of this experience came the rapid rise of the Knights of Labor, embracing all occupations together and skilled and unskilled alike in solidarity under the banner "Universal Brotherhood of Labor."

With the return of prosperity these trades again found their footing. Their unions revived and often prospered. Their rules were secured often within highly competitive trades, as we have seen. Even within the ranks of the Knights of Labor a craft spirit reared its head, as separate crafts went their various ways in national assemblies of their own, to the great distress of the so-called fundamentalist bearers of the Order's original faith. The creation and growth of the A.F. of L. in the last half of the 1880s marked the triumph of craft particularism.

A more formidable challenge faced the trade unions in the form of the large industrial corporation. Rich enough to withstand long strikes, employing vast numbers of laborers and helpers whom the unions ignored, using advanced and specialized machinery to undermine their reliance on craftsmen, such huge companies were destroying the unions which faced them, at the very time the A.F. of L. was waxing strong in industries dominated by small entrepreneurs. The Cambria Iron Works forced its rollers and all other trades (6,000 men in all) to forswear their unions in 1874. Western Union broke up the mighty telegraphers in 1883. The great Chicago meat packing houses disposed of their unions for almost twenty years to come in 1886, as did the vast McCormick Harvesting Machine Company. Carnegie Steel after six months of combat in 1892 put an end to the proudest lodge of the Amalgamated Iron and Steel Workers, the one in Homestead, Pennsylvania.

Clearly the craft unions could not cope with the vast modern factory and the multi-plant firm. Even the remarkable upsurge of the A.F. of L., between 1898 and 1903 failed to establish a significant, lasting grip on steel, meat packing, farm equipment, electrical appliances, textiles and other domains of big enterprise.

The intricate division of labor in such factories replaced the traditional dichotomy of craftsman vs. laborer with a new continuum of grades of workers, all subject to a steadily-growing degree of managerial supervision, whose earnings were ranged over a broad set of rather small gradations determined by such variables as training, responsibility, physical exertion, individual output—the kinds of functions contemporary job evaluation attempts to cope with. Those workers whose tasks did require a high degree of skill were divided into too many distinct groups to allow any one of them to control the life of the plant, or even its own work, to any significant degree. In the McCormick Harvesting Machine Company of the early 1880s, Iron Molders Lodge No. 23 dominated the life of the entire factory. In large textile mills at the very same period beamers, mule spinners, blockers, denim weavers, jacquard weavers, and innumerable other skill groups were easily mastered one at a time by the employers on wage questions and could scarcely have dreamed of controlling even their own special parts of the productive process the way iron molders or iron rollers did.

In such large-scale industries by the dawn of the twentieth century there was simply no denying the argument that craft unionism had become technologically obsolete. A.F. of L. leaders, committed to the craft form of organization after 1898 as a matter of doctrine, tried to secure their position by deals with employers, protecting present contracts at the expense of expansion, shielding craftsmen where possible at the expense of the laborers. In some instances, for example the iron molders of Philadelphia, where scarcely one-fourth those in the trade were true journeymen eligible for union membership by 1903, the union held wages down and hours up for their own members in order to allow those foundries which still employed full-fledged craftsmen to compete with their rivals who were more advanced technologically. In other cases, like the shoe lasters of New England, once the union had failed to maintain trade standards against newly-developed machine processes, it abruptly abandoned its militancy (including in this case the socialist outlook of its leadership) and tried to survive by offering its members costly insurance schemes. Day by day such unions became more bureaucratic, more conservative, more openly contemptuous of the common herd in the factories. It was this degradation of craft unionism at the end of the century that made possible the rise of the I.W.W.

So much for practice. I have argued that the craftsmen exercised in fact an important, if limited, form of workers' control in the late nineteenth century, and that such control was dependent on both the fact that they (not the employers) were the masters of technique and the fact that their trade unions, through which that control was exercised in a deliberate, collective manner, were engaged in relentless struggle to maintain and extend the limits of that control. This struggle made the craftsmen the vanguard of the late 19th century working class movement. Finally, I have noted that the progress of capitalism was undermining the strength of the craftsmen. In the most advanced factories and industries, the workers were bit by bit losing that struggle.

How were these conditions reflected in the ideology of the craftsmen? First, no spokesmen of the labor movement between 1860 and 1890 looked upon capitalism as a desirable, or even a permanent, fact of life. In the speeches and writings of the workers' leaders of this epoch, the goal of the labor movement was invariably described as the emancipation of the workers from the wages system. This was as true of the American Federation of Labor in its early days as it was of the Knights of Labor, the Socialist Labor Party, the International Workingmen's Association, and the anarchists. For most craftsmen, however, resistance to the wages system was envisaged more as a reformist objective than as a revolutionary one. They looked upon the *capitalists* as the subversive element of society. The rich were destroying the foundations of the great Republic born of the Revolution of 1776. The businessmen were overturning Christian virtue with their new materialistic religion of greed. As the President of the Massachusetts State Federation of Labor lamented in 1894: "But it seems that the word of God has almost been forgotten now, and the mighty dollar rules the world."

This is an important distinction. The demand of the I.W.W. for abolition of the wages system was not new. But the I.W.W. looked upon capitalism as the rotten old regime which had to be overthrown. The nineteenth century craftsmen had seen capitalism as a new force which was rapidly undermining their country's glorious traditions of liberty and equality. The workers' task was not to overthrow the government and social order, but to protect them from the Robber Barons. Listen to the words of George McNeill, intimate colleague of Samuel Gompers and prominent figure in both the A.F. of L. and the Knights of Labor:

> These extremes of wealth and poverty are threatening the existence of the government. In the light of these facts, we declare that there is an inevitable and irresistible conflict between the wage-system of labor and the republican system of government—the wage-laborer attempting to save the government, and the capitalist class ignorantly attempting to subvert it.

Note that the root of the problem was not the corruption of political life which so vexed upper-class reformers, but control of the job. "It is ridiculous to imagine that the wage workers can be slaves in employment and yet achieve control at the polls," argued Gompers in 1894. "There never yet existed coincident with each other autocracy in the shop and democracy in political life."

Even where workingmen made extensive use of the language and concepts of middle-class reformers, they infused those concepts with a meaning quite different from what the middle class had in mind. Education, temperance, self-help, and self-improvement were spoken of as often and as highly by McNeill, Gompers, Jarrett, and company as ever they were by Josiah Strong, E. L. Godkin, or President Cleveland, but never did labor reformers see such efforts as alone sufficient to elevate their status or as alternatives to class struggle. Nor did the words have the same implications for them as for their middle-class users, as a single example may show.

Educational reformers and some eminent economists, from Horace Mann through Edward Atkinson, John Eaton, and Edward Bemis, accepted wholeheartedly what today would be called the doctrine of "human capital," that better educated workers are more productive workers, that investment in schooling directly augments the national wealth. Senator Blair of New Hampshire, author of a scheme for a national compulsory system of elementary education, shared this view, and was, therefore, delighted to hear President Jarrett of the iron workers talk about the value of education. Senator Blair pressed Jarrett on the point:

> "Then your theory is that the more intelligent a man is the more work he will be able to do?" he asked.
>
> "Yes," came the trade unionist's reply. "But you will not understand me to assume that the more physical, manual labor he will perform. What I do believe is that the more a man's intelligence is improved the better he learns how to do his work with more ease to himself and in better fashion."

Education for Jarrett was part and parcel of the struggle for control and for emancipation, not a technique to make the workers fit more smoothly into their employers' designs. The contrast becomes most vividly clear when one reads George McNeill's portrayal of what Gompers had called "autocracy in the shop":

> The bell that calls the weary, half-paid worker from his needed rest, taunts him with each resounding stroke. The machinery that renders his skill and time of less value to himself and more to his master, becomes the hated instrument of torture; its monotonous hum keeping time to his groans and curses. The mill, the mine, the foundry and the round-house stand like giants, ever ready to swallow up his substance. With such feelings constantly present in the hearts of the laborers, unused to thought, disciplined only to act, what wonder that violence should spread like an epidemic from station to station, from mine to mine, and from factory to factory. What wonder that in this war life was destroyed? The man who, for his class, dares death for freedom's sake, must needs look upon the man who takes his place as giving aid and comfort to the enemy. It is war, and cries of 'peace, peace,' when there is no peace, will only lull the thoughtless into treacherous sleep.

Still this doctrine of emancipation, despite its apocalyptic rhetoric could be put to uses which were far from revolutionary. In July, 1894, during the famous Pullman strike, a special meeting of the A.F. of L. Executive Council *rejected* a plea for a general strike to help the embattled railroad workers. Explaining its action in a manifesto ringing with thunderous denunciation of the capitalists, the Council summoned all workers to stand by their trade unions in these words: "so that in the ever-present contest of the wealth-producers to conquer their rights from the wealth-absorbers, we may by our intelligence and persistency, the earnestness of our purpose, the nobility of our cause, work out through evolutionary methods the final emancipation of labor."

If this was the outlook of reformist craftsmen, how did *radical* workmen envisage their emancipation? The answer is that they approached the problem with a marked syndicalist bias, as a question of workers' control of production, as an extension of their own daily experience. If, as I have argued, their strength lay in the productive process and the employers' in property, clearly the emancipation of labor meant that the workers should acquire the property too. As early as the 1860's printers, iron molders, coopers, shoemakers, tailors, and even coal miners experimented with cooperative production (just as more archaic handicrafts had already been doing for thirty years before that). The idea was simple. They did not need a boss to tell them how to perform their work. They needed only capital. The problem of accumulating capital led many of them, by common sense, to the proposition that the State should advance the funds. (Shades of Ferdinand Lassalle!) Thus, an iron heater from Birmingham, Alabama, told a Senate committee in 1883:

> I think the best thing that could be done for the South would be for Congress to appropriate money to start mills that could be run by skilled workmen on a fair percentage of interest to the government. We would show them that we have got talent enough to run a rolling-mill at less cost than these capitalists claim is required. We claim that they are eating up the profits with percentages and big salaries, and that they want to cheat us out of our hard-earned money to pay these big salaries and to put us in a position so that we can never educate our children, . . . so that we can never get out into society in any respectability.

What could be more simple? Save the worker's respectability and the consumers' money by getting rid of the useless, profit-mongering boss. The idea was echoed by several other craftsmen before the committee. A telegraphers' leader asked the State to loan capital to his union in order to start a national telegraph company run by the operators. The plan could serve as an example to be followed by other industries, he argued. In reply to a Senator's protest against "government in business," the telegrapher stressed: "The government would not be doing any kind of work. These organizations of [workers in] different industries would be the recognized contractors for the performance of their several kinds of work."

The platform of the Central Labor Union of New York City, an assembly of representatives of that city's trade unions, carried the argument to its logical conclusion. Urging workers' organizations to "keep pace with the progress of the age and with the march of advanced ideas," the platform declared: "Organizations of trade and labor unions are the only means to put a check to the evil outgrowths of the prevailing system, and they contain the seed for a new and better system."

This idea that the trade union was socialism in embryo appealed so strongly to American workers that even those who espoused the doctrines of such European thinkers as Johann Most and Ferdinand Lassalle, who were hostile to trade unions, modified those theories in a syndicalist direction. Most arrived in America in 1881, found the ranks of the Socialist Labor party rent by a dispute over fusion with petit bourgeois reformers and highly susceptible to anarchist ideas (on both sides of the schism, in fact). By the time of the Pittsburgh anarchist congress of 1883, he was the most influential individual in American revolutionary ranks. Yet in Chicago, where his organization enjoyed the bulk of its numerical strength, Albert Parsons, August Spies, and the other local anarchist leaders rejected both Most's contempt for trade unions and his gospel of propaganda by deed. They participated actively and eagerly in the city's trade union movement and sacrificed their lives in the mass struggle for the eight-hour day. Parsons and Spies justified their line in this way:

> The International recognizes in the trade union the embryonic group of the future "free society." Every Trade Union is, *nolens volens*, an autonomous commune in the process of incubation. The Trades Union is a necessity of capitalist production and will yet take its place by superseding it under the system of universal free co-operation. No, friends, it is not the unions but the methods which some of them employ with which the International finds fault, and as indifferently as it may be considered by some, the development of capitalism is hastening the day when all Trades Unions and Anarchists will of necessity become one and the same.

An apparent and possibly significant exception to my thesis appeared in the Far West. The center of working-class revolutionary activity in California and the Rocky Mountains was a secret conspiratorial group which assumed the name International Workingman's Association. Between 1882 and 1887 this body embraced many leaders of trade unions and of the Knights of Labor, but it never envisaged the trade union as a revolutionary agency or as the institution to operate a socialist economy. In Marxist fashion it struggled for what it called "a system of governmental co-operation in all matters of mental, moral and physical construction and elevation," as a necessary prelude to "perfect anarchy." Atop this Marxist perspective it superimposed tactics in the heritage of Blanqui. It used trade unions simply as offices from which to recruit a dedicated minority who were to be educated, drilled, and armed to seize state power and dispossess the bourgeoisie.

There is no doubting that the I.W.A. had a strong working-class base for a time. Yet the contrast between its outlook and that of other organizations described here may not be so striking as it first appears, for the I.W.A. was largely the creation of one man, the lawyer Burnette G. Haskell, who saw himself as the H.M. Hyndman of America. When he abandoned the organization, it quickly collapsed. The seeds of revolutionary elan which he had planted in the Far West obviously bore fruit in the I.W.W. itself. Here is a problem in the transmission of ideology which deserves much more thorough treatment than any historian has yet attempted. The I.W.A.'s domain a generation later was the very heartland of the I.W.W.

Quite different is the story of the Socialist Labor Party, the most durable of all American revolutionary groupings. (It is still with us.) Here the syndicalist bias I am describing appeared in its most remarkable form. Heavily based on German immigrants, the S.L.P. drew on both Marx and Lassalle for its theory. For the most part, Marx provided its analysis of capitalist economics, Lassalle contributed its moral critique of capitalism and its conception of the organic state as the coming socialist order. But the party membership was constituted almost entirely of skilled workers and trade union members. The dominant faction at its founding in 1876 believed that all its efforts should be devoted to the building up of trade unions—that political action should wait until it could rest on a firm base of economic organization.

The dramatic strikes which swept the nation the next year provided a splendid opportunity for the party to carry out its appointed task. Especially impressive was its role in St. Louis, where the party organized and led a five-day general strike. When an upsurge of working-class political activity followed the strikes, however, the party succumbed to the temptation to leap into the maelstrom of electoral maneuvers. This reversal of line drove a number of important figures out of the S.L.P. over the next few years, either to the anarchists (like Parsons and Spies) or to devote themselves exclusively to their unions (like Adolph Strasser and Peter J. McGuire).

Those who remained with the party nevertheless saw the socialist future in the image of their trade unions. Time permits a look at only one document—the most widely read piece of party literature, *The Co-operative Commonwealth*. Its author was Laurence Gronlund, who had been prominent in the St. Louis leadership of 1877.

Gronlund's critique of the wages system is thoroughly Lassallean. Though he uses Marx to explain surplus value, the main thrust of his attack on capitalism is aimed at the system's immorality. He depicts capitalism as the only society ever to make a virtue of greed. The cooperative commonwealth, he promises, will substitute mutuality for egotism. It will be an organic order, "an impersonal Power, coeval with human nature: The STATE." Gronlund even espouses the iron law of wages, Lassalle's central argument against trade unions.

But then he abandons Lassalle abruptly. Trade unions assume a central position in the whole edifice of Gronlund's thought. First, they educate workers in the spirit of collectivism, representing the first decisive step toward the new morality. Second, they provide "the lever by means of which the new ideas are to move society"—though this point is not elaborated. Finally, he portrays the unions as the basic units for the administration of the co-operative commonwealth. The State governs all, yes, but the State itself is a composite of syndical elements. Each trade is to govern itself, subject to the general planning and direction of a National Board of Administrators, made up of elected representatives of the various industries. American workers had given even Lassalle a syndicalist twist.

This style of thinking was so pervasive that it deserves to be called the American style of socialism. The cooperative commonwealth was imagined simply as the world governed by union meetings. The concept developed without the help of intellectuals, on the basis of the craftsmen's personal experience of controlling the productive process, in a society whose great minds were fiercely hostile to any form of workers' power. As Big Bill Haywood was to say: "Socialism is so plain, so clear, so simple that when a person becomes an intellectual he doesn't understand socialism."

When America did produce its own great socialist thinker, Daniel DeLeon, his intellect gave systematic form to the ideas the workers had created for themselves. "The reason for a political party unfits it to 'take and hold' the machinery of production," he wrote. "The mission of unionism is to organize and drill the Working Class for final victory—to 'take and hold' the machinery of production, which means the administration of the country."

Note

Reprinted courtesy of New York University and the Tamiment Library and the Robert F. Wagner Labor Archives.

CHAPTER 10

Workers' Control of Machine Production in the Nineteenth Century

Labor History 17 (Fall 1976): 484–509

"In an industrial establishment which employs say from 500 to 1000 workmen, there will be found in many cases at least twenty to thirty different trades," wrote Frederick Winslow Taylor in his famous critique of the practices of industrial management which were then in vogue.

> The workmen in each of these trades have had their knowledge handed down to them by word of mouth. . . . This mass of rule-of-thumb or traditional knowledge may be said to be the principal asset or possession of every tradesman . . . [The] foremen and superintendents [who comprise the management] know, better than anyone else, that their own knowledge and personal skill falls far short of the combined knowledge and dexterity of all the workmen under them. They recognize the task before them as that of inducing each workman to use his best endeavors, his hardest work, all his traditional knowledge, his skill, his ingenuity, and his goodwill—in a word, his "initiative," so as to yield the largest possible return to his employer."[1]

Big Bill Haywood put the same point somewhat more pungently, when he declared: "The manager's brains are under the workman's cap."[2]

Both Taylor and Haywood were describing the power which certain groups of workers exercised over the direction of production processes at the end of the nineteenth century, a power which the scientific management movement strove to abolish, and which the Industrial Workers of the World wished to enlarge and extend to all workers. It is important to note that both men found the basis of workers' power in the superiority of their knowledge over that of the factory owners. It is even more important to note that they were referring not to "preindustrial" work practices, but to the factory itself.

The richly impressive work of Herbert Gutman in this country, E.P. Thompson in England, and others[3] has already unveiled to us the profound changes forced by the advent of industrial capitalism upon people's values and expectation, work habits, and sense of time, as well as the persistence with which working people clung to their traditional, spasmodic, task-oriented styles of work and to a social code which was less tightly disciplined, less individualistic and less exploitative than that which industrialization was imposing upon them. These studies have directed our attention to the experiences of the first generation of industrial workers, or, in the case of Gutman's conception, to the persistence of that "first-generation" experience over more than a century of American life.

My concern here, however, is not with the encounter of industrial with "pre-industrial" ways, but rather with the patterns of behavior which took shape in the second and third generations of industrial experience, largely among workers whose world had been fashioned from their youngest days by smoky mills, congested streets, recreation as a week-end affair and toil at the times and pace dictated by the clock (except when a more or less lengthy layoff meant no work at all).[4] It was such workers, veterans, if you will, of industrial life, with whom Taylor was preoccupied. They had internalized the industrial sense of time, they were highly disciplined in both individual and collective behavior, and they regarded both an extensive division of labor and machine production as their natural environments. But they had often fashioned from these attributes neither the docile obedience of automatons, nor the individualism of the "upwardly mobile," but a form of control of productive processes which became increasingly collective, deliberate and aggressive, until American employers launched a partially successful counterattack under the banners of scientific management and the open shop drive.

Workers' control of production, however, was not a condition or state of affairs which existed at any point in time, but a struggle, a chronic battle in industrial life which assumed a variety of forms. Those forms may be treated as successive stages in a pattern of historical evolution, though one must always remember that the stages overlapped each other chronologically in different industries, or even at different localities within the same industry, and that each successive stage incorporated the previous one, rather than replacing it. The three levels of development which appeared in the second half of the nineteenth century were those characterized by 1) the functional autonomy of the craftsman, 2) the union work rule, and 3) mutual support of diverse trades in rule enforcement and sympathetic strikes. Each of these levels will be examined here in turn, then in conclusion some observations will be made on the impact of scientific management and the open shop drive on the patterns of behavior which they represented.

The functional autonomy of craftsmen rested on both their superior knowledge, which made them self-directing at their tasks, and the supervision which they gave to one or more helpers. Iron molders, glass blowers, coopers, paper machine tenders, locomotive engineers, mule spinners, boilermakers, pipe fitters, typographers, jiggermen in potteries, coal miners, iron rollers, puddlers and heaters, the operators of McKay or Goodyear stitching machines in shoe factories, and, in many instances, journeymen machinists and fitters in metal works exercised broad discretion in the direction of their own work and that of their helpers. They often hired and fired their own helpers and paid the latter some fixed portion of their own earnings.

James J. Davis, who was to end up as Warren Harding's Secretary of Labor, learned the trade of puddling iron by working as his father's helper in Sharon, Pennsylvania. "None of us ever went to school and learned the chemistry of it from books," he recalled. "We learned the trick by doing it, standing with our faces in the scorching heat while our hands puddled the metal in its glaring bath."[5] His first job, in fact, had come at the age of twelve, when an aged puddler devised a scheme to enable him to continue the physically arduous exertion of the trade by taking on a boy (twelve-year-old Davis) to relieve the helper of mundane tasks like stoking the furnace, so that the helper in turn could assume a larger share of the taxing work of stirring the iron as it "came to nature." By the time Davis felt he had learned enough to master his own furnace, he had to leave Sharon, because furnaces passed from father to son, and Davis' father was not yet ready to step down. As late as 1900, when Davis was living at home while attending business college after having been elected to public office, he took over his father's furnace every afternoon, through an arrangement the two had worked out between themselves.[6]

The iron rollers of the Columbus Iron Works, in Ohio, have left us a clear record of how they managed their trade in minute books of their local union from 1873 to 1876. The three twelve-man rolling teams, which constituted the union, negotiated a single tonnage rate with the company for each specific rolling job the company undertook. The workers then decided collectively, among themselves, what portion of that rate should go to each of them (and the shares were far from equal, ranging from 19¼ cents, out of the negotiated $1.13 a ton, for the roller, to 5 cents for the runout hooker), how work should be allocated among them, how many rounds on the rolls should be undertaken per day, what special arrangements should be made for the fiercely hot labors of the hookers during the summer, and how members should be hired and progress through the various ranks of the gang.[7] To put it another way, all the boss did was to buy the equipment and raw materials and sell the finished product.

One cannot help being impressed by the fact that the Columbus iron rollers were conducting the operations of the firm in precisely the way J. T. Murphy and the Sheffield Workers' Council demanded that shop stewards should operate British industries in 1918, the union contracting with the employer to do the whole job, then performing that job without interference from employers.[8] But to make that analogy is to run too fast. The iron rollers of Columbus were not raising revolutionary demands, but pursuing commonplace practices. On the other hand, the practices themselves were both historically quite new (a "pre-industrial" iron roller is a contradiction in terms), subject to incessant attacks by employers, and defended by the craftsmen's own disciplined ethical code.

Three aspects of the moral code, in which the craftsmen's autonomy was protectively enmeshed, deserve close attention. First, on most jobs there was a stint, an output quota fixed by the workers themselves. As the laments of scientific management's apostles about workers "soldiering" and the remarkable 1904 survey by the Commissioner of Labor, *Regulation and Restriction of Output*, made clear, stints flourished as widely without unions as with them.[9] Abram Hewitt testified in 1867 that his puddlers in New Jersey, who were not unionized, worked 11 turns per week (5 1/2 days), made three heats per turn, and put 450 pounds of iron in each charge, all by arrangement among themselves. Thirty-five years later a stint still governed the trade, though a dramatic improvement in puddling furnaces was reflected in union rules which specified 11 turns with five heats per turn and 550 pounds per charge (a 104% improvement in productivity), while some nonunion mill workers followed the same routine but boiled bigger charges.[10]

Stints were always under pressure from the employers, and were often stretched over the course of time by the combined force of competition among employers and improving technology. In this instance, productivity under union rules expanded more than three percent annually over three and a half decades. But workers clung doggedly to the practice, and used their superior knowledge both to determine how much they should do and to outwit employers' efforts to wring more production out of them. In a farm equipment factory studied in 1902, for example, the machine shop, polishing department, fitting department and blacksmith shop all had fixed stints, which made each group of workers average very similar earnings despite the fact that all departments were on piecework. In the blacksmith shop, which unlike the others had no union rule fining those who earned too much, workers held down the pace by refusing to replace each part they removed from the heaters with a cold one. They emptied the heaters entirely, before refilling them and then waited for the new parts to heat up.[11] Similarly, Taylor's colleague Carl Barth discovered a planer operator who avoided exceeding the stint while always looking busy, by simply removing the cutting tool from his machine from time to time, while letting it run merrily on.[12]

"There is in every workroom a fashion, a habit of work," wrote efficiency consultant Henry Gantt, "and the new worker follows that fashion, for it isn't respectable not to."[13] A quiver full of epithets awaited the deviant: 'hog,' 'hogger-in,' 'leader,' 'rooter,' 'chaser,' 'rusher,' 'runner,' 'swift,' 'boss's pet,'[14] mention some politer versions. And when a whole factory gained a reputation for feverish work, disdainful craftsmen would describe its occupants, as one did of the turret lathe works, as comprised half "of farmers, and the other half, with few exceptions, of horse thieves."[15] On the other hand, those who held fast to the carefully measured stint, despite the curses of their employers and the lure of higher earnings, depicted themselves as sober and trustworthy masters of their trades. Unlimited output led to slashed piece rates, irregular employment, drink and debauchery, they argued. Rationally restricted output, however, reflected "unselfish brotherhood," personal dignity, and "cultivation of the mind."[16]

Second, as this language vividly suggests, the craftsmen's ethical code demanded a "manly" bearing toward the boss. Few words enjoyed more popularity in the nineteenth century than this honorific, with all its connotations of dignity, respectability, defiant egalitarianism, and patriarchal male supremacy. The worker who merited it refused to cower before the foreman's glares—in fact, often would not work at all when a boss was watching. When confronted with indignities, he was expected to respond like the machinist in Lowell, who found regulations posted in his shop in 1867 requiring all employees to be at their posts in their work clothes when the first bell rang, to remain there until the last bell, and to be prevented from leaving the works between those times by locked doors:

> Not having been brought up under such a system of slavery, [he recalled,] I took my things and went out, followed in a few hours by the rest of the men. Thinking perhaps that it might be of some benefit to the rest, I remained with them on the strike. They went back to work with the understanding that the new rules should not apply except in regard to the doors being locked. A few days after I went for my pay and it was politely handed me without the trouble of asking for it.[17]

Finally, "manliness" toward one's fellow workers was as important as it was toward the owners. "Undermining or conniving" at a brother's job was a form of hoggish behavior as objectional as running more than one machine, or otherwise doing the work that belonged to two men. Union rules commanded the expulsion of members who performed such "dirty work," in order to secure employment or advancement for themselves. When the members of the Iron Heaters and Rollers Union at a Philadelphia mill learned in 1875 that one of their brothers had been fired "for dissatisfaction in regard to his management of the mill," and that another member had "undermined" the first with the superintendent and been promised his rolls, the delinquent was expelled from the lodge, along with a lodge member who defended him, and everyone went on strike to demand the immediate discharge of both excommunicates by the firm.[18]

In short, a simple technological explanation for the control exercised by nineteenth-century craftsmen will not suffice. Technical knowledge acquired on the job was embedded in a mutualistic ethical code, also acquired on the job, and together these attributes provided skilled workers with considerable autonomy at their work and powers of resistance to the wishes of their employers. On the other hand, it was technologically possible for the worker's autonomy to be used in individualistic ways, which might promote his own mobility and identify his interests with those of the owner. The ubiquitous practice of subcontracting encouraged this tendency. In the needle trades, the long established custom of a tailor's taking work home to his family was transformed by his employment of other piece workers into the iniquitous "sweat shop" system.[19] Among iron molders, the "berkshire" system expanded rapidly after 1850, as individual molders hired whole teams of helpers to assist them in producing a multitude of castings. Carpenters and bricklayers were lured into piece work systems of petty exploitation, and other forms of subcontracting flourished in stone quarrying, iron mining, anthracite mining, and even in railroad locomotive works, where entire units of an engine's construction were let out to the machinist who filed the lowest bid, and who then hired a crew to assist him in making and fitting the parts.[20]

Subcontracting practices readily undermined both stints and the mutualistic ethic (though contractors were known to fix stints for their own protection in both garment and locomotive works), and they tended to flood many trades with trained, or semi-trained, workers who undercut wages and work standards. Their spread encouraged many craftsmen to move beyond reliance on their functional autonomy to the next higher level of craft control, the enactment and enforcement of union work rules. In one respect, union rules simply codified the autonomy I have already described. In fact, because they were often written down and enforced by joint action, union rules have a visibility to historians, which has made me resort to them already for evidence in the discussion of autonomy per se. But this intimate historical relationship between customary workers' autonomy and the union rule should not blind us to the fact that the latter represents a significant new stage of development.[21]

The work rules of unions were referred to by their members as "legislation."[22] The phrase denotes a shift from spontaneous to deliberate collective action, from a group ethical code to formal rules and sanctions, and from resistance to employers' pretentious to control over them. In some unions the rules were rather simple. The International Association of Machinists, for example, like its predecessors the Machinists and Blacksmiths' International Union and the many machinists' local assemblies of the Knights of Labor, simply specified a fixed term of apprenticeship for any prospective journeyman, established a standard wage for the trade, prohibited helpers or handymen from performing journeymen's work, and forbade any member from running more than one machine at a time or accepting any form of piece work payment.[23]

Other unions had much more detailed and complex rules. There were, for example, sixty-six "Rules for Working" in the by-laws of the window-glass workers' Local Assembly 300 of the Knights of Labor. They specified that full crews had to be present "at each pot setting," that skimming could be done only at the beginning of blowing and at meal time, that blowers and gatherers should not "work faster than at the rate of nine rollers per hour," and that the "standard size of single strength rollers" should "be 40x58 to cut 38x56." No work was to be performed on Thanksgiving Day, Christmas, Decoration Day or Washington's Birthday, and no blower, gatherer or cutter could work between June 15 and September 15. In other words, during the summer months the union ruled that the fires were to be out.[24] In 1884 the local assembly waged a long and successful strike to preserve its limit of 48 boxes of glass a week, a rule which its members considered the key to the dignity and welfare of the trade.[25]

Nineteenth-century work rules were not ordinarily negotiated with employers or embodied in a contract. From the 1860s onward it became increasingly common for standard *wages* to be negotiated with employers or their associations, rather than fixed unilaterally as unions had tried earlier, but working rules changed more slowly. They were usually adopted unilaterally by local unions, or by the delegates to a national convention, and enforced by the refusal of the individual member to obey any command from an employer which violated them. Hopefully, the worker's refusal would be supported by the joint action of his shop mates, but if it was not, he was honor bound to pack his tool box and walk out alone, rather than break the union's laws. As Fred Reid put the point so well in his description of nineteenth-century Scottish miners' unionism: "The strength of organized labour was held to depend upon the manliness of the individual workman."[26]

On the other hand, the autonomy of craftsmen which was codified in union rules was clearly not individualistic. Craftsmen were unmistakably and consciously group-made men, who sought to pull themselves upward by their collective boot straps. As unions waxed stronger after 1886, the number of strikes to enforce union rules grew steadily. It was, however, in union legislation against subcontracting that both the practical and ideological aspects of the conflict between group solidarity and upwardly mobile individualism became most evident, for these rules sought to regulate in the first instance not the employers' behavior, but that of the workers themselves. Thus, the Iron Molders Union attacked the "berkshire" system by rules forbidding any of its members to employ a helper for any other purpose than "to skim, shake out and to cut sand," or to pay a helper out of his own earnings. In 1867, when 8,615 out of some 10,400 known molders in the country were union members, the national union legislated further that no member was allowed to go to work earlier than seven o'clock in the morning.[27] During the 1880s the Brick Layers' Union checked subcontracting by banning its members from working for any contractor who could not raise enough capital to buy his own bricks. All building trades unions instructed their members not to permit contractors to work with tools alongside with them. The United Mine Workers limited the number of helpers a bituminous miner could engage, usually to one, though the employment of several laborers by one miner remained widespread in anthracite mines through the first World War. The Carpenters and the Machinists outlawed piece work altogether, for the same purpose. The Amalgamated Iron and Steel Workers required the companies to pay helpers directly, rather than through the craftsmen, and fixed the share of tonnage rates to which helpers were entitled.[28] All such regulations secured the group welfare of the workers involved by sharply rejecting society's enticements to become petty entrepreneurs, clarifying and intensifying the division of labor at the work place, and sharpening the line between employer and employee.

Where a trade was well unionized, a committee in each shop supervised the enforcement in that plant of the rules and standard wage which the union had adopted for the trade as a whole. The craft union and the craft local assembly of the Knights of Labor were forms of organization well adapted to such regulatory activities. The members were legislating, on matters on which they were unchallenged experts, rules which only their courage and solidarity could enforce. On one hand, the craft form of organization linked their personal interests to those of the trade, rather than those of the company in which they worked, while, on the other hand, their efforts to enforce the same rules on all of their employers, where they were successful, created at least a few islands of order in the nineteenth century's economic ocean of anarchic competition.

Labor organizations of the late nineteenth century struggled persistently to transform workers' struggles to manage their own work from spontaneous to deliberate actions, just as they tried to subject wage strikes and efforts to shorten the working day to their conscious regulation. "The trade union movement is one of reason, one of deliberation, depending entirely upon the voluntary and sovereign actions of its members," declared the executive Council of the AFL.[29] Only through "thorough organization," to use a favorite phrase of the day, was it possible to enforce a trade's work rules throughout a factory, mine, or construction site. Despite the growing number of strikes over union rules and union recognition in the late 1880s, the enforcement of workers' standards of control spread more often through the daily self-assertion of craftsmen on the job than through large and dramatic strikes.

Conversely, strikes over wage reductions at times involved thinly disguised attacks by employers on craftsmen's job controls. Fall River's textile manufacturers in 1870 and the Hocking Valley coal operators in 1884, to cite only two examples, deliberately foisted severe wage reductions on their highly unionized workers in order to provoke strikes. The owners' hope was that in time hunger would force their employees to abandon union membership, and thus free the

Table 1. Strike Trends, 1881–1905

Year	Number of Strikes (1)	Workers Involved (,000) (2)	Percent Wage Strikes (3)	Percent Ordered by Unions (4)	Percent Sympathy Strikes (5)	Number Sympathy Strikes (6)
1881	471	101	79.8	47.3	0.8	2
1882	454	121	75.4	48.5	0.9	3
1883	478	122	77.2	56.7	0.6	2
1884	443	117	74.1	54.2	2.0	6
1885	645	139	72.9	55.3	3.1	20
1886	1432	407	63.0	53.3	2.9	37
1887	1436	273	54.8	66.3	4.7	71
1888	906	103	55.2	68.1	3.8	34
1889	1075	205	59.0	67.3	6.1	67
1890	1833	286	50.9	71.3	9.9	188
1891	1717	245	48.9	74.8	11.5	204
1892	1298	164	50.4	70.7	8.9	117
1893	1305	195	58.8	69.4	4.5	62
1894	1349	505	63.7	62.8	8.8	120
1895	1215	286	69.6	54.2	0.6	7
1896	1026	184	57.6	64.6	0.6	7
1897	1078	333	66.2	55.3	0.7	9
1898	1056	182	63.0	60.4	0.8	9
1899	1797	308	59.4	62.0	1.5	29
1900	1779	400	59.0	65.4	1.5	29
1901	2924	396	46.6	75.9	2.4	71
1902	3162	553	51.2	78.2	2.6	87
1903	3494	532	51.5	78.8	2.4	88
1904	2307	376	42.2	82.1	3.7	93
1905	2077	176	44.5	74.7	2.7	61

Sources: The number of strikes and the number of workers involved (1 and 2) are taken from U.S. Commissioner of Labor, *Twenty-First Annual Report* (1906), 15, Wage strikes as a percentage of all strikes (3) is from J. H. Griffin, *Strikes* (1939), 76. The percentage of strikes ordered by unions, the percentage of all strikes represented by sympathetic strikes, and the number of sympathetic strikes (4, 5, and 6) are from Florence Peterson, *Strikes in the United States, 1880–1936* (1937), 32, 33.

companies' hands to change production methods.[30] As the treasurer of one Fall River mill testified in 1870: "I think the question with the spinners was not wages, but whether they or the manufacturers should rule. For the last six or eight years they have ruled Fall River."[31] Defeat in a strike temporarily broke the union's control, which had grown through steady recruiting and rule enforcement during years which were largely free of work stoppages.

The third level of control struggles emerged when different trades lent each other support in their battles to enforce union rules and recognition. An examination of the strike statistics gathered by the U.S. Commissioner of Labor for the period 1881–1905 reveals the basic patterns of this development.[32] Although there had been a steady increase in both the number and size of strikes between 1881 and 1886, the following 12 years saw a reversal of that growth, as stoppages became both smaller and increasingly confined to skilled crafts (except in 1894). With that change came three important and interrelated trends. First, the proportion of strikes called by unions rose sharply in comparison to spontaneous strikes. Nearly half of all strikes between 1881 and 1886 had occurred without union sanction or aid. In the seven years beginning with 1887 more than two-thirds of each year's strikes were deliberately called by a union, and in 1891 almost 75 percent of the strikes were official.

Secondly, as strikes became more deliberate and unionized, the proportion of strikes which dealt mainly with wages fell abruptly. Strikes to enforce union rules, enforce recognition of the union, and protect its members grew from 10 percent of the total or less before 1885 to the level of 19–20 percent between 1891 and 1893. Spontaneous strikes and strikes of laborers and factory operatives had almost invariably been aimed at increasing wages or preventing wage reductions, with the partial exception of 1886 when 20 percent of all strikes had been over hours. The more highly craftsmen became organized, however, the more often they struck and were locked out over work rules.

Third, unionization of workers grew on the whole faster than strike participation. The ratio of strike participants to membership in labor organizations fell almost smoothly from 109 in 1881 to 24 in 1888, rose abruptly in 1890 and 1891 (to 71 and 86 respectively), then resumed its downward trend to 36 in 1898, interrupted, of course, by a leap to 182 in 1894.[33] In a word, calculation and organization were the dominant tendencies in strike activity, just as they were in the evolution of work rules during the nineteenth century. But the assertion of deliberate control through formal organization was sustained not only by high levels of militancy (a persistently high propensity to strike), but also by remarkably aggressive mutual support, which sometimes took the form of the unionization of all grades of workers within a single industry, but more often appeared in the form of sympathetic strikes involving members of different trade unions.

Joint organization of all grades of workers seemed most likely to flourish where no single craft clearly dominated the life of the workplace, in the way iron molders, brick layers, or iron puddlers did where they worked. It was also most likely to appear at the crest of the waves of strike activity among unskilled workers and operatives, as is hardly surprising, and to offer evidence of the organizational impulse in their ranks. In Philadelphia's shoe industry between 1884 and 1887, for example, the Knights of Labor successfully organized eleven local assemblies, ranging in size from 55 to 1000 members, each of which represented a different craft or cluster of related occupations, and formulated wage demands and work rules for its own members. Each assembly sent three delegates to District Assembly 70, the highest governing body of the Knights for the industry, which in turn selected seven representatives to meet in a city-wide arbitration committee with an equal number of employers' representatives. Within each factory a "shop union" elected by the workers in that plant handled grievances and enforced the rules of the local assemblies, aided by one male and one female "statistician," who kept track of the complex piece rates.[34]

There is no evidence that local assemblies of unskilled workers or of semi-skilled operatives ever attempted to regulate production processes themselves in the way assemblies of glass blowers and other craftsmen did. They did try to restrict hiring to members of the Knights and sometimes regulated layoffs by seniority clauses. For the most part, however, assemblies of operatives and laborers confined their attention to wages and to protection of their members against arbitrary treatment by supervisors.[35] On the other hand, the mere fact that such workers had been organized made it difficult for employers to grant concessions to their craftsmen at the expense of helpers and laborers. Consequently, the owners were faced simultaneously with higher wage bills and a reduction of their control in a domain where they had been accustomed to exercise unlimited authority.

Moreover, workers who directed important production processes were themselves at times reluctant to see their own underlings organized, and frequently sought to dominate the larger organization to which their helpers belonged. A case in point was offered by the experience of the Knights of Labor in the garment industry, where contractors were organized into local assemblies of their own, supposedly to cooperate with those of cutters, pressers, tailors, and sewing machine operators. Contractors were often charged with disrupting the unionization of their own employees, in order to promote their personal competitive advantages. Above all, they tried to discourage women from joining the operators' assemblies. As the secretary of a St. Louis tailors' local assembly revealed, contractors who were his fellow Knights were telling the parents of operators that "no dissent [*sic*] girl belong to an assembly."[36]

On the other hand, the experience of the Knights in both the shoe and garment industries suggests that effective unionization of women operatives was likely to have a remarkably radicalizing impact on the organization. It closed the door decisively both on employers who wished to compensate for higher wages paid to craftsmen by exacting more from the unskilled, and on craftsmen who were tempted to advance themselves by sweating others. In Philadelphia, Toronto, Cincinnati, Beverly, and Lynn both the resistance of the manufacturers to unionism and the level of mutuality exhibited by the workers leapt upward noticeably when the women shoe workers organized along with the men. Furthermore, the sense of total organization made all shoe workers more exacting in their demands and less patient with the protracted arbitration procedures employed by the Knights. Quickie strikes became increasingly frequent as more and more shoe workers enrolled in the Order. Conversely, the shoe manufacturers banded tightly together to destroy the Knights of Labor.[37]

In short, the organization of all grades of workers in any industry propelled craftsmen's collective rule making into a more aggressive relationship with the employers, even where it left existing styles of work substantially unchanged. The other form of joint action, sympathetic strikes, most often involved the unionized skilled crafts themselves, and consequently was more directly related to questions of control of production processes. When Fred S. Hall wrote in 1898 that sympathetic strikes had "come so much in vogue during the last few years,"[38] he was looking back on a period during which organized workers had shown a greater tendency to walk out in support of the struggles of other groups of workers than was the case in any other period in the history of recorded strike data. Only the years between 1901 and 1904 and those between 1917 and 1921 were to see the absolute number of sympathetic strikes approach even *one-half* the levels of 1890 and 1891.

There were, in fact, two distinct crests in the groundswell of sympathetic strikes. The first came between 1886 and 1888, when a relatively small number of disputes, which spread by sympathetic action to include vast numbers of workers, caught public attention in a dramatic way. The Southwest railways strike of 1886, the New York freight handlers dispute of 1887, and the Lehigh coal and railroad stoppages of 1888 exemplified this trend. None of them, however, primarily involved control questions, in the sense they have been described here.

The second crest, that of 1890–92, was quite different. It was dominated by relatively small stoppages of organized craftsmen. In New York state, where the Bureau of Labor Statistics collected detailed information on such stoppages until 1892 (and included in its count strikes which were omitted from the U.S. Commissioner of Labor's data because they lasted less than a single day or included fewer than six workers), the number of establishments shut by sympathetic strikes rose from an average of 166 yearly between 1886 and 1889 to 732 in 1890, 639 in 1891, and 738 in 1892. Most of them involved the employees of a single company, like the 15 machinists who struck in support of the claims of molders in their factory or the four marble cutters who walked out to assist paper hangers on the same site. A few were very large. When New York's cabinet makers struck to preserve their union in 1892, for example, 107 carpenters, 14 gilders, 75 marble cutters and helpers, 17 painters, 23 plasterers, 28 porters, 12 blue stone cutters, 14 tile layers and helpers, 32 upholsterers, 14 varnishers, 149 wood carvers, and others walked out of more than 100 firms to lend their support.[39]

Eugene V. Debs was to extoll this extreme manifestation of mutuality as the "Christ-like virtue of sympathy," and to depict his own Pullman boycott, the epoch's most massive sympathetic action, as an open confrontation between that working-class virtue and a social order which sanctified selfishness.[40] It is true that the mutualistic ethic which supported craftsmen's control was displayed in its highest form by sympathetic strikes. It is equally true, however, that the element of calculation, which was increasingly dominating all strike activity, was particularly evident here. As Fred S. Hall pointed out, sympathetic strikes of this epoch differed sharply from "contagious" strikes, which spread spontaneously like those of 1877, in two respects. First, the sympathetic strikes were called by the workers involved, through formal union procedures. Although figures comparing official with unofficial strikes are not available, two contrasting statistics illustrate Hall's point. The construction industry was always the leading center of sympathetic strikes. In New York more than 70 percent of the establishments shut by sympathetic action between 1890 and 1892 were involved in building construction. On the other hand, over the entire period of federal data (1881–1905) no less than 98.03 percent of the strikes in that industry were called by unions.[41]

Second, as Hall observed, the tendency toward sympathetic strikes was "least in those cases where the dispute concerns conditions of employment such as wages and hours, and [was] greatest in regard to disputes which involve questions of unionism—the employment of only union men, the recognition of the union, etc."[42] The rise of sympathetic strikes, like the rise of strikes over rules and recognition, was part of the struggle for craftsmen's control—its most aggressive and far-reaching manifestation.

It is for this reason that the practice of sympathetic strikes was ardently defended by the AFL in the 1890s. Building trades contracts explicitly provided for sympathetic stoppages. Furthermore, at the Federation's 1895 convention a resolution carried, directing the Executive Council to "convey to the unions, in such way as it thinks proper, not to tie themselves up with contracts so that they cannot help each other when able." The Council itself denied in a report to the same convention that it opposed sympathetic strikes. "On the contrary," it declared, "we were banded together to help one another. The words union, federation, implied it. An organization which held aloof when assistance could be given to a sister organization, was deserving of censure," even though each union had the right to decide its own course of action.[43]

On the other hand, not all unions supported this policy by any means. Under the right conditions it was just as possible for work processes to be regulated by the rules of a craft union which stood aloof from all appeals to class solidarity, as it was for an individual craftsman to identify his functional autonomy to his employer's interests through subcontracting. Precisely such a solitary course was proudly pursued by the locomotive engineers and firemen. In general, where a union was strong enough to defy its employers alone and where no major technological innovations threatened its members' work practices, it tended to reach an accommodation with the employers on the basis of the latter's more or less willing recognition of the union's work rules.

Two examples will suffice. One appeared in stove molding, where eight years of protracted strikes and lockouts followed the National Stove Founders' Defense Association's 1882 denunciation of the "one-sided cast-iron rules" of the Molders' Union, from which it envisaged "no appeal except through a bitter struggle for supremacy." But the molders' indispensable mastery of the art of casting satiny smooth stove parts, their thorough organization, and their readiness to strike again and again enabled the Molders Union to prevail with little help from other unions. In 1890 the employers' Defense Association signed a national trade agreement, which provided for arbitration of all disputes and tacitly accepted the union's authority to establish work rules.[44] In sharp contrast to machinery molders, who often joined machinists, boiler makers, and other metal tradesmen in strikes, participation by stove molders in sympathetic strikes was practically unheard of.

Similarly, brick layers and stone masons proved eminently capable of defending themselves, seldom found their rules seriously challenged, and consequently felt little need for joint action with other trades, except during campaigns for shorter hours. The forceful but conservative form of craft control which they represented is evident not only in the refusal of the Bricklayers' and Masons' International Union to send representatives to New York City's Board of Walking Delegates or to affiliate with the AFL, but also in the reluctance of its members to engage in sympathetic strikes. Between 1890 and 1892 only four New York firms were shut by bricklayers and four by stone masons in sympathetic actions. By way of contrast, during the same three years sympathetic strikes by carpenters in that state closed 171 firms and similar stoppages by cloakmakers another 152.[45]

Furthermore, employers in many industries banded together in the early 1890s to resist sympathetic strikes, union rules and union recognition with increasing vigor and effectiveness. Sympathetic lockouts were mounted by employers' organizations to deny striking workers alternative sources of employment or financial support. Legal prosecutions for conspiracy in restraint of trade, including use of the Sherman Anti-Trust Act against the Workingmen's Amalgamated Council of New Orleans for the city-wide sympathetic strike of 1892, and court-ordered injunctions provided supplementary weapons. In this setting, unionized craftsmen suffered a growing number of defeats. Whereas less than 40 percent of the strikes of 1889 and 1890 had been lost by the workers, 54.5 percent of the strikes of 1891 and 53.9 percent of those of 1892 were unsuccessful. This level of defeats was by far the highest for the late nineteenth century, and would not be approached again until 1904.[46] The losses are all the more remarkable when one recalls that these were record years for union-called strikes (as opposed to spontaneous strikes), and that throughout the 1881 to 1905 period strikes called by unions tended to succeed in better than 70 percent of the cases, while spontaneous strikes were lost in almost the same proportion. The explanation for the high level of defeats in calculated strikes of 1891 and 1892 lies in the audacity of the workers' demands. Official strikes over wages remained eminently successful. The fiercest battles and the bitterest losses pivoted around union rules and recognition and around sympathetic action itself.

Consequently, trade unionists began to shy away from sympathetic strikes in practice, despite their verbal defenses, even before 1894. The statistical appearance of a crescendo of sympathetic strikes in 1894 followed by an abrupt collapse is misleading. Hall suggests that crafts other than the building trades were becoming hesitant to come out in sympathy with other groups, especially with workers from other plants, from 1892 onward. Although the New York data ends that year, it seems to bear him out in an interesting way. The total number of sympathetic strikes in New York was as great in 1892 as it had been in 1890. On the other hand, 67 percent of those strikes had been in the building trades in 1890, as compared to 69 percent in 1891 and 84 percent in 1892. One wishes the figures had continued, so as to reveal whether the small numbers of such strikes after 1895 were confined to construction. In any event, even in 1892 more than 100 of the 120 establishments outside of the building trades which were hit by sympathetic strikes were involved in a single conflict, that of the cabinet makers. And the workers ultimately abandoned that battle in total defeat. In this context the resurgence of such strikes in 1894 appears as an aberration. Indeed, the Pullman boycott and the bituminous coal strike together accounted for 94 percent of the establishments shut by sympathy actions in the first six months of that year.[47]

In short, historians have, on the whole, been seriously misled by Norman J. Ware's characterization of the period after the Haymarket Affair as one of "*Sauve qui peut!*"[48] As craftsmen unionized, they not only made their struggles for control increasingly collective and deliberate, but also manifested a *growing* consciousness of the dependence of their efforts on those of workers in other crafts. They drew strength in this struggle from their functional autonomy, which was derived from their superior knowledge, exercised through self-direction and their direction of others at work, and both nurtured and in turn was nurtured by a mutualistic ethic, which repudiated important elements of acquisitive individualism. As time passed this autonomy was increasingly often codified in union rules, which were collectively "legislated" and upheld through the commitment of the individual craftsmen and through a swelling number of strikes to enforce them. Organized efforts reached the most aggressive and inclusive level of all in joint action among the various crafts for mutual support. When such actions enlisted all workers in an industry (as happened when women unionized in shoe manufacturing), and when they produced a strong propensity of unionized craftsmen to strike in support of each other's claims, they sharply separated the aggressive from the conservative consequences of craftsmen's autonomy and simultaneously provoked an intense, concerted response from the business community.

In an important sense, the last years of the depression represented only a lull in the battle. With the return of prosperity in 1898, both strikes and union organizing quickly resumed their upward spiral, work rules again seized the center of the stage, and sympathetic strikes became increasingly numerous and bitterly fought. Manufacturers' organizations leapt into the fray with the open shop drive, while their spokesmen cited new government surveys to support their denunciations of workers "restriction of output."[49]

On the other hand, important new developments distinguished the first decade of the twentieth century from what had gone before. Trade union officials, who increasingly served long terms in full-time salaried positions, sought to negotiate the terms of work with employers, rather than letting their members "legislate" them. The anxiety of AFL leaders to secure trade agreements and to ally with "friendly employers," like those affiliated with the National Civic Federation, against the open shop drive, prompted them to repudiate the use of sympathetic strikes. The many such strikes which took place were increasingly lacking in union sanction and in any event never reached the level of the early 1890s.[50]

Most important of all, new methods of industrial management undermined the very foundation of craftsmen's functional autonomy. Job analysis through time and motion study allowed management to learn, then to systematize the way the work itself was done. Coupled with systematic supervision and new forms of incentive payment it permitted what Frederick Winslow Taylor called "*enforced* standardization of methods, *enforced* adoption of the best implements and working conditions, and *enforced* cooperation of all the employees under management's detailed direction."[51] Scientific management, in fact, fundamentally disrupted the craftsmen's styles of work, their union rules and standard rates, and their mutualistic ethic, as it transformed American industrial practice between 1900 and 1930. Its basic effect, as Roethlisberger and Dickson discovered in their experiments at Western Electric's Hawthorne Works, was to place the worker "at the bottom level of a highly stratified organization," leaving his "established routines of work, his cultural traditions of craftsmanship, [and] his personal interrelations" all "at the mercy of technical specialists."[52]

Two important attributes of the scientific management movement become evident only against the background of the struggles of nineteenth-century craftsmen to direct their own work in their own collective way. First, the appeal of the new managerial techniques to manufacturers involved more than simply a response to new technology and a new scale of business organization.

It also implied a conscious endeavor to uproot those work practices which had been the taproot of whatever strength organized labor enjoyed in the late nineteenth century. A purely technological explanation of the spread of Taylorism is every bit as inadequate as a purely technological explanation of craftsmen's autonomy.[53]

Second, the apostles of scientific management needed not only to abolish older industrial work practices, but also to discredit them in the public eye. Thus, Taylor roundly denied that even "the high-class mechanic" could "ever thoroughly understand the science of doing his work," and pasted the contemptuous label of "soldiering" over all craft rules, formal and informal alike.[54] Progressive intellectuals seconded his arguments. Louis Brandeis hailed scientific management for "reliev[ing] labor of responsibilities not its own."[55] And John R. Commons considered it "immoral to hold up to this miscellaneous labor, as a class, the hope that it can ever manage industry." If some workers do "shoulder responsibility," he explained, "it is because certain *individuals* succeed, and then those individuals immediately close the doors, and labor, as a class, remains where it was."[56]

It was in this setting that the phrase "workers' control" first entered the vocabulary of the American labor movement. It appeared to express a radical, if often amorphous, set of demands which welled up around the end of World War I among workers in the metal trades, railroading, coal mining, and garment industries.[57] Although those demands represented very new styles of struggle in a unique industrial and political environment, many of the workers who expressed them could remember the recent day when in fact, the manager's brains had been under the workman's cap.

Notes

Reprinted courtesy of *Labor History*.

The research for this study was assisted by a fellowship from the John Simon Guggenheim Memorial Foundation.

1. Frederick Winslow Taylor, *The Principles of Scientific Management* (Norton Library Edition, New York, 1967), 31, 32.

2. William D. Haywood and Frank Bohn, *Industrial Socialism* (Chicago, n.d.), 25.

3. Herbert G. Gutman, "Work, Culture, and Society in Industrializing America, 1815–1919," *American Historical Review* 78 (June 1973): 531–588; E.P. Thompson, "Time, Work-Discipline, and Industrial Capitalism," *Past and Present* 38 (Dec. 1967): 56–97; E.J. Hobsbawm, "Custom, Wages and Work-load in Nineteenth Century Industry," in Hobsbawm, *Labouring Men* (1964): 344–370; Gregory Kealey, "Artisans Respond to Industrialism: Shoemakers, Shoe Factories and the Knights of St. Crispin in Toronto," Canadian Historical Association, *Historical Papers* (June 1973): 137–157; Paul G. Faler, "Workingmen, Mechanics, and Social

Change: Lynn, Massachusetts, 1800–1860" (unpublished PhD diss., University of Wisconsin, 1971); Bruce Laurie, "The Working People of Philadelphia, 1827–1853" (unpublished PhD diss., University of Pittsburgh, 1971); David Montgomery, "The Shuttle and the Cross: Weavers and Artisans in the Kensington Riots of 1844," *Journal of Social History* 5 (Spring 1972): 411–446.

4. The question of industrial generations has been treated in American history largely in terms of leaders. See David Montgomery, *Beyond Equality: Labor and the Radical Republicans, 1862–1872* (New York, 1967), 197–229; Warren R. Van Tine, *The Making of the Labor Bureaucrat: Union Leadership in the United States, 1870–1920* (Amherst, 1973), 1–32. For a more fundamental social analysis, see Leopold H. Haimson, "The Russian Workers' Movement on the Eve of the First World War," unpublished paper, presented at the American Historical Association convention, 1972; Michelle Perrot, *Les Ouvriers en Greve: France, 1871–1890* (Paris, 1974), I, 312–395.

5. James J. Davis, *The Iron Puddler: My Life in the Rolling Mills and What Came of It* (Indianapolis, 1922), 91.

6. Ibid., 85, 92–3, 96, 114, 227. The issue of promotion of helpers to puddlers' furnaces provoked strikes by helpers against puddlers in the 1870s. See John H. Ashworth, *The Helper and American Trade Unions* (Baltimore, 1915), 83, 93–4.

7. Minute Books, Lodge No. 11, Rollers, Roughers, Catchers and Hookers Union (Columbus, Ohio), July 14, 1873-April 28, 1876 (William Martin Papers, University of Pittsburgh library).

8. Ernest Mandel, ed., *Controle ouvrier, conseils ouvriers, autogestion, anthologie* (Paris, 1970), 192–97. See also Carter Goodrich, *The Frontier of Control* (New York, 1921).

9. Frederick Winslow Taylor, "Shop Management," *Transactions of the American Society of Mechanical Engineers*, XXIV (1903): 1337–1456; U.S. Commissioner of Labor, *Eleventh Annual Report*, "Regulation and Restriction of Output" (Washington, 1904).

10. United Kingdom, Parliament, *Second Report of the Commissioners Appointed to Inquire into the Organization and Rules of Trades Unions and Other Associations* (Parliamentary Sessional Papers, 1867, xxxii c3893), 2; "Restriction of Output," 243.

11. "Restriction of Output," 198–199.

12. U.S. Commission on Industrial Relations, *Final Report and Testimony Submitted to Congress by the Commission on Industrial Relations* (64th Cong., 1st sess., Washington, DC, 1915), 893–94.

13. Henry L. Gantt, *Work, Wages, and Profits* (second revised edition, New York, 1919), 186.

14. "Restriction of Output," 18.

15. P.A. Stein to *Machinists' Monthly Journal*, XV (April 1903): 294.

16. See "What One Trade Has Done," *John Swinton's Paper*, March 23, 1884. Cf., Peter N. Stearns, "Adaptation to Industrialization: German Workers as a Test Case," *Central European History* 3 (Dec. 1970): 303–331.

17. Massachusetts Bureau of Statistics of Labor, *Report of the Bureau of Statistics of Labor for 1871* (Boston 1871): 590–591.

18. Associated Brotherhood of Iron and Steel Heaters, Rollers and Roughers of the United States, "Report on Communications. The Year's Term Having Closed July 10th, 1875," Feb. 25, 1875. For more on "dirty work" and "one man-one machine" rules, see "Amalgamated Association of Iron and Steel Workers," *Proceedings* (1877): 52, 75; "Restriction of Output," 101–05, 226–27.

19. On the origins of "sweating" in the needle trades, see Conrad Carl testimony, U.S. Congress, Senate Committee on Education and Labor, *Report of the Committee of the Senate upon the Relations between Labor and Capital* (Washington, DC, 1885), I, 413–21; Louis Lorwin, *The Women's Garment Workers* (New York, 1924), 12–23.

20. Ashworth, 67–72; Robert A. Christie, *Empire in Wood: A History of the Carpenters' Union* (Ithaca, NY, 1956), chapter 5; Paul Worthman, "Black Workers and Labor Unions in Birmingham, Alabama, 1897–1904," *Labor History* X (Summer 1969): 374–407; Jacob H. Hollander and George E. Barnett, *Studies in American Trade Unionism* (New York, 1912), 147–48; *The Iron Age* LXXXXI (Jan. 30, 1913): 334; *Machinists' Monthly Journal* XVI (April, 1904): 321.

21. Cf., Benson Soffer, "A Theory of Trade Union Development: The Role of the 'Autonomous' Workman," *Labor History* 1 (Spring 1960): 141–63.

22. The Typographers still call their rule book the Book of Laws. See Selig Perlman, *A Theory of the Labor Movement* (New York, 1928), 262–72; Seymour Martin Lipset, Martin A. Trow, and James S. Coleman, *Union Democracy* (Garden City, NY, 1962), 160–226.

23. "Restriction of Output," 101–8; Charles B. Going, "The Labour Question in England and America," *Engineering Magazine* XIX (May, 1900): 161–76; Hollander and Barnett, 109–52.

24. By-Laws of the Window Glass Workers, L.A. 300, Knights of Labor (Pittsburgh, 1899), 26–36.

25. "What One Trade Has Done," *John Swinton's Paper*, March 23, 1884.

26. Fred Reid, "Keir Hardie's Conversion to Socialism," in *Essays in Labour History, 1886–1923*, eds. Asa Briggs and John Saville (London, 1971), 29. See also Montgomery, *Beyond Equality*, 142–53; David A. McCabe, *The Standard Rate in American Trade Unions* (Baltimore, 1912).

27. *Proceedings of the Eighth Annual Session of the Iron Molders' International Union* (Philadelphia, 1867), 10, 14, 40–41; Ashworth, 36, 38, 68.

28. See above, note 20.

29. Samuel Gompers, "The Strike and Its Lessons," in John Swinton, *A Momentous Question. The Respective Attitudes of Labor and Capital* (Philadelphia and Chicago, 1895), 311.

30. See Philip T. Silvia, Jr., "The Spindle City: Labor, Politics and Religion in Fall River, Massachusetts, 1870–1905" (unpublished PhD diss., Fordham Univ., 1973), chapter 3; Jon Amsden and Stephen Brier, "Coal Miners on Strike: The Transformation of Strike Demands and the Formation of the National Union in the U.S. Coal Industry, 1881–1894," forthcoming in *The Journal of Interdisciplinary History*; Andrew Roy, *A History of the Coal Miners* (Columbus, Ohio, 1902), 220–242.

31. Massachusetts Bureau of Statistics of Labor, *Report*, 1871, 5.

32. See Table 1.

33. John H. Griffin, *Strikes: A Study in Quantitative Economics* (New York, 1939), 107. A splendid discussion of the increasing role of calculation in nineteenth-century strikes may be found in Perrot, *Les ouvriers en grève*, I, 101–180; II, 424–85, 574–606.

34. Augusta E. Galster, *The Labor Movement in the Shoe Industry, with Special Reference to Philadelphia* (New York, 1924), 49–57.

35. See, for example, the agreement between Carpet Weavers' National Assembly No. 126, K. of L. and E. S. Higgins & Co., in New York Bureau of Statistics of Labor, *Fourth Annual Report*, 1886 (Albany, 1887), 256. Much more research is needed on the demands of unskilled workers, but note the sharp contrast in the types of demands presented by craftsmen and laborers when each group met separately during the Bethlehem Steel Strike. U.S. Congress, Senate, *Report on the Strike at the Bethlehem Steel Works* (Senate Document No. 521, Washington, DC, 1910), 26–32.

36. Abraham Bisno, *Abraham Bisno, Union Pioneer* (Madison, 1967), 77–78, 135–37; John W. Hayes Papers (Catholic University of America), LA 7507, LA 2567, LA 10353. The quotation is from Gustive Cytron to John Hayes, Nov. 1, 1893. Hayes Papers, LA 10353. See Ashworth, passim, on the domination of helpers' unions by locals of craftsmen.

37. Galster, 55–57. See also Alan C. Dawley, "The Artisan Response to the Factory System: Lynn, Massachusetts, in the Nineteenth Century" (unpublished PhD diss., Harvard Univ., 1971); Kealey, 145–47; James M. Morris, "The Cincinnati Shoemakers Lockout of 1888," *Labor History* 13 (Fall 1972): 505–19.

38. Fred S. Hall, *Sympathetic Strikes and Sympathetic Lockouts* (New York: Columbia University Studies in History, Economics and Public Law, No. 26, 1898), 29.

39. New York B. L. S., *Report*, 1890, 936–49, *Report*, 1891, Part II, 732–45; *Report*, 1892, 124–39.

40. Debs, "Labor Strikes and Their Lessons," in Swinton, *Momentous Question*, 324–25.

41. U. S. Commissioner of Labor, *Twenty-First Annual Report* (Washington, DC, 1906), 21–2, 33–4, 81–2. The calculation of the percentage of New York sympathetic strikes involving the building trades are my own, from the New York B. L. S. data.

42. Hall, 33.

43. Levasseur, *The American Workman* (Baltimore, 1900), 237–39; Hall, 102–103. The quotations from the AFL are in Hall, 102–03.

44. Hollander and Barnett, 226–31. The quotation is on p. 226. The trade agreement is reprinted on pp. 230–31.

45. John R. Commons, *Trade Unionism and Labor Problems* (First Series, Boston, 1905), 66–7; Philip Taft, *The A.F. of L. in the Time of Gompers* (New York, 1957), 25, 29, 251. On sympathetic strikes in New York, see above, note 39.

46. Hall, 36–51, 70–78; John T. Cumbler, "Labor, Capital, and Community: The Struggle for Power," *Labor History* 15 (Summer 1974): 395–415; Almont Lindsay, *The Pullman Strike* (Chicago, 1942), 122–46, 203–73; Edwin E. Witte, *The Government in Labor Disputes* (New York and London, 1932), 26–31: 61–82; Gerald G. Eggert, *Railroad Labor Disputes: The Beginnings of Federal Strike Policy* (Ann Arbor, 1967),

81–191; United States v. Workingmen's Amalgamated Council of New Orleans, et al., 54 Fed. 994 (1893); Florence Peterson, *Strikes in the United States, 1880–1936* (Washington: U.S. Dept. of Labor Bulletin No. 651 Aug., 1937), 34.

47. Hall, 37–38.

48. Norman J. Ware, *The Labor Movement in the United States, 1860–1895* (New York and London, 1929), xii.

49. Clarence E. Bonnett, *Employers' Associations in the United States: A Study of Typical Associations* (New York, 1922); *Commons, Trade Unionism and Labor Problems, passim*; "Restriction of Output."

50. See Van Tine, 57–112; Mark Perlman, *The Machinists: A New Study in American Trade Unionism* (Washington, DC, 1956), 20–36, 48–50.

51. Taylor, 83.

52. F. J. Roethlisberger and W. J. Dickson, *Management and the Worker: Technical vs. Social Organization in an Industrial Plant* (Cambridge: Harvard University Business Research Studies, No. 9, 1934), 16–17. Cf., Harry Braverman, *Labor and Monopoly Capital: The Degradation of Work in the Twentieth Century* (New York and London, 1974).

53. For basically technological interpretations of scientific management, see David Landes, *The Unbound Prometheus* (New York, 1969), 290–326; Samuel Haber, *Efficiency and Uplift: Scientific Management in the Progressive Era, 1890–1920* (Chicago and London, 1964); Hugh G. J. Aitken, *Taylorism at Watertown Arsenal: Scientific Management in Action, 1908–1915* (Cambridge, Mass., 1960).

54. U. S. Congress, House of Representatives, *Hearings before the Special Committee of the House of Representatives to Investigate the Taylor and other Systems of Shop Management* (3 vols., Washington, D.C., 1912), 1397.

55. Brandeis, "Brief before the I. C.C., January 3, 1911," in Daniel Bloomfield, *Selected Articles on Employment Management* (New York, 1922), 127.

56. John R. Commons and others, *Industrial Government* (New York, 1921), 26.

57. See Arthur Gleason, "The Shop Stewards and Their Significance," *Survey* XLI (Jan. 4, 1919): 417–22; Carter Goodrich, "Problems of Workers' Control," *Locomotive Engineers Journal* LVII (May 1923): 365–67, 415; Evans Clark, "The Industry Is Ours," *Socialist Review* IX (July 1920): 59–62; David Montgomery, "The 'New Unionism' and the Transformation of Workers' Consciousness in America, 1909–1922," *Journal of Social History* 7 (Summer 1974): 509–29.

CHAPTER 11

The "New Unionism" and the Transformation of Workers' Consciousness in America, 1909–22

From *Journal of Social History* 7, no. 4 (Summer 1974): 511–529

Andre Tridon, correspondent of *La bataille syndicaliste* in the United States, had little concern for theoretical debates among syndicalists, industrialists, Socialists and "pure and simple" unionists. The "New Unionism," said he, "is the practice which will enable the workers to assume as a return for their labor the full control of the various industries."[1] This emphasis on practice and control suggests that syndicalist tendencies among American workers may have reached far beyond the limited influence of the Industrial Workers of the World, and that the customary image of the I.W.W. as representing conduct and aspirations far removed from the "mainstream" of American labor development may be misleading. To test these implications of Tridon's view this essay will first examine the patterns of working-class behavior in the years 1909 to 1922, then explore the causes of that behavior. Along the way it will try to shed some light on the question widely voiced in Wobbly circles in 1911: "Why don't the I.W.W. grow?"

The I.W.W. was born just as a massive upsurge in trade union strength had been brought to an abrupt halt. Between 1898 and 1903 the American economy had enjoyed an extraordinary boom resulting from the reconstruction of urban commercial centers with reinforced concrete and structural steel, the emergence of a host of new industries based on products and processes created in research laboratories of the previous decade, ranging from chemicals to electrical machinery, and an extensive quest for the resources of the tropical world, the value of which was largely revealed by those laboratories. In this setting financial houses sponsored mergers among competing manufacturing firms, which gave birth to most of the twentieth century's leading corporations. The same upsurge generated so strong a demand for labor that skilled workmen had been able to force General Electric, United States Steel, International Harvester, the Morgan interests in anthracite and the Big Four meat packers of Chicago, not to mention the smaller employers of the building trades, machine tool industry, boot and shoe manufacture and northern textiles, to deal at least momentarily with numerous craft unions.

The economic downturn of 1903–04 changed this situation dramatically. The great steel corporation, having seriously limited union influence in the 1901 strike, began to pick off union outposts in the South, Great Lakes shipping and bridge erection, in preparation for dealing the *coup de grace* to all unions within its writ in 1909. Harvester and the meat packers disposed of union annoyance in 1904, and eastern metal working shops began universally to ignore the rules of the machinists' union and to substitute handymen and specialists for journeymen.[2] Outside the metropolitan centers of the land, all unionism but that of miners was "stopped in its tracks"[3] by Citizens' Alliances and other mobilizations of the local middle classes sponsored by employers' associations to rid their communities of strikes and union restrictions on production.

But the craft unions, checked at flood tide by an aroused Babbittry, had already been tamed in their own conduct by the bitter social conflicts of the 1890s. The quest for binding trade agreements to secure their industrial positions had induced their leaders to suppress sympathy strikes, which had been the mainspring of their growth in earlier decades. Most unions, furthermore, had come to rely on the union label as their primary organizing instrument. By bestowing labels on companies with which they signed agreements, union leaders offered employers a talisman to promote their sales in working-class markets (as with overalls, beer or machinists' instruments) or to distinguish wares of high quality from mass produced articles (as with cigars or shoes). "The union label," observed Brewery Workers' editor W.E. Trautmann, "is practically the manufacturers' label."[4]

It was such unionism which roused the ire of the men and women who assembled in July, 1905 to found the I.W.W. Agreeing that "trade lines have been swallowed up in a common servitude of all workers to the machines which they tend,"[5] the delegates decided to organize workers from the bottom up, enlisting first the unskilled and using their enthusiasm and power to pull the more highly skilled workers into action. This meant that the I.W.W. had to replace the craft unions' meticulous caution with dramatic tactics. It would scorn large strike funds, relying instead on mass appeals for aid, on the workers' own spirit of sacrifice and on short strikes. It would reject all reliance on negotiations, labels, written contracts, trade autonomy and benefit funds, and it would summon the workers to leave the decrepit "American Separation of Labor" and enlist in the new revolutionary union.[6]

In the ensuing four or five years little came of these great hopes. The I.W.W. seemed determined to devour itself in internecine bickering. Leaders of the

A.F. of L. union which had borne the most intense raids from the I.W.W., the Machinists, could assure their members by the end of 1906 that the rival organization had reached the end of its career. What "went up like a rocket," they crowed, "came down like a stick."[7] In fact, the most massive struggle of the period, set off in 1907 when 36 unions of the New Orleans Dock and Cotton Council closed the port of the Crescent City to help the Brewery Workers challenge a jurisdictional award of the A.F. of L., had borne many attributes of an I.W.W. battle—a general strike based on the power of the "unskilled," black-white unity explicitly and decisively asserted, Marxist leadership and bitter worker hostility to the A.F. of L., but the Wobblies had played no greater part in it than the organization of some support meetings.[8]

Despite its peculiar attributes of being set in the deep South and engaging strikers more against the A.F. of L. than against capital, the New Orleans strike did portend things to come. In the last quarter of 1907 the economy was struck by a crisis of such severity that the average level of unemployment for the ensuing year was 16.4 percent of the nation's non-farm employees.[9] Then between July, 1909 and the summer of 1910 the economy revived vigorously, before sinking back into the doldrums for all of 1911. With the upturn came the beginning of a decade of strikes of unprecedented scale and continuity.

In New York a militant nucleus of workers enrolled in the Ladies Garment Workers broke sharply with the union label tradition by calling general strikes, first of the city's entire shirtwaist industry then of cloak and suit manufacture. Strikers at the Pressed Steel Car Company near Pittsburgh called in I.W.W. organizers to assist them. The great armaments works of Bethlehem Steel was brought to a halt when blast furnace laborers quit work in sympathy with machinists, who had struck to protest Sunday work.[10]

In Philadelphia, efforts by the city government to break the streetcarmen's union provoked in quick succession a strike of motormen, violent crowd action against scabs, which saw 298 cars wrecked and more than 500 people arrested, a sympathy stoppage which spread from the knitting mills of the Kensington district across the city and ultimately a general strike involving 146,000 workers at its peak and directed by the A.F. of L.'s Central Labor Union for twenty days.[11] The Socialist editors of the *New York Call* saw in this upsurge a challenge to the established practices of the union movement and the electoral orientation of their party alike:

> Such strikes as that of McKees Rocks, the shirtwaist makers' strike of this city, and now the Philadelphia strike are witnesses of the incapacity of the conservative and "constructive" labor leaders, as well as of the fighting spirit which animates the working masses . . . The working masses are just as ready to fight the capitalists by means of the strike as by means of the ballot.[12]

The mass involvement, direct challenge to managerial authority and contempt for accepted A.F. of L. practice workers exhibited in 1909–10 were to remain the outstanding characteristics of American labor struggles, not episodically but continuously for the next dozen years. That most large strikes of the epoch ended in total defeat for the workers testifies both to the audacity of the strikers' pretentions and to their willingness to act in defiance of warnings from experienced union leaders that chances of victory were slim. In fact, large scale strikes erupted whenever the level of unemployment fell off sufficiently to give the strikers a ghost of a chance of success. The critical level of unemployment seems to have been as high as nine percent of the non-farm labor force. At any jobless rate below that level, the ratio of strikers to industrial workers shot up.[13]

From mid-1910 until the first quarter of 1912, however, the economy sagged consistently, and unemployment rose above the 13 percent mark, despite a short-lived false recovery early in 1911. Major strikes were few, though one of them, that of the shopmen on the Illinois Central Railroad, was to be a major landmark in the history of American syndicalism. No great strikes were staged against wage reductions, largely because major corporations followed the lead of U.S. Steel in scrupulously avoiding wage cuts. They sought rather to reduce unit costs of production by the widespread promotion of new efficiency schemes and to capitalize on heavy unemployment by "the weeding out of the less efficient workmen."[14] Socialist party votes surged upward, and party members captured leading positions in the Machinists and the Mine Workers, but direct action in basic industry was at a minimum.[15]

Even before the first clear signs of revival in 1912, the woolen mills of Lawrence were closed by the I.W.W.'s famous strike against one group of companies which had assumed that the state of the labor market would allow them to reduce wages (in conjunction with a small reduction of hours mandated by law). The textile workers' revolt spread across New England and New Jersey during the ensuing 18 months, focusing its fire increasingly on the new stretch-out and premium pay schemes. By April, 1913 *Iron Age* complained that the country was gripped by an "epidemic of strikes."[16] Most of the walkouts were brief, spontaneous and local and were sparked by unskilled workers, like those at Studebaker and Firestone Rubber. Republic Steel avoided trouble by raising its common labor rate for the first time since May, 1910 from 17 cents to 19½ cents an hour. In New York the most wretchedly paid garment workers, the 10,000 women who sewed kimonos, wrappers and other "white goods," staged a fierce and successful strike for union recognition.[17]

By the end of 1913 both the prosperity and the workers' militancy had subsided. *Iron Age* commented that "a year of blight" had opened with the "most buoyant activity ever known," and closed in an atmosphere of business uncertainty.[18] Unemployment stood at brutally high levels for a year and a

Table 1. Strike Trends in the United States, 1900–1925

Year	Strikes and lock-outs (1)	Workers involved (000) (2)	Strikers as % of all workers (3)	Index of control strikes (4)	Unemployed as % of nonfarm employees (5)
1900	1,899	568	4.9	182	12.6
1901	3,012	564	4.7	320	10.1
1902	3,240	692	5.6	328	8.6
1903	3,648	788	6.2	375	9.0
1904	2,419	574	4.3	296	12.0
1905	2,186	302	2.2	249	9.5
1906	629[a]	74[b]	5.1[b]		3.0
1907	680[a]	94[b]	6.3[b]		6.0
1908	315[a]	28[b]	1.9[b]		16.4
1909	452[a]	65[b]	4.1[b]		11.6
1910	604[a]	218[a]	11.4[a]		11.6
1911	511[a]	112[a]	5.8[a]		13.0
1912	575[a]	138[a]	7.0[a]		9.0
1913	567[c]	337[c]	24.4[c]		8.2
1914	1,204			81	14.7
1915	1,593	640	3.7	109	15.6
1916	3,789	1,600	9.2	225	9.1
1917	4,450	1,227	6.9	312	8.2
1918	3,353	1,240	6.8	220	2.4
1919	3,630	4,160	22.5	269	2.4
1920	3,411	1,463	7.8	214	8.6
1921	2,385	1,099	5.7	144	19.5
1922	1,112	1,613	8.3	93	11.4
1923	1,553	757	3.8	150	4.1
1924	1,249	655	3.3	121	8.3
1925	1,301	428	2.1	133	5.4

[a]Massachusetts, New York, and New Jersey figures.
[b]Massachusetts and New York only.
[c]New York and New Jersey only.

Sources: The number of strikes and lockouts (1) and the number of workers involved (2) are from Florence Peterson, *Strikes in the United States, 1880–1936* (U.S. Dept. of Labor, Bulletin No. 651), 21; U.S. Bureau of the Census, *Historical Statistics of the United States, Colonial Times to 1957* (Washington, 1960), 99; Massachusetts Bureau of Statistics of Labor, *Reports, 1901–16*; New York Dept. of Labor, *Bulletin No. 66* (Nov., 1914); New Jersey Bureau of Industrial Statistics, *Reports, 1901–16*; U.S. Census Bureau, *Census of Manufactures, 1914 Abstract* and *Census of Manufactures, 1919 Abstract*. No strike data was gathered by the federal government from 1906 through 1914.

The number of "all workers" on which column (3) is based is the number of "manual and service workers" minus the number of "private household workers," from *Historical Statistics*, 74. Annual figures were estimated from the decadal figures of the census.

The index of control (4) is the ratio of the total number of strikes each year for recognition, union rules, sympathy and miscellaneous, to the number of such strikes in 1886, taken as 100. The data used are from Peterson, 33, 39.

Figures on unemployment (5) are from Stanley Lebergott, *Manpower in Economic Growth* (New York, 1964), 512.

half, and strikes were largely confined to long unionized sectors, such as coal mines and the building trades.

Then came the Allies' war orders, and with them all economic inhibitions to direct action were removed. The "munitions strikes," as they were called by the U.S. Bureau of Labor Statistics, swept out of New England across the whole northeastern part of the country in the hot summer of 1915. Metal trades replaced building trades as the most strike-prone occupations. Small and middling sized towns, the scene of the Open Shop Drive's earlier triumph, replaced big cities as the location of most work stoppages. Moreover, of the 179 strikes of machinists recorded for 1915, only 43 had union support.[19] In the ten-day closing of the whole complex of firms controlled by Westinghouse in the East Pittsburgh area, the Machinists and other A.F. of L. unions were repudiated by the 40,000 strikers, despite the fact that the tumultuous strike had been initiated by tool and die makers. The most prominent spokesmen of the strikers had Socialist party, Socialist Labor party and I.W.W. affiliations.[20]

Despite the uneven impact of the war orders on the economy and the persistence of serious unemployment through 1916, the strike fever spread to many other industries. For the seven years following 1915, the ratio of strikers to all industrial and service employees remained *constantly* on a par with the more famous strike years of 1934 and 1937. The declaration of war had only a minor impact on this militancy. Each year of American participation more than a million workers struck, more, that is, than had ever struck in any year before 1915. The soaring cost of food, and especially government orders diluting wheat flour with corn meal, added fuel to the fire. Food riots flared in March, 1917, when New York women attacked grocery stores and marched on the Waldorf-Astoria hotel demanding bread. In Philadelphia troops killed one woman and wounded nine others, breaking their occupation of the city's marketplace.[21]

The 6,205 recorded strikes between April 6, 1917 and November 11, 1918 tended to be short and took on more of an outlaw quality than ever in the face of the A.F. of L.'s official pledge not to strike. With unemployment down to 1.4 percent, workers improved their incomes as much by moving from job to job as they did by striking. It was common for workers to accept six to eight jobs in a single day of searching, then to report to the most promising one. An annual factory turnover rate "of 1,600 to 2,000 percent was by no means phenomenal," observed Professor L.C. Marshall.[22] On the other hand, the most ambitious claims of workers, the eight-hour day and control over their conditions of work, could not be obtained by individual action. They provoked the most intense, and the most chronic, collective conflicts.

The second decade of the twentieth century was the decisive period in the battle for the eight-hour day, which American workers had been waging since the 1860s. At the start of the decade only eight percent of the country's workers had regular schedules of 48 hours a week or less. Almost 70 percent of them worked more than 54 hours weekly. By 1919, however, 48.6 percent had the 48-hour week, and less than 26 percent still put in more than 54 hours.[23] The machinists of Trenton, whose strike for a nine-hour day in 1914 had been drowned in the unemployed of Philadelphia, shut their city's machine shops for three months at the end of 1915 to demand an *eight-hour* day. When their employers yielded to the union, they found "practically all" of the strikers had found jobs elsewhere.[24] According to the National War Labor Board, 1,026,703 workers had achieved the eight-hour day between 1915 and 1917 alone, before the Board instituted its "basic eight-hour day." Most dramatic of all was the accomplishment of the silk, cotton and woolen mill hands of the North. In 1910 the state of Massachusetts had legislated a 58-hour week for textile workers, the first reduction since the law of 1874 had established the 60-hour week. Nine years later the 48-hour week was the norm in all three industries.[25]

Such gains cannot be understood simply as the logical fruit of technological progress and rising productivity. In fact, there is evidence to suggest both that output per man-hour declined during the war years and that some restoration of longer hours accompanied rising productivity in the twenties.[26] A survey by the National Industrial Conference Board of five major industries in 1919 and 1920 found employers overwhelmingly of the opinion that the more mechanized an industry was, the more *difficult* it was for employers to compensate for reductions of hours by increases in hourly output, and consequently the greater the resistance of employers to such reductions.[27] Certainly the intense opposition of metal trades firms to demands for the eight-hour day in the strikes of 1916 (when some 600 strikes were called on May 1st alone) indicated their full agreement with the editorial resolve of *Iron Age*, "that the unparalleled situation which has made victory in Europe turn not only upon sheer tonnage in steel projectiles, but upon the metal-cutting capacity of American machine tools, must not be allowed to settle for years to come so important an issue as the eight-hour machine shop day."[28]

Every bit as provocative of conflict as the battle for the eight-hour day, but far less richly rewarded in long term effects, was the effort by workers to establish collective control over their conditions of work. A measure of control struggles other than those for eight hours may be constructed by lumping together such strike issues as enforcement of work rules, union recognition, discharge of unpopular foremen or retention of popular ones, regulation of layoffs or dismissals, and actions of sympathy with other groups of workers. An index of the frequency of these control strikes since 1881 reveals that they became especially prominent in three periods: 1901–04, 1916–20 and 1934–41.[29]

The control strikes of 1901–04 basically involved the titanic and mostly unsuccessful effort of the craft unions to secure a firm hold within the congealing structure of monopoly capitalism. Many similar efforts appeared in the

1916–20 period, when unions like the United Brotherhood of Carpenters and Joiners and the International Association of Machinists took advantage of the buoyant labor market to renew their efforts to operate in the old way. Much more distinctive and significant were the extensive efforts of workers both inside and outside the old unions to exert new forms of collective control. Even the recognition struggles of older unions, however, could trigger new forms of struggle. Five city-wide general strikes plagued the government between September 1917 and April 1918: in Springfield, Illinois; Kansas City, Missouri; Waco, Texas; and two in Billings, Montana. The Billings strikes were called to aid embattled building tradesmen, Kansas City's was to help laundry workers, and the others were in support of streetcar motormen and conductors.[30]

In the four years following the armistice, control strikes persisted at high levels, while the phrase "workers' control," seldom heard before that time, became a popular catchword throughout the labor movement. Union membership in the United States was two and a half times the level of 1910, an increase not far below the threefold rise for the world's twenty leading industrial nations as a whole.[31] The Machinists union alone had grown from 54,000 members under predominantly conservative leadership in 1910 to 331,450 members under a Socialist administration by 1919.[32] Both the United Mine Workers, now over 400,000 strong, and the increasingly unified coalition of 16 unions among the 1,850,000 railway workers had committed themselves officially to immediate nationalization of their particular industries, with future direction to be shared by the employees and consumer groups. When the railroad brotherhoods and shopcraft unions tested the sentiment of their members on the so-called Plumb Plan in 1920, 90 percent of the workers voting favored a strike to make Congress enact the nationalization scheme.[33]

Among the 4,160,348 workers who participated in strikes in 1919 every conceivable type of demand was raised: wage increases to catch the soaring cost of living, reductions of hours to 44 a week in the needle trades and 40 in metropolitan building trades, recognition of unions and shop committees, joint negotiation with councils of related unions in particular plants, shipyards or communities, defiance of governmental decrees and, on July 4th through 9th, freedom for Tom Mooney. In Seattle the committee directing the city's general strike declared:

> Labor will not only SHUT DOWN the industries, but Labor will REOPEN, under the management of the appropriate trades, such activities as are needed to preserve public health and public peace. If the strike continues, Labor may feel led to avoid public suffering by reopening more and more activities.
>
> UNDER ITS OWN MANAGEMENT.
>
> And that is why we say we are starting on a road that leads—NO ONE KNOWS WHERE![34]

The new mood among workers shattered the Socialist party and subjected the A.F. of L. to extreme stress. As J.B.S. Hardman noted: "the war emphasized the power of money, of industry, the significance of leadership, of direct action. And the Socialist party had nothing to offer but advice to use the franchise intelligently."[35] Samuel Gompers, in turn, organized an "All-American" committee of labor leaders to stage rallies against "bolshevism, I.W.W.ism and red flagism in general."[36] Editorially he warned his flock: "History records few ideas more tragic and fantastic than the idea of government by direct action. The strike itself is a weapon too sacred and too valuable to be used for any other than its legitimate purpose."[37]

In 1920, consequently, 7.4 percent of the strikes and 58 percent of the strikers were without union sanction. The insurgent strike of 60,000 Illinois coal miners and another of 25,000 railroad switchmen were the best known of these conflicts.[38] They also marked a return to the center of the American labor scene of the alliance of railroad workers and coal miners which had been the germ of most nineteenth-century mass strikes.[39] But the upward spiral of unemployment, starting in the summer of 1920 and rising to 20 percent through 1921, put a damper on this insurgent behavior.

The main thrust of official union efforts during the 1921–22 depression was to preserve contracts and work rules, even at the expense of wage reductions.[40] Workers, in turn, tended to close ranks around their organizations and hence to strengthen the hand of incumbent leaders. In 1922 less than one-tenth of one percent of the 1,613,000 strikers were out without union authorization. Yet the year began with almost 40,000 packing house workers on strike and progressed to a summertime state of war in American basic industries. The strikes were not numerous, but they were huge, protracted, desperate battles. Fully 400,000 railroad shopmen, 600,000 coal miners and 60,000 textile workers struck in vain attempts to preserve union organization against the employers' American Plan offensive.[41]

In summary, then, direct action had been, not the exclusive property of the I.W.W., but the main theme of a dozen years of fierce class conflict in America. During those years a secondary theme of workers' control had recurred incessantly and become increasingly explicit. It is small wonder, therefore, that avowedly syndicalist groupings of workers were numerous, some of them inside the A.F. of L. The Cloth Hat and Cap Makers and the Sheet Metal Workers of New York put no faith in trade agreements or union labels and bestowed absolute power on shop committees, coordinated by executive boards of avowed revolutionaries.[42] The Jewelry Workers, sparked by an alliance of Jewish Socialists and Italian syndicalists, boasted their shop autonomy and the direct action which had won them a 44-hour week as early as 1916.[43] Another Italian-Jewish axis gave similar orientation to the local of the Structural Iron Workers which dealt with New York's ornamental iron shops.[44]

All these unions were made up of skilled craftsmen and dealt with very small employers. A Parisian syndicalist would have understood them well.[45] But all of them stood outside the world of modern large-scale industry, where the direct-action currents of these twelve years were concentrated. The more significant appearance of New Unionism *within* basic industry was attributed by Vice-President P.J. Conlon of the Machinists to the spread of new managerial practices which, he claimed, stimulated a response of "sabotage, syndicalism, passive resistance" on the workers' part. "We did not hear of any of these things," he argued, "until we heard of scientific management and new methods of production."[46]

Conlon's view merits careful examination because American manufacturing had, in fact, been drastically transformed since the 1890s not only in its financial structure and market relationships by the consolidation of competing firms and the formation of ubiquitous trade associations, but also in the internal organization of the production process itself. The cutting edge of the internal reform was described by Frederick Winslow Taylor as "the deliberate gathering in on the part of those on management's side of all of the great mass of traditional knowledge, which in the past has been in the heads of the workmen, and in the physical skill and knack of the workman, which he has acquired through years of experience."[47]

Although the particulars of the process varied substantially from one industry to another, employers in every major industry sought to develop an engineering staff, academically educated for its new role, which could plan and direct the flow of production on the basis of systematic research in both the properties of materials used in production and the logical sequence of productive operations, then assign each worker a very specific task in that sequence, based on time and motion studies, and finally, induce the worker to perform that task as assigned by a carefully structured system of incentive payments. By this innovation, the power of the craftsmen which had rested on their superior knowledge of their work relative to their employers was undermined, and the traditional dualism of craftsmen operating the machinery while laborers fetched and carried was remodeled into a continuum of specialized machine tenders performing functions which required only minor variations in training and agility, and all of which were directly under the detailed supervision of a swarm of managerial officials.[48]

Three important consequences for workers flowed from the combination of corporate consolidation and the adoption of new efficiency schemes. The first was the divorce between the technical and social systems of control in the factory, which Roethlisberger and Dickson were to discover in the famous Hawthorne experiments.[49] Some degree of worker restriction of output remained, but on a guerrilla basis, as defiance of management's will and instructions, as sabotage. The small informal work group persisted, not as an agency of explicit control, as it had been under craft unionism, but as a submerged, impenetrable obstacle to management's sovereignty. The steel mill laborers of Whiting Williams's gang had "not the slightest interest in what [their work] means or how it affects the operations of the mill around them . . . It is all just a matter of doing as little work as the boss will allow." Their favorite saying was, "What the hell!"[50]

Secondly, the more thoroughly business rationalized itself, the more extreme became the chaos of working-class life. Even the frail safeguards of employment stability that union rules and standard rates had represented were swept away, while the urgent need of heavily capitalized corporations to operate only at full capacity made job tenure increasingly spasmodic for many workers. Hence weavers could be ordered to run twelve looms in place of eight because, "there's plenty waitin' at the gates for our jobs."[51] Henry Ford could enforce any tempo of work he wished because, when he announced the famous five-dollar day in January, 1914, 10,000 men rioted at the plant gates, fighting each other for the jobs.[52] At a national conference on unemployment that year, the secretary of the Chicago Unemployment Commission reported that conditions were no worse than usual. That was the tragedy, he continued, unemployment was now chronic and endemic to the economy.[53] The typical unemployed male, a conference the next year concluded, was neither the casual laborer nor the craftsman, but the specialist, whom scientific management had spawned. In New York only 21 percent of the unemployed had been in the United States fewer than five years. Fifty-five percent of them had been here more than ten years.[54] The jobless were not marginal men, but an indispensable part of "rationalized" industry.

Third, the oligopolistic power of the new corporation provided it with a new capacity to administer prices on the basis of long-range planning for company development. Simultaneously, the rapid growth of the urban population reversed the nineteenth-century trend of constantly falling food prices. These two factors contributed to an upward drift in the cost of living, which averaged 2.4 percent annually from 1896 through 1912. With the coming of the war the rate of increase soared upward.[55] As a result, even though major corporations increasingly adhered to a policy of maintaining stable wages through crisis periods, thus avoiding mass revolts against wage cuts, real earnings were, in fact, constantly falling. Every period of relatively full employment, therefore, was marked by strikes of lower paid workers over wages.

The combined impact of these three developments generated two distinct currents of working-class struggle, which often tended to fuse during and after the war years: one arising from the craftsmen and the other from operatives and laborers. The more skilled workers took advantage of every period of low unemployment to attack certain elements of the new managerial methods directly. During the war they mounted a widespread revolt against premium pay systems, dilution of skills and the stop watch, especially in metal-working plants where, Taylor had boasted, little overt protest had greeted the introduction of those devices.[56] Anxious to maintain uninterrupted war production, the National War Labor Board had even agreed to the abolition of incentive pay systems in some large companies, at the very time top A.F. of L. leaders were consummating their celebrated reconciliation with the Taylor Society.[57] Numerous strikes for job classifications with standard rates directly challenged the individualized wage rates which employers had come to believe were inevitable reflections of the variety of machine tending tasks and necessary inducements to individual exertion. The Board consistently refused to support such sweeping changes in company practices as the demand for classifications entailed.

Furthermore, the enormous expansion of tool-room work which attended the shift from the use of all-around machinists to specialized operators in metal works made the manufacture of jigs and fixtures itself a production line function, carried on in large plants by hundreds of men, who were called tool makers but who had very heterogeneous work assignments and earnings (ranging from 38 to 90 cents per hour). Consequently, in the munitions strikes the "tool makers" were the stormy petrels. Their demand for a standard tool-room rate was the most difficult issue for government agencies to mediate. Ostensibly a wage demand, it challenged the basic fabric of the new managerial methods.

Bridgeport, Connecticut, where some 120 local firms subcontracted for the Remington Arms Company, which directly employed 18,000 men and women in a 21-building plant erected in the first eight months of 1915, was a seething cauldron of such conflicts from the summer of 1915 onward. Strikes for the eight-hour day, wage increases and overtime pay, abolition of premiums, equal pay regardless of sex on all jobs where women were substituted for craftsmen, an end to discrimination and intimidation against union members, secure draft deferments and recognition of shop committees were endemic to this boom town. The preeminence of tool makers in these actions brought the city's District 55 of the I.A.M. under the leadership of an erstwhile Wobbly, Samuel Lavit and his radical colleagues. The refusal of the National War Labor Board to uphold their demand for seven standardized job classifications (where there were more than 250 known wage rates) provoked a total strike at Remington and most contractors in September 1918, which was broken only when President Wilson personally ordered all who failed to return to work barred from any war employment for a year. A city-wide council of shop delegates, created by the government to ease the crisis atmosphere, quickly fell under the leadership of Lavit, and was repudiated by the employers. By January 1919 when the local machinists staged rallies against lay-offs, their leaders cast off the non-political guise they had carefully assumed through America's participation in the fighting. Louise Bryant, just returned from Russia with John

Reed, was the featured speaker, and union petitions demanded "co-operative ownership and democratic management of industry."[58]

The Bridgeport struggles, with their clear emphasis on control questions, were led by skilled workers, in fact by a craft union (the I.A.M.). The second current of workers' activity, however, that which arose from laborers and operatives, was prompted primarily by wage questions, that is to say by the rising cost of living. The resistance of these workers to speed up and management's authority tended to take the form of continuous, covert, self-organization by small informal groups at work.[59] On the other hand, the very occurrence of strikes among them shattered the myth of immigrant docility and revealed that the new industrial discipline had promoted a sense of raw injustice and common cause among, as well as within, the various ethnic communities of foreign born. The experience of immigrant machine tenders, furthermore, made both the craft divisions of the A.F. of L. and its traditional commitment to self-help appear ludicrous.[60]

Consequently, revolts of immigrant operatives offered a fertile field for the work of revolutionary activists, provided those activists could circumvent the Socialist party's official fixation on electoral activity.[61] The mass picketing and endless succession of huge rallies which characterized such strikes lent themselves to an energizing sense of collective power and invited revolutionary rhetoric. When, for example, 2,000 Lithuanians, Poles and Hungarians walked out of the pipe threading, finishing and furnace departments of National Tube in Pittsburgh in 1912, the leadership of their daily meetings and parades quickly fell to Fred Merrick, a local Socialist journalist, and several of his party comrades. More than a thousand strikers marched across a bridge over the Monongahela to stand outside the company office, while Merrick and their committee negotiated the settlement.[62]

As this pattern of action recurred time and again, some well-tested and charismatic radicals became veritable folk heroes: William Z. Foster, William D. Haywood, Arturo Giovanitti and especially Carlo Tresca, one man who actually incarnated the conservative's fantasy of the agitator who could start an uprising with a speech. During the strikes of immigrants, local authorities went to extraordinary lengths to exclude such men from the mill towns and to dominate the mass meetings themselves. In Ipswich, Massachusetts, the local citizens of standing mobilized vigilante forces to control rallies of Greek and Polish cotton-mill strikers in 1913, jailed all the Socialist and Wobbly activists who came to town and lured native workmen back to their jobs with patriotic appeals. In the strike of Bayonne oil refinery workers, Sheriff Kinkead literally seized command, first by flamboyantly jailing 80 Bergoff detectives and the company superintendent on riot charges to gain credibility with the strikers while his deputies discretely lured Frank Tannenbaum and other Wobblies onto company property, beat them brutally and expelled them from town, then persuaded a mass meeting to accept a settlement he had worked out with Standard Oil.[63] In Passaic in 1919 police officers sat on the platform and censored speeches, while a representative of the Department of Labor denounced the strike leaders sent by the Amalgamated Clothing Workers and cajoled strikers into the A.F. of L. When Anthony Capraro, a leader of the 1919 Lawrence strike, succeeded in smuggling Tresca into the city past the police dragnet, the police retaliated by taking Capraro into the countryside and beating him within an inch of his life.[64]

Such repression, however, does not provide a sufficient explanation of the I.W.W.'s failure to grow apace with the rising militancy of industrial workers. Paradoxically, the greater the scope and intensity of struggles in the northeast grew, the more exclusively the I.W.W.'s attention became riveted on timber and agricultural workers of the south and west. Conversely, individual Wobblies of industrial areas collaborated ever more closely with mill town locals of the Socialist party, which were charting their own courses in direct action without guidance (or even in the face of hostility) from their party's national executive.[65]

Two reasons for the small role of the I.W.W. as such in the New Unionism suggest themselves. First, it became increasingly apparent that the immigrant machine tenders wanted something more from their organizations than oratory and strike leadership. As their aspirations to regulate working conditions and shorten hours grew stronger, their desire for durable, open, recognized unions grew with them. The enthusiastic responses of immigrant packing-house workers and steel workers to Foster's organizing committees revealed this desire clearly.[66] The steady growth of the language federations of the Socialist party, from 15,340 members in 1912 to 23,000 in 1915 and 56,680 by 1919 and the great effectiveness of the Ladies Garment Workers among Jews in New York and of the United Shoe Workers among Italians in Lynn and Poles in Chicago, both unions being led by militant Socialists, bore testimony to the appeal of revolutionary leadership coupled with businesslike organization among foreign-born workers.[67] After 1916, however, the lodestone of the leftward movement among immigrants clearly became the Amalgamated Clothing Workers. So effective was the fusion of Jewish and Italian workers, on which that union and its satellite, the Amalgamated Textile Workers, rested, that by 1919 even Giovanitti and Tresca had put the I.W.W. behind them and were devoting all their energies to the Amalgamated.[68]

Second, the contempt of the Wobblies for craft unions all too easily became contempt for the more skilled workers. "I do not care the snap of my finger whether or not the skilled workman joins this industrial movement," Haywood had said in 1905. "When we get the unorganized and unskilled laborer into this organization, the skilled worker will of necessity come here for his own protection."[69] This contempt in turn explains the absence of any reference to "workers' control" at the founding convention of the I.W.W., aside from the recurring theme that under socialism workers would assume direct management of their industries.[70] As the munitions strikes revealed, fights for the deliberate collective regulation of production were most likely to arise from the ranks of workers who had exercised such regulation in the memorable past, that is, from craftsmen. Despite the fact that the progress of scientific management had ruled out the possibility of their restoring control in its traditional form (the journeyman machinist, pledged to union rules, making the product his way), the machinists of Bridgeport had formulated by the summer of 1918 their own clear alternative to the way management directed the factories: a plan based on the eight-hour day, standard job classifications and shop committees energized by a militant machinists' union. This counterplan, distilled from countless strike meetings, provided the substance behind the rhetoric of their 1919 appeal for "collective participation of the workers in the control of the industry."[71] Without such widely shared aspirations and collectively formulated plans, Louis Fraina had argued six years earlier, syndicalism easily degenerates into a "slavery to means," a fixation on militant tactics, or even a cult of violence.[72]

The potential significance of craftsmen's struggles had been grasped, however, by the North American Syndicalist League, and the shopmen of the Illinois Central Railroad and Harriman lines provided their favorite case in point. These workers had been noted both for the prevalence of Socialist politics among them and for their craft exclusiveness. Their lodges cast overwhelming votes at the 1903 I.A.M. convention for resolutions favoring the cooperative commonwealth and against resolutions to admit handymen to the union.[73] Here were political Socialists of the type any good syndicalist would mock. Yet in 1911, the very year the bloc of Socialist party candidates swept the elections for top offices in the I.A.M., these shopmen launched a strike which was to last for four years and pit them as insurgents against the union's new leaders.

The spur was the spread of time study and incentive pay to railroad car shops, which had long been strongholds of traditional unionism. When organized craftsmen in the I.C.'s two largest shops (Chicago and Paducah, Kentucky) observed new timecards and stopwatches appearing around them, they began on their own initiative to protest to local superintendents through joint committees of the several trades. Meeting top-level resistance from the railroad, the shopmen convened an unofficial meeting in Memphis, where they formed a "system federation" to speak jointly for locals of the machinists, steam fitters, carmen, sheet-metal workers, boiler makers, blacksmiths, painters, laborers and (cruelest blow to the company of all) clerks.

A parallel movement spread out of Kansas City along the Union Pacific and other lines controlled by the Harriman interests, which the I.C. linked to Chicago and New Orleans. Together the new systems' federations demanded the abolition of premium pay schemes, time study, personnel records, and dilution of skills. When the railroads involved refused to deal with the unions except through the separate national offices of the different crafts, as they had done in the past, the federations called a strike of more than 16,000 workers, to which the seven national unions gave reluctant support.[74]

The railroads deluged the strikers with injunctions and drew strikebreakers from the heavy ranks of unemployed, and from the "clerks, druggists, soldiers, street car drivers, motormen . . . [and] young men that wanted to learn a trade," in towns along their lines.[75] Gunplay blazed around the tracks and shops for four years, 553 strikers were jailed and 1,069 lost their homes before the unions officially called off the strike, over the angry protests of its leaders.[76] Subsequently I.C. executives complained that clerks who had returned to work showed a marked aptitude "in removing and concealing records, in removing cards from cars, and in exchanging cards on cars so that the utmost confusion resulted from their action."[77]

The strike had revealed a readiness among some craft unionists of long standing to fuse all grades of workers in open confrontation with scientific management. William Z. Foster of the newly established Syndicalist League used the strike to illustrate the foolishness of the I.W.W.'s dual unionism and the significance of a "militant minority" among unionized workmen. Max Dezettel, James Cannon and Earl Browder were three of the League's supporters in Kansas City, a storm center of the conflict and the cradle of the Communist Party in the West.[78] The strikers themselves pushed their unions into a convention at Kansas City in 1912, where they created a Federation of Federations to coordinate the efforts of all railway shopmen and to agitate for a general strike over the whole western railroad district.[79]

In short, both the control struggles of skilled workers and the wage strikes of laborers and machine tenders had opened new vistas to millions of workers by 1920. In fact, the basic challenges to which employers responded with the American Plan were those of preventing the convergence of the two currents of working-class activity and defusing control demands with an appearance of worker participation in management. But the transformation of consciousness which generated these challenges by enrolling five million into unions and infusing into their ranks a widespread aspiration to direct the operation of railroads, mines, shipyards, and factories collectively, was itself the product of a decade of continuous struggle, the new forms of which resulted from management's reorganization of industry. Only when that transformation was well under way, and only when the strong unionization of workers in basic industries it made possible had been achieved, did the challenge Joseph Schlossberg hurled to the 1920 convention of the Amalgamated Clothing Workers become meaningful:

> It is now our responsibility to establish order in the industry in the place of the chaos created by the employers when they had things their own way.[80]

Notes

Reprinted courtesy of Oxford University Press and the *Journal of Social History.*

1. Andre Tridon, *The New Unionism* (New York, 1914), 17.

2. David Brody, *Steelworkers in America: The Nonunion Era* (Cambridge, 1960), 50–79; Luke Grant, *The National Erectors' Association and the International Association of Bridge and Structural Ironworkers* (Washington, 1915); Robert Ozanne, *A Century of Labor-Management Relations at McCormick and International Harvester* (Madison, 1967), 44–70; David Brody, *The Butcher Workmen, A Study of Unionization* (Cambridge, 1964); Clarence E. Bonnett, *Employers' Associations in the United States: A Study of Typical Associations* (New York, 1922); Jacob H. Hollander and George E. Barnett, *Studies in American Trade Unionism* (New York, 1912), 109–52.

3. President C.W. Post of the Citizens' Industrial Alliance, quoted in Selig Perlman and Philip Taft, *History of Labor in the United States, 1896–1932* (New York, 1935), 136.

4. *Proceedings of the First Convention of the Industrial Workers of the World, Founded at Chicago, June 27-July 8, 1905* (New York, 1905, hereafter cited as *I. W.W. Proceedings*), 123. See also Marguerite Green, *The National Civic Federation and the American Labor Movement, 1900–1925* (Washington, 1956); James Weinstein, *The Corporate Ideal in the Liberal State, 1900–1918* (Boston, 1968); Philip S. Foner, *History of the Labor Movement in the United States* (4 vols., New York, 1947–1965), III, 32–110.

5. "Manifesto," in *I. W.W. Proceedings*, 4.

6. Vincent St. John, *The I. W.W., Its History, Structure and Methods* (Chicago, 1919); Foner, IV, 36–39, 114–71.

7. *Machinists' Monthly Journal* XVIII (Dec 1906): 1108–11. Hereafter cited as *M.M.J.*

8. Oscar Ameringer, *If You Don't Weaken* (New York, 1940), 194–223; James Leonard to Frank Morrison, June 2, June 6, June 9, July 7, July 14, Sept. 1, Sept. 29, 1907 (John Mitchell Papers, Box A3–49); New Orleans *Daily Picayune*, July 13, 1907; Foner, III, 250–53.

9. *Iron Age*, 92 (Dec. 4, 1913), 1294, hereafter cited as *I.A.*; Stanley Lebergott, *Manpower in Economic Growth* (New York, 1964), 512.

10. Louis Levine, *The Women's Garment Workers* (New York, 1924), 144–95; Melvyn Dubofsky, *When Workers Organize: New York City in the Progressive Era* (Amherst, 1968), 49–66; John N. Ingham, "A Strike in the Progressive Era: McKees Rocks, 1909," *The Pennsylvania Magazine of History and Biography* XC (July 1966): 353–77; U.S. Congress, Senate, *Report on the Strike at the Bethlehem Steel Works*, Senate Document 521 (Washington, 1910).

11. Perlman and Taft, 343–48; Edward Levinson, *I Break Strikes! The Technique of Pearl L. Bergoff* (New York, 1935), 89–104.

12. Editorial, New York *Call*, March 7, 1910.

13. See Table 1.

14. Editorial, *I.A.*, 93 (April 23, 1914), 1018–19. See also ibid., 88 (Sept. 21, 1911), 607; Judge Gary's speech, Ibid., 87 (Jan. 19, 1911), 208–10.

15. James Weinstein, *The Decline of Socialism in America, 1912–1925* (New York,

1967), 93–119; John H.M. Laslett, *Labor and the Left: A Study of Socialist and Radical Influences in the American Labor Movement, 1881–1924* (New York, 1970), 161–64, 214–18.

16. *I.A.*, 91 (April 17, 1913), 954.

17. Melvyn Dubofsky, *We Shall Be All: A History of the Industrial Workers of the World* (Chicago, 1969), 286–87; *I.A.*, 92 (Sept. 11, 1913), 572; Levine, 227–31.

18. *I.A.*, 93 (Jan. 1, 1914), 13.

19. *Monthly Labor Review* II (April 1916): 13–26. Hereafter cited as *M.L.R.*

20. Dianne Kanitra, "The Westinghouse Strike of 1916" (unpublished M.A. paper, University of Pittsburgh, 1971).

21. *International Socialist Review* XVI (April 1917): 582–87; Joseph T. Makarewicz, "The Impact of World War I on Pennsylvania Politics, with Emphasis on the Election of 1920" (unpublished doctoral dissertation, University of Pittsburgh, 1972).

22. Leon C. Marshall, "The War Labor Program and Its Administration," *Journal of Political Economy* XXVI (May 1918): 429.

23. *M.L.R.* XVII (Dec. 1923): 82–5.

24. Bureau of Industrial Statistics of New Jersey, *Thirty-Ninth Annual Report* (Camden, 1916), hereafter cited as *N.J.B.I.S.*, 1916, 225; *N.J.B.I.S.*, 1914, 227–40.

25. Alexander M. Bing, *Wartime Strikes and Their Adjustment* (New York, 1921), 60–61, 178, 181; Susan M. Kingsbury, *Labor Laws and Their Enforcement, with Special Reference to Massachusetts* (New York, 1911), 90–125.

26. Robert Ozanne, *Wages in Practice and Theory: McCormick and International Harvester, 1860–1960* (Madison, 1968), 108–11.

27. Paul H. Douglas, C.N. Hitchcock, and W.E. Atkins, *The Worker in Modern Economic Society* (Chicago, 1923), 361–62.

28. *I.A.*, 96 (Oct. 14, 1915), 884–85.

29. See Table 1.

30. Bing, 30.

31. Frank Tannenbaum, *The Labor Movement: Its Conservative Functions and Social Consequences* (New York, 1921), 147.

32. Mark Perlman, *The Machinists: A New Study in American Trade Unionism* (Cambridge, 1961), 33, 51.

33. Douglas, Hitchcock and Atkins, 562–63; Nationalization Research Committee, United Mine Workers of America, *How to Run Coal* (New York, 1922); Glenn E. Plumb and William G. Roylance, *Industrial Democracy: A Plan for Its Achievement* (New York, 1923); William Z. Foster, *The Railroaders' Next Step* (Chicago, 1921); John G. Randall, Jr., *The Problem of Group Responsibility to Society* (New York, 1922), 227.

34. History Committee of the General Strike Committee, *The Seattle General Strike* (reprinted as *Root and Branch* pamphlet 5, 1972), 4.

35. J.B.S. Hardman, ed., *American Labor Dynamics, in the Light of Post-War Developments* (New York, 1928), 21. Cf. Weinstein, *Decline*, 177–233.

36. *The Tailor*, April 8, 1919.

37. "Direct Action Loses," *American Federationist* (Oct. 1919): 962–64.

38. Sylvia Kopald, *Rebellion in Labor Unions* (New York, 1924), 50–177. The percentage figures of insurgent strikers are my own.

39. Jeremy Brecher, *Strike!* (San Francisco, 1972), 69–96, 243–44.

40. Vertrees J. Wyckoff, *The Wage Policies of Labor Organizations in a Period of Industrial Depression* (Baltimore, 1926); Royal E. Montgomery, *Industrial Relations in the Chicago Building Trades* (Chicago, 1927), 233–309.

41. *M.L.R.* XIV (May 1922): 183; Ibid., XVI (June 1923): 231–39.

42. Interviews with Max Zuckerman, Gen. Secy., Cloth Hat and Cap Makers of America, March 3, 1919 and David Brodsky, Pres. Local 137 Sheet Metal Workers, March 11, 1919 (David J. Saposs Papers, Box 22).

43. Interview with Samuel E. Beardsley, Organizer Local Union No. 1, Jewelry Workers Union, Feb. 19, 1919; D.J. Saposs, "Jewish Unions," typescript (Saposs Papers, Box 21).

44. Interviews with Harry Jones, Secy.-Tres., Int. Assn. of Bridge and Structural Iron Workers, Jan. 23, 1919, and Sol Broad, Bus. Agt., Jewish Local, I.A.B. & S.I.W., March 6, 1919 (Saposs Papers, Box 22).

45. See Peter N. Stearns, *Revolutionary Syndicalism and French Labor: A Cause without Rebels* (New Brunswick, 1971), 19–33.

46. U.S. Commission on Industrial Relations, *Final Report and Testimony*, 64th Cong., 1st sess., Senate Doc. No. 415 (Washington, 1916, hereafter cited as C.I.R.), I, 874.

47. Frederick W. Taylor, "Testimony," 49, in Taylor, *Scientific Management, Comprising Shop Management: The Principles of Scientific Management Testimony Before the Special House Committee* (New York, 1947).

48. See Ibid.; Robert F. Hoxie, *Scientific Management and Labor* (New York, 1915); Hugh G.J. Aitken, *Taylorism at the Watertown Arsenal: Scientific Management in Action, 1908–1915* (Cambridge, 1960).

49. F.J. Roethlisberger and W.J. Dickson, *Management and the Worker: Technical vs. Social Organization in an Industrial Plant* (Cambridge, 1934).

50. Whiting Williams, *What's On the Worker's Mind, By One Who Put on Overalls to Find Out* (New York, 1921), 20.

51. Leon Stein and Philip Taft, eds., *Workers Speak: Self Portraits* (New York, 1971), 30.

52. *I.A.*, 93 (Jan. 8, 1914); Keith Sward, *The Legend of Henry Ford* (New York, 1968), 52–60.

53. *American Labor Legislation Review* IV (May 1914): 225.

54. Ibid., V (Nov., 1915), 486, 487. See also Don D. Lescohier, *The Labor Market* (New York, 1919).

55. Lebergott, 524, 528.

56. *C.I.R.*, I, 772–73.

57. E.G., *N.W.L.B.* Administrative Files Box 54 (General Electric); Docket No. 22 (Bethlehem Steel), Record Group 2, National Archives. On the reconciliation, see Milton J. Nadworny, *Scientific Management and the Unions, 1900–1932* (Cambridge, 1955).

58. N.W.L.B. Case File 132, R.G. 2, N.A. On the Remington plant, see *I.A.* 96 (Oct. 14, 1915): 296–303.

59. See Stanley B. Mathewson, *Restriction of Output among Unorganized Workers* (New York, 1931).

60. William M. Leiserson, *Adjusting Immigrant and Industry* (New York, 1924), 169–233.

61. Paul Buhle, "Debsian Socialism and the 'New Immigrant' Worker," in William O'Neill, ed., *Insights and Parallels: Problems and Issues of American Social History* (Minneapolis, 1973), 249–77.

62. *Survey* XXVIII (July 6, 1912): 487–88; (Aug. 3, 1912): 595–96.

63. J.S. Biscay, "The Ipswich Strike," *International Socialist Review* XIV (Aug. 1913): 90–92; *N.J.B.I.S.* (1915): 210–31.

64. Interview with Matthew Pluhar, Pres. Ind. Textile Workers Union, Passaic, April 3, 1919 (Saposs Papers, Box 21); Nat Hentoff, ed., *Essays of A.J. Muste* (Indianapolis, 1967), 71–73.

65. Foner, IV, 462–72; Frederick A. Barkey, "The Socialist Party in West Virginia from 1898 to 1920: A Study in Working Class Radicalism" (unpublished PhD dissertation, University of Pittsburgh, 1971), 106–56, 180–86.

66. William Z. Foster, *The Great Steel Strike and Its Lessons* (New York, 1920); William M. Tuttle, "Labor Conflict and Racial Violence: The Black Worker in Chicago, 1894–1919," *Labor History* X (Summer 1969): 408–32.

67. Buhle, 267–68; Levine, 233–41; interview with C.P. Dean, Bus. Agt. Joint Council No. 9, United Shoe Workers of America, Dec. 24, 1918 (Saposs Papers, Box 21).

68. Interviews with David Wolf, Gen. Treas., Amalgamated Clothing Workers of America, Feb. 27, 1919 and Frank Blanco, Gen. Organizer, A.C.W.A., March 29, 1919 (Saposs Papers, Box 21); Muste, 59–83.

69. Quoted in Foner, IV, 37.

70. The only explicit reference to workers' control was in Haywood's speech to the ratification meeting. *I.W.W. Proceedings*, 579.

71. Petition for the Creation of National Labor Agencies, N.W.L.B. Case File 132, R.G.2, N.A.

72. Louis Fraina, "Syndicalism and Industrial Unionism," *International Socialist Review* XIV (July 1913): 25–28.

73. *M.M.J.* XV (July 1903): 590–91.

74. *C.I.R.* X, 9697–10048; Carl E. Person, *The Lizard's Trail. A Story of the Illinois Central and Harriman Lines Strike of 1911 to 1915 Inclusive* (Chicago, 1918); William Z. Foster, *Pages from a Worker's Life* (New York, 1939), 146–48; *M.M.J.*, 1911–16.

75. *C.I.R.* X, 9918.

76. Ibid., X, 9877–78.

77. Ibid., X, 9705.

78. *The Agitator*, May 15, 1912; Ibid., April 15, 1912; William Z. Foster and Earl C. Ford, *Syndicalism* (Chicago, n.d.); Theodore Draper, *The Roots of American Communism* (New York, 1957), 308.

79. Person, 42–63.

80. Quoted in Evans Clark, "The Industry Is Ours," *Socialist Review* IX (July 1920): 59.

PART V

After *The Fall*

David Montgomery concluded his most ambitious and synthetic book, *The Fall of the House of Labor* (1987), with a portrait of a working class under duress following the postwar strike defeats and "the tight repression of the Coolidge era." With an underlying tone of pessimism, he noted that "all but a radicalized handful of workers reported quietly to whatever jobs they managed to hold, discarding their wartime aspirations." The labor movement, though larger than before the war, "was like a great ship becalmed in a shark-infested sea." But, in quintessentially Montgomery fashion, his final paragraph affirmed that "no historical resolution of the conflict between wage labor and capital, however, has enjoyed a permanent lease on life." And in less than a decade, amid economic collapse, a resurgent worker militancy would reopen a question Frank Walsh had posed in 1916: How might workers create "a democracy, industrious and political, based on enduring justice"?[1]

In a set of essays published over the course of the next twenty-five years, Montgomery wrestled with the continuities and discontinuities of the 1920s and 1930s. In the process he would complicate and deepen our understanding of the years in which the foundations were laid for the enhanced state capacity manifested in the New Deal and for the worker activism that enabled the changes in labor relations and politics that would push the US closest to its own version of social democracy. These essays still crackle with new insights and fresh understandings that offer an agenda for future research on these pivotal decades.

Several themes rise from the essays that bear especially close attention. Montgomery was struck by the continuities in workers' demands for enlargement of the state's responsibility for stabilizing the labor market and securing relief from periodic surges in unemployment, whether through Jacob Coxey's vision of public work relief, the garment workers' work rationalization schemes, or New Deal programs like Federal Emergency Relief Administration (FERA) or the Works Progress Administration (WPA). He was always attuned to workers' agency in defending and securing their access to workplace rights and their claims to a fairer distribution of the fruits of their labor. Even for the becalmed 1920s, he documented the survival of traditions of collective action and a left still capable of organizing massive protests, for instance in defense of Sacco and Vanzetti. A leadership seasoned by survival in the 1920s drew on the lessons of the postwar strike defeats to provide guidance for the NRA strikes of 1934.

Montgomery was always mindful of shifting social identities and structures that shaped political and industrial action whether it was the role of women in local textile strikes, the social hierarchies within immigrant enclaves, or the youthfulness and educational background of the new cadre of CIO organizers. Deploying social history of a changing working class, he complicated and enriched the history of shifts in New Deal public policy and institutional innovation. Although he was attentive to the debates about the institutional constraints that came with the CIO and the New Deal labor legislation,[2] he did not get trapped in the terms of that debate. He sought not so much a middle ground as an alternative way of understanding the pragmatic "adaptation of political strategies to the new power relationships within which workers were transforming their own lives."

In the final essay written before his death and published posthumously, Montgomery deftly surveyed the history of depressions in the US enlivened by accounts of the social impact of unemployment on diverse communities of working people, the shifting currents of public policy at local, state, and federal levels, and, most vividly, the actions of workers themselves to remedy the conditions brought on by depression. As in so much of his scholarship during his career, international and comparative threads are intimately woven into the American context.

Notes

1. David Montgomery, *The Fall of the House of Labor: The Workplace, the State, and American Labor Activism, 1865–1925* (Cambridge and New York: Cambridge University Press, 1987), 464.

2. For the debate over the constraints or opportunities posed by the CIO and the Wagner Act, see the so-called "Brody/Lynd" debate, in, for instance, David Brody, *Workers in Industrial America: Essays on the Twentieth Century Struggle*, 2nd ed. (New York: Oxford University Press, 1993) and the essays in Staughton Lynd, ed., *"We Are All Leaders": The Alternative Unionism of the Early 1930s* (Urbana: University of Illinois Press, 1996).

CHAPTER 12

Thinking about American Workers in the 1920s

From *International Labor and Working-Class History* 32 (Fall 1987): 4–22

Labor historians' abiding interest in manifestations of working-class solidarity needs to be related at all times to analysis of the formation and reconstructions of bourgeois hegemony. All industrialized countries experienced declining strike activity and trade union membership between 1921 and 1933, although the patterns of subsidence and occasional revival of industrial confrontations were quite different in Germany or England from those evident in France or the United States. So stark was the contrast within the United States between the decade Irving Bernstein called "the lean years" and "the turbulent years" that followed, that historians have been prone to separate the twenties and thirties into two distinct periods for study. In this essay I wish to explore some of the more continuous lines of social and political developments between the world wars that deserve the attention of historians of the working class, to suggest some international aspects of U.S. experience, and to identify topics that appear to be in special need of further research.

Sidney Fine's perceptive account of the policies and beliefs to which the leading executives of the General Motors Corporation adhered when confronted by rising union membership and eventual sit-down strikes in the thirties clearly reveals a continuity of managerial powers, principles, and practices dating back at least to the post-World War I years. Management was to cultivate and defend "loyal employees"; a closed shop agreement with a union would decisively undermine that objective and consequently had to be avoided at all costs. Efficient production methods required not only systematic analysis and assignment of work tasks and foremen selected, trained and guided as the front line of management, but also planned use of wage incentives.

Although executives of the company needed to maintain incessant communication with both their employees and the local elites of the communities in which they were located, they were also determined to avoid any "outside" interference in their direction of the enterprise. The autonomy of the enterprise was the *sanctum sanctorum* of interwar management. As Ronald Schatz, Nelson Lichtenstein, Katherine Stone, Karl Klare, Christopher Tomlins, and Fine himself have argued—and as Sumner Slichter revealed in 1940—even when business leaders were obliged to sign contracts with unions in the thirties, they did not surrender any of their long-established objectives. And, indeed, CIO leaders who were veterans of the struggles that had followed World War I were quick to offer reassurances to employers that union recognition did not threaten these basic principles of management.

The principles of modern management had been disseminated through industry and engineering journals, efficiency societies, technical institutes, business schools, employers' associations, the wartime activities of government agencies, and the postwar crusades against "waste" so ardently and consistently organized by Secretary of Commerce Herbert Hoover. Wartime full employment had unleashed not only soaring levels of turnover, but also seven continuous years of the highest levels of strike activity recorded in the history of the United States (1916–22). These were the years when welfare capitalism (the so-called American Plan) enjoyed its greatest vogue. Pensions, holidays, sporting and musical clubs, Americanization classes, safety committees, and in-plant concerts, sermons, dances, and exhibits of consumer durables available through installment payments became commonplace. Pay and benefits linked to length of service, managerial plans for reduction of the workforce that privileged the older and more skilled workers, and—in clothing, food processing and other seasonal industries—conscious manipulation of inventories to reduce the level and frequency of layoffs were of special importance in cultivating the much prized "loyalty" of employees to the firm.

As Sanford Jacoby has shown, such liberal innovations became less common after 1923, when strikes became few and chronically high levels of unemployment retarded turnover. Thereafter, training of foremen, a reassertion of the authority of production managers, and careful handling of layoffs dominated the practice of up-to-date firms. Nevertheless, most of the new benefits linked to seniority remained in effect, at least until the Great Depression forced a drastic reduction in labor costs.

All in all, American management in the 1920s enjoyed an international reputation for organizing efficient production by faithful employees comparable to that of their Japanese counterparts in the 1980s. To be sure, Stanley B. Matthewson's informative if impressionistic study *Restriction of Output among Unorganized Workers* (1930) found workers turning "payment plans, designed as incentives to increased production [into] incentives to restriction" and concluded that increases in output produced by Taylor's methods had been meager in comparison with what he had predicted. Nevertheless, when managers discovered workers restricting output, they blamed themselves and called in not only time-study men, but also industrial psychologists to recommend remedies. It was in the 1920s that the concept of "alienation" reentered learned discourse, from which it had been largely absent since the eclipse of utopian socialism. It was revived by Elton Mayo, Ordway Tead, Hendrik de Man and other students of social psychology, who argued that it was the immediate and remediable conditions of employment and social life that estranged workers from their own work, not private ownership of the means of social production.

Canada's Minister of Labour W. L. Mackenzie King had made an influential contribution to this discussion in 1914, when John D. Rockefeller, Jr. had asked his advice in resolving the bloody coal miners' strike in Colorado without recognizing the United Mine Workers. King had suggested that the Colorado Fuel and Iron Company institute its own plan for consultation between representatives chosen by the workers and the local managers, as the only way to ensure "that cordial cooperation which is likely to ensure industrial efficiency" and to provide the company "a maximum of publicity with a minimum of interference with all that pertains to the conditions of employment." Although the Colorado Industrial Plan that was created pursuant to King's recommendations was by no means America's first company union, no previous plan had exerted a comparable influence on public opinion and business thinking. Its influence was soon magnified by the initiatives of the National War Labor Board and other government agencies, which promoted shop committees in enterprises vital to the war effort as a mechanism for reducing strikes and implementing the agencies' rulings on wages and hours. Most postwar employee representation plans (ERPs) were actually instituted under government direction, but corporate executives fought to convert them into something akin to "the Rockefeller plan" by excluding government examiners and wage standards and trade unionists from influence over the operation of the plans.

The executives of America's leading manufacturing corporations, who met periodically at the Yama Farms Inn from 1919 to 1937 and styled their informal gatherings on the Special Conference Committee, agreed on the cultivation of ERPs as one of their most important common objectives. A report issued in 1929 summing up the experience of ERPs covering 1.5 million workers, however, emphasized the conclusion that the "plans which have the highest measure of success are those in which responsible executives have taken an active and continuing interest and to which they have furnished guidance." Such plans, they noted, furnished "an effective means through which management can exercise its normal function of leadership over the working force."

In 1914 Mackenzie King proposed to Rockefeller an imaginative project which aptly defined the Special Conference Committee's agenda for dealing with labor in the twenties. When the war ended, King predicted, heavy unemployment and deflation would undermine the conditions unions had won for their members, so that gaining recognition from employers would become "less pressing as an immediate end" for union leaders than the maintenance of "standards already existing." In that context, unions might "come to regard as their friends and allies companies and corporations large enough and fair enough to maintain these standards of their own accord." Large corporations, which had preserved their own freedom from union or governmental interference, would uphold standards of wages and working conditions to which unions could appeal in their battles with smaller and more competitive companies. This is the formula that historians of the "corporate liberalism" interpretation of business' policies have misconstrued as a greater willingness to deal with unions in the ranks of efficient oligopolistic enterprises than was found among smaller companies in day-to-day confrontation.

A comparative study of American and European employers' associations is needed. Theda Skocpol has argued that the achievement of coordination within industries, without the emergence of an effective voice for business leadership as a whole, remained decisive not only in what Hoover called the associational activities of the twenties, but also in defining the National Recovery Administration (NRA) and subsequently in preventing a coordinated business response to the New Deal. Not only was the organization of business' interests confined to an industry-by-industry basis, but also the capacity of government to stand above those parochial influences was so limited that even the prewar measures of the New Deal for the most part left businessmen regulating industrial life. Skocpol's thesis warns historians attracted by new varieties of Marxism that, in the United States, the relative autonomy of the state was slight at best before 1940.

President Wilson had rejected various proposals from administration officials for planned reconversion of the economy to a peacetime basis and explained to Congress that there was no "general scheme of 'reconstruction'" that "we could force our spirited businessmen and self-reliant laborers to accept with due pliancy and obedience." Nevertheless, two general policies proclaimed first by the Wilson administration and subsequently by that of Harding enjoyed strong support from the electorate: bring down prices and defend social order. In the United States, as in Canada, England, and continental Europe, a powerful "public interest" supported government attacks on inflation and on disruptions of life's daily routine. Even before Harding won the voters' hearts with promises of "normalcy," Wilson's advisors had warned the president that an appeal to labor such as had won him re-election in 1916 would now lose more Democratic votes than it would win. Wilson resisted the pay claims of railroad workers and miners in 1919 with the argument that prices needed to fall, and would do so unless pushed upward by higher wages.

In all industrial countries public authorities had also developed considerable experience in mobilizing society against massive industrial action. Civilian volunteers could move critical supplies, strikers could be threatened with conscription, trucks could be activated to replace struck railroads, and soldiers could be used not only to disperse strikers, but also to replace them temporarily. The familiar truism that "you can't mine coal with bayonets" had lost some of its punch, just at the time when the "mass strike" had become a common event rather than a revolutionary's dream. The spirit of self-proclaimed "society" mobilized for action against rebellious workers was neatly captured by a banner that was unfurled in Winnipeg during a massive demonstration of middle-class men and former army officers against the city's 1919 general strike. It read: "We will maintain/Constituted authority, law and order/ Down with the high cost of living/To Hell with the alien enemy/God save the King."

To beat back the strike wave of 1919–22, therefore, public authorities used powers of coercion that had not been available to the nineteenth-century state. Wartime regulatory agencies were revived to combat the demands of coal miners and railroad workers in 1919 and 1920 and to force seamen to accept the conditions of work proclaimed by the shipowners and the navy despite the fierce maritime strike of 1921. Industrial courts with authority to outlaw strikes were established by law in Kansas and Colorado and strongly supported in the legislatures of New York and other states. Eighteen states passed laws against "criminal syndicalism," which not only prohibited many types of strikes, but also often authorized the temporary imprisonment without charge of people suspected of fomenting industrial unrest. Throughout the decade, and in the thirties as well, municipal regulations concerning the use of public space and disorderly conduct and the "red squads" of city police forces remained the instruments most commonly used to inhibit union activity. Representatives of the Federal Mediation and Conciliation Service considered it their duty to ferret out and deport alien agitators who had encouraged strikes.

Although the level of strike activity subsided rapidly after 1922, strikes lasted longer on average than did strikes in the 1930s. The stoppage of bituminous coal miners in 1927–28 was so protracted that the number of worker-days lost by disputes in 1927 surpassed that of any other subsequent year until 1945, except for 1937. The proportion of workers involved in strikes each year, however, fell steadily to 0.8 percent in 1930, the lowest level recorded by the Bureau of Labor Statistics since 1883. In this context Secretary of Commerce Hoover revived the legacy of Mackenzie King and asserted that there were "some things worse in the development of democracy than strikes and lockouts." Compulsory arbitration, industrial courts, and judicial orders reducing wages in inefficient and marginal companies hindered "the real development of self-government in industry," he said, and were "less effective as a stimulus to improved relations among men than is discussion and a system of voluntary settlement of differences." To be sure, Congress enacted a new law in 1926 to regulate labor relations on the railroads, which had faced six threats of nationwide strikes between 1916 and 1922. Moreover, coal strikes brought on federal investigating commissions, and the government of New York state was deeply involved in the reordering of the garment industry. In both those industries, where unions remained influential, the primary thrust of government activity after 1922 was the reduction of "waste" and inefficiency, rather than the dictation of terms of employment. While court injunctions routinely hobbled strike activity against small firms, the members of the Special Conference Committee speaking from the economy's commanding heights echoed Secretary Hoover's warnings against "state invasion" of industrial life. They shared his faith in the resolution of labor problems at the enterprise level.

Combined and Uneven Decline

The differences among economic sectors and in levels of concentration of economic power were as important for working-class experience and trade union development as they were for the policies, or lack of policies, of government and industry.

The primary sector was in a global crisis, as prices of agricultural goods and minerals fell steadily. For Africa and much of Latin America, the twenties may have been a more blighted economic period than the thirties, or at least the second half of the thirties. Prices of food and raw materials fell, while those of manufactured goods improved and held steady between 1923 and 1929, to the benefit of the urbanized world. A.J.P. Taylor's comment that "Great Britain could as it were, afford both higher unemployment and a higher standard of living at the same time," suggests a line of inquiry for historians of the United States. "Dollar diplomacy" may have been indispensable to the success of the American Plan.

The domestic face of this phenomenon was painfully familiar to coal miners, whose numbers fell from 704,000 in 1923 to 439,000 in 1940. Intense price competition among the operators, to whom the government had returned full control of the mines, coupled with the long-familiar determination of steel producers and railroads to hold down the cost of coal, undercut the Central Competitive Field agreement, which the United Mine Workers of America (UMWA) had restored on the eve of the war. Output expanded very rapidly in the coalfields of West Virginia, which bloody union defeats during the 1920–22 depression had left nonunion, encouraging employers in the Central Competitive Field to attack, ignore, and eventually repudiate the terms of their union contracts. Having stood its ground on the famous slogan "no backward step" throughout the decade, and fought in 1922–23 and 1927–28 the longest industry-wide strikes in American history, by 1930 the UMWA (long the largest union in the AFL) found itself virtually without members. New mines mechanized loading from the start, while older mines introduced undercutting and loading machines that rapidly reduced their labor force. This had an especially calamitous impact on black miners, who were largely confined to handloading. Despite the sudden revival of the coal miners' union in 1933 and its prominence in shaping New Deal legislation and the creation of the CIO, the long-term downward trend in employment continued as total mining output, which had remained stable between 1923 and 1929, now fell off as well.

Agriculture lost even more workers in a trend that was reversed briefly in the worst years of the depression and then resumed through the New Deal. Between 1920 and 1929, the number of people who left farms for the urban world numbered 19,436,000. Their ties to rural life often remained strong, so that many returned to the land. They were joined in that movement by immigrants who bought farms abandoned by native American farmers, especially in Pennsylvania and New England. In all, 13,140,000 urban residents moved to farms during the decade. The two-way flow left a net urban migration averaging about 620,000 people a year, which supplied workers in abundance for the incessantly expanding and contracting numbers of jobs at the bottom of the industrial hierarchy. The relative stability of employment, which welfare capitalism offered the more experienced and skilled workers during the twenties, was possible only because of the flexibility provided by this unskilled force in meeting the unstable demands of the market.

This migration is best known for its role in the making of a black working class in northern cities. What needs close examination in this process are the tightly circumscribed patterns of industrial employment of Afro-Americans in the North that left them constituting one-fifth or more of the labor force in certain companies (Armour, U.S. Steel) and virtually none in others (G.E., Remington-Rand). These patterns had complex effects on black workers' strategies for improving their lot during the thirties. Moreover, the full effects of the Great Depression, which actually reduced the total number of black workers in manufacturing between 1930 and 1940, left them a highly visible segment of the long-term unemployed during and after 1937.

Even while the famous exodus from the land was underway, highly capitalized forms of agriculture based on migratory wage labor were becoming increasingly important in the fruit, vegetable, and cotton producing valleys of California, in the sugar beet and fruit production of the Great Lakes region, and in onion growing areas of lower Ohio. In 1926, sugar beet farming in Michigan alone employed 40,000 Mexicans and Chicanos, who had been recruited mostly in Texas by the seven great sugar processing companies and distributed among farmers who raised beets on contract to those companies. Total immigration from Mexico exceeded 150,000 (the quota for all of Europe) in 1928. Although many of the immigrants entered the auto, steel, and packinghouse industries, most of them supplied America's increasingly large force of migrant agricultural wage laborers. Their widespread purchase of used automobiles and trucks by the end of the decade had left them less submissive to contractors than rail transportation had forced them to be. These were the workers, in fact, who initiated the strike wave of the thirties—in the cotton, fruit, and vegetable fields of California between 1930 and 1934. An important discontinuity was also to be found here. Although the vast majority of the migratory workers of the twenties and most of the strikers had been Mexicans, they largely returned or were forced to return (a question of serious historical controversy) to their homeland after 1930 and were replaced in the fields primarily by Anglos from the ranks of expropriated farmers, the destitute of Appalachia, and the urban unemployed.

Northern textile production suffered a continuous decline. In a decade of struggles textile workers both in older centers of cotton manufacture and in those towns that had developed huge silk and woolen mills on the eve of the war (Lawrence, Passaic, and Paterson) had won both real wage gains and a reduction of working hours from 58 to 48 or even 44 hours per week. Efforts of employers to revoke these gains had led to the great strikes of 1922 and had been only partially successful. Cotton manufacturers, therefore, accelerated the movement south, bringing weaving (especially of fabrics for the new automobile and tire industries) into a region whose spinning mills had already dominated the nation's output of cotton yarn by 1914. Mill closings plagued New England throughout the twenties and thirties. Meanwhile, much clothing manufacture left highly unionized centers like New York, Philadelphia and Rochester, for rural locations and towns located in the anthracite coalfields. These changes prompted Sumner Slichter's observation that in the absence of bursts of organizing struggles, the unionized sector of industry tends inexorably to decline, as production shifts toward nonunion areas.

Four interrelated consequences flowed from this tendency, all of which have received some attention from historians and economists in the past. First, even while the general level of strikes fell off, clothing and textile centers of unionism in the North remained theaters of intense industrial conflict as employers tried to drive down labor costs, intensify production, and obtain a free hand to weed out employees they considered inefficient or undesirable at the beginning of each new production season. Communists, socialists, anarchists, and One Big Unionists continued to exert an important influence on local union activity in strike-prone areas like Passaic, Paterson, New York, and New Bedford.

Second, the success of the Ladies' Garment Workers, Amalgamated Clothing Workers, shoe workers, and various Philadelphia weavers and knitters' unions in surviving bitter strikes and lockouts in 1921 with their contracts and short hours intact, confronted their leaders with an urgent need to help the hard-pressed employers stay in business afterwards. These were the unions that led the way in encouraging the adoption of scientific management by the bosses. The ambivalent and often confused responses of groups on the left to this development deserve close attention, such as Steven Fraser has given to the men's clothing industry. Increasingly bureaucratized unions promoted standardization of tasks, as well as workers' education and political action.

Third, some rank-and-file revolts against union leadership in these industries took the form of a challenge by native American workers to immigrant officers. Gladys Palmer found that in the case of Philadelphia-region carpet and knitting mills, they were even led by the Ku Klux Klan. The whole question of how new migrants from the countryside perceived unions, when they encountered them, deserves close attention. Consider the decisive rejection of the CIO by General Motors workers in Anderson, Indiana, and even by the sitdown strikers in Hershey, Pennsylvania, late in the thirties. Crucial as the experience of the new immigrants and their children was in the remaking of the American working class, the "typical American working man," (57 percent of the total) as Colston Warne observed in 1920, lived in a city with a population of 200,000 or less, had "not travelled far from the place of his birth," was born to parents who were immigrants from northern Europe, and had been educated in American schools.

Finally, the relocation of production in cotton textiles also shifted the geographic centers of strike militancy. The famous strikes of 1929–30 erupted in the South (in Elizabethton, Gastonia, and Marion) just as the driving force behind the 1934 national strike in textiles came from the southern mills. Although the AFL proclaimed a southern organizing drive with great fanfare in 1927, its self-presentation as an agency of social harmony and industrial efficiency won the hearts of neither the workers nor the employers of Dixie. When southern textile workers organized, and when southern-born workers played a prominent role in the earliest locals of the auto workers' union, they clearly marched to a different drummer than the AFL provided.

Many important questions of continuity and discontinuity of experience emerge from these observations. Among them is the extent to which the largest strikes and the most successful unionizing drives of the NRA period (1933–35) appeared among workers who already had deeply rooted union experience (dockers, sailors, coal miners, clothing workers, textile workers, construction workers, and railroad workers) and in industries that had been in decline since the end of the war. To be sure, over-the-road truck drivers represented the most dramatic growth sector of the American economy and had no union heritage of their own. Nevertheless, intra-city drivers had often sustained craft unions (of milk, coal, and laundry drivers) through the twenties and had built the Teamsters into one of the AFL's most important unions by 1930. The famous Minneapolis strike of 1934 was organized by Trotskyists, who used their base of power within established craft locals to reach out to long-haul drivers and warehousemen. Should we then look at the strikes of 1933–34 as a re-run of 1919–22, with important continuities of industrial base, styles of organization, and leadership?

By way of contrast, the unionizing of 1936–41 was located largely in the growth industries of the twenties—those related to automotive transport and electrification. In the latter, workers could draw upon rich union experience from the first twenty years of the century but also faced as sophisticated a management as American industry had to offer and a proliferation of different types of work and workers within the same companies and even plants. In auto work, life was more homogeneous, and management had long relied on high hourly wages, highly seasonal employment, and harsh discipline to keep its workers in line rather than on welfare capitalism. Unions had to establish a base in smaller firms that fabricated components and in tool-and-die shops before they could assault the three giants. Steel seems to have blended the two patterns. The 1933–34 drive, which signed up workers more rapidly than the CIO later did, duplicated the strategies of 1918–19, but could not overcome the resistance of the union's officials and the federal government to a strike. The 1936–37 campaign quickly overwhelmed the Pittsburgh region, which had been in decline since the twenties, and the industry's least innovative company, U.S. Steel. The companies known as "Little Steel" were more closely tied to growth sectors of the economy, especially auto production, and to steel's newer regional centers. They also proved more combative. Perhaps the main continuity from the World War epoch on the union side was the leading personalities of the Steel Workers' Organizing Committee, their conviction that steel had to be struck as an industry, not firm by firm, and their haunting memory that workers had never won such a strike.

The notion that the great watershed in union practice came around 1935, not before, and that unions in 1933 and 1934 were largely picking up the pieces of their shattered efforts during the war years should not be pushed too far, because the history of working-class practice permits no such neat partitions. Nevertheless, it does help us to understand the amazing speed of union growth under the NRA and its relationship to the stabilization of declining industries. It also helps to explain the profound shift in the relationship between the union movement and the state accomplished by the New Deal, and especially by the Wagner Act (1935). That shift has been perceptively analyzed by Christopher Tomlins as marking the end of a self-legitimizing and self-directed trade union movement proudly independent of (although often attacked by) the state. As Tomlins also reminds us, however, the resurgence of the AFL after 1937, using strategies and appeals it had elaborated without success during the Coolidge prosperity and quickly outstripping the membership growth of the CIO, indicates that established patterns of unionism did not simply fade away with the appearance of National Labor Relations Board (NLRB) certification elections. On the contrary, by 1940 decisions of the courts and of the NLRB had become increasingly accommodating to AFL practice and needs. It was World War II that made the trends in union-government relations initiated by the Wagner Act irreversible.

Union versus State Invasion

If we are to understand the policies of the AFL during the interwar decades, we must bear in mind two aspects of the legacy of World War I. First, although the trade union movement had suffered decisive defeats by the end of 1922, its membership remained larger and its contracts in many sectors more secure than they had been in 1913. National Bureau of Economic Research calculations of union membership as a percentage of potential membership indicate that union density rose from 10.3 percent in 1913 to a peak of 16.7 percent in 1920, a level not reached again until 1940. By 1923, union density had been hammered down to 11.3 percent (3.4 million members as compared with 2.6 million in 1913), then gradually subsided, with the decline of industries where unions had remained strong, to 9.3 percent on the eve of the Great Depression, and tumbled to 7.3 percent before the new growth began in 1933. Even at the 1933 level the absolute number of members remained 8 percent higher than it had been in 1913, a tenacity that compares well at least with England, where union membership had fallen by 1933–34 back to what it had been in 1913. That comparison, of course, does not take into account the greater absolute strength of unions in Britain, where unions lost more members between 1920 and 1926 than American unions had ever enrolled.

The point of this numbers exercise is that the AFL had by no means been eliminated from American economic life during the twenties. Often new members in mass production industries had been lost very quickly through a rapid succession of strike defeats and through the closing of industries like shipbuilding. Others were lost only after protracted battles, like the meat packing, textile, coal, and railroad strikes of 1922. Nevertheless, the surviving strength of the unions revealed that the solidarities workers had displayed in those strikes had not been futile. The legacy of those struggles was more perverse. It took the form of beleaguered unions clinging to minority sectors of their industries, surrounded by a hostile open-shop environment, and governed by ruthless suppression of dissent within their own ranks. A membership matching that of 1913 might still have been there; the combativeness, diversity, and optimism were not.

Second, all trade unionists had become vividly aware of the power of the state during the war, and many of them had come to believe that this power might be harnessed by labor to transform America in a more egalitarian direction. Vigorous union mobilization of voters for the re-election of President Wilson in 1916 had unleashed aspirations for public ownership of railroads and mines, national health insurance and old-age pensions, legal prohibition of the dismissal of workers for union membership, a federal program of housing construction, and legal enforcement throughout each industry of conditions negotiated between unions and employers' associations. When John L. Lewis ran against Gompers for president of the AFL in 1921, he identified his candidacy with all of these ideas. Postwar strike defeats not only cost the unions the new members, who had lent these proposals vigorous support, but also taught the surviving leaders to expect little of benefit to workers from the federal government. None of the once-popular statist reforms received even a serious hearing at any AFL conventions between 1923 and 1932. Indeed, their espousal was taken as a sign of disloyalty to the federation.

The justly famous resolution, Industry's Manifest Duty, adopted by the AFL at its 1923 Portland convention, had called upon industry and labor, as two organized "functions" of modern society, to collaborate for the improvement of living conditions in such a way as to ward off the peril of "state invasion" of economic life. Such collaboration was possible, John L. Lewis explained in his book, *The Miner's Fight for American Standards* (1925), because "the men and the ownership have a common interest in resisting the onslaught of the irresponsible elements which dominate the industry in regions where labor is virtually enslaved." The internal discipline of the unions and the experience of their long-tenured officers, President Johnston of the machinists argued, constituted a "very valuable asset at the disposal of those who would now help solve some of our serious industrial problems." Their role was not to combat the social order. On the contrary, AFL President William Green declared that "the so-called 'irrepressible conflict' between the employers and the employees can be terminated" by "good judgement and reciprocal concessions."

By the time the AFL Executive Council announced its New Wage Policy in 1925, the notion of collaboration between the economy's organized functional elements had been expanded into a grandiose vision of the end of poverty and social conflict in America. The goals expressed by Hoover and King emerged as union demands. The conception of social power, like that of Industry's Manifest Duty, was impressively similar to the "pluralistic" concepts of sovereignty championed by political theorists from Harold Laski on the left to John N. Figgis on the Catholic right. As Selig Perlman noted at the time, the AFL's new doctrine also resembled the resolution adopted by Germany's Free

Trade Unions in 1922. Their Leipzig resolutions had declared that the ability of organized workers to share in the direction of the economy was more important than the ownership of the means of production, and that unions could transform society by means of a "spiritual infusion" of their values and standards into the existing structure of power. Hyacinthe Dubreuil, reformist leader of France's Confédération Générale du Travail, also proclaimed in 1921 that class struggle had served its purpose: the creation of new institutions, standards, and possibilities of collaboration. When Dubreuil visited the United States late in the decade, he hailed Henry Ford as "a sort of organizer of a socialist type of production." Ford's various enterprises, he added, promised to transform the whole fabric of social life: "There should be leisure, music and poetry—the five-day week, the old-fashioned dances, and a hospitable inn beside the road."

The AFL coupled its New Wage Policy to craft unionism to determine the criteria by which its executive council would decide what behavior would and would not be tolerated within the House of Labor in the twenties and the thirties. Writer Benjamin Stolberg sarcastically contrasted the evolution of the AFL to demands from the left for better class struggle through industrial unions. The AFL's program, he wrote, strove to keep unions "pure" by giving up their old "simplicity." The communists, he added, wanted to abandon craft purity for the sake of the old simplicity, so that unions "would be 'militant' and dumb."

Revolutionaries and Reformists

Revolutionary movements of the twenties deserve a more careful analysis than Stolberg's comment suggests or space permits here. The mass struggles and soaring popular hopes before 1922 had politicized large numbers of workers. What happened to those workers and their relationship to their neighbors when the tide of mass struggle ebbed? Part of the answer we know from available memoirs: they threw themselves into building parties and inner-party struggles. It is important to recall, however, that regardless of the legends that both communists and their foes bequeathed to us, the communists did not become the dominant group on the American left until the mid-1930s.

The persistent strength of the Socialist party in many communities and unions, the widespread appeal of the One Big Union movement in 1919–20 and its continuing role in Lawrence, Glace Bay, and western Canada, the remarkable continuities between the International Labor Defense and post-1927 Trotskyism, the virtually forgotten "Bukharinites" who gathered around Diego Rivera and Bertram Wolfe, the anarchists who remained a force to be reckoned with in the International Ladies' Garment Workers throughout the factional battles of the twenties, the IWW whose brief resurgence in

1923 gave it more members then than it had ever had before the war, the farmer-laborites who retained a strong base throughout the Northwest and became the second party of Minnesota and Manitoba, and the contingents of intellectuals in search of a third party that were constantly formed and reformed between 1919 and 1938, all must take their places in the panorama of the twenties. Institutions like the Federated Press, the International Labor Defense, the American Fund for Public Service (Garland Fund), and the *Labor Age* encouraged interaction and some cooperation among all these groups. As Gabriella Ferruggia has demonstrated, the *New Masses* after its founding in 1926 revived the open experimentation for which its prewar predecessor had been famous. Its large editorial collective, which included no more than two communists, pursued its quest for proletarian literature and art remarkably free of any party's direction, in part because the intensely workerist orientation of the Communist party in the twenties left it with little interest in the arts.

Moreover, an important group of self-styled progressives remained active in Brookwood College, in the Workers Education Bureau of America, on the staff of *Labor Age*, and in the leadership of many local unions and city central labor unions, as well as in the national leadership of the Amalgamated Clothing Workers and the Full Fashion Hosiery Workers. They had concluded from the defeats of 1919–22 that unionization of mass production industries would require both a new style of union activity and a more hospitable political environment. They had spearheaded effective intervention in the congressional and state elections of 1922 through the Conference for Progressive Political Action, only to see that organization disband after Robert La Follette's presidential campaign of 1924. Thereafter, they pinned their hopes on workers' education to train cadre for future union efforts and to prepare organized workers to assume active roles in the management of their own industries. There is an interesting topic for research in the transformation of the meaning of "workers' control" in these circles from an immediate collective seizure of power in the factory to training, as educator Horace Kallen put it, to enter "into the tasks and problems of management."

As early as 1927, however, a more aggressive theme was heard in workers' education circles. Abraham Muste and his colleagues at Brookwood concluded that the attempt to broaden and energize the labor movement through amalgamation of related craft unions had met with decisive defeat, and that the time had come to create new industrial unions. This line of argument not only brought the wrath of the AFL down upon Brookwood, but it also anticipated by a year the communists' initiative in forming the Trade Union Unity League. Although the fruits of this activity were to be reaped only in the thirties, the editors of *Labor Age* had also welcomed such initiatives as labor research and publicity bureaus, a labor radio station in Chicago, a victorious strike in

Passaic, and a series of meetings and seminars held by black trade unionists for the purpose of increasing their influence in the movement.

Unlike the periods before and after the Coolidge prosperity, this multifarious left-wing activity had little impact outside the circles of its participants, because there were few large popular struggles with which it might connect. A demand to free "class war prisoners," who had been jailed during and since the war period, enjoyed enough support, however, to generate what may have been the biggest strike movement ever led by the IWW, in May 1923. After several months of agitation for "General Amnesty or General Strike," following the release of Eugene Debs from jail, Wobblies coupled the local grievances of loggers, dockers, seamen, oil workers, and building tradesmen to their own political appeal and brought out workers from San Pedro to Philadelphia in a staccato fire of short strikes.

Four years later the struggle to save Sacco and Vanzetti from electrocution also stirred work stoppages and demonstrations across the country in a wave of protest that historians fascinated with the response of intellectuals to the case have failed even to chronicle. In western Pennsylvania, where the demonstrations erupted in the midst of the protracted coal miners' strike, police raids on meetings and prosecutions of workers absorbed almost all the energies of the International Labor Defense. Even Mackenzie King's thirteen-year-old ERP at Colorado Fuel and Iron did not stop the company's Chicano, Slavic, Greek, and Italian miners from striking for two days for Sacco and Vanzetti at the behest of the IWW.

Assimilation, Consumerism, and Unemployment

As the Sacco and Vanzetti struggle made clear, however, the potential mass base for the left now lay primarily in the communities of recent immigrants. So too did the potential electoral support for a welfare state. The two promises were simultaneously fulfilled during the New Deal. Maurice Isserman's study of the Communist party in the Popular Front period revealed the phenomenon of assimilation through opposition. In a larger sense, that process provided a central theme of working-class experience between the wars.

The closing of immigration by the quota and national origins laws had a greater impact on working-class life than any other government measure since the emancipation of the slaves. The act of 1924 assigned national quotas within an overall annual limit of 150,000 Europeans in such a way as to virtually exclude newcomers from southern and eastern Europe, banned all Asian workers whatsoever, and left free entry from North America, thus permitting the circular flow of Mexicans. Although Samuel Gompers, John R. Commons, and others saluted the law as the measure that would end competition for jobs and make fulfillment of the AFL's new Wage Policy possible, most employers found they could obtain all the new workers they needed from Ireland, the American countryside, Mexico, Quebec, and the Canadian Maritimes. Interestingly, few Germans came despite the large quota they were allocated.

The law did mean that communities of southern and eastern Europeans rapidly became more sedentary, were haunted by immigration officials in search of illegal entrants (who deported tens of thousands of people each year), and lived with daily reminders that the president, Congress, and most literary opinion of the United States had declared their presence undesirable. Most historians of immigration agree that it was the children of the immigrants, educated in schools where their "foreignness" was underscored while their desires were attuned, not to what their parents had left behind but by what they saw around them, who most keenly felt the unending insult. At home, Ewa Morawska has argued, they respected their parents, but at work they chafed under the foreman and the stop watch. They tended to perceive class through an ethnic lens (as did Anglo-Saxons at the top of the social ladder). The trial and execution of Sacco and Vanzetti encapsulated all their grievances. When they struck at Bethlehem Steel ten years later, Morawska relates, the dominant theme of their protest was: "You are not going to call us 'Hunky' no more."

Within the increasingly sedentary immigrant communities, the influence of professional and business strata had also grown significantly. Officers of fraternal organizations were drawn from their ranks much more heavily than they had been before the war. Immigrant lawyers, grocers, bankers, and real estate agents had been made more visible by their roles in wartime patriotic and Americanization campaigns, by their association with newly created or enlarged nation states in Europe, and by the links they provided their communities with corporate employment offices, political parties, local governments, and chambers of commerce. Simultaneously, access to the ranks of ethnic elites became more difficult. The clientele on which their businesses were based had ceased to grow significantly and, indeed, was seriously challenged by fashions and the sales of large-scale merchandisers.

Consequently, it was quite possible for immigrant leaders to become important figures in the Republican and Democratic parties, both of which celebrated business success as the primary purpose of political life, while the mass of immigrant workers were estranged from politics. Voter participation fell in the twenties to the lowest level since the 1830s in all parts of the country, although the decline was most serious by far in the South. Nevertheless, when Alan Lichtman compared the correlation between voter preferences and incomes in the Republican triumph of 1928 and the Democratic sweep of 1932, he concluded that the depression "did not appreciably widen the gap between economic classes that already existed in the 1920s." Roosevelt's victories may have rested on the mobilization of low-income voters who had sat out the elections of the twenties, rather than on the substitution of new economic divisions in the electorate for older cultural ones.

These considerations underscore the importance for historians of coming to grips with working-class living standards, unemployment, and consumerism in a systematic way. Chris Waters's investigations of incomes and expenditures during the twenties has reminded us about just how limited the material resources available to workers were at a time when almost half of the world's manufacturing output was generated within the boundaries of the United States. Despite the AFL's New Wage Policy and Hoover's prediction that the end of poverty was in sight, Morawska contends that in the Johnstown of 1925 "the majority—almost two-thirds of the male- and female-headed workingclass households who had persisted in town since 1900—existed on a collective annual income of less than $1,600, which was below the threshold of a 'good life' as seen by the immigrants."

Of special importance to workers was the chronically high level of unemployment throughout the Coolidge prosperity. To be sure, unemployment did not reach the levels endured by Germany and England at the same time, although it was worse than in France. Studies done by the National Resources Committee in the late 1930s may prove especially valuable for researchers, because they were focused directly on the supply and experience of wage earners and the impact of new technologies. David Weintraub estimated for the committee that between 10 and 13 percent of the "man-years" of work available went unemployed each year between 1923 and 1929, compared to 25 percent in 1921, 47 percent in 1933, and only 6 percent in 1920.

A virtually static demand for workers in production was offset by a steady upswing in the service sector, so that the latter absorbed 30 percent of the worker-years in 1920, 38 percent in 1929, and 42 percent in 1935, according to Weintraub. That trend, which accelerated greatly after 1922, meant that unemployment in 1921–22 was more severe than it was in late 1929 and 1930. More important, the growing spheres of employment shaped the work experience of women far more directly than they did those of men, for whom the most important change was the movement out of agriculture. As early as the census of 1920, more than 25 percent of all female employees were in clerical or sales work, slightly more than the proportion in manufacturing (24 percent), and significantly more than the historically dominant category of women's employment, domestic service (18 percent). Few if any lines of gender demarcation within manufacturing jobs changed between the wars. Although gender segregation was no less strict in the office and the store, working people were keenly aware of the rapid growth of employment there. Education in high school was especially important for young women who sought such jobs. And many of the companies were prepared to employ married women, whom most manufacturers did not want. The proportion of wage-earning women who were married rose from 22.8 percent in 1920 to 28.8 percent in 1930, and it continued to rise during the depression despite loud public protests against married women's employment.

How these changes, coupled with the rapid decline in the number of children in the average family, reshaped the experience, expectations, and sense of self of working-class women who came of age between the wars is a question that the researches of Susan Porter Benson, Ileen DeVault, Judith Smith, and John Modell have begun to open up for us. As is the case with so many of the issues raised by the twenties, we are reminded by these authors not to define as important only those changes in working-class life that resulted in someone's throwing up a picket line.

Similarly, the question of unemployment itself raises three interrelated problems. First is the question of how workers coped with joblessness in a time and country that had no unemployment insurance, in which reduced labor turnover made the search for new employment harder than it had previously been, in which industries like automobiles, rubber, construction and clothing remained highly seasonal, and in which advanced age remained a major barrier to employment while the average age rose rapidly. Youths may not have been as hard-hit then as they are today, but the new migrants from the countryside, who occupied the least secure positions in industry, tended to be young adults.

Second, the jobless in all countries between the wars tended to be uninterested in, if not hostile toward, unions. Job security arrangements for members, on which AFL unions laid special stress in the twenties, appeared to others as obstacles to finding work. Moreover, the AFL shunned even discussion of government insurance for the unemployed from 1923 to 1932. Unemployment compensation represented precisely the "outside" interference with the business of wage earners that the federation was determined to avoid. According to the AFL, unions should ensure their own members (which very few did) and negotiate with employers to even out production in order to reduce layoffs (which some managed to do). Neither plan helped the man or woman who had no source of income. This was the issue that produced the first great policy revolt within AFL ranks during the thirties.

Third, chronic unemployment provided the climate in which management's most effective efforts to cultivate loyal employees thrived. Employers' associations could not only blacklist unruly workers, but could also find jobs for those in need who seemed trustworthy. Company managers retained trained and tested employees during reductions of the workforce by shifting them into the jobs of newer and usually less skilled workers who were let go. Many firms, sometimes under pressure from unions but often not, tried to plan inventories in advance in order to stabilize the number of people needed over relatively long periods of time. When major reductions of output were unavoidable, many companies tried to reduce the work week for all (often after dismissing unmarried young men and women), although managers often thought that this practice bought workers' loyalty at a heavy cost in efficiency. Layoffs, after all, were the ideal time to weed out less productive members of the force, and very short working days inhibited a steady flow of work. From the point of view of most workers, however, nothing better defined a "good job" than dependability.

Nevertheless, we must not simply deny the importance of improved material conditions of life and "consumerism" in shaping both the relative quiescence of the twenties and the reformism of the thirties. Automobiles, radios, gas stoves, and running water became increasingly important in the lives of those who had jobs in the thirties as well as the twenties. The presence of such amenities informed both the personal, family-oriented quest for a better life that appeared to be the only realistic option available to most workers during the Coolidge years and the demands of industrial unionism in the next decade. As we think about this domain of consumption, however, it is important to be guided by three considerations. First, through cooperatives, union labels, boycotts, and efforts to commandeer the mass media, the workers' movement waged its own battles within the sphere of consumption between the wars. Second, the relationship between the depressed agricultural and primary goods sector and the urban world with its swelling manufacturing productivity and growing orientation toward services made possible the coexistence of higher living standards and higher levels of unemployment than workers had known before the war.

Third, a society in which the earning of wages had become by far the dominant way of obtaining a livelihood had made the struggle for control of the use of time decisive in the confrontation of classes. Consumerism dominated social life only because consumption was *not* the guiding purpose of production. "If the aim of production were use-value," as Gerald A. Cohen has written, "much less use-value would be sought, produced, and consumed than is in fact produced and consumed." The determination of business and government to shape workers' use of their time in the interest of capital accumulation (or "economic growth") remained as important for New Deal depression policy as it had been for Hoover's resistance to state invasion of the economy during the twenties. After all, the productive capacity of the American economy by 1920 was more than sufficient to have secured everyone a comfortable existence without either feverish toil or unemployment, if that had been the purpose to which it was directed.

Note

Reprinted courtesy of Cambridge University Press and *International Labor and Working-Class History*.

Selected Bibliography

Adamic, Louis. *Dynamite: The Story of Class Violence in America.* New York, 1931.

Benson, Susan Porter. *Counter Cultures: Saleswomen, Managers, and Customers in American Department Stores, 1890–1940.* Urbana, Ill., 1986.

Bodnar, John. *Workers' World: Kinship, Community, and Protest in an Industrial Society, 1900–1940.* Baltimore, 1982.

Bodnar, John, Roger Simon, and Michael Weber. *Lives of Their Own: Blacks, Italians, and Poles in Pittsburgh, 1900–1960.* Urbana, Ill., 1982.

Brandes, Stuart. *American Welfare Capitalism, 1880–1940.* Chicago, 1976.

Brody, David. *Workers in Industrial America: Essays on the Twentieth Century Struggle.* New York, 1979.

Bukowczyk, John. "The Transformation of Working-Class Ethnicity: Corporate Control, Americanization, and the Polish Immigrant Middle Class in Bayonne, New Jersey 1915–1925." *Labor History* 25 (Winter 1984): 53–82.

Corbin, David. *Life, Work, and Rebellion in the Coal Fields: The Southern West Virginia Miners, 1880–1922.* Urbana, Ill., 1981.

Daniel, Cletus. *Bitter Harvest: A History of California Farmworkers, 1870–1941.* Ithaca, NY, 1981.

Daniel, Pete. *Breaking the Land: The Transformation of Cotton, Tobacco, and Rice Cultures Since 1880.* Urbana, Ill., 1985.

DeVault, Ileen A. "Sons and Daughters of Labor: Class and Clerical Work in Pittsburgh, 1870s-1910s" (PhD diss., Yale University, 1985).

Edwards, Paul K. *Strikes in the United States, 1881–1974.* Oxford, England, 1981.

Ewen, Stuart. *Captains of Consciousness: Advertising and the Social Roots of the Consumer Culture.* New York, 1976.

Ferruggia, Gabriella. "Radical Intellectuals and the Workers' (Communist) Party in the United States: *New Masses* and *The Daily Worker*, 1926–1928." *Storia Nordamericana* 2 (1985): 5–34.

Fine, Sidney. *Sit-Down: The General Motors Strike of 1936–37.* Ann Arbor, 1969.

Foster, William Z. *Misleaders of Labor.* Chicago, 1927.

Frank, Dana. "'At the Point of Consumption': Seattle Labor and the Politics of Consumption, 1919–1927" (PhD diss., Yale University, 1988).

Gambs, John. *Decline of the I.W.W.* New York, 1932.

Goodrich, Carter L. *The Miner's Freedom: A Study of the Working Life in a Changing Industry.* Boston, 1925.

Gordon, David M., Richard Edwards, and Michael Reich. *Segmented Work, Divided Workers: The Historical Transformation of Labor in the United States.* New York, 1982.

Gottlieb, Peter. *Making Their Own Way: Southern Blacks' Migration to Pittsburgh, 1916–30.* Urbana, Ill., 1987.

Guerin-Gonzales, Camille. "Cycles of Immigration and Repatriation: Mexican Farm Workers in California Industrial Agriculture, 1900–1940" (PhD diss., University of California, Berkeley, 1985).

Hardman, J.B.S. *American Labor Developments in the Light of Postwar Developments.* New York, 1928.
Hareven, Tamara. *Family Time and Industrial Time: The Relationship Between the Family and Work in a New England Industrial Community.* New York, 1982.
Hareven, Tamara, and Randolph Langenbach. *Amoskeag: Life and Work in an American Factory-City.* New York, 1978.
Isserman, Maurice. *Which Side Were You On? The American Communist Party During the Second World War.* Middletown, Conn., 1982.
Jacoby, Sanford. *Employing Bureaucracies: Managers, Unions, and the Transformation of Work in American Industry, 1900–1945.* New York, 1985.
Kessler-Harris, Alice. *Out to Work: A History of Wage-Earning Women in the United States.* New York, 1982.
Keyssar, Alexander. *Out of Work: The First Century of Unemployment in Massachusetts.* New York, 1986.
Kleppner, Paul. *Who Voted? The Dynamics of Electoral Turnout, 1870–1980.* New York, 1982.
Lequin, Yves. "Social Structures and Shared Beliefs: Four Worker Communities in the 'Second Industrialization.'" *International Labor and Working-Class History* 22 (Fall 1982): 1–17.
Lichtman, Alan J. *Prejudice and the Old Politics: The Presidential Election of 1928.* Chapel Hill, 1979.
Lorwin, Lewis. *The American Federation of Labor: History, Policy, and Prospects.* Washington, D.C., 1933.
Lorwin, Lewis. *The Women's Garment Workers: A History of the International Ladies' Garment Workers' Union.* New York, 1924.
Lynd, Robert S., and Helen S. Lynd. *Middletown: A Study in Contemporary American Culture.* New York, 1929.
Maier, Charles. *Recasting Bourgeois Europe: Stabilization in France, Germany, and Italy in the Decade after World War I.* Princeton, NJ, 1975.
Matthewson, Stanley B. *Restriction of Output among Unorganized Workers.* Carbondale, Ill., 1969.
Mayo, Elton. *The Human Problems of Industrial Civilization.* Boston, 1946.
Montgomery, David. *The Fall of the House of Labor: The Workplace, the State, and American Labor Activism, 1865–1925.* New York, 1987.
Morawska, Ewa. *For Bread with Butter: Life-Worlds of East Central Europeans in Johnstown, Pennsylvania, 1890–1940.* New York, 1987.
Palmer, Gladys. *Union Tactics and Economic Change.* Philadelphia, 1932.
Perlman, Selig. *A Theory of the Labor Movement.* New York, 1928.
Preston, William. *Aliens and Dissenters: Federal Suppression of Radicals, 1903–1933.* Cambridge, Mass., 1963.
Schatz, Ronald W. *The Electrical Workers: A History of Labor at General Electric and Westinghouse, 1923–1960.* Urbana, Ill., 1983.
Skocpol, Theda. "Political Response to Capitalist Crisis: Neo-Marxist Theories of the State and the Case of the New Deal." *Politics and Society* 10 (1980): 155–201.

Slichter, Sumner. *Union Policies and Industrial Management.* Washington, DC, 1941.
Smith, Judith E. *Family Connections: A History of Italian and Jewish Immigrant Lives in Providence, Rhode Island, 1900–1940.* Albany, NY, 1985.
Soule, George. *Prosperity Decade: From War to Depression, 1917–1929.* New York, 1947.
Tomlins, Christopher I. *The State and the Unions: Labor Relations, Law, and the Organized Labor Movement in America, 1880–1960.* New York, 1985.
Trotter, Joe William, Jr. *Black Milwaukee: The Making of an Industrial Proletariat, 1915–45.* Urbana, Ill., 1985.
Walling, William English. *American Labor and American Democracy.* New York, 1926.
Weinstein, James. *The Corporate Ideal in the Liberal State, 1900–1918.* Boston, 1968.

CHAPTER 13

Labor and the Political Leadership of New Deal America

From *International Review of Social History* 39, no. 3 (December 1994): 335–360

Summary

This essay examines the relationship between popular initiatives and government decision-makers during the 1930s. The economic crisis and the reawakening of labor militancy before 1935 elevated men and women, who had been formed by the workers' movement of the 1910s and 1920s, to prominent roles in the making of national industrial policies. Quite different was the reshaping of social insurance and work relief measures. Although those policies represented a governmental response to the distress and protests of the working class, the workers themselves had little influence on their formulation or administration. Through industrial struggles, the Committee for Industrial Organization (CIO) mobilized a new cadre, trained by youthful encounters with urban ethnic life, expanding secondary schooling and subordination to modern corporate management, in an unsuccessful quest for economic planning and universal social insurance through the agency of a reformed Democratic Party.

The political and industrial conflicts of the 1930s reshaped both the role of the United States government in economic and social life and the character and influence of the labor movement in ways that formed essential features of the polity for the next forty years. The importance of this transformation made the relationship between government policy decisions and the growing labor movement a subject of intense public controversy at the time, and it has continued to generate disputes among historians to this day.

President Franklin D. Roosevelt, while annotating an early edition of his own papers, had depicted the new industrial unions as both a beneficiary of his government and a tribulation to it. Introducing messages related to the steel strike of 1937, he wrote:

> Labor was having its growing pains. Labor, which had been subjected to so much exploitation in the past, was just beginning to find its power under the new impetus of favorable legislation and a sympathetic Government. It had not quite grown up to such power. In some quarters irresponsible leadership had developed [. . .] From familiar circles came the old cry of the Tories: "Something drastic must be done to curb labor [. . .]"[1]

Much of the subsequent disagreement among historians might be considered as an exegesis on the President's statement. What David Brody has called the "liberal conception of industrial-union history" focused its attention on the role of Roosevelt's "favorable legislation and a sympathetic Government" in making rapid union growth possible and on the conservative reaction to industrial militancy that had sharply curtailed both union growth and reform legislation by the end of the decade.[2] A contrary position, well represented by a new anthology of essays edited by Staughton Lynd, has interpreted the "favorable legislation" itself as a reluctant response by the Roosevelt government to labor militancy. More important, it also depicts not only the government's action, but also the institutionalization of the industrial union impulse in the Committee for Industrial Organization (CIO) as deliberate and effective containment of more radical impulses among the workers (what Roosevelt called "irresponsible leadership"). From this point of view, the establishment of unions which defined their jurisdictions by industry and which negotiated binding contracts with businesses fragmented the community-wide solidarities from which workers had drawn strength during the early 1930s, while the legislative reforms of 1935–1936 (often called by historians the Second New Deal) undermined a growing movement for a labor party and tied the emerging union movement to the Democratic Party. Moreover, despite the angry identification of strikes and unions with Communist insurgency by contemporary conservatives, these historians assess the policies pursued by the Communist party during the Popular Front era as having served only to assist the process of cooptation.[3]

Although David Brody pays tribute to the "new questions" that have been posed by these revisionists, he nevertheless charges that they have not shown that "it could have been otherwise"—that real alternatives existed to "the union course that was actually taken."[4] While the debate over historical assessment of paths not taken remains open, however, other historians have enriched the controversy by posing questions of a different order. From one direction, Lizabeth Cohen has argued that a "culture of unity," fashioned by urban immigrant life and mass consumerism made the New Deal possible. In her view the interaction between the working class and the state viewed from the base involved much more than just industrial conflict. From quite the opposite direction,

Theda Skocpol and others have stressed the "relative autonomy of the state," and argued that policy-makers played their own creative roles that cannot be understood simply as reacting to social conflict and popular demands.[5]

The extent of my own agreement and disagreement with each of these positions will become evident in the pages to come. Let me assert at the outset, however, that one promising clue to resolving the disputes has been offered by Steven Fraser's biography of Sidney Hillman, a leading figure in both the industrial unions and the government.

"From the vantage point of rising new trade union, managerial, and political elites," wrote Fraser, "the CIO was a quintessentially political creature [,] whose origins and fate were entirely bound up with the rising and receding of the 'second New Deal.'"[6] His argument suggests that both the institutions and the cadre of the labor movement were more intimately tied to government policymakers of the period than is suggested by either the image of the "relative autonomy of the state" in formulating policy or that of industrial turmoil, which the state sought to pacify by concessions. It also suggests that the workers' movement of the epoch generated new governmental leaders at the local, state, and national levels, and that the critical support offered the New Deal administration by the American version of the Popular Front was not so much a betrayal of revolutionary impulses inspired by Moscow's foreign policy as an adaptation of political strategies to the new power relationships within which workers were transforming their own lives. It may prove useful to follow that line of argument, while directing attention to what was happening in factories and neighborhoods, as well as to policy formation in Washington.

This essay will examine the relationship between popular initiatives and government decision-makers during the 1930s. It will begin with a consideration of the role of the economic crisis and the reawakening of labor militancy before 1935 in elevating men and women who had been formed by the workers' movement of the 1910s and 1920s to prominent roles in the making of industrial policies. It will then turn to the reshaping of social insurance and work relief measures and argue that, although those policies represented a governmental response to the distress and protests of the working class, the workers themselves had little influence on their formulation or administration. Finally, it will scrutinize the way the Committee for Industrial Organization (CIO) mobilized a new cadre, trained by youthful encounters with urban ethnic life, expanding secondary schooling and subordination to modern corporate management, in an unsuccessful quest for economic planning and universal social insurance through the agency of a reformed Democratic Party.

In the United States, as in Mexico, reorientation of the ruling party toward social reform required the formation of a new union movement. Unlike Mexico, however, the United States remained the theater of intense electoral competition. A groundswell of new voters, largely of eastern and southern

European ancestry, had broadened the urban base of the Democratic Party beyond its traditional Irish-German constituency, while African Americans bargained during the 1930s with both major parties for government jobs and open access to public accommodations in the North, and also mobilized campaigns for voting rights in southern industrial centers in alliance with the new unions. Conversely, as the Lynds discovered when they revisited Muncie, Indiana, in 1935–1936, a siege mentality had unified the Protestant middle class under the Republican banner. The nation's opposing camps confronted each other with rival 1936 Labor Day parades in Aliquippa, Pennsylvania, where Jones and Laughlin had its finest steel mill. Morning festivities featured company union loyalists, businessmen's lodges, and the McKinley Republican Club. They were challenged in the afternoon by adherents of the Steel Workers' Organizing Committee, thousands of coal miners and craft unionists, affiliates of the International Workers Order, and representatives of the local Farmer-Labor Party, all marching to the beat of a United Mine Workers' drum and bugle corps behind portraits of President Roosevelt.[7]

Agencies created in Washington to encourage employers' recognition of industrial unions, especially the National Labor Relations Board (NLRB) and the LaFollette Civil Liberties Committee, empowered local groups of workers to exercise their own initiatives for their own purposes. The experience of the mid-1930s taught millions of workers that the police powers of the state could be used to unleash popular initiatives, as well as to repress them. Intense reaction by business and conservative groups against workers' uses of their newly won collective power, coupled with the abrupt collapse of the economy in late 1937, brought widespread victories of the Right in the federal and state elections of 1938, checked the growth of the CIO, and encouraged Congress and the administration to refrain from additional reform legislation and to trim expenditures for relief projects. Supreme Court rulings declaring the replacement of employees who were engaged in "economic strikes" (1938) and the punishment of sit-down strikers (1939) permissible under the Wagner Act were supplemented by a wave of state legislation to restrain strikes and union practices.[8] America's great hour of worker-driven political reform had lasted no longer than that of France.

Unions and Industrial Policy

Both the leadership of the American Federation of Labor (AFL) and their more radical rivals within the workers' movement formulated their policies for dealing with the Great Depression on the basis of their own experience during the epoch of World War I. The proportion of the labor force engaged in strikes every year between 1916 and 1922 had been far greater than that generated by the strike waves of 1934 and 1937. Moreover, the percentage of the working class that had enrolled in unions in 1920 was not to be equaled again until 1940, when conditions of war mobilization again prevailed. Not only had AFL and independent unions momentarily secured a large membership in heavy industry, as well as a more durable constituency in the skilled trades, but a self-styled bloc of "progressives" within the AFL had advocated national old-age pensions, unemployment and health insurance, a federal program of housing construction, legislation to prohibit the dismissal of workers for union membership, pacts committing unions to mutual strike support, national ownership of coal mines and railroads, and union participation in the Conference for Progressive Political Action.[9]

By the end of the depression of 1920–1922 unions had been expelled from mass production industries, total union membership had fallen by nearly 40 percent, and the AFL's progressives had largely been relegated to the workers' education movement. Nevertheless, total union membership at its lowest ebb during the 1920s remained greater in proportion to the size of the labor force than it had ever been before the war (or than it is in the private sector in 1993), and the gap between union and non-union wages in manufacturing, mining and construction was the greatest it had ever been.

Unions continued to negotiate trade agreements primarily with relatively small employers, who serviced local markets. Municipal licensing regulation of construction, entertainment, conveyance and food service often contributed to the local strength of unions and tightened their bonds to urban politicians. Moreover, even when they were beleaguered by injunctions and open shop campaigns, officers of AFL unions knew that during and since the war the government had endowed them with a quasi-official status. Whenever they were challenged by the Industrial Workers of the World, the One Big Union, the Trade Union Educational League, or smaller unaffiliated Left-led unions, both local police and federal authorities could be relied upon to attack their rivals and confer with the "legitimate" unions of the AFL. In a word, the conservative practitioners of "tried and true" craft unionism did have something tangible to defend against what the teamsters' Daniel Tobin called "the rubbish at labor's door" in the 1930s.[10]

When the depression devastated the economy, therefore, the journal of the AFL's International Brotherhood of Electrical Workers editorialized that the federal government should consider "organized workers as assets to the state." The editor explained: "If [the government] can come into a vision of organized workers—labor unions—as technical instruments of production, as arms of the state to police and enforce fair laws—then the nation may well be on the road to a new and better prosperity."[11]

The aspiration to employ trade unions, which workers had created by their own efforts, as instruments of government-sponsored rationalization of the market behavior of business had taken shape not only among the electricians, whose exertions were converting American industry and residences to electrical power and wiring the huge dams that both Hoover and Roosevelt presented to the public as symbols of their recovery programs, but also among both union leaders and industrialists in the coal, garment and textile industries. As Stanley Vittoz has argued, in those three incurably competitive industries, labor costs were decisive determinants of prices, and unions had been a significant presence at least since the turn of the century. It was in the same industries that the Communist Party (as earlier the IWW and OBU) was able to organize major strikes: witness the textile workers' strikes in Passaic, New Bedford and Gastonia, the strikes of the National Miners Union in Kentucky, New Mexico and Pennsylvania, and the historic strike of the International Ladies' Garment Workers in New York City under Communist leadership in 1926.

In both bituminous coal and women's clothing crushing strike defeats suffered by AFL unions during 1926 and 1927 had ironically left the victorious employers helpless to deter cost-cutting by their competitors, which dragged all prices relentlessly down and threatened even the mightiest firms with ruin after 1929. In June 1931 Frank E. Taplin, President of the North American Coal Corporation, circulated an open letter to his fellow mine owners, admonishing them that "the situation is even worse [now] than when we dealt with the Union." He asked them to consider carefully "whether it is better to operate with a well-regulated Union which has a legitimate right to exist," or to compete with "a lot of price-cutting, wage-cutting operators," in the unrestrained way that "fills the mines with Communists."[12]

The election of 1930 returned a Congress that was prepared to enact the major legislative demands of the AFL. The Norris-LaGuardia Act restricted the use of injunctions against unions and put an end especially to court orders which had prohibited union recruiting of miners who had signed a pledge not to join a union, as a condition of employment. The Davis-Bacon Act required the payment of the "prevailing wage" (which usually meant union wage) in construction work contracted by the federal government. Senator James Davis, who had been Secretary of Labor under President Calvin Coolidge, was soon joined by such fellow Pennsylvanians as Joseph Guffey and Henry Ellenbogen, in depicting the Sherman Anti-Trust Act as the primary obstacle to the development of cartels which could stabilize prices and of unions strong enough to enforce the same wage standards on all members of those cartels. They were a bipartisan group, so it is small wonder that in 1932 the national labor committees of the Republican, Democratic and Socialist parties were all headed by presidents of AFL unions (William Hutcheson, Daniel Tobin and Emil Rieve).

The culmination of their efforts was the National Industrial Recovery Act of 1933, which enjoyed its most consistent support from unions and major employers in clothing, coal mining and textiles (especially northern). That major piece of New Deal legislation, however, also owed much to a broader conception of the role of government in reshaping industrial relations, which had taken root during the 1920s in the cluster of intellectuals who gathered around the decade's "New Unions," especially the unaffiliated Amalgamated Clothing Workers of America (ACWA). Created in 1914 by a secession of primarily Jewish and Italian workers from the AFLs United Garment Workers, the ACWA grew to control major centers of men's clothing production, despite incessant attacks from the AFL (and in Baltimore the IWW), frequent treatment as an "outlaw union" by the courts, and a concerted attempt by employers to stamp it out in 1921. It became, along with the smaller Full Fashion Hosiery Workers, the lodestone of left-liberal hopes during the Harding and Coolidge years, when the rest of the trade union movement had lapsed, in Selig Perlman's apt phrase, into a "curious blending of 'defeatism' with complacency."[13]

Not only was the leadership of the ACWA graced by some of the ablest men and women ever to hold union office in the United States (like Sidney Hillman, Joseph Schlossberg, Bessie Abramowitz, Augusto Bellanca, J. B. S. Hardman, and Aldo Cursi), but the New Unionism they symbolized combined vigorous commitment to workers' education, a labor party, comprehensive social insurance, government assistance to collective bargaining, and friendly ties to Soviet Russia (especially during its New Economic Policy) with an innovative quest for both union standards and higher productivity. That quest drew into the Amalgamated's orbit a constellation of social scientists and social engineers, including Morris Cooke, Mary Van Kleeck, Wesley Mitchell, Leo Wolman and Ordway Tead, along with business leaders like Edward Filene and Henry Dennison, for whom stimulation of mass consumption was a more compelling objective than absolute mastery over their own employees. Together they cultivated what Steven Fraser calls "microregulation" of the economy: securing high earnings, raising productivity, evening out seasonal patterns of layoffs, introducing company-based unemployment insurance, policing the behavior of subcontractors, and creating a nucleus of experienced arbitrators, whose decisions introduced an element of predictability into industrial relations. In localities where no employers' association existed to deal with the union, the ACWA organized one.[14] Consequently, the New Unionism was one major contributor to the assembling and training of the cadre of the New Deal.

NRA Codes and Popular Initiatives

The most important agency through which workers exercised their own initiatives and generated new political leadership was the industrial union. As many historians have agreed, the resurgence of trade unionism unleashed by the National Industrial Recovery Act in 1933 and 1934 was most successful in industries with long-established union traditions and prominent business leaders who regarded the NRA Codes and even strong unions as necessary to check ruinous price competition. Moreover, the national officers of the unions which benefited most from the Act, such as the mine workers, men's and women's clothing workers, textile workers (who emerged strong in the North, though defeated in the South), teamsters, longshoremen, seamen and building trades, had been securely established in office since the World War I epoch and had learned from those years to press for government policies hospitable to union growth, and to operate cautiously within the terrain those policies permitted. Even the central labor unions of Detroit, Akron, Bridgeport, Bessemer and other cities, that played major roles in mobilizing local solidarity in support of new unions, had usually been dominated by the same individuals for years. Many of them were old socialists, like Detroit's Frank X. Martel, who seemed to rekindle some of the ardor of their own youth.[15]

The most famous strikes of 1934, those of the Pacific Coast maritime workers, Minneapolis truckers and Toledo Auto-Lite workers, were led by Communists, Trotskyists and Musteites, who drew on the political vision and organizational experience of their revolutionary parties to defy established union leaders and to project new personalities into positions of lasting influence. Even the organizing campaigns that were most carefully managed by veteran AFL officials, however, also unleashed popular mobilizations in areas that had long been quiescent and churned up new activists, who challenged local elites and established union leaders all over the land.

For example, the rapid organization of eighty-seven locals in Alabama by the United Mine Workers (UMWA) inspired the local Communist Party to abandon its nearly defunct National Miners' Union in favor of rank-and-file committees of UMWA members. Miners struck in defiance of the union's leadership against the low wage scales authorized by the NRA bituminous coal code in the South and also against the widespread practice of subcontracting, by which operators evaded many code provisions. Although a strike of 15–20,000 miners against the regional differential in February 1934 was unsuccessful, subcontracting was ended. Local Communist Party membership rose to more than 500 in spite of fierce police repression, while strikes in laundries, iron mines, and packinghouses, coupled with incessant struggles in support of relief recipients, set the stage for a May Day parade of more than 5,000 participants, who were brutally attacked by Birmingham's police and some 1,500 White Legionnaires. Since almost all local Communists were black workers, few of them were able to rise to eminence even in the CIO, let alone local government, in the segregated South. But with the help of party schools some became prominent trade unionists, like Henry O. Mayfield, Joe Howard, Ebb Cox and Hosea Hudson. More important, as Robin Kelley has shown, the women's auxiliaries of the unions came to rival the unions themselves in membership and activism, especially through their battles to place families of strikers on relief rolls and to register African Americans as voters.[16]

In the anthracite region of eastern Pennsylvania, where especially autocratic districts of the miners' unions had survived more than a decade of declining markets and chronic unemployment, class solidarity in the NRA context upset established relationships of local economic and political power. The subcontracting system, which made some union miners exploiters of others, had survived the recognition of the United Mine Workers and even a large strike against the practice led by the IWW among the largely Italian laborers of the Old Forge region in 1916. Although the United Mine Workers had enjoyed a virtual closed shop and union dues check-off since that time, a wildcat strike against subcontracting in 1933 spread rapidly through the northern region, encompassing Wilkes-Barre, Old Forge and Scranton. Because President Lewis had decreed that any local officer who entertained a strike motion would be expelled, the miners learned to take strike votes with no one on the podium and no debate. When UMWA officials attempted to drive members back to work, the informal leaders of the strike (most of whom had earlier been friendly to the Communist NMU, but not party members) organized a new union, the Anthracite Miners' Union of Pennsylvania.

As was the case in the Alabama coal fields, unemployed councils and organizations of miners' wives and daughters were especially prominent in mobilizing strike support. Wilkes-Barre added an unusual twist: its school children struck classes in sympathy with their fathers. Within two months, however, the anthracite strike was broken, when thirty leaders were imprisoned for violating an injunction (despite the Norris-LaGuardia law), the president of the rebel union was killed by a bomb mailed to his home, and a German-born anarchist was executed on very dubious evidence that he had sent the bomb. Activists from the defeated union then joined with the Communists to field a Luzerne County Labor Party ticket for the 1934 elections.[17]

The nation-wide textile strike in September 1934 renewed mass action in the region. The anthracite fields were unusually highly urbanized for a North American coal mining region, and during the second and third decades of the twentieth century they had attracted many textile (especially silk) mills, which employed women from miners' families. The 1934 strike was especially fiercely fought at the large, paternalistic Duplan mills of Hazleton, but the women who regularly assaulted scabs and bombarded that factory with rocks also formed motorized flying squadrons to dispense the same treatment to mills in Wilkes-Barre, Scranton and other towns. A huge rally convened by Hazleton's Central Labor Union in the auditorium of St. John's Greek Catholic school resulted in a general Labor Holiday called by all unions of the region on 12 September. Twenty thousand workers marched through the town's streets behind banners of their unions and unemployed councils, to the cadence of three popular orchestras and bands provided by the UMWA and war veterans' organizations.[18]

The virtual unanimity of the Hazleton holiday and the marchers' consistent praise for the NRA provided clear evidence that the established unions had embraced the popular movement, and that it would be the Democratic Party that swept the polls in November, leaving the new labor party hardly 5 percent of the region's vote. Nevertheless, one more incident in the little town of Kelayres, south of Hazleton, suggested the dimensions of the upheaval involved in the triumph of the Democrats.

Lizabeth Cohen, John Bodnar, Gary Gerstle, John Bukowczyk, Cecelia Bucki and other historians have scrutinized the consolidation of immigrant fraternal organizations, business and political leadership that followed the virtual closing of immigration from eastern and southern Europe by the National Origins Act of 1924. All of them have observed, as Louis Adamic had done back in the 1930s, that immigrant self-help efforts were bankrupted by the Great Depression, and that even the business and professional strata of immigrant communities appealed for federal relief, showing no nostalgia whatever for the "rugged individualism" preached by President Herbert Hoover. Just as common hatred for Prohibition had turned ethnic leaders toward the Democrats, so the economic crisis made them spur on the Democrats' turn to what Hoover had condemned as "state invasion" of economic life.[19]

It was the distinctive contribution of Ewa Morawska, however, to note that the closing down of new immigration had also curbed the expansion of immigrant elites, leaving established business, clerical, and professional leaders fiercely protective of their domains and encouraging their rivals within the ethnic communities (both petit bourgeois and worker) to challenge their hegemony with populist and pan-ethnic appeals, that often earned the most favorable response among the American-educated youth.[20] In Kelayres, where most men worked (when there was work) for the Lehigh and Wilkes-Barre Coal Company, the Bruno family, whose progenitors had come to the mines from Cosenza in Calabria in the late 1880s, ruled the town in the shadow of the corporation until 1934. By the time the depression broke, various Brunos ran a hotel, a cigar factory, a general store, the local bank, and the local Republican Party. Among the cousins could be found the tax assessor, a school director, the high school's principal, two justices of the peace, a county detective, an officer of the Coal and Iron Police, and a poor relief director.

Unease with the Brunos' regime turned to rage when the economic crisis prompted various members of the family to foreclose mortgages on homes and stores of other townspeople, deny relief funds to the needy while pilfering money for themselves, and use the school buses to transport bootleg beer. It was, in fact, aggrieved shopkeepers who first mobilized neighbors (with Ukrainian, Slovak, Irish and Polish, as well as Italian names) to challenge the Brunos, first inside the Republican Party, and then with the eager support offered them by the state's Democrats. Hostilities mounted to the point where Bruno women would not go to church unarmed. The night before the elections, a large angry parade behind an American flag and banners hailing President Roosevelt was fired on from the Brunos' residential enclave. Five men were killed instantly, and twenty more men, women and children were seriously injured. State police entering the Bruno homes found an arsenal of weaponry, as well as slot machines, and escorted fourteen leaders of the town's Republican Party out to stand trial for murder. Election day broadcasts by the Democratic Party trumpeted news of the massacre perpetrated by the Republicans. Some 20,000 people attended the funeral, where they heard the victorious Democratic gubernatorial candidate George Earle proclaim that the victims had "died in the trenches of the New Deal."[21]

In short, a fixation on the well-known surge of votes toward the Democrats in neighborhoods dominated by immigrants and their descendants can mask political upheavals within those communities that were brought to a crescendo by the 1933–1934 strike wave. The forging of a New Deal coalition, which has been so eloquently described by Lizabeth Cohen's account of Chicago, was often a far less benign process than she has depicted. Victorious Democratic candidates (or New Deal Republicans like Fiorello LaGuardia and Vito Marcantonio) may have been securely rooted in their ethnic communities, but they also had to challenge entrenched leaders within those communities. As Gary Gerstle has shown in the case of Woonsocket and Hyman Berman in that of Minnesota, it was the renewed economic distress and conservative reaction of 1938–1939 that allowed older ethnic leaders their moment of revenge, usually behind appeals to anticommunism, ethnic nationalism and antisemitism.[22]

Social Insurance and Social Workers

Emergency relief for the unemployed and the Social Security Act of 1935 brought significant benefits to many workers, but both the prior history of state legislation and the decisions of the federal government during the 1930s served to minimize the role of workers' organizations in shaping policy or providing administrative personnel. Early in the twentieth century the American Association for Labor Legislation had assembled academics and other reformers, who wished to devise governmental measures to protect working people against the hazards of industrial life. During the brief but highly visible depression of 1914–1915, the association's carefully crafted proposals for publicly funded insurance against old age, sickness and unemployment, similar to measures that had recently been adopted by Britain's parliament, won the support of many state branches of the AFL and serious consideration by legislative commissions in several states, especially Massachusetts.

Nothing came of these efforts. By the early 1920s proposals for governmentally regulated and funded social insurance had met with defeat in state legislatures or in the courts. The electorate (which had shriveled to an all-time low) adamantly favored lower taxes, and the managers of major industrial firms, which had successfully fought off unionization of their employees, clearly preferred to introduce pensions, health benefits, stabilization of employment and even dismissal pay for long-term employees (which more than 300 firms had instituted before the Great Depression) on their own initiative and for their own employees. Management considered such benefits a means to encourage the loyalty of workers to the enterprise and an antidote to the insurance offered by ethnic fraternal lodges and trade unions. Government insurance threatened not only to increase the tax burden, but also to invade the domain of managerial discretion in the direction of the firm and the cultivation of loyal employees.[23]

In this context the state of Wisconsin played a role in the development of social insurance comparable to that of the ACWA in "micro-regulation" of the economy. The Socialist-led State Federation of Labor provided an important lobby, as did its counterpart in Pennsylvania, but the measures introduced into the legislature were developed by scholars from the University of Wisconsin (most famous among them John R. Commons), who carefully tailored the proposals to minimize the opposition of business and taxpayers. The funds were contributed by potential beneficiaries, rather than general state revenues, and in the case of unemployment insurance, companies which maintained their own reserve funds avoided taxation. Of the six states which enacted old age pensions before 1928, two had them ruled unconstitutional (Pennsylvania and Arizona), and only Montana and Wisconsin had actually paid out benefits. Four years later Wisconsin passed the country's first unemployment benefits law. "When the New Deal came," Theda Skocpol has argued, "'Wisconsin experts' were uniquely well positioned to be called to Washington, D.C." and influence "the formulation and implementation of the Social Security Act."[24]

Their influence did not go unchallenged in Congress. The Rank and File Conference of AFL activists, with the Communist painter Louis Weinstock its secretary-treasurer, had developed an alternative plan for comprehensive social insurance financed by general revenues, which was introduced into the House of Representatives in 1934 by Ernest Lundeen of Minnesota's Farmer-Labor Party. For the rest of the decade the Lundeen bill enjoyed the support of the Workers' Alliance, all local labor parties and the CIO. A poll conducted by the *New York Post* in 1935 found respondents favoring the proposal over the administration's social security bill by a ratio of one hundred to one. During the subsequent debate, the administration, according to Edwin Witte who headed the staff of the President's Committee on Economic Security, used the Lundeen bill "as a scarecrow to get action on its bill."[25]

The aim of the Lundeen bill was to guarantee a minimum standard of living for every resident of the United States. As Mary Van Kleeck of the Russell Sage Foundation, who had redrafted Lundeen's bill in 1935, told Congress: *"Social insurance should not be split into categories."* It provided for social insurance against all loss of wages, whether through unemployment, part-time work, sickness, old age, or maternity and for all "workers and farmers without discrimination because of age, sex, race, or color, religious or political opinion, or affiliation, whether they be industrial, agricultural, domestic, or professional workers, for all time lost." The bill received the enthusiastic endorsement of executive secretary T. Arnold Hill of the Urban League, because its uniform benefits and universal coverage, which were absent from the administration's bill, had "special meaning for Negro workers."[26]

Most innovative of all was the Lundeen bill's provision that social insurance should be administered, under general rules prescribed by the Secretary of Labor, by "commissions composed of the rank and file of workers' and farmers' organizations." No idea was further from the mind of the Roosevelt administration than the use of workers' organizations to administer social insurance funds, the way trade unions in Belgium, Sweden and England administered government unemployment compensation, or placing representative workers on the staff of administrative agencies, as German health insurance had done since Wilhelmine times. Quite the contrary. New Deal policy-makers and Congress preferred old age pensions and unemployment compensation funded entirely by contributions of employers and employees, with no benefits to be paid out until an adequate reserve fund had been accumulated (two years later). They were also to be administered by civil servants. Although the CIO called the Social Security Act of 1935 "a step in the right direction," all its vigorous lobbying between 1944 and 1948 to revive the Lundeen bill, reincarnated as the Murray-Wagner-Dingall bill, failed to prod the government toward universal social insurance.[27]

The Social Security Act contained another provision, which underscored labor's remote influence on social welfare policy: it returned control of all relief expenditures other than work projects to the states. Since all states except South Carolina and Georgia had enacted mothers' pensions (sometimes called widows' pensions) before the coming of the New Deal, the law made federally-aided but state-administered Aid to Dependent Children the basic national system of poor relief, rather than the universal income guarantees proposed by Lundeen.

The favored form of relief had its origin in campaigns mobilized at the turn of the century by the General Federation of Women's Clubs, National Congress of Mothers and National Consumers' League, for public funds to enable widowed and impoverished mothers to care for their own children, without swelling the ranks of the lowest-paid wage earners. Their demand for "mothers' pensions" was launched from White House conferences, it secured the endorsement of the AFL and influential fraternal lodges, and it overwhelmed the opposition of private charity organizations, which had feared a restoration of the municipal "outdoor relief" that they had stamped out by protracted struggle in the nineteenth century. So difficult did politicians find it to resist the appeal to motherhood and the family circle, that the twenty states which enacted mothers' pensions between 1911 and 1913 did so by nearly unanimous tallies. By 1920 twenty more states had followed suit, and in 1931 all but two had joined the ranks.[28]

This was the form of relief that was systematized by the New Deal and passed on to our own times. As it turned out, however, the women's organizations had been more successful in securing the enactment of mothers' pensions than they were in shaping their implementation. Tax-shy state legislatures authorized such paltry appropriations that widows were more likely to be on waiting lists than receiving benefits, and the actual pensions were so small that beneficiaries had to supplement them by stealthily taking in work that paid far less than women's wages in factories, stores or offices. More important for the long run, professional social workers, often from the very agencies that had opposed the laws in the first place, assumed the task of determining which applicants displayed life styles that would make them worthy of the state benefits. Largely through the growing influence of the National Conference of Social Work, the men and women who administered both public benefits and private charities increasingly adhered to the same professional code. They regarded with contempt all signs of "sentimentalism" in dealing with the poor.[29]

The cadre for the New Deal's relief administration was drawn from the ranks of the professional social workers, led by those who came with Harry Hopkins from the state of New York to staff the Federal Emergency Relief Administration (FERA). In the memory of American workers, no act of the New Deal evokes a warmer response than the massive scale of its relief effort. From the vantage point of the social work profession, however, the FERA was, in William Brock's words, "a government by experts at the expense of elected amateurs. It was a government by outsiders: outside the political system, outside the bureaucratic establishment, and belonging to a profession that had yet to win public recognition."[30]

By the time Aid to Dependent Children was returned to the states in 1935 (under the direction of the new Social Security Administration rather than the female-staffed Children's Bureau), the National Conference of Social Work approved the transfer of responsibility, confident that its standards would now prevail in every state without Harry Hopkins' oversight. Branches of the Workers' Alliance subsequently waged many protests about the size and rules of relief allocations to women, some of them successful. But they could only protest. Unlike the Wagner Act, which empowered workers to fashion and use their own agencies, the administration of poor relief remained outside of the workers' grip. More research is needed before one can say how often and under what circumstances the united Communist-Socialist organization for the unemployed, the Workers' Alliance, was able to cultivate local relief officials friendly to its point of view. It is clear, however, that many a recipient shared the sentiments of one who wrote to the Minneapolis Workers' Alliance: "I myself would have liked nothing better than in broad daylight to heave bricks of patent dynamite into the windows of bureaus and agencies that are supposed to be established for the benefit of unemployed girls."[31]

While relief for women was remanded to state authorities, where professional social workers held sway, relief for men was directed toward work projects, whose relationship to the labor movement was more complex. Jobless men had often been employed on municipal construction before the Civil War, but bourgeois reformers had largely eliminated the practice during the last third of the nineteenth century. Labor organizations, including the AFL, raised the cry for public employment with every downturn of the economy from 1893 onward. At the same time that the AFL rejected contributory social insurance, it adopted in 1915 an elaborate program for public works, municipal lodging for homeless men and repeal of state vagrancy laws. Faced with the devastating depression of 1929, the federation revived those demands, while placing its greatest hopes in work-sharing plans voluntarily instituted by unions and by major employers, and in its persistent but unsuccessful campaign for legislation to establish a thirty-hour work week.[32]

When the FERA in 1934 channeled some 4,000,000 adults from the ranks of its 27,000,000 relief recipients into work projects, therefore, the labor movement endorsed the action. Its main concerns were to establish pay differentials based on skill and to prevent projects from competing with unionized private construction firms. By the time the Works Progress Administration (WPA) was created in 1935 the challenge of generating public sector jobs, which would be socially useful without throwing other people out of private employment, had elevated the agency to a crucial role in the thinking of advocates of national economic planning. "If a thousand jobless workers in a community are to be employed on public projects," wrote the WPA's labor relations director Nels Anderson, "the problem is, first, to ascertain the type of work they can do and then to apply it to work the community would like to have done."[33]

The schools, port facilities, dams, murals, plays, and historical research and restoration undertaken by the WPA not only enriched American life, but also gave the government a very different economic role from that required by planning through business cartels (as with the NRA) or by fiscal policy. Small wonder the conservative Congress of 1939 slashed its appropriations, investigated its projects, abolished wage differentials based on skill, imposed a loyalty oath on employees, and compelled the dismissal of everyone who had been in its employ for eighteen months. In 1943 Congress abolished both the WPA and the National Resources Planning Board, sparing only those planning agencies that were directly related to the war emergency.[34]

Labor's relationship to WPA administrators varied by locality from hostility to such intimacy as enabled the CIO to enroll thousands of steel workers dismissed during the 1937 recession directly into the WPA. In turn, the Workers' Education Division of the WPA assigned unemployed teachers to develop study programs for unions. In general, it was the Workers' Alliance that battled constantly against reductions in the WPA's budget or pay scales, helped workers register, became as familiar as the furniture in the agency's offices, hailed the vision of a planned economy, and led the extraordinary strikes of WPA workers against the cutbacks of 1939. In fact, Trotskyists complained that the preference of the Workers' Alliance for consultation over direct action had given that organization "the character of a *company union*" for the Roosevelt administration.[35]

The CIO and the State

Although rank-and-file militancy propelled the industrial union impulse, and workers who were committed to creating some form of labor party and an industrial order whose priorities were set by social needs, rather than market imperatives, kept the cause alive after the bitter set-backs suffered by unions in the auto, steel, and textile industries in 1934, it was the Second New Deal (1935–1936) that gave birth to the Committee for Industrial Organization. The angry debates over industrial unionism, multi-craft strikes, racial discrimination and social insurance at the 1935 convention of the AFL aligned those union leaders who were afterwards to announce the formation of the CIO, and who were, in Steven Fraser's words, "connected by a thousand threads to a newly emergent managerial and political elite," which was transforming the political and industrial life of the country, against an "AFL old guard [which] not only lacked those strategic and managerial connections and objectives, but moreover often adamantly opposed [. . .] essential elements of the New Deal–CIO agenda."[36] The contrast makes it clear why the CIO not only tapped—indeed came to personify—the reform impulses of the epoch, but also why it simultaneously unleashed grassroots creativity and steered the impulses it nurtured toward a program of governmental economic planning, guided by a reformed Democratic Party—a program totally at odds with the traditions of working-class radicalism in the United States.

The staff of the NLRB, and especially Thomas Emerson and the other young liberal lawyers of its Review Division, worked intimately with CIO unions. So did that of the LaFollette Civil Liberties Committee, which exposed to public scrutiny the arsenals assembled by great corporations, their links to right-wing paramilitary and assassination units, and their techniques of mobilizing public opinion against strikers. During the first three years after the Wagner Act had been ruled constitutional, 81 percent of the more than one million secret ballots cast in certification elections favored unionization. Craft unionists were understandably indignant when board decisions favored large, inclusive bargaining units, applied the principle of majority rule to set aside agreements reached by craft unions and employers, and otherwise helped CIO unions win 75 percent of the early elections. Quite clearly, it had been the enactment of the Wagner Act that convinced John L. Lewis and his colleagues who formed the CIO that the hour had struck for the successful unionization of mass production industries. In their view, the reshaping of the union movement and the reshaping of government's economic role went hand in hand.[37]

Lewis, who had but five years earlier supported Hoover for reelection, made the connections explicit in October 1937:

> Time was, before the depression, when the representative labor leader would have said "Guarantee labor the right to organize and we shall do the rest." Now he knows that modern mass production industry [is] uncoordinated, uncorrelated and over-capacitated. With the guarantee of the "right to organize," such industries may be unionized, but, on the other hand, better living standards, shorter working hours, and improved employment conditions for their members cannot be hoped for unless legislative or other provisions be made for economic planning and for price, production, and profit controls. Because of these fundamental conditions, it is obvious to industrial workers that the labor movement must organize and exert itself not only in the economic field but also in the political arena.[38]

The 300 delegates to the convention of CIO activists to which Lewis spoke went on to call not only for freedom to assemble peaceably, strike, and bargain collectively, but also for Congress to enact the Lundeen social insurance bill, for federal licensing of corporations to guarantee their operation in conformity to established social standards, for expanded WPA projects to secure the "right to work," for state action to stimulate housing construction, for stabilization of farm prices, and for legislation to end monopoly control over radio communication.[39]

Those delegates were the offspring of the ethnic communities in the nation's industrial centers, and they had been taught the realities of economic life by the vast corporate enterprises for which they worked and the scientific management practiced there. The partial revival of industrial output between 1933 and 1937 had found major employers as ardently committed as they had been in the 1920s to a relentless quest for higher productivity, intense and systematic supervision, avoidance of overt reduction of hourly wages, and the cultivation of loyal employees. Spurred on by the legal obligation to permit collective bargaining under the NRA codes, companies had reinvigorated employee representation plans on such a scale that by the time the Wagner Act outlawed employer sponsorship of those plans, some 2,500,000 workers had been enrolled in them. By early 1937, when the total value of manufacturing production had reached and surpassed that of 1928, output per worker-hour was 22 percent higher. Hourly real wages averaged 36 percent higher. At the same time, unemployment still stood at more than 14 percent of the labor force, and almost 10 percent had been out of work a year or more.[40]

As Richard J. Jensen has demonstrated, the depression enabled managers to be very selective in hiring and retaining workers, and they made the most of their opportunity. Those who held jobs tended to be highly trained both through schooling and in their own specialties on the job, long-term employees but not older than 45, and men (and increasingly women) with families to support. Between 1933 and 1939 factories hired some 400,000 workers a month with remarkable consistency, but could and did choose new employees carefully. Those who had earned high wages elsewhere were the most likely to be selected. Those who had completed more than eight years of school were heavily favored, even in the hiring of unskilled workers (a remarkable development, considering how widespread illiteracy had been among common laborers twenty years earlier). So few northern companies outside of railroads, steel and meat packing hired any black workers for production jobs that those which hired any tended to hire many (like Ford Motor Company), and were well known for that reason among African Americans nationally. Among the hundreds of firms surveyed by the WPA in the highly diversified industry of Philadelphia, Atlantic Refinery, Franklin Sugar, Westinghouse, Diston Saw and Midvale Steel stood out as those that *did* have black production workers.[41]

In stark contrast to the ethnic diversification of the work-force during the century's first two decades and during the 1940s, the combined impact of the restriction of European immigration, corporate hiring policies during the depression, and the continuous growth of secondary education tended to homogenize the industrial work-force. These developments intensified the impact of mass consumerism and the insecurity of industrial life, with which Lizabeth Cohen has made us familiar, in preparing urban communities to produce what she has called the "CIO's culture of unity."[42]

Stanley Vittoz argues correctly that "business opposition to the Wagner Act was probably more unified than its response—positive or negative—to any other single piece of New Deal legislation."[43] No sooner had the Act been passed than eighty-three injunction proceedings were filed in courts to restrain its operation. The fact remains, however, that the CIO brought United States Steel, General Motors and General Electric under contract before the Supreme

Court had ruled the Act constitutional and allowed the NLRB to function. During the first two years of the board's operation, it issued ninety-five cease and desist orders against employers: only four resulted in compliance. During the decisive General Motors sit-down strike, John L. Lewis made it clear to Michigan's Governor Frank Murphy that he had no interest in an election by the workers on the question of union certification. "The important thing," he declared, "is we have enough men to close the plants and we have closed them." Moreover, even after the board began conducting frequent certification elections in 1937, CIO unions more often than not won recognition simply through threat of strikes.[44]

What mattered most to workers was that the publicity and reinstatement of dismissed activists produced by the board, coupled with the relief benefits provided strikers' families by governors like Murphy and Earle, and Supreme Court rulings which used the Wagner Act as a legal basis for striking down municipal ordinances that barred union activity in public spaces and proclaiming picketing a form of speech protected by the constitution, expanded the social space within which workers could mobilize during the last half of the decade. By comparison, board and court rulings channeling that mobilization into contractual relations with employers appeared to most workers to be but a temporary set-back. Although the number of such rulings mounted rapidly after 1937, their restrictive implications did not become fully apparent until after World War II.[45]

Successful unionization of major companies often brought in its wake an abrupt overturning of the local government in smaller factory towns. In the autumn elections following the recognition of the CIO by United States Steel seventeen towns in the Pittsburgh region threw out Republican regimes that had governed them since early in the century and replaced them with labor-oriented Democratic administrations. Elmer J. Maloy, who became mayor of Duquesne, and John Mullen of Clairton, had both achieved prominence within the company's employee representation plan, before assuming leading positions in the Steel Workers Organizing Committee. Both had to oust entrenched and ineffective Democratic organizations in primaries, before they could go on to replace Republican mayors, who had served the steel corporation like invulnerable autocrats. Not only did the new administrations disarm the mill police and assist local unionization, they also eagerly solicited WPA projects, which had been shunned by their predecessors. The new atmosphere in the mill towns also inspired local black youth to refuse any longer to accept racial segregation in the communities' movie theaters and ice cream parlors.[46]

The political innovations inspired by the CIO were ardently opposed not only by discomfited local business, ethnic and political leaders, but also by the officialdom of the AFL. The older labor federation remained by far the larger of the rival labor bodies, and in the late 1930s it grew more rapidly than the CIO. In contrast to the CIO's membership, which was concentrated in highly capitalized manufacturing firms, that of the AFL was more diverse. It included, among others, construction workers, waitresses, office employees, sailors, railroad maintenance workers and truck drivers. The federation's most aggressive unions, the electricians, machinists and teamsters, continued to be dominated by craftsmen employed by smaller employers who serviced local markets, but those unions also effectively competed with the CIO for the support of mass production workers in the aircraft, armaments and electrical products industries, while sizable groups of textile and automobile workers left the CIO for the AFL in 1938 and 1939. Nationwide, when the CIO reached its early membership peak in 1937, the AFL outnumbered it by better than two to one. In Chicago, a union stronghold, there were five AFL members for every one worker in the CIO in 1939.[47]

The active cooperation of AFL officials, like John Frey, in investigations of the CIO by the House Committee on Un-American Activities, and the federation's decision in 1938 to withhold endorsement from any candidate for public office who accepted the support of the CIO contributed significantly to the conservative electoral triumph of that year, to the downfall of Minnesota's Farmer-Labor Party and to crippling divisions within the American Labor Party of New York.[48] To mollify the larger labor federation, President Roosevelt appointed William M. Leiserson to the NLRB in April 1939, with an explicit mandate to "clean up the mess" of favoritism to the CIO and "Communist influence." Leiserson's eminence as a scholar friendly to patterns of collective bargaining which had grown out of historic trade union methods, rather than government design, made him acceptable to the AFL. As its leaders had hoped, Leiserson reoriented board rulings to accommodate institutionalized craft union practices, encourage stable contractual relations between unions and employers, and strengthen the capacity of leaders to restrain job actions initiated by the rank-and-file. Within two years he had also witnessed with satisfaction the departure of lawyer Thomas Emerson, and also of the board's leading champions of industrial unionism, Nathan Witt, Edwin S. Smith, and chairman Harry A. Madden.[49]

At the same time, the government's decisive role in reshaping industrial relations and the CIO's close ties to New Deal administrators in Washington and in state capitals pressed Left-wing parties which clung to their traditional strategy of mobilizing a mass movement openly arrayed against capitalism and independent of the existing major parties increasingly to the margins of political life. On the Pacific Coast, where mass unionism had developed most rapidly, unbending champions of the revolutionary syndicalist heritage, like Harry Lundberg of the Seamen's Union and Ralph Chaplin (author of the song "Solidarity Forever") fought vigorously, even physically, in the ranks of the AFL against the new CIO. In Minnesota, where the Farmer-Labor Party dominated the state government, Trotskyist leaders of the teamsters union organized large demonstrations against that party's popular front orientation after Barcelona's May 1937 events. Their calls for expulsion of Stalinists from the party won the endorsement of some of its most honored founders. They could not stem the tide of support for the New Deal, however, because the most important reforms instituted by the state government had all come to depend on money from Washington, while the Republican state senate blocked more radical measures.[50]

Consequently, the CIO greeted coldly attempts to challenge the growing conservatism that gripped the country after 1937 by reviving the movement for a national farmer-labor party. The Communist Party itself responded to the growing tide of anticommunism by identifying its own program closely with that of the CIO and cultivating personal ties with individual union leaders. The distinguishing features of the party's position were reduced to its foreign policy and its unrelenting denunciation of "Trotskyites." Although Communist-led unions continued to rely on vigorous mobilization of shop floor activists, the party's shop units and shop papers, which had been catalysts of such many struggles before 1938, were abandoned.[51]

When C. Wright Mills examined the country's union officials at the end of World War II, he discerned important contrasts between the generation produced by the New Deal experience and their predecessors. Whereas 42 percent of the union officers surveyed in 1924 had proclaimed their affiliation with some party other than the Republicans and Democrats, in 1944 less than 10 percent did. In every corner of the land new activists had emerged out of the struggles of the 1930s. They were predominantly youthful. At the 1939 convention of the United Electrical Workers-CIO only one member of the General Executive Board and no member of the staff was over 35 years old. In contrast to the unions that had been well established by the 1920s, few of the officers of the newer unions were foreign born. Immigrants who had played major roles organizing their workmates often considered it to the unions' advantage to have "American boys" represent them to the public. Sons and daughters of twentieth-century immigrants shared the spotlight with colleagues of Irish and German ancestry, many of whom had first gained prominence by guiding company unions, of which they had been officers, into the CIO.[52]

The new cadre were products of inter-war decades in which almost half the nation's youth completed high school, and many even had a taste of college education, before the depression drove them from the classroom. Indeed, many of them remembered the schools of the 1920s as a cultural battleground for children of immigrants. Both the Mexican American Movement and its larger successor, *El Congresso Nacional de los Pueblos de Habla Español*, which were energized by the CIO, Mexico's nationalization of its oil, and the Spanish Civil War, drew heavily on educated cadre, whose school experience had been especially bitter. Mills found in 1946 that the average schooling of CIO leaders was slightly over twelve years, in contrast to nine years for officers of older craft unions. Nevertheless, education provided by unions and Left parties had often transformed activists' view of the world. As Cleophas Williams, a black longshoreman from San Francisco, remembered the California Labor School: "It was a beautiful experience to see how you could be in concert with other workers to improve your lot, and not be out there saying 'You got to hustle, hustle, hustle, and get ahead, son.'"[53]

The new activists, for all their militancy, enlightenment and workplace base of power, matured within statist orbit of the New Deal and the CIO. By the end of the decade there was no other serious game in town.

Notes

Reprinted courtesy of Cambridge University Press and the *International Review of Social History.*

1. *The Public Papers and Addresses of Franklin D. Roosevelt, With a Special Introduction and Explanatory Notes by President Roosevelt.* 1937 Volume. *The Constitution Prevails* (New York, 1941), 272–274.

2. Arthur M. Schlesinger Jr., *The Age of Roosevelt: The Coming of the New Deal* (Boston, 1959); Irving Bernstein, *Turbulent Years: A History of the American Worker, 1933–1941* (Boston, 1970); Jerold S. Auerbach, *Labor and Liberty: The La Follette Committee and the New Deal* (Indianapolis, 1966).

3. Staughton Lynd, ed., *"We Are All Leaders": The Alternative Unionism of the Early 1930s* (Urbana, 1996); Mike Davis, *Prisoners of the American Dream: Politics and Economy in the History of the American Working Class* (London, 1986); Elizabeth Faue, *Community of Suffering and Struggle: Women, Men, and the Labor Movement in Minneapolis, 1915–1945* (Chapel Hill, NC, 1991); Peter Rachleff, *Hard-Pressed in the Heartland: The Hormel Strike and the Future of the Labor Movement* (Boston, 1993).

4. David Brody, *Workers in Industrial America: Essays on the Twentieth Century Struggle*, 2nd ed., (New York, 1993), p. 151.

5. Lizabeth Cohen, *Making a New Deal: Industrial Workers in Chicago, 1919–1939* (New York, 1990); Michael Goldfield, Theda Skocpol and Kenneth Finegold, "Explaining New Deal Labor Policy," *American Political Science Review* 84 (December 1990): 1298–1317. See also, Michael Goldfield, "Worker Insurgency, Radical Organization, and New Deal Labor Legislation," *ibid.* 83 (December 1989): 1257–1282.

6. Steven Fraser, *Labor Will Rule: Sidney Hillman and the Rise of American Labor* (New York, 1991), 329.

7. *Beaver Valley Labor History Journal* 1 (September 1979): 4; Robert S. Lynd and Helen Merrell Lynd, *Middletown in Transition: A Study in Cultural Conflict* (New York, 1937), 402–486. On the Right of the 1930s, see Robert F. Burk, *The Corporate State and the Broker State: The Du Ponts and American National Politics,*

1925–1940 (Cambridge, Mass., 1990); Geoffrey S. Smith, *To Save a Nation: American Countersubversives, the New Deal, and the Coming of World War II* (New York, 1973).

8. Harry A. Millis and Emily C. Brown, *From the Wagner Act to Taft Hartley: A Study of National Labor Policy and Labor Relations* (Chicago, 1950), 316–322. The relevant Supreme Court cases were *NLRB v. Mackay Radio and Telegraph Co.* 304 US 333 (1938) and *NLRB v. Fansteel Metalurgical Corporation* 306 US 240 (1939).

9. David Montgomery, *The Fall of the House of Labor: The Workplace, the State, and American Labor Activism, 1865–1925* (Cambridge and New York, 1987), 403–407, 417–424.

10. David Montgomery, "Thinking about American Workers in the 1920s," *International Labor and Working-Class History* 32 (Fall 1987), 4–24; Stanley Vittoz, *New Deal Labor Policy and the American Industrial Economy* (Chapel Hill and London, 1987), 18–19.

11. Quoted in Grace Palladino, *Dreams of Dignity, Workers of Vision: A History of the International Brotherhood of Electrical Workers* (Washington, DC, 1991), 151. The vocabulary of this resolution is that of the famous 1923 resolution of the AFL, "Industry's Manifest Duty," but that resolution had warned against "state invasion" of economic life. See Montgomery, "Thinking," 15–16.

12. Vittoz, *New Deal Labor Policy*, 43–49. The quotation from Taplin is on p. 64. Taplin's argument was also the theme of Michael Musmanno's novel (later movie), *Black Fury*.

13. Selig Perlman, *A Theory of the Labor Movement* (New York, 1928), 232.

14. Fraser, *Labor Will Rule*, 261–277.

15. Warren R. Van Tine, *The Making of a Labor Bureaucrat: Union Leadership in the United States, 1870–1920* (Amherst, Mass., 1973) examines the emergence of long-term leadership, but its reinvigoration has been best captured by Cecelia F. Bucki, "The Pursuit of Political Power: Class, Ethnicity, and Municipal Politics in Interwar Bridgeport, 1915–1936" (unpublished PhD dissertation, University of Pittsburgh, 1991), and by such biographies as Fraser, *Labor Will Rule*; Melvyn Dubofsky and Warren Van Tine, *John L. Lewis: A Biography* (New York, 1977); and Christopher H. Johnson, *Maurice Sugar: Law, Labor, and the Left in Detroit, 1912–1950* (Detroit, 1988).

16. Robin D. G. Kelley, *Hammer and Hoe: Alabama Communists during the Great Depression* (Chapel Hill, NC, 1990), 60–69. The Communist Party's decision to supplement its dual unions in favor of aggressive work within the AFL had been reached in July 1933 at an Extraordinary National Conference in New York, two years before the Seventh World Congress of the Comintern. James R. Prickett, "Communists and the Communist Issue in the American Labor Movement, 1920–1950" (unpublished PhD dissertation, University of California, Los Angeles, 1975), 142–161.

17. Steve Nelson, James R. Barrett, and Rob Ruck, *Steve Nelson: American Radical* (Pittsburgh, 1981), 167–173; Christopher Sterba, "Textile Labor Conflict in the Anthracite: The General Labor Holiday in Hazleton, Pennsylvania, September 12,

1934" (unpublished paper, cited by permission of author), 19; Patrick M. Lynch, "Pennsylvania Anthracite: A Forgotten IWW Venture, 1906–1916" (unpublished MA thesis, Bloomsburg State College, 1974).

18. Sterba, "Textile Labor Conflict," 29–37.

19. Cohen, *Making a New Deal*; John Bodnar, *Immigration and Industrialization: Ethnicity in an American Mill Town, 1870–1940* (Pittsburgh, 1977); Gary Gerstle, *Working-Class Americanism: The Politics of Labor in a Textile City* (Cambridge and New York, 1989); John J. Bukowczyk, *And My Children Did Not Know Me: A History of the Polish Americans* (Bloomington, Ind., 1987), 65–84; Bucki, "Bridgeport"; Louis Adamic, *My America, 1928–1938* (New York and London, 1938).

20. Ewa Morawska, *For Bread with Butter: The Life-Worlds of East Central Europeans in Johnstown, Pennsylvania, 1890–1940* (Cambridge and New York, 1985), 252–265.

21. John Cerullo and Gennaro Delana, "The Kelayres Massacre," *Pennsylvania Magazine of History and Biography* 57 (July 1983): 331–361. The quotation is on p. 337.

22. Gerstle, *Working-Class Americanism*, 230–259; Hyman Berman, "Political Antisemitism in Minnesota during the Great Depression," *Jewish Social Studies* 38 (Summer-Fall 1976): 247–264. Oddly, Cohen, *Making a New Deal*, has little to say about either the local officials or Congressional representatives elected by Chicagoans during the New Deal era.

23. Theda Skocpol, *Protecting Soldiers and Mothers: The Political Origins of Social Policy in the United States* (Cambridge, Mass. and London, 1992), 161–310; Montgomery, *Fall of the House of Labor*, 410–416, 438–457; Ronald W. Schatz, *The Electrical Workers: A History of Labor at General Electric and Westinghouse, 1923–60* (Urbana, Ill., 1983), 11–24; Cohen, *Making a New Deal*, 160–211. On voters and taxes, see Bucki, "Bridgeport," 244–267, 371–379.

24. Roy Lubove, *The Struggle for Social Security, 1900–1935* (Cambridge, Mass., 1968), 164–170; Skocpol, *Protecting Soldiers and Mothers*, 157–158, 198, 237.

25. Quoted in Kenneth Casebeer, "The Workers' Unemployment Insurance Bill: American Social Wage, Labor Organization, and Legal Ideology," in Christopher L. Tomlins and Andrew J. King, eds., *Labor Law in America: Historical and Critical Essays* (Baltimore and London, 1992), 250.

26. Casebeer, "Workers' Unemployment Bill," 250, 232, 247.

27. *Ibid.*, 232; Faue, *Suffering and Struggle*, 149; Nelson, Barrett, and Ruck, *Steve Nelson*, 160; Herbert Harris, *American Labor* (New Haven, 1939), 403–405, 410n; Alan Derickson, "Health Security for All? Social Unionism and Universal Health Insurance, 1935–1938," *Journal of American History* 80 (March 1994): 1333–1356; *Final Proceedings of the Eighth Constitutional Convention of the Congress of Industrial Organizations*, November 18, 19, 20, 21, 22, 1946 (n.p., n.d.): 81–83. On European social insurance, see George Steinmetz, "Workers and the Welfare State in Imperial Germany," *International Labor and Working-Class History* 40 (Fall 1991): 18–46; James E. Cronin and Peter Weiler, "Working-Class Interests and the Politics of Social Democratic Reform in Britain, 1900–1940," *ibid.*, 47–66.

28. Skocpol, *Protecting Soldiers and Mothers*, 321–479. On the campaign against outdoor relief in the nineteenth century, see David Montgomery, *Citizen Worker: The Experience of Workers in the United States with Democracy and the Free Market during the Nineteenth Century* (Cambridge and New York, 1993), 71–82.

29. Skocpol, *Protecting Soldiers and Mothers*, 520–522; William R. Brock, *Welfare, Democracy, and the New Deal* (Cambridge and New York, 1988), 27–49. For a perceptive analysis of professionalization, see Regina G. Kunzel, *Fallen Women, Problem Girls: Unmarried Mothers and the Professionalization of Social Work, 1890–1945* (New Haven, 1993).

30. Brock, *Welfare, Democracy*, 174.

31. *Ibid.*, 259–260; "Leah" to *United Action*, 16 September 1935, quoted in Faue, *Suffering and Struggle*, 63. See Meridel Le Sueur, *The Girl* (Minneapolis, 1978). There were instances of workers being elected to poor boards, but they seem to have been less numerous than such elections had been during the late nineteenth century.

32. Alexander Keyssar, *Out of Work: The First Century of Unemployment in Massachusetts* (Cambridge and New York, 1986); Benjamin Kline Hunnicutt, *Work without End: Abandoning Shorter Hours for the Right to Work* (Philadelphia, 1988), 147–250; Hany A. Millis, *How Collective Bargaining Works: A Survey of Experience in Leading American Industries* (New York, 1942), 213, 223.

33. Nels Anderson, *The Right to Work* (New York, 1938), 135.

34. James Patterson, "Comparative Welfare History: Britain and the United States, 1930–1945," in *The Roosevelt New Deal: A Program Assessment Fifty Years After*, ed. Wilbur Cohen (Austin, Tex., 1986), 136.

35. David Montgomery and Ronald Schatz, "Facing Layoffs," in Montgomery, *Workers' Control in America* (Cambridge and New York, 1979), 146–147; Faue, *Suffering and Struggle*, 154–164; Nell Irvin Painter, *The Narrative of Hosea Hudson: His Life as a Negro Communist in the South* (Cambridge, Mass., 1979), 296–302; Morris Llewellyn Cooke and Philip Murray, *Organized Labor and Production: Next Steps in Industrial Democracy* (New York, 1940), 227; Art Preis, *America's Permanent Depression: The Truth about Unemployment* (New York, n.d.), 18.

36. Fraser, *Labor Will Rule*, 335–336.

37. *Ibid.*, 349–352, 404; Goldfield, "Worker Insurgency," 1268; Dubofsky and Van Tine, *Lewis*, 211–232.

38. Quoted in Harris, *American Labor*, 408.

39. *Ibid.*, 410–411. On radio communications, see Robert W. McChesney, *Telecommunications, Mass Media, and Democracy: The Battle for the Control of U.S. Broadcasting, 1928–1935* (New York, 1993).

40. Richard C. Wilcox, "Industrial Management's Policies Toward Unionism," in Milton Derber and Edwin Young, eds., *Labor and the New Deal* (Madison, Wis., 1957), 288; Richard J. Jensen, "The Causes and Cures of Unemployment in the Great Depression," *Journal of Interdisciplinary History* 19 (Spring 1989): 557–559.

41. *Ibid.*, 563–571; Walter Licht, *Getting Work: Philadelphia, 1840–1950* (Cambridge, Mass. and London, 1992), 44–55; Zaragosa Vargas, *Proletarians of the North: A History of Mexican Industrial Workers in Detroit and the Midwest, 1917–1933*

(Berkeley, 1993), 105–112; Yale researchers found a strong preference of New Haven employers for white workers. E. Wright Bakke, *The Unemployed Worker: A Study of the Task of Making a Living without a Job* (New Haven, 1940), 247–248.

42. Cohen, *Making a New Deal*, 333–349.

43. Vittoz, *New Deal Labor Policy*, 149–150.

44. Karl E. Klare, "Judicial Deradicalization of the Wagner Act and the Origins of Modern Legal Consciousness, 1937–1941," *Minnesota Law Review* 62 (1978): 275, 286; John L. Lewis, quoted in Sidney Fine, *Sit-Down: The General Motors Strike of 1936–1937* (Ann Arbor, 1970), 256.

45. A good discussion of the restrictive rulings, which assessed their early impact more severally than I do, is James B. Atleson, *Values and Assumptions in American Labor Law* (Amherst, Mass., 1983), 19–66. The Supreme Court decisions on public space and free speech are *Hague v. CIO* 307 US 469 (1939) and *Thornhill v. Alabama* 310 US 88 (1940).

46. For most of this information I am deeply indebted to an unpublished paper by Eric Leif Davin of the University of Pittsburgh, "The Littlest New Deal: SWOC Takes Power in Steeltown, A Possibility or Radicalism in the Late 1930s." See also George Powers, *Cradle of Steel Unionism: Monongahela Valley, Pa.* (East Chicago, Ind., 1972).

47. Christopher L. Tomlins, "AFL Unions in the 1930s: Their Performance in Historical Perspective," *Journal of American History* 65 (March 1979): 1021–1042; Barbara Warne Newell, *Chicago and the Labor Movement: Metropolitan Unionism in the 1930s* (Urbana, Ill., 1961), 205, 208.

48. David Milton, *The Politics of U.S. Labor: From the Great Depression to the New Deal* (New York and London, 1982), 117–120; Daniel Nelson, *American Rubber Workers and Organized Labor, 1900–1941* (Princeton, NJ, 1988), 223–233; Gerald Meyer, *Vito Marcantonio: Radical Politician, 1902–1954* (Albany, NY, 1989), 25–26; Fraser, *Labor Will Rule*, 430–440.

49. Christopher L. Tomlins, *The State and the Unions: Labor Relations, Law, and the Organized Labor Movement in America, 1880–1960* (Cambridge and New York, 1985), 201–224.

50. Bruce Nelson, *Workers on the Waterfront: Seamen, Longshoremen, and Unionism in the 1930s* (Urbana, Ill., 1988), 202–244; Faue, *Suffering and Struggle*, 111, 134–145; Millard L. Gieske, *Minnesota Farmer-Laborism: The Third Party Alternative* (Minneapolis, 1979), 244–261: Paul Buhle, *Marxism in the United States: Remapping the History of the American Left* (London, 1987), 146–147.

51. Mark Naison, "Remaking America: Communists and Liberals in the Popular Front," in *New Studies in the Politics and Culture of U.S. Communism*, eds. Michael E. Drown, Randy Martin, Frank Rosengarten and George Snedeker (New York, 1993), 65–69; Steve Rosswurm, ed., *The CIO's Left-led Unions* (New Brunswick, NJ, 1992).

52. Party affiliations are my calculations, based on figures in C. Wright Mills, *The New Men of Power: America's Labor Leaders* (New York, 1948), 183; United Electrical, Radio, and Machine Workers of America, *Proceedings, Fifth Convention* (New York, 1939), 87; Maurice Isserman, *Which Side Were You On? The American*

Communist Party During the Second World War (Middletown, Conn., 1982), 9–14; Schatz, *Electrical Workers*, 80–101.

53. Richard A. Varbero, "Philadelphia's South Italians in the 1920s" in Allen F. Davis and Mark H. Haller, eds., *The Peoples of Philadelphia: A History of Ethnic Groups and Lower-Class Life, 1790–1940* (Philadelphia, 1973), 255–275; Lynd and Lynd, *Middletown in Transition*, 230–241; Mario T. Garcia, *Mexican Americans: Leadership, Ideology, and Identity, 1930–1960* (New Haven, 1989), 145–165; Garcia, *Memories of History: The Life and Narrative of Bert Corona* (Berkeley, 1994); Richard J. Altenbaugh, *Education for Struggle: The American Labor Colleges of the 1920s and 1930s* (Philadelphia, 1990); Cleophas Williams quoted in Howard Kimeldorf, *Reds or Rackets? The Making of Radical and Conservative Unions on the Waterfront* (Berkeley, 1988), 147.

CHAPTER 14

Working People's Responses to Past Depressions

In *Workers in Hard Times: A Long View of Economic Crises*, edited by Leon Fink, Joseph A. McCartin, and Joan Sangster (Urbana: University of Illinois Press, 2014)

Since the founding of the Republic, working men and women have been all too familiar with alternating periods of boom times and hard times, with seasonal unemployment, with marked differences in availability of jobs among various parts of the country, and with general depressions abruptly precipitated by overproduction of wares or by bank panics. Not all downturns struck with the same severity. The crisis of the early 1840s pitched nine state governments into default (primarily in the rapidly expanding cotton kingdom), while the depression that began in 1873 sent ten state governments into default over the ensuing eleven years. The sharp collapse between the spring of 1907 and the spring of 1908 so crippled the economy that for many months more immigrants left the United States for their homelands or other countries than disembarked here, while the depressions of 1873–79, 1893–98, and 1929–40 set the stage for fundamental restructuring of industrial, agricultural, and political life.[1]

Vigorous economic expansion between the mid-1820s and the crisis of 1837 (augmented by rising tariffs and by chronic surpluses in federal budgets) stimulated massive sales and transportation of slaves from the Southeast to the booming Cotton Belt. They also attracted a swelling tide of immigration from Europe and migration of rural women to seek wages in port cities and in scattered mill towns. These boom years gave rise to numerous strikes and to the formation of effective trade unions, especially in the thriving ports of Philadelphia and New York. Representatives of fifty occupations in Philadelphia, ranging from dock laborers, handloom weavers, and suburban factory operatives at the poorer end of the income scale to bookbinders, cabinet makers, and butchers at the upper end, contributed monthly dues to citywide delegate bodies (called the Trades' Union) to help finance each other's strikes and the city's famous general strike for a ten-hour day in 1835.[2] Prominent leaders of the Trades Unions in both cities became heavily involved in municipal politics.

The depression that had gripped much of the nation by the summer of 1837 crushed most unions, emptied their formerly lucrative treasuries and left little possibility of successful strikes. As one prominent Philadelphian confided to his diary in 1842:

> The streets seem deserted, the largest houses are shut up and to rent, there is no business, there is no money, no confidence & little hope, property is sold every day by the sheriff at a 4th of the estimated value of a few years ago, nobody can pay debts, the miseries of poverty are felt by both rich & poor.[3]

By the mid-1840s, however, a renewal of capital inflows from Europe, resurgence of canal and railroad construction, conquest of half the previous territory of Mexico, and a flood of German, Irish, and other immigrants opened the way to almost three decades of rather steady increases in per capita output—to be sure, punctuated by half a dozen relatively brief recessions and a severe manufacturing downturn between 1857 and 1861, not to mention a civil war. The 1850s represented a nodal point in this transformation. The iron ship, the telegraph, railroad trunk lines, gold rushes, and enactment by several states of general incorporation laws lent a modern flavor to the era. Most noteworthy, at some point between the census of 1850 and that of 1860 the number of people over ten years of age who were counted as wage laborers (in the United States which was still dominated by agricultural landowners) came to surpass the number of those counted as slaves.[4] The subsequent destruction of slavery by the Civil War enabled the census of 1870 to classify as wage earners more than half of the men and women then listed as "gainfully employed."[5]

In the autumn of 1873, the overinvestment in railroad expansion led the banking house of Jay Cooke to collapse—the bank whose sales of 5–20 bonds to both small investors and large financial institutions from the earliest days of the Civil War onward had decisively funded the Union war effort and earned Cooke the reputation of the financier who rallied ordinary people to save the imperiled Union. Prices and wages fell to historically unprecedented levels after Cooke's failure, devastating the standards once upheld by even the strongest unions, like those of Pennsylvania's anthracite miners and New England's shoe workers, and ultimately in July 1877 unleashing a wave of strikes that swept along the country's major railroad lines from Maryland to California and prompting President Hayes to proclaim a state of insurrection and dispatch troops from the South and the West to put down strike activity.[6]

By the spring of 1879 the economy had resumed its expansion, vigorously until 1882 and sporadically thereafter, with rising manufacturing and agricultural output producing intense business competition, falling prices, many business failures, and (usually ineffective) efforts by competing businesses to bolster prices by means of trusts and pools. Most important for the working class, the level of immigration had soared as soon as the economy recovered from the 1870s depression, bringing 2,855,000 newcomers to the United States between 1880 and 1885.

Germans came to dominate working-class life in Detroit, St. Louis, Chicago, and elsewhere in the Old Midwest. Because most immigrants were of working age, the labor force grew much faster than the total population. The number of female wage earners also rose sharply, while their most common occupations gradually changed, first from domestic service to factory work, and then at the turn of the century to office and sales work. Simultaneously, farm families were more likely to intensify their own toil than to hire additional hands. Many farmers, black and white, either worked seasonally in manufacturing, lumber, or transportation or gave up farming altogether and often moved step by step to town. In brief, the key to industrial growth in the late nineteenth century was more people devoting more of their lives to working harder than ever before.[7]

Alexander Keyssar's study of unemployment in Massachusetts during the last half of the nineteenth century concluded that occasional joblessness had become a commonplace experience for these wage earners, and that textile-manufacturing communities suffered the most severe fluctuations in levels of employment. For most people, however, three or four months without a reliable job simply led them to move someplace else. A city like Houston provided more varied opportunities for picking up at least some casual job, though as cities became more congested it became increasingly difficult for inhabitants to feed themselves with gardens, livestock, or orchards. Credit from local grocers was often the most likely form of relief, though many employers were known to cut wages rather than lay people off (at least keeping their more skilled work men). Moreover, by the early 1880s trade-union benefit funds and loans from fraternal organizations sustained many of the better-paid craftsmen, and union traveling cards helped many get established in more promising locations. One consequence of these practices was a growing spread between the earning levels of people in skilled trades and those of laborers and machine operatives (wider than the differentials then found in Europe). This divergence set the stage for a major assault on the high pay scales during and after the 1890s.[8] For most families, however, three or four months without a reliable job simply led them to rely for survival on women's ingenuity and/or moving someplace else.[9]

From the 1850s onward, the questions of who should aid the jobless poor and which impoverished women and men deserved any aid at all became increasingly controversial issues. A commissioner of the New York State Board of Charities declared in the 1870s: ""The policy of the law should be to treat as criminal those who levy upon the public for support while able to earn their own living."[10] According to an influential 1880s treatise on law, because no one was required by law to be a productive citizen, the criminal offense was becoming a "public burden."[11] Reformers of public charities sought to privatize poor relief and apply their own strict standards to the determination of who among the poor was truly deserving and who was simply shiftless and pretending to be in need. By the 1870s, the Association for Improving the Condition of the Poor had come to lead the crusade to privatize and systematize the distribution of alms. Their efforts had a special impact on poor women. One must add, however, that urban society in this country then spawned such a variety of religious, fraternal, trade-union, and other institutions offering some assistance, not to mention local customs that induced working men to patronize stores and bars run by widows, as to limit the effectiveness of the association.[12]

It also became increasingly common during periods of high unemployment for urban workers to demand that municipal governments create work projects that would provide some income to the unemployed—especially to men. In turn, the marked increase in voter-participation rates after about 1840 prompted urban political leaders to pay increasing attention to working-class voters. Moreover, many recent immigrants brought with them experience of Europe's revolutions of 1848—and especially of the emergency workshops then established in response to workers' demands in Paris.[13]

Western European workers, especially in the Rhineland, had also momentarily been granted the right to hold their meetings in city halls. It was not astonishing, therefore, that New York's Board of Aldermen granted the trade delegates and social reformers who formed New York's Industrial Congress in 1850 permission to conduct their meetings in the Supreme Court room of City Hall. Delegates assembled there demanded regular use of the meeting rooms, the creation of public baths, a reading room for public use, and a labor exchange where workers could meet potential employers.[14]

By 1852, however, Tammany Hall had secured control of the Industrial Congresses, inducing delegates from trade unions to exclude politicians, land reformers, and representatives of cooperatives from their assemblies. Nevertheless, the severe unemployment that afflicted New York during the antebellum recession of 1857–59 prompted Mayor Fernando Wood to institute widespread public-works projects, among them improving Central Park.

To be sure, Wood was a most unusual mayor. He is most famous for his proposal that New York City secede from the union in 1861 and become a neutral free city.[15] During the latter half of the century, however, working people around the land often appealed to municipal authorities for work relief when jobs had disappeared from the private sector. Those in New Albany and Evansville, Indiana, had some success with their towns' Know-Nothing administrations in the 1850s, as did the black members of the Knights of Labor in Richmond in the 1870s and the immigrants mobilized by Social Revolutionaries facing Mayor Carter Harrison's regime in Chicago during the 1880s. As mines and mills failed around Denver in the early 1890s, the city's Trades and Labor Assembly established Camp Relief which provided clothing and shelter in a tent colony governed by its own inhabitants, and the Maverick Restaurant, which fed 550 people a day.[16] Mayor William Shelton of New Haven, Connecticut, in 1877 had summed up the argument that the city government should be the employer of last resort:

> [H]umanity should prompt a liberal provision for giving [jobless residents] a partial employment until our industries assume their normal condition, as the condition of the laboring classes is a sad one. The distribution of labor should be general among those out of employment. To keep a set of men continually work, to the exclusion of others equally worthy at a time like this is morally wrong; a change should be made every week, and no favoritism shown except to those in great need.[17]

By no means did all local political leaders share Shelton's view. Boss Tweed's regime in New York had borrowed heavily from European banks and poured the funds so obtained into the development of mid-Manhattan, and also into Catholic and other charities to aid the poor. In the early 1870s the foreign banks called in their loans, while a mobilization of the propertied electorate and Protestants irate over Catholic influence overthrew Tweed's government. Its successors in City Hall pared public expenditures to the bone, even during the protracted depression that struck the country in 1873 while the city's larger factories began to leave Manhattan for more spacious surroundings and lower rents.[18] When jobless workers gathered in Tompkins Square in 1874 to demand work from the city they were brutally assaulted by municipal police.[19]

The hardened lines of ideological confrontation had already been evident in the division between advocates and foes of other efforts of working people to improve the accessibility and terms of employment. During a national economic slump in the immediate aftermath of the Civil War, state legislatures in Illinois, Missouri, California, Wisconsin (in 1867), and Pennsylvania (in 1868) enacted laws making eight hours "a legal day's work" though a major strike in Chicago starting May 1, 1867, and aiming to force the state's employers actually to close after eight working hours ended without success. In the same year the legislature of Massachusetts rejected bills to shorten the hours for women and children, though in 1874 it did outlaw the employment of women for more than ten hours a day, and thus forced a general reduction of work hours in the state's large textile industry.

In the South, plantation areas experienced considerable turmoil over the terms of work during the summer of 1867, while black dock workers in Mobile and Charleston engaged in strikes, and some southern branches of the Union League encouraged freedmen to boycott conservative planters, seize crops if they were defrauded, slow down work, and squat on planters' land.[20] But even the gatherings of the Union Leagues in the South soon became centers of stormy controversy. When black delegates to the League conference in Richmond demanded confiscation and partition of plantations, they were shouted down by the white delegates. Most prominent black elected officials also opposed confiscation and advised assembled freedmen to rely on hard work, frugality, and steady habits to improve their lives. Nevertheless, one black laborer at the Richmond League meeting who spoke passionately in favor of confiscation of estates was greeted with thunderous applause from his colleagues.[21]

During the same postwar year, the *New York World* had warned its readers of the perils awaiting the nation if political leaders endorsed the legislative demands of working people. The columnist wrote: "When the government, that is the taxing power, represents the poverty of the community, and not its property, there will be a constant tendency to rob property of its rights." This was true, he added, whether the poor were black or white. They will have government "squandering prodigality," becoming "wasteful and corrupt."[22] Later, in 1892, a learned commentary on criminal law written by Joel Bishop made the point clear: "There is, in just principle, nothing which a government has more clearly the right to do than to compel the lazy to work; there is nothing more absolutely beyond its jurisdiction than to fix the price of labor."[23]

In contrast, workers' remedies for unemployment focused on mutual assistance and on their influence on local and state governments. All the platforms and declarations of principles adopted by most international unions and by the Knights of Labor stressed the ways workers should behave toward each other: solidarity, brotherhood, and sisterhood.[24] Between the founding of the National Labor Union in 1867 and the demise of its successor the Industrial Congress, in 1874, labor's legislative demands on the federal government focused on the freedom to form trade unions on the creation of a national ("greenback") currency that would provide entrepreneurs and farmers with higher prices and ready access to loan capital, on attempts to protect the Homestead Act against large land grants to corporations, and on a legal eight-hour day for federal employees.[25] The eight-hour standard was actually made federal law in 1868 and was even strengthened during President Grant's reelection campaign in 1872, but it was rendered toothless by subsequent Supreme Court decisions.

During the spasmodic economic growth of the 1880s, however, labor advocates, often in tandem with Farmers' Alliances, did develop a growing list of demands for action by Washington, among them the creation of a bureau of labor statistics, postal savings banks, and public ownership of railroads and of coal, iron, gold, and other mines.[26] It was, however, the response of Coxey's Army and other mobilizations of the unemployed during the catastrophic depression that followed the crisis of 1893 that formulated and popularized demands for federal action aimed directly at revitalizing the economy and generating jobs. Jacob Coxey was a prosperous businessman whose thinking was rooted in the post-Civil War greenback movement. When Coxey announced his plan in April 1894 for a march on Washington to arrive on May 1, he specifically endorsed bills introduced by Senator W. A. Peffer of Kansas for the printing of five hundred million dollars in legal tender notes to fund the building of roads by workers who were to be paid not less than $1.50 for an eight-hour day. Coxey also called for states and localities to deposit non-interest-bearing bonds with the U.S. treasury to finance the building of "their own market houses, public libraries, museums, engine houses, schoolhouses, and public halls, where people can come and discuss all questions that interest them . . . own and build their own electric light plants, waterworks, street railroads, and other public improvements that . . . promote the advancement of the whole people."[27]

The famous march set out from Massillon, Ohio, on Easter Sunday, 1894, and crossed Pennsylvania and Maryland preceded by an African American flag bearer and usually with 50 to 200 men participating, regularly inspired by sermons about Jesus's works "viewed from the purely humanitarian standpoint." In some communities, like Beaver Falls, Pennsylvania, local inhabitants greeted them warmly, while in others, like Allegheny City and Hagerstown, they were met with hostility. Kaufman's department store in Pittsburgh welcomed the marchers with a contribution of three hundred pairs of shoes and three hundred vests. In Frederick, Maryland, the sheriff kept them under surveillance, only to be denounced by local citizens who contributed generously to the marchers. In the steel towns of the Monongahela Valley, which had lately been shaken by the Homestead strike, the friendly reception was tumultuous.[28]

Other marchers set out from Seattle, Denver, Birmingham, Grand Rapids, and elsewhere. The ranks of some of them swelled at times to more than two thousand and some marchers in Butte and Council Bluffs seized trains, rousing the ire of Attorney General Richard Olney. National Guard units were called out eight times against various groups of marchers. Some California marchers crossed Arizona on trains its members had commandeered. The Knights of Labor in Chicago endorsed the jobless army (though the city council barred approaching members from the city).[29] Coxey's Army did reach Washington by May 1, but Coxey and other leaders were not permitted to address Congress, and they were arrested when they tried to speak on the capitol lawn. Nevertheless, several Congressmen did introduce "Coxey bills" for federal public works. None passed.[30] But the legacy of marching on Washington for jobs and public assistance survived to become a regular feature of subsequent depressions.

The stormy decade of the 1890s is best remembered by historians of labor for the titanic battles such as the Homestead strike and the Pullman boycott and the huge strikes of coal miners in the Midwest and in southern Colorado which were spread from pit to pit by the strikers marches, the total shut down of textile mills in Lawrence and Fall River, the frequency with which immigrants in the lowest pay grades joined strikers from the most skilled ranks, and the solidarity exhibited between black and white dockers in 1892. Time and again, the courts enjoined such solidarity, making this a critical epoch in the development of labor law, while federal or state authorities mobilized their armed forces to enforce such rulings.[31]

By the 1890s, the United States added more value to its national income by manufacturing than did any other nation in the world. It also exported unequaled quantities of agricultural products. By 1900, a handful of countries in Western Europe and North America accounted for some 80 percent of the manufactured goods of the world.[32] Those countries in turn had partitioned most of the rest of the world into colonies and spheres of influence. They poured resources into the development of naval power, like the Great White Fleet that President Theodore Roosevelt was to send around the world and the Japanese flotilla that crushed Russia's Pacific power in 1904. Subsidies provided by rival European powers to their respective merchant and passenger fleets made it possible for immigrants to sail to the Western Hemisphere at fares far cheaper than immigrants from Asia had to pay, forcing the Asians into resurgent forms of indentured servitude.[33] Military confrontations, like the Anglo-French standoff in the Sudan, Italy's invasions of Ethiopia and later of Libya, German seizure of Shandong from China, and the destruction of the Spanish Empire by the United States, all contributed to making fear of pending world war the primary concern of the Socialist International as the new century dawned.[34]

The depression of the 1890s deserves close comparison with our own times. The decline of sales began in mining and commercial agriculture, the major shippers for the vast railway network. The railroads' loss of revenues precipitated the failure of the giant British banking house Baring Brothers, which in turn provoked British investors to unload U.S. stocks and the New York Stock Exchange to collapse. By the end of 1893, 491 American banks and over fifteen thousand other commercial institutions had failed. Gold was drained out of the U.S. Treasury at an unprecedented rate, receipts from the highly protective tariff shriveled, and the huge Civil War pensions enacted by the previous Republican administration and Congress commandeered more than 40 percent of federal expenditures.[35] President Grover Cleveland stood like Horatio at the bridge, prepared to sacrifice his presidency and his party's control of Washington and to endure in secret a painful operation so that he might slash government expenditures, pare down the tariff, fight off incessant opposition efforts to remonetize silver, and save the gold standard—to him and to his admirers, the ultimate emblem of Euro-American civilization and bulwark of unfettered global commerce. By early 1895, when the rapid flow of gold out of Washington threatened the federal government with default, only the intervention of a consortium of banks assembled by J.P. Morgan saved the government—the last time in history the private sector rescued the public sector. As Cleveland's resolve made starkly evident, pegging national currencies to gold imposed a tight discipline on the "free market" of every industrialized country. Gunboats and marines were soon to be deployed to impose similar budgetary discipline on less-developed countries (or, to use the language of Theodore Roosevelt, those who were less "civilized").[36] Cleveland's determination shaped his negative responses to all measures intended to expand the currency, to the Pullman boycott, and to Coxey's Army.

The economic crisis also opened the way to effective consolidation of the country's business structure. During the decade 1895–1905, most of the major corporations that were to dominate the U.S. economy until the 1970s were created. One thinks of U.S. Steel, Westinghouse, General Electric, International Harvester, Armour, and Standard Oil (all soon to be joined by General Motors), whose eternal life we older folks long took for granted. Unsuccessful strikes in steel, meat packing, and farm equipment had left large-scale industry overwhelmingly nonunion by 1910.[37]

The consolidation and revitalization of industrial capitalism at the turn of the century was international in scope. The French economist Leon Dupriez calculated that the average annual change in physical output per capita for advanced industrial countries as a group between 1895 and 1913 was double what it had been between 1880 and 1894.The United States, which had already emerged during the 1880s as the world's leading industrial producer increased its output even more than its leading rivals, England, Germany, and France. Although most manufacturing and construction firms remained relatively small and privately owned as the twentieth century dawned, the average worker in manufacturing now worked for one of the new giant enterprises. By 1909 fully 62.2 percent of all wage earners in manufacturing were employed by only 4.8 percent of the firms.[38] As *Iron Age* reported in 1912, "millions of dollars in specifications for special and semi-special machinery, and the newest types of high-power, high-speed and standard tools" reshaped production processes, with the result, according to the 1910 Census of Manufactures, that the value added per worker had grown by more than 40 percent, whereas the number of wage earners in American manufacturing had risen 37 percent between 1899 and 1909."[39]

The framework of business life that emerged from the depression of the 1890s lasted with important modifications in federal relief measures, in labor law, and in social insurance until the 1970s. It also reshaped working-class life, the labor movement, and responses to depressions for the next three-quarters of a century.

Space will not allow us to discuss the growing popularity after the 1890s of social ownership of industry and of the numerous municipal-reform movements, the appeal of direct action (around the world after Russia's 1905 revolution), both through the IWW and outside of it, or Americans' part in the transnational Great Upheaval of strikes dominated by unskilled workers between 1910 and the recession of 1913, or the wartime and postwar upsurge of labor unions in the economy's dominant corporations. In the prosperous months of these decades, workers not only launched spectacular strikes but also simply quit their jobs in astonishing numbers. (Ford suffered a quit rate of 415 percent in 1912–13). Big companies undertook major efforts to retain their experienced employees, with growing success during the 1920s. The median quit rate in manufacturing fell to 30 percent by 1929, and less than 15 percent in 1936–37.[40]

The New Deal experience was a remarkable example of American Exceptionalism. The depression pushed most European and South American governments to the right—either to durable conservative coalitions (Britain) or to outright dictatorships. The moment of Popular Front influence (France, Belgium, Spain) proved brief. As Daniel Rodgers has observed:

> The institution of new social insurance systems came virtually to a halt in the early 1930s. Canadian Conservatives pushed through an unemployment insurance act on the New Deal example in 1935, only to be voted out of office and watch their Liberal successors nullify the measure in the courts. The Swedish unemployment benefits act of 1934 was a belated subsidarist measure. New Zealand's Social Security Act of 1938 eschewed insurance principles altogether. Only in the United States was there a major push forward in social insurance during the Depression decade.[41]

In addition to the innovations enacted by federal and state governments, working men and women often intervened on their own initiative to secure and improve their own livelihoods—sometimes successfully, sometimes not. Let us look briefly at some such actions undertaken during the second round of the Great Depression, 1937–39. The union movement, though crushed in most basic industries during the earlier depression years of 1920–1922, had revived vigorously, aided by the New Deal. Its total membership by 1940 would surpass that of 1920, its previous record high. But it was also evident that an upward leap in worker productivity had lifted output per worker by 1935–36 above the previous high of 1928, even though the level of unemployment remained high, especially for older, youthful, and nonwhite men and women. Then, late in 1937, a sharp downturn in orders for capital goods encouraged many companies large and small to revive their anti-union policies, while also contributing to the sharp rightward turn of the electorate in 1938. Many workers concluded that capital had gone on strike against the New Deal, and many advocated a planned economy. But it also challenged millions of workers to use their new unions to voice immediate answers to the resurgence of unemployment.[42]

The Steel Workers Organizing Committee found its employed membership literally cut in half in the final months of 1937, as did the important St. Louis district of the United Electrical Workers. Both unions fought successfully to arrange for laid-off members to be instated immediately on relief rolls, without going through welfare agencies. In major industrial centers like Pittsburgh and Tarentum, union officers and activists won the power to manage local relief rolls directly. Other local unions fought for and won the power to place unemployed members directly onto the rolls of the Works Progress Administration (WPA). When a newly conservative Congress in 1939 terminated all non-manual WPA relief work, required a loyalty oath of all WPA employees, and prescribed a one month dismissal of everyone who had been on WPA rosters for more than a year and a half, CIO locals in Minnesota and the famous Trotskyist-led local of the Teamsters threw their support behind a strike by WPA members—one of the strongest of many WPA strikes across the country. The unemployed refused to go to work![43]

Moreover, it was during and after the 1930s that the principle that seniority should govern layoffs and promotions was elevated from an occasional union or company practice to a basic tenet of working-class morality. Some building trades and other unions with effective hiring halls fixed quotas of workers older than fifty-five whom contractors had to retain during any reduction of force. The aim was to prevent a threatened elimination of older workers from trades whose unions had rarely interfered with employers' decisions to fire individual workers, so long as the dismissal was not for union activity, and any replacement was a union member paid union scale. At the other extreme, major locals of the United Electrical Workers, like that at Westinghouse in East Pittsburgh, fought for an unqualified seniority principle even before the union had been certified, but they were so staggered by the numbers of people dismissed in 1937 that they changed their demand to a general reduction of weekly hours and no layoffs. But when the short time they had won dragged on for month after month, the local shifted to a complex plan calling for a reduction of weekly hours to thirty-six in any affected division, followed by dismissing anyone with less than a year's seniority, followed by further stair-step reductions if needed, and finally by department negotiations if things got even worse than that. Control of layoffs and recall according to seniority was far better than leaving all choices up to the management, but it was hardly a cure for unemployment.[44]

Our own time calls for still more imaginative responses. Manufacturing and agriculture have yielded place to public employment, service work, and clerical jobs as the dominant sources of employment. Stimulus efforts introduced by one major country risk disrupting those undertaken by competitors. In the United States, profits and subsidies accumulated by companies are far more likely to be invested in labor-saving equipment than in employment of more people. Most important, figures released by the United Nations in the late 1990s revealed that 78 percent of all manufacturing employees in the world are now employed outside of the industrial powers that had dominated the world economy before 1970. Both government measures and workers' collective efforts to restore declining incomes must now take an international shape.[45]

Notes

Reprinted courtesy of University of Illinois Press.

Unfortunately, David Montgomery passed away before he was able to submit a final version of this paper. Joseph McCartin edited his original contribution with assistance from Edward Montgomery, and in a few instances, they added details to footnotes, whose citations were incomplete at the time of Professor Montgomery's death.

1. Carmen N. Reinhart, "This Time Is Different Chartbook: Country Histories on Debt, Default, and Financial Crises," Working Paper 15815, National Bureau of Economic Research Cambridge, Mass., March 2010, accessed June 5, 2013, http://www.nber.org/papers/w15815.

2. David Montgomery, "The Shuttle and the Cross: Weavers and Artisans in the Kensington Riots of 1844," *Journal of Social History* 5 (Spring 1972): 411–46; Bruce Laurie, *Working People of Philadelphia, 1800–1850* (Philadelphia: Temple University Press, 1980); Sean Wilentz, *Chants Democratic: New York City and the Rise of the American Working Class, 1788–1850* (New York: Oxford University Press, 1984); Christine Stansell, *City of Women: Sex and Class in New York, 1789–1860* (New York: Knopf, 1986).

3. Stephen G. Fisher, *A Philadelphia Perspective: The Diary of Sidney George Fisher Covering the Years 1834–1871*, ed. Nicholas B. Wainwright (Philadelphia: Historical Society of Pennsylvania, 1967), 134–35.

4. David Montgomery, *Citizen Worker: The Experience of Workers in the United States with Democracy and the Free Market during the Nineteenth Century* (New York: Cambridge University Press, 1993), 13, n. 1; Joseph G. Baldwin, *Flush Times of Alabama and Mississippi: A Series of Sketches*, 2nd ed. (New York: D. Appleton and Co., 1854).

5. David M. Gordon, Richard Edwards, and Michael Reich, *Segmented Work, Divided Workers: The Historical Transformation of Labor in the United States* (New York: Cambridge University Press, 1982).

6. J. A. Dacus, *Annals of the Great Strikes in the United States* (Chicago: L. T. Palmer and Co., 1877); Philip S. Foner, *Great Labor Uprising of 1877* (New York:

Monad Press, 1977); Michael J. Perman, *Road to Redemption: Southern Politics, 1869–1879* (Chapel Hill: University of North Carolina Press, 1984).

7. David Montgomery, *Fall of the House of Labor: The Workplace, the State, and American Labor Activism, 1865–1925* (New York: Cambridge University Press, 1987), 46–57; Alice Kessler-Harris, *Out to Work: A History of Wage-Earning Women in the United States* (New York: Oxford University Press, 1982); John Mack Faragher, *Sugar Creek: Life on the Illinois Prairie* (New Haven, Conn.: Yale University Press, 1986); Tera R. Hunter, *To 'Joy My Freedom: Southern Black Women's Lives and Labors after the Civil War* (Cambridge, Mass: Harvard University Press, 1997); Estelle Feinstein, *Stamford in the Gilded Age* (Stamford, Conn.: Stamford Historical Society, 1974); Jacqueline Dowd Hall, *Like a Family: The Making of a Southern Cotton Mill World* (Chapel Hill: University of North Carolina Press, 1987).

8. Alexander Keyssar, *Out of Work: The First Century of Unemployment in Massachusetts* (New York: Cambridge University Press, 1983), chaps. 3 and 5; David Montgomery and Marcel van der Linden, eds., August Sartorius von Waltershausen, *The Workers' Movement in the United States, 1879–1885* (New York: Cambridge University Press, 1998); Shelton Stromquist, *A Generation of Boomers: The Pattern of Railroad Labor Conflict in Nineteenth-Century America* (Urbana: University of Illinois Press, 1987); Peter Bischoff, "D'un atelier de moulage á un autre: les migrations des mouleursoriginaires des Forges du Saint-Maurice et la segmentation du marché du travail nord-américain, 1851–1884," *Labour/Le Travail* 40 (Fall 1997): 21–73.

9. S. J. Kleinberg, *The Shadow of the Mills: Working-Class Families in Pittsburgh, 1870–1907* (Pittsburgh: University of Pittsburgh Press, 1989).

10. Quoted, in Amy Dru Stanley, *Bondage to Contract: Wage Labor, Marriage, and the Market in the Age of Slave Emancipation* (New York: Cambridge University Press, 1998), 104.

11. *Ibid.*, 106.

12. Kleinberg, *Shadow of the Mills*; Montgomery and van der Linden, eds., Sartorius von Waltershausen, *The Workers' Movement in the United States, 1879–1885*.

13. On voter turnout, see Paul Kleppner, *The Third Electoral System, 1853–1892: Parties, Voters, and Political Cultures* (Chapel Hill: University of North Carolina Press, 1979). On Paris workshops and Rhineland uprisings, see P.H. Noyes, *Organization and Revolution; Working-Class Associations in the German Revolutions of 1848–1849* (Princeton, NJ: Princeton University Press, 1966).

14. Wilentz, *Chants Democratic*; Carl Frederick Wittke, *The Utopian Communist: A Biography of Wilhelm Weitling, Nineteenth Century Reformer* (Baton Rouge: Louisiana State University Press, 1950).

15. Iver Bernstein, *New York Draft Riots: Their Significance for American Society and Politics in the Age of the Civil War* (New York: Oxford University Press, 1990).

16. Peter J. Rachleff, *Black Labor in the South: Richmond, Virginia, 1865–1890* (Philadelphia: Temple University Press, 1984), 161–62; Todd DePastino, *Citizen Hobo: How a Century of Homelessness Shaped America* (Chicago: University of Chicago Press, 2003); Carlos C. Closson Jr., "The Unemployed in American Cities," *Quarterly Journal of Economics* 8 (January 1894): 168–217, 257–58.

17. Mayor's Address, *City Year Book for the City of New Haven, 1877* (New Haven: City of New Haven, 1877), 23.

18. Montgomery, *Citizen Worker*, 141–43; Bernstein, *New York Draft Riots.*

19. David Montgomery, *Beyond Equality: Labor and the Radical Republicans, 1862–1872* (Urbana: University of Illinois Press, 1981), 320–31; Herbert Gutman, "The Failure of the Movement by the Unemployed for Public Works in 1873," *Political Science Quarterly*, 80 (1965): 254–76.

20. Heather Cox Richardson, *Death of Reconstruction: Race, Labor, and Politics in the Post-Civil War North, 1865–1901* (Cambridge, Mass.: Harvard University Press, 2001), 37–56; Michael W. Fitzgerald, "Union League Movement in Alabama and Mississippi: Politics and Agricultural Change in the Deep South during Reconstruction" (PhD dissertation, University of California Los Angeles, 1986).

21. Richardson, *Death of Reconstruction*, 55.

22. Quoted in *ibid.*, 59.

23. Joel Bishop, *New Commentaries on the Criminal Law*, vol. 1 (Chicago: T. H, Flood, 1892), 273–74.

24. See, for example, George McNeill, *Labor Movement: The Problem of To-day* (Boston: A. M. Bridgman and Co., 1887), 483–96.

25. Andrew Cameron, editorial, *Workingman's Advocate* 25 (March 1865).

26. See, for example, "Nine Things Needed," *John Swinton's Paper* 14 (October 1883).

27. Henry Vincent, *Story of the Commonweal* (Chicago: W.B. Conkey Co., 1894), 52–53; Carlos A. Schwantes, *Coxey's Army: An American Odyssey* (Lincoln: University of Nebraska Press, 1965).

28. Vincent, *Story of the Commonweal*, 69–105 (quotation on 69); see also, DePastino, *Citizen Hobo.*

29. Vincent, *Story of the Commonweal*, 174, 181.

30. Montgomery, *Citizen Worker*, 56–57.

31. Christopher L. Tomlins, *The State and the Unions: Labor Relations, Law, and the Organized Labor Movement in America, 1880–1960* (New York: Cambridge University Press, 1985); William E. Forbath, *Law and the Shaping of the American Labor Movement* (Cambridge Mass.: Harvard University Press, 1991).

32. By way of contrast, in 1800, 3.3 percent of the world's manufacturing output had been fabricated in China (roughly the same as Europe including Britain) and almost 20 percent in India. Mike Davis, *Late Victorian Holocausts: El Niño Famines and the Making of the Third World* (New York: Verso, 2001), 294.

33. David Northrup, *Indentured Labor in the Age of Imperialism, 1834–1922* (New York: Cambridge University Press, 1995), 8–9, 156–61; Stanley Engerman, "Servants to Slaves to Servants: Contract Labour and European Expansion," in *Colonialism and Migration; Indentured Labour before and after Slavery*, ed. P. C. Emmer (Dordrecht, Neth.: M. Nijhoff, 1986), 263–94.

34. David Montgomery, "Workers' Movements in the United States Confront Imperialism: The Progressive Era Experience," *Journal of the Gilded Age and Progressive Era* 7 (January 2008): 7–42.

35. On veterans' pensions, see Theda Skocpol, *Protecting Soldiers and Mothers: The Political Origins of Social Policy in the United States* (Cambridge, Mass.: Harvard University Press, 1992). On the simultaneous extensive but unsuccessful campaign for reparations for former slaves, see Mary Frances Berry, *My Face Is Black Is True: Callie House and the Struggle for Ex-Slave Reparations* (New York: Alfred A. Knopf, 2005).

36. Horace Samuel Merrill, *Bourbon Leader: Grover Cleveland and the Democratic Party* (Boston: Little Brown, 1957); Nick Salvatore, *Eugene V. Debs: Citizen and Socialist* (Urbana: University of Illinois Press, 1982); John Sproat, *"The Best Men": Liberal Reformers in the Gilded Age* (New York: Oxford University Press, 1968), 170–203; Theodore Roosevelt, "Fourth Annual Message . . . December 6, 1904," in *A Compilation of the Messages and Papers of the Presidents*, vol. 15 (New York: Bureau of National Literature, 1914), 7053–54; Lloyd C. Gardner, Walter F. LaFeber, and Thomas J. McCormick, *Creation of the American Empire* (Chicago: Rand McNally, 1976).

37. James Livingston, *Origins of the Federal Reserve System: Money, Class, and Corporate Capitalism, 1890–1913* (Ithaca, NY: Cornell University Press, 1986), 83–99.

38. *Ibid.*, 56–57. See also Daniel Nelson, *Managers and Workers: Origins of the New Factory System in the United States, 1880–1920* (Madison: University of Wisconsin Press, 1975), 3–10. Compare that figure with 1995, when only 19 percent of the country's workers were employed by firms with more than five hundred employees.

39. Gordon, Edwards, and Reich, *Segmented Work*, 103; Nelson, *Managers and Workers*, 9; *Iron Age* 89 (18 April 1912): 1004.

40. David Montgomery and Ronald Schatz, "Facing Layoffs," in David Montgomery, *Workers' Control in America: Studies in the History of Work, Technology, and Labor Struggles* (New York: Cambridge University Press, 1979), 140.

41. Daniel T. Rodgers, *Atlantic Crossings: Social Politics in a Progressive Age* (Cambridge, Mass.: Harvard University Press, 1998), 435.

42. Walter Licht, *Getting Work, Philadelphia, 1840–1950* (Cambridge, Mass.: Harvard University Press, 1982).

43. Montgomery and Schatz, "Facing Layoffs," 144–47.

44. *Ibid.*, 146–51.

45. Catherine Rampell, "Companies Spend on Equipment, Not Workers," *New York Times*, 10 June 2011, A1. For a provocative proposal for stimulus on an international basis, which was devised by Germany's Free Trade Unions (Social Democratic) shortly before Hitler stamped it out, see Vladimir Woytinsky, "International Measures to Create Employment: A Remedy for the Depression," *International Labour Review* 25.1 (January 1932): 1–22 (quotations on 20 and 21). The article was brought to my attention by Jeremy Brecher.

PART VI

The Move to Global and Comparative Study

David Montgomery was an internationalist at heart. It shaped his political activism and guided his teaching—his PhD students at Pittsburgh invariably prepared a field in "*Comparative* Labor History." He immersed himself in British labor history during the two-year sojourn with Edward Thompson at Warwick University. He edited a key journal in the field, *International Labor and Working-Class History* (*ILWCH*), during a crucial period in its development. His scholarship and lecturing in US labor history were widely known around the world—in Europe, in Brazil, in Japan, and elsewhere. Although his pioneering research and writing primarily focused on the United States, his scholarship was always inflected with transnational comparisons. Later in his career he turned to new transnational areas of research with a focus on American empire and on American trade unions as both its handmaidens and opponents. This approach has since emerged as a major influence in the field. The essays in this section reflect that new departure. They offer suggestive threads and pose critical questions for those working in the burgeoning field of "global labor history."

In these essays and others Montgomery wrestled with twin problems: the shifting posture of organized labor—specifically the AFL—with respect to American imperial expansion in the twentieth century and the racialized character of class formation in the U.S. and Europe's settler colonies, where slavery imprinted wage labor and the state and employers were active agents in shaping the racial landscape of class relations.

In the first essay, "Empire, Race and Working-Class Mobilizations," Montgomery burrowed deeply into the historical reinvention of race as a global phenomenon imprinted by slavery and its aftermath in the United States, the Caribbean, colonial settler states, and Europe. State coercion but also liberal reform performed crucial supportive tasks for regimes in which racial hierarchies imbued class formation and conflict. He warned against romanticizing the struggles of ex-slaves or colonial wage laborers to achieve economic independence or national autonomy, but he also documented the crucial role played by women in those struggles. He called for historians to analyze the "contingent and variable meanings of race" in the context of black and white workers' efforts to find common ground. Ultimately, he was impressed at the beginning of the twenty-first century with "the boiling discontent of subordinated races and classes, which will make the new world empire's triumphal free marketism even more short lived than the political barriers the Great Powers erected a century ago."

In the second essay, "Workers' Movements in the US Confront Imperialism: The Progressive Era Experience," published in 2008, he reminds us of the internationalist orientation of the American Federation of Labor, first as part of a wider anti-imperial chorus when the American empire came of age at the turn of the twentieth century and, later, as a loyal proponent of American interventionism whether in Puerto Rico, Mexico, Canada, or in the "Great War" in Europe. In his view, labor's posture was not simply that of an imperial handmaiden but was interventionist in its own right. Gompers and his allies sought to inoculate labor movements globally, especially those in the Americas, against the virus of industrial unionism and socialism. That project was an extension of the AFL's own preoccupation with its continuing war against these tendencies domestically, whether the vestiges of its old nemesis, the Knights of Labor, or the still threatening influence of the Industrial Workers of the World. Like so much of his scholarship, the essay offers both a richly textured analysis of key cases—Canada, Puerto Rico, and Mexico—and a sharply focused lens on the counter currents of opposition, whether manifested in Canada's One Big Union, the ambiguous posture of Santiago Iglesias in Puerto Rico, or the trans-border revolutionary activism of Ricardo Flores Magón.

CHAPTER 15

Empire, Race, and Working-Class Mobilizations

In *Racializing Class, Classifying Race: Labour and Difference in Britain, the USA and Africa*, edited by Peter Alexander and Rick Halpern (New York: St. Martin's Press, 2000)

Working-class mobilizations in England, South Africa and the United States have exhibited remarkable differences and remarkable similarities during the last 150 years. The purpose of this essay is to explore the relationship between the different trajectories of working-class movements in those three corners of the Atlantic world during the twentieth century and the changing patterns of imperial domination and rule, with the hope of formulating meaningful questions about the relationship of empire, race and class in modern life. Such an effort can build on decades of research into the diverse ways in which working women and men have burrowed their own enclaves of collective power into a global economy driven by the accumulation of wealth and shaped by market relations and military might. History remains a collective project, no matter how much pleasure and profit we may derive from controversies among ourselves.

To understand the lives and struggles of working people we must be prepared to think on three levels: local, national and global. The local setting is where workers have pursued their personal goals in familiar contexts, identified friend and foe through everyday encounters, and forged, or failed to forge, collective action. This is precisely why the best social history of the last generation has concentrated research on particular localities (often to the exasperation of its critics). Even when we research localities, however, we often encounter patterns of migration that link working people's behaviour and aspirations at their sites of employment to regions from which they have come, be they nearby native reserves or distant homelands. For black women and men who toiled in white households, the periodic journey between home and work, or even from kitchen to dining room within the employers' residence, was a trip from one racial context to another. Moreover, for sailors, who were the first to engage in wage labor on a large scale, the locus of their action included not only a ship navigating the high seas, but also ports of call which might be in several continents. In each of those ports local authorities might have enforced a different type of racial hierarchy. We are obliged, in short, to devote close attention to just what types of localities framed the action of each group of workers.

The national synthesis has long provided the favourite domain of historians of labor movements and of political action. It is at the level of the nation-state that governmental power framed economic activity in Britain, the United States and South Africa (although not in important parts of the colonial world, such as the Dutch East Indies and India), and it is at that level that the organized power and mere presence of the working class have most obviously influenced state policy. Much of our discussion will compare the political and social consequences of class and racial confrontations in different nation-states. But we must also concern ourselves with the role of class struggles in informing workers' sense of their own nationality and in creating new states. Conversely, state power has played a decisive role in shaping the meaning of race, the character of labor movements and the content attributed to the term "working class" in popular discourse. The global dimension has already surreptitiously slipped into my argument through the reference to migration. Under modern capitalism an ethnically homogeneous working class has been practically a contradiction in terms. On the eve of the Great War strike initiators on the Witwatersrand, in Pennsylvania and in Arizona had to address the miners in several different languages. Moreover, global as well as national product markets and labor markets have been forged, and continue to be forged, by governmental edicts and military force, as well as by economic pressures.

The hegemony created by the power of the United States during the twentieth century has differed from the British Empire by involving far less direct colonial administration. The heartland of the United States' dominion lay in Latin America and the Caribbean. Nevertheless, the crucial role of the conquest of northern Mexico and of Native American peoples in shaping the ascendance of the United States reminds us of three considerations, which are relevant to any country we might study. The first is that race has seldom confronted workers as a simple dichotomy of black and white. Mexicans who had long inhabited the conquered region or who moved into it after it had been annexed by the US, and European migrants, who varied from Cornish to Greek and Finn, interacted with laborers and merchants from China's Taishan province, Japan's Hiroshima prefecture, the Philippines and Samoa.[1]

Second, people repeatedly reinvented races in the context of these encounters. This was *not* simply a question of European immigrants adopting "whiteness." For example, David Montejano has demonstrated that the racial self-definition of Mexicans changed over the course of a century and often varied from region to region. Moreover, for Mexicans in rural Texas, whether or not they were "treated as white" reflected the dissimilar class structures of particular ranch and farm counties, in much the way that the social and legal implications of being called "coloured" in Cardiff or Salford varied over time with British imperial maritime and immigration policies.[2]

The revolutionary epoch that spanned the years between 1775 and 1815 was of critical importance not only in the "making of the English working class," but also in forging a new sense of the interplay of citizenship, slavery and complexion. Sylvia Frey has shown that the presence of slavery left an indelible imprint on the rhetoric, political alignments and military strategies of the American Revolution. Once the colonies had won their liberty, their political and intellectual leaders had to reconstruct the institutional and ideological underpinnings of chattel slavery, while they also imported thousands of new slaves from Africa. Subsequently, Haiti's struggles for independence and emancipation left their mark on the way the whole Atlantic world thought about citizenship and race. But let me just suggest a different example. When more than 1,000 American seamen were incarcerated in Britain's Dartmoor prison in 1814, during a war of little diplomatic significance but enormous ideological importance in the history of American democratic ideas, the republican white prisoners demanded that their monarchist jailers segregate them from the scores of black fellow seamen—and they got their way.[3]

Third, the experience of self-styled whites in the conquered territory suggests the importance of settler consciousness. Empire promised working people of the conquering nation the possibility of escape from the class oppression they suffered at home through the subordination or annihilation of previous inhabitants of the conquered territories. This promise was of decisive importance in the elaboration of "the wages of whiteness" in antebellum America and Labouristic Australia, as well as in the readiness of British workers to enlist in the imperial cause.

The sailor Larry in Herman Melville's 1849 novel *Redburn* expressed the fantasy that saturated radical Democratic rhetoric in the United States of escaping one's own oppression by lording it over the imagined lawless domains of darker people:

> "And what's the use of bein' *snivelized*?" he said to me one night during our watch on deck; "snivelized chaps only learns the way to take on 'bout life, and snivel. You don't see any Methodist chaps feelin' dreadful about their souls; you don't see any darned beggars or pesky constables in *Madagasky*,

> I tell ye; and none o' them kings there gets their big tose pinched by the gout. I might have been a great man in Madagasky; it's too darned bad! Blast Ameriky, I say."[4]

Joseph Conrad explored the role of that delusion in the origins of modern imperialism. A basic theme of his writings was that Larry's fantasy could turn the poor man into a ruthless advanced guard of the very civilization he had sought to escape, free from the social obligations and scrutiny he had faced at home, and inflicting terrible suffering on the people he encountered, while leaving himself flirting with insanity. Carolyn Brown's research into the coal mines of Nigeria has produced a memorable image of this relationship: the "hammock boys," who carried white supervisors back and forth each day between their residences and their places of work.[5]

Settler colonies assumed a complex role in the way the Second International regarded imperialism. Both Karl Kautsky and Bureau Secretary Emile Vandervelde distinguished between productive colonies (*Arbeitskolonien*), where European labour could advance socialist goals, and colonies of exploitation, which had been created by the lust of capital for accumulation but were inhabited by "backward" peoples. As the socialist movement came to grips after 1899 with news of immigrants' strikes and native resistance, it struggled to reconcile its faith in Europe's role as vanguard of civilization with the movement's hostility to wars of conquest and competition for empire. The socialist press in Europe denounced the "Gold War" waged by the capitalists in South Africa and advocated a "return" of India and Egypt to self-rule. As for other colonies, Vandervelde wrote, the goal of the International should be:

> to expand the autonomy of the indigenous community step by step, to give them back possession of the soil, to suppress all forms of coerced labor, and, in general, to support all efforts and movements that aim to free the natives from slavery and to make them independent.[6]

Imperialism's Reincarnation for the Twentieth Century

Formal and informal empires have defined the realm of possibility for working people in both imperialist countries and the portions of the world that those countries dominated. Vandervelde's program of action both identified some basic features of the world order that emerged at the beginning of this century and evaded others. Only a few years earlier, W.E.B. Du Bois had suggested a quite different point of departure in his famous 1903 aphorism: "The problem of the twentieth-century is the problem of the color-line, the relation of the darker to the lighter races of men in Asia and Africa, in America and the islands of the sea."[7] But Thomas Holt recently has argued that the "problem" cannot be *reduced* to "race." Said Holt: "The development of racist thought was not a natural outgrowth of the legacy of slavery; it arose in part from the seemingly nonracist (or racially neutral) premises of liberal ideology."[8]

Let us look more closely at the turn of the century, so that we might better understand the circumstances that transformed both "racist thought" and "liberal ideology." At the end of the 1890s decades of protracted price decline, culminating in a world-wide depression, gave way to a spectacular leap in worker productivity and a wave of business consolidation in the highly industrialized countries. Mines, plantations, and railways in the lands of the "darker races" attracted investment capital and ambitious workers away from the North Atlantic areas that had been blighted by sluggish performance and fierce confrontations between capital and labor. While cities of the Northern Hemisphere hid grinding poverty behind their displays of unprecedented wealth, the colonies became, in another phrase from Du Bois, "the slums of the world."[9] In both domains, the gospel of separate development of the races enjoyed ardent acclaim in intellectual life and practical application in segregation laws, Native Land Acts and municipal zoning regulations.[10]

Political leadership in the industrial powers intervened vigorously in domestic economic and social life, while lavishing expenditures on military and naval strength. As Karl Polanyi summarized the transformation: "society took measures to protect itself" from the "self-regulating economy," which had grown to threaten the annihilation of its "human and natural substance." The new measures were summarized by an official British report on the coal mines of India in 1937 as the "world-wide trend away from the competitive ideal towards formulas of public control."[11]

The transformation Polanyi described was in its springtime when all of society's measures of self-protection converged in Britain's "Liberal landslide" of 1906. Historians of the welfare state have hailed the old age pensions enacted by parliament during the ensuing half decade, along with unemployment insurance, eight-hour day for miners, health insurance through approved societies and expanded welfare services as the advent of citizen-entitlements in the Anglo-Saxon world. Students of labor movements have celebrated this same election for the improved legal framework for trade union action enacted on the eve of the voting and the subsequent emergence of the Labour Party as an organized parliamentary bloc.[12]

Henry Pelling raised challenging questions about the famous election of 1906. He noted that most working-class voters and most trade unions proved unenthusiastic about both the Liberal welfare proposals and expansion of the navy and the empire. His depiction of Gladstone, "the most popular leader among the working class," as "more hostile than almost anyone else to the extension of the power of the state," and favouring reconciliation with the Afrikaners, whom Britain had defeated in the recent war, bears a remarkable resemblance to the appeal of William Jennings Bryan for the American Federation of Labor in 1908. The walls and fences of urban Britain had been festooned during the election campaign with menacing depictions of Chinese, dramatizing the Liberals' protest against the recruitment of indentured workers from China for South Africa's mines.[13]

Pelling's view of the victorious Liberals as committed to "the repudiation of the consequences of the South African war" has considerable merit, and it evokes comparison with the sometimes tacit, often explicit, endorsement by America's Bryan and Wilson Democrats of the spread of segregation laws in southern states. Ardent appeals to London by Africans to overturn the Act of Union and the Native Land Act were rebuffed by Britain's Liberal government.[14] Nevertheless, a view from South Africa reveals that far more was at work than simply British reconciliation with Afrikaner racism.

Shula Marks and Stanley Trapido, and more recently Saul Dubow, have pointed out that Sir Alfred Milner and his young colleagues of the so-called "kindergarten," whose careful research and planning guided the formation of the new South African state and its labor policies in mining and agriculture, had been educated at Oxford in the neo-Hegelianism of T.H. Green. That doctrine, which was still an important part of the academic curriculum during the 1940s, inspired many progressives on both sides of the Atlantic to view the state as a creative force for the common good. The "kindergarten's" way of thinking was cut from the same cloth as that of the authors of the pioneering Liberal welfare legislation. As Sidney Webb asked: "What is the use of talking about Empire, if here, at its very centre, there is always to be found a mass of people, stunted in education, a prey to intemperance and congested beyond the possibility of realizing in any true sense either social or domestic life?"[15]

To be sure Milner often faced powerful opposition within South Africa from both British immigrant workers and Afrikaners, and he was censured by the Liberals in parliament on the eve of the 1906 election for authorizing the whipping of Chinese workers by mine supervisors. Nevertheless, his plan to introduce 60,000 Chinese workers under three-year contracts to work in Witwatersrand mines was designed to break the independence and reduce the wages of *black* miners. The effort to put an end to conditions that, mining companies complained, had produced a "shortage" of African workers was a complete success. Even the electoral victory of the Afrikaner nationalist *Het Volk* (People's) Party in 1907 resulted not in the abrupt expulsion of the Chinese, but in government agreement to their phased withdrawal, in exchange for augmented recruitment of poor whites. When English-speaking miners subsequently struck against an increase in the tempo of work, the strikers were replaced by Afrikaner scabs, while Africans and Chinese continued to labor alongside whatever white men appeared at the mine face.[16]

The common intellectual origins of reform in the metropolis and in the colonies did not mean that the same formulas would apply to all locations. British authorities explained policy differences in the language of race. Thus, as early as 1895 Colonial Secretary Joseph Chamberlain advocated both a constitutional style of union between England and those of her overseas domains where white settlers could govern themselves, and direct control of crown colonies where other races predominated. "It would appear to me absurd," said Chamberlain, "to apply to savage countries the same rules which we apply to civilized portions of the United Kingdom."[17]

Milner had been every bit as explicit when he explained the racial implications of his proposals:

> The position of the whites among the vastly more numerous black population requires that even their lowest ranks should be able to maintain a standard of living far above that of the poorest section of the population in a purely white country.[18]

One cannot help being impressed ninety years later at the long-term success of this policy. Nevertheless, neither the history of South African public policy nor that of welfare state development in Britain and the United States can be understood as simply the fulfilment of the social vision shared by Milner and his contemporaries. The fierce class struggles that raged between 1909 and 1926 left their stamp on the statecraft of all three countries. In South Africa the strikes of white miners were treated very differently by the state from those of black miners, but both white and black strikes left their mark on the policies of the government and of mining corporations. The crushing of the 1922 Rand Revolt by the military and air power of Smuts' government broke the back of white working-class rebellion and culminated in bloody massacres of African residents of mining communities, but it also paved the way for the electoral victory of the Labour-Nationalist coalition scarcely two years later. It was that coalition, not the social engineering of Milner's kindergarten, that produced the economic and social legislation of interwar South Africa: the "civilizing" of major sectors of the economy through reservation of specified jobs for whites, tariffs to encourage domestic manufacturing, and subsidies and marketing legislation designed to promote Afrikaner farming. South Africa's new Conciliation Act, which provided a legal framework for white trade unions, was the counterpart in timing and spirit to America's Railway Labor Act of 1926.[19]

The coalition's legislation also helped the mining companies accomplish the remarkable feat of preventing any increase in the earnings of African workers for almost half a century. The profitability—some would say the very survival—of South Africa's gold mining and the resuscitation of white agriculture depended not only on state assistance to whites, but also on an equally effective *suppression* of the wages of Africans. That effort too had global ramifications: it was part of the remarkable resurgence of labor coerced by penal sanctions *after* the abolition of slavery.

Unfree Wage Labor

In both the United States and the West Indies former slaves struggled to secure economic independence from their former owners through obtaining land of their own, claiming possession of plantation homes and gardens, whether or not all (or even any) family members were in the planter's employ, and enforcing their claims through both political associations and crowd action, in which men and women played visibly different roles. Their quest for peasant proprietorship has captured the attention of many historians, but not all have interpreted that quest in the same way. Eric Foner, writing about the West Indies, associated peasant proprietorship with isolation from markets and innovation, holding up Haiti as his prime example. Thomas Holt has argued that in Jamaica black peasants sought out areas where they could combine market gardening with wage labor, and that they moved quickly into the production of market goods, as well as subsistence crops. In a word, black men and women did insert themselves somewhat advantageously into the new framework of local and global capitalism. Similarly, Africans seized opportunities opened by early mine development on the Rand to grow commercial crops, before the 1913 Natives Land Act separated white-owned lands from isolated black reservations. African men, especially Zulu, also dominated household and laundry work, before pass laws herded them into the mines.[20]

These rural struggles are of great importance for our research for several reasons. First, they remind us that in the formation of African-American and colonial working classes the development of wage labor often did *not* entail radical separation from the land. We must look for ways in which men and women combined rural households and at least partial self-subsistence with wage labor, sometimes under conditions of people's own choosing, but increasingly under harsh options framed by the state. Planters often found that labor was most abundant at harvest time—when the work was the most arduous, we might note, but also when earnings were best. Conversely, in the American South, at least, the work of freed people that was most directly associated with their own aspirations for autonomy was women's work in and around the household, in stark contrast to the devaluation and "pastoralization" of women's unpaid labor in Euro-American society, which Jean Boydston has analysed so tellingly.[21]

In many areas, however, women's work within the household also earned money. Look again at *All God's Dangers*, Theodore Rosengarten's narrative of a successful black farmer in Alabama and consider the array of income-earning tasks undertaken by Hannah Shaw, who did *not* go to the cotton fields or to white women's kitchens: she sold honey, eggs, butter, vegetables and quilts, while also serving as her husband's legal adviser. Sugata Bose's conclusion regarding Bengal has validity far beyond the borders of India: capitalist development "rested heavily on the forcing up of labor intensity within family units actually tilling the land."[22]

Richard Roberts has demonstrated that in West Africa the increase of peasant cotton production brought with it a steady *expansion* of domestic weaving and spinning, rather than simply exports of raw cotton to the textile mills of England and France. A harsher aspect of the gendered link between peasant proprietorship and wage earning has been noted by John Higginson in the Belgian Congo. Men from the Lomami region often went to the copper mines in quest of wages, with their ultimate objective being to buy more wives, who could raise cotton for sale. Robert Shenton has observed that "much of the writing of the last two decades on the changing position of African women under colonial rule has been focused on the battle between men and women over control of women's labor and productive assets such as land."[23]

Second, as the discussion of African cotton production suggests, in many regions the great leap in commercial production of primary products, which called forth in turn state planning and coercion to produce a native wage labor force, occurred a long time *after* the abolition of slavery. Diamonds and gold in South Africa, tobacco in Sumatra and rubber in the Congo, not to mention the flourishing of settler agriculture in Kenya, all belonged to the new imperialism. Systematic employment of convict labor was an integral element in the development of coal mining, railway construction and turpentine extraction in America's New South, and the number of convicts employed grew rapidly in the 1880s and 1890s. The quest for a labor force that was both inexpensive and available at the behest of mining and agricultural capital also brought forth the new array of master-and-servant legislation in the colonies, in some cases more than half a century after the end of chattel slavery, and also after penal sanctions for refusal to work had been abolished in Britain by the famous Act of 1875, and in the United States by protracted popular struggle in the antebellum North and by Congressional overturning of the postwar Black Codes in the South. Although the Portuguese had abolished slavery in Angola in 1869, it was not until 1902 that their imperial legislation declared all Africans vagrants by nature and legally obliged to work.[24]

Moreover, both agricultural production for export and colonial coal, gold, and diamond mining incorporated and transformed styles of employment that antedated wage labor. The 125,000 workers in India's Jharia coalfields during the 1920s, for example, have been described by Dilip Simeon as "'low' caste, female and tribal." They moved about incessantly but were bound by obligations of debt and piece-rated family labor to contractors, in a complex network of subinfeudation that stretched from the coalfields to often distant homes. Intense controversies developed among administrators and nationalist intellectuals as to whether "traditional" practices should be abolished or treasured. British managers of mines in India argued that "*the ethical standard of aborigines and semi-savages is hardly compatible with the principle of the minimum wage.*" Champions of "native customs" within the British elite marshalled such arguments against what they denounced as the "Westernizing" thrust of the India Congress Party and the African National Congress.[25]

Finally, we must probe the role of workers struggling within post-slavery regimes in the forming of nationalisms and of Pan-Africanism. Dealing with this question requires as much caution as is needed to study the relationship between industrial workers and socialism. Although trade unions in the colonial setting and struggles for national independence have been shaped by different social dynamics and often conflicting objectives, it has also often happened that each form of struggle opened political space for the other. For example, India's independence movement during the early years of the Second World War inspired British maritime authorities to grant important concessions to the wage demands of Indian seamen, who manned British vessels. More often it was the case that important strikes, like those of Jamaica's workers in 1938, pushed the question of independence for colonies into public discussion in the metropolitan country.[26] Conversely, Frantz Fanon has argued that the task of state-building after the achievement of independence invariably (or at least frequently) led to suppression and isolation of the new nations' trade union movements.[27]

I wish to draw attention at this point, however, to a rather different question: to the formulation of race, class and nation in working people's language of struggle. Consider the battle-cry of Paul Bogle during the rebellion of 1865 in Jamaica's Morant Bay: "It is now time for us to help ourselves—skin for skin . . . war is at us, my black skin. War is at hand."[28] His appeal to "black skin" was constructed, as Benedict Anderson would argue was the case with nationalism generally, "in terms of historical destinies, while racism dreams of eternal contaminations, transmitted from the origins of time through an endless sequence of loathsome copulations: outside history."[29] Bogle sought to create a sense of national unity based on the racial vocabulary white masters had created, to make someone else's language his own by populating it "with his own intention, his own accent," to use the words of Mikhail Bakhtin.[30]

Evelyn Brooks Higginbotham, while endorsing Bakhtin's usage, also reminds us that race "not only tends to subsume other sets of social relations, namely gender and class, but it suppresses its own complex interplay with the very social relations it envelopes."[31] Bogle's call to the Maroons to join forces with Jamaica's former slaves, we might note, failed to overcome historic differences and suspicions, leaving the battle to peasant families and sugar workers. Even the most persuasive discourse can collide with the real world.[32]

But Higginbotham's warning about succumbing to the "metalanguage of race" also brings to mind the provocative argument of Kevin Gaines about the class content of the uplift rhetoric, with which African American leaders challenged racial oppression at the turn of the century. "A rising race must be aristocratic," W.E.B. Du Bois wrote in 1901, "the good cannot consort with the bad—not even the best with the less good."[33] As Gaines observed: "the middle-class character of the emphasis on positive representations of educated, assimilated blacks of sterling character was interdependent on the image of the so-called primitive, morally deficient lower classes," with its emphasis on dance halls, prostitution and gambling.[34]

Higginbotham's admonition draws our attention to what to my mind is the most valuable element of postmodernist analysis: its concern with the diverse and often conflicting narratives through which people who are differently situated in society construct their experience. This approach, rather than simply deconstructing the texts of dominant discourse, builds creatively upon labor historians' attention to the "traditions, value-systems, ideas, and institutional forms"[35] through which working men and women handled their daily experience with capitalist relations of production. It is important for our purposes to recognize that popular cultures have been more than a residue of traditional norms, but are nurtured by both work experience and social relations outside the workplace, that they are often expressed in nonverbal forms, and they have been employed by working people in a creative interaction with the dominant discourse of their time and place. Within the vast domain of modern capitalism and empires, at least, we are never dealing with what Aileen Kraditor called "autochthonous cultures," impervious to the teachings of bourgeois reformers and radicals alike.[36]

Robin Kelley and Tera Hunter in the United States and Charles van Onselen in South Africa have stressed the importance of such evidence as body language, cursing, loud talking, music and dance, all of which could provoke the revenge of the authorities. They have also noted the importance of "dance halls and blues clubs" as places "that enabled African Americans to take back their bodies, to recuperate, to be together." Kelley adds that often "the most intense skirmishes between such blacks and authority erupted during and after weekend gatherings."[37] As Earl Lewis has put it: African Americans "congregated" in a segregated society.[38] Such observations also remind us sharply that what mattered personally to working men and women was often quite different from what was couched in the programs of labor or nationalist movements.[39]

Finally, let us note that creating a national identity involved not just an act of imagination, but also collective deeds. Julie Saville's path-breaking work on Reconstruction South Carolina has highlighted the role of self-organized paramilitary processions (even to and from cotton fields), platoons of new voters marching miles to the polls, and ritualized group confrontations with white authorities in the process through which men and women, who had lately been the property of different masters, became "a people." This transformation had been put into words by two handwritten documents found by a policeman on the streets of New Orleans in 1863 and signed simply "A Colored Man." The author proclaimed war aims of his people, which were not those of the United States: "we care nothing about the union[.] we have been in it Slaves over two hundred and fifty years," but he added, "when we are free men and a people we will fight for our rights and liberty." He concluded with a dazzling and defiant inversion of the political discourse then pronounced in Washington:

> we are the Blackest and bravest race the president Says there is a wide Difference Between the black Race and the white race But we Say that white corn and yellow will mix by the taussles but the black and white Race must mix by the root as we are so well mixed and has no tassels—freedom and liberty is the word with the Colored people.[40]

Imperialism and Internationalism

To ask what it meant for black and white (and other) races to "mix by the roots" and what such mixing had to do with the mobilization of different groups of working people for "freedom and liberty" is to pose the historical problem of human agency in the interaction of race and class. It is also a question that has evoked sharply opposing interpretations from different historians.

Much of the discussion recently has turned on the relationship between white racism and class consciousness. The best recent work has highlighted not only the frequent violent actions of whites against people of colour who were successful in business or who aspired to participate in political and social activity that whites considered their exclusive inheritance, but also the frequent shaping of class struggles around the militant demand of white workers for better treatment than employers accorded workers of other races. Consider the way white women hired for domestic labor in Johannesburg households insisted that their role was to supervise the black men, with whom they made beds and cleaned floors. Or the fact that it was a socialist preacher, Alexander Irvine, then investigating peonage in Alabama mines, who protested when the Italians with whom he was travelling were seated in a car marked "coloured." His ire rose when he asked a black porter, was there not a law on "the separation of the races" and was met with the reply: "Dere sho' is boss, but you ain't races. You is jes Dagoes, ain't you?"[41]

Persuasive analyses of the material and psychic advantages that white workers have gained, and continue to gain, by virtue of their complexions, of the saturation of workers' movement rhetoric with white supremacy doctrines in pre-Civil War America, and of the effective designation of Chinese as the class enemy in mobilizing trade union and labor party strength in many countries bordering the Pacific Ocean, have converged to change the tone of historical studies of working-class culture from one of celebration to one of denunciation. Herbert Hill's conclusion that trade unions are inherently racist has inspired both critiques of historical portraits of interracial collaboration as romantic myths and Bruce Nelson's ominous conclusion that democratic unionism does not lead to democratic social practice: to empower white rank-and-filers is to unleash racism.[42]

Such studies have served us well by drawing attention sharply to the racialized nature of class. It is important, however, not to allow that realization to close off examination of the specific circumstances that have encouraged or prevented various levels of collaboration and even solidarity among workers of different races. If we fail to probe the meaning of racialized encounters to the people directly involved and the ways in which workers' own conduct and programs could, did and will in the future make a difference between reinforcing white supremacy and challenging it, we have thrown the whole burden of changing the world onto peoples of colour, with perhaps some noble white radicals as a cheering section.

When American soldiers marched into the Mexican city of Saltillo in 1847, they were greeted by a woman from New Jersey, who worked in a Mexican textile mill. "Americans I am glad to see you," she exclaimed. "I have seen but one white man in eight months, a negro from New Orleans."[43] Her greeting not only dramatized the contingency of race (which could be recounted through thousands of such tales), but also underscored the importance of local meanings. When Laura Tabili examined the 1930 protest in Salford's union hall against the employment of six Arabs, she found that the incident was resolved when a committee of two white and two black seamen satisfied itself that the Arabs were "local men." She also shows us that the same British port cities that saw whites assaulting racially mixed neighbourhoods in 1919 also produced frequent marriage between British women and colonial seamen and consequently kin networks that criss-crossed racial lines. Some of them also nurtured the inter-racial Seamen's Minority Movement.[44]

Tabili's work is especially important, however, for the ways it reminds us of the role of the state, business and union policies in shaping the racializing of class. Similarly, Thomas Sugrue has quite properly protested that "in the current historiography on race relations and labor, employers are almost entirely missing."[45]

The Great Depression reshaped state and empire in ways that were remarkably different in the United States, Britain and South Africa. Permit me to focus my remarks here on the experience of the United States. I do so both because the decisive economic power of the United States, as producer of more than 40 percent of the world's value added by manufacture during the 1920s and as creditor to the other imperialist powers after 1914, meant that the collapse of New York securities markets brought the world economy down to ruin, but also because Depression era struggles in the United States can illuminate the relationship between working-class agency and race.

The American industrial unions of the 1930s were created during a period of such heavy unemployment that employers could be very choosy about the workers they hired. One consequence was an unprecedented homogenization of the industrial labor force, at the very time the new unions publicly repudiated racial and ethnic barriers to membership. Factory hirings averaged about 400,000 workers a month between 1933 and 1939. Those who were hired were overwhelmingly men (and increasingly women) with families to support, who were white, between the ages of 25 and 45, and graduates of more than eight years of schooling. Those who were specialists at the occupations to be filled and who had earned the highest wages on their previous jobs were the most favoured. Not only did the absolute number of black workers in manufacturing decline between 1930 and 1940, but a WPA survey of some 1,500 firms in Philadelphia's highly diversified industry found that only five—Atlantic Refinery, Franklin Sugar, Westinghouse, Diston Saw and Midvale Steel—had any black production workers.[46]

The United States had responded to the Depression with much the same turn toward autarchy that was evident elsewhere in the world. The New Deal's domestic reforms would have been impossible had the United States not broken with the world gold standard. Nevertheless, important features of American political life during the 1930s differed remarkably from those of most other industrial powers and of South Africa: party rivalries for office remained vigorous, Right-wing nationalism was confined to the role of opposition, and official policy encouraged workers of all races in manufacturing and mining to unionize.[47]

The revival of trade union strength is of special relevance to our investigation. American workers had gone through the 1920s with a union movement that was so widely committed to segregation as to make the unions that did not exclude or separate members of colour those in need of explanation.[48] The accommodations surviving unions had made by the end of the anti-union onslaught of 1919–22 resemble those Tabili found in the conservative British sailors' union. As Eric Arnesen has shown, the interwar legislative victories of railway unions empowered white workers often at the expense of black employees. Moreover, even in 1946, after union membership had exceeded

13 million workers, more than 7.5 million workers belonged to the American Federation of Labor. Most of its affiliates, including the electricians, machinists and teamsters who sparked the federation's growth, either barred non-whites from membership or consigned them to a subordinate status.[49]

Nevertheless, the new unions of the 1930s were involved in rather different racial dynamics from those that had shaped their precursors. All unions of the rival Congress of Industrial Organizations were publicly committed to enrolling everyone working in their industries, regardless of race or sex. On the West Coast fierce battles between the two federations were openly fought over race policy, especially in aircraft and shipbuilding. In the Southeast, African Americans provided most of the CIO's early recruits on riverfronts, in tobacco factories and in iron mines. The early defeat of unionism in the all-white textile industry magnified the importance of black workers in what union growth the region did experience.[50]

Within the automobile and steel industries, where large numbers of black and Chicano workers were employed, skilled white workers tended to hold aloof from the new unions, except in those auto and tool-making enterprises where whites constituted virtually the entire workforce. In one steel mill after another it was the black workers and those of recent immigrant stock who carried the day for the industrial unions, while the tonnage men, who had constituted most of the union members before 1919, clung to company-sponsored Employee Representation Plans, even at times after the CIO had been recognized.[51]

Looking specifically at Michigan automobile firms during the postwar decade, Thomas Sugrue observed that company policies created job categories and hiring pools that either excluded black workers almost entirely, as in the case of Chrysler and many General Motors affiliates, or reserved huge numbers of the most punishing job assignments for them, as in the case of Ford. All auto companies vehemently opposed proposals for a state fair employment practices law until lobbying by allied African-American and CIO organizations overcame their resistance in 1956. Most important of all, between 1947 and 1958 the Big Three transferred their operations wholesale out of Detroit to twenty-five new plants located in virtually all-white suburban areas.[52]

White workers exercised their own important initiatives in this process. The resistance of skilled tradesmen to the admission to their ranks of anyone who was not white was vigorous and successful, just as recurrent threats by those craftsmen to quit the United Auto Workers earned them special treatment by the union's leaders. Residents of the white suburbs in which new branch plants were built frequently resorted to violence against African Americans who attempted to move into the neighbourhoods. As John McGreevy has demonstrated, Catholic parishes formed community boundaries that were especially resistant to penetration, despite the postwar rise in appeals by Catholic clergy and lay intellectuals for inter-racial harmony.[53]

The story in the packinghouse industry played out somewhat differently. The crushing defeats of 1919–22 had left many workers wary of risking their jobs once again in the union cause. Those in better positions, like the older Polish women in Swift's sliced bacon department, openly feared that union victory would turn their jobs over to African Americans. It was black workers who spearheaded the new unionization in Chicago, despite the fact that their share of jobs in the city's packinghouses had fallen from 31.2 percent to 19.6 percent between 1930 and 1940. Consequently, the United Packinghouse Workers established a reputation for combating racism both on and off the job that no other national union could match—until the Chicago stockyards went out of business in the 1950s. It is important to add, however, that this achievement was accomplished by an alliance between black members and a left-wing minority of whites. It was supported, or at least tolerated, by the majority of white workers only when and to the extent that the union was successful in improving economic conditions. When union activists attacked residential segregation, however, they were openly, even violently, opposed by many white members.[54] Careful study of the packinghouse experience can tell us much about the impact and limits of workers' own activity in challenging the racialization of class.

A very influential book by Lisabeth Cohen has popularized the concept of the "CIO's Culture of Unity," which enabled the goals of the new labor movement to be discussed in non-racial terms. Labor-oriented cultural expressions of the 1930s and 1940s depicted "Americans" as "working men and women of many races and nationalities."[55] In stark contrast to South Africa's 1938 Great Trek commemoration, visions of history sponsored by the Roosevelt administration challenged Anglo-Saxon cultural supremacy in a way that framed in discourse an alliance between children of immigrants and African Americans. New Deal radio broadcasts such as "Let Freedom Ring" (1937), "Americans All, Immigrants All" (1938), and "Freedom's People" (1941–42), slotted programs about black Americans into the formula of "a nation of nations." Not only did that metaphor reflect the lines of support enjoyed by the CIO in heavy industry, but it had also been previewed by the 1926 Catholic Eucharist Congress in Chicago, when cardinals announced they had met "thousands of Chicagoans of foreign birth or extraction," among them African Americans.[56]

Contradictions within the "culture of unity" were made evident in the streets of America's cities by the Italian invasion of Ethiopia. Mussolini's escalating demands against Ethiopia and his invasion of that country in October 1935 had galvanized African American popular opinion like no previous foreign event since emancipation. Roi Ottley of the *Amsterdam News* observed that the teachings of black nationalists pervaded the conversation of black New Yorkers as never before. Moreover, the military assault in East Africa came hard on the heels of ardent "Don't Buy Where You Can't Work" campaigns and the Harlem riot of 1935, in which the ubiquitous Italian store and bar keepers of Harlem were often singled out as targets.[57]

At the same time, Mussolini's invasion swelled the pride of Italian Americans. An editor of *Il Progresso Italo-Americano* explained that pride concisely:

> The Italians of America, who have known in the past the saddest bitterness, the Italians of America who have been so long in a world where Italians are looked down upon, today can raise their heads high and say to all the others: Hats off.[58]

Italian American joy over the new international stature of their ancestral land turned into open enthusiasm for fascism after 6 May 1936, the day the Italian army entered Addis Ababa. Thousands of couples renewed their wedding vows at special Catholic masses using iron wedding bands, so that they could contribute their gold rings to the imperial cause. The mayors of Philadelphia and Paterson banned Italian victory parades, however, fearing bloody racial confrontation between two peoples, both of whom provided important constituencies of the new industrial unions.

The conflict in Harlem precipitated by the Ethiopian war not only dramatizes the tensions within the New Deal coalition, but also brings us back to the interaction of local, national and global history in shaping the classification of race and the racialization of class. The experience was not unique. Japan's invasion of China catapulted the left-leaning Chinese Hand Laundry Alliance into sharp confrontation with the established leadership of New York's Chinatown, while in San Francisco it precipitated the unionization of Chinese-American women at the National Dollar Stores—the first open participation of Asians in an AFL union. Protests against the Munich Pact cemented the alliance between Chicago's Slavic fraternal organizations and the CIO, just as subsequent Soviet conduct in Poland later disrupted it. Cardenas' reforms in Mexico, and especially the nationalization of American oil companies, strengthened the Left and the CIO among Chicanos in Texas and California.[59]

The links between local actions and the reshaping of world imperialism assumed both informal and institutional forms, which also deserve close attention. The interracial character and intercontinental role of maritime workers did not end with the nineteenth century. It persists in our own age of container ports, despite their isolation far out from urban centres, which has removed the ships and their crews from view. Out of sight, out of mind. We easily convince ourselves that the cargoes of a global economy somehow move about like our papers, in cyberspace.[60]

The Baku Congress of the Peoples of the East not only summoned European workers to "form a close alliance with the working masses of the entire East, of the entire world," but also proclaimed the necessity "to set up soviets even where there are no urban workers." Revolution in the Russian empire had forged a physical link between insurgent industrial cities and insurgent Asia. Comintern chairman Zinoviev assured the delegates that "only weeks will be needed before our Red Army stretches out its red hand once more toward Warsaw," advancing war "against the imperialists around the world."[61] Even though the revolutionary assault on the world order had been hurled back decisively on all fronts by 1927, the maritime world provided another geographic web for revolutionary activity. It was a seamen's journal, the *Negro Worker*, printed in Hamburg, Copenhagen, or wherever the police had not shut it down, through which the Comintern explicitly addressed people of African ancestry. Its first editor, George Padmore, quickly captures the attention of any historian who may be examining the Pan-African, world trade union, or Communist movements.[62]

Those international links assumed a new importance during and after the Second World War. The war itself unleashed popular struggles and heightened workers' aspirations in both the metropolitan countries and their colonies in ways that proved difficult, if not impossible, for the governing authorities to contain. The defeat of the Axis powers, the achievements of the partisans and the electoral triumph of the Labour Party in Britain appeared to working people on both sides of the Atlantic to herald a new era, free from the destitution, repression, murderous racism and fear of impending war that had characterized the 1930s. In the United States a wave of postwar strikes matched the scale of those that had followed the First World War but produced very different results. The new industrial unions turned back corporate efforts to reassert "management's prerogatives" in the workplace and won major wage increases, which were of special benefit to lower-paid workers. Emboldened by its newfound strength, delegates to the CIO's 1946 convention adopted the most audacious program in its history. They demanded statutory prohibition of racial discrimination and democratization of the American South as a "Down Payment on the Four Freedoms": comprehensive economic planning, including price controls; governmental allocation of basic raw materials designed to direct production towards the needs of working people; exclusive government control of all uses of nuclear power; and United Nations control of atomic weapons. Although none of these proposals became law until the civil rights legislation of the 1960s, they articulated the working-class hopes that were soon to be snuffed out by the Cold War and channeled into the consumerism of the 1950s.[63]

Even more formidable was the rising tide of national independence struggles, which swept across the war-weakened empires of Britain, France and the Netherlands. General strikes in Nigeria and Sierra Leone, armed struggles in the Philippines and declarations of independence by Indonesia and Vietnam challenged Winston Churchill's reassurance that the principles of the Atlantic Charter applied only to Europe. Although the Cold War left its ugly and all-too-often bloody imprint on the Third World's experience of independence, it could not halt the process of decolonization. The independence of India and Pakistan in 1947, the Bandung Conference of 1955 and the independence of Ghana two years later signaled the demise of the colonial empires which had appeared to be invincible half a century earlier.[64] Faced with the revolt against colonialism, the political and intellectual leaders of the United States repudiated the ideology of white supremacy that had guided empire- and state-building at the turn of the century. Anti-colonial movements and the appeal of Soviet communism in nations which the United States sought to incorporate into its political and economic orbit, campaigns by African Americans in all parts of the country against both legal and *de facto* discrimination and the decisive role of urban political coalitions in presidential elections produced executive orders, court rulings and ultimately legislation, which prohibited racial discrimination and made verbal commitment to racial equality a crucial component of the "liberal consensus." By the end of the 1950s the hegemonic discourse castigated openly racist arguments as archaic and parochial.

In 1948, the very year the electoral triumph of Daniel Malan's Nationalists secured the future of apartheid in South Africa for more than four decades to come, the Democratic Party in the United States committed itself to a comprehensive program of civil rights. Strom Thurmond's Dixiecrats, who left the party, protesting (quite accurately) that it had betrayed its historic commitment to white supremacy, initiated years of forceful but ultimately futile "interposition" by Southern state governments against federal desegregation efforts. Neither that defensive effort nor the widespread popular support that bolstered the presidential campaigns of Alabama's George Wallace in 1964, 1968 and 1972, however, could restore the open celebration of white supremacy to the honoured status in national and international political discourse that it had enjoyed in the heyday of Woodrow Wilson and Jan Christian Smuts.[65]

The war and postwar years initiated a remarkable racial recomposition of the working class in both the United States and Britain. During the war the Depression's homogenizing effect on America's industrial labour force was reversed. Over the ensuing three decades a veritable depopulation of the Southern countryside made African Americans one of the most urbanized segments of the population. By the 1970s they constituted more than 20 percent of the country's manufacturing and service workers. As their numbers in industry grew, so did their demands for access to more skilled jobs and to union leadership. Moreover, the doors to immigration had by then once again been partially opened. Immigrants from Asia and Latin America arrived in numbers that surpassed those of European newcomers in the late nineteenth century. The gradual shift of union leaders from support of the racial privileges of white members to endorsement of their newer members' demands and actions, which Satnam Virdee has found in England between the 1950s and 1970s, has a familiar ring to observers of the corresponding experience in the United States. By the elections of 1964 and 1968 major unions in the United States had come to identify George Wallace's appeal to their white members as a menace to the unions' own futures, which had to be combated vigorously, for the sake of the unions' political alliance with the Democratic Party and liberal organizations.[66]

Almost a century after the Liberal landslide of 1906, therefore, imperialism has assumed a very different shape from the one that was congealing at that time. One sphere of influence encompasses the globe, "unleashing market forces" is its watchword, workers' movements have been humbled within the most highly industrialized countries, and the Soviet revolution is gone. Racism has simultaneously become the target of almost universal verbal condemnation and assumed an increasingly formidable presence in social and political practice. In former colonies state-building has become the preeminent concern, circumscribing both the space allowed workers' movements and economic policies. The most eminent intellectuals have repudiated their earlier faith in public control of economic life and staked their hopes for social improvement on profit-making enterprise. Even Jamaica's Michael Manley confessed before his death:

> I kept thinking that you could make the world economy submit to a system of political management to safeguard against injustice and inequity. I didn't realize the forces of production are too powerful, and their inherent logic too irresistible, to be made subservient to political barriers on a permanent basis.[67]

In short, at the end of the century of the colour bar the dialogue of race and class has not been resolved, but it is being subsumed into new forms of domination and conflict. But we mistake the nature of both past and future social struggle if we relegate the study of exploitation and class struggles to the historians' dustbin. To take that course is to write the past in the image of the shopping-mall present, to accept the new world order as natural and inevitable, and to close our eyes to the classification of race. It is also to ignore the boiling discontent of subordinated races and classes, which will make the new world empire's triumphal free marketism even more short lived than the political barriers that the Great Powers erected a century ago.[68]

Notes

Reprinted courtesy of Palgrave-Macmillan Press and Springer/Nature Publishers.

1. Howard Lamar, "From Bondage to Contract: Ethnic Labor in the American West, 1600–1890," in *The Countryside in the Age of Capitalist Transformation: Essays in the Social History of Rural America*, eds. Steven Hahn and Jonathan Prude (Chapel Hill and London, 1985), 293–324.

2. David Montejano, *Anglos and Mexicans in the Making of Texas, 1836–1986* (Austin, 1987), 7; Laura Tabili, *"We Ask for British Justice": Workers and Racial Difference in Late Imperial Britain* (Ithaca and London, 1994).

3. Sylvia Frey, *Water from the Rock: Black Resistance in a Revolutionary Age* (Princeton, 1991); W. Jeffrey Bolster, *Black Jacks: African American Seamen in the Age of Sail* (Cambridge, MA and London, 1997), 105–6. See also C.L.R. James, *The Black Jacobins: Toussaint L'Ouverture and the San Domingo Revolution* (New York, 1963); David B. Davis, *The Problem of Slavery in the Age of Revolution, 1770–1823* (Ithaca and London, 1975).

4. Herman Melville, *Redburn, His First Voyage* (Anchor Books Edition, Garden City, New York, 1957), 96. The destructive potential of this fantasy for both races is explored carefully in John A. McClure, *Kipling and Conrad: The Colonial Fiction* (Cambridge, MA and London, 1981). Similarly, Japanese American nationalists assured fellow inmates in the Manzanar concentration camp during the Second World War that after the war there would "be plenty of opportunity in Malaya, East Indies and Australia where you'll be able to live like kings." Brian Masaru Hayashi, *"For the Sake of Our Japanese Brethren": Assimilation, Nationalism, and Protestantism among the Japanese of Los Angeles, 1895–1942* (Stanford, California, 1995), 144.

5. McClure, *Kipling and Conrad*, 90; Carolyn Brown, "Becoming 'Men,' Becoming 'Workers': Race, Gender and Workplace Struggle in the Nigerian Coal Industry, 1938–1948" (unpublished paper, presented at Racializing Class, Classifying Race—A Conference on Labour and Difference in Africa, USA and Britain, St. Anthony's College, University of Oxford), 11–13 July 1997. See also the brief but vivid description of colonists' pretensions in Benedict Anderson, *Imagined Communities: Reflections on the Origin and Spread of Nationalism* (London and New York, 1983), 137–39.

6. Emile Vandervelde, "Die Sozialdemokratie und das Kolonial Problem," II: "Die belgischen Sozialisten und die Congofrage," *Die Neue Zeit* 27 (1909), quoted in Preben Kaarsholm, "The South African War and the Response of the International Socialist Community to Imperialism between 1896 and 1908," in Frits van Holthoon and Marcel van der Linden, eds., *Internationalism in the Labour Movement, 1830–1940* (2 vols., Leiden, 1988), I, 62. My translation from Vandervelde's German text.

7. W.E.B. Du Bois, *Souls of Black Folk: Essays and Sketches* (Premier Americana edition, Greenwich, Conn., 1961), 23.

8. Thomas C. Holt, *The Problem of Freedom: Race, Labor, and Politics in Jamaica and Britain, 1832–1938* (Baltimore, 1992), xix.

9. Eric J. Hobsbawm, *Industry and Empire: The Making of Modern English Society, 1750 to the Present Day* (New York, 1968), 171; Brinley Thomas, *Migration and Economic Growth, A Study of Great Britain and the Atlantic Economy* (Cambridge, Mass., 1954); Paul A. Baran and Paul M. Sweezy, *Monopoly Capital: An Essay on the American Economic and Social Order* (New York and London, 1966), 90–108; W.E.B. Du Bois, *Color and Democracy: Colonies and Peace* (New York, 1945), 17.

10. The political scientist Ernest W. Burgess worried that the industrial city nurtured "areas of demoralization, or promiscuity, and of vice." Like many of his peers,

he proposed segregation as the remedy, because "segregation offers the group, and thereby individuals who compose the group, a place and role in the total organization of city life. Segregation limits development in certain directions, but releases it in others." Ernest W. Burgess, "The Growth of the City: An Introduction to a Research Project," in *The City*, eds. Robert E. Park, Ernest W. Burgess and Roderick D. McKenzie (Chicago, 1967. First published 1926), 59.

11. Karl Polanyi, *The Great Transformation* (New York and Toronto, 1944), 3; the Burrows Report, quoted in Dilip Simeon, "Coal and Colonialism: Production Relations in an Indian Coalfield, c. 1895–1947," *International Review of Social History* 41 Supplement 4 (1996), 106.

12. E.G. Maurice Bruce, *The Coming of the Welfare State* (London, 1961), 133–96; T.H. Marshall and Tom Bottomore, *Citizenship and Social Class* (London and Concord, Mass., 1992). It is fashionable among critical legal historians, if misleading, to depict this moment as one of fundamental divergence between the labor movements of Britain and the United States. See, for example, William E. Forbath, *Law and the Shaping of the American Labor Movement* (Cambridge, Mass., 1991); Victoria C. Hattam, *Labor Visions and State Power: The Origins of Business Unionism in the United States* (Princeton, NJ, 1993).

13. Henry Pelling, "The Working Class and the Origins of the Welfare State," in Pelling, *Popular Politics and Society in Late Victorian Britain* (London, 1968), 1–18, and "British Labour and British Imperialism," in *ibid.*, 98. Pelling adds that efforts by Conservatives to counteract this sentiment by denouncing the immigration of Jews from Russia into England attracted few workers' votes outside London's East End. Joseph L. White discusses the weakness of the Liberal-Labour appeal to Lancashire cotton workers in *The Limits of Trade Union Militancy: The Lancashire Textile Workers, 1910–1914* (Westport, Conn., and London, 1978), 146–61.

14. Pelling, *Popular Politics and Society*, 17; John W. Cell, *The Highest Stage of White Supremacy: The Origins of Segregation in South Africa and the American South* (Cambridge and New York, 1982), 266–67; C. Vann Woodward, *Tom Watson, Agrarian Rebel* (New York, 1938); Elliott Rudwick, *Race Riot at East St. Louis, July 2, 1917* (New York, 1972); Nell Irvin Painter, *Standing at Armageddon: The United States, 1877–1919* (New York and London, 1987), 278–79. Paul H. Buck hailed this epoch as the final healing of the wounds of Civil War. Buck, *The Road to Reunion, 1886–1900* (New York, 1937), 294–320.

15. Shula Marks and Stanley Trapido, "Lord Milner and the South African State," *History Workshop* 8, no. 3 (1979), 50–80. The quotation is on p. 55.

16. *Ibid.*, 58–65, 73; Saul Dubow, "Colonial Nationalism, the Milner Kindergarten and the Rise of 'South Africanism,' 1902–1910," *History Workshop Journal* 43, no. 2 (1997), 58. Dubow, *Segregation and the Origins of Apartheid in South Africa* (London, 1989).

17. Quoted in Holt, 332.

18. Quoted in Marks and Trapido, 66. This perspective informed the work of the Transvaal Indigency Commission. See Dubow, "Colonial Nationalism," 65. It was shared by champions of the all-white textile industry in America's New South.

See Alan Tullos, *Habits of Industry: White Culture and the Transformation of the Carolina Piedmont* (Chapel Hill, NC, 1989).

19. Cell, 64–81; Jeremy Kirkler, "The Inner Mechanisms of a Racial Massacre"; Dunbar Moodie, "Profitability, Respectability and Challenge: (Re)gaining Control and Restructuring the Labour Process While Maintaining Racial Order on the South African Gold Mines, 1913–1922"; Deborah Posel, "The Office of van der Merwe: The Politics of Patronage and Labour Relations in the Apartheid Civil Service"; Eric Arnesen, "The Death Knell of Jim Crow Unionism? Race, Law and Railroad Labor in Mid-Twentieth Century America" (all presented at the conference, Racializing Class, Classifying Race). In the United States government officials who had crushed the railway strike of 1922 were also repudiated at the polls, opening the way to the act of 1926. Colin J. Davis, *Power at Odds: The 1922 National Railroad Shopmen's Strike* (Urbana, Ill., 1997); David Montgomery, *The Fall of the House of Labor: The Workplace, the State, and American Labor Activism, 1865–1925* (Cambridge and New York, 1987), 435–37.

20. Eric Foner, *Nothing But Freedom: Emancipation and its Legacy* (Baton Rouge and London, 1983), 29–38; Holt, 156; Cell, 215–19; Charles van Onselen, *Studies in the Social and Economic History of the Witwatersrand, 1886–1914* (2 vols., Harlow, 1982), I, 1–24, II, 1–110.

21. Holt, 156–63; Jeanne Boydston, *Home and Work: Housework, Wages, and the Ideology of Labor in the Early Republic* (New York and Oxford, 1990), 142–63.

22. Theodore Rosengarten, *All God's Dangers: The Life of Nate Shaw* (New York, 1974); Bose quoted in Samita Sen, "Unsettling the Household: Act VI (of 1901) and the Regulation of Women Migrants in Colonial Bengal," *International Review of Social History* 41 Supplement 4 (1996), 135. See also Julie Saville, *The Work of Reconstruction: From Slave to Wage Labor in South Carolina, 1860–1870* (Cambridge and New York, 1994), 130.

23. Allen Isaacman and Richard Roberts, eds., *Cotton, Colonialism, and Social History in Sub-Saharan Africa* (Portsmouth, NH, 1995); John Higginson, *A Working Class in the Making: Belgian Colonial Labor Policy, Private Enterprise, and the African Mineworker, 1907–1951* (Madison, Wisc., 1989), 107–8; Robert Shenton, review of Isaacman and Roberts, *International Labor and Working-Class History* 51:1 (1997), 256.

24. W. Kloosterboer, *Involuntary Labour Since the Abolition of Slavery: A Survey of Compulsory Labour throughout the World* (Leiden, 1960), 194, 67; Frederick Cooper, *From Slaves to Squatters: Plantation Labor and Agriculture in Zanzibar and Coastal Kenya, 1890–1925* (New Haven and London, 1980); Alex Lichtenstein, *Twice the Work of Free Labor: The Political Economy of Convict Labor in the New South* (London and New York, 1996); Karin A. Shapiro, "The Tennessee Coal Miners' Revolts of 1891–92: Industrialization, Politics, and Convict Labor in the Late Nineteenth-Century South" (PhD dissertation, Yale University, 1991); Daniel Letwin, *The Challenge of Interracial Unionism: Alabama Coal Miners, 1878–1921* (Chapel Hill, NC, 1997); Daphne Simon, "Master and Servant," in *Democracy and the Labor Movement*, ed. John Saville (London, 1954), 160–200; David Montgomery, *Citizen Worker: The*

Experience of Workers in the United States with Democracy and the Free Market during the Nineteenth Century (New York and Cambridge, 1993), 25–51. Charles van Onselen suggests that master-servant law was applied by Johannesburg magistrates primarily against whites, and with light sanctions, while pass laws provided the draconian sanctions against Africans. Van Onselen, II, 34–35.

25. Dilip Simeon, "Coal and Colonialism: Production Relations in an Indian Coalfield, c. 1895–1947," *International Review of Social History* 41 Supplement 4 (1996), 83–108. The quotations are on pp. 89 and 103, with italics in the original. See McClure, 28–29 on the celebration of the "true India" by Orientalists in the British elite. White American steam shovel and crane operators on the Panama Canal advised Samuel Gompers that black Jamaican laborers were unfit for an eight-hour day. T.J. Dolan to S. Gompers, 6 September 1906, quoted in Julia Greene, "The Strike at the Ballot Box: Politics and Partisanship in the American Federation of Labor" (PhD dissertation, Yale University, 1990), 249.

26. Tabili, *We Ask for British Justice*, 162–66; Holt, 387–91.

27. Frantz Fanon, *The Wretched of the Earth*, translated by Constance Farrington (New York, 1968), 118–28.

28. Quoted in Holt, 262.

29. Anderson, *Imagined Communities*, 136.

30. Quoted in Evelyn Brooks Higginbotham, "African-American Women's History and the Metalanguage of Race," *Signs* 17, no. 1 (1992), 267.

31. *Ibid.*, 255.

32. Holt, 295–302.

33. Du Bois, "The Black North," quoted in Kevin K. Gaines, *Uplifting the Race: Black Leadership, Politics, and Culture in the Twentieth Century* (Chapel Hill, NC, and London, 1996), 165. Cf. Du Bois's declaration of 1888: "Bismark was my hero." The Chancellor's mastery of the process that created a nation "out of a mass of bickering peoples . . . foreshadowed in my mind the kind of thing that American Negroes must do." Quoted in Paul Gilroy, *The Black Atlantic: Modernity and Double Consciousness* (Cambridge, Mass., 1993), 35.

34. Gaines, 75, 158.

35. E.P. Thompson, *The Making of the English Working Class* (New York, 1966), 10. James E. Cronin argues that the methodological distance between Thompson's work and that of Gareth Stedman Jones, Joan Scott and other advocates of the linguistic turn has been exaggerated by the latter. Cronin, "Neither Exceptional nor Peculiar: Towards the Comparative Study of Labor in Advanced Society," *International Review of Social History* 38 (1993), 59–75, note 10. A particularly perceptive scrutiny of "narratives" can be found in James Gray Pope, "Labor's Constitution of Freedom," *The Yale Law Journal* 106 (1997), 941–1031.

36. Aileen S. Kraditor, *The Radical Persuasion: Aspects of the Intellectual History and the Historiography of Three American Radical Organizations* (Baton Rouge and London, 1981), 297–321.

37. Robin D.G. Kelley, "'We Are Not What We Seem': Rethinking Black Working-Class Opposition in the Jim Crow South," *Journal of American History* 80, no.

1 (1993), 84, 86; Tera W. Hunter, *To 'Joy My Freedom: Southern Black Women's Lives and Labors after the Civil War* (Cambridge, Mass., and London, 1997), 168–86. See also Gilroy, 75–85.

38. Earl Lewis, *In Their Own Interests: Race, Class, and Power in Twentieth-Century Norfolk, Virginia* (Berkeley, 1991), 91–92.

39. The *Alltagsgeschichte* current among historians of Germany has been constructed largely around this principle. See, for example, Alf Lüdtke, "Polymorphous Synchrony: German Industrial Workers and the Politics of Everyday Life," *International Review of Social History* 38 (1993), 39–84. For an innovative study of the interaction of personal life and movement life, see Horst Groschopp, *Zwischen Bierabend und Bildungsverein: Zur Kulturarbeit in der deutschen Arbeiterbewegung von 1914* (Berlin, 1985).

40. Ira Berlin, ed., *The Black Military Experience*, Series II of *Freedom: A Documentary History of Emancipation, 1861–1867* (Cambridge and New York, 1982), 155, 154.

41. Van Onselen, II, 23–27; Alexander Irvine, *From the Bottom Up*, quoted in Kathryn J. Oberdeck, "Popular Narrative and Working-Class Identity: Alexander Irvine's Early-Twentieth-Century Literary Adventures," in Eric Arnesen, Julie Greene and Bruce Laurie, eds., *Labor Histories: Class, Politics, and the Working-Class Experience* (Urbana, Ill., 1998).

42. Bruce Nelson, "Class, Race and Democracy in the CIO: The 'New' Labor History Meets the 'Wages of Whiteness,'" *International Review of Social History* 41 (1996), 351–74. Among the pioneering works in this exploration are Alexander Saxton, *The Indispensable Enemy: Labor and the Anti-Chinese Movement in California* (Berkeley, 1971); Alexander Saxton, *The Rise and Fall of the White Republic: Class Politics and Mass Culture in Nineteenth Century America* (London and New York, 1990); Herbert Hill, "Myth-Making as Labor History: Herbert Gutman and the United Mine Workers of America," *International Journal of Politics, Culture, and Society*, 2:1 (1988), 49–127; Hill, "The Problem of Race in American Labor History," *Reviews in American History*, 24:2 (1996), 196–208; Herbert Hill and James E. Jones, Jr., eds., *Race in America: The Struggle for Equality* (Madison, Wisc., 1993); Theodore W. Allen, *The Invention of the White Race, vol. 1: Racial Oppression and Social Control* (London, 1994); Noel Ignatiev, *How the Irish Became White* (New York and London, 1995); David R. Roediger, *The Wages of Whiteness: Race and the Making of the American Working Class* (London and New York, 1991). Political implications of this development are explored by Staughton Lynd, "History, Race, and the Steel Industry," *Radical Historians Newsletter* 76:1 (1997), 1, 13–16.

43. David B. Hill diary, 16 November 1846, quoted in Paul W. Foos, "Mexican Wars: Soldiers and Society in an Age of Expansion, 1835–1855" (PhD dissertation, Yale University, 1997), 489.

44. Tabili, *We Ask for British Justice*, 1–2, 149–59. In Port Darwin, Australia dockside workers of Aborigine, Malay, Chinese, and Filipino backgrounds were supported by local unions and included in wage awards in the 1930s, provided they had been locally born.

45. Thomas J. Sugrue, "Segmented Work, Race-Conscious Workers: Structure, Agency and Division in the CIO Era," *International Review of Social History* 41 (1996), 403.

46. Richard J. Jensen, "The Causes and Cures of Unemployment in the Great Depression," *Journal of Interdisciplinary History* 19, no. 3 (1989), 553–83; Walter Licht, *Getting Work: Philadelphia, 1840–1950* (Cambridge and London 1992), 30–31, 45–46, 51–53; E. Wright Bakke, *The Unemployed Worker: A Study of the Task of Making a Living Without a Job* (New Haven, Conn., 1940), 247–48.

47. Nancy J. Weiss, *Farewell to the Party of Lincoln: Black Politics in the Age of FDR* (Princeton, NJ, 1983); Earl Lewis, *In Their Own Interests: Race, Class, and Power in Twentieth-Century Norfolk, Virginia* (Berkeley, 1991), 110–98; Joe W. Trotter and Earl Lewis, *African Americans in the Industrial Age: A Documentary History, 1915–1945* (Boston, 1996); Raymond Wolters, *Negroes and the Great Depression: The Problem of Economic Recovery* (Westport, CT, 1970); Linda Gordon, *Pitied But Not Entitled: Single Mothers and the History of Welfare, 1890–1935* (New York, 1994); Gwendolyn Mink, *Wages of Motherhood: Inequality in the Welfare State, 1917–1942* (Ithaca, 1995); David Montgomery, "Labor and the Political Leadership of New Deal America," *International Review of Social History* 39 (1994), 335–60; Eric J. Hobsbawm, *The Age of Extremes: A History of the World, 1914–1991* (New York, 1996), 85–141.

48. Sterling D. Spero and Abram L. Harris, *The Black Worker: The Negro and the Labor Movement* (New York, 1931); Dana Frank, *Purchasing Power: Consumer Organization, Gender, and the Seattle Labor Movement, 1919–1929* (Cambridge and New York, 1994); Charles H. Wesley, *Negro Labor in the United States, 1850–1925; A Study in American Economic History* (New York, 1927).

49. Eric Arnesen, "'Like Banquo's Ghost, It Will Not Down': The Race Question and the American Railroad Brotherhoods, 1880–1920," *American Historical Review*, 99:4 (1994), 1601–33; U.S. Bureau of the Census, *Historical Statistics of the United States: Colonial Times to 1970* (2 vols., Washington, DC, 1975), I, 177. (The Bureau of Labor Statistics figures showing a larger CIO membership are based on exaggerated claims.)

50. Christopher L. Tomlins, "AFL Unions in the 1930s: Their Performance in Historical Perspective," *Journal of American History* 65:4 (1979), 1021–42; Robert H. Zieger, *The CIO, 1935–1955* (Chapel Hill and London, 1995); Michael K. Honey, *Southern Labor and Black Civil Rights: Organizing Memphis Workers* (Urbana, 1993); Steve Rosswurm, ed., *The CIO's Left-led Unions* (New Brunswick, NJ, 1992); Jacquelyn Dowd Hall, et al., *Like a Family: The Making of a Southern Cotton Mill World* (Chapel Hill and London, 1987).

51. James D. Rose, "Shop Floor Representation without a Union: Skilled Workers, US Steel, and the Employee Representation Plan during the 1930s" (unpublished paper, quoted by permission of the author); Nelson Lichtenstein, *The Most Dangerous Man in Detroit: Walter Reuther and the Fate of American Labor* (New York, 1995), 47–131; Prudence Cumberbatch, "For Liberty and Victory: Blacks, Unions, and the Bethlehem Company, 1937–1945" (unpublished seminar paper, Yale University, 1993); Peter Gottlieb, *Making Their Own Way: Southern Blacks'*

Migration to Pittsburgh, 1916–30 (Urbana, 1987); Dennis C. Dickerson, *Out of the Crucible: Black Steelworkers in Western Pennsylvania, 1875–1980* (Albany, 1986).

52. Thomas J. Sugrue, "Segmented Work, Race-Conscious Workers: Structure, Agency and Division in the CIO Era," *International Review of Social History* 41 (1996), 402; Sugrue, "Crabgrass-Roots Politics: Race, Rights, and the Reaction against Liberalism in the Urban North, 1940–1964," *Journal of American History* 82:3 (1995), 551–78; Zaragosa Vargas, *Proletarians of the North: A History of Mexican Industrial Workers in Detroit and the Midwest, 1917–1933* (Berkeley, 1993).

53. Sugrue, "Segmented Work," 403; Sugrue, "The Structures of Urban Poverty: The Reorganization of Space and Work in Three Periods of American History," in Michael B. Katz, ed., *The "Underclass" Debate: Views from History* (Princeton, 1993), 111–12; John T. McGreevy, *Parish Boundaries: The Catholic Encounter with Race in the Twentieth Century Urban North* (Chicago and London, 1996). McGreevy also reminds us: "Simply invoking the talisman of "class" to explain racial tension . . . is inadequate," he argued. "Even the most working-class Catholic neighbourhoods contained a core of physicians, lawyers, city government officials, and police officers, and Catholics were significantly more likely than white Protestants or Jews to structure social networks along religious, and not simply occupational, lines" (107). The contrast between white workers' emphasis on class on the job and on race in defining neighborhoods is a central theme of David Halle, *America's Working Man: Work, Home, and Politics among Blue Collar Property Owners* (Chicago and London, 1984).

54. Rick Halpern, *Down on the Killing Floor: Black and White Workers in Chicago's Packinghouses, 1904–1954* (Urbana, Ill., 1997); Roger Horowitz, *"Negro and White, Unite and Fight!" A Social History of Industrial Unionism in Meatpacking, 1930–90* (Urbana, Ill., 1997); Shelton Stromquist, *Solidarity and Survival: An Oral History of Iowa Labor in the Twentieth Century* (Iowa City, 1993). The figures on black packinghouse workers in Chicago are from Catherine Lewis, "Trade Union Policies with Regard to the Negro in the Slaughtering and Meatpacking Industry in Chicago" (MA thesis, University of Chicago, 1946), 74–77.

55. Lizabeth Cohen, *Making a New Deal: Industrial Workers in Chicago, 1919–1939* (Cambridge and New York, 1990), 323–60; Michael Denning, *The Cultural Front: The Laboring of American Culture in the Twentieth Century* (London and New York, 1996), 126–36.

56. Barbara D. Savage, "Broadcasting Freedom: Radio, War, and the Roots of Civil Rights Liberalism, 1938–1948" (PhD dissertation, Yale University, 1995); McGreevy, *Parish Boundaries*, 34. For all its limitations, this representation contrasted sharply with the Amos 'n' Andy image and brought to the networks representations of black America advised and written by black intellectuals. Cf. the critique of Warren Sussman, *Culture as History: The Transformation of American Society in the Twentieth Century* (New York, 1984), 80, 205–12.

57. This discussion and what follows is based, unless otherwise indicated, on Nadia Venturini, *Neri e italiani ad Harlem: Gli anni Trenta e la guerra d'Etopia* (Rome, 1990). See also William R. Scott, *The Sons of Sheba's Race: African Americans*

and the Italo-Ethiopian War, 1935–1941 (Bloomington, Ind., 1993); Joseph E. Harris, *African-American Reactions to the War in Ethiopia, 1936–1941* (Baton Rouge, La., 1994). In 1895 black workers in Sao Paulo, who were being displaced by Italian immigrants, had clashed sharply with the newcomers over Italy's earlier invasion of Ethiopia. George Reid Andrews, "Black Workers in the Export Years: Latin America, 1880–1930," *International Labor and Working-Class History* 51: 1 (1997), 13, 19.

58. Quoted in Venturini, 138. My free translation.

59. Renqiu Yu, *To Save China: To Save Ourselves: The Chinese Hand Laundry Alliance of New York* (Philadelphia, 1992); Judy Yung, *Unbound Feet: A Social History of Chinese Women in San Francisco* (Berkeley, 1995), 209–22; John J. Bukowczyk, *And My Children Did Not Know Me: A History of the Polish-Americans* (Bloomington, 1987), 80–89; Margaret Collingwood Nowak, *Two Who Were There: A Biography of Stanley Nowak* (Detroit, 1989); Mario T. Garcia, *Mexican Americans: Leadership, Ideology, and Identity, 1930–1960* (New Haven and London, 1989), 145–86; Mario T. Garcia, *Memories of Chicano History: The Life and Narrative of Bert Corona* (Berkeley, 1994), 59–66, 94–96.

60. See Allan Sekula, *Fish Story* (Dusseldorf, 1995).

61. John Riddell, ed., *To See the Dawn: Baku, 1920—First Congress of the Peoples of the East* (New York and London, 1993), 68, 72, 49.

62. James R. Hooker, *Black Revolutionary: George Padmore's Path from Communism to Pan-Africanism* (New York, 1967), 18–28; Penny M. von Eschen, *Race against Empire: Black Americans and Anticolonialism, 1937–1957* (Ithaca and London, 1997), 48–52; Tabili, *We Ask for British Justice*, 158–59; Bruce Nelson, *Workers on the Waterfront: Seamen, Longshoremen, and Unionism in the 1930s* (Urbana, Ill., 1988), 1–38; Fernando Morais, *Olga: A Vida de Olga Bernario Prestes, Judia Communista Entregue a Hitler pelo Governo Vargas* (Sao Paulo, 1986), 202–32.

63. "What Are We Fighting For?" *Steel Labor*, 28 May 1943, pp. 6–7; *Final Proceedings of the Eighth Constitutional Convention of the Congress of Industrial Organizations, November 18, 19, 20, 21, 22, 1946, Atlantic City, New Jersey* (n.p., n.d.), 36–43, 59–60, 73–87; Georges Gurvitch, *The Bill of Social Rights* (New York, 1946).

64. Von Eschen, *Race Against Empire*, passim.

65. John Egerton, *Speak Now against the Day: The Generation before the Civil Rights Movement in the South* (New York, 1994), 471–512; Dan T. Carter, *The Politics of Rage: George Wallace, The Origins of the New Conservatism, and the Transformation of American Politics* (New York, 1995).

66. Satnam Virdee, "Racism and Resistance in British Trade Unions, 1948–1979," in Peter Alexander and Rick Halpern, eds., *Racializing Class, Classifying Race: Labour and Difference in Britain, the USA, and Africa* (New York, 2000), 122–49.

67. Obituary for Michael Manley, *New York Times*, 8 March 1997.

68. See James Petras, "Latin America: The Resurgence of the Left," *New Left Review* 223:1 (1997), 17–47; *NACLA Report on the Americas*, 30 July/August, 1997).

CHAPTER 16

Workers' Movements in the United States Confront Imperialism

The Progressive Era Experience

From *Journal of the Gilded Age & Progressive Era* 7:1 (Jan. 2008): 7–42

Summary

In 1898, the American Federation of Labor feared that colonial expansion would militarize the republic and undermine the living standards of American workers.[1] Subsequent expansion of industrial production and of trade union membership soon replaced the fear of imperial expansion with an eagerness to enlarge the domain of American unions internationally alongside that of American business. In both Puerto Rico and Canada important groups of workers joined AFL unions on their own initiative. In Mexico, where major U.S. investments shaped the economy, anarcho-syndicalists enjoyed strong support on both sides of the border, and the path to union growth was opened by revolution. Consequently, the AFL forged links there with a labor movement very different from itself. Unions in Mexico became tightly linked to their new government, while World War I drove the AFL's leaders into close collaboration with their own. The Pan-American Federation of Labor was more a product of diplomatic maneuvering than of class solidarity.

During the last forty years, historians of the labor movement in the United States have focused their attention on the local places of work and residence. Rightly so. We have learned much about our social and political life from such studies. Nevertheless, at no point during the twentieth century could union or socialist movements ignore the *global* economic networks that shaped workers' lives. By 1900, the handful of countries in North America and Europe that accounted for more than 85 percent of the world's manufacturing output had effectively divided the rest of humanity into their respective spheres of influence and colonies. Moreover, some 55 million Europeans and more than 30 million people from India, China, and Java had migrated overseas between 1820 and 1920. Most of them traveled on shipping lines built by countries competing for world power, and most of them went, temporarily or permanently, to destinations where the Great Powers needed their labor.[2]

When leaders of trade unions and socialist parties in Europe and North America discussed the economic transformation of the globe taking place around 1900 before their very eyes, they couched issues in terms of the impact on *domestic* affairs: the use of soldiers from the ranks of the poor (especially conscripts) in colonial wars, naval construction, the rising tax burden, and migration (or the perceived threat of migration) from and to the colonies. The wars and rumors of war in Asia, Africa, and the Middle East from 1894 to 1904 greatly intensified these concerns and produced innumerable cartoons of workers staggering under the burden of cannons and warships.[3] The 1900 May Day Manifesto of the International Socialist Bureau highlighted these issues: "It is war all over the globe. War budgets rise and rise . . . More is spent on rifles, cannons, barracks, ships than is paid in wages to millions of workers; millions of men are put under arms, to massacre, to destroy, to burn, to steal, to kill."[4]

The purpose of this essay is to consider how the questions of war and empire looked to activists in U.S. labor organizations. Although the press and individual members of the Socialist Party and the Industrial Workers of the World (IWW) frequently devoted attention to workers' struggles in other lands, it was the American Federation of Labor (AFL) that most actively acquired members outside the boundaries of the United States and involved itself directly in the country's foreign affairs (at least until the antiwar campaigns of the Socialist Party after 1914).[5] Around 1900, the AFL was highly critical of the expansionist policies of the U.S. government. Fewer than twenty years later it had come not only to support those policies, but also even to participate actively in their execution—though in the case of Mexico often also urging Woodrow Wilson's administration to pursue particular courses of action. In very important ways, actions taken by AFL leaders were responding to those of the socialists and the IWW as well as to the domestic and international upsurge in worker support for direct action, sympathetic strikes, and all-inclusive organization, of which the IWW was but the highly visible tip of the iceberg. Moreover, not all these initiatives and developments originated in the United States by any means. We must also consider the actions of workers in countries that were targets of U.S. investment and colonization. I will devote special attention to the influence on the AFL of workers in Canada, Puerto Rico, and Mexico.

The American Federation of Labor had been more categorically opposed to the annexation of colonies in 1900 than were most European socialist and labor parties and the International Socialist Bureau. To be sure, AFL convention delegates had resolved their "hearty sympathy" with Cubans fighting for "the right of self-government" in 1896.[6] Going to war against Spain was another matter, however: In 1898, most of the labor and socialist press warned against a resort to arms.[7]

Labor's sympathy for Cubans was tempered by fear of war and militarism, echoing that often expressed by the Socialist International. Both the regular army and state national guards had been called out to break strikes again and again during the 1890s. Troops suppressing the Coeur d'Alene, Homestead, and Pullman strikes had attracted national attention, while the 1897 massacre of Slavic strikers at Lattimer Mines, Pennsylvania, and the 1898 confrontations at Virden and Pana, Illinois, coincided with the Federation's convention debates about war and imperialism. AFL president Samuel Gompers had declared back in 1892 that "membership in a labor organization and the militia at one and the same time is inconsistent and incompatible."[8]

Early in 1899, Gompers went so far as to "look forward to the time" when workers would enforce peace, if diplomats failed to do so, "by the dock laborers refusing to handle goods that are to be used to destroy their fellow men, and by the seamen of the world, united in one organization, while willing to risk their lives in conducting the commerce of nations, absolutely refusing to strike down their fellow men." In 1916 he would explicitly repudiate those words.[9]

The end of the short war of 1898 and the prospect of annexing the Philippines and Puerto Rico reopened the whole discussion. Gompers made a widely publicized speech to the Chicago Peace Jubilee, in which he warned:

> There is even now a strife going on among the nations of the earth for the partition and possession of Eastern countries. Let us take the Philippines, and we shall be in the midst of the conflicts. We shall have to follow the monarchical policy of large standing armies, with immense navies . . . [and] we will come to that point against which the genius of our institutions revolts—compulsory military duty.[10]

Within days of the signing of the Treaty of Paris ending the Spanish-American War in December 1898, delegates to the AFL convention adopted a resolution ardently opposing the "new and far-reaching policy, commonly known as 'imperialism' or 'expansion,'" which "if ratified by the United States Senate will . . . seriously threaten the perpetuity of our Republic."[11]

Three features of the AFL's 1898 debate are worth noting. First, the only negative interventions came from delegates who were social democrats. The socialist leader from Cleveland, Max Hayes, argued that the controversy over imperial expansion had been invented by politicians and plutocrats, and that trade unionists should have "nothing to do with it." They should instead concentrate their efforts on creating a cooperative commonwealth. Despite their objections, however, the socialists did not vote against the resolution.[12]

Second, both Gompers, in an earlier address to a National Conference on Foreign Policy, and most delegates who took the floor during the convention debate emphasized the danger of annexing lands populated by "servile races" and "a semi-barbaric population." The prospects of massive migrations of Filipinos and Chinese into the continental United States as well as the competition from goods produced in colonies haunted the discussion. Delegate John Kirby of a federal labor union in Ouray, Colorado, expressed his opposition to the recent annexation of Hawaii: "We cannot elevate the inhabitants to our standard, but will drag our people down to their level. If the products of those countries are brought in, it will remove our products from competition." Stuart Reid of the International Association of Machinists drew on the experience of his native British Isles: "The people of India did interfere with our movement: machinery was shipped to that country and coolies were put to work, and as a result reduced the wages below a living standard."[13]

More than one historian has argued that racist hostility toward immigrants and peoples of color explains the unions' foreign policy stance.[14] That explanation contains an important element of truth, but it is inadequate to account for the evolving policies of the labor movement. Racism flourished on both sides of the debates about imperialism and trade unionism. Consider Harrison Gray Otis, editor of the *Los Angeles Times*, who had invested heavily in land and development in both Southern California and Mexico. He crusaded relentlessly in his highly influential newspaper against *both* Chinese immigrants and labor unions. Otis had proudly served as a brigadier-general in charge of volunteers who battled the independence fighters of the Philippines, and he subsequently cultivated in print the ominous image of Chinese, Japanese, and Mexicans blended into the "Bronze Menace," against which white Americans had to stand guard. While keeping ever in mind the formidable influence of white racism in the labor movements of the United States, Canada, and Europe, we must look elsewhere for an adequate explanation of AFL policies regarding empire. As Barbara Fields has pointed out, racist arguments have often been marshaled on all conflicting sides of debates over economic and political policies.[15]

Third, the National Business League had sponsored the Peace Jubilee where Gompers had made his famous speech.[16] When Gompers joined the newly formed Anti-Imperialist League late in 1898, so did Andrew Carnegie, Edward Atkinson, Henry Villard, George F. Peabody, and former president Benjamin Harrison.[17] Moreover, as will be argued below, the National Civic Federation, which brought business and union leaders together in quest of common interests, became an important theater for discussion of overseas colonies and commerce.

Indeed, both the arguments advanced against the annexation of colonies and those in favor of the policy have a familiar ring in the twenty-first century.

Opponents contended that capital would flow to the colonies, where it would be possible to fabricate products so cheaply that they would undercut jobs and wages in the United States. As Gompers often put it, living standards could be raised only by manufacturing goods at home for consumption by workers who were motivated by the expectations of "civilized" men and women and paid union wages.[18] Joining the battle for empire would bring no benefits for American workers, but only burden them with taxes, oligarchic rule, resurgent immigrant contract labor, and incessant calls to arms.

Champions of imperialism replied that colonies would provide markets to absorb the domestic overproduction. Colonies would also increase the United States' access to raw materials and food products and lower the cost of living. All the while, racially defined immigration policies and enforcement of laws against contract labor could make it possible to restrain residents of the colonies from moving to the United States. And indeed, the Supreme Court ruled in 1901 in the so-called Insular Cases that the constitution does *not* follow the flag.[19] Moreover, William Randolph Hearst, whose newspapers were read avidly by many workers, vigorously opposed Gompers on the question of colonies. Hearst argued that the troops needed to hold colonies would probably be provided mainly by "natives of the islands," while imperial expansion would create career opportunities for American workers who "have brains, energy and a determination to be something more prosperous than a day laborer."[20] The famous naval theoretician A. T. Mahan added that no country that wished to survive as a great power in the modern world could stay out of the race for colonies. He warned that continued adherence to the ideals of Jeffersonian democracy would prove fatal to America in an age when the Great Powers were redrawing the political and economic map of the world.[21]

During the opening years of the twentieth century, it seemed that these conflicting arguments were being reconciled. The diplomatic historian William Appleman Williams and his followers have persuasively singled out two defining features of an emerging consensus on foreign policy. First, as a review of the world's commerce, published by the U.S. State Department in 1899, argued: "The enlargement of foreign consumption of the products of our mills and workshops has . . . become a serious problem of statesmanship."[22]

Moreover, the attention of American business and the U.S. government then focused on the Western Hemisphere. Consequently, it was easy to understand why Secretary of State Richard Olney had proclaimed in 1895, in regard to the Americas: "Today the United States is practically sovereign on this continent, and its fiat is law upon the subjects to which it confines its interposition."[23] Around 1900, 50 percent of this country's direct investments abroad were placed in Latin America—overwhelmingly in Mexico—and another 33 percent were in Canada.[24] Although the investments in Mexico were concentrated in ranch lands, railroads, petroleum, and minerals, the $175 million of U.S.

capital invested in Canada at the time went not only into timber and minerals, but also heavily into manufacturing. General Electric, Westinghouse, National Cash Register, and American Asbestos were among those who had established branch plants north of the border.[25] As Gregory S. Kealey has argued, the industrial upsurge at the turn of the century "combined with Canada's high tariff wall and preferential access to British empire markets to create the world's first major branch plant economy."[26] Small wonder some of the same business leaders who had joined Gompers in the Anti-Imperialist League simultaneously promoted the cause of closer ties between what they called the Anglo-Saxon nations of North America.[27]

As if to quiet Gompers' fears for the home economy, the United States enjoyed spectacular industrial growth, as did Western Europe and Russia. The French economist Leon Dupriez has calculated that the average annual increase in physical output per capita for the advanced industrial countries as a group between 1895 and 1913 was double what it had been from 1880 to 1894. The United States, which had already emerged during the 1880s as the world's leading producer of manufactured goods, increased its output even more rapidly than its leading rivals, England, Germany, and France. Not only was immigration increasing America's labor force rapidly, output per worker was growing even faster.[28]

Even more important for the AFL, between 1897 and 1904 trade union membership in the United States had more than *quadrupled*, growing from 440,000 to 2,067,000—in percentage terms the greatest upward leap in U.S. history. The proportion of workers in private industry who belonged to unions in early 1904 was greater than it is today. And the AFL had for the first time consolidated its position as the country's dominant labor organization—encompassing 81 percent of all union members.[29]

Trade union resurgence after 1897 also stimulated widespread public discussion of possible ways to make America's industrial relations less bloody. Among many related developments was the formation of the National Civic Federation, through which prominent corporate leaders met with AFL officials in quest of possible terms of peaceful contractual coexistence between labor and capital. In my opinion, these discussions had precious little effect on actual industrial practice.[30] But they *did* provide an important forum in which business and union leaders discussed foreign and colonial policy.

There were also thousands of workers who rejected both the Civic Federation's pursuit of harmony between the classes and the AFL's vision of gradually improving workers' lives by means of union contracts. The founding convention of the IWW in 1905 brought together delegates with many different political views, but all of them were determined to rid the world of capitalism, not to polish its rough edges. As the preamble to the IWW's constitution said, its goal was to organize "the workers of the world as a class, take possession of the earth and the machinery of production, and abolish the wage system."[31]

The Wobblies held militarism and all forms of nationalism in contempt. They argued that craft unions could do no more than improve life for a fortunate few among the workers, and in fact were not very good even at that. Only the mobilization of all workers, regardless of occupation, race, or gender, could be effective in improving the conditions of life. Both short-term objectives and the ultimate overthrow of capitalism, they proclaimed after their 1908 convention, could be achieved only by direct action: "industrial action directly by, for, and of the workers themselves, without the treacherous aid of labor misleaders or scheming politicians."[32]

The IWW took shape under distinctly North American conditions, but it reflected a widespread belief, inspired in workers' movements especially by the Russian Revolution of 1905, that exploitation and tyranny could be brought down by mass strikes. That faith was incorporated in the basic principles of the anarcho-syndicalist unions of France, Italy, and Spain (all of which had more members than the IWW) and of smaller unions elsewhere in Europe. It also inspired new labor organizations and mass strikes in Argentina, Brazil, Uruguay, and Chile, as well as the strikes of 1906 in the Mexican copper mining, textile, and railroad industries.[33]

To be sure, demands for social reform in the United States and elsewhere came from many directions, some of which pointed toward political action, rather than away from it. For example, working people gave widespread support to "municipal socialism"—intervention by city governments to improve housing, provide services, and hold down streetcar fares (a burning issue in the United States). Both locally oriented movements such as Britain's Independent Labour Party and "impossiblist" socialists who scoffed at entitlement programs emanating from national governments, such as the Guesdeists in France, sought control of city governments. In the United States, Progressive Era struggles for municipal services were powerfully supported and often led by recent immigrants and by socialists.[34]

At the same time, the mobilization of state power for formal and informal empire also encouraged an expansion of government's role in the domestic economy. Let one example suffice. Building the Panama Canal was a vast government undertaking. The Socialist editor of the *Machinists' Monthly Journal* could scarcely contain his enthusiasm. The creation of the canal, the reconstruction of two cities, the erection of ports and quays, and the containment of contagious diseases and mosquitoes provided a model of what state enterprise had "done for the nation at large far superior to work done under private contract." Moreover, the wages, hours, housing, recreation facilities, and health services supplied by the federal government's Isthmian Canal Commission provided a model for proper treatment of workers—at least for the five to six thousand white citizens of the United States who were engaged in the operation (workers on the "gold roll"). The 45,000 workers on the "silver roll," primarily black men and women from the Caribbean, but also East Indians, Italians, Venezuelans, and even Spaniards, were not only paid much less but were also left to fend for themselves and were barred from entering facilities reserved for "whites."[35]

The example of the canal influenced others in addition to white socialist machinists. It aroused enthusiasm for municipal ownership among businessmen. Nowhere was this more evident than in Seattle, a city catapulted to importance because of its location on the great circle routes from Panama City to Asia. The city expanded and modernized its port facilities as a public project, while powerful reform coalitions broke railroad control of local politics and floated bond issues to improve the physical environment and shut down "vice." Its University of Washington became the pinnacle of the Philippine's educational system.[36] Such developments around the imperialist world led socialists such as William English Walling and Emile Vandervelde, secretary of the International Socialist Bureau, to warn that public enterprise and state ownership did *not* constitute socialism. On the contrary, they argued, modern capitalism's expansion of the state had to be overcome by socialist revolution.[37]

As political philosopher Herbert Croly argued in 1909, the Spanish-American War "and its resulting policy of extra-territorial expansion . . . availed, from the sheer force of the national aspirations it aroused, to give a tremendous impulse to the work of national reform and it indirectly helped to place in the Presidential chair [Theodore Roosevelt] who . . . represented both the national idea and the spirit of reform."[38]

In this new political environment, both Gompers and Carnegie quietly quit the Anti-Imperialist League, and protests against annexing colonies simply disappeared from AFL proceedings.[39] Instead, AFL leaders reoriented their efforts toward spreading their style of unionism throughout North America.

The AFL and Canada

Major American international unions grew in Canada, cheek-by-jowl with the expansion of branch plants of American corporations. Their growth was assisted by the nature of the border between the United States and Canada, the most permeable in the world. Especially since the 1870s, both English-speaking and French-speaking Canadians had migrated south in such numbers as to repopulate the textile and shoe factories of New England and to constitute more than a quarter of Detroit's foreign-born population. Thousands of British, Italian, and Finnish immigrants who came through Montreal subsequently moved southward, while seasonal Italian railroad workers traveled through the

Port of New York to Montreal and then to jobs in Canada's western provinces. It was commonplace for immigrants to return to Canada when work became slack in the United States, so that personal and economic contacts across the border assumed a continuing importance in family life. Moreover, from the 1890s to 1914, more people entered the rapidly growing far western provinces of Canada from the United States than moved the other way.[40]

Both the Knights of Labor and AFL craft unions had recruited many members in Ontario, Quebec, and Atlantic Canada since the 1880s. It was commonplace for labor activists and elected leaders on one side of the border to have been born on the other side. Labor organizations in the two countries also shared a venomous hostility toward Chinese immigrants (supplemented in the Canadian case by opposition to immigrants from India). Immigrants from the British Isles had often brought with them important trade union experience and sometimes even British unions, such as the Amalgamated Society of Engineers, a bitter rival to the International Association of Machinists, which had important branches in Ontario, Michigan, and Illinois (and which participated in the founding convention of the IWW in 1905). Many recent immigrants from Britain came with a strong commitment to industrial unionism and to socialist politics. Their influence was to be especially evident in the strike wave of 1919 and in particular in the Montreal shipyards strike and the general sympathetic strikes of Seattle, Toronto, Amherst, and Winnipeg.[41]

The Knights of Labor survived the depression of the 1890s somewhat better in Canada than it did in the United States. Three-fourths of its remaining local assemblies were found in Quebec. There were also numerous autonomous Canadian trade unions. But the most spectacular union growth in Canada at the opening of the twentieth century was to be found in the local membership of international unions, such as the carpenters, bricklayers, printers, shoe workers, iron molders, and mine workers, with headquarters in U.S. cities such as Indianapolis, Chicago, and New York and which were affiliated with the American Federation of Labor. Although those international unions often had some Canadian officers, their most effective support came from rank-and-file craftsmen in more than 1,000 local unions (in 1902), who felt strengthened by the financial resources, benevolent funds, and traveling cards provided by the internationals. Locals of the internationals, together with assemblies of the Knights and purely Canadian unions were represented in the Trades and Labor Congress of Canada, which had been created in 1883 and acquired the name TLCC in 1892. All groups agreed that the parliamentary system and confederation structure of the Canadian state required a Canadian institution distinct from but not necessarily in conflict with the AFL.[42]

Consensus did not extend beyond that point. AFL leaders were determined to drive the remaining Knights of Labor assemblies out of Canadian city assemblies and to bring the many independent unions under the wing of the Federation. That effort faced ardent hostility not only from the powerful and pro-British Conservative Party and from Quebec's Catholic hierarchy, which denounced AFL leaders as foreigners and Masons, but also from many Canadian unionists who thought they should be allowed to run their own affairs. Ralph Smith, a coal miner born in England who had close ties to the governing Liberal Party in British Columbia and was president of the TLCC from 1898 to 1902, argued that Canadian labor could wield a strong influence only if all components of the nation's movement worked together. He enjoyed especially strong support in the bilingual area around Ottawa and Hull. Smith's outspoken opponent was John Flett, a carpenter from Hamilton, Ontario, whom Gompers had appointed salaried organizer for Canada and who helped bring 140 new local unions into the AFL in 1900 alone.[43]

Their dispute was brought to a head by the AFL's growing reliance on union labels as an organizing device. The use of union labels was especially contentious in the important shoe industry of Quebec, where workers were involved in a wave of strikes and lockouts during 1900 and 1901 while adhering to a variety of different unions. The New England-based Boot and Shoe Workers International Union, led by the former socialist John F. Tobin (himself born in Guelph, Ontario), sought to bring all the manufacturers involved in the conflicts under his union's label. His effort failed to impress the province's shoe workers, who knew that their industry was protected from American competitors by a high tariff, and he enraged the militant shoe lasters of Montreal by undermining support for their craft strike.[44]

The stage was thus set for the decisive September 1902 convention of the TLCC in Berlin, Ontario (renamed Kitchener during World War I). It was the largest labor convention Canada had yet produced, and floor battles were furious from the start. The AFL's advocates carried the crucial votes with better than two to one margins. Flett replaced Smith as president. The constitution was changed to bar from affiliation with the TLCC not only the Knights of Labor but also all unions with possible jurisdictional conflicts with the AFL internationals. Gompers wrote in triumph that the interests of the labor movement were "identical" regardless of "arbitrary geographic lines."[45]

Gompers' foes in Canada reacted swiftly, but they proved unable to reverse the fateful work of the Berlin Congress. The upper house of the Canadian parliament passed a bill making it a criminal offense for foreigners to encourage or provoke a strike in Canada, but TLCC leaders mobilized Liberal Party votes in the lower house and defeated the bill. Union leaders who had unsuccessfully advocated allowing all Canadian labor organizations into the TLCC quickly formed a rival National Trades and Labor Congress (soon renamed the Canadian Federation of Labor). Despite the widespread reluctance of many city trades councils to expel unions not chartered by the AFL, however, the international unions encompassed more than 88 percent of all Canadian union locals by 1914. The most effective alternatives then clustered around two poles. One was revolutionary syndicalism, represented first by the Industrial Workers of the World and after 1919 by the One Big Union. The other was found in the largest center of nationalist unions: Quebec. There, unions that rejected the AFL were gradually but systematically gathered, under the guidance of the Catholic Church and in a political context of increasingly intense Catholic nationalism, into a movement guided by Papal encyclicals and a chaplain in each local, the *Confédération des Travailleurs Catholiques du Canada*.[46]

In short, the Canadian experience suggests that while their resolutions against annexing colonies remained on the books, AFL unions, like important business leaders, were expanding their own economic reach beyond this country's borders. By the 1905 convention of the AFL, Gompers could assert his contempt for the newly founded IWW and proudly declare:

> Our limits are no longer from Maine to California, from the Lakes to the Gulf, but we include the whole of the United States, Canada, Hawaii, Cuba, Porto Rico, Mexico, the Philippines, and British Columbia. Our international unions deserve support in this growth and in bringing . . . an example to the rest of the world.[47]

And what was that example? Autonomous craft unions engaged in a carefully guided quest for contractual relations with employers or groups of employers, symbolized, where possible, by the union label on the employers' wares. Strong trade unions, able to carry out effective, coordinated strikes but restraining spontaneous strikes and sympathetic strikes, were the necessary precondition of cooperation with "the more intelligent among the employers," Gompers continued.[48]

Moreover, it was not only *industrial* peace that was nurtured by the strength of organized labor, but also the peace of the world. Since 1900, AFL convention resolutions had insisted that the "preservation of peace in the world devolves more and more upon organized labor, whose voice is ever becoming more potent in the formation of public opinion, that supreme tribunal before which both monarch and merchant must inevitably bow." But in contrast to the resolutions of the Socialist International, which continued to link the danger of war explicitly to the clash of imperial ambitions, the warnings against annexations and militarism, spoken so loudly by the AFL in 1898, simply faded away. In their place was a celebration that "the labor movement of the United States and Canada is one," as Gompers put it in his 1904 report to the convention, "that the labor movement of the United States and Porto Rico is one," and that collaboration with the unions of Britain and the British Empire was on the rise and providing an example that might spread to continental

Europe. "We have heard a great deal about peace, about international peace," Gompers continued, "but I can conceive of no peace that will be lasting unless it is based upon the federation of the working men of the civilized world."[49]

Lurking behind these bold claims were two unspoken questions. First, in its relations with European unions, international labor secretariats, and the International Federation of Trade Unions, AFL leaders insisted adamantly on the autonomy of every national labor movement. How was that insistence to be reconciled with the decisions of the Berlin Congress and with the new claim that wherever American business went, U.S.-based unions would also go?[50] The second question was what role labor movements within the economic spheres and colonies of the Great Powers (or what Gompers called the "civilized world") should play in shaping global struggles for social reform and peace. Workers in Puerto Rico and Mexico brought both of those questions sharply to the attention of the AFL. In both those countries, though each in a different way, nationalist struggles against foreign domination powerfully shaped workers' mobilizations for social reform at home.

The AFL and Puerto Rico

In Puerto Rico, urban artisans had created their own movement during the last years of Spanish rule. Among the immigrant craftsmen who had launched the periodical *Ensayo Obrero* on May 1, 1897, were the men who would lead the union movement until the 1930s: Santiago Iglesias, Eduardo Conde, and Ramón Romero Rosa.[51] Like the anarchists in Europe, they castigated organized religion for numbing workers' minds, and they placed universal secular education high on their agenda of demands. The autonomous island government, which Spain had authorized early in 1897, soon punished the journal with fines and jailed Iglesias for disrespect toward Catholic education.[52]

The hacienda owners and creole professionals who led the autonomous government under Spain continued to dominate the island's politics under early U.S. rule. Prominent among them was Luis Muñoz Rivera. He aspired on one front to remove Spanish-born merchants and civil officials from control and to replace them with native Puerto Rican leaders. He also hoped, as he wrote in 1891, to arouse the masses, "breaking the ice of their indifference and lighting the sacred fire of patriotism in their hearts." Like other patriotic leaders he despised the workers' movement as inimical to "the great Puerto Rican family."[53]

The U.S. law that instituted limited self-government in 1901 was the product of expert investigations and lengthy Congressional hearings, in true Progressive Era style.[54] Scholarly advisors in Washington depicted Puerto Ricans as people retarded by centuries of Catholic monarchism, which had left their gentry arrogant patriarchs, their poor women subject to male tyranny but often without husbands, and their male laborers dissolute and undisciplined. Consequently, military authorities had instituted civil marriage in 1899, and three years later one of the first acts of the new legislature permitted women to divorce abusive husbands—a right which women quickly put to widespread use.[55]

The new regime took power amid economic desolation, caused by a worldwide collapse of the price of coffee—then the island's most valuable export. A large, mobile wage-earning class had already been generated by the abolition of slavery, completed in 1873, and by the subsequent spread of coffee and sugar plantations. Now those workers and their families could welcome abolition of the hated "*regimen de la libreta*" (obligatory pass books which certified workers' places of employment and employers' permission to travel), while they also faced ruinous unemployment and slashed wages. Thousands emigrated to seek work—to Hawaii, Cuba, Panama, and the continental United States.[56]

Between 1898 and 1901, the island had erupted in strikes, and workers created a federation of unions, whose most prominent leader was Santiago Iglesias.[57] His personal story reveals as much about the workings of imperial government as it does about the difficult relationship between workers' struggles and national independence movements.

Born in Spain, Iglesias apprenticed as a cabinetmaker and migrated at the age of fourteen to Havana, where he became involved in workers' study *circles* and in the Cuban struggle for independence until military authorities forced him to flee to Puerto Rico. There, Muñoz Rivera's autonomous government put him in jail, as we have seen, but he escaped when U.S. troops landed.[58] Subsequently, Iglesias participated prominently not only in the founding conventions of the union federation and of the new *Partido Obrero Socialista*—he called himself a socialist all his life—but in a San Juan reform rally, he also came out in favor of annexation: *Somos anexionistas? Si.*[59]

Iglesias traveled north and made personal contact with both the new Socialist Party of America and La Resistencia, the militant union of Cuban and Puerto Rican cigar makers in New York.[60] Those connections helped him bring moral and financial support to strikers in Puerto Rico. The island's government responded by arresting Iglesias and seven other strike leaders, charging them under an old Spanish law with "conspiracy to raise the price of labor." Iglesias jumped bail, came again to the United States, and appealed for help to the 1900 convention of the AFL. Trade unionists at the convention were infuriated by the reappearance of the hated labor conspiracy doctrine, which they thought America had buried.[61] A reporter from the *Louisville Courier Journal* wrote that "the most heated and most interesting debate of the convention" developed around a motion to organize the workers of Puerto Rico "before American capitalists go in there and attempt to control native labor at the prices now paid for it." They appropriated money to help organize the island's workers and persuaded the unions of cigar makers, tobacco workers, longshoremen, and carpenters to take part in the struggle and to translate their constitutions into Spanish. Gompers then commissioned Iglesias as a general organizer for the AFL.[62]

More intriguing, Gompers appealed on behalf of Iglesias to President Theodore Roosevelt. The president's personal secretary, George Cortelyou, was a leader of the National Civic Federation, which was then seeking to harmonize relations between labor and capital in the United States. Cortelyou wrote to the colonial governor assuring him that Iglesias was "endorsed by Mr. Gompers," who had requested Iglesias be "left free to carry out the objects of his mission." U.S. attorney general Philander C. Knox then persuaded the Supreme Court of Puerto Rico to overturn the workers' sentences and to rule that "any Spanish law in Porto Rico, [which impairs the right of free assembly] has lost its force and become a nullity with the change of sovereignty."[63]

Workers' rights to organize and strike had been vindicated by intervention from the North in defiance of Muñoz Rivera and his fellow *hacendados* and in the context of popular misery and upheaval. For the next decade, the labor federation continued to denounce the "statements made in favor of independence of Puerto Rico" by Muñoz Rivera's party as "only the aspiration and thirst for dominion over the producing masses, to secure places and to strangle in the throat of the people the blessed freedom that now exists in Puerto Rico."[64]

The AFL's activity in Puerto Rico reflected its general move away from the opposition to colonial expansion expressed in 1898. In 1902, the year of the Berlin Congress's decisions reigning in the autonomy of Canadian unions, Gompers appointed Ed Rosenberg, a Norwegian-born officer of the Sailors Union of the Pacific, as salaried organizer for Hawaii and the Philippines with authority to organize workers there into unions affiliated with the AFL.[65] When U.S. forces invaded Haiti in 1915 and rewrote Haiti's constitution and land laws, took control of revenue collection, and established a new police force with American officers, making Haiti a colony in all but name for nineteen years, the AFL uttered not a word of protest.[66]

It is crucial to understanding Puerto Rico, however, to recall that its major employers in 1900 were *not* foreigners. For a time, Spanish-born merchants continued to dominate much of the island's commerce and money lending. But that condition changed rapidly under American rule, and correspondingly dissent from Iglesias's views on U.S. annexation grew in labor's ranks. As early as 1905, the primary participants in strikes were no longer the artisans and port workers of San Juan, but the largely seasonal workers in tobacco and sugar, where many of the largest enterprises had recently been created by investors from the North. Among them were James B. Duke's American Tobacco Company and the Porto Rico Sugar Company, owner of five plantations with 7,000 acres of cane. When nearly 14,000 workers struck that company and other sugar centrals of the Ponce region demanding 75 cents a day, the

U.S. district court of Puerto Rico imposed on Iglesias *not* an archaic Spanish conspiracy indictment but a modern American injunction.[67] As tensions continued to mount in the sugar regions, the island's appointed executive council and the elected House of Delegates agreed in 1910 to create a special police force empowered by the government but paid and directed by companies and *hacendados* who requested them, along the lines of Pennsylvania's infamous Coal and Iron Police.[68]

Trade union activists in the sugar regions, who were involved in yet another surge of strikes in 1915, persuaded the labor federation to establish a new socialist party. Although Iglesias was elected the party's president, local party sections often denounced their country's domination by U.S. capital. Their denunciations grew louder early the next year, when police dispatched to the Arecibo region by Governor Arthur Yager arrested many strikers and killed several. When Gompers protested to President Woodrow Wilson that the workers' constitutional rights had been violated, Wilson defended Yager as just and patriotic. The convergence between socialist and nationalist aspirations was clearly evident at the new party's 1919 convention, when delegates openly and ardently debated whether to fight for national independence or to appeal to the democratic pretensions of the United States against the domination of Puerto Rican elites. In the end, Iglesias's position prevailed: that independence should come, if at all, only after social democracy had been won at home. What is truly remarkable about the 1919 debate, however, is that speakers on both sides of the question (including Iglesias) referred to the example of revolutionary Russia to support their positions.[69]

It is noteworthy that the trade union body headed by Iglesias, the *Federación Libre de los Trabajadores* (FLT), while affiliated with the AFL, exercised sufficient autonomy to create its own political party. More important, the desolate condition of the island's agriculture between the world wars undermined trade union power, making the Socialist Party the tail that wagged the trade-union dog. Seeking to secure some legislative benefits for workers, not to mention appointments to government office, the party joined in coalition with the Republican Party, which was committed to the quest for statehood. This alliance made the Socialists partners in governing the colony from 1924 to 1940. A party with a platform devoted to organizing workers' own collective power on the job against "the plutocracy" and "under the banner of the socialist ideal" governed in coalition with representatives of some of the island's most powerful business interests.[70]

As if the Great Depression had not brought enough misery to Puerto Rico, as it did throughout the Caribbean, a furious hurricane swept the island in 1932. The haunting refrains of Rafael Hernández's famous song "*Lamento Borincano*" evoked both the people's distress and a growing animosity toward Yankee companies that had devoured their land. Strikes by women in tobacco and clothing in 1933 met both police violence and student support. The Nationalist Party, under the charismatic leadership of Pedro Albizu Campos, shook the political landscape not only by vigorous electoral activity but also by turbulent street demonstrations as well as the murder of the island's chief of police.

Iglesias's labor federation sought to stabilize working conditions through master collective bargaining agreements for each of the island's major industries. The sugar workers' contract evoked furious protests from union members because it provided no wage increase and ignored local struggles over the task system of payment and hours of work. Their strike spread from plantation to plantation, while Iglesias and other FLT leaders tried to cajole or command workers to return to their jobs. In response, strikers called on Albizu Campos for help, and his oratory made strike meetings resound with demands for independence. As the next elections revealed in 1936, however, the discourse of national sovereignty had not won many adherents among those mobilized in the name of wages, hours, and local control ("*un peso y ocho horas*" were words sung across the sugar fields), but workers were to desert the Socialist Party and the FLT in ever growing numbers. After Iglesias died in 1939, the party fell apart.[71]

Nevertheless, nationalist agitation did contribute heavily to a basic realignment of Puerto Rican politics. In 1936, Albizu Campos and six colleagues were sentenced to the Atlanta penitentiary for conspiracy to murder the police commandant. The following March, a nationalist parade in Ponce was met with police gunfire, leaving nineteen people dead (including two police) and at least 100 wounded. While the main opposition party, long committed to island autonomy, disintegrated in the aftermath of the massacre, up in New York City, Congressman Vito Marcantonio, representing the eastside Italian-Puerto Rican community, became a vocal champion of Puerto Rican independence and of the imprisoned Albizu Campos, in addition to social reform.[72]

A new party headed by Luis Muñoz Marin (son of Luis Muñoz Rivera) rose out of the crisis to dominate the island's political life. After initially calling for independence with social justice, he had by 1940 proclaimed that social justice was the issue, not the island's legal status. As war mobilization reinvigorated the economy, Muñoz Marin worked, often in tandem with the new U.S. governor Rexford Tugwell, to strip sugar companies of their massive holdings, distribute land to smallholders, erect state factories, and ultimately to negotiate self-government in most domestic affairs, while still under U.S. rule, in the form of the *Estado Libre Asociado* (Commonwealth).

In the new imperial relationship, Puerto Rico remained firmly annexed to the United States while it was rapidly transformed into a branch plant economy in the name of Operation Bootstrap. The labor movement envisaged by Gompers and Iglesias had been marginalized. The *Confédération General de los Trabajadores*, established in 1940, shaped a new militancy, first among sugar workers then in other domains. Its president was a member of the inner circle of Muñoz Marin's party.[73]

The AFL and Mexico

By that time, however, the focal point of entanglement with imperialism for the American labor movement had clearly become Mexico. In stark contrast to Canada and Puerto Rico, there was no popular support among workers in Mexico for joining the international unions of the AFL. Moreover, under the regime of Porfirio Diaz any union or strike activity faced brutal repression, though railroad brotherhoods (not affiliated with the AFL) did wield some power on the railroads of northern Mexico, as preserves of locomotive engineers and dispatchers who had come from the United States along with the railroad companies. After 1905, there was some IWW activity involving both Mexicans and Anglo immigrants in the Tampico oil fields, but the crucial links of Mexico's workers' movement to the IWW were not organizational, but ideological. The most influential organization involved in the strikes that shook the Diaz regime in 1906 was the *Partido Liberal Mexicano* (PLM), whose commitment to revolutionary workers' action aimed at bringing down capitalism had much in common with the Wobblies' beliefs.

Nevertheless, the labor movement that took shape during Mexico's revolutionary struggles ultimately did so under the wing of the victorious General Venustiano Carranza. Correspondingly, the resurgent American Federation of Labor allied itself ever more closely with the Wilson administration in Washington and with its foreign policies. Consequently, the links formed between officers of the two national labor movements between 1916 and 1924 were shaped as much by international diplomacy as they were by questions of trade union strategies and affiliations.

The United States had annexed half the former area of Mexico by 1848, and at the turn of the century, modern capitalist development—especially railroads—had transformed the border region. In Texas, it had brought a flood of white farmers to the region north of the Rio Grande, where they had displaced the surviving *Mexicano ranchero* elite from both its economic and its political dominance of the borderland. Anglo political reformers for the first time imposed legal segregation on neighbors of Mexican ancestry.

South of the Rio Grande, the major railroads, built rapidly after 1880, were extensions of U.S. lines. Between 1900 and 1911, almost 40 percent of all foreign investment from the United States went into Mexico—into its railroads, mines, and oil. Throughout Mexico, foreigners owned virtually all industry, except the brewery and steel mill in Monterrey, while Spaniards, Turks, and Chinese dominated wholesale and retail commerce. The ruthless military forces of Porfirio Diaz safeguarded all these enterprises. Consequently, as the Revolution made evident, even the Mexican bourgeoisie had few qualms about expropriating capitalists whom they hoped to replace.[74]

Moreover, there was virtually a free-trade zone linking the United States with the northern states of Mexico-Sonora, Chihuahua, Coahuila, and Durango. Revolutionary leaders Madero, Obregon, Villa, Orozco, and Carranza stemmed from that region. The workers of those northern states tended to be very mobile, many alternating between farm labor and mines and between one side of the border and the other. As Emilio Zamora has argued, before 1915, the largest number of Mexicans entering the United States went to Texas, and somewhere between 50 percent and 75 percent of the new arrivals returned to Mexico each year. This regional society and its revolution were very different from the cohesive villages found in Morelos to the south, which produced Zapata and the agrarian revolt, and also from San Luis Potosi, which had nurtured the earliest intellectual opposition to the Diaz regime.[75]

Working-class activists also crossed the border constantly, salting Mexico with people familiar with the American Federation of Labor, Industrial Workers of the World, and Socialist Party of America. Locomotive engineers, dispatchers, and conductors were overwhelmingly Yankees. Job examinations were given in English! Many of them belonged to U.S. railroad brotherhoods until President Francisco Madero broke their grip in 1912 by requiring workers running Mexican trains to speak Spanish.[76]

Many Mexican political groups had officers or even headquarters in Texas, Missouri, and California. Foremost among those groups was the *Partido Liberal Mexicano* (PLM) led by Ricardo Flores Magón. Although this party and its newspaper *Regeneración* ardently advocated land reform and civil liberties, it also discretely encouraged anarcho-syndicalism.[77] Members of the PLM played prominent roles organizing strikes by copper miners in Cananea, Sonora, and Clifton-Morenci, Arizona, and in the 1905 to 1907 effort to reshape an AFL federal labor union in Laredo, Texas, into a city-wide organization of all Mexican workers. PLM members later helped initiate the futile IWW invasion of Baja California and provided at least inspiration for the *Sediciocos* who raided three Texas border towns during the summer of 1915 in support of the Plan de San Diego. That proclamation called for "Social Revolution" and the transfer of arable land to "the proletarians." In response to those attacks, the Texas Rangers and white vigilante groups unleashed a reign of terror against local Mexicans, which in turn inspired many to flee for safety into war-torn Mexico itself.[78]

As historian James Cockcroft has persuasively argued, major strikes of miners, textile workers, and railroad workers in 1906 marked the beginning of open revolt against the Diaz regime. The PLM had been founded in San Luis Potosi in 1901 and as its name suggests originally favored political liberties, competitive capitalism, and removal of the Church from public life. Repression radicalized the party, and by the time Magón and his comrades had been released from prison and had established headquarters in Laredo, they had committed the movement to armed insurrection, libertarian socialism, and return of the land to the despoiled peasants. The famous strike at the complex of copper, gold, and silver mines in Cananea, owned by the well-connected American William C. Greene, was organized out of Douglas, Arizona, by PLM activists and was subsequently crushed by the Arizona Rangers, who crossed the border under the command of a former officer of Roosevelt's Rough Riders. The strikers enjoyed strong support from the Western Federation of Miners and the newly formed IWW, though they actually organized on a community basis, not as an industrial union (similar to Canada's One Big Union rather than the IWW).[79]

Magón and his compatriots were harassed constantly by the William Howard Taft administration as well as by Mexican authorities, and they were forced to move headquarters several times. Ricardo Flores Magón was imprisoned nine times in Mexico and the United States, and he died in Fort Leavenworth in 1923, despite efforts of the new Mexican government to secure his release. But his legal battles enjoyed the support of Missouri's progressive governor, Joseph W. Folk, as well as Samuel Gompers, prominent Socialist Party members such as Mother Jones and Eugene V. Debs, and Magón's attorney, Job Harriman of Los Angeles. By 1910, Socialist magazines and newspapers published a steady diet of articles linking the oppression of Mexican workers and peasants to American business interests. John Turner's expose *Barbarous Mexico* (1910), first published in serial form, had become basic reading for the American left.[80] Earlier, in 1908, when President Theodore Roosevelt sought to clamp down on Mexican revolutionaries by proposing legislation to allow censorship of mail and to expand the secret service, Congress voted his proposals down.[81]

Francisco I. Madero's military uprising against Diaz in 1911 drew much support away from the *Magónistas*. Although much of the business and agricultural elite had benefited from Diaz's solicitation of capital from the United States, a deep and prolonged Mexican economic crisis, triggered in 1907 by a financial crisis in the United States, had undermined the middle class and roused even wealthy men like Madero to battle for political liberties and constitutional government. When Magón denounced Madero's lack of a social program, reminding his readers that "governments are protectors of the rich," and encouraged an armed incursion into Baja California by his followers and hundreds of Wobblies (among them, briefly, Joe Hill), Gompers and other AFL leaders proclaimed their support for Madero—most assertively after the new Mexican president had legalized free speech, strikes, and trade unions (measures the Taft administration greeted with hostility). Eugene Debs,

Mother Jones, and the socialist *New York Call* joined in that support, all of them arguing that Mexico had to pass through bourgeois democracy before it could be ready for socialism.[82]

After the armies of Venustiano Carranza won control of much of the country in 1914, with no clear ideology other than nationalism, their commanders turned local buildings over to workers' unions in the towns they occupied. Foreign-owned companies employed most of the unions' members. The *Casa del Obrero Mundial* (House of the World Worker) soon attracted the active support of many PLM veterans and declared its major weapon to be the "direct action of worker against capitalist." The *Casa* was founded in 1912, and it briefly became the pilot of widespread strikes, only to be fiercely repressed by the regime of General Victoriano Huerta (1913–14). Nevertheless, the failure of PLM-led military efforts, including those in Baja California, coupled with the brutal suppression inflicted on workers by the Huerta government, left the Casa susceptible to enticements to organize some 7,000 workers in 1915 into six Red Battalions fighting under Carranza's command. The general's adamant opposition to the occupation of Vera Cruz by U.S. military and naval forces had already won many workers to his banner.[83]

The price the Red Battalions had to pay for Carranza's material assistance was to join Carranza's assault on Emiliano Zapata, in the name of the "struggle against reaction." This was a fateful development: The workers' movement and the agrarian revolution had become enemies. Dissident members of the *Casa* fled to Morelos, among them their most eminent public intellectual, Antonio Diaz Soto y Gama, who became Zapata's chief theoretician and a bitter enemy of the urban working class.[84]

When desperate conditions of life provoked a new wave of strikes in 1916, Carranza dissolved the Red Battalions, turned on the Casa, commandeered many of the new union headquarters, and ordered military courts to imprison arrested strike leaders—something many of his army commanders refused to do. He also unleashed what he intended to be an annihilation campaign against Zapata.[85]

At almost the same time, the constitutional assembly meeting at Aguascalientes finished work on its labor code, article 123. It was the most comprehensive governmental declaration of workers' rights the world had ever seen. In addition to guaranteeing the eight-hour day and rights to organize and strike, it specified equal pay for both sexes and rest periods for working mothers, guarantees of housing, old age and sickness care, government supervision of contracts to work in foreign countries, prohibition of peonage, and more. All this from a convention where there were only two trade unionists.[86]

As the new constitution revealed, this was revolution from above. The new *Confederación Regional Obrera Mexicana* (CROM), which arose out of the rubble of the 1916 repression and the hopes inspired by the new constitution, was closely allied to the Carranza government. Many of its officers had worked in the United States and had been members there of trade unions or the IWW or both. In 1918, the anarcho-syndicalists of Mexico City (*Federación de Sindicatos Obreros del Distrito Féderal*) also affiliated with the CROM, bringing with them many admirers of the IWW. Although the CROM continued to employ the discourse of syndicalism, modified to advocate "multiple action" rather than direct action, its success, if not its survival, depended on its support from the government.[87]

Luis Morones and other officers of Mexican labor organizations persuaded the AFL Executive Council to petition President Wilson to recognize Carranza's regime and later to join the CROM in joint efforts to prevent war between their two countries after General John J. Pershing had led U.S. troops into northern Mexico in futile pursuit of Francisco Villa. Gompers wrote to AFL officers in California of the need to establish "closer fraternal relations between the labor movements of our two countries that are necessary to protect the wage-earners in our future commercial and industrial developments."[88]

Gompers' letter referred specifically to the 1915 Pan-American Financial Conference, which had been promoted by President Wilson. Gompers had urged the administration in vain to include trade unionists as representatives of "human welfare" in the commissions authorized by that conference to promote economic integration in the Americas. He had argued specifically that union labels constituted one of the instruments of modern commerce. At that year's AFL convention in San Francisco, Santiago Iglesias presented a report calling for solidarity among the trade unions of the Americas in response to the reorganization of business that had been made possible by the opening of the Panama Canal and encouraged by the recent financial conference. The AFL convention, which had been marked by bitter divisions over war preparedness, accepted his report unanimously.[89]

Socialists, who later supported Wilson's war against Germany, heavily influenced Gompers' policies and his links to Mexican unions. Among them were John Murray, former correspondent in Mexico for the *New York Call*, James Lord of the AFL's Mining Department, Santiago Iglesias, and the Romanian-born Roberto Haberman, who managed to hold membership simultaneously in the International Association of Machinists, the Drug Clerks Union of Mexico City, and the cooperative movement of Yucatan.[90]

Moreover, just as the CROM was tied to Carranza's government, so the AFL increasingly linked itself to that of Wilson in both domestic and foreign affairs. Wilson had enjoyed some labor support during his first presidential campaign, but by the election of 1916, he enjoyed a margin of support among working-class votes without precedent in the history of presidential elections. Secretary of Labor William B. Wilson had come from the AFL's largest union, the United Mine Workers of America. Under his guidance, the new U.S.

Conciliation Service mediated 1,780 labor disputes between 1915 and 1919 and encouraged employers to negotiate with unions chartered by the AFL and to shun the IWW and other groups which he and the Federation deemed "outlaw." As preparedness for war took center stage in 1916, he sponsored a series of joint meetings between cabinet members and the AFL's executive council, and then successfully proposed Gompers' appointment to the Council of National Defense. Major strikes for the eight-hour day in the spring of 1916 and the threat of a nationwide railroad strike on the eve of a presidential election had yielded a statutory eight-hour day on the railroads (the Adamson Act). After Congress declared war on Germany, the Wilson administration appointed many union officials to agencies created to mobilize the economy and muster public support for a war that initially faced widespread public opposition.[91]

Nevertheless, wartime industrial conditions triggered huge strikes during 1917, especially in mining and lumbering, as if to mock the no-strike pledge Gompers had pronounced on his own initiative. Worse yet, the IWW not only provided leadership to many of those strikes, but in the Arizona mining region especially, also organized stable locals of thousands of workers. Among the members in Bisbee, Jerome, Morenci, and elsewhere were many Mexicans. Nevertheless, as IWW activist and future Communist leader Ludwig Lore wrote: "It is not the 'outlaw' worker any longer, the migratory nomad, but the stationary worker with a permanent home and family who constitutes a goodly part of the IWW membership." When Bisbee vigilantes rounded up more than 1,200 strikers and deported them to the desert in July, an army census of the victims found almost half of them to be U.S. citizens, even though most of them were foreign born.[92]

Brutal treatment of strikers by enraged and armed local residents was by no means restricted to Arizona. It was precisely the resurgent strength of the IWW in 1917, colliding with appeals by local businessmen and editors to patriotic fury, that unleashed violent assaults and murders inflicted on Wobblies across the West. State and federal governments followed suit with indictments and deportations, culminating in the mass trial of 133 actual and alleged IWW leaders. Meanwhile, many well-known AFL unions, as well as unaffiliated newcomers like the Amalgamated Clothing Workers, increased their memberships dramatically. Wartime full employment overcame workers' fear of dismissal, and participation in strikes soared to all-time record highs—war or no war—while new government agencies often resolved major disputes in favor of the workers, who could now couch their demands in the vocabulary of wartime.[93] The AFL's collaboration with the federal government may have violated its proclaimed self-reliance and "voluntarism," but its reward was vigorous growth in membership and in influence.

These pressures and opportunities provided the context for the AFL's controversial alignment with President Wilson's foreign policy, including his moves towards intervention in World War I. Although Gompers had joined Mexican union leaders and many socialists and progressives at home in urging the President to curb his military ventures of 1914 and 1916 inside revolutionary Mexico, he had shared Wilson's hopes that Madero and later Carranza would bring constitutional government to their country. Moreover, by April 1917, Wilson had stationed marines in Haiti, Santo Domingo, and Nicaragua, and annexed the Virgin Islands—all with no protest from the AFL. It was, however, the approaching war with Germany that drew AFL leaders into active participation in war mobilization. By the time of the turbulent AFL convention of 1915 in San Francisco, Executive Council members in control of the platform gaveled down vociferous opponents of military preparedness and their hooting supporters in the balcony, while Gompers took the floor to declare:

> I am a pacifist . . . and I had hoped that we would get away from the war idea. But when I saw the way the trade unionists of each European nation rallied to their colors in this war, I had to agree the old Biblical sentiment, "Love thy neighbor as thyself,["] had been shot to pieces. We want to see the people of the United States thoroughly trained so that they may control their military and naval forces in the interests of peace, democracy and humanity.[94]

Gompers lent unstinting support to Wilson's war effort and then to the League of Nations.[95] As the invectives that convention delegates hurled at each other in San Francisco made evident, however, many workers sharply opposed his policies. Just as the war had increased union membership by 1920 to levels not to be reached again until 1940, so it had stimulated the aspirations, discontent, and sense of power among those members. Gompers remarked to his colleague and confidant James Duncan of the Granite Cutters: "Our movement is passing through a critical stage. The struggles, the sacrifices, the enthusiasm, the highly nervous strain induced by the World War, have brought about a state of almost mental hysteria."[96]

The rebellious mood Lore had praised and Gompers feared manifested itself in political as well as economic life. Versailles and the other treaties ending the war had left the British, French, and Japanese empires not only intact but enlarged, with Italy the only empty-handed ally, and had left Eastern Europe ablaze with nationalist conflicts and social revolution. One immigrant group after another protested what seemed to its members a mockery of the Fourteen Points. Labor's dissidents demanded direct intervention by working people in foreign affairs—"democratic diplomacy." A workers' convention, which drafted demands for a pending strike at five General Electric plants shortly after the armistice, included in its demands the release of all imprisoned antiwar dissidents and radicals in the United States and the inclusion of labor representatives as half their country's delegates to the Versailles peace conference. Critics of President Wilson and of Gompers found their most articulate voice in the Chicago Federation of Labor and its newspaper, the *New Majority*. Just as that journal advocated industrial democracy at home, so it demanded direct participation in foreign policy by working people. A famous *New Majority* cartoon of 1919 depicted working men and women approaching the door of the peace conference and captioned: "You could not make War without us—you cannot make Peace without us."[97]

As was the case with Winnipeg's *Western Labour News* and the *Seattle Union Record*, the *New Majority* depicted "nationalist rebellions" as "part of the class struggle, not a distraction from it." The Chicagoans resolved that they would not "be satisfied with a League of Imperialist governments dominated by an international League of money bosses."[98] They applauded the self-determination accorded to Poles, Yugoslavs, and other peoples in Europe, but they insisted that Ireland, India, Egypt, and Mexico be accorded the same right. They found a champion in Frank Walsh of Missouri, who not only quit the National War Labor Board, but also threw his efforts into a League of Oppressed Peoples. As Alan Dawley has argued, "The immediate postwar period deserves to be remembered as the most significant moment of anti-imperialism since the beginning of the century."[99]

In the elections of 1918 and 1920, it was the Republicans who capitalized most effectively on popular discontent with Wilson's government. Business leaders and Republicans rallied voters against immigrants, radicals, and trade unions, while labor's wartime influence in the government faded quickly into memory. AFL delegates walked out of the 1919 President's Industrial Conference after they could not even get adopted a resolution favoring labor's right to organize. The embattled Wilson administration did not invite them back to the second industrial conference.[100]

Revolutionary upheavals around the world had also induced the diplomats assembled in Paris to enshrine the eight-hour day and other labor standards in the peace treaties and to create the International Labor Organization to oversee their enforcement. Those same upheavals, however, had by 1923 produced not one international union congress, but four. The social-democratic International Federation of Trade Unions dating from 1900 had survived, but it was now confronted by a Communist-led Red International of Labor Unions, an anarcho-syndicalist International Workingmen's Association, and an International Federation of Working Women.[101]

Labor Solidarity in the Americas?

It was in this turbulent context that the AFL and the CROM took the initiative to create a Pan-American Federation of Labor. Pursuant to the decision of its 1915 convention, Gompers and other AFL officials met in Washington with

Luis Morones and others of the CROM and a separate group from Yucatan. After that meeting, two of the delegates from Yucatan set out to enlist support from other countries in Latin America, but the only favorable response came from one union in Cuba. That was hardly surprising. The labor organizations formed in Argentina, Brazil, Uruguay, and Chile starting in 1905 were more akin to the IWW than to the AFL or the CROM. In fact, the maritime workers and artisans who created the first nationwide labor organization in Chile (1919) actually named themselves a branch of the Industrial Workers of the World. For international solidarity, the Chileans sent their delegates to the 1922 congress of the anarcho-syndicalist International Workingmen's Association in Berlin, Germany, as did unions in Argentina, Brazil, and Uruguay. One union in Yucatan even replied to the AFL's invitation by stating that a mutual assistance organization should be worldwide, not Pan-American.[102]

Consequently, only two national movements took part in the founding convention held in the important Texas border railroad junction of Laredo just days after the armistice had taken effect in Europe, both of them operating in close collaboration with their respective governments. In fact, the official call for the meeting had been issued only after the United States had formally recognized Carranza's government, while President Wilson and his Committee on Public Information had secretly provided the funding.[103] Even so, there was plenty of tension in the air. The Tampico section of the IWW had withdrawn from the CROM in protest against meeting with the AFL, and president Frank Duffy of the powerful Carpenters Union had ardently objected on behalf of the AFL's Catholic members to Gompers' dealings with Mexico's anticlerical revolutionaries.[104]

The opening statement from Morones called on the AFL to open all of its unions to membership for workers of Mexican origin and to come to the aid of the many IWW and other political prisoners in the United States. But AFL unions were then collaborating closely with President Wilson's government to exclude the IWW from the copper mines and the maritime world and also with the Canadian government to fight the One Big Union in Nova Scotia and in the western provinces.[105] Consequently, Gompers responded with a ringing denunciation of the IWW as an opponent of the Allied war effort and an enemy of trade unionism. He also defended the authority of every constituent AFL union to make its own membership rules, and he proposed that both federations collaborate to limit immigration into the United States.[106]

The sticking point was Texas. The Texas Federation of Labor was dominated by trade unionists who shared the virulent racism that flourished in their state during the war years and the early 1920s. Fort Worth was a storm center of hostility. There, Anglo and black workers had marched together on city hall to demand that civic leaders "rid the city of cheap Mexican labor."[107] The heartland of *Mexican* participation in the AFL was Laredo itself, where unions of

Mexican track workers thrived. Clemente Idar, son of a pioneering organizer on the Mexican National Railway, was a prominent advocate of both racial integration and trade unionism along strict craft lines. Idar did succeed over the years in integrating some Mexican workers into the Texas Federation, and he succeeded most notably in working together with the Mexican government to keep Mexican workers on both sides of the border from crossing picket lines during the historic nationwide 1922 strike of the railroad shopcraft unions.[108]

Gompers in turn lobbied Washington to resume full diplomatic relations with Mexico and to cede to that country the control that its new constitution asserted over its own natural resources. Gompers and his successor as AFL president, William Green, consistently opposed the efforts of American oil and mining interests to persuade the administrations of Warren Harding and Calvin Coolidge to intervene militarily in Mexico on their behalf. In return, Gompers persuaded the CROM not to affiliate with the Amsterdam-based International Federation of Trade Unions. At a joint conference of the AFL and CROM in El Paso in the fall of 1923, the Mexican and American federations jointly proclaimed the "Monroe Doctrine of Labor." It declared their shared hostility to any efforts by either "the Red Internationale of autocratic Moscow [or] any other internationale" to violate the "sovereignty" of labor in the Western Hemisphere.[109]

In less than a quarter of a century, the AFL had been transformed from a vehement foe of imperial expansion into an active promoter of alliances with those unions in Mexico, Canada, and Puerto Rico that were *not* committed to social revolution. The change began with efforts by the AFL to extend its reach beyond the boundaries of the United States, wherever American business went. A second phase emerged during the First World War. For a few years, the Federation also participated in formulating government policy and enjoyed the shelter that federal agencies provided for trade union growth. At the same time, Mexico had changed from a country where unions had been forbidden into one with a labor congress (the CROM) that supported the government and was in turn nurtured and restrained by that government—though in some places, union activity independent of the CROM actually increased during the 1920s. The AFL in turn lent its support to the rise to power of Plutarco Elías Calles, solicited the aid of the International Federation of Trade Unions as well as the U.S. Navy in blocking shipments of arms to Calles's enemies in 1923, and arranged the following year's convention of the Pan-American Federation to meet in Mexico City at the time of his inauguration. Gompers died in El Paso upon his return from that gathering.[110]

To sum up, at the end of the 1890s, the labor movement of the United States expressed profound anxiety that the division of the world into colonial spheres dominated by the Great Powers threatened world peace as well as the ability of trade unions to improve the lot of working people within the domestic economy. During the next twenty years, however, spectacular growth in the domestic economy and in union membership helped persuade leaders of the AFL quietly to abandon their opposition to the annexation of colonies, while major constituent unions incorporated many workers in Canada and Puerto Rico into their ranks and successfully opposed nationalist currents within the movements of both countries. Moreover, the Wilson administration provided at least some assistance to AFL efforts to construct its own countervailing power to that of business. From 1915 to 1919, militant struggles by workers both benefited from the converging efforts of government and union bureaucrats and often overran the boundaries prescribed by that collaboration. When the country went to war, top union leaders openly jettisoned their historic quest for peace through the common efforts of workers in many lands, and they provided wholehearted support not only to the government's mobilization for war, but also to proselytizing around the globe for its war aims.

Revolutionary Mexico presented a challenge of decisive importance. Starting with the copper, textile, and railroad strikes of 1906, Mexican workers' struggles (including those north of the border) displayed closer kinship to the teachings of the Industrial Workers of the World than to those of Samuel Gompers. Moreover, commanders of revolutionary armies (with the major exception of the intensely provincial Zapatista agrarian movement) appealed to nationalism, rather than social reform. Between 1915 and 1917, however, forces under Carranza's command offered workers' organizations sporadic assistance and the glowing promises incorporated in the new constitution.

AFL initiatives toward alliance with the new Mexican labor movement were guided by the Federation's adherence to President Wilson's foreign policy goals, which also helped secure funding for AFL activities in Latin America. Together, two labor federations, each tied to its respective government, created the Pan-American Federation of Labor, which was to play but an occasional role in strike and organizing activity but which concentrated its efforts on defusing conflicts between the two countries (especially over U.S. companies' claims to oil and mineral rights), securing the ascendancy of a regime in Mexico friendly to its dominant labor organization, and excluding communist, socialist, and syndicalist internationals from the Western Hemisphere. In short, the AFL had changed from a foe of imperial power to a participant in its exercise.

Notes

Reprinted courtesy of Cambridge University Press and the *Journal of the Gilded Age and Progressive Era.*

1. I am deeply indebted to the Initiative on Labor and Culture at Yale University, the Tamiment Institute, the Ashley Fellowship program at Trent University, and the University of Massachusetts Graduate Student Conference for their assistance

in the research and development of this essay. Grace Palladino, Michael Denning, Shana Redmond, Zaragosa Vargas, and Blanca Silvestrini de Pacheco have provided especially helpful research information and comments. I am also grateful to Julie Greene and an anonymous reader for the journal for their comments on an earlier draft of this essay.

2. Frank Thistlethwaite, "Migration from Europe Overseas in the Nineteenth and Twentieth Centuries," *XI Congrés international des sciences historique, Rapports V. Histoire Contemporaine* (Stockholm, 1960), 32–60; Sidney Mintz, *Sweetness and Power: The Place of Sugar in Modern History* (New York, 1985), 126–47; Jan Breman, *Labour Migration and Rural Transformation in Colonial Asia* (Amsterdam, 1990), 13–14; David Northrup, *Indentured Labor in the Age of Imperialism, 1834–1912* (New York, 1995), 26–31, 107–12; Mary A. Renda, *Taking Haiti: Military Occupation and the Culture of U.S. Imperialism, 1915–1940* (Chapel Hill, 2001), 10, 117, 148–49; Stanley Engerman, "Servants to Slaves to Servants: Contract Labor and European Expansion" in *Colonialism and Migration: Indentured Labour before and after Slavery*, ed. P.C. Emmer (Dordrecht, 1986), 263–94.

3. Georges Haupt, comp., *Bureau socialiste international: Comptes rendus des réunions, manifestes, et circulaires* (Paris, 1969), 1: 26–28, see esp. note 4 on 27–28; Partha Sarathi Gupta, *Imperialism and the British Labour Movement, 1914–1964* (London, 1975).

4. Haupt, *Bureau socialiste*, 29–31. My translation of the quotation on p. 30. "C'est la guerre sur tout le globe. Les budgets de la guerre montent, montent . . . On dépense en fusils, canons, casernes, flottes, plus qu'on ne paye en salaries á des millions et encore des millions d'hommes, on massacre, on détruit, on incendie, on viole, on tue."

5. See Alexander Trachtenberg, *American Socialists and the War* (New York, 1917); James Weinstein, *The Decline of Socialism in America, 1912–1925* (New York, 1967).

6. *American Federation of Labor: History, Encyclopedia, Reference Book* (Washington, 1919), 192. See also Samuel Gompers, *Labor and the Common Welfare*, comp. and ed. Hayes Robbins (New York, 1919), 224–25.

7. Philip S. Foner, *History of the Labor Movement in the United States* (New York, 1955), 2: 405–12; Ray Ginger, *The Bending Cross: A Biography of Eugene Victor Debs* (New York, 1947), 203; Daniel De Leon, "A Word to the Proletariat of Spain," *Daily People*, Mar. 20, 1898, quoted in Stephen Coleman, *Daniel De Leon* (New York, 1990), 59.

8. David Montgomery, *Citizen Worker: The Experience of Workers in the United States with Democracy and the free Market during the Nineteenth Century* (New York, 1993), 103; Philip S. Foner, *Militarism and Organized Labor, 1900–1914* (Minneapolis, 1987), 24, 27, 36.

9. Gompers, *Labor and the Common Welfare*, 228–29.

10. "An Address at the Chicago Peace Jubilee (Oct. 18, 1898)" in *Samuel Gompers Papers*, vol. 5, ed., Stuart B. Kaufman, Peter J. Albert, and Grace Palladino (Urbana, 1996), 20–29, qts. on 22–23.

11. AFL, Proceedings, 1898, in *Gompers Papers*, 5: 43, 46.

12. *Ibid.*, 5: 44–46.

13. "An Address at the National Conference on the Foreign Policy of the United States, Saratoga, N.Y." in *Gompers Papers*, 5: 6; AFL Proceedings, 1898, in *Gompers Papers*, 5: 44, 46. Arguments similar to those of Reid were frequently expressed in the British Trades Union Congress, especially by delegates from textile unions. See Gupta, *Imperialism and the British Labour Movement*, 43–49.

14. See, for example, Gwendolyn Mink, *Old Labor and New Immigrants in American Political Development: Union, Party, and State, 1875–1920* (Ithaca, NY, 1986); Jack Scott, *Yankee Unions Go Home: How the AFL Helped the U.S. Build an Empire in Latin America* (Vancouver, 1978), 141–44.

15. W. Dirk Ratt, *Revoltosos: Mexico's Rebels in the United States, 1903–1923* (College Station, TX, 1981), 15, 258–59; Louis Adamic, *Dynamite: The Story of Class Violence in America*, rev. ed. (Gloucester, MA, 1963), 203–9; Michael Kazin, *Barons of Labor: The San Francisco Building Trades and Union Power in the Progressive Era* (Urbana, 1987), 202–5; Scott, *Yankee Unions*, 147; Barbara J. Fields, "Slavery, Race and Ideology in the United States of America," *New Left Review* 118 (May/June 1990): 95–118. Eugene V. Debs argued against annexation of the Philippines, Puerto Rico, and Cuba in 1898, but he favored admitting Hawaii, because those islands were "composed in a degree of Caucasians, and . . . already have an established government." Nick Salvatore, *Eugene V. Debs, Citizen and Socialist* (Urbana, 1982), 226–27.

16. "Chicago Peace Jubilee," *Gompers Papers*, 5: 29n1.

17. Robert L. Beisner, *Twelve Against Empire: The Anti-Imperialists, 1898–1900* (New York, 1968).

18. See Dana Frank, *Buy American: The Untold Story of Economic Nationalism* (Boston, 1999), 47–55.

19. *Downes v. Bidwell*, 182 U.S. 244 (1901) in Henry Steele Commager, *Documents of American History* (New York, 1947) 2: 193–98. See also Scott, *Yankee Unions*, 129–31.

20. Hearst's reply to Gompers in the *New York Evening Journal* in *Gompers Papers*, 5: 64–66, quotes on 65 and 64n2. Hearst sponsored the film *Patria* in collaboration with the Navy Department. It warned of the peril of a joint Japanese-Mexican invasion of California. Ratt, *Revoltosos*, 266–68.

21. A. T. Mahan, *The Interest of America in Sea Power* (1897; Port Washington, NY, 1970), 183.

22. William Appleman Williams, *The Tragedy of American Diplomacy*, rev. ed. (New York, 1962), 41.

23. Commager, *Documents*, 2: 170. For an excellent review of recent studies of U.S. imperialism, see Julie Greene, "The Labor of Empire: Recent Scholarship on U.S. History and Imperialism," *Labor: Studies in Working Class History of the Americas* 1 (Summer 2004): 113–29.

24. François Houle, "La crise et la place du Canada dans la nouvelle division international du travail" in *Le Canada et la nouvelle division internationale du travail*, ed. Duncan Cameron and François Houle (Ottawa, 1985), 84.

25. Jacques Rouillard, *Les syndicates nationaux au Québec de 1900 a 1930* (Quebec 1979), 39. On investments in Mexico, see James D. Cockcroft, *Intellectual Precursors of the Mexican Revolution, 1900–1913* (Austin, 1968), 18–23.

26. Gregory S. Kealey, "The Writing of Social History in English Canada, 1970–84" in Kealey, *Workers and Canadian History* (Montreal, 1995), 137.

27. Rouillard, *Syndicats nationaux*, 39–40.

28. David M. Gordon, Richard Edwards, and Michael Reich, *Segmented Work, Divided Workers: The Historical Transformation of Labor in the United States* (New York, 1982), 103; Daniel Nelson, *Managers and Workers: Origins of the New Factory System in the United States, 1880–1920* (Madison, 1975), 9; *Iron Age*, Apr. 18, 1912; David Montgomery, *Fall of the House of Labor: The Workplace, the State, and American Labor Activism, 1865–1925* (New York, 1987), 214–18; Scott, *Yankee Unions*, 148–50.

29. Montgomery, *Fall of the House of Labor*, 5–6.

30. *Ibid.*, 262–81.

31. Joyce L. Kornbluh, *Rebel Voices: An I. W. W. Anthology* (Ann Arbor, 1972), 13. This refers to the 1908 wording of the IWW preamble.

32. *Ibid.*, 35. See also Melvyn Dubofsky, *We Shall Be All: A History of the Industrial Workers of the World* (Chicago, 1969); *Proceedings of the first Convention of the Industrial Workers of the World* (New York, 1905).

33. S. Fanny Simon, "Anarchism and Anarcho-Syndicalism in South America," *Hispanic American Historical Review* 26 (Feb. 1946): 38–59; Hobart Spaulding, *Organized Labor in Latin America: Historical Case Studies of Urban Workers in Dependent Societies* (New York, 1977), 59; Wayne Thorpe, "El Ferrol!, Rio de Janeiro, Zimmerwald, and Beyond: Syndicalist Internationalism, 1914–1918," *Revue Beige de Philologie et d'Histoire* 84 (2006): 1005–24.

34. On municipal socialism, see Shelton Stromquist, *Reinventing "The People": The Progressive Movement, the Class Problem, and the Origins of Modern Liberalism* (Urbana, 2006), 30–31, 76–86; Joan Wallach Scott, "Social History and the History of Socialism: French Socialist Municipalities in the 1890s," *Le Mouvement Social* 111 (Apr.-June 1980): 145–53; E. P. Thompson, "Homage to Tom Maguire" in *Essays in Labour History*, ed. Asa Briggs and John Saville (London, 1967), 276–316; David Montgomery, "Racism, Immigrants, and Political Reform," *Journal of American History* 87 (March 2001): 1266–69.

35. *Machinists Monthly Journal* quoted in Julie Greene, "As I Am a True American: White U.S. Workers, Race, Empire, and Citizenship in the Canal Zone, 1904 to 1914," unpublished paper presented at the OAH annual convention, Apr. 4, 2003; Greene, *"The 13th Labor of Hercules": The United States and the Building of the Panama Canal 1903 to 1915* (New York: forthcoming), cited by permission of the author; Greene, "Spaniards on the Silver Roll: Labor Troubles and Liminality in the Panama Canal Zone, 1904–1914," *International Labor and Working-Class History* 66 (Fall 2004): 78–98.

36. Richard C. Berner, *Seattle 1900–1920: From Boomtown, Urban Turbulence, to Restoration* (Seattle, 1991), 76, 110–53. On the University of Washington, see

Dorothy Fujita-Rony, *American Workers, Colonial Power: Philippine Seattle and the Transpacific West, 1919–1941* (Berkeley, 2003), 61–67.

37. William English Walling, *Socialism As It Is: A Survey of the World-Wide Revolutionary Movement* (New York, 1913); Emile Vandervelde, *Socialism Versus the State*, trans. Charles H. Kerr (1914; Chicago, 1919).

38. Herbert Croly, *The Promise of American Life*, ed. Arthur M. Schlesinger, Jr. (1909; Cambridge, MA, 1965), 169. See also Howard Gillette, Jr., "The Military Occupation of Cuba, 1899–1902: Workshop for American Progressivism," *American Quarterly* 25 (Oct. 1973): 410–25.

39. Jim Zwick, "The Anti-Imperialist League and the Origins of Filipino-American Oppositional Solidarity," *Amerasia Journal* 24 (Summer 1998): 65–85; Robert D. Johnston, *The Radical Middle Class: Populist Democracy and the Question of Capitalism in Progressive Era Portland* (Princeton, 2003), 35–37. The platforms of the Democratic Party continued to advocate independence for the Philippines in 1904, 1908, and 1912. Grayson L. Kirk, *Philippine Independence: Motives, Problems, and Prospects* (New York, 1936), 38–39.

40. Nora Faires, "Leaving the 'Land of the Second Chance': Migration from Ontario to the Great Lakes States in the Nineteenth and Early Twentieth Centuries" (unpublished paper in possession of the author); Bruno Ramirez, *On the Move: French-Canadian and Italian Migrants in the North Atlantic Economy, 1860–1914* (Toronto, 1991); Tamara K. Hareven and Randolph Langenbach, *Amoskeag: Life and Work in an American Factory City* (New York, 1978); Donald Avery, *"Dangerous Foreigners": European Immigrant Workers and Labour Radicalism in Canada, 1896–1932* (Toronto, 1979); Carlos A. Schwantes, *Radical Heritage: Labor, Socialism, and Reform in Washington and British Columbia, 1885–1917* (Seattle, 1979); Marie Sarah-Jane Mathieu, "Jim Crow Rides This Train: The Social and Political Impact of African American Sleeping Car Porters in Canada, 1880–1939" (PhD diss., Yale University, 2001).

41. Gregory S. Kealey and Brian D. Palmer, *Dreaming of What Might Be: The Knights of Labor in Ontario, 1880–1900* (Cambridge, 1982); Kealey, "1919: The Canadian Labour Revolt" in Kealey, *Workers and Canadian History* (Montreal, 1995), 289–326; Norman Penner, ed., *Winnipeg 1919: The Strikers' Own History of the Winnipeg General Strike*, 2nd ed. (Toronto, 1975); David J. Bercuson, *Fools and Wise Men: The Rise and Fall of the One Big Union* (Toronto, 1978); Bercuson, "The One Big Union in Washington," *Pacific Northwest Quarterly* 69 (July 1978): 127–34.

42. Rouillard, *Syndicats Nationaux*, 12–41; Robert H. Babcock, *Gompers in Canada: A Study in American Continentalism before the First World War* (Toronto, 1974), 38–71; Stuart B. Kaufman, Peter J. Albert, and Grace Palladino, eds., *Samuel Gompers Papers*, vol. 4 (Urbana, 1992), 471–472.

43. Rouillard, *Syndicats Nationaux*, 31–36; Babcock, *Gompers in Canada*, 61–76. Flett could speak no French.

44. Rouillard, *Syndicats Nationaux*, 56–59. Both Tobin and Gompers appealed to large strike rallies without speaking French. On the origins of the Boot and Shoe

Workers and its union label policy, see Mary H. Blewett, *Men, Women, and Work: Class, Gender, and Protest in the New England Shoe Industry, 1780–1910* (Urbana, 1988).

45. Rouillard, *Syndicats nationaux*, 74–82, quote 79; Babcock, *Gompers in Canada*, 85–97; "Excerpts from the Minutes of a Meeting of the Executive Council of the AFL" in *Samuel Gompers Papers*, vol. 6, ed. Stuart B. Kaufman, Peter J. Albert, and Grace Palladino (Urbana, 1997), 134–36.

46. Babcock, *Gompers in Canada*, 111–42; Rouillard, *Syndicats Nationaux*, 157–204. In the very different context of the 1960s, that Catholic union movement was to be transformed into the militant and intensely political *Confédération des Syndicats Nationaux*. See Jacques Rouillard, *Histoire de la CSN, 1921–1981* (Montreal, 1981).

47. AFL, *Report of Proceedings of the Twenty-Fifth Annual Convention, 1905* (Washington, 1905), 17.

48. *Ibid.*, 18.

49. The 1900 resolution is quoted in Philip Taft, *The A.F. of L. in the Time of Gompers* (New York, 1957), 422. AFL, *Report of the Proceedings of the Twenty-Fourth Annual Convention, 1904* (Washington, 1904), 8.

50. For discussions of the AFL's insistence on national autonomy in the world trade unionism, see Taft, *A.F. of L.*, 418–26; Bernard Mandel, *Samuel Gompers: A Biography* (Yellow Springs, OH, 1963), 331–33.

51. Igualdad Iglesias de Pagan, *El Obrerismo en Puerto Rico: Época de Santiago Iglesias (1896–1905)* (San Juan, Puerto Rico, 1973), 35–41; Angel G. Quintero Rivera, *Patricios y plebeyos: burgueses, hacendados, artesanos y obreros: Las relaciones de clase e en el Puerto Rico de cambio de siglio* (Rio Piedras, Puerto Rico, 1988), 247–69. Igualdad Iglesias's biography of Santiago Iglesias has proven especially useful because it reproduces many movement texts at considerable length. For a revealing sample of Ramón Rivera's writing, see Angel Quintero Rivera, *Workers' Struggle in Puerto Rico: A Documentary History*, trans. Cedric Belfrage (New York, 1976), 17–39.

52. Iglesias, *Obrerismo*, 37.

53. Iglesias, *Obrerismo*, 194. My translation of Muñoz Rivera's passage, written in 1891: "*todavia no hemos sacudir a esas masas, rompriendo el hielo de su indiferencia y encendiendo en su curazón el sacra fuego del patriotismo*." Quintero Rivera, *Patricios y Plebeyos*, 260.

54. Maria Dolores Luque de Sánchez, *La Occupación Norteamericana y la Ley Foraker (La Opinión Publica Puertorriqueña), 1898–1904* (Rio Piedras, Puerto Rico, 1980), 138. For a useful discussion of historians' controversies over Puerto Rican reception of the U.S. invasion, see Luis Martinez-Fernandéz, "Puerto Rico in the Whirlwind of 1898: Conflict, Continuity, and Chance," special issue on War of 1898, *OAH Magazine of History* 12 (Spring 1998): 24–29.

55. Luque de Sánchez, *La Occupación Norteamericana*, 95–133; Eileen J. Findlay, "Love in the Tropics: Marriage, Divorce, and the Construction of Benevolent Colonialism in Puerto Rico, 1898–1910" in *Close Encounters of Empire: Writing the Cultural History of U.S.-Latin American Relations*, ed. Gilbert M. Joseph, Catherine C. LeGrand, and Ricardo D. Salvatore (Durham, NC, 1998), 147, 153–54, 158–59. Within a decade, popular tales came to include the theme of dangerously

free women who earned their own livings and were defiant toward men. Lillian Guerra, *Popular Expression and National Identity in Puerto Rico: The Struggle for Self, Community, and Nation* (Gainesville, FL, 1998), 38–39, 194–96.

56. Laird W. Bergad, *Coffee and the Growth of Agrarian Capitalism in Nineteenth-Century Puerto Rico* (Princeton, 1983), 198–209; Igualdad Iglesias, *Obrerismo*, 57–58, 101–2, 135; Guerra, *Popular Expression*, 181–83, 200–209; Blanca Silvestrini de Pacheco, *Los Trabajadores Puertorriqueño y el Partido Socialista (1932–1940)* (Rio Piedras, Puerto Rico, 1978), 17–18.

57. Iglesias, *Obrerismo*, 48–49, 73–77.

58. *Ibid.*, 21–24, 47–48. The U.S. military commander did interrogate Iglesias but released him upon concluding that Iglesias was not a supporter of anarchist propaganda by deed. Several prominent statesmen were assassinated by anarchists between 1896 and 1901, among them President William McKinley.

59. *Ibid.*, 50. On the SLP, see 73–76. Actually, the organization formed in 1899 was the Federation Regional de los Trabajadores de Puerto Rico (FLT). The FLT broke away later in the year and reorganized when the original group declared its support for the island's Republican Party. Iglesias went to Washington in 1899 and testified on behalf of the FLT in favor of annexation. Luque de Sanchez, *La Occupación Norteamericana*, 57.

60. Iglesias, *Obrerismo*, 101–6; Cesar Andreu Iglesias, ed., *Memoirs of Bernardo Vega: A Contribution to the History of the Puerto Rican Community in New York*, trans. Juan Flores (New York, 1984), 84–85.

61. For a study that emphasizes the importance of conspiracy cases to the AFL, see Victoria C. Hattam, *Labor Visions and State Power: The Origins of Business Unionism in the United States* (Princeton, 1993).

62. "Excerpts from Accounts of the 1900 Convention of the AFL in Louisville, Ky," in *Gompers Papers*, 5: 278–81, qt. on 280.

63. George Cortelyou to Gov. William H. Hunt, Oct. 19, 1901, Cortelyou Papers, Series 1, Box 2, Letterbook 5, 323, Library of Congress. I am indebted to Grace Palladino for this information. See also William G. Whittaker, "The Santiago Iglesias Case, 1901–1902: Origins of American Trade Union Involvement in Puerto Rico," *The Americas* 24 (Apr. 1968): 378–93; Iglesias, *Obrerismo*, 118–32, 166–82; Iglesias, *Bernado Vega*, 92–96; Santiago Iglesias to Gov. Hunt, Nov. 9, 1901, and Iglesias to Gompers, Nov. 12, 1901, Gompers Papers, microform, reel 53, 513–15, 520–21.

64. Quintero Rivera, *Workers' Struggle*, 62–63. AFL-style union practice had already created tensions within the Puerto Rican labor movement. See Arturo Bird-Carmona, "Between the Insular Road and San Juan Bay: The Cigar World of Puerta de Tierra" (PhD diss., University of Iowa, 1998), 109–13.

65. "From Edward Rosenberg," in *Gompers Papers*, 6: 4–5; Kazin, *Barons of Labor*, 29–30, 52.

66. Renda, *Taking Haiti*, 310–11.

67. Bird-Carmona, "Insular Road," 58–79, 170–83; "An Excerpt from an Article in the *Washington Star*," in *Gompers Papers*, 6: 423–29.

68. Quintero-Rivera, *Workers' Struggle*, 52–53.

69. Quintero-Rivera, *Patricios*, 110–79; Quintero-Rivera, *Workers' Struggle*, 86–112; Arturo Bird-Carmora, *"A Lima y Machete": La Huegla Cañera de 1915 y la Fundación del Partido Socialista* (Rio Peidras, Puerto Rico, 2001); "To Woodrow Wilson" in *Samuel Gompers Papers*, vol. 9, ed. Peter Albert and Grace Palladino (Urbana, 2003), 410–11.

70. Francisco A. Scarano, *Puerto Rico: Cinco Siglos de Historia* (Santafé de Bogota, Colombia, 1993), 654–58, 670–92. The quotations are from the 1919 party program, reproduced in *ibid.*, 655. Between 1919 and 1924, several AFL state federations, especially in the Midwest and Canada, also helped create political parties.

71. Silvestrini, *Los Trabajadores Puertorriqueños*, 59–127, 148–57, song on 73; Ruth Glasser, *My Music Is My Flag: Puerto Rican Musicians and Their New York Communities, 1917–1940* (Berkeley, 1993), 163–68; Scarano, *Puerto Rico*, 701; Sidney W. Mintz, *Taso: trabajador de la caña* (Rio Piedras, Puerto Rico, 1988), 178–84; this is a translation of Mintz, *A Puerto Rican Life History* (Westport, CT, 1974) with a bibliography and chronology by Francisco A. Scarano.

72. Scarano, *Puerto Rico*, 694–701; Gerald Meyer, *Vito Marcantonio: Radical Politician, 1902–1954* (Albany, 1989), 150–55. A Nationalist interpretation of these events can be found in Rubén Berrios Martínez, *La Independencia de Puerto Rico: Razón y Lucha* (Mexico City, 1983), 104–11, 184–89.

73. Scarano, *Puerto Rico*, 718; cf. Steven Fraser's interpretation of the relationship between the New Deal and the CIO in *Labor Will Rule: Sidney Hillman and the Rise of American Labor* (New York, 1991). For a clear, concise discussion of the partial success of Operation Bootstrap and the subsequent collapse of Puerto Rico's economy in the 1970s, see Rafael Bernabe, "Puerto Rico's New Era: A Crisis in Crisis Management," *NACLA Report on the Americas* 40 (Nov./Dec. 2007): 15–20.

74. David Montejano, *Anglos and Mexicans in the Making of Texas, 1836–1986* (Austin, 1987); Frank Tannenbaum, *Peace by Revolution: Mexico qfter 1910* (New York, 1966), 226–30; Benjamin Heber Johnson, *Revolution in Texas: How a Forgotten Rebellion and Its Bloody Suppression Turned Mexicans into Americans* (New Haven, 2003); Jesus Silva Herzog, *Un Ensayo sobre la Revolución Mexicana* (Mexico City, 1946); David M. Pletcher, *Rails, Mines, and Progress: Seven American Promoters in Mexico, 1867–1911* (Ithaca, NY, 1958); Friedrich Katz, *Secret War in Mexico: Europe, the United States, and the Mexican Revolution* (Chicago, 1981), 226–29, 558; Michael David Snodgrass, "The Birth and Consequences of Industrial Paternalism in Monterrey, Mexico, 1890–1940," *International Labor and Working-Class History* 53 (Spring 1998): 115–36.

75. Katz, *Secret War*, 127–28; Emilio Zamora, *The World of the Mexican Worker in Texas* (College Station, TX, 1993), 17. John Womack, Jr., *Zapata and the Mexican Revolution* (New York, 1968); Cockcroft, *Intellectual Precursors*, 91–116.

76. Richard Ulrich Miller, "American Railroad Unions and the National Railways of Mexico: An Exercise in Nineteenth-Century Proletarian Manifest Destiny," *Labor History* 15 (Spring 1974): 239–60.

77. Zamora, *Mexican Worker*, 110–23, 140.

78. Vernon H. Jensen, *Heritage of Conflict: Labor Relations in the Nonferrous Metals Industry up to 1930* (Ithaca, NY, 1950), 365–68, 408–19; Andrea Yvette Huginnie, "'Strikitos': Race, Class, and Work in the Arizona Copper Industry, 1870–1920" (PhD diss., Yale University, 1991); Johnson, *Revolution in Texas*, 71–143; James R. Green, *Grass-Roots Socialism: Radical Movements in the Southwest, 1895–1943* (Baton Rouge, 1978). Differing versions of the Plan de San Diego are presented in Johnson, *Revolution in Texas*, 79–82, and James A. Sandos, *Rebellion in the Borderlands: Anarchism and the Plan of San Diego, 1904–1923* (Norman, OK, 1992). On Mexican fears that IWW activity in Baja California represented a Yankee annexationist threat, see Lowell Blaisdell, *Desert Revolution: Baja California, 1911* (Madison, 1962), 13–20.

79. Cockcroft, *Intellectual Precursors*, 4, 91–119 (the 1906 program of the PLM is reproduced on 239–45); Begoña Hernández y Lazo, *Huelga de Cananea* (Mexico City, 1985); W. Dirk Raat, *Revoltosos: Mexico's Rebels in the United States, 1903–1923* (College Station, TX, 1981), 65–91.

80. Cockcroft, *Intellectual Precursors*, 127, 147; Raat, *Revoltosos*, 41–52, 115–17, 126–27, 162–63; Blaisdell, *Desert Revolution*, 169–72, 198–200; Ethel Duffy Turner, *Revolution in Baja California: Ricardo Flores Magón's High Noon* (Detroit, 1981).

81. Raat, *Revoltosos*, 162–203.

82. Cockcroft, *Intellectual Precursors*, 18–42, 205–6, qt. on 181; Katz, *Secret War*, 48; Raat, *Revoltosos*, 212–14.

83. Tannenbaum, *Peace by Revolution*, 123, 155–57; Katz, *Secret War*, 273; Cockcroft, *Intellectual Precursors*, 223–25. On Carranza's nationalism, tempered by fear of war with the United States, see Katz, *Secret War*, 134–35.

84. John Womack, *Zapata and the Mexican Revolution* (New York, 1970), 193–96, 200–202; Cockcroft, *Intellectual Precursors*, 113–14.

85. Katz, *Secret War*, 293–94; Womack, *Zapata*, 288–300.

86. Tannenbaum, *Peace by Revolution*, 232–42, 165–72.

87. Harvey A. Levenstein, *Labor Organizations in the United States and Mexico: A History of Their Relations* (Westport, CT, 1971), 11, 64–70; John Lear, *Workers, Neighbors, and Citizens: The Revolution in Mexico City* (Lincoln, NE, 2001).

88. Katz, *Secret War*, 313–14; Tannenbaum, *Peace by Revolution*, 137; Zamora, *World of the Mexican Worker*, 173–75; Sinclair Snow, *Pan-American Federation of Labor* (Durham, NC, 1964), 9–17; Gompers to M. Grant Hamilton, Sept. 27, 1915 in *Gompers Papers*, 9: 327; Excerpts from the Minutes of a Meeting of the Executive Council of the AFL in *ibid.*, 9: 436–43.

89. Gompers to William McAdoo, July 2, 1915, in *Gompers Papers*, 9: 296–300; Snow, *Pan-American*, 56–59.

90. Ronald Radosh, *American Labor and United States Foreign Policy* (New York, 1969), 40–43, 58–71; Snow, *Pan-American*, 11–18; Solon DeLeon, ed., *American Labor Who's Who* (New York, 1925), 286, 310.

91. Montgomery, *Fall of the House of Labor*, 356–59, 370–410; John S. Smith, "Organized Labor and the Government in the Wilson Era," *Labor History* 3 (Fall 1962), 265–86; Joseph A. McCartin, *Labor's Great War: The Struggle for Industrial Democracy and the Origins of Modern American Industrial Relations, 1912–1921*

(Chapel Hill, 1997); Melvyn Dubofsky, "Abortive Reform: The Wilson Administration and Organized Labor, 1913–1920" in *Work, Community, and Power: The Experience of Labor in Europe and America, 1900–1925*, ed. James E. Cronin and Carmen Sirianni (Philadelphia, 1983), 197–220; Dubofsky, *We Shall Be All*, 369–75, 384–91.

92. Ludwig Lore, "The IWW Trial," *Class Struggle*, Sept.-Oct. 1918, 381; Dubofsky, *We Shall Be All*, 385–87; Cf. Alan Dawley, "Internazionalismo e antimperialismo al tempo dell'IWW" in *Wobbly! L'industrial Workers of the World e il Suo Tempo*, ed. Bruno Cartosio (Milan, 2007), 228. See also Austin Lewis, "New Labor Movement in the West," *Class Struggle*, Sept.-Oct. 1917, 1–10; Tatsuro Nomura, "Who Were the Wobblies? The Defendants of the Chicago IWW Trial of 1918: Collective Biographies," *Journal of the Aichi Prefectural University* (Twentieth Anniversary Number, 1986), 135–50 (made available to me by Professor Ferdinando Fasce).

93. David Montgomery, "Nationalism, American Patriotism, and Class Consciousness among Immigrant Workers in the United States in the Epoch of World War I" in *"Struggle a Hard Battle": Essays on Working-Class Immigrants*, ed. Dirk Hoerder (DeKalb, IL, 1986), 327–51; Dubofsky, *We Shall Be All*, 382–97; William Preston, Jr., *Aliens and Dissenters: Federal Suppression of Radicals, 1903–1933* (New York, 1963); Office of Naval Intelligence, "Investigation of the Marine Transport Workers and the Alleged Threatened Combination between Them and the Bolsheviki and Sinn Feiners," Dec. 23, 1918, Department of Labor, Chief Clerk's File 20/580, RG 174, National Archives.

94. *San Francisco Chronicle*, Nov. 19, 1915, in *Gompers Papers*, 9: 344–46, qt. on 346. It was the same convention that had adopted the resolution to build solidarity among unions of the Americas. See also, Walter LaFeber, *Inevitable Revolutions: The United States in Central America* (New York, 1983), 53; Frank L. Grubbs, Jr., *Struggle for Labor Loyalty: Gompers, the AF of L, and the Pacifists, 1917–1920* (Durham, NC, 1968).

95. See Radosh, *Labor and Foreign Policy*, 103–84; Grubbs, *Labor Loyalty: Gompers, Labor and the Common Welfare*, 211–92.

96. Samuel Gompers to James Duncan, May 4, 1920, qtd. in Smith, "Labor and Government," 282. On the aspirations and strikes unleashed by the war, see Montgomery, *Fall of the House of Labor*, 330–410.

97. Montgomery, *Fall of the House of Labor*, 375–438, GE demands on 447; Elizabeth McKillen, "Ethnicity, Class, and Wilsonian Internationalism Reconsidered: The Mexican American and Irish-American Left and U.S. Foreign Relations, 1914–1922," *Diplomatic History* 25 (Fall 2001): 553–87, qt. on 578.

98. Elizabeth McKillen, *Chicago Labor and the Quest for a Democratic Diplomacy* (Ithaca, NY, 1995), 51.

99. Dawley, "Internazionalismo e antimperialismo," 231. My translation from the Italian: "*l'immediato primo dopoguerra merita di essere ricordato come il momento piú significativo dell'antimperialismo negli Stati Uniti dopo l'inizio del secolo.*"

100. McCartin, *Labor's Great War*, 191–94.

101. Gary Cross, *A Quest for Time: The Reduction of Work in Britain and France, 1840–1940* (Berkeley, 1989), 129–49; Denis MacShane, *International Labour and*

the Origins of the Cold War (Oxford, 1992), 21–42; Reiner Tosstorff, *Profintern: Die Rote Gewerkschafts Internationale, 1920–1937* (Paderborn, Germany, 2004), 130–64; Geert van Goethem, "An International Experiment of Women Workers: The International Federation of Working Women, 1919–1924," *Revue Belge de Philologie et d'Histoire* 84 (2006): 1025–47.

102. Simon, "Anarchism and Anarcho-Syndicalism in South America," 38–59; Snow, *Pan-American*, 28–29, 33–34; Hobart Spaulding, *Organized Labor in Latin America: Historical Case Studies of Urban Workers in Dependent Societies* (New York, 1977), 59. Spaulding argues that the IWW in Chile "never built a mass base" and was overshadowed by the Catholic labor federation, which was captured in 1919 and in 1921 by socialists affiliated with the Communist International.

103. Snow, *Pan-American*, 28–30, 45–46; Radosh, *Labor and Foreign Policy*, 352; Levenstein, *Labor Organizations*, 21–65, 73–74.

104. Levenstein, *Labor Organizations*, 33, 68–71.

105. Dubofsky, *We Shall Be All*, 382–91; David J. Bercuson, *Fools and Wise Men: The Rise and Fall of the One Big Union* (Toronto, 1978), 110–20; Babcock, *Gompers in Canada*, 111–42.

106. Snow, *Pan-American*, 9–30, 41–46, 53–55; Zamora, *World of the Mexican Worker*, 17–18.

107. Zamora, *World of the Mexican Worker*, 45.

108. *Ibid.*, 61–63, 80–81, 110–13, 162–71; Snow, *Pan-American*, 114–15; Gregg Andrews, *Shoulder to Shoulder? The American Federation of Labor, The United States, and the Mexican Revolution* (Berkeley, 1991), 2–90, 118; Colin Davis, *Power at Odds: The 1922 National Railroad Shopmen's Strike* (Urbana, 1997), 70, 147.

109. Levenstein, *Labor Organizations*, 101–6, 129; *New York Times*, Oct. 16, 1925, qtd. in Andrews, *Shoulder to Shoulder*, 4.

110. Snow, *Pan-American*, 114–15; James D. Cockcroft, *Mexico: Class Formation, Capital Accumulation, and the State* (New York, 1983), 110–33; Paul Friedrich, *Agrarian Revolt in a Mexican Village* (Chicago, 1977); Jocelyn Olcott, *Revolutionary Women in Postrevolutionary Mexico* (Durham, NC, 2005). After Gompers' death, discussions between the AFL and the CROM focused largely on limiting immigration from Mexico to the United States. They produced many AFL convention resolutions demanding the exclusion of immigrants but only ineffective verbal agreements between the two labor federations. Levenstein, *Labor Organizations*, 117–23.

PART VII

Political Interventions

Known primarily as a labor historian, Montgomery was also a critical voice on contemporary American politics, especially related to working-class life and the role of the labor movement. He emerged from military service at the end of World War II as a socialist and although his political perspective certainly evolved, he maintained these values throughout his life. In his career as an academic historian, he continued to actively and publicly support the labor movement, especially the United Electrical Workers, with which he had longstanding ties. In these essays he discusses the political implications of his scholarly work. They convey his critical analysis at four distinct moments in the recent history of the United States.

"What's Happening to the American Worker" was published as a pamphlet in 1970 by a group of radical scholars and activists associated with the New Left publication *Radical America*. It was a moment when many young people were looking to rank and file workers and their strikes as paths toward social transformation. Montgomery and some others in the intellectual movement that produced the "New Labor History" represented a link between the Old Left of the postwar era and the New Left of the late sixties and 1970s. With a blend of history and contemporary social criticism, this essay captured a transitional moment for American workers and the unions they had built. Drawing on his own work experience and political activism and on a subtle understanding of the historical trajectory of corporate capitalism, Montgomery affirmed that "as always, the workers will have to find their own way," grounded in a class consciousness kept alive by their "daily experience at work." He spoke directly to a new and sometimes skeptical activist generation and drew their attention to the historical "trademark" of workers' response to social crisis—"direct action."[1] His teaching and mentorship

Cover of "What's Happening to the American Worker," *Radical America* pamphlet, 1970.

at the University of Pittsburgh and Yale brought him into direct contact with this younger generation of radicals, while his continuing involvement with the labor movement offered them a crucial vantage point for understanding unions and labor politics.

In 1984 Montgomery took an active role in support of clerical and technical workers at Yale who had organized and struck for better wages and conditions. His foreword to a book Yale graduate employees wrote[2] placed the strike in the broader context of attacks on unions in the 1970s and 1980s and the successful strategies Yale unionists followed to win a contract in this beleaguered environment. In personal terms, this short piece and Montgomery's role in the strike reflected his continuing involvement with labor struggles over the course of his career.

"Yesterday's Wisdom, Changing Situations, and New Initiatives in the American Labor Movement" is the text for a talk Montgomery gave at Notre Dame University's Higgins Labor Program in 1990. The lecture series was named for Joseph Molony, a district leader and later a vice president of the United Steelworkers of America. Speaking amid widespread attacks on the labor movement, he asked if there were lessons for the moment in labor's past. Drawing his ideas from a papal encyclical as well as labor publications, he questioned society's total reliance on market values as the basis for social organization and posed instead socialist and Christian notions of social equality and solidarity as an alternative.

"Challenges Facing Historians of the Working Class," a talk delivered around 2000, represents Montgomery's clearest discussion of labor historiography in this volume. Assessing the field at a moment when his variety of materialist social history was under attack by postmodernists, Montgomery reflected critically on the ways "linguistic" analysis can enrich a materialist perspective. Based on new scholarship that drew on both traditions, he was generally optimistic about future directions of labor history as a field. Characteristically, he drew on African American, immigrant, Latinx, and women's and gender history as constitutive of the American working-class experience and identified emerging trends in the field that reflect a new international orientation, a broader conception of "work," continuing interest in local study, and attentiveness to the role of the state.

Notes

1. David Montgomery, "What's Happening to the American Worker," *Radical America* pamphlet (Madison, WI, 1970), 13, 19, 24.

2. Toni Gilpin, Gary Isaac, Dan Letwin and Jack McKivigan, *On Strike for Respect: The Clerical & Technical Workers' Strike at Yale University (1984–85)* (Chicago: Charles H. Kerr, 1988).

CHAPTER 17

What's Happening to the American Worker

Radical America pamphlet, Madison, WI: 1970, 1–27

American socialists cannot hope to develop a valid theoretical perspective for our times without an accurate assessment of the present aspirations of this country's industrial workers. Without such a foundation, radical analysis of imperialism, monopoly capital, the subjugation of women, and Third World struggles, impressive as much of it might be, bears an eerie resemblance to good Nineteenth Century Mugwump critiques of the sins of the trusts: the illiberal and parochial lower classes are assumed to be reaction's mass base, and the stockholder's meeting or academic assembly provides the ideal forum for progressive agitation.

This essay will not attempt to depict the proper role for those of us who are not workers to play in helping to guide current tendencies in working class thinking toward a socialist vision. It will attempt the much more modest task of suggesting where those tendencies are now headed in the absence of such guidance, or, more accurately, with a minimum of socialist guidance (for some conscious radicals survived even the 1950s in America's mines, mills, and loading docks). In a word, the article is designed more to enlighten intellectuals about workers than to suggest how intellectuals might help enlighten workers. There is no possibility of rebuilding a mass socialist movement in America if those engaged in that effort accept the assumption that Harvey Swados described so well, that the "worker has died out like the passenger pigeon," or if "he is still around, he is just like the rest of us—fat, satisfied, smug, a little restless, but hardly distinguishable from his fellow TV-viewers of the middle class."[1]

Recently the GE strike, the Wallace campaign, massive confrontations over lily-white hiring practices in the building trades, and the murder of Jock

Yablonski have rudely reminded America's intellectuals that the country still has industrial workers, and that those workers still have their grievances.

To some extent the intellectual must be forgiven his ignorance. The labor leader did nothing to correct the image of the contented worker. On the contrary, union officials themselves appeared more often than not as posh and prosperous suburbanites preaching their "team" and "mutual trusteeship" programs to increase labor productivity and improve the employer's competitive position, racing off on government junkets to the far corners of the earth arm-in-arm with the CIA to help hold down the efforts of working people in other lands to improve their lot, loudly endorsing every twist and turn of the Government's most belligerent and reckless Cold War policies—not to recoil even at the futile slaughter of their own members' sons in the bloody jungles of Vietnam.

To outsiders, be they intellectuals, blacks, or poor whites, the labor unions appeared more often than not as conservative, even openly crooked champions of petty privilege, content to watch the ratio of organized workers to the total labor force (already well below one in three) slip lower each year, fearing to raise the feeblest public protest when their brothers in the building trades flagrantly collaborated with contractors to exclude black men from membership and jobs, and satisfied to dissipate their vast political power in petty personal deals without the faintest shadow of even a local labor program against which they could test candidates.

To their own members the leaders of such unions looked little better. More than half of America's union members are now under 40 years old. One-fourth are under 30. If ever they do get themselves down to a local meeting, what do they hear about? The Bad Old Days. How rough it was before the union came, when those members were but kids, or not even born. What about them? The answer given by David McDonald is all too typical. Defeated in the 1965 election for the presidency of his union he consoled himself with the thought that "there was little left to seek for my steelworkers except for periodic wage adjustments. We'd done it all."[2]

Think of it: the union had done all there was to be done. Certainly no one could deny that the American worker of today enjoys immensely more of the comforts and security of life than his counterpart of a century ago. And no one acquainted with the history of the last hundred years should doubt that what the worker has gained he won for himself the hard way, through his union struggles.[3]

But before we accept Brother McDonald's self-satisfied judgment, I want you to listen to two statements, written 80 years apart. The first is from the pen of George McNeill, a leading figure in both the Knights of Labor and the early AF of L, writing on the meaning of the labor movement in 1887. The second consists of a series of comments made to Harvey Swados by his fellow automobile workers in 1957.

First McNeill summing up the grievances of the workers in 1887:

> The bell that calls the weary, half-paid worker from his needed rest taunts him with each resounding stroke. The machinery that renders his skill and time of less value to himself and more to his master becomes the hated instrument of torture, its monotonous hum keeping time to his groans and curses. The mill, mine, the foundry, and the roundhouse stand like giants, ever ready to swallow his substance. With such feelings constantly present in the hearts of the laborers, unused to thought, disciplined only to act, what wonder that violence should spread like an epidemic from station to station, from mine to mine, and from factory to factory.[4]

Now compare that voice from the past with voices of the present—three quotations from men who worked with Harvey Swados:

> Before starting work: "Come on, suckers, they say the Foundation wants to give away more than half a billion this year. Let's do and die for the old Foundation."
>
> During the rest period: "Ever stop to think how we crawl here bumper to bumper, and crawl home bumper to bumper, and we've got to turn out more every minute to keep our jobs, when there isn't even any room for them on the highways?"
>
> At quitting time (this from older foremen, whose job is not only to keep things moving, but by extension to serve as company spokesmen): "You're smart to get out of here. . . . , I curse the day I started, now I'm stuck. Any man with brains that stays here ought to have his head examined. This is no place for an intelligent human being."[5]

Almost a century elapsed between the first statement and the last three, but some basic facts of life had remained unchanged. The worker was and is an instrument bought and used by other men for their purposes. His attitude toward his work was and is, to use Swados's words again, "generally compounded of hatred, shame, and resignation."[6]

Perhaps one thing has changed. George McNeill sustained himself with a dream of a beautiful future which the workingmen themselves were to bring about in America. "In this movement of the laborers toward equity," he wrote, "we will find a new revelation of the old gospel, when the Golden Rule of Christ shall measure the relations of men in all their duties toward their fellows, in factory and workshop, in the mine, in the field, in commerce . . . (then) the new Pentecost will come, when every man shall have according to his needs."[7]

There is no such faith to sustain today's worker. Some will say: "It makes the time go quicker and easier when I keep thinking about that turkey farm I'd like to buy." The fantasies of others are less benign: "You get the feeling, everybody gets the feeling, whenever the line jerks everybody is wishing: 'Break down, baby.'"[8]

Basically, today's worker survives by splitting his life into two watertight compartments, his job and his home. The job is the place of bondage to which he submits in search of money. The home is where he hopes somehow to make life worthwhile with the goods that money will buy. Just go any day and stand by the time clock as the shift ends. See the men lined up with timecards in hand, waiting out the countdown for quitting time, then watch the mad dash to the parking lot for freedom and life. Then you will know what I mean.

But hold on a minute. Conditions on the job are certainly not the same as they were in McNeill's day. Two social forces have wrought great changes: the union and scientific management.

The successful spread of unionism to nearly 18,000,000 workers has significantly raised the income level not just of the members, but of millions of other workers for whom union scales have set industrial standards. Where unions have done their jobs at all seriously, they have provided their members with a precious sense of security. They supply a basic line of defense against abuse and arbitrary discharge, downgrading or suspension by management. They have put an end to industry's traditional practice of slashing wages at every downturn of the business cycle. They have done away with "packinghouse hiring," secured for the worker at least a minimum workday if he is called in, and even forced auto, steel, meat packing, and other industries to cut down on seasonal layoffs.

So important is this role of the union that, though most workers grouse about their leaders and their dues, stay away from meetings, and in fact take no part whatever in the life of the union, they have proven again and again in every major industry that they are ready to sustain strikes for many months rather than see their unions' power reduced. Jack Barbash was right when he wrote in 1961:

> For perhaps the largest number of union members the union serves a function, not a mission. The primary function of the union as these rank-and-filers see it is protection from unbridled rules of management. If he is not totally involved in the union, (the worker) does not, however, lack a deep-rooted perception of the protective function of the union.[9]

It has only been in the last 25 years that American big business has been content to curb unions rather than try to destroy them. The contrast between the two stormiest strike years in the nation's history shows the change. In 1919, 4,000,000 workers hit the bricks in the face of absolute refusal by capital to recognize their unions. They were crushed, and the next decade was the great age of the open shop "American plan" and the company union. When 4,500,000 organized workers struck in 1946, management chose not to challenge their determination to have unions, but rather to fence in the unions with the Taft-Hartley Law's prohibitions against secondary boycotts, sympathy strikes, political action, and radical leadership. In short, direct face-to-face collective bargaining was accepted, while actions of class solidarity were forbidden by law.

Since then it has been clear to the workingman that his union is officially tolerated, but always under a cloud of suspicion in the press, Congress, and law courts, and subject to an ever-increasing array of legislative restrictions. He knows that in the eyes of middle-class America his union is still not quite legitimate. Seeing school boards and hospital authorities resist the spread of unions to their workers today on the very same grounds and in the very same way Little Steel and General Motors did a generation ago, the worker senses that his own union is still far from secure. Down in Uniontown, Pennsylvania, coal miners and laundry workers proved the point by staging sympathy strikes to support the unionizing efforts of their brothers in the hospital.

Side by side with the major, if insecure, improvement the union has brought in the worker's life must be placed the somewhat contrary impact of scientific management. The gospel of management reform preached by Frederick Winslow Taylor and his associates at the beginning of this century has directly touched every American worker, the union men and those missed by the unions alike. Through systematic application of industrial engineering American industry has achieved staggering levels of productivity, discarded the Nineteenth Century notion that low labor costs could be achieved only by low wages, and made possible a drastic improvement in the people's living standards even without any significant improvement in the shares distributed to wages and profits.

On the other hand, the American worker has paid a heavy social and psychological price for this progress. The essence of scientific management, as seen by Taylor himself, was to take the "initiative," the control over how the job was done, away from the worker and put it in the hands of management. Taylor described his method as "the deliberate gathering in on the part of those on management's side of all of the great mass of traditional knowledge, which in the past has been in the hands of the workman, and in the physical skill and knack of the workman, which he has acquired through years of experience."[10]

In other words, management picked the workers' brains, took from them their knowledge of how the job was done, then distilled that knowledge into engineering formulas that could be taught in college and handed it back to the workers in the form of orders. Taylor's associate Frank Gilbreth, pioneer of time-and-motion studies, instructed workers in "the one right way" to perform every assigned task. Another colleague, Henry Gantt, made it clear: "Learning to obey orders is often the hardest part of the workman's task."[11]

Let me make myself perfectly clear here. To introduce a systematic approach into the organization of production should have been an unqualified boon to the workers. Imagine the industrial engineer and the production worker pooling their knowledge, pulling in harness together and linking their different skills in common effort. Not only would production shoot up, but work itself would be all-absorbing—yes, even interesting and enjoyable. But that is not what happened. Today the factory is the scene of a battle of wits between the worker and the industrial engineer. The time-study man is the symbol of everything the worker hates. The main cause of wildcat strikes is not the demand of management that the workers produce, but its demand that they obey. "Management's right to manage" is the holy of holies of American industry.

The reason for the conflict is very simple and is well understood by every workingman. The industrial corporation exists to make a profit for its owners. No matter how eloquently the industrial engineers may claim to apply impartial, "objective" standards, they are hired by the company to increase those profits. Consequently, the employer insists that the power to make decisions about production must rest exclusively with him.

As George Romney said when he headed the Automobile Manufacturers' Association: "If the management representatives must talk to the union representatives before they can act or make a decision, then management has lost its management function."[12]

Perhaps the worker will be permitted to file a grievance about the orders given him, but while that grievance is winding its torturous way through proper contractual channels to an arbitrator, the worker involved must continue to do what he was told. How seldom it is today that a shop steward can even settle a grievance on the shop floor. Once the power to stop or slow down production was taken from the steward by the union contract and the company instructed the foreman to refer all grievances to the personnel office, the worker's protest against the decisions of "expert" engineers was referred to "expert" negotiators. The worker found himself right back where he started from. Somebody else makes the decisions about his fate.

The crux of the matter is that in the corporation of today, the greater role a man plays in making a decision, the less likely he is to be personally affected by that decision. The plant manager does not lay himself off when he installs new machines. And this "line of command" is justified today by the cult of the expert and the myth of complexity. The worker is told that only trained specialists can decide such issues. The clearest statement of this doctrine came from Frederick Winslow Taylor himself. Listen to what he said in 1912, and think of how this ideology pervades factories, schools, and government today:

> I can say, without the slightest hesitation, that the science of handling pig-iron is so great that the man who is fit to handle pig-iron as his daily work cannot possibly understand that science; the man who is physically able to handle pig-iron and is sufficiently phlegmatic and stupid to choose this for

> his occupation is rarely able to comprehend the science of handling pig-iron; and this inability of the man who is fit to do the work to understand the science of doing his work becomes more and more evident as the work becomes more complicated, all the way up the scale. I assert, without the slightest hesitation, that the high-class mechanic has a far smaller chance of ever thoroughly understanding the science of his work than the pig-iron handler has of understanding the science of his work . . . that the man who is fit to work at any particular trade is unable to understand the science of that trade without the kindly help and co-operation of men of a totally different kind of education.[13]

This process of removing from the worker control over his work, then compounding the crime by labeling him too dumb to understand it anyway, is right now being carried to its ultimate development with the spread of automation. The historical process is quite clear. First Taylor and his colleagues studied the workers and learned from them how industrial jobs were done. Then they reduced that information to mathematical formulas which could be learned in engineering school and claimed only the trained engineer was capable of mastering such knowledge. It was World War II which added the next step, for in the search for a means to track high-speed aircraft for ground fire control, men learned that machinery can be directed by means of electronic impulses. Since any information which can be expressed in logical terms, such as a mathematical formula, can be translated into electronic impulses, it became clear that machines could be directed by computers. The worker's brain, it seemed, could be replaced by an electronic brain, and the expert assumed the task of programming that mechanism.

The worker now finds he needs a higher level of education than ever before to master the technical intricacies of his job, but he is denied the right to use his own mind to control what he is doing. He must anxiously watch his machine respond to the commands someone else programmed into it. Said one tape-controlled machine operator at Allen-Bradley:

> You have to keep your eyes and ears on it all the time. You have to know when a switch will fail or a fuse will blow and the thing will still be working. You have to be able to read blueprints better than you did on an ordinary machine. When the fuse blows, the table will move but the spindle won't be working. You never know what the machine is going to do—before you did.[14]

This combination of the high degree of technical competence required by his job with the trivial nature of the decisions he is allowed to make lies at the heart of the workers' discontent today. The worker is keenly aware that he is no fool. He knows he can still outsmart the engineers on his own job, that he has his own private way of doing the job that is often better than the assigned way—or at least allows him some say in what he is doing, like banking parts, doubling up cuts, or sharing tasks on an assembly line with a buddy. Many workers will recognize this experience of a Westinghouse boring mill hand:

> A lot of times the programmer will come down and you'll say: "What tools do you think I should use?" He'll say: "Let's use this tool, let's use that tool." And actually, he's picking up more from me than I am from him because I've been here 26 years.[15]

It is this daily experience at work which keeps alive the worker's class consciousness. Everything in his home environment, the press, the television, the installment-plan living, invites him to join the middle-class "consensus." The American Dream of opportunity and independence is dangled before him daily. But the instant he hits that time clock, Mr. Big lets him know: "Your ass belongs to me." For the next eight hours the lines of authority, the lines of class, are sharply imprinted on every moment.

Many workers try to reconcile the two ends of their lives by devoting their lives to the goods they can buy. The desperate quest for meaning through houses, cars, and TVs drives them back to moonlight on a second job, so that there is never enough time to enjoy what they have bought. Many others lapse into self-hatred and self-contempt, believing that if they only had brains or "gumption" they could escape the trap of factory labor. They are failures, and since they have been taught any man worth his salt in America can get ahead, the fault must be their own. "The social order is thus protected," as Ely Chinoy said, "only at the psychological expense of those who have failed."[16]

The only alternative is to attack "the social order," and the brutal Red purges which followed both world wars have shown what troubles that course can bring on their heads. Furthermore, most workers genuinely see no alternative that looks to them any better. A Milwaukee IAM shop steward spoke for millions when he expressed his dilemma this way:

> First of all, I think capitalism is the best system and I am in full agreement with that. I would rather live under this than any other form of government working. But, it seems that companies put as the most important thing their product, stockholders, and things like that. And I say that what is produced is merely a product made of metal or wood or something like that. And actually, the people working there have feelings and souls and one thing and another.[17]

The common response to this dilemma is to lapse into cynicism. This attitude is above-all evident among the younger workers of today, those whose whole lives have been experiences in powerlessness and aimlessness and who have been so inundated with advertising and propaganda from the day of their births that they have developed a fine immunity to any kind of appeal for any cause whatever.

Many of the older workers, scarred by memories of their hunger and their struggles of the '30s, say the cure for youth's complacency would be a "good five-cent recession." In the words of a 53-year-old shop steward from International Harvester:

> I think the working people, they need a good whipping once to appreciate what they had, and to appreciate their union. Right now it don't seem that they appreciate it. Now, let's get back to the way people feel. They feel that they pay their three-dollar-a-month dues, they shouldn't have to attend meetings. They elect a steward, he will do their fighting for them, he'll do their arguing for them, he'll go to the meetings, he'll go back and tell them what went on, why should they bother about it? That's just about the feeling of a lot of people . . . And I would say that a good whipping once in a while would do them a hell of a lot of good.[18]

But younger workers turn a deaf ear to such warnings of the Bad Old Days—"pie in the sky talk" they call it, in a curious reversal of the older meaning of that phrase. Their minds are on their mortgages and their installment payments. They will volunteer for any amount of overtime in the frantic effort to meet their monthly bills. Any work stoppage threatens them, interest rates threaten them, taxes threaten them, urban redevelopment threatens them. If they are white, they believe blacks threaten them. All these are seen as menacing the comforts they have worked so hard to put into their homes, and it is only for the sake of those comforts that they submit to the daily indignities from The Man at work. Herman's Hermits caught this mood when they sang: "The man with the cigar, I hope he doesn't push me too far." Here is an audience to cheer when George Wallace proclaims:

> I think there's a backlash in this country against the theoreticians who look down their nose at the steelworker and the paper worker and the communications worker and the beautician and the barber and the policeman and the fireman and the little businessman and the clerk and the farmer, and say you don't have intelligence enough to know how to get up in the morning and when to go to bed at night, and people are tired of theorists running their country.[19]

If the Wallaceite reaction is to be understood clearly, two points must be kept in mind. First, while Wallace recognizes and plays upon the workers' sense of alienation, his own program promises only to lead them deeper than ever into the social morass which alienated them in the first place. He parades before the workers second-rank or even imaginary enemies: the bureaucrat, the theoretician, the hippie. Mr. Big himself is never mentioned. How silent Wallace remained during the GE strike. He identifies "The Establishment" with Harvard and Washington, not with General Motors and US Steel. Quite the contrary, he leaps to the defense of the very "property rights" which shield management's prerogatives to command and compel the worker to obey. Aware of the worker's fantasy of escaping to a turkey farm or a little business of his own, Wallace lures the workers deeper into this dream world to identify their own aspirations, as we saw, with "the farmer" and "the little businessman." Here is the demagogue in his classic role, playing on the grievances of the people in order to bind them even more closely to the social order which created those grievances. The leaders of the AFL-CIO sensed this fraudulent quality to Wallaceism in 1968, and quite properly attacked the Alabama Governor by exposing how badly he measured up against a genuine labor political program.

Second, as popular as the Alabama racist undoubtedly is in so many white working-class neighborhoods, his popularity has a remarkable tendency to disappear just when Wallace needs it most, on election day. I do not think this means his strength has been overrated. Quite the contrary, it means that when the ballots are cast, the workers are swayed by other threats which propel them back to the regular Democratic ticket. Those threats stem directly from the work situation, and in 1968 they were summed up in the person of Richard M. Nixon.

Nixon meant two things to the workers. The first was a freer hand to employers to attack union power. Workers correctly anticipated that the Republicans would stiffen corporate resistance to labor. Remember Jack Barbash's point: the worker does not feel "totally involved in the union," but he does have "a deep-rooted perception of the union's protective function." Without it, he would stand utterly helpless before Mr. Big.

The other reason to fear Nixon was that he represented unemployment. There is some irony in this situation. Roosevelt and the Keynesians have by now pretty well convinced workers that depressions can be avoided by means of intelligent government action. The rank-and-file fully supports leaders of the AFL-CIO when they react instantly to the slightest downturn of the economy with calls for expansionist fiscal and public-works policies. But if most workers no longer think that crises of overproduction are simply unavoidable features of capitalism, if they believe government action can prevent them, the logical corollary is that government action can also create them. They think Eisenhower did just that in 1958. They also know that Nixon's economic advisors believe in a "little unemployment" as the only cure for inflation. To put it bluntly, they believe there is middle-class pressure in favor of putting workers out of work, and Nixon wants that middle-class vote.

These are the fears which led countless Wallace supporters to vote for Humphrey when the chips were down. The truly reliable voting supporters of

Wallace were found in the upper middle class—prosperous and well-educated bigots, whose second choice would certainly have been Nixon himself, and for whom Spiro Agnew is now the knight in shining armor.

Both of these observations suggest that the American workers' sense of their own identity and their own interests as a class remain a potent force in American life, that the current sociological vogue of dividing our society into a middle class (comprising the effective labor force) and an alienated poverty culture (attached to the world of welfare) is totally misleading. Furthermore, it is right at the place of work, where the sense of class is strongest, that American workers right now are responding to the present crisis, not with a new ideology or an elaborate political program, but with that form of practice which has historically been their trademark—direct action.

American labor has no mass-based Communist or Social Democratic party, no widely espoused ideology of a New Jerusalem, no intellectuals to speak on its behalf. It has, consequently, long been obliged to express all its needs and aspirations through union action. In this sense, the famous Industrial Workers of the World, radical as they may have been, were simply manifesting the elementary facts of American life. In our present social order, dominated as it is by the military and industrial complex, computer control, and the elitist ideology of The Expert, the workingman is able to influence his own fate only by direct action. I repeat the point I made earlier: in today's corporation—let me say, in today's America—the greater the role a man plays in making a decision, the less likely he is to be affected by that decision. Those who decide that inflation must be fought by a hard line against wage increases and by "a little unemployment" will never suffer either a wage-freeze or unemployment themselves. Those who are assigned the task of suffering can reverse the "enlightened" decisions of the elite only by mass action.

Here is the significance of the General Electric strike, easily the most far-reaching struggle to be undertaken by American labor since 1946. The myth of labor's affluence was shattered by these 147,000 strikers averaging less than $7,000 a year during a period when the Department of Labor said $10,500 was needed for a moderate standard of living. In the doctrines of its former director of employee relations, Lemuel Boulware, GE manifested the last word in the Divine Right of Management. Even a US Court of Appeals had declared in 1969 that the Boulware policies "amounted to a declaration . . . that not only the union but the process of collective bargaining itself might be dispensed with."[20]

The workers' response in the months just past took the form of a nationwide strike, mass picketing (often in defiance of injunctions) in mill towns throughout the land, the total repudiation of a back-to-work drive which used every device in the employers' book, and frequent instances of co-operation between university students and workers—something America had scarcely heard of since the 1930s. In GE's many new Southern runaway plants, the unions became the center of community life. Sympathy strikes became commonplace, despite Taft-Hartley. The 1300 workers of United Shoe Machinery in Beverly, Massachusetts, whose local union had never had a strike of its own, struck for 19 days rather than make parts for GE. Such grass-roots solidarity brought unity at the top, in the form of close co-operation among the 14 major unions involved. This co-operation embraced AFL-CIO unions, the auto workers and teamsters of the Alliance for Labor Action, and the UE. Perhaps the most significant index of what happened was the return of the UE from its 20-year-old exile to an honored position of leadership, publicly acknowledged by the other unions.

The upshot was that GE was forced to bargain. The terms of settlement (in my judgment quite good) were not as important as the fact that this corporation had for the first time in more than 20 years been prevented from imposing its will—had been forced by direct action to come to terms with its workers. So infectious was the new spirit that the IUE reversed its own 20-year-old practice (embodied in its constitution) and allowed its members to vote on the agreement. Its biggest local, Schenectady 301, in fact voted no.

The new unionism which checked General Electric has many other manifestations today. As always, the keys to the vitality of a union movement are the extent to which it is engaged in organizing new recruits and the strength of its shop stewards. New organizing drives today are successfully reaching out in two directions: to white-collar workers and to service workers. In both areas mass picketing and militant, democratic unionism prevails. The sight of school teachers, hospital workers, and garbage men going off to jail for violating injunctions is becoming routine. The teachers are demonstrating that arbitrary authority is as common, and as intolerable, in educational hierarchies as it is in factories.

Hospital workers have been in the forefront of service employees. They too have brought old truths home to Americans. Despite Daniel Moynihan they have made it clear that the basic cause of poverty is low pay. Despite all the efforts of anti-poverty programs and university projects to upgrade the poor, unions like Local 1199 have shown that what the poor need is upgraded jobs. The fact that about a fourth of all full-time, year-round, non-white male workers earn less than $3500 per year is not the result of missing fathers or some mysterious quality of the black psyche, but the result of the pay American industry provides for the work they do. Service workers are learning that the only way the decision-makers, faced with middle-class protests over high taxes and service costs, will do anything about those pay scales, is if the workers use their organized power to make them do it. From Atlanta and Memphis to Pittsburgh that's what's happening.

While the strike of white hospital workers at Uniontown shows that poverty is no respecter of color, there is no doubt that a great impetus has been given these new organizing drives by the black liberation movement. To see the interaction between the black community and the labor movement only in terms of black struggles against unions is very misleading. The fact that black America is made up overwhelmingly of industrial and service workers makes it inevitable that the new sense of militancy and dignity in the black community should influence increasingly the behavior of the union movement itself. Through black caucuses, revolutionary union movements like the one at Dodge, and introduction into collective bargaining of tactics developed on the civil-rights front this influence is already being felt. In such areas as Pittsburgh's hospitals, black workers are clearly leading the way for the whites to follow. It is safe to say that the more effective black workers are in these new organizing efforts, the more the white workers will be tempted to join them rather than oppose them.

The revitalizing of the shop stewards and other elected local officers as the direct spokesmen of the rank-and-file on the job manifests itself in several ways. The Steelworkers' current struggle to extend incentive payments in the teeth of defiant corporate opposition is clearly reinvigorating local union activity in this area. The whole thrust of management practice today is away from incentives toward such schemes as measured day work to allow absolute management control over rates of output and to perfect the integration of the workers' activity with the automated sectors of the plant. By pushing hard in the opposite direction, the United Steelworkers, willy nilly, are mounting a battle for workers' control which has the strength of clearly meaning money in the pocket for every worker involved.

More apparent to the outsider is the current rash of wildcat strikes (usually over the manning of jobs, as in Sharon, Pennsylvania), sympathy strikes (like the shutting down of J & L to support the trainmen), and strikes in defiance of union officials (like that of the mailmen). In all these efforts the local and steward level of leadership is clearly asserting itself. In fact, the spread of conglomerates, or of super-corporations, and perfection of automation are bound to give increasing importance to wildcat and quickie strikes, just as they have already increased the incidence of pacts among unions for industry-wide strikes at the other end of the scale. If all grievances are saved up for the contract negotiations once every two or three years, the modern corporation can easily prepare itself to hold out for months, to use supervisory personnel to man automated equipment, and to invoke government aid against the threat to national defense such massive strikes involve. On the other hand, precisely such automated corporate giants are peculiarly vulnerable to brief, unexpected work stoppages which can easily disrupt their intricate, computerized scheduling.

President Nixon knows it, too, and the new array of legislation his Administration is preparing is aimed directly at these emerging types of worker actions. Most drastic and most revealing of all is his proposal that workers be forbidden by law from voting on contract settlements. Remember how recently the thrust of anti-union propaganda in this country was that labor unions were too dictatorial and that the rights of members had to be protected by such measures as Landrum-Griffin? Now the same voices are crying that labor unions are too democratic—the members upset the decisions of the experts!

We are witnessing the reassertion of old truths about the relations among social classes, truths as old as the industrial revolution, truths which no amount of extolling of the "consumer economy" can change. But the new shape of our society (computer control, the conglomerate corporation, the black revolution, the women's liberation movement, the student revolt over the style of life, Wallaceism) is certain to give the new syndicalism attributes never before seen in the American labor movement. As always, the workers will have to find their own way. The leaders of the AFL-CIO could articulate their members' grievances and show how they form a coherent whole reaching from the lunacy of Vietnam through the defiance by US Steel of the arbitrator's incentives award to the underpaid employment of the ghetto. But they won't. Here is another old truth. Carl Sandburg said it 34 years ago:[21]

> The people will live on.
> The learning and blundering people will live on.
> They will be tricked and sold and again sold
> And go back to the nourishing earth for rootholds,
> The people so peculiar in renewal and comeback,
> You can't laugh off their capacity to take it.
> The mammoth rests between his cyclonic dramas.
> . . .
> This old anvil laughs at many broken hammers.
> There are men who can't be bought.
> The fireborn are at home in fire.
> The stars make no noise.
> You can't hinder the wind from blowing.
> Time is a great teacher.
> Who can live without hope?
> In the darkness with a great bundle of grief
> the people march.
> In the night, and overhead a shovel of stars for
> keeps, the people march:
> "Where to? What next?"

Notes

1. Harvey Swados, "The Myth of the Happy Worker," *A Radical's America* (Boston, 1962), 112.

2. David McDonald, *Union Man* (New York, 1969), 324.

3. See Robert Ozanne, *Wages in Practice and Theory: McCormick and International Harvester, 1860–1960* (Madison, Wisconsin, 1968), chapter 4.

4. George McNeill, *The Labor Movement: The Problem of Today* (New York, 1887), 460–461.

5. Swados, 118–119.

6. *Ibid.*, 112.

7. McNeill, 468–469.

8. Ely Chinoy, *Automobile Workers and the American Dream* (Garden City, New York, 1955), 71, 94.

9. Jack Barbash, *Labor's Grass Roots* (New York, 1961), 200.

10. Frederick Winslow Taylor, "Testimony Before the Special House Committee," 40, in Taylor, *Scientific Management, Comprising Shop Management, Principles of Scientific Management, Testimony Before the Special House Committee* (New York, 1947). Each of the three books bound together has separate pagination.

11. Henry Gantt, *Work, Wages and Profits*, 2nd ed., (New York, 1919), 156.

12. Quoted in Neil Chamberlain, *The Union Challenge to Management Control* (New York, 1948), 3.

13. Taylor, "Testimony," 49.

14. *UE Guide to Automation and New Technology* (New York, 1969), 20.

15. *Ibid.*, 23.

16. Chinoy, 129-130.

17. Sidney M. Peck, *The Rank and File Leader* (New Haven, 1963), 301.

18. *Ibid.*, 121.

19. Quoted in *Guardian*, September 21, 1968.

20. "GE Versus American Labor," *Labor Today* IX (January-February 1970): 6.

21. Carl Sandburg, "The People, Yes," *Complete Poems* (New York, 1950), 615, 617.

CHAPTER 18

Foreword to *On Strike for Respect*

In *On Strike for Respect: The Clerical and Technical Workers' Strike at Yale University, 1984–85*, edited by Toni Gilpin, Gary Isaac, Dan Letwin, and Jack McKivigan (Chicago: Charles H. Kerr, 1988)

How can working people win today? What should they try to win? The story of the unionization and strike of clerical and technical employees at Yale University helps us answer both those questions.

Since the mid-1970s the American labor movement has been battered by plant closings, company demands for concessions, systematic destruction of industry-wide agreements and of pattern bargaining, renegotiations of signed contracts under threats of bankruptcy, and reorganizations of international trade by multinational corporations, whose speculative designs show no interest whatever in the welfare of American workers and communities. Real earnings ceased to grow, and middle-income jobs became increasingly scarce, so that each passing year has seen inequalities of income become more glaring. After 1980 the assault was intensified, as the government dismantled regulatory agencies that had formerly provided some security for workers' health and for the union standards, revamped the National Labor Relations Board and the Civil Rights Commission to strengthen employers' hands, and ruthlessly smashed the air traffic controllers' union as a signal to the whole country that a new era had arrived. Every day in every way the government and the media celebrate these developments as a triumph of individualism, of the unfettered market, and of new prosperity for the fortunate few.

The clerical and technical employees at Yale challenged this new era head-on. They did so by breathing new life into the beleaguered labor movement. They joined a major AFL-CIO union, filed for and won an NLRB certification election, went on strike, and successfully negotiated a first contract. All those things had been accomplished by other workers many times before. They represent the established practice of modern unionism in the United States. What was new in the Yale struggle was the workers' sense of organization, their goal of equality, and their spirit of solidarity. All three were rooted in the daily lives of the people involved, and all three represented a repudiation of Reaganite ideology.

Organization came first. The hundreds of activists who made Local 34 tick knew that a union is organized not once, but every day. The need of the hour was not simply to sign people up, but to make them active members of elaborate networks of action and discussion that reached into every corner of the enterprise. The endless round of lunchtime gatherings, the consultations between negotiating committee members and their departmental constituents, and the lively debates on picket lines were what allowed two thousand women and men to decide what they wanted and how they were going to get it. Organization overcame the isolation and helplessness of individuals. The demands arose out of the organization.

The union's demands stressed equality: standard rates for clearly defined tasks, equal pay for jobs of comparable worth, and ladders of progression that all employees could ascend together. The money demands were designed to end the systematic underpayment of jobs filled mainly by women, to rebuild that threatened middle-income group of earners, and to make a respectable retirement possible. Invigorating all these demands was the battle-cry of "respect." Women and men, white, black, Hispanic, and Asian employees together sought treatment and earnings that reflected their contributions to the University.

Their goals were won through solidarity. First and foremost, came the daily manifestations of unity in their own ranks and the unstinting support offered the clerical and technical employees by Yale's service and maintenance workers. Sharing strike benefits with each other, walking the lines day after day, mobilizing large and enthusiastic demonstrations, and going to jail together, the strikers infused the University with a mood of mutual concern and support. They reached out to New Haven residents, to students, and to other employees of the University, involving all of them in strike activities. After the end of the strike the victorious members of Local 34 charted a three-point plan of action for the future: to build the union continuously in every department, to make New Haven a union town, and to ally themselves with black workers in South Africa and the campaign for divestment of Yale's funds from that country.

The U.S. labor movement has been beaten down and revived again many times during the last 150 years. Its revivals have always been animated by a sense of organization, equality, and solidarity similar in some ways to the one recounted in this book. Today, however, those principles have assumed added meaning. They are indispensable to union success in this grim epoch. Beyond that, they also provide the keys to a necessary redefinition of labor's goals. Only when working people are organized into unions they control can they even decide what they want. Only through solidarity can they hope to win it. Many similar struggles throughout the land will be required if American working men and women are to chart a path toward a community life based on their needs and welfare. As the members of Local 34 learned early in their battle: no union, no matter how large, militant, and resourceful, is big enough to stand alone.

Note

Reprinted courtesy of C. H. Kerr Publishing Company.

CHAPTER 19

Yesterday's Wisdom, Changing Situations, and New Initiatives in the American Labor Movement

Unpublished manuscript, October 11, 1990, David Montgomery Papers, New York University, Tamiment Library and Robert F. Wagner Labor Archives

This lecture series was established to help the present generation and future generations "better understand the principles of industrial unionism as articulated by Joseph P. Molony." The principles of industrial unionism provide a timely question for us to consider in the autumn of 1990. Our country seems to have turned its back on the beliefs which Joseph Molony articulated by word and by deed, from his youthful efforts to bring an effective union to his fellow workers in Buffalo's steel mills to his battle for industry-wide standards in the copper mines of the American West.

The challenge of understanding the origins, historic application, and present meaning of the principles of industrial unionism assumes a peculiar shape today. Few of the familiar signposts that have guided, or misguided, our labor movement during the past century remain standing today. We are experiencing, all at one and the same time, stunning testimony to the collective power of working people in action, tightened governmental restraints on union activity in both the United States and Europe (and routine murder of trade unionists in Latin America), and the trumpeting of loud hosannas to the unrestrained pursuit of corporate and personal profit by every medium of communication of ideas.

First, the bright side: The concerted struggles of millions of ordinary and very extraordinary women and men have checked the upward spiral of nuclear weaponry, opened prospects for a more democratic polity from South Africa and eastern Europe to Chile and Nepal, and ended the epoch of the Cold War. Here at home workers have demonstrated a willingness to strike for endless months and have often enjoyed solidarity from other unions and sympathizers of a type most commentators had thought vanished from American life after the 1940s. At Pittston, NYNEX, Boeing, and Colt the strikers won. So did the Janitors for Justice in Los Angeles.

Nevertheless, the legacy of PATCO and of twelve years of concession bargaining still dominates the domestic scene. Traditional anti-union weapons like injunctions, private security forces, and "permanent replacements," have been vigorously revived. They have been supplemented by an arsenal of new armor: bankruptcy filings, decertification elections, out-sourcing, "temporary" employees numbering in the millions, privatization of public services, attacks on prevailing wage requirements for government contracts, and racketeering suits by employers against effective strike actions. Such weapons old and new have made almost any strike hazardous. They have brutally prolonged the battles against Eastern Airlines and Greyhound, and they destroyed good unions at Phelps Dodge, International Paper, and Hormel.

The ideological justification for this magnification of corporate power has been celebration of what is mystifyingly called "the free market." To restore America's competitive edge, to accelerate economic growth, and to bring the blessings of democracy to the rest of the world, we are told, it is necessary to "unleash enterprise" and restore "flexibility" to the workplace.

Even the democratic struggles of peoples in other lands are interpreted for us in this vein. "In Eastern Europe, It's the Sale of the Century," proclaimed the *New York Times*. "Assets of over $100 billion are available for profit-minded investors."[1] We are supposed to believe that the collapse of communist regimes proves that no economy can prosper unless it is directed by men who are guided by the quest for their own enrichment.

Our press would have us believe that the ordinary citizens of Eastern Europe and the Soviet Union are eager to dispense with all social ownership and social direction of economic activity as speedily as possible: five hundred days to the free market! And voices of new government officials are often quoted, hailing Margaret Thatcher as the oracle of economic reform. For example, Nikolai Petrakov, an advisor to President Gorbachev on economic affairs, proclaimed: "When I criticize the Government program in terms of its compensation for rising prices of bread and meat, it is because it is a subversion of the market principle. People should not be paid because they eat bread and meat but because they work."[2] The quest for full shelves in the stores seems to have overruled every historic protest ever mouthed by a socialist, or a trade unionist, or a Christian, that human beings are the subjects of economic activity, not simply its instruments, and that work is the basis of community life and welfare, not simply means to individual self-aggrandizement.

What options does this paradoxical combination of democratic initiatives and market delusions leave the American labor movement? Does yesterday's wisdom contain any guideposts at all for tomorrow's actions? To answer such questions, we need to reconsider those principles of industrial unionism for which Molony stood. They may be summed up in three words: solidarity, organization, and equality. Solidarity, because people who are employed by others for wages have no effective power to influence their society and government, or even their conditions of work, as isolated individuals. Their strength comes from standing by each other. Their social power comes from the human bondings that create common interests.

Organization, because only deliberate action and purposeful debate can give effective shape to solidarity. Organization enables people to decide together what they want, to make use of their numbers and their strategic locations in the economy and society in order to achieve those goals, and to finance and sustain themselves during the long battle that invariably faces ordinary people when they set out to improve their own lot. It is precisely because workers cannot wield effective power without organization that the battle for democracy inside the union movement is so important.

Equality, because that secures the community toward which we strive. Although no major labor organizations have ever advocated that each individual worker receive the same material goods as each other person, arbitrariness, favoritism, and cruel extremes of personal fortunes have always been anathema to working people. Molony's own United Steelworkers found more than 50,000 different job titles and wage rates in the American steel industry, when they won their first contracts. The union set out at once to rationalize the wage structure, first by filing thousands of grievances, then by creating a joint evaluation committee to fix a small number of justifiable labor grades and job titles for the industry nationwide. In 1946 the Steelworkers waged the largest strike in American history to that time. Their goal was a flat 17 1/2 cents-an-hour increase for everyone. Unlike the percentage increases that characterized union settlements after 1950, this style of across-the-board raise compressed wage differentials. And it was quickly followed by major bargaining efforts to raise the wage levels of the South to those of the North.

But those achievements of the Steelworkers in the 1940s need to be set in their historical context. We must remember that workers have embodied the principles of organization, solidarity, and equality in a variety of different organizational forms in the past, and they are bound to develop still different forms in the future. If we want to look for guideposts to help the struggle for democratic self-rule evade the waiting claws of the multinational corporations, it may be worthwhile to consider not only how Molony's Steelworkers came into being, but also what other forms of modern trade unionism came before and after that time.

During the last one hundred years union strength has grown in three waves, each of which overlapped with the decline of the preceding wave. Moreover, each phase was dominated by different groups of workers and different styles of unionism. Today all three types of unionism still play important roles, but all are on the defensive and searching for a path to revival.

The first continuous trajectory of union growth lasted from 1897 to 1947. It featured a modified version of the nineteenth-century trade union, and its enduring centers were in construction, railroading, and coal mining (despite the disastrous setbacks for miners in the late 1920s). Other significant unions, though considerably weaker ones, were then found in intracity trucking, printing trades, food services, and longshore. Union membership was determined by occupation, rather than by place of employment, and trade agreements were negotiated more often with associations of employers than with individual firms. No government agency determined the jurisdiction or bargaining unit of the early unions. Such questions were settled by the unions themselves.

Although these unions pioneered in the battle for safety legislation and workers' compensation, their primary political goal was to stop government interference through injunctions, police action, and enforcement of yellow-dog contracts, with the workers' own exercise of collective economic power. Their decisive victories in Congress preceded the New Deal: the Norris-LaGuardia anti-injunction act (1932), the Davis-Bacon prevailing wage law (1931), and the Railway Labor Act of 1926.

Even at the nadir of the Great Depression less than 64% of construction workers were union members. By 1947 union membership encompassed 87% of construction workers, 65% of all mine workers, and 91% of railroad workers. A major obstacle to total unionization was the racial exclusion practiced by many of the building and railroad unions themselves.

During the next twenty years (1947–67), however, these unions suffered catastrophic losses—especially building trades, where union density fell to 41% in 1966, less than half the 1947 level.[3] While the labor force had increased by almost two-thirds, postwar construction of suburbia was a spawning pool for open shop firms (as well as for residential racial segregation underwritten by federal mortgage practices). The building trades made little effort to resist the trend, concentrating their attention instead on retaining control of large urban commercial construction, and in the process reinforcing the unions' own exclusive hiring practices. Here was a source of bitter conflict between the AFL-CIO and the civil rights movement.

By the 1970s anti-union contractors had developed sufficient size and strength to challenge the unions in the heartland of urban commercial construction. Tens of thousands of contractors, who combined in the name of the "merit shop," were encouraged by efforts of the Nixon administration to restrain building costs, by the newly established Business Roundtable, and especially by the Reagan recession of the early 1980s. In 1985 only 22% of America's construction workers were union members.

Similar combinations of industry development outside the unionized heartland, decades of inert leadership, and growing attacks from employers had also by then driven union membership among miners of all sorts down to 15%. By 1985, however, a process of renewal was evident in both mining and the building trades. Molony himself had helped create the industry-wide coalition of unions in the copper mines, which conducted a successful nine-month strike in 1967 and 1968. The revival of the coal miners is a familiar story. It began with the black lung associations of the 1960s, drew new strength from the murder of Jock Yablonski, and evolved through the Miners for Democracy to restructuring of the UMWA and the creative leadership of Richard Trumka, to Camp Solidarity and to the victory over Pittston Coal.

New initiatives in the building trades have attracted less popular attention, but they are no less important than those in mining. Through affirmative action programs, membership books and apprentice programs major trades have been opened to many thousands of workers from minority groups, who had previously been shut out of unionized commercial construction. National and local union leaders have often joined with contractors to promote union construction and have involved themselves directly in the process of bidding for job contracts. Many of the trades have cultivated more active membership participation in union affairs and in organizing drives. The study of labor history and the goals of the movement has often become an integral part of the training they offer apprentices.

In Massachusetts the building trades mobilized an unprecedented and successful public campaign to preserve the state's prevailing wage law during a 1988 referendum. The Massachusetts trades enlisted the support of many community groups in the campaign, among them the Minority Contractors Association—a development that would have been inconceivable before the breakdown of the unions' own discriminatory practices. In fact, the very act of publicly searching for allies was a novel experience: for the trades, and the campaigns of many unions to recruit new members (including the "salting" of construction sites with rank-and-file organizers) have restored in some (though by no means all) localities the vibrancy of nineteenth-century construction unionism.[4]

The unionism in construction, mining, and railroading which I have described had fashioned its basic mode of operation before Joseph Molony even arrived in the United States. Unionism in the manufacturing sector, where he worked, followed a different course from that of the older organizations, in its ascent, in its decline, and in its search for renewal.

Less than 8% of workers in manufacturing were union members in 1931, despite intense, if sporadic, surges in union strength during the preceding half century. Titanic struggles in steel, textiles, meat packing, ship building, farm equipment, and electrical manufacturing between 1918 and 1922 had all ended in defeat for the workers, leaving the women and men of the clothing industry and some textile mills lonely keepers of the union flame. After 1933, however, unions not only returned to the scenes of their earlier efforts, but also secured beachheads in auto, rubber, and aircraft. They expanded and continued growing even after the crafts had begun their decline, to reach their peak density (42%) in 1953. Most of the new union contracts in manufacturing were won by unions in the Congress of Industrial Organizations, though some AFL affiliates opened their doors to mass production workers and grew rapidly—especially the Machinists, the Teamsters, and the Brotherhood of Electrical Workers.

The new unions were inseparable from the political coalition that brought America the New Deal. Their members were the driving force behind federal emergency relief, the Wagner Act, the WPA, social security, and minimum wages. During the war the CIO tied its aspirations for an expanded New Deal to the mobilization of the economy. It formed the Political Action Committee, under the leadership of Sidney Hillman, in order to help reelect President Franklin D. Roosevelt in 1944, as well as to defeat special enemies of labor and elect friends in Congressional and state campaigns. Many historians have agreed with Bert Cochran that "the PAC was a powerhouse," of decisive importance in several industrial states, which was soon imitated by the American Federation of Labor, and which "laid the foundation for the modern labor bloc in American politics."[5]

The United Steelworkers poured money and salaried staff into its 1944 campaign, with dramatic impact in wards where steel workers and their families resided. Moreover, the union incessantly linked the achievement of its social goals to the Grand Alliance against the Axis. In May 1943, *Steel Labor* featured a dramatic centerfold demanding a "substantial down payment on the Four Freedoms," starting with democracy in the American South and national planning for postwar prosperity.[6]

A cry went up from the business world that management had lost its "right to manage" to an alliance between the new unions and Washington. The *Iron Age* headlined an editorial on the eve of the 1946 elections, "Who Shall Plan, You or Uncle Sam?" In a preview of today's cult of the free market (and one that was partially successful in its own time), Frederick A. Hayek's attack on planning and the welfare state, *The Road to Serfdom* was featured in bookstores and college curriculums across the land.[7]

By 1946 the ideological struggle over the nation's future policies was at flood tide. The CIO had expanded its political demands to include national health insurance, national child-care facilities, prohibition of racial or sex discrimination, government construction of homes, voting rights for Afro-American and Chicano citizens, and national economic planning. Determined opposition from the Dixiecrats and Republicans defeated all those measures. Instead,

Congress enacted the restrictive Taft-Hartley law, while the CIO's ties to the Democrats carried it headlong into support of the Cold War and expulsion of dissident member unions on charges of "Communist domination."

Although the CIO contributed mightily to the Democratic electoral victory of 1948, the political tide did not turn in its favor. Despite their campaign promises to repeal Taft-Hartley, the Democrats brought to the floor in Congress in 1949 a bill which actually retained several restrictive features of the new law, and then failed to muster the votes to pass even that. After the outbreak of the Korean War repeal efforts singled out only specific features of the law. Union practice soon accommodated itself to the strictures of the law (except in the building trades), just as dominant union ideologies adhered to Cold War anticommunism.

Consequently, not only did the United States emerge from the 1940s with the leanest excuse for welfare state of any industrialized country, but its industrial unions had also ceased to espouse any fundamental expansion of the government's role in directing economic and social development.[8] Nevertheless, they did establish national standards through pattern bargaining, which flattened regional wage differentials, doubled average real family incomes during the three postwar decades, and placed most union members in the ranks of home-owners.

Although the employers' counterattack got under way during Eisenhower's "rolling readjustment" of 1958–60, it was not until the late 1970s with the global migration of capital, increasing foreign competition, and the relocation of industry out of the unionized Rust Belt, that business routinely employed the now-familiar arsenal of anti-union weapons, and union membership was driven down to 25% of the manufacturing work force. Non-union shops came to set wage patterns (Iowa Beef style), average family incomes went into decline, and homelessness challenged home ownership as the hallmark of the American Standard of Living.

In every industrial union a debate over the path to revitalization is now in progress. On one side stand the many union leaders who have been persuaded by their fear of plant closings, interminable strikes and decertification elections, or by their own members' tangible lack of faith in their leadership, to tie their fates as closely as possible to whatever companies will still recognize them. "Non-adversarial" relationships look good when the company seems to hold all the trump cards, and also when the possibility of the firm's economic failure is very real. On the other side stand advocates of policies to rekindle rank-and-file militancy in the factories and community coalition in the neighborhoods and in the chambers of local government. Their hope is not just to retard the tide of concessions and closings, but also over the long haul to energize a new social mobilization that will change the path of the country's economic and political development.

The outcome of that debate will not be settled exclusively within the industrial unions. As union power in manufacturing subsided, a third wave of unionism gathered force in public employment. Unions in this sector have had extremely broad and overlapping jurisdictions, and government agencies have played the decisive role in determining bargaining units. Moreover, unionism has been inseparably linked to the size, health, and character of the public sector itself. The historic enclaves of unionism in municipal firefighting, police, and maintenance work were dramatically overshadowed by the militancy of schoolteachers and sanitation workers during the 1960s. Employees of hospitals and universities, where ownership was private but government funding decisive, also engaged in strikes, which could be won only by alliances with civil rights, feminist, and community groups, and by dramatic demonstrations and civil disobedience. President Kennedy's executive order of 1962 reversed the thrust of the Truman-era decrees that had kept federal civil servants out of unions, and opened the door to unionism among employees at all levels of government. By 1965 union density in the public sector had surpassed that in private industry, and by 1975 40% of government employees were union members.

Although public sector employees constitute almost one-third of all union members today, their numbers have also been reduced during the last decade by the combined impact of tax revolts, privatization, contracting out of jobs, and the intense hostility of many elected officials. State and city governments on whom Reagan's New Federalism has dumped both higher expenditures and lower revenues have time and again demanded concessions and staff reductions from the unions they faced—even from unions that had recently supported the election campaigns of officials they now face angrily across the table. Unions like AFSCME in Philadelphia, the Pennsylvania Social Service Union, the Texas State Employees (CWA), and the Service Employees in Los Angeles have responded by mobilizing the electorate and recipients of public aid in defense of the threatened public sector. They have mixed job actions with lobbying, arbitrations, public appeals, and well-planned strikes to block dismantling of government services.[9] Public sector unionism is and will remain intensely political, in every sense of the word.

To sum up: the American union movement has experienced three overlapping waves of growth and decline—one located primarily in construction, mining, and railroading, a second in manufacturing, and a third in the public (and quasi-public) sector. Each wave featured a different style of unionism, and each manifested a different relationship between unions and the government. In all three sectors of the movement the current crisis has led to widespread questioning of established practices and the conventional wisdom.

At each moment in the past when the labor movement has increased its influence in public affairs, renewed its vitality in areas of earlier defeats, or broken out into domains that had previously been nonunion, it has tapped into the reservoir of the everyday thoughts and experience of working men and women, where the principles of solidarity, organization, and equality are nourished. It is also the case, however, that each moment of renewal of the labor movement has required the overturning of some established leaders and institutions of the movement itself. The democratic impulses of our time do not consider anything on this earth sacred, and especially not those people or agencies who speak in the workers' name.

No lessons from the past enable us to predict the future, except to say that labor unions in neither the West nor the East will ever again be the way they were in the days of Kennedy and Khrushchev. There is certainly nothing in the past of human experience, however, to suggest that the current mania for the free market will enjoy a long life. Too many workers in our land lament what they call "the disappearance of the middle class." And too many workers in Eastern Europe have already seen store shelves filled—at prices none of them can afford.

Neither the Soviet coal miners fresh from their nation-wide strike nor the American counterparts whom they visited at Camp Solidarity last spring spoke in the language of competitive individualism. The Soviet miners were astonished to hear the vocabulary of class struggle used by the Americans, who were actual miners, not party *apparatchniki*, but they admired the Americans' determination to defend the union their fathers had built. In fact, so great was the visitors' admiration that their parting wish was that they might create back home something for their children similar to the union built by the Americans' parents.

We are already witnessing three significant developments, which hint at the future shape of labor struggles: a renewed appreciation by trade unions of their relations to the communities in which they function, a battle to reimpose social standards, both national and international, on the labor market, and a direct incursion by workers' organizations into domains that corporate management now jealously guards as its exclusive domain.

The sense of community has been manifested in several ways. First, from the grass roots to the headquarters of the AFL-CIO the necessity of coalitions with non-union groups is now accepted, and community activists who were shunned in union halls two decades ago are now invited to participate in both political campaigns and strike support. Press attention has been focused on coalition activity in Washington, like the defeat of Bork's nomination to the Supreme Court, and the growing campaign for national guarantees of health care for all.

I would like to draw attention, however, especially to the many coalitions which have been organized at the local level. In Connecticut and New Mexico, for example, well organized and persistent joint efforts of labor, civil rights, feminist, and environmentalist groups have seriously changed the political complexion of state legislatures. Struggles against plant closings have grown into efforts to rebuild regional economies, as in the Tri-State Conference on Steel or the Naugatuck Valley Project in Connecticut. The Naugatuck Valley Project, which has chapters in six towns, has been sustained primarily by local Catholic and Protestant churches, the United Auto Workers, the Connecticut Citizens' Action Group, and the worker-owned Seymour Specialty Wire Company, which it helped create, but it is also supported by the region's chamber of commerce. Through local solidarities and careful planning the project has partially reversed the damage inflicted on the valley by transnational corporations.

"Jobs for Justice" actions have united local allies with union members from different internationals and from all three historic sectors of the labor movement in mutual strike support. Workers have pledged "I'll Be There" at least five times a year in solidarity with other workers in town. The effects have been especially important in smaller cities, like New Haven. A great exception to that rule has been Los Angeles, where the thousands of people mobilized in the name of Justice for Janitors met, first, a brutal attack by the police, then a sweeping victory at the bargaining table.[10]

The fight for national and even international standards is evident in the auto workers' New Departure movement, the struggle of the Mine Workers to preserve the integrity of national contracts, joint bargaining by multiple unions with General Electric and Westinghouse, and some beginnings of international cooperation among unions. The fight for standards has also stimulated legislative campaigns (most effective at the state level) for comparable worth, parental leave, plant closing, and occupational health bills. The declining quality and spiraling cost of medical care has reopened the question of a national health plan, and even attracted important support among employers. Whether the efforts involve collective bargaining, governmental action, the mobilization of non-governmental social groups, or (as is often the case) all three fronts at once, they all aim at creating at least a minimum level of social entitlements, which workers deserve simply because they are human beings.

Moreover, both the end of Cold War barriers and the global movements of capital and goods have made Americans increasingly aware that their fate is tied to the conditions and struggles of working people in other lands. We all need to ponder the words of Pope John Paul II: "While in the past *the 'class' question* was especially highlighted as the center of [the quest for social justice], in more recent times it is *the 'world' question* that is emphasized."[11] Learning the meaning of international solidarity will be a new experience for American trade unionists. In the past, industrial unionism at its best forged unity among workers of all national backgrounds who found themselves in the United States. That is no longer enough. We must now build working ties across national boundaries to match the power of transnational corporations. We must learn how high our stakes are in the battles of Third World peoples for social justice.

Finally, successful mobilizations of craft, industrial, and public service unions to meet the challenges of our day have invariably led workers' organizations to venture deeply into the terrain once clearly marked Management Prerogatives. The four-year strike at Colt Firearms ended with the employees becoming part owners through a state-financed purchase of the plant. Public employees' unions have responded to threats of privatization by their own initiatives to improve delivery of services. The machinists resisted mismanagement of Eastern Airlines first by challenging the plundering of the company by directors representing banks and aircraft companies, and then dumping Frank Lorenzo.

All these instances of the democratic upheaval of our times have challenged frontally the notion that those who occupy the top offices of corporate management possess and deserve some kind of exclusive entitlement to making decisions that shape the lives and fortunes of millions of other people. The managers of our largest enterprises are quick to proclaim their own social responsibilities. What they resist is anyone else telling them what those responsibilities are. Their ideologists celebrate a dynamic economy of allegedly irresistible change, but they find it inconceivable that the rights of ownership and management, which were only defined during the last century and a half, might also be changed. On the contrary, they take refuge behind the myth of the free market to announce that history has ended, and they have won.

The democratic upheaval of our time suggests to me that history has only begun, and that quite a different future can emerge from the increasingly fierce social conflicts of our times. Today's labor struggles for community needs and social standards follow in that path. The industrial unionism of Joseph Molony's time linked the goals of workers' control, production for use, and a vibrant public sector serving community needs. In defiance of corporate insistence that the world be reshaped to satisfy "the needs of the economy," labor's new campaigns also point toward conscious redirection of economic activity to create a more livable world.

Notes

Reprinted courtesy of New York University, Tamiment Library and Robert F. Wagner Labor Archives.

1. *New York Times*, May 22, 1990, D1, D5.
2. *New York Times*, September 14, 1990, A3.
3. All data on union density—here and below—are taken from Leo Troy, "The Rise and Fall of American Trade Unions: The Labor Movement from FDR to RR," in Seymour M. Lipset, *Unions in Transition* (San Francisco, 1986), 87 (table 7).

4. *Labor Research Review*, 12: *Up Against the Open Shop: New Initiatives in the Building Trades* (Chicago, 1988); "Toning Up Union Muscles," *Engineering News Record* (April 26, 1990), 36–40.

5. Cochran, 242, 243. Cochran's evaluation does slight the precedents of AFL political action in the 1906 and 1980 elections and the Conference for Progressive Political Action in 1922.

6. Mark McColloch, "Consolidating Industrial Citizenship: The USWA at War and Peace, 1939–46," in Paul F. Clark, Peter Gottlieb, and Donald Kennedy, eds., *Forging a Union of Steel* (Ithaca, NY, 1987), 83–84; "What Are We Fighting For?" *Steel Labor*, May 28, 1943, 6–7.

7. Clark, Gottlieb, and Kennedy, 98; Frederick A. Hayek, *The Road to Serfdom* (Chicago, 1944).

8. In 1964, the Executive proposed a legislative program to combat poverty significantly different from the CIO's program of 1946. It proposed a 35-hour week, job training and public works, an equal employment opportunities bill, an increased minimum wage, Medicare and increased social security, increased food stamp allotments, an urban renewal program, and tax cuts to stimulate economic growth. Out of these proposals the Johnson administration included only work training, the EEOC, and the tax cut in its proposals to Congress. The next year Medicare was also adopted. *AFL-CIO News*, Feb. 22, 1964.

9. *Labor Research Review*, 15: *Privatization and Contracting Out* (Chicago, 1990).

10. Good accounts of coalition movements can be found in Jeremy Brecher and Tim Costello, eds., *Building Bridges: The Emerging Grassroots Coalition of Labor and Community* (New York: Monthly Review Press, 1990).

11. Pope John Paul II, *On Human Work* (Boston: St. Paul Editions, n.d.), 9.

CHAPTER 20

Challenges Facing Historians of the Working Class

Unpublished manuscript, c. 2000, David Montgomery Papers, New York University, Tamiment Library and Robert F. Wagner Labor Archives

If you want to write the history of working people, you must be prepared from the start to wrestle with sources that require careful and imaginative use, to encounter frequently professional colleagues who consider any interest in class struggles to be *passé* and to engage in relentless controversies with fellow labor historians and with influential people in the labor movement itself about the topics you engage, the methods you use, and the conclusions you reach. There is nothing new about this. All historians of working people and their movements have hammered at the door of a skeptical, if not hostile, historical profession. That was true of the labor journalists of the nineteenth century who wrote the first, pioneering accounts of their own movement, the reform-minded labor economists who introduced the subject to the academic world at the turn of the century, the New Deal liberals and the Marxists who recounted the influence of workers' mass struggles on the country's political development, and the so-called New Labor historians, who were inspired by popular mobilizations to win civil rights and end the Vietnam war to explore the roles of human agency in shaping history and of working-class cultures in shaping human agency. They all knew that the subject about which they wrote was inescapably political, and inescapably contentious. So be it.

College courses on the history of American labor proliferated in history departments between the 1960s and the 1980s, then and only then. Job postings specifically for labor historians virtually disappeared in the wake of the rapid exodus of manufacturing from the continental U.S., the Reagan revolution in the country's political agenda, and the collapse of Soviet communism. Who wanted to bother with workers anymore? Moreover, celebrated scholars on the academic cutting edge transformed historical interest in popular culture into postmodernism. Under the influence of Foucault and Derrida, they argued that domination pervaded all relationships, and that subjugation and submission were constituted in discourse. In academic journals the favorite concepts used by labor historians to analyze everyday experience—class, exploitation, capital accumulation—were themselves denounced as discursive modes of gender and racial subordination.

It is evident by now that the linguistic turn had a devastating impact on the study of European labor history. Many eminent Europeanists in this country have transferred their attention to new research interests. Some editorial board members of *International Labor and Working-Class History* fought mightily to change the title and the purview of that influential journal, before they resigned from the board. Among historians of the American working class, the outcome of the philosophical controversies has been more positive in my opinion. Analysis of the ways in which power pervades all aspects of human behavior and sensitivity to the ways in which rhetoric—words—shape people's actions has proved to be especially valuable in reframing our thinking about gender and about "whiteness."

Although influential practitioners of postmodernism like Patrick Joyce, Joan Scott, and Christopher Tomlins, present themselves as leading a war of extermination against historical materialism, many materialists have learned valuable lessons from them and incorporated sophisticated tools of linguistic analysis into interpretations of working-class life and struggles which those materialists continue to root in experience and exploitation. There is a real world out there. But we can improve our understanding of that reality by also striving to grasp the ways men and women of the past have imagined it, and also the history of the concepts we employ.

An outstanding example of materialist interpretation enriched by linguistic analysis can be found in Julie Saville's 1994 book, *The Work of Reconstruction: From Slave to Wage Labor in South Carolina, 1860–1870*. While Saville is keenly aware of the tight boundaries that federal policies and northern-based planters, as well as their former owners and the Ku Klux Klan, described around freed peoples' aspirations, she scrutinizes carefully and persuasively the everyday struggles that shaped the meaning of wage labor and sharecropping in practice. Hers was not a story of laws and ideas constituting social life while facing "resistance" (to use a term that is all too popular and often all too vague), but rather one of incessant collective and individual struggle at the point of production, in family affairs, and in the use of state power over who owed precisely what to whom in the new contractual relationships. We cannot grasp what happens at work or the changing nature of wage labor, by reading only court cases, important as they are in framing power.

The nature of this struggle is illuminated by careful scrutiny of the words of contending parties—if you will, of texts. But Saville makes it clear that

African Americans knew well the rhetoric of dominant white political groups, yet infused their own meaning into that vocabulary. She also finds that freed people's frequent recourse to the written word in petitions and letters produced narratives that were not autobiographical but collective. Moreover, she writes, "Outside the centers of resistance to restoration [of plantations], popular agitation for land often spoke in an indirect idiom of song, dance, religious enthusiasms, and the interpretation of omens."[1]

The basic reason that historians who continue to insist on the reality of experience have been able successfully to adopt analytical techniques from those who deny that reality is that the influence of E. P. Thompson, C. L. R. James, and Antonio Gramsci had long since guided the most influential historians of American labor away from reductionist economic explanations and toward the close scrutiny of working people's speech, gestures, and codes of conduct at work and in the neighborhood, where keys to understanding working-class agency were to be found. Culture was already the centerpiece of Herbert Gutman's agenda and influence. Saville has demonstrated that the best methods of analyzing social power and conflict produced during Gutman's heyday can be richly augmented by devoting close attention to: 1) the ways participants in social conflicts imbibed, but also interpreted and reframed the dominant discourse, and also 2) to changing relationship between public and private power—that is to say, to the nature of state power at different points in history.

One way to discern what course new research in our field is taking is to look at *Dissertation Abstracts* and see which topics have been favored in recent years. The heading "labor history" yields 296 titles for 1997, 314 titles for 1998, and 173 titles for 1999. The college labor history courses which proliferated during the last two decades are evidently still stirring interest. True, many of the dissertations listed turn out to be in economics, sociology, or literature, but even they do not suggest that working people have been forgotten by graduate students. But what subjects have attracted those whom we would classify as historians?

The first thing that catches my eye is that, despite the shriveling up of European labor history studies, studies of workers in Asia, Africa, and Latin America are flourishing, perhaps as never before. Abundant and sometimes splendid research is being lavished on the workers of China and Japan. An example of special interest to us has been produced by Elson Boles at SUNY-Binghamton. He examined the way silk production in Japan and silk textile manufacture in Paterson, New Jersey, were transformed after 1880 by new trade policies adopted by both governments. The upshot was not only the famous strikes of Paterson (remember Gutman), but also the Chichibu revolt of 1883 in Japan.[2]

The second is the continuing influence of gender studies in reshaping our notions of what working-class history is all about. More than a dozen recent dissertations investigate ways in which both governmental and non-governmental provisions of poor relief and social insurance have been designed to reinforce prescribed familial roles. Linda Gordon and Alice Kessler-Harris are among the established scholars who have highlighted these questions for young researchers.

Moreover, gendered analysis has reminded us that although large manufacturing units dominated the organizing strategy of this country's industrial unionists and of revolutionaries for the first half of this century, they never employed the majority of wage earners. Workers in clerical and service occupations have now taken center stage in the interests of historians, as well as of activists. Many if not most of them have been women throughout this century. Dorothy Sue Cobble's important book on waitress unionism, *Dishing It Out,* has led us to question the whole dichotomy of craft versus industrial unionism, around which most writing of labor history has been structured since at least 1905.[3] Similarly, historians who have devoted close attention to paid household workers, like Tera Hunter, Kim Phillips, and Varpu Lindström-Best, have all noted the decisive community roles of those women both in recreational and religious life of their communities and in political struggles, such as battles against racial discrimination in employment, voter registration, and Finnish socialist activity.[4]

Third, both government policy and international links of trade, debt, and migration have attracted much attention in recent dissertations. The New Labor History of the 1970s had encouraged studies of local history. It was at the community level that working-class culture was most likely to be revealed (as in Gutman's studies of Paterson), that workers' political impact was most evident (as in Leon Fink's *Workingmen's Democracy*), and that the whole panorama of class interaction could most easily be portrayed (as in Iver Bernstein's *New York Draft Riots of 1863* and Karin Sawislak's *Smoldering City: Chicagoans and the Great Fire, 1871–1874*). Such works often came under attack for underestimating the impact of the federal government on local life and for failing to explore the decisive role of the judiciary in shaping the nature of state power in the U.S. The battle cries of critics were to "bring the state back in" and to recognize the "constitutive" role of law.

The fact remains that community studies remain popular as dissertation topics. Looking closely at an industrial city over time or at the formation and development of neighborhoods of migrants continues to be not only a popular undertaking, but often a rewarding one. I find it noteworthy, however, that the late nineteenth century, the favorite epoch of the Gutman generation, has virtually disappeared from view except among historians writing about black or Asian workers. The twentieth century has simply taken over.

Fourth, the two topics that encompass the largest number of recent dissertations are government and the working class (especially the rise and demise of social insurance measures) and the roles of gender and racism in shaping public policy toward workers. Institutional histories of unions continue to appear, though in reduced numbers and clearly focused on the 1930s and beyond. Especially welcome, in my view, is the attention recently showered on steel workers, whose union, after all, stood at the center of the CIO's organizing agenda and of its power structure.

Judith Stein's magisterial work, *Running Steel, Running America* shows how all these topics can be brought together effectively.[5] Stein examines steel workers and their union during the years since the 1940s, when black workers effectively battled to break into new jobs, often with government help, at the same time that deliberate government encouragement of iron and steel production in other countries, for foreign policy purposes, made jobs rapidly disappear. The interaction was especially evident in Birmingham, Alabama where the civil rights movement crested during 1962 and 1963 in the aftermath of the closing of the region's mills and mines. Like Thomas Sugrue's insightful study of racism in Detroit, Stein forces us to incorporate public policy and the power of corporate leadership into our scrutiny of whiteness within the working class.[6]

Fifth, my interest in Stein's book on steel workers also brings us to another prominent and encouraging characteristic of recent dissertations. Close to a dozen of them frame working-class experience in an international context. Coming to grips politically with the global economy has inspired some historians to situate local struggles globally. This tendency has manifested itself in a variety of ways—all of which deserve encouragement.

Research on immigrants has benefited from this tendency in at least two ways. First, the old dichotomies—push vs. pull, assimilation vs. cultural retention—have been augmented by a growing interest in the impact of the backward and forward flow of people and of earnings on the Old Country, as well as on the United States and on other immigrant destinations. The monumental research conducted by Donna Gabaccia and Fraser Ottanelli, and also by Bruno Ramirez, on the world-wide diaspora of Italians has set an example for others to follow.[7] So have Peter Rachleff's work on the Croatian Fraternal Union and Nora Faires' scrutiny of white and black Canadian immigrants in Michigan. Similarly, Winston James's book on Afro-Caribbean radicals in American politics, *Holding Aloft the Banner of Ethiopia,* has not only drawn our attention to the extent of twentieth-century black immigration, but also revealed its crucial importance in the history of the Left in both this country and the British Empire.[8]

The best historians of migration across the Pacific have long since shown us how to treat the Pacific rim as a unit for investigation and have produced rich insights into community building, women's lives, and racism. They have also drawn our attention to the role of state power and of imperial domination in determining who migrated where and under what conditions, and this is a subject demanding much closer scrutiny by Americans. Unfree labor returned in a variety of guises in the tropical and semi-tropical world often decades after the abolition of chattel slavery in the same regions. It was as important to the development of modern corporate capitalism as was large scale industry. To be sure, "contract labor" often appeared in trade union rhetoric as a metaphor for non-white labor. But while we need to deconstruct that rhetoric, we also need much more research into the reality, which Sidney Mintz described so graphically: "the link between sweated, tropical colonial labor and nonwhite-labor was preserved, largely undisturbed by the end of slavery."[9]

Finally, we have only begun to break new ground in the study of nationalism and internationalism in the American labor movement. Dana Frank's *Buy American* has not only revealed the persistence of union struggles over trade policy and tariff protection from the American Revolution to the present day but has done so with a style of presentation that attracts readers from circles far broader than just the academic world. Her book makes especially important reading for union activists today. She shows how both protection and free trade have served to tie unions to employers' interests and to deflect demands for economic policies based on working people's needs. To take another example, five years ago Elizabeth McKillen published a study of the efforts of the Chicago Federation of Labor, during its most progressive years around World War I and its aftermath, to mobilize mass involvement in quest of a democratic foreign policy. Chicago labor vigorously challenged Woodrow Wilson's attempt to reconstruct imperialist domination of the world by arousing workers' support for revolution in Ireland, Russia, Mexico, and India.[10]

Although half a dozen dissertations and some valuable new books explore the foreign policies of the AFL and the CIO, the establishment of NAFTA has made the history of interaction between the U.S. and Mexican workers especially important. Historians of Mexican immigrants have increasingly often devoted close attention to their encounters with established Mexican-American communities and also to the long history of U.S. domination of the economy of northern Mexico. The work of David Gutierrez, Gilbert Gonzalez, and Camille Guerin-Gonzalez comes quickly to mind.[11] I hope not too much time will pass before the publication of Dan La Botz's 1998 dissertation on the role of refugee American resisters to World War I in helping found and shape the early Communist Party of Mexico.[12] But it is the CIO epoch that remains almost a blank page in our knowledge of interaction between the two countries' labor movements. And the records from which that can be done are not in Moscow, but in the US and in Mexico.

Finally let me note that the global vision which is now enriching our understanding of local and national working-class life and struggles is currently informing new insights into the history of slavery and of the way African American workers and political leaders have interpreted their world. For at least three centuries black activists in the United States and those traversing Atlantic ports have depicted this country's racism as an American variant of world-wide oppression. Just as the conditions under which black sharecroppers entered Birmingham's mines and mills or ventured north to Cleveland were fashioned by international capital flows, as well as by local white supremacy, so the great voice of Pan-Africanism, George Padmore, appeared regularly in many major African American newspapers during the 1940s until Cold War demands for patriotic loyalty forced those journals to treat "civil rights" exclusively as a domestic moral dilemma.[13] Consider how often black working people approvingly described an activist in their ranks as "a race man—a communist and a Garveyite." They let intellectuals bother themselves with the contradiction they found there.

But this international perspective on the writing of American labor history has posed one major problem with which we have only begun to deal. Defining labor history as the history of wage earners makes it easy to envisage the basic trajectory of our subject in Bruce Laurie's apt phrase "artisans into workers," or perhaps to start our labor history courses with the great strikes of 1877. But as C.L.R. James, among others, argued more than half a century ago, the first concentrations of large numbers of producers brought from distant areas to work under close supervision producing commodities for export, rather than for their own consumption, were slaves brought from Africa.[14] Although some of us must concentrate our research energies on some types of working people and others on different histories, the fact remains that we must learn, and have yet to learn, how to integrate those divergent but interacting stories of exploitation, migration and struggle. That does not mean simply adding more paragraphs—akin to the practice Ava Baron described as "add women and stir."[15] It does mean pursuing all of our investigations with an analytical framework and a research sensitivity that incorporates the many dimensions capitalism's incessant change—accumulation, empire, and creative destruction as they have been evident in workers' experience, identity, accomplishments, and tragic defeats. Only then will we not only understand our world better, but perhaps even help change it.

Notes

Reprinted courtesy of New York University and the Tamiment Library and the Robert F. Wagner Labor Archives.

1. Julie Saville, *The Work of Reconstruction: From Slave to Wage Labor in South Carolina, 1860–1870* (Cambridge and New York: Cambridge University Press, 1994), 86.

2. Elson E. Boles, "Rebels, Gamblers, and Silk: Agencies and Structure of the Japan-United States Silk Network, 1860–1890" (unpublished PhD diss., State University of New York at Binghamton, 1998).

3. Dorothy Sue Cobble, *Dishing It Out: Waitresses and Their Unions in the Twentieth Century* (Urbana and Chicago: University of Illinois Press, 1991); Dorothy Sue Cobble, "Organizing the Postindustrial Work Force: Lessons from the History of Waitress Unionism," *Industrial and Labor Relations Review* 44 (April 1991): 419–36.

4. Tera R. Hunter, *To 'Joy My Freedom: Southern Black Women's Lives and Labors After the Civil War* (Cambridge and London: Harvard University Press, 1997); Kimberly L. Phillips, *Alabama North: African-American Migrants, Community, and Working-Class Activism in Cleveland, 1915–45* (Urbana and Chicago: University of Illinois Press, 1999); Varpu Lindström-Best, *Defiant Sisters: A Social History of Finnish Immigrant Women in Canada* (Toronto: Multicultural History Society of Toronto, 1988).

5. Judith Stein, *Running Steel, Running America: Race, Economic Policy, and the Decline of Liberalism* (Chapel Hill and London: University of North Carolina Press, 1998).

6. Thomas J. Sugrue, "Crabgrass-Roots Politics: Race, Rights, and the Reaction Against Liberalism in the Urban North, 1940–1964," *Journal of American History* 82 (September 1995): 551–78. Thomas J. Sugrue, *Origins of the Urban Crisis: Race and Inequality in Postwar Detroit* (Princeton: Princeton University Press, 1996).

7. Donna R. Gabaccia, "Worker Internationalism and Italian Labor Migration, 1870–1919," *International Labor and Working-Class History* 45 (Spring 1994): 63–79; Bruno Ramirez, *On the Move: French-Canadian and Italian Migrants in the North Atlantic Economy, 1860–1914* (Toronto: McClelland & Stewart, 1991).

8. Winston James, *Holding Aloft the Banner of Ethiopia: Caribbean Radicalism in Early Twentieth-Century America* (London and New York: Verso, 1998).

9. Sidney W. Mintz, *Sweetness and Power: The Place of Sugar in Modern History* (New York: Viking Penguin, 1985), 71.

10. Elizabeth McKillen, *Chicago Labor and the Quest for a Democratic Diplomacy, 1914–1924* (Ithaca and London: Cornell University Press, 1995).

11. David C. Gutierrez, *Walls and Mirrors: Mexican Americans, Mexican Immigrants, and the Politics of Ethnicity* (Berkeley, Los Angeles, London: University of California Press, 1995); Gilbert G. Gonzalez, *Labor and Community: Mexican Citrus Worker Villages in a Southern California County, 1900–1950* (Urbana and Chicago: University of Illinois Press, 1994); Camille Guerin-Gonzalez, *Mexican Workers and American Dreams: Immigration, Repatriation, and California Farm Labor, 1900–1939* (New Brunswick: Rutgers University Press, 1994).

12. Dan La Botz, "American War Resisters and Communists in Mexico, 1917–27" (PhD diss., University of Cincinnati, 1998).

13. Penny M. von Eschen, *Race Against Empire: Black Americans and Anticolonialism, 1937–1957* (Ithaca and London: Cornell University Press, 1997).

14. C.L.R. James, *Black Jacobins: Toussaint L'Ouverture and the San Domingo Revolution* (New York: Random House, 1963).

15. Ava Baron, ed., *Work Engendered: Toward a New History of American Labor* (Ithaca and London: Cornell University Press, 1991), 8.

A David Montgomery Bibliography

Works ordered chronologically within each section.

Books

Beyond Equality: Labor and the Radical Republicans, 1862–1872. New York: Knopf, 1967; reprinted, University of Illinois Press, 1981.

Workers' Control in America: Studies in the History of Work, Technology, and Labor Struggles. Cambridge and New York: Cambridge University Press, 1979.

Rapporti di Classe nell'America del Primo 900, with an introduction by Elisabetta Benenati Marconi and Vittorio Foa. Turin: Rosenberg e Sellier, 1980.

El Control Obrero en los Estados Unidos. Madrid: Ministerio de Trabajo y Seguridad Social de Espana, 1985.

The Fall of the House of Labor: The Workplace, the State, and American Labor Activism, 1865–1925. Cambridge and New York: Cambridge University Press, 1987.

The American Civil War and the Meanings of Freedom. Oxford, UK: Clarendon Press, 1987.

Citizen Worker: The Experience of Workers in the United States with Democracy and the Free Market during the Nineteenth Century. Cambridge and New York: Cambridge University Press, 1993.

August Sartorius von Walterhauseen. *The Workers' Movement in the United States.* Edited by David Montgomery and Marcel van der Linden in collaboration with Jan Gielkens and Gregory Zieren. Translated by Harry Dorst. Cambridge and New York: Cambridge University Press, 1998.

(With Horace Huntley) *Black Workers' Struggle for Equality in Birmingham.* Urbana, IL: University of Illinois Press, 2004.

Articles and Essays

Flaherty, Amos [David Montgomery]. "The Great Northern Strike of 1894: When Gene Debs Beat Jim Hill." *The People Together* (1958), edited by Meridel Le Sueur.

"Radical Republicanism in Pennsylvania, 1866–1873." *Pennsylvania Magazine of History and Biography* 85 (October 1961): 439–457. Reprinted in *Radical Republicans in the North: State Politics during Reconstruction*. Edited by James C. Mohr. Baltimore and London: Johns Hopkins University Press, 1976.

"The Working Classes of the Pre-industrial American City, 1780–1830." *Labor History* 9 (Winter 1968): 3–22. Reprinted in Katz, Stanley N., and S. I. Kutler, eds. *New Perspectives on the American Past*. 2nd edition. Boston: Little Brown and Company, 1972; Irwin Unger, D. Brody, and P. Goodman, eds. *The Record of American History: Interpretive Readings*. Waltham, Mass.: Xerox College Publishing Company, 1971; Mohl, Raymond A., and N. Betten, eds. *Urban America in Historical Perspective*. New York: Weybright and Talley, 1970; Bobbs-Merrill reprint in American History No. H-447.

"What's Happening to the American Worker." *Radical America* Pamphlet. Madison, Wisconsin, 1970.

"The Shuttle and the Cross: Weavers and Artisans in the Kensington Riots of 1844." *Journal of Social History* 5 (Summer 1972): 411–46; Reprinted in Stearns, Peter N., and Daniel Walkowitz, eds. *Workers in the Industrial Revolution: Recent Studies in the United States and Europe*. New Brunswick, NJ: Transaction Books, 1974; Nash, Gary B., ed. *The Private Side of American History*. New York: Harcourt, Brace, Jovanovich, 1975; Pessen, Edward, ed. *The Many Faceted Jacksonian Era*. Westport, Conn.: Greenwood Press, 1978.

"The Conventional Wisdom." *Labor History* 13 (Winter 1972): 107–136.

"The War and the Worker." In *Many Pasts: Readings in American Social History*, edited by Herbert G. Gutman and Gregory S. Kealey. Englewood Cliffs, NJ, 1973.

"The 'New Unionism' and the Transformation of Workers' Consciousness in America, 1909–22." *Journal of Social History* 7, no. 4 (Summer 1974): 510–29.

"Labor in the Industrial Era." *U.S. Department of Labor Bicentennial History of the American Worker*. Edited by Richard Morris. Washington, DC: Government Printing Office, 1976.

"Workers' Control of Machine Production in the Nineteenth Century." *Labor History* 17 (Fall 1976): 485–509.

(with Ronald Schatz) "Facing Layoffs." *Radical America* 10 (March-April 1976): 15–28. Republished in Montgomery, *Workers' Control in America*. Cambridge: Cambridge University Press, 1979.

"Gutman's Nineteenth Century America." *Labor History* 19 (Summer 1978): 416–439.

"*Les artisans et la conscience de classe ouvrière: Nouveaux recherches aux États-Unis*." *Labour/Le Travailleur* 3 (1978): 233–242.

"*Quels Standards? Les ouvriers et le réorganisation de la production aux États-Unis* (1900–1920)." *Le Mouvement Social* 102 (January-March, 1978): 101–127.

"The Past and Future of Workers' Control." *Radical America* 13 (November-December 1979): 7–24.
"To Study the People: The American Working Class." *Labor History* 21 (Fall 1980): 485–512.
"The Irish and the American Labor Movement." In *Ireland and America, 1776–1976*, edited by David N. Doyle and Owen Dudley Edwards. Westport, CT: Greenwood Press, 1980; Translated and reprinted as "*Na Gaeil agus Gluaiseacht an Lucht Oibre*," in S. O. *Annrachain, Go Meiriceá Siar*. Dublin, 1979, 138–153.
"Strikes in Nineteenth-Century America." *Social Science History* 4 (Winter 1980): 81–104.
"Labor and the Republic in Industrial America, 1860–1920." *Le Mouvement Social* 111 (April–June 1980): 201–15.
"Work." In *Encyclopedia of American Economic History*, edited by Glenn Porter, 974–987. New York: Charles Scribner's Sons, 1980.
"Violence and the Struggle for Unions in the South, 1880–1930." In *Perspectives on the American South*, edited by Merle Black. New York: Gordon and Breach, 1981.
"New Tendencies in Union Struggle and Strategies in Europe and the United States, 1916–1922." In *Work, Community, and Power: The Experience of Labor in Europe and America. 1900–1925*, edited by James E. Cronin, and Carmen Sirianni, 88–116. Philadelphia: Temple University Press, 1983.
"*Nacionalizmus, amerikai patriotizmus, és osztálytudat a bevándorolt munkások között az Egyesült Államokban az első világháború időszakában*." *Tőrténelmi Szemle* 83 (1983): 255–280.
The Irish Influence in the American Labor Movement. Lecture published by the Cushwa Center for the Study of American Catholicism, Notre Dame, Ind., 1984.
"Immigrants, Industrial Unions, and Social Reconstruction in the United States, 1916–1923." *Labour/Le Travail* 13 (Spring 1984): 101–113.
"Nationalism, American Patriotism, and Class Consciousness among Immigrant Workers in the United States in the Epoch of World War I." In *"Struggle a Hard Battle": Essays on Working-Class Immigrants*, edited by Dirk Hoerder, 327–353. DeKalb: Northern Illinois University Press, 1986.
"*State e sindicato nelle politiche del lavoro*." In *Ripensere Roosevelt*, edited by Tiziano Bonazzi and Maurizio Vaudagna, 188–209. Milan: Franco Angeli, 1986.
"Thinking about American Workers in the 1920s." *International Labor and Working-Class History* 32 (Fall 1987): 4–24.
"William H. Sylvis and the Search for Working-Class Citizenship." In *Labor Leaders in America*, edited by Melvyn Dubofsky and Warren Van Tine, 3–29. Urbana: University of Illinois Press, 1987.
"Marxism and Utopianism in the USA." [extended review essay of Paul Buhle, *Marxism in the United States: Remapping the History of the American Left* (London: Verso/Haymarket, 1987)]. *New Left Review* 164, (July 1987): 123–128.
"Gutman's Agenda for Future Historical Research." *Labor History* 29, no. 3 (1988): 299–312.
"Class, Capitalism, and Contentment." In "Symposium on *The Fall of the House of Labor*," *Labor History* 30 (Winter 1989): 125–137.

"Strikes of Machinists in the United States." In *Strikes, Wars, and Revolutions in an International Perspective: Strike Waves in the Late Nineteenth and Early Twentieth Centuries*, edited by Leopold H. Haimson and Charles Tilly, 269–288. New York: Cambridge University Press, 1989.
"Citizenship and Justice in the Lives and Thoughts of Nineteenth-Century American Workers." *Tanner Lectures on Human Values* XIII. Salt Lake City, Utah, 1992, 175–259.
"Industrial Democracy or Democracy in Industry? The Theory and Practice of the Labor Movement, 1870–1925." In *Industrial Democracy in America: The Ambiguous Promise*, edited by Nelson Lichtenstein and Howell John Harris, 20–42. New York: Cambridge University Press and Woodrow Wilson Center Press, 1993.
"Labor and the Political Leadership of New Deal America." *International Review of Social History* 39 (December 1994): 335–360.
"Wage Labor, Bondage, and Citizenship in Nineteenth Century America." *International Labor and Working-Class History* 48 (Fall 1995): 6–27.
"Planning for Our Futures." In *Audacious Democracy: Labor, Intellectuals, and the Social Reconstruction of America*, edited by Steve Fraser and Joshua B. Freeman, 64–72. Boston: Houghton Mifflin, 1997.
"Epilogue: The Pullman Boycott and the Making of Modern America." In *The Pullman Strike and the Crisis of the 1890s: Essays on Labor and Politics*, edited by Richard Schneirov, Shelton Stromquist and Nick Salvatore, 233–249. Urbana: University of Illinois Press, 1999.
"Empire, Race, and Working-Class Mobilizations." In *Racializing Class, Classifying Race: Labor and Difference in Britain, the USA and Africa*, edited by Peter Alexander and Rick Halpern. New York: St. Martin's Press, 2000.
"Racism, Immigrants, and Political Reform." *Journal of American History* 87 (March 2001): 1253–74.
"Workers' Movements in the United States Confront Imperialism: The Progressive Era Experience." *Journal of the Gilded Age and Progressive Era* 7 (January 2008): 7–42.
"Working Peoples' Response to Past Depressions." In *Workers in Hard Times: A Long View of Economic Crises*, edited by Leon Fink, Joseph A. McCartin, and Joan Sangster. Urbana, IL: University of Illinois Press, 2014.

Shorter Works

"The Evolution of the Society of American Foresters, 1934–1937, as Seen in the Memoirs of H. H. Chapman." *Forest History* 6 (Fall 1962): 2–9.
"Spontaneity and Organization: Some Comments on Jeremy Brecher's *Strike!*" *Radical America* 7 (Nov.–Dec., 1973): 70–80.
"The New Urban History." *Reviews in American History* 2 (December 1974): 498–504.
"Goodwyn's Populists." *Marxist Perspectives* 1 (Spring 1978): 166–173; Reprinted in *The Common People of the Postwar South*. Edited by Edward Magdol. Westport, CT: Greenwood Press, 1980, 337–343.

"The Farmer-Labor Party's Legacy to the Socialist Left." *In These Times*, October 8–14, 1980, 18–19; Reprinted in *Working for Democracy: American Workers from the Revolution to the Present,* edited by Paul Buhle and Alan Dawley. Urbana, IL: University of Illinois Press, 1985.

"E.P. Thompson: History as Human Agency." *Queen's Quarterly* 87 (Summer 1980): 267–272; Reprinted in *Monthly Review* 5 (October 1981): 42–48.

"Introduction," to *Labor and the World Social Structure*, edited by Immanuel Wallerstein. Berkeley, Cal.: Sage Publications, 1983, 9–16.

Response to Harold Benenson, "Victorian Sexual Ideology and Marx's Theory of the Working Class." *International Labor and Working-Class History* 25 (March 1984): 24–29.

"Labor." *Miami Herald*, September 2, 1984, 1E, 5E.

"Afterword," to Mary C. Grimes. *The Knights in Fiction: Two Labor Novels of the 1880s*. Urbana: University of Illinois Press, 1986.

"Haymarket Centennial: The Wounds Remain." *In These Times*. April 30–May 6, 1986.

"Trends in Working-Class History." *Labour/Le Travail* 19 (Spring 1987): 13–22.

"Foreword," to Toni Gilpin, Daniel Letwin, and Jack McKivigan. *On Strike for Respect: The Strike at Yale of 1984–85*. Chicago: Charles H. Kerr, 1988.

"*Prefazione*," to Simonetta Ortaggi Cammarosano. *Il Prezzo del Lavere: Torino e l'Industria Italiana nel Primo '900*. Turin: Rosenberg & Sellier, 1988, 9–13.

"Introduction," to *Class, Community and the Labour Movement: Wales and Canada. 1850–1930*, edited by Deian R. Hopkin and Gregory S. Kealey, 1–6. Society for Welsh Labour History and Canadian Committee on Labour History, 1989.

"Introduction," to K. B. Gilden. *Between the Hills and the Sea*. Ithaca, NY: ILR Press, 1989.

"Capitalism, Race, Democracy and Reconstruction." *Radical History Review* (1990): 153–160.

"Unions and the Control of Economic Activity." *Democratic Left* 18 (September-October 1990): 5–6, 8.

"The Limits of Union-Centered History: Response to Howard Kimmeldorf." *Labor History* 32 (Winter 1991): 110–116.

"Afterword." In *The River Ran Red: Homestead, 1892*, edited by Fania Weingartner and David Demarest. Pittsburgh: University of Pittsburgh Press, 1992.

"Foreword," to Irving Richter. *Labor Struggles in America: A Participant's View of 1945–1947*. Cambridge University Press, 1994.

"Labour History's Mission and Method." *Saothar: Journal of Irish Labour History* 21 (1996): 91–95.

"Introduction." In *The Cold War and the University: Towards an Intellectual History of the Cold War*. New York: New Press, 1996.

"Foreword." In *Cogs in the Classroom Factory: The Changing Identity of Academic Labor*, edited by Deborah M. Herman and Julie M. Schmid. Westport, CT: Praeger, 2003.

"Workers and Diplomacy." *Diplomatic History* 34, no. 4 (September 2010): 727–731.

"Law and the Shaping of the American Labor Movement: Government by Injunction." In *American Labor Struggles and Law Histories*, edited by Kenneth Casebeer. Durham, NC: Carolina Academic Press, 2011.
"The OAH in St. Louis: The Protest." In *The Organization of American Historians and the Writing and Teaching of American History*, edited by Richard S. Kirkendall, 351–356. New York: Oxford University Press, 2011.
"Class, Gender and Reciprocity: An Afterword." In Benson, Susan Porter, and David Montgomery. *Household Accounts: Working-Class Family Economies in the Interwar United States*. Ithaca: Cornell University Press, 2015, 171–75.
"Carry It On." In *Civic Labors: Scholarly Activism and Working-Class Studies*, edited by Dennis Deslippe, Eric Fure-Slocum, and John W. McKerley. Urbana: University of Illinois Press, 2016.

Interviews

"*'Ma dove eravate, voi comunisti, negli anni '20?' Stavamo nelle corali degli immigranti, e li nacque il Cio.' La nuova storia di una classe operaia. Un colloquia con Montgomery e Mason.*" Interview by Ester Fano. *Il Manifesto* (May 4, 1979).
"Unions Will Expand Role, Stiffen as Labor Enters Its Second Century: Ideas for the Eighties." Interview by Clarke Thomas. *Pittsburgh Post-Gazette* (November 30, 1981).
"*Sindicato, ti ricordi la II Internationale.*" Interview by Piero *Lavatelli. L'Unita* (November 27, 1981).
"Once upon a Shop Floor: An Interview with David Montgomery." Interview by Paul Buhle and Mark Naison. *Radical History Review* 23 (Spring 1980): 37–53; Reprinted in MAHRO, *Visions of History*. New York: Pantheon Books, 1983.
"Class Act: An Interview with David Montgomery." Interview by James R. Barrett. *Labor Studies in Working-Class History of the Americas* 1, no. 1 (2004): 23–54.

Index

DAVID MONTGOMERY (1927–2011) was the Farnam Professor of History at Yale University. His books include *The Fall of the House of Labor: The Workplace, the State, and American Labor Activism, 1865–1925.*

SHELTON STROMQUIST is an emeritus professor of history at the University of Iowa. He is the author of *Claiming the City: A Global History of Workers' Fight for Municipal Socialism.*

JAMES R. BARRETT is an emeritus professor of history at the University of Illinois, Urbana-Champaign. He is the author of *History from the Bottom Up and the Inside Out: Ethnicity, Race, and Identity in Working-Class History.*

The University of Illinois Press
is a founding member of the
Association of University Presses.

Composed in 11.5/13 Adobe Garamond
with Gotham display
by Jim Proefrock
at the University of Illinois Press
Manufactured by Versa Press, Inc.

University of Illinois Press
1325 South Oak Street
Champaign, IL 61820-6903
www.press.uillinois.edu

FSC
www.fsc.org
MIX
Papier | Fördert gute Waldnutzung
FSC® C083411

Kolibri 360 GmbH
Ferdinand-Jühlke-Straße 7
99095 Erfurt, Deutschland
produktsicherheit@kolibri360.de